## 4 ► Diverse content helps you SEE YOURSELF in the text and connect with your audience.

The qualities that make you who you are—your background, your accent (everyone has one!), your abilities, your culture, your interests, your identity—are all assets to you as a speaker and a learner. *Speak Up!* is consciously designed as a space where you can bring your whole self to your learning and see yourself reflected in the materials you use.

With a wide variety of images and topics included in each chapter, *Speak Up!* gives you the tools you need to craft speeches that have personal meaning *and* resonate with the many diverse people in your audience. Concrete strategies include ways to consider gender identity, disability status, and other demographics during audience analysis; tips for using the singular "they" (and other methods for incorporating gender-neutral language into your speech); and suggestions for considering neurodiversity alongside nonverbal delivery.

The Washington Post/Getty Images

## 5 ► *Speak Up!* encourages you to RAISE YOUR VOICE.

*Speak Up!* encourages you to find your voice and speak up on issues you are passionate about.

As one of the only public speaking texts with an entire chapter dedicated to speaking for social change (Chapter 21: Civic Engagement), *Speak Up!* includes concrete, practical, nonpartisan tips about how you can use the concepts you're learning in this class to advocate for what's most important to you.

# Speak Up!

## A GUIDE TO PUBLIC SPEAKING

### Sixth Edition

**Douglas M. Fraleigh**

*California State University–Fresno*

**Joseph S. Tuman**

*San Francisco State University*

*With Illustrations by*
**Peter Arkle**

**bedford/st.martin's**

Macmillan Learning

Boston | New York

**Joe**

*For my wife, Kirsten: With every new edition of* Speak Up!, *there are more reasons to appreciate your love and, above all, your patience with my taking over so much of the dining room table to write.*

**Doug**

*To my family, the source of inspiration for all of my writing.*

**For Bedford/St. Martin's**

*Vice President, Editorial, Macmillan Learning Humanities:* Leasa Burton
*Senior Program Director for Communication:* Erika Gutierrez
*Marketing Manager:* Melissa Rodriguez
*Director of Content Development, Humanities:* Jane Knetzger
*Senior Development Editor:* Christina Lembo
*Development Editor:* Kimberly Roberts
*Director of Media Editorial:* Adam Whitehurst
*Senior Media Editor:* Julia Domenicucci
*Media Editorial Assistant:* Erin Peraza
*Marketing Manager:* Melissa Rodriguez
*Senior Director, Content Management Enhancement:* Tracey Kuehn
*Senior Managing Editor:* Lisa Kinne
*Senior Content Project Manager:* Peter Jacoby
*Senior Workflow Project Manager:* Paul Rohloff
*Production Supervisor:* Robert Cherry
*Director of Design, Content Management:* Diana Blume
*Design Services Manager:* Natasha A. S. Wolfe
*Interior Design:* Jerilyn DiCarlo
*Cover Design:* William Boardman
*Text Permissions Associate:* Maisie Howell
*Photo Permissions Editor:* Allison Ziebka-Viering
*Photo Researcher:* Cheryl Dubois, Lumina Datamatics, Inc.
*Director of Digital Production:* Keri deManigold
*Advanced Media Project Manager:* Sarah O'Connor Kepes
*Project Management:* Lumina Datamatics, Inc.
*Editorial Services:* Lumina Datamatics, Inc.
*Composition:* Lumina Datamatics, Inc.
*Printing and Binding:* Lakeside Book Company

Manufactured in the United States of America.

1 2 3 4 5 6     27 26 25 24 23 22

*For information, write:* Bedford/St. Martin's, 75 Arlington Street, Boston, MA 02116 (617-399-4000)

ISBN 978-1-319-44853-0

# BRIEF CONTENTS

# CONTENTS

## LANGUAGE AND DELIVERY

## 12 LANGUAGE AND STYLE   *283*

## TYPES OF PUBLIC SPEAKING

## 15 MEDIATED PUBLIC SPEAKING   *367*

# 20 GROUP COMMUNICATION *513*

# 21 CIVIC ENGAGEMENT *539*

# COVERAGE IN *SPEAK UP!*, SIXTH EDITION

## Correlated with NCA's Learning Outcomes in Communication

*Note:* This table aligns with the 2018 learning outcomes of the National Communication Association (NCA).

| NCA Outcome Correlation Grid | |
|---|---|
| **NCA Outcome** | **Relevant Coverage in *Speak Up!*** |
| **LOC #1:** Describe the communication discipline and its central questions | Chapter 1: Introducing Public Speaking introduces public speaking and its place within the larger communication discipline. Subsequent chapters address core communication competencies like responsible listening, speaking ethically, intercultural awareness, and argument construction. |
| **LOC #2:** Employ communication theories, perspectives, principles, and concepts | The authors have grounded their book in current communication scholarship, backing up its practical advice with key scholarly concepts. These include *linear and transactional speaking* (Ch. 1), the *classical canons of rhetoric* (Ch. 2), *source credibility* (Ch. 7), *Monroe's motivated sequence* (Ch. 17), *logical fallacies* (Ch. 18), and more. |
| **LOC #3:** Engage in communication theory | The book discusses a variety of critical approaches to communication, including theories related to the evolution of public speaking (Ch. 1), speech anxiety (Ch. 2), and means of persuasion (Ch. 18), among others. |
| **LOC #4:** Create messages appropriate to the audience, purpose, and context | Chapter 5 is an in-depth discussion of audience analysis, including size, demographics, prior exposure, and disposition, while Chapters 2 and 6 cover a speech's rhetorical purpose. |
| **LOC #5:** Critically analyze messages | Chapter 4 includes coverage of critiquing and constructively criticizing speeches as a listener, and Chapter 1 discusses the role of critical thinking in public speaking. |

PRINCIPLES FOR DIVERSE, EQUITABLE, INCLUSIVE, AND CULTURALLY RESPONSIVE AND SUSTAINING (DEI+CRS) LEARNING MATERIALS

| NCA Outcome | Relevant Coverage in *Speak Up!* |
|---|---|
| **LOC #6:** Demonstrate the ability to accomplish communicative goals (self-efficacy) | Chapter 2: Developing Your First Speech walks students through the process of developing a speech, addressing the various steps and potential barriers that they might encounter along the way, including methods of overcoming speech anxiety. In the sixth edition, the Speech Choices case study feature includes questions that prompt students to consider their own speech choices during each phase of the speechmaking process, thereby encouraging metacognitive reflection about which choices produce the most effective results. |
| **LOC #7:** Apply ethical communication principles and practices | Chapter 3: Speech Ethics discusses various codes of ethics (absolute, situational, and culturally relative), and covers the ethics of communicating truthfully, acknowledging the work of others, and using sound reasoning—as well as the process of ethical listening. |
| **LOC #8:** Utilize communication to embrace difference | Chapter 5: Audience Analysis includes material on analyzing audience demographics to encourage inclusive and thoughtful communication, keeping in mind age, gender identity, sexual orientation, race and ethnicity, disability status, religious orientation, socioeconomic background, and political affiliation. Inclusive language, examples, and visual images are incorporated throughout the text. Chapter 12: Language and Style discusses strategies for using respectful language in a speech—words, phrases, and expressions that are courteous and don't reflect bias against other cultures or individuals. |
| **LOC #9:** Influence public discourse | Chapter 21 on civic engagement discusses in detail how public speaking can and should influence public discourse. Strategic and ethical discourse is emphasized in Chapters 17 and 18 on persuasion. |

## PRINCIPLES FOR DIVERSE, EQUITABLE, INCLUSIVE, AND CULTURALLY RESPONSIVE AND SUSTAINING (DEI+CRS) LEARNING MATERIALS

A textbook is more than just a curated collection of scholarship—it is a community of voices who contribute to it, an editorial process that hones it, and ultimately, a dialogue with the students and instructors who encounter it. So what voices are included in your learning materials? What standards are being used to combat bias? What methods are being used to help students see themselves in the material? At Macmillan Learning, we hear you. That is why we are opening up our process and products to be more transparent. At the heart of this transparency is putting into words and sharing with you how we define our editorial work: our principles for diverse, equitable, inclusive, and culturally responsive and sustaining learning materials.

Macmillan Learning's process for developing learning materials is grounded in three principles:

1. Diverse voices in an inclusive development process
2. Editorial standards that combat bias
3. Learning rooted in lives, experiences, and culture

### Principle 1. Diverse Voices in an Inclusive Development Process

Learning materials reflect the voices that are included in the development process. Effective textbooks are the product of diverse and inclusive communities, built at every stage of development, from author voices and editorial decisions to the review program and input from students and instructors.

- **Cultural Inclusivity.** We see authors' own cultural backgrounds and cultural self-awareness as assets in the development of learning materials.
- **Diverse Scholarship.** By regularly revising and updating our texts, we are able to incorporate new scholars from a variety of backgrounds to provide a diverse, inclusive, and equitable approach to scholarship in our learning materials.
- **Review Program.** Since 2018, Macmillan Learning's editors in communication have included specific questions about diversity, inclusion, and educational equity in review programs, where the publisher collects input from instructors and users in the development of learning materials.

- **Editorial Board.** The Editorial Board consists of a group of experts and advocates for inclusive learning, which has convened multiple times since 2018 to guide the development of particular titles and to lead changes to our overall publishing process.
- **Transparency.** Part of inclusion is transparency, which means inviting the larger community of instructors, students, and others into a conversation to improve learning materials—this project is part of this effort.

Participants in the DEI+CRS Editorial Board
From left to right: Reproduced with permission of Bryan M. Dewsbury and the University of Rhode Island; photo by Nora Lewis. Photo by Lucy Kramer; reproduced with permission of Jill and Lucy Kramer. Dorien Martin. Photo by Ryan Kennedy; photo provided courtesy of Tenisha Baca. Photo by Kellie Bradshaw; photo provided courtesy of Danielle Harkins. Courtesy Tasha Davis. Photo by Norma Piña; photo provided courtesy of Rody Randon. Courtesy Timothy Brown. Photo by University of Georgia Office of Public Service and Outreach; courtesy of Tina Harris. Photo courtesy of Myra Washington. Reproduced with permission of Molly J. Scanlon.

## Principle 2. Editorial Standards That Combat Bias

A successful publishing process relies on critical self-reflection to bring to light implicit bias that can exclude or harm a student's educational experience. Key checkpoints and standards ensure that critical self-reflection is fundamental to the development process, in order to create an inclusive, positive learning experience for all students and instructors.

- **Development Checklist.** All editors at Macmillan Learning now check their work against a content development checklist, developed in early 2020, which codifies a set of editorial practices to help eliminate bias and foster inclusive pedagogy.
- **Style/Usage Guidelines.** In fall 2020, Macmillan Learning worked to create its first ever Diversity, Equity, & Inclusion Usage Guidelines, whose purpose is to educate and provide a decision-making tool for editors and content managers about words or terms that may come up in work across disciplines.
- **Illustration Guidelines.** Photos, art, and cartoons are some of the most powerful media in learning materials, and our editors follow several sets of guidelines to combat bias and promote inclusion when choosing them.

## Principle 3. Learning Rooted in Lives, Experiences, and Culture

Education is a communicative process, and classrooms are sites of intercultural exchange. Knowledge is constructed through that communication and exchange. Inclusive and culturally responsive and sustaining learning materials are not merely opening up access to education, they are constitutive of education itself.

- **Positive Modeling.** Learning is the product of effectively modeling behavior for students, and students need relatable models who can reflect their diversity.

**SPEECH CHOICES**

A CASE STUDY: *RAFAELA*

*Let's check in with Rafaela to see how she is integrating audience analysis into her speech preparation.*

As Rafaela continued to think about her idea for a speech about women running for office, she decided to interview several women in her class to get their perspective. She discovered that three women had been in student government before and two considered it a valuable experience. One student said it helped build her résumé when applying to college; the other said it gave her a helpful perspective of what it was like to be in charge. None of the women had received much encouragement, but they had run anyway because it was important to them personally.

- **Inclusive Examples.** Because knowledge is contextual it is important that learning materials situate concepts and skill formation within real-world, contemporary, and diverse contexts that challenge and engage students to drive learning.
- **Relevant Application.** The aim of education is ultimately self-development, and aligning content to students' college, career, and life goals helps them develop as self-efficacious learners.

## DEI AT MACMILLAN LEARNING

Our DEI strategy and program work to make Macmillan Learning a more diverse, inclusive, and equitable company. Our goal is to support and advance our principles for developing diverse, equitable, inclusive, and culturally responsive and sustaining learning materials for all.

To learn more, visit: macmillanlearning.com/college/us/content /developmentmatters.

**Douglas M. Fraleigh** is the University Assessment Coordinator and a professor in the Communication Department at California State University-Fresno. He has often taught public speaking in the General Education program and the Honors College at Fresno State and chaired the university's Oral Communication Core Competency Assessment. He previously served as chair of the Communication Department. His teaching and research interests include freedom of speech, argumentation, and public discourse. He is coauthor of *Let's Communicate: An Illustrated Guide to Human Communication* and *Freedom of Expression in the Marketplace of Ideas*. Before becoming chair, he was active in speech and debate coaching at Fresno State, Cornell, UC Berkeley, and California State University, Sacramento. He holds a Juris Doctor from UC Berkeley and BA from CSU Sacramento. When not busy teaching, writing, and administrating, he looks forward to running, reading, family time (especially plays and sporting events), and hanging out with his dogs.

Photo credit: Nancy Fraleigh

**Joseph S. Tuman** is a full professor with tenure and a former chair of the Department of Communication Studies at San Francisco State University, where he received the Jacobus tenBroek Society Award, a statewide award in California for excellence in teaching. He has also taught at the University of California at Berkeley, the New School for Social Research, and the University of Paris II, where he lectured about comparative American and French laws pertaining to freedom of speech. Additionally, he served at a NATO facility (COE/DAT—Centre of Excellence, Defense Against Terrorism) in Ankara, Turkey, where he taught new NATO members about interpretation of and counter messaging against terrorist groups' use of social media. Professor Tuman has published widely in the field of communication studies (including *Let's Communicate: An Illustrated Guide to Human Communication*) and authored books on political communication in campaigns and social media use by terror groups. Tuman has appeared regularly on local and national network television and radio as a political analyst since 1984. He has served on the boards of several nonprofits in Oakland, and in 2014 he was one

Photo credit: Joseph Tuman

of the leading candidates in the mayoral race. Currently, he serves as a public ethics commissioner for the Oakland Public Ethics Commission, while continuing to serve as an academic advisor and expert analysist to senior level NATO staff regarding terrorism and social media. In his spare time, Tuman is an avid triathlete and marathoner.

Photo credit: Peter Arkle

**Peter Arkle** is a freelance illustrator who grew up in Scotland and received a BA in illustration from St. Martin's School of Art and an MA from the Royal College of Art (both in London). His clients include magazines (*The New Yorker*, *Sierra*, *Time*, and *Popeye* in Tokyo), newspapers (the *New York Times*, the *Asahi Shimbun*, and the *Wall Street Journal*), Scotch whisky makers (anCnoc Highland Single Malt Whisky), and other enterprises that keep his life interesting. To see more of Peter's work, please visit peterarkle.com.

As longtime teachers of public speaking and former coaches of forensics, we have spent more than seventy combined years teaching students about the power of speech in their own lives and its value in shaping our society. In creating the first edition of *Speak Up!*, we distilled our best practices while transmitting our passionate commitment to the craft of public speaking. Our goal was to create a product that would grab students' attention while meeting the teaching and learning needs of students, colleagues, and friends across the communication discipline.

We recognized that covering the vast field of public speaking—from classical rhetoric and contemporary theory to the specific steps of researching, preparing, and delivering a speech—can be a tremendous challenge, especially given the time constraints of any course. Instructors need teaching materials that are comprehensive yet flexible enough to work with a variety of teaching styles. At the same time, students want a book that is engaging, fun, and affordable.

Keeping these challenges in mind, we came up with a three-part plan. First, we would make sure to include both traditional and compelling content. The organization would seamlessly integrate with instructors' syllabi, and the accessible language and current examples would engage students. Second, we would team up with the brilliant Peter Arkle to develop illustrations that would illuminate concepts visually, working synergistically with the written text. Professors have since confirmed that these are smart, pedagogically effective learning tools, and students have told us that the fun images actually motivate them to read more of the text. Third, we would aim to be affordable for students, and with our current digital packages, we now have more price-friendly options than ever.

We have continued to emphasize these goals in every revision, even as we make changes that reflect and respond to the experiences of today's students. For our sixth edition, in particular, we wanted to make changes that would take advantage of unique features of *Speak Up!*, while also expanding coverage of recent developments and events that have had a significant impact on the public speaking environment.

One significant change we've made is to incorporate photos into the text along with *Speak Up!*'s signature illustrations. The illustrations work hand-in-hand with the written text to explain key concepts and engage students in the chapter material, while the photos depict public speakers in a variety of contexts and real-world speech situations—and together, they represent one of the strongest art programs available in a public speaking text today.

The sixth edition also includes an expanded discussion of mediated public speaking. At the time the fifth edition published, some students were taking public speaking courses online, but this was not a universal experience. Then came the COVID-19 pandemic, and suddenly nearly all public speaking courses were virtual—as were many workplace meetings and community events. Although face-to-face public speaking opportunities are increasing once again as the pandemic subsides, colleges, workplaces, and organizations will continue to use mediated forums as a significant channel of communication, and students will need to build skills to communicate in mediated environments just as they do in in-person settings. Therefore, we have substantially revised Chapter 15 on Mediated Public Speaking, which incorporates new and updated concepts such as strategies for managing videoconferencing fatigue and tips for connecting with audience members, and we have woven additional examples of mediated public speaking into chapters throughout the text.

Just as mediated communication has changed a great deal in a short time, so has civic engagement, which has become an increasingly important avenue for social justice. Recent demonstrations calling for justice for George Floyd were some of the largest in U.S. history, and members of Generation Z have been more likely to become engaged in their communities than other cohorts. We want to encourage students to find their voices and speak up on issues they are passionate about, which is why we've incorporated current examples of civic engagement throughout the text, and updated Chapter 21: Civic Engagement to illustrate—in a concrete and practical manner—how the concepts learned in a public speaking class can be applied to advocacy in the public square. We've also added a new annotated sample speech on banned books to Chapter 21, and a video of this speech is available in Achieve, Macmillan's online learning system.

In addition to key content updates for the sixth edition, we wanted to add resources that would help students better understand the process of developing and presenting a successful speech. Each edition of *Speak Up!* has emphasized the idea that effective speeches are the result of a series of good choices. To help bring this idea to life for students, we have revised and personalized our Speech Choices feature, which uses a case study to follow student Rafaela as she goes through each stage of developing her speech. Keeping Rafaela's experiences in mind, we have added new questions to this feature that ask students to analyze their *own* choices as they use the chapter content to develop their speeches.

Finally, we wanted to ensure that the digital platform accompanying *Speak Up!* was as current and helpful as possible, so this sixth edition is now available with Achieve, Macmillan Learning's state-of-the-art online learning system. With Achieve, instructors can access an expanded array of videos—including professionally-filmed video of the sixth edition's new speech on banned books, video of Ukrainian President Volodymyr Zelensky's compelling 2022 address to the U.S. Congress, and a full-length sample speech about women running for office based on the book's Speech Choices feature—as well as activities and adaptive quizzing. Our full suite of instructor and assessment resources—including an instructor's manual, test bank, and lecture slides—is also available.

# NEW TO THIS EDITION

**Achieve for *Speak Up!*** sets a new standard for driving student learning in your public speaking course with powerful learning content, engaging activities, and actionable insights and analytics. Achieve brings together an interactive e-textbook, speech videos, LearningCurve adaptive quizzing and other assessments, learning activities, and extensive instructor resources—all within a new, enhanced technology platform carefully built over the past five years.

**A fully revised Chapter 15 (Mediated Public Speaking) prepares students to thrive in an age of virtual presentations.** New and updated topics include the pandemic's influence on mediated communication, strategies for managing videoconferencing fatigue, interactive features of videoconferencing technology, and tips related to vocal variety, eye contact, and connecting with audience members.

**An updated Chapter 21 (Civic Engagement)** incorporates new research about both the resurgence of civic engagement during the COVID-19 pandemic and the declining quality of public discourse, along with cutting edge examples that include Derrick Palmer and Christian Smalls's work to unionize Amazon, Mila Kunis's Oscars speech on the war in Ukraine, and disability justice advocate Stacey Park Milbern's speech style. The chapter includes **a new annotated persuasive speech** on banned books designed to model a presentation delivered at a school board meeting. A new professionally-filmed video of this speech is available on the Achieve digital platform.

**An increased emphasis on diverse perspectives, images, and experiences helps students see themselves in the text.** The sixth edition includes new and expanded coverage of topics such as gender identity, disability status, and other demographics (Chapter 5), the singular *they* as a method for incorporating gender-neutral language into a speech (Chapter 12), and neurodiversity and nonverbal delivery (Chapter 13). In addition, vibrant new images representing a wide variety of people and experiences are integrated throughout.

**Newly added photos help to bring concepts to life.** As a complement to *Speak Up!*'s custom drawn, pedagogically-powerful illustrations, the sixth edition includes newly added photos that depict real people in real speech situations. In *Speak Up!*, written explanations and accompanying visuals reinforce and work together to clarify key ideas, offer inspiration, and help students internalize what they need to do to create a successful speech.

**New speeches and videos address timely topics.** The sixth edition includes the full text of Ukrainian President Volodymyr Zelensky's compelling 2022 address to the U.S. Congress, as well as a new community engagement–focused persuasive speech on banned books and school libraries. Both speeches are fully annotated in the text and available in video form on Achieve.

**A revised and personalized Speech Choices case study feature** helps students apply what they learn from the experiences of speech student, Rafaela, to situations they encounter in their own lives. New to this edition, questions at the end of each vignette prompt students to consider their own speech choices during each phase of the speechmaking process and encourage metacognitive reflection about which choices produce the most effective results.

# ACKNOWLEDGMENTS

We would like to offer special thanks to Joan Feinberg, former copresident of Macmillan Learning, and Denise Wydra, former president of Bedford/St. Martin's, for convening the meeting that gave birth to this project, providing an exceptional team of editorial and developmental support, and seeing multiple editions of our book all the way through to completion. We offer our warmest thanks to Senior Program Director for Communication Erika Gutierrez for working with us for over fifteen years to select, refine, and implement new ideas, innovations, and features through what will now be six editions of *Speak Up!* We would also like to thank Macmillan Learning's Vice President of Editorial Leasa Burton and Executive Development Manager Susan McLaughlin. Shepherding any textbook from manuscript to production is a daunting task, even more so when working with an innovative idea that creates new challenges. We appreciate their enthusiasm and professionalism. Finally, we would like to thank Simon Glick. Simon played a major role in the creation of our first edition and we always greatly enjoyed collaborating with him.

It was also an absolute pleasure to continue our collaboration with professional artist Peter Arkle. Peter's ability to depict our ideas in pictures is simply amazing. His illustrations are a large part of what makes this text provocative, fun, and engaging.

For the sixth edition of *Speak Up!*, we were very pleased to have Christina Lembo join the team as our Senior Development Editor. Christina did an outstanding job working with us to develop and implement the incorporation of photos into our book, providing excellent editorial suggestions for achieving our goals for sixth edition revisions, and coordinating all the logistics required to get our book out on time. Development Editor Kimberly Roberts also deserves a huge round of thanks for her focus, enthusiasm, and attention to detail in managing the assessments accompanying the text. We are very thankful to the incredible professionals who guided the production and design of *Speak Up!*, including Senior Design Services Manager Natasha Wolfe. Senior Content Project Manager Peter Jacoby expertly guided the process from manuscript through pages, delivering page proofs with great efficiency and helping us with the tricky business of making each page look its best. Senior Workflow Project Manager Paul Rohloff kept production on track, and the team at Lumina Datamatics put in the hard and careful work needed to turn hundreds of manuscript pages with hundreds of illustrations and photos into a finished product, as did Director of Rights and Permissions Hilary Newman, Permissions Associate Maisie Howell, and Permissions Editor Allison Ziebka-Viering, who lined up permissions for the book's new photos and sample speeches. We also thank Senior Media Editor Julia Domenicucci, Media Editorial Assistant Erin Peraza, and Advanced Media Project Manager Sarah O'Connor Kepes for all their work developing Achieve for *Speak Up!* This will be a valuable resource for both instructors and students.

Beyond collaborating with the many people who helped to produce this book, we have been fortunate to work with a crackerjack marketing team. We love working with Marketing Manager Melissa Rodriguez, who helped develop our marketing and sales message.

We want to thank Nancy Fraleigh of Fresno City College, Steve Vrooman of Texas Lutheran University and Chrys Egan of Salisbury University, who authored the instructor materials for earlier editions of the text.

In addition, we would like to thank Dr. Monica Summers and Dr. Chadley James for sharing their expertise with us as we revised Chapter 1 in this sixth edition.

We are also grateful to the many reviewers who gave us feedback on *Speak Up!* and helped us make it even better. The input of our colleagues in the public speaking profession played a central role in our decisions for revising the prior edition, and they offered both validation for what was working and constructive suggestions for improvement. For the sixth edition, we would like to thank Amy Arellano, Boise State University; Cameron Basquiat, College of Southern Nevada; Barbara Ruth Burke, University of Minnesota, Morris; Chantele S. Carr, Estrella Mountain Community College; Christy N. Carter, Harper College; Natalie Dudchock, Jefferson State Community College; Keeli H. Fawcett, Appalachian State University; Diane M. Ferrero-Paluzzi, Iona College; Jeffrey W. Fox, Northern Kentucky University; Matthew Bruce Ingram, Dakota State University; Peggy Kendall, Bethel University; Cynthia Langham, University of Detroit Mercy; Christopher M. Leland, Azusa Pacific University; Douglas J. Marshall, Southern University at New Orleans; Jermaine Martinez, Northern Arizona University; Stephanie Poole Martinez, Saint Edward's University; Shellie Michael, Volunteer State Community College; Daniel McRoberts, Northcentral Technical College; Mumba Mumba, Lewis and Clark Community College; D. Carolina Ramos, Laredo Community College; and Dawn Pfeifer Reitz, Pennsylvania State University Berks.

We would like to thank our own speech teachers and forensics coaches for their contributions to our development as public speakers and teachers. We thank our faculty colleagues for their support and understanding as we balance teaching, writing, and other academic responsibilities. We are grateful for the many students and forensics team members who have worked with us to develop and present speeches over the past thirty-nine years, and we hope that our book will help a new generation of students gain public speaking skills and confidence.

Our friendship began at the 1977 Governor's Cup Speech and Debate Tournament in Sacramento, California. This is our seventh major book project, and it continues to be both a privilege and a pleasure to write together. Our families have been exceptional at supporting our work and serving as sounding boards for ideas. Our kids—Douglas, Helen, Nate, and Whitney—have their own careers and families now, but we continue to value their strategic input (and input from their significant others) as we make revisions. For thirty-plus years our wives, Kirsten and Nancy, have encouraged and supported our writing and contributed valuable ideas to our projects. Needless to say, their love, patience, and intelligence have sustained and focused us through all our collaborations. We appreciate the opportunity to continue to share ideas and write with each other—something we will do long after *Speak Up!* is (hopefully) in its tenth edition.

Douglas M. Fraleigh
Joseph S. Tuman

Achieve for *Speak Up!* sets a new standard for driving student learning in your public speaking course by way of powerful learning content, engaging activities, and actionable insights and analytics. Achieve brings together all of the features that instructors and students loved about our previous platform, LaunchPad—interactive e-book, LearningCurve adaptive quizzing and other assessments, interactive learning activities, and extensive instructor resources—all within a new, enhanced technology platform carefully built over the past five years.

macmillanlearning.com/achieve

## PROVEN STUDENT SUCCESS

Macmillan Learning's Learning Science & Insights team has conducted extensive research to inform the development of Achieve. Their research has shown that students who use more of their courses' assignments and have higher grades on those assignments in Achieve also have higher exam scores.[*] In addition:

- 88% of students said Achieve was easy to use.
- 82% of students agreed that Achieve helped them develop, practice, and apply skills associated with their course.
- 80% of instructors agree that Achieve helped students improve their knowledge of the course material.

To learn more about Learning Science & Insights, please visit: **macmillanlearning .com/learning-science**.

## BENEFITS

### Powerful Learning Content

**E-book.** Macmillan Learning's e-book is an interactive version of the textbook that offers highlighting, bookmarking, and note-taking. Students can download the e-book to read offline, or to have it read aloud to them. Achieve allows instructors to assign chapter sections as homework.

---

[*]Based on a survey of Achieve users in the fall of 2021 with over 200 instructor and over 3,000 student responses

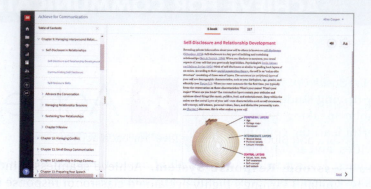

**Adaptive Quizzing.** LearningCurve Adaptive Quizzing provides personalized question sets and clear feedback based on each student's correct and incorrect answers—offering an easy way for students to prepare for class by reviewing the e-book and then assessing their understanding of the key concepts.

**Video.** A powerful video program in Achieve allows students to identify and reflect on actual public speaking strategies played out in both real and simulated contexts. Achieve includes a complete video collection with exemplars and needs improvement examples, using current, in demand clips from high-quality sources, with original content. Accompanying assessment makes these video activities assignable, with results reporting to the Achieve gradebook. All videos are closed-captioned.

## Engaging Activities

**Instructor Activity Guides.** Instructor Activity Guides provide instructors with a structured plan for using Achieve's active learning opportunities in both face-to-face and remote learning public speaking courses. Each guide offers step-by-step instructions—from pre-class reflection to in-class engagement to post-class follow-up. The guides include suggestions for discussion questions, group work, presentations, and simulations, with estimated class time, implementation effort, and Bloom's taxonomy level for each activity.

**iClicker Classroom Response System.** Achieve seamlessly integrates iClicker, Macmillan Learning's highly acclaimed classroom response system. iClicker can help make any classroom—in person or virtual—more lively, engaging, and productive.

**Instructor Resources.** Achieve provides a full suite of instructor resources to foster active learning, all in one place. For *Speak Up!* these include the Instructor's Resource Manual, lecture slides, iClicker slides, and more.

## Actionable Data and Insights

**Summative Assessment.** Chapter quizzes and test bank questions provided in Achieve allow students to demonstrate what they've learned. The test bank contains thousands of questions meticulously checked against the updated content of the text. Instructors can assign out-of-the-box exams or create their own by:

- Choosing from thousands of questions in our database
- Filtering questions by type, topic, difficulty, and Bloom's level
- Customizing multiple-choice questions
- Integrating their own questions into the exam

Exam/quiz results report to a Gradebook that lets instructors monitor student progress individually and classwide.

**Learning Objectives, Reports, and Insights.** Achieve's Insights and Reports provide powerful analytics—viewable in an elegant dashboard—that offer instructors a window into student progress against learning objectives and facilitate lessons that are specifically tailored to students' needs.

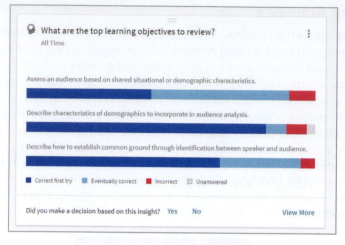

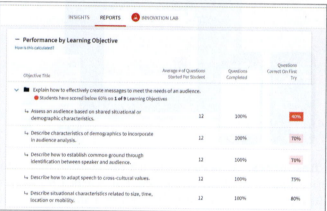

**Reflection and Goal-Setting Surveys.** These checkpoint surveys help the instructor learn how students are doing beyond just their grade achievement to target interventions and accommodations that can help them achieve more in the course.

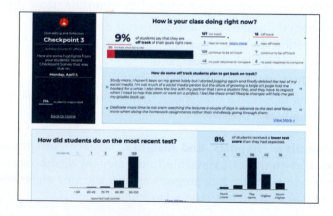

## Enhanced Platform

**Next-Generation Technology.** Achieve provides a cleaner, more intuitive, mobile-friendly interface. Designed for the Cloud, it has better monitoring tools and enables faster response to issues, allowing us to improve on our uptime. It is generally more scalable and extensible, so it can support future products and customer needs.

**Integration.** Achieve can be integrated with the tools of your choice—including the iClicker Student Response system or your LMS (Blackboard, Canvas, D2L, or Moodle). For more information, visit macmillanlearning.com/solutions/LMS -Integration or speak with your local sales representative.

**Accessibility.** Macmillan Learning strives to create products that are usable by all learners and meet universally applied accessibility standards. For more information, visit: macmillanlearning.com/accessibility.

**Learn More:** macmillanlearning.com/achieve
**Customer Support:** macmillanlearning.com/Contact-Us/Training-and-Demos
**Ordering Information:** store.macmillanlearning.com or contact your local sales representative

# INTRODUCING PUBLIC SPEAKING

**1**

> ❝With public speaking, you can advocate for what is important to you.❞

Simone Biles was no stranger to performing on some of the world's largest stages. As a gymnast, she had thrilled countless spectators in packed arenas and viewers watching on TV as she won Olympic medals. On September 15, 2021, however, she faced a daunting challenge. Along with gymnasts McKayla Maroney, Maggie Nichols, and Aly Raisman, Biles spoke to the Senate Judiciary Committee about the FBI's failure to properly investigate former Olympic and National Team doctor Larry Nasser—a man accused of sexually abusing hundreds of athletes who is currently serving a sixty-year prison sentence. Each of the four gymnasts courageously shared her story and provided powerful testimony, calling on the Senate Committee to hold accountable all who enabled the doctor's abuse.

It was not easy to speak up in this forum. Biles told the committee that she could "imagine no place that I would be less comfortable right now than sitting here in front of you, sharing these comments."[1] Sexual victimization is largely unreported, yet Biles said that she felt compelled and empowered to speak out: "I sit before you today to raise my voice so that no little girl must endure what I,

◀ **Public Speaking in Action.** Olympic gymnast Simone Biles told the Senate Judiciary Committee that she felt compelled and empowered to share her experiences.   Bloomberg/Getty Images

the athletes at this table, and the countless others who needlessly suffered under Nassar's guise of medical treatment . . . continue to endure today."[2] By having the courage to speak out about her experiences, she showed other victims that they are not alone.

Public speaking may be challenging for many reasons—apprehension about being in front of an audience, anxiety caused by a lack of preparation, or (as in the case of Biles) the context of the situation you are in. But Simone Biles's testimony also provides a compelling example of the *importance* of public speaking, and the power involved in making your voice heard. Whether you are addressing a national audience or a local one, public speaking is a vital skill for anyone looking to inform, influence, or persuade others. That's why the goal of *Speak Up!* is to help you learn to overcome any challenges and be prepared to speak, especially when it is really important for you to express your message.

Because there are likely to be many times in life when it is important to speak out, public speaking is highly useful in school, at work, and beyond. Each year, the National Association of Colleges and Employers (NACE) surveys employers to determine the competencies college graduates need for career readiness. One key competency is communication, including public speaking skills and the ability to express ideas understandably to coworkers and the public. That being said, a NACE survey noted that less than half of the employers surveyed rated recent college graduates as proficient in communication.[3] A public speaking course helps you master skills that will enable you not only to advance in your career but also to excel in other courses (especially your major) *and* make valuable contributions in other areas of your life—such as by taking an active role in the community.

Of course, for reasons noted above, you may find the thought of giving a speech terrifying. If so, you're not alone. A survey by Randolph H. Whitworth and Claudia Cochran found that public speaking is Americans' number one fear, and another researcher noted that many people find it "even scarier than rattlesnakes."[4] But you *can* learn to master public speaking—just as most people learn to read, ride a bicycle, or keep up with the latest technology. In our fifty-plus years of teaching public speaking, we've seen thousands of students gain confidence and lose their fear of public speaking as they acquire experience with it.

This book walks you through the steps you need to follow in order to create and deliver an effective speech—one that will get a favorable response from your listeners. In the chapters that follow, we explain each step in clear terms and show you how to make smart choices at each stage of the speech preparation process. We supplement these explanations with illustrations and photos designed to help you grasp and remember key points, while often entertaining you in the process.

But before we jump into the process of preparing and delivering an effective speech, we use this chapter to explore the field of public speaking, beginning

with an examination of the process itself. We then take a closer look at the benefits of studying public speaking, survey its rich tradition, and finally consider contemporary trends in the study of public speaking.

## WHAT IS PUBLIC SPEAKING?

What is public speaking, exactly? When done effectively, this activity has several characteristics that distinguish it from other types of communication.

### Public Speaking Features Communication between a Speaker and an Audience

In public speaking, the speaker does most of the talking, while the audience primarily listens. However, that does not mean audience members don't respond to what they're hearing. Audience members may smile, frown, or look puzzled. Talented speakers recognize these signals and modify their message if needed—for example, clarifying a point when they notice confused expressions on their listeners' faces. Audience members might even respond with more than just silent facial expressions. For instance, they may applaud the speaker or shout out words of encouragement and appreciation if they're pleased with or excited by the speaker's message. Or they may boo or heckle the speaker if they disagree with the message. However, in public speaking, even the most energetic interjections are usually brief. For the majority of the speech, the speaker "has the floor."

## Public Speaking Is Audience Centered

In public speaking, presenters choose their messages with the audience's interests and needs in mind. Good speakers consider what topics would be appropriate for their audience on a particular occasion. They also develop their messages in a way that their audience will find interesting and understandable.

For example, suppose you recently got hired as a product developer at a furniture company. You've asked to meet with members of the company's management team to discuss a new line of dorm furniture that you'd like to launch. At the meeting, your goal will be to persuade your listeners to approve funding for this new furniture. In preparing your speech, you determine what members of the management team care about most: the company's profitability—its ability to increase revenue while reducing costs. With that in mind, you develop explanations for how the proposed campaign will enhance profitability ("This new line will increase sales by 10 percent over the next two quarters, cut our expenses by 5 percent, and lead to a 6 percent increase in profitability"). You make sure to avoid marketing-style language ("This new design is bold and provocative") because you know that such language will hold little interest for your business-oriented listeners.

## Public Speaking Emphasizes the Spoken Word

Speakers can supplement their speeches with pictures, charts, videos, handouts, objects, or even a live demonstration. However, public speakers devote most of their time to *speaking* to their audience. The spoken word plays the central role in their message, although speakers use gestures, posture, voice intonation, eye contact, other types of body language, and even presentation aids to heighten the effect of their words.

## Public Speaking Is Usually a Prepared Presentation

Few public speakers simply walk up to the lectern or podium and make up their talk on the spot. The best speakers choose their topic in advance, carefully consider what they might say about that topic, and then select the best ideas for the audience they will be addressing. They organize those ideas, choose their words carefully, and practice delivering the speech before the big day. Even people who suspect that they may be called on to deliver an impromptu speech—for example, at a community-service awards dinner—know how to quickly piece together a few comments as they step to the front of the room; that way, they have an idea of what they will say when they begin their speech.

## YOU ARE A PUBLIC SPEAKER WHEN

## YOU ARE NOT A PUBLIC SPEAKER WHEN

# WHY STUDY PUBLIC SPEAKING?

As you make your way through life—completing your degree, advancing in your career, establishing yourself in a neighborhood or community—you will sometimes find yourself in situations in which you need to express your ideas to others. By studying and practicing public speaking, you can learn to deliver effective presentations in each of these contexts. Public speaking skills give you the power to share your ideas and bring about needed change in the world around you.

Public speaking skills can also come in handy in everyday situations. As you become more comfortable with public speaking, you will find yourself more confident about asking a question at a meeting or speaking up when hanging out with new people. You will also be equipped to speak on the fly if you are asked to give a toast, accept an award, or make a presentation at the last minute.

## Using Public Speaking as a Student

Of course, you'll need to start practicing your public speaking skills to get through this class. But the skills you acquire by working your way through this book will help you as you complete your degree and participate in additional educational opportunities throughout your life. Those later opportunities may include adult-education workshops, higher-level degrees, or professional development courses. Instructors in all types of courses may ask students to stand up on the first day of class and introduce themselves as well as explain what they hope to get out of the class. You can check out an example of this type of presentation in the Speech Choices feature at the end of the chapter.

---

▼ **Speaking Up on Campus.** Juvanie Piquant, a student leader at the City University of New York, speaks out against a proposed tuition hike. Erik McGregor/Getty Images

Many instructors also require students to deliver oral presentations on research projects and other coursework. Students with strong public speaking skills can share their findings more effectively than those with a limited background in presenting speeches. Think about students who have given oral presentations in your classes. Most likely you've noticed that those who give thoughtfully crafted and skillfully delivered presentations make a better impression on the instructor *and* the rest of the class. Equally important, the information they offer is probably more useful to listeners than the information delivered by less skilled speakers.

As you approach graduation, your college may require you to deliver an oral presentation to show what you have learned. For example, engineering majors might have to explain their senior project to a panel of local construction managers, or business majors might have to pitch an idea for a product to a faculty committee. Colleges are increasingly having students submit an ePortfolio of their work as a way to assess student learning, often requiring them to upload an oral presentation, among other assignments.[5]

Public speaking skills also enhance your ability to participate in campus activities. If you belong to an organization or a club, team, sorority, or fraternity, you may want to speak out at a group meeting or represent your group before the student senate or other campus organizations. When you present an effective speech to these audiences, you boost your chances of achieving your goal—whether it's persuading your sorority to take up a new social cause or convincing the student senate to fund a campus job fair related to your major.

## Using Public Speaking in Your Career

A knack for public speaking is one of the most important assets you can possess in the workplace. A 2021 NACE survey found that almost three-fourths of the employers responding said that they look for verbal communication skills on job applicants' résumés.[6] Employees agree that communication skills are important. In the survey "Making the Grade? What American Workers Think Should Be Done to Improve Education," 87 percent of the 1,014 U.S. adult workers surveyed rated communication skills as very important for performing their jobs.[7]

The importance of public speaking is not limited to careers that might first come to mind, such as law or politics. As Dr. Mónica Feliú-Mójer, director of communications and outreach for CienciaPR, notes, members of the scientific community regularly present talks and interact with diverse audiences. This requires "transmitting your message clearly and concisely," "engaging your audience," and answering the "why does it matter" question.[8] No matter which career path you choose, you'll almost certainly need public speaking skills. Consider the following examples:

- A firefighting trainer needs to provide more advanced workshops for firefighters as wildfires in the United States reach record numbers. Yet due to the COVID-19 pandemic, face-to-face training is restricted in many areas. The trainer develops virtual training presentations so that these vital workers can continue to gain the skills they need.

- A city engineer addresses an angry crowd of citizens at a city council meeting following a news report that a heavily traveled local bridge has safety issues. The engineer calmly reassures the public that repairs will be made immediately and describes the repairs in a way that the audience can understand.

- An information technology professional creates a podcast for a company's sales force, explaining how to use a new software app to track prospective customers.

As another example, baseball Hall of Famer Lou Gehrig was planning to major in engineering at Columbia University before the Yankees came calling, and neither of those career paths are typically associated with public speaking. Nevertheless, he delivered one of the most compelling presentations in American history. After being diagnosed with amyotrophic lateral sclerosis (ALS), he was honored in a ceremony at Yankee Stadium. His eloquent remarks, sometimes called "Baseball's Gettysburg Address," are perhaps even more memorable than his four Most Valuable Player awards.[9] If you'd like to view it, search for "Gehrig's Farewell Address" on YouTube.

## Using Public Speaking in Your Community

Beyond work or school, you may wear many different hats in your community. You might be active in service organizations, athletic leagues, clubs, religious groups, or political committees. If you're a parent, you may find yourself taking on leadership roles in your children's schools, sports teams, clubs, or other activities. You may also decide to get involved in a social cause you feel passionate about. In each of these endeavors, public speaking skills can help you.

For example, Tammy Duckworth, a Black Hawk helicopter pilot, received a Purple Heart for being wounded in action after her aircraft was hit by a grenade near Baghdad, Iraq, in 2004. When she returned to the United States, she decided to enter public service. Ms. Duckworth was appointed to a Department of Veterans Affairs post, where she advocated for veterans' issues, such as therapy for post–traumatic stress disorder. She next used her public speaking skills on the campaign trail, earning election to the House of Representatives twice and then to the Senate in 2016. She continues to be a passionate advocate for veterans and for women's rights. Because Senate rules require in-person voting, Ms. Duckworth made history when she cast a vote on the Senate floor, accompanied by her newborn daughter, Maile.[10]

To play an active role in issues that concern you, you will also need to speak out. The health of a democratic, self-governing society like ours depends on **civic engagement**, or active public participation in political affairs and social and community organizations. Public speaking skills facilitate civic engagement. College students who actively participate in public discussion or political activities are more likely to be confident in their ability to make a difference in their communities.[11]

▲ **Speaking Up in the Community.** Sen. Tammy Duckworth introduces rock star Joe Walsh at a VetsAid benefit concert. Paul Morigi/Getty Images

Throughout life, you may also be asked to speak in less formal situations—for example, by offering a wedding toast or presenting an award to a friend or colleague who is retiring. In each of these cases, the skills you learn in a public speaking class will help ensure that others hear and respect your views.

## PUBLIC SPEAKING: A HISTORICAL TRADITION

For centuries, people around the world have studied the art and practice of public speaking and used public address to inform, influence, and persuade others. As far back as the fifth century BCE, all adult male citizens in the Greek city-state of Athens had a right to speak out in the assembly and vote on proposals relating to civic matters. Sometimes as many as six thousand citizens attended these meetings.[12] Indeed, the ancient Greeks were the first people to think formally about and teach **rhetoric**, the craft of public speaking. Socrates and Plato are two of the best-known examples of these rhetoricians. And in the fourth

century BCE, the Greek scholar Aristotle wrote *Rhetoric*, a systematic analysis of the art and practice of public speaking that still influences the study of the subject today. The study of public speaking also arose in first-century BCE Rome, where senators vehemently debated the issues of the day. Cicero, a Roman politician, was a renowned orator and a prolific writer on rhetoric, while another noteworthy Roman rhetorician, Quintilian, emphasized the ideal of an ethical orator—the good person speaking well.

The tradition of public speaking is not limited to Greece and Rome: it's been practiced in many regions throughout history. From the time of Confucius in the fifth century BCE until the end of the third century BCE, China enjoyed an intellectual climate whose energy rivaled that of ancient Greece.[13] Scholars traveling throughout China passionately advocated a variety of systems of political and economic philosophy. In fifteenth-century western Africa, traveling storytellers recited parables and humorous stories, while in northeastern Africa, Islamic scholars embarked on lecture tours attended by large crowds.[14] On feast days in one African kingdom (near present-day Mali), it was traditional for a bard to dress in a bird's-head mask and deliver a speech encouraging the king to live up to his predecessors' high standards.[15] In seventeenth-century India, a speaker's words were valued over other means of communication, and inscribed versions of the messages were referred to as "treasure houses of the Goddess of Speech."[16]

Indigenous Peoples in North America prized oratory, too; indeed, many deemed oratorical ability a more important leadership quality than bravery in battle.[17]

The United States also has a rich history of public speaking. During the Great Awakening of the 1730s and 1740s, preachers sought to revive waning religious zeal in the colonies, often preaching in fields to accommodate the many listeners. During the American Revolution in the second half of the eighteenth century, colonists took to the streets to passionately denounce British policies and call for independence. In the 1770s and 1780s, political leaders in each of the states energetically debated the merits of ratifying the U.S. Constitution and the Bill of Rights.

In the nineteenth century, public speaking became a hallmark of American society, as people debated political issues, expanded their knowledge, and even entertained one another. Political debates drew particularly large and enthusiastic crowds, such as the debates between Abraham Lincoln and Stephen Douglas during the Illinois Senate election. More than fifteen thousand people gathered to hear the contenders in Freeport, Illinois—a town with just five thousand residents.[18]

The antislavery movement of this time also used public speaking to drive major social change. Frederick Douglass, a formerly enslaved person who moved audiences with his depictions of life under slavery, counted among the most compelling antislavery speakers. Women also actively participated in the American Anti-Slavery Society, holding offices and delivering public lectures. Angelina Grimké was one of these eloquent orators, who won audience members' commitment to the antislavery cause with graphic descriptions of the abuse experienced by enslaved people that she witnessed while growing up in South Carolina. Other women—such as Elizabeth Cady Stanton, Susan B. Anthony, and Lucy Stone—took leadership roles in the women's suffrage movement, which arose in the mid-1800s and continued into the early 1900s. These able orators used fiery speeches to convince Americans that women deserved the right to cast a ballot at the polls—a radical notion at the time.[19]

During the twentieth century, public address continued to play a key role in American and world affairs, especially from political leaders throughout both world wars and the Great Depression. In August 1963, 250,000 people gathered near the Lincoln Memorial in Washington, D.C., to hear Martin Luther King Jr. deliver his "I Have a Dream" speech, an address that instantly excited the imaginations of people around the world.[20] In June of that same year, President John F. Kennedy traveled to Berlin to speak to an audience of over 400,000, voicing his support for those blocked in by the Berlin Wall—built by East German leaders after World War II to prevent immigration to the West. Kennedy famously showed his solidarity with Berliners by declaring "Ich bin ein Berliner" (I am a Berliner). Twenty-four years later, President Ronald Reagan traveled to the Brandenburg Gate in Berlin and challenged Russian leader Mikhail Gorbachev with the iconic words, "Mr. Gorbachev, tear down this wall!" The wall was finally opened in 1989.

Speaking out remains an important tool for advocacy in the twenty-first century. Within minutes of the June 26, 2015, ruling that the Constitution guaranteed marriage equality, a crowd gathered outside the U.S. Supreme Court building, where lead plaintiff Jim Obergefell addressed supporters and the Washington,

## PUBLIC SPEAKING: AN ENDURING LEGACY

D.C., Gay Men's Chorus sang the national anthem. And after the murder of George Floyd on May 25, 2020, many speakers delivered passionate speeches during protests and rallies demanding justice for Mr. Floyd and other victims of police violence. One example was Youa Vang, who had lost her own son, Fong Lee, to police violence in 2006. Speaking in her native language at a Hmong for Black Lives rally, she noted that many in the Black community had supported her after Fong's death and called for her own community to demand justice for George Floyd.[21]

Today, new means of digital communication (social media, smartphones, videoconferences) allow people to use technology to connect with distant audiences almost instantly. When public gatherings were restricted due to the COVID-19 pandemic, many speeches were necessarily delivered virtually. For example, when National Women's Soccer Team Captain Megan Rapinoe addressed a congressional committee on Equal Pay Day in 2021, she spoke via video. A survey of experts in technology, communications, and social change by Pew Research and Elon University found a consensus that even after the pandemic, "larger segments of the population will rely on digital connections" in a "'tele-everything' world."[22] Nevertheless, thousands and sometimes hundreds of thousands of people continue to come to in-person rallies to hear speakers address issues

ranging from women's rights to immigration to gun policy. From presidential State of the Union addresses to Academy Awards acceptance speeches to town hall presentations, public speaking before a live audience remains an important part of our social fabric. Furthermore, even when your presentation is virtual, using fundamental public speaking skills remains essential—though you will face unique challenges when using technology to speak out. You will learn more about mastering these challenges in Chapter 15 on mediated public speaking.

## PUBLIC SPEAKING: A DYNAMIC DISCIPLINE

Clearly, public speaking has a long history, and many of the principles taught by ancient scholars such as Aristotle are still relevant today. However, it's also a dynamic discipline that has evolved to reflect changes in society. In this section, we highlight several of these major changes—new ways of depicting the public speaking process, ever-expanding channels for communication, greater awareness of audiences' diversity, new emphasis on the importance of critical thinking in preparing a speech, and increasing attention to ethics in public address.

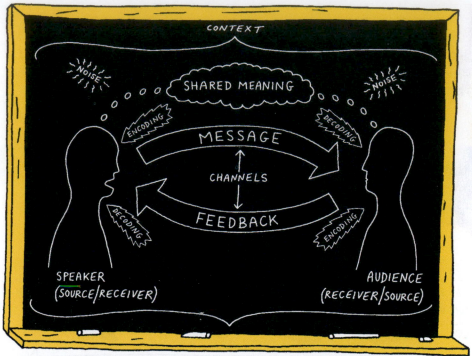

## A MODEL OF COMMUNICATION

## From Linear to Transactional: Evolving Views of the Public Speaking Process

At the dawn of the modern communication disciplines, scholars viewed all forms of communication—including public speaking—as a linear process. In their view, a speech was a one-way flow of ideas from speaker to audience. That is, speakers "injected" listeners with their ideas, much as a doctor injects a patient with a vaccine.

A linear model includes several key elements. Specifically, a person with an idea to express is the **source**, and the ideas that this person conveys to the audience constitute the **message**. The source must **encode** the message, which involves choosing **verbal** and **nonverbal symbols** to express the ideas. Verbal symbols are the words that the source uses. Nonverbal symbols are the means of making a point without the use of words, such as hand gestures, eye contact, and facial expressions. In a particularly poignant example of nonverbal communication, activist X González remained silent for six-plus minutes during a speech at the Washington, D.C., March for Our Lives rally—the length of the mass shooting that took the lives of seventeen of their classmates at Marjory Stoneman Douglas High School.

The source communicates the encoded message through a **channel**, the medium of delivery. For example, to deliver their message, speakers can use their voices to address a small group, rely on a microphone or the broadcast

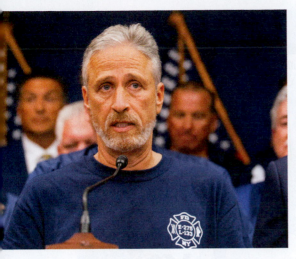

▲ **We Are Both Channels.** At left, comedian Jon Stewart takes a serious approach, speaking to a live audience after passage of the 9/11 Victims' Compensation Fund Act. At right, an Elvis impersonator officiates a vow renewal ceremony virtually.

SOPA Images/Getty Images; Ethan Miller/Getty Images

airwaves to give a speech to a huge crowd, or even podcast a speech so that it can be heard at different times in different locations. Increasingly, speeches can be experienced through different channels. Presentations for TED, 99U, and the Moth, for example, can be viewed live and also accessed online.

In the linear model, sources communicate their message to one or more **receivers**, who try to make sense of the message by decoding. To **decode**, receivers process the source's verbal and nonverbal symbols and form their own perception of the message's meaning.

**Noise** (also called **interference**) is a phenomenon that disrupts communication between source and receiver. Noise may be caused by external sources (for example, when a speech is drowned out by a fleet of jets roaring overhead). But noise can also originate internally—within the source or the source's listeners. For instance, a student giving an oral presentation in class might forget key elements of her speech if she is preoccupied with a recent argument with a coworker. Meanwhile, her audience members might have difficulty focusing on her message if they, too, are distracted by their own thoughts and concerns, such as a push alert on their smartphone.

Today, scholars have modified this view to consider communication—including public speaking—to be transactional and not a one-way activity. Although many of the elements of the linear model remain in play, a **transaction** is a communicative exchange in which all participants continuously send *and* receive messages.[23] For example, suppose you're about to deliver a speech. As you organize your notes at the lectern, you notice a man yawning in the front row of your audience. In this case, the man is both a receiver of your message

and a sender of his own message: "I hope you're not planning to talk for two hours."

Participants in a public speaking transaction can also send and receive messages by providing **feedback** in the form of verbal or nonverbal responses. An audience member who shouts "That's right!" in response to a compelling point in a speech is giving feedback. People listening to a speech can also provide nonverbal feedback. For example, an audience member can lean forward to express interest, nod vigorously to show agreement, fold her arms to signal disagreement, or adopt a puzzled look to convey confusion. Audiences may use the like or comment feature to provide feedback during a virtual speech.

In the transactional model of communication, the participants in a public speaking exchange seek to create **shared meaning**—a common understanding with little confusion and few misinterpretations.[24] Good public speakers don't merely try to get their point of view across to their audience. Instead, they strive to improve their own knowledge, seek understanding, and develop agreements when they communicate with others.[25]

For example, suppose an audience member nods when the speaker says, "Hackers took personal data from more than 530 million Facebook user profiles in 106 countries and posted it on a public site."[26] The speaker must assume the role of *receiver* and decode the message behind that nod. The nod could mean either "I agree" or "Well, duh, we all know that. Move on!" To better decode the message, a speaker may look for additional cues, such as signs of understanding or boredom on the faces of other audience members. Imagine that the speaker

## SHARED MEANING

determines that the nod conveys agreement that this potential loss of privacy is a serious problem. They might respond by saying, "Because we agree that using Facebook can put our privacy at risk, let's take a look at how we can protect ourselves." Audience members then smile and nod. Now, audience and speaker have created shared meaning.

## New Technologies, New Channels

For thousands of years, public speaking was conducted exclusively face-to-face. Whether it was our ancient ancestors planning a hunt around a campfire or Susan B. Anthony calling for equal rights for nineteenth-century women, speaker and audience were at the same location.

The rise of new communication technologies changed this, providing speakers with ever-expanding options for bringing their message to an audience. In 1923, Calvin Coolidge delivered the first presidential address broadcast on radio, and just twenty-four years later, President Harry S. Truman delivered the first televised presidential address.[27] In the late twentieth century, the development of the Internet introduced even more channels for public speaking and many more continue to be developed today.[28] Speakers can now present live speeches to remote audiences using technologies such as Zoom, Google Meet, or RingCentral. During the COVID-19 pandemic, you probably participated in remote learning at your college or high school using these types of technologies. Communicators can also create podcasts or make digital recordings of their speeches available on platforms such as YouTube.

Although technological innovation presents many options for speakers to reach audiences, face-to-face public speaking is unlikely to go the way of the passenger pigeon or landline phone anytime soon. If you, like most of us, have had a text message misinterpreted, then you know the risks of remote communication firsthand. The connection that is created when speaker and audience are physically present is very powerful. As Mina Chang, CEO of Linking the World, explained, "Prioritization of speed over face time grossly underestimates the power of human interaction and the importance of face-to-face communication." This is because "you do business with people, not entities. The beauty of communication is found in the nuance that's only felt in face-to-face conversations."[29]

## Awareness of Audiences' Diversity

Effective public speakers consider the diversity of their audience members and craft a message that respects the diversity of that audience and of society as a whole. There are multiple dimensions of diversity to consider, including age, gender identity, ethnicity, disability status, and sexual orientation. We elaborate on how speakers should take diversity into account when crafting and presenting their message throughout this text (for example, see Chapter 5, Audience Analysis), but we look at a couple of specific examples here to begin.

**Gender identity** is one dimension of diversity. The Human Rights Campaign defines gender identity as "one's innermost concept of self as male, female, a blend of both or neither."[30] A wide variety of people, including those who identify as **nonbinary** (not identifying as exclusively male or female) may use pronouns other than *he/him* or *she/her*. For example, the singer Demi Lovato uses the pronouns *they/them*, because these pronouns allow them "to feel most authentic and true to the person I both know I am and still am discovering."[31] Lovato used Twitter to share a video disclosing this decision.

**Ethnicity**, another dimension of diversity, refers to the cultural background that is usually associated with shared religion, national origin, and language. By **cultural background**, we mean the values, traditions, and rules for living that are passed from generation to generation.[32] Culture is learned, and it influences all aspects of a person's life, including not only religion and language but also behaviors such as food choices, dress, and ways of communicating with others.

---

▼ **Demi Lovato Shares Their Gender Identity via Video.** Demi Lovato selected a mediated channel, a Twitter video, to explain how their pronouns best reflect their identity. This choice let Lovato reach a wide audience, with over 7 million views.

**Demi Lovato** ✔
@ddlovato

Every day we wake up, we are given another opportunity & chance to be who we want & wish to be. I've spent the majority of my life growing in front of all of you... you've seen the good, the bad, & everything in between.

▶ 7.1M views                                    1:09 / 1:28

3:10 AM · May 19, 2021

In the United States, public speakers have increasingly needed to consider the range of cultures represented by their audience members as the nation has grown more culturally diverse. The U.S. Census Bureau calculates a diversity index, which indicates the chance that any two people in the country who are chosen at random will be from different ethnic or racial groups. In 2020 that index was 61.1 percent, meaning that about three of every five pairs of people will be from different groups—an increase from 54.9 percent in 2010.[33] This diversity is likely to continue increasing over time. According to the Pew Research Center, based on current immigration patterns, 88 percent of U.S. population growth through 2065 will be from immigrants and their descendants. Immigrants to the United States are coming from diverse nations, with China, Mexico, India, and the Philippines contributing the most people in 2018.[34]

Effective public speakers must be sensitive to the diversity of their audience. This means they avoid biased language and ethnic jokes, and they use appropriate terms to refer to audience characteristics such as gender identity, ethnicity, and physical ability. Savvy speakers make an effort to recognize the diversity in their audience and customize their presentation so it will be interesting and meaningful to each of the people or groups who are represented.

## Emphasis on Critical Thinking

In addition to encouraging greater attention to diversity awareness, scholars of public speaking have begun emphasizing the importance of critical-thinking skills for speakers who are preparing presentations. **Critical thinking** refers to the analysis and evaluation of ideas based on reliability, truth, and accuracy. When you are engaged in critical thinking, you carefully evaluate the evidence and reasoning presented in the message.[35] You also are open-minded about your own ideas and assumptions and subject them to the same analysis that you apply to others' viewpoints.

Before you present ideas to an audience, you should feel confident that those ideas are reasonable. Rather than assuming that your beliefs are true, suspend judgment and consider other perspectives. For example, suppose you are interested in speaking about a law that requires companies to pay for new countermeasures to keep customers' personal data safe from hackers. You could research the perspectives of information technology professionals, businesses affected by the law, consumer protection organizations, legal scholars, and economists. Carefully consider the ideas of each group, and modify your opinions when new ideas make sense.

To use critical thinking, you would also evaluate the probable truth of the claims you plan to make. Anybody can make a claim, but not all claims are based on careful analysis. For example, if you are researching the ability of new technology to keep information safe from hackers, the views of a highly regarded cybersecurity consultant are more likely to be accurate than those of an angry customer who posted a rant on social media.

CRITICAL THINKING MEANS EVALUATING THE IDEAS OF OTHERS AND YOUR OWN ASSUMPTIONS

## A Focus on Free, Engaged, and Ethical Communication

Public speaking also involves careful consideration of the rights and responsibilities that come into play when individuals are free to express their ideas in a public forum. **Freedom of expression**—the right to share one's ideas and opinions free from government censorship—is vital in a democratic society, where self-governance depends on both the free flow of information and open debate.

Actively exercising your freedom of speech through civic engagement is equally essential to a democratic society. Supreme Court justice Louis Brandeis, one of the most eloquent defenders of freedom of expression, wrote that the founders of this nation believed that "the greatest menace to freedom is an inert people; that public discussion is a political duty; and that this should be a fundamental principle of the American government."[36] The National Communication Association has endorsed this principle, too, by including "Influence Public Discourse" as a learning outcome for communication students.[37] We saw this principle in action at the beginning of the chapter, with the compelling example of Simone Biles, McKayla Maroney, Maggie Nichols, and Aly Raisman. It is our hope that you will use the knowledge and experience you gain from studying public speaking to "Speak Up!" on issues that are important to you. Chapter 21 focuses on this vital skill.

Although you are guaranteed the right to express your ideas freely, as a public speaker you also have a responsibility to express your ideas ethically. **Ethics**

refers to a group's shared beliefs about what behaviors are correct or incorrect. Protecting freedom of expression and encouraging the ethical use of that right are increasingly important concerns in the field of public discourse. The principles endorsed by the National Communication Association include the following:

- "We advocate truthfulness, accuracy, honesty, and reason as essential to the integrity of communication."
- "We endorse freedom of expression, diversity of perspective, and tolerance of dissent to achieve the informed and responsible decision making fundamental to a civil society."[38]

Concerns about free expression and ethics are not a new consideration in public speaking. In the first century CE, the Roman rhetorician Quintilian argued that parents and teachers should strive to produce "the good person speaking well." That is, communicators should be virtuous, moral, and focused on the public good, in addition to being effective orators.[39] Today, as unethical communication has increased in the United States, people have stepped up their demands for ethical public speaking. Americans are tired of politicians, lawyers, and multimillionaire CEOs who blatantly lie to the public. Recent polling indicates Americans' low level of trust in society's major institutions—not only the usual suspects, such as big business and politicians, but also the Supreme Court, technology companies, and the medical system.[40] The online world also has led to new modes of unethical communication, such as trolling (posting incendiary comments to start arguments), catfishing (misrepresenting one's identity to online contacts), and disseminating fake news (spreading falsified or "grossly distorted" news stories).[41]

Consequently, ethics have begun playing an increasingly prominent role in the study of communication, as well as in other disciplines. As it turns out,

## SPEECH CHOICES

### A CASE STUDY: *RAFAELA*

What can you do to prepare and present an effective speech? What practices might hold you back? Throughout this book, we'll consider Rafaela—a college student enrolled in her first public speaking class. We'll follow Rafaela as she moves through every step in the speechmaking process, from picking a topic to working on her delivery. You can use her ideas and try to avoid her pitfalls as you prepare your own speeches. At the end of the book, you can see Rafaela's final outline and speech.

To introduce Rafaela let's take a look at the introductory biographical speech she had to give on the second day of class. It was to be a five-minute speech, and the instructor left it up to each person how much detail to share about themselves. Rafaela decided to keep some of her information basic—she'd mention her major and the fact that she wanted to go into sports medicine—but she would also share a few more personal tidbits, including that she researches her family history for fun, attends church on the weekends, and loves using Instagram to keep up with her favorite female comedians. Rafaela made a few cuts when her speech ran long during a practice run-through, and she ended up finishing up in under five minutes—just about right.

 **YOUR TURN:**

Now that you've seen how Rafaela's choices influenced her speech, it's time to consider similar choices you'll need to make for a speech of your own. Making speech choices involves asking and answering a series of questions related to your assignment. In the case of an introductory speech, those questions might include the following:

- How formal does my self-introduction need to be?

- What should I talk about? Are there specific questions our instructor asked us to address? What's the most interesting or relevant information I can share with the class to help them get to know me?

- How much time will I have to speak? How can I make sure I won't run long or short?

Making choices in response to questions like these will help you craft an introductory speech that meets your instructors' requirements—*and* stays faithful to your ideas and interests.

there's far more to public speaking than just presenting your message in a way that induces your audience to agree with you and take the actions you have advocated. You must also treat your listeners ethically. That means telling the truth, helping your audience make a well-informed decision about your topic, avoiding manipulative reasoning, and incorporating research materials properly in your speech. We discuss ethical public speaking further in Chapter 3.

**With public speaking, you can advocate for what is important to you.** In this chapter, we introduced the field of public speaking. Key elements of public speaking are communication between speaker and audience, a focus on the audience by the speaker, an emphasis on the spoken word, and a prepared presentation. We also examined the benefits of mastering public speaking—in the classroom, on the job, in the community, and in everyday situations.

Next, we turned to the rich tradition of public speaking, citing examples from across time and from around the world.

We also examined the ways in which public speaking as a discipline has evolved to reflect changes in society. We provided examples of several contemporary developments in the field—new ways of viewing the public speaking process; the effects of changing technologies; an emphasis on understanding an audience's diversity; the usefulness of critical thinking when planning a speech; and the importance of protecting, exercising, and making ethical use of freedom of expression.

## Key Terms

| | | |
|---|---|---|
| civic engagement *11* | channel *16* | gender identity *21* |
| rhetoric *11* | receiver *17* | nonbinary *21* |
| source *16* | decode *17* | ethnicity *21* |
| message *16* | noise (interference) *17* | cultural background *21* |
| encode *16* | transaction *17* | critical thinking *22* |
| verbal symbol *16* | feedback *18* | freedom of expression *23* |
| nonverbal symbol *16* | shared meaning *18* | ethics *23* |

## Review Questions

1. Describe the four basic characteristics that distinguish public speaking from other forms of communication.
2. Name and explain three ways in which becoming a competent public speaker can positively affect your life and career.
3. Define *civic engagement*, and explain how it is an important part of democratic self–government.
4. Describe the historical tradition of public speaking. Offer some examples of rhetoric playing a role in world events.
5. What is the transactional model of communication? How does it differ from the linear model?
6. How is new technology changing the nature of public speaking?
7. Why is it important to consider diversity when analyzing an audience?
8. In what ways can you employ critical thinking in a public speaking situation?
9. Why is it important for speakers to behave ethically?

## Critical Thinking Questions

1. In what ways might becoming a more effective and confident speaker affect your life? How could it affect your performance in your classes? Help you in your career? Enable you to make a difference in your community?
2. What kinds of public speaking situations are you exposed to on a daily basis? What kind of feedback do you provide to the speakers? How might this feedback affect each speaker's message?
3. How would you prepare for a speech assignment if you were going to deliver it in a classroom? Would your preparation change if you were recording your speech at home and posting it on YouTube?
4. Consider your public speaking class as an audience. In what ways are the people in the group alike? In what ways are they diverse?
5. In the 1970s, many women began using *Ms.* as an alternative to *Mrs.* or *Miss.* How is the use of *they/them* for nonbinary people similar to the change to *Ms.*? Are there ways the later change is different?
6. Think of a time you believed that a speaker was being honest with the audience and another time when you thought a speaker was being dishonest. What differences between the two speakers led you to these conclusions?
7. Name one person whom you believe to be an effective public speaker. What are the main characteristics that make that speaker effective?

## Activities

1. Review the illustration "A Model of Communication" on page 16. Then think of an example where a speaker's message could be misinterpreted. Answer the following questions: What was the speaker's message? How might an audience member decode a different message from the one that the speaker intended? What feedback might that audience member give to the speaker? Could the speaker clarify their idea to help create shared meaning?
2. In small groups, develop a list of situations in which you could suddenly be called on to give an unanticipated speech. For example, the occasion might be a wedding toast, a tribute at the retirement party of a favorite teacher, a presentation of an award, or a plea to the city council about an issue that concerns you. Have each group member select one situation and prepare a brief (one-minute) speech to deliver to the group.
3. Consider a career of interest to you. Then identify a scenario for that career in which you may be called on to speak. Jot down two or three main ideas that you would express in that speech.
4. Search for and watch soccer star Megan Rapinoe's speech at the White House on Equal Pay Day, March 24, 2021. What diverse audiences do you think Rapinoe was addressing in her speech?

# DEVELOPING YOUR FIRST SPEECH

> **Preparation and perseverance are the keys to a successful speech.**

On August 28, 1963, tens of thousands of Americans traveled huge distances to join the March on Washington for Jobs and Freedom. Gathering at the Lincoln Memorial, they sang protest songs and hymns and listened to speeches by civil rights leaders.[1] After nearly three hours, the final orator stood at the lectern and addressed an audience of about 250,000 people.[2]

With the Lincoln Memorial as a backdrop, the speaker, Martin Luther King Jr., told the audience, "I have a dream . . . a dream big enough to include all Americans."[3] The dream that King shared—one in which people would "not be judged by the color of their skin but by the content of their character"—had his listeners cheering and weeping as he concluded his address. Covered by major television networks and newspapers, the speech captured the imaginations of people around the world. In the aftermath of the March on Washington, Congress passed civil rights legislation that banned discrimination in public facilities, in laws or practices pertaining to voting rights, and by employers.

King's "I Have a Dream" speech has won renown among speech scholars as the greatest oral presentation of the twentieth century. A gifted public speaker, King won his first oratorical contest when he was just fifteen years old.[4] Yet he

---

◄ **Dr. King at the March on Washington.** Even gifted and experienced speakers invest time preparing and practicing their speeches. Bettmann/Getty Images

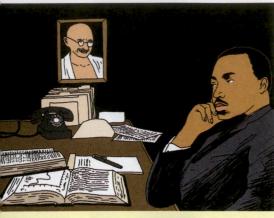

still diligently prepared for the March on Washington speech, putting even more care into it than he'd put into any of his previous public addresses.[5] Indeed, he typically invested much time in speech preparation, writing multiple drafts of his Nobel Peace Prize acceptance speech and spending as many as fifteen hours preparing a typical Sunday sermon.[6]

The careful attention that King gave to preparing his addresses illustrates an important lesson that can benefit all public speakers, whether they have experience or are new to public speaking: preparation and perseverance are the keys to a successful speech. We have found that students who have a well-organized plan for speech preparation—and who devote enough time to following that plan—become more effective speakers than those who rely solely on natural talent and confidence.

In this chapter, we provide a preview of the speech preparation process. We begin by discussing the importance of preparation. Next, we cover five major considerations you should keep in mind while preparing a public address. We then lay out steps you can follow to deliver a successful speech early in the term. Finally, we discuss a common challenge of public speaking—speech anxiety—and offer tips for minimizing it.

## WHY PREPARE?

For beginning speakers, preparation is crucial. The more rigorously you prepare your speech, the more likely you'll avoid three common problems that inexperienced public speakers typically encounter:

- *Leaving too little time for planning and practicing.* Students who wait until the last minute to develop their speeches usually deliver weaker addresses than their better-prepared classmates. Why? If you put off your assignment until just before the due date, you can't plan or practice your presentation. And without a plan or sufficient practice, you risk losing track of your thoughts while delivering your speech.

- *Focusing on length rather than quality.* Beginners sometimes focus more on meeting time requirements than on developing their ideas. They write down the first thoughts that come to mind or simply insert chunks of researched material. They don't consider what information might be most interesting, useful, or convincing to their listeners, nor do they try to organize their ideas in a way that their audience can easily follow. The result? A disjointed, lackluster presentation.

- *Failing to follow the assignment.* A speech may impress a classroom full of beginning speakers if it's delivered well and includes interesting details. Yet it will not succeed if it fails to meet your instructor's assignment regarding such matters as which topics are acceptable, how the speech should be organized, and how many sources are required. Make sure to clarify such expectations before preparing your speech.

Fortunately, you don't have to succumb to these challenges. This chapter introduces steps of the speechmaking process that will help you avoid these stumbling blocks and deliver a successful speech.

You waited until the last minute.

You focused on length, not quality.

You did not follow the assignment.

## THE CLASSICAL APPROACH TO SPEECH PREPARATION

The speech preparation process that we outline in this book is based on principles of rhetoric that have been taught and learned for over 2400 years. As we noted in Chapter 1, Aristotle wrote a systematic analysis of rhetorical practices in the fourth century BCE. Cicero (106–43 BCE)—a Roman lawyer, a politician, and one of history's most famed orators—elaborated on these concepts. During this time, rhetoric was a highly prized skill that citizens used to present and defend their ideas in public forums.

▲ **Cicero's Rhetoric in Action.** In this artistic depiction, Cicero addresses the Roman Senate, accusing the politician Catiline of conspiring to overthrow the Roman Republic. DEA PICTURE LIBRARY/Getty Images

In his treatise *De inventione*, Cicero maintained that effective speakers attend to five key matters while preparing a speech—*invention*, *arrangement*, *style*, *memory*, and *delivery*. Contemporary scholars refer to these five concepts as the **classical canons of rhetoric**. These five canons form the basis of speech preparation to this day. Here, we take a closer look at each one:

- **Invention** is the generation of ideas for use in a speech, including both the speaker's own thoughts on the topic and ideas from other sources. Speakers generate a large number of ideas for their speeches and then choose those that will best serve their purpose in an ethical manner. Talented speakers select the best ideas for a particular speech based on their analysis of their audience, their choice of topic and purpose, the research they conduct, and the evidence they gather.

- **Arrangement** refers to the structuring of ideas to convey them effectively to an audience; today, we refer to this as *organization*. Most speeches have three main parts—an introduction, a body, and a conclusion—with the body serving as the core of the speech and containing the main points. Effective speakers arrange the ideas in the body so that the message will be clear and memorable to the audience.

- **Style** is the choice of language that will best express a speaker's ideas to the audience. Through effective style, speakers state their ideas clearly, make their ideas memorable, and avoid bias.

- **Memory** (also known as *preparation*) is somewhat analogous to practice and refers to the work that speakers do to remain in command of

their material when they present a speech.[7] This canon originally emphasized techniques for learning speeches by heart and creating mental stock-
piles of words and phrases that speakers could inject into presentations
where appropriate.[8] In contemporary settings, speakers seldom recite
speeches from memory; instead, they rely on notes to remind themselves
of key ideas that they can deliver conversationally.

- **Delivery** refers to speakers' use of their voice and body during the actual
  presentation of a speech. A strong delivery—one in which the speaker's
  voice, hand gestures, eye contact, and movements are appropriate for the
  audience and setting—can make a powerful impression. Chapter 13 covers
  delivery skills in detail.

The five canons—invention, arrangement, style, memory, and delivery—
inform the steps you will follow to prepare and deliver an effective speech. Next,
we discuss how to use these principles to craft a speech. The material in this
chapter serves two purposes. First, it introduces you to the steps in the preparation process for any speech. Second, it covers information about each step
that will help you prepare for a speech that has been assigned early in the term,
before you have covered the later chapters in more detail.

## PREPARING AND DELIVERING YOUR FIRST SPEECH

It's happened: you've just begun this course, and already your instructor has
assigned your first speech. Often, this first assignment is designed to be an

## COMMON FIRST SPEECH ASSIGNMENTS

icebreaker—a speech introducing a classmate, for example, or a talk about your-self. Such assignments are usually focused on giving students an opportunity to speak in front of the class in a low-pressure situation as well as a chance to get to know one another better. Other instructors may begin with a more sub-stantive assignment, such as a three- to five-minute speech describing a hero in your community or an artifact that is significant to your culture. In either case, because the speech comes early in the term, you will not be expected to be famil-iar with all the concepts in this book. However, your instructor will have covered some of these topics and will expect to see you apply them in your presentation.

This section provides a quick guide to preparing and delivering your first speech. By following each of these steps, you should be able to pull together a workable speech and deliver it on the appointed day. Refer to your assignment description or ask your instructor which of these steps you will be responsible for, and emphasize them in your preparation. If you'd like to know more about any of these steps, use the following table to find the corresponding section and chapter where each step is discussed in more detail.

| If you want to know more about | Go to |
| --- | --- |
| analyzing your audience | Ch. 5 |
| selecting a topic for your speech | Ch. 6 |
| determining your speech's rhetorical purpose | Ch. 6, pp. 147–48 |
| creating a thesis statement | Ch. 6, pp. 152–54 |
| determining your main points | Ch. 9, pp. 213–16 |
| developing supporting materials | Chs. 7–8 |
| organizing the body of your speech | Ch. 9, pp. 216–19 |
| outlining the body of your speech | Ch. 11 |
| organizing and outlining the introduction and conclusion | Ch. 10 |
| incorporating transitions | Ch. 9, pp. 225–26; Ch. 11, p. 264 |
| considering word choice | Ch. 12 |
| considering presentation aids | Ch. 14 |
| practicing your speech | Ch. 13, pp. 315–17 |
| delivering your speech | Ch. 13 |
| delivering mediated presentations | Ch. 15 |

## Analyze Your Audience

Speeches should always be given for the benefit of the audience—whether to inform, persuade, or mark a special occasion. **Audience analysis** is the process of learning about an audience's interests and backgrounds in order to create a speech that meets their needs. It is important to learn about the audience members (or make educated guesses) before you select a topic and choose the ideas you will use to develop your topic.

At this early point in the course, you may not be able to conduct a detailed, formal analysis of your audience. However, you may have spoken with classmates or heard them share information during class about their interests and backgrounds. In addition, you and the other students will likely have shared experiences in class and in the larger college or university environment. Use your knowledge of these shared experiences to anticipate your listeners' attitudes and interests.

If you feel you need to do more to analyze your audience, here are some questions you could direct toward several classmates:

- Do you have favorite sports teams, activities, and traditions on campus? Have you experienced difficulties related to the college experience, such as problems with technology during virtual classes, insufficient outlets for charging mobile devices in classrooms, or difficulty in signing up for required classes?
- Are you active in community service? Do you know any organizations or classes on campus that promote community service?
- What year are you in school? Do you live on campus, commute, or attend virtually? Do you work to finance your education?

Jot down responses to these questions, as well as your own thoughts about topics that may interest your classmates.

## Select Your Topic

Your **topic** is the subject you will address in your speech. The topic for your first speech will depend on the assignment your instructor has given you. Typical assignments include informing the class about an interesting issue you studied in another course, telling the class about a pet peeve, or sharing a cultural tradition with your audience.

To choose a topic, list as many possibilities as you can, and then use your audience analysis to select one that you think would most appeal to your listeners—and yourself. When you personally care about the topic, you'll invest more time in preparing and practicing your speech. Your interest in the topic will also shine through while you deliver your speech, which will further engage your audience.

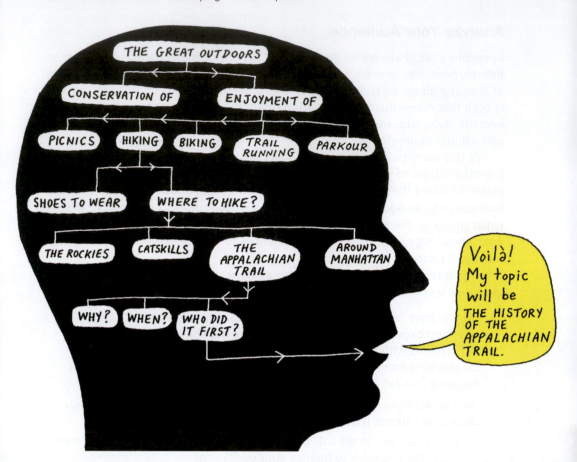

Make sure to avoid overused topics—such as the drinking age, steroids in sports, abortion, or the "art" of making a perfect peanut butter and jelly sandwich. All instructors have lists of "reruns" that they would prefer not to sit through again. If you do choose a topic that is often presented in student speeches (for example, the death penalty or legalization of marijuana), make sure to take a fresh perspective or approach. If you have any doubts whatsoever about whether your topic is appropriate, be sure to check with your instructor.

Finally, consider ways to narrow your topic. Most topics are too broad to cover in a five- or ten-minute presentation. You would run out of time long before you could discuss everything there is to know about your major, culture, or favorite sport. Select one or more *aspects* of your topic that you think will most interest your audience and that you can also cover in the available time for your speech. For example, instead of trying to describe your entire culture, you might focus your topic on how your family or neighborhood celebrates a particular holiday.

## Determine Your Speech's Rhetorical Purpose

Every speech must have a **rhetorical purpose**—a primary goal for the speech. Speeches typically have one of the following objectives:

- *Informing:* Increasing your audience's understanding or awareness of your subject
- *Persuading:* Trying to influence your audience's beliefs or actions with respect to your subject
- *Marking a special occasion:* Commemorating events, such as graduations, memorial services, weddings, awards ceremonies, and holidays

The rhetorical purpose you choose focuses the content of your speech. This is because each idea you develop needs to support the purpose you've selected. For classroom speeches, your instructor may specify a rhetorical purpose. If it is not specified, determine the purpose yourself. How? Decide whether you

---

▼ **A Presenter Displays Kiki the Cat.** A speech on robot pets will address different information depending on the speech's rhetorical purpose. For example: how robot pets improve the lives of dementia patients (informative); gift a robot pet to a friend or family member (persuasive); today we honor the person who led the drive to provide robot pets to memory care patients (special occasion). ROBYN BECK/Getty Images

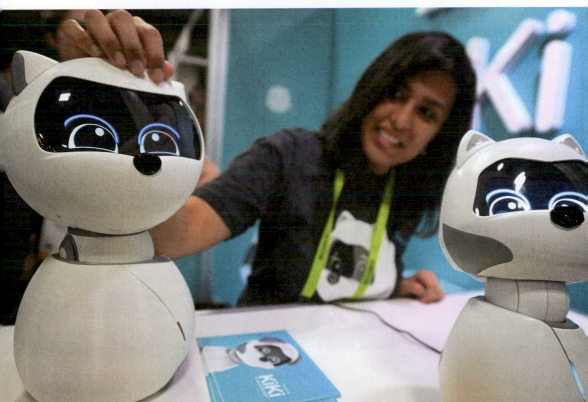

want your audience members to understand, believe, feel, or do something in particular about your topic after they listen to your speech. For instance, one student who was concerned about a regional drought wanted to persuade audience members to practice water conservation techniques in the residence halls.

## Create a Thesis Statement

After you've selected your topic and identified your rhetorical purpose, draft a thesis statement for your speech. The **thesis statement** (sometimes called the *central idea* or *topic statement*) is a single sentence that sums up your speech's main message and reflects your narrowed topic and rhetorical purpose. Basically, the thesis statement should convey your speech's bottom line, enabling audience members to understand the essence of your overall message. Here are some examples of thesis statements:

- "New Year celebrations in my culture include three unique traditions." (informs)
- "You should try the Green Mediterranean Diet for 30 Days." (persuades)
- "We honor Krista, Felicia, and Nadia as this year's top campus advisers." (marks a special occasion)

## Determine Your Main Points

**Main points** are the major ideas you will emphasize in your presentation. By calling attention to these points, you help your audience understand and remember the most important ideas from your speech. If you fail to do so, listeners will have difficulty following and retaining your speech's message.

To determine main points, begin by making a list of ideas you might like to cover. These ideas can come from what you already know and from research you do on your topic. After making your list, select main points by considering which ideas would be most interesting to your audience and would best help listeners obtain a deeper understanding of your topic.

Each main point you select must also support your thesis statement. Otherwise, your audience may conclude that you're straying off course and may lose interest or become confused.

## Develop Supporting Materials

Once you've selected your main points, develop **supporting materials**—information that bolsters and fleshes out the claims made in each of those points. There are several types of supporting materials, including examples, definitions, testimony, statistics, narratives, and analogies. You can generate supporting materials internally by brainstorming and externally by conducting research.

**Brainstorming** is the process of quickly listing every idea that comes to mind—without evaluating its merits—in order to develop a substantial list of ideas. To brainstorm potential supporting materials, ask yourself questions such as, "What do I know about my topic?" and "What do I think is most important or interesting about this topic?" List all the responses to these questions that spring to mind. Your goal is to create a diverse list of many possible ideas, not to make a final decision about which ones you will use.

**Research** is the process of gathering information from libraries, quality online sources, and interviews with authorities on your topic. Through research, you obtain information from experts that will enhance your understanding of the topic and strengthen your speech's credibility. Even if your instructor requires less research for your first speech than for later assignments, you should still do a little research to answer any questions you have about your topic area.

As you research, be sure to save a copy of any useful material you unearth. Also record the **citation**—the key information about each research source—so that you can use it in your outline and your speech. Be sure that you have the following information for your sources:

- *The author:* The writer or sponsoring organization of a book, an article, or an online entry
- *The author's credentials on the subject:* The author's job title, relevant education or job experience, or academic or institutional affiliation
- *The name of the source:* The title of a book, the title of an article and the name of the periodical or newspaper it ran in, or the name of a person you interviewed

## BUILDING A SPEECH WITH SUPPORTING MATERIALS

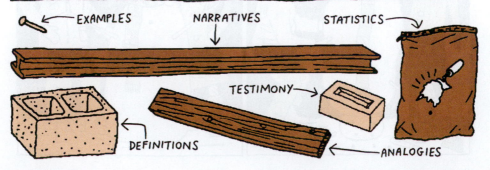

- *The publication date:* The copyright date for a book you used, the publication date of a periodical or newspaper you researched, the date you accessed a website, or the date you conducted an interview
- *The page(s)* on which you found relevant information in a printed source or the URL of an online source

After brainstorming and researching supporting materials for your main points, select the supporting materials that would most interest your listeners and help them grasp what you're saying about your topic.

## Organize and Outline the Body of Your Speech

A speech should be well organized, meaning that your ideas are structured in a way that enables the audience to follow your message easily. To organize your speech, draft an **outline**. Your outline will contain the text of your speech in complete sentences or briefer phrases (depending on what your instructor prefers).

A speech outline has three major parts—the introduction, the body, and the conclusion. The **body** is the core of your speech and is where you present your main message about your topic. For this reason, we recommend outlining the body of your speech before outlining the introduction, even though the body will follow the introduction when you actually deliver the speech.

To create a full-sentence outline for the body of your speech, first express each of the main points you've selected as a single sentence that states a key idea you're planning to emphasize. Then number each main point with a Roman numeral. It is common to have between two and five main points, although your instructor may ask you to develop a single main point for your first speech.

ALWAYS BUILD THE BODY FIRST—IT'S THE CORE OF YOUR SPEECH (AND YOUR SNOWMAN)

Next, create subpoints from the supporting materials you have gathered through brainstorming and research. **Subpoints** explain, prove, or expand on your main points. In your outline, indicate each subpoint with a capital letter, and indent each under its corresponding main point.

An important principle of outlining is **subordination**. Each main point must relate to your thesis, and each subpoint must relate to the main point that it supports. If you include additional supporting material under any subpoint (a sub-subpoint, so to speak), it must relate to that subpoint; be sure to indicate any sub-subpoints with Arabic numerals. Here are both generic and specific examples of how subordination might look in a typical outline:

I. Main Point 1
  A. Subpoint
  B. Subpoint
    1. Sub-subpoint
    2. Sub-subpoint
II. Main Point 2

I. Robot pets benefit many different groups of people.
  A. They are a great alternative for renters whose leases disallow pets.
  B. They are very useful in memory care facilities.
    1. Robot pets provide comfort to patients.
    2. Robot pets are useful in therapy.
II. Robot pets are easy to use.

## Outline Your Introduction and Conclusion

The **introduction** to your speech serves several vital purposes, each of which is the basis for one major section of the introduction, as shown in the following list (your instructor may require a specific combination or order of these elements):

I. *Attention-getter.* Start your speech with a brief story, quotation, striking fact or statistic, or humorous incident that grabs listeners' attention while also hinting at what your speech will cover.
II. *Thesis statement.* In a single sentence, convey the topic and purpose of your speech.
III. *Show the audience what's in it for them.* In one or two sentences, summarize why audience members should listen to your speech. Will you provide information they need to know? Information they will want to share with friends and family?
IV. *Establish your credibility.* To show that you are a believable source of information on your topic, indicate any relevant expertise, experience, or education that you have.
V. *Preview your main points.* To help the audience understand where you will be going in your speech, list each main point using no more than one sentence per point.

The **conclusion** of your speech summarizes what you have said and leaves the audience with a memorable impression of your presentation. There are two main parts to a conclusion:

I.  *Summary of your main points.* Briefly recap the major points you made during your speech.

II.  *Clincher.* End with a closing sentence or paragraph that leaves your audience with a vivid memory of your speech. A clincher may be related to the introduction (for example, supplying a happy ending to a story you began in the attention-getter), or it may consist of a statement or quotation that characterizes the content of your speech.

## Incorporate Transitions

After you've outlined the body, introduction, and conclusion, you will want to create transitions to connect the parts of your speech. A **transition** is a sentence that indicates you are moving from one idea to another. Transitions are especially helpful in the following places:

- Between the introduction and your first main point
- Between each main point
- Between the final main point and the conclusion

Here are some examples of transitions:

- "First, let's talk about . . ." (*transition from introduction to first main point*)
- "Now that we've considered . . . , let's move on to . . ." (*transition between two main points*)
- "This completes our discussion of . . ." (*transition from final main point to conclusion*)

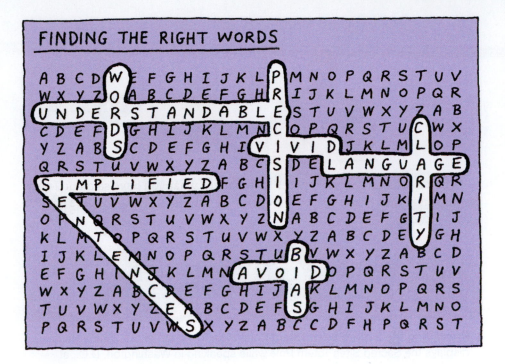

## Consider Your Word Choice

Reread your entire outline, this time carefully considering the language you will use to express your ideas. Effective **word choice** (or **diction**) can help make your speech much more memorable and engaging for listeners. When preparing your speech, select words that your audience will understand, use precise terms to express your ideas, and choose language that makes your speech come alive. Focus on simplifying your sentences (remember, audience members cannot reread parts of your speech if they become confused). Finally, be sure to avoid biased language that may hurt others or damage your credibility.

## Consider Presentation Aids

A **presentation aid** is anything beyond the speech itself that your audience members can see or hear that helps them understand and remember your message. Traditional aids include actual objects (such as the Lummi Nation Totem Pole in the photo shown on the next page) or models (for example, a physical model of a DNA molecule), video and audio recordings (such as short clips to compare the music of Olivia Rodrigo and Camila Cabello), drawings, photographs, charts, maps, and graphs. PowerPoint presentations or other electronic slide shows are also common aids.

▲ **Presenting the Sacred Sites Totem Pole.** Phreddie Lane of the Lummi Nation displays the Sacred Sites Totem Pole while speaking in Washington, D.C., at the end of a two-week national tour in support of protecting sacred lands. Jemal Countess/Getty Images

Each presentation aid needs to support the point that you are developing. For example, if you want your audience to appreciate the differences between birdcalls, an audio recording that clearly demonstrates those differences would be entirely relevant. In addition, take care that audio aids are loud and clear and that visual aids are uncluttered and large enough for your audience to see from all points in the room.

## Practice Your Speech

After drafting your outline, make sure to practice your speech. With practice, you'll feel more confident about your presentation—and more comfortable talking in front of your classmates. This comfort level will enable you to use **extemporaneous delivery**, which involves using only notes for reference rather than reading your speech to the audience word-for-word.

Speech practice is a "best practice" of successful public speakers. Dr. Jill Bolte Taylor's TED talk "My Stroke of Insight," which provides her insights as a brain scientist experiencing a stroke, had almost twenty-eight million views as of October 2021.[9] Dr. Taylor practiced two hundred times before delivering her speech.[10]

Of course, not everybody can practice a speech two hundred times. Nevertheless, it is important to practice delivering your speech several times, until the

content begins to feel familiar. When practicing, time your speech to make sure that it is not too long or too short. When you create your notes, be sure that the words are large enough so that you can easily glance down and find your place while you are presenting. You may refer to your notes when you need to refresh your memory, but you should generally be looking at the audience as you speak.

Finally, consider the environment in which you'll be presenting your speech and use that knowledge to inform how you practice. Instead of delivering your speech in person, for example, your assignment may call for a **mediated presentation**. This means you will use technology to deliver your message rather than speaking to the audience face-to-face. In cases like this, be sure to practice with the necessary technology ahead of time so you can do your best to avoid technical difficulties.

## Deliver Your Speech

The moment has come: you're watching a classmate wrap up their speech, and you're next in line. As you begin to present, keep the following guidelines in mind:

- *Project your voice.* Speak loudly and slowly enough that your audience can easily hear what you are saying.
- *Maintain an even rate of speaking.* Many speakers tend to rush through a speech, particularly if they are nervous. Speak at a rate that enables you to pronounce the words clearly, allowing the audience to follow your speech.
- *Convey interest in your topic.* Maintain energy and variety in your speaking voice so that you build audience enthusiasm for your speech.
- *Maintain eye contact.* Try to make eye contact with people in each section of the room during an in-person presentation. During a recorded presentation, be sure you are regularly looking at the camera.

Each speech you deliver is a learning experience. Your instructor (and perhaps your classmates) will offer feedback after your presentation. Use these suggestions to prepare future speeches; you'll soon see your public speaking skills improve.

## OVERCOMING SPEECH ANXIETY

As you begin to prepare for your first speech, you may experience some nervousness about speaking in front of an audience. If so, you're not alone. Although the claim that people fear public speaking more than death may be an urban legend, almost everyone—from college students to the public at large—feels nervous about speaking before an audience.[11] The symptoms of **speech anxiety**—the worry or fear that some people experience before giving a talk (also called **stage fright**)—can take a wide variety of forms. Some people experience the stereotypical sensation of butterflies in the stomach, as well as sweaty palms and a dry mouth. Others endure nausea, hyperventilation, and downright panic.

A little nervousness can actually be a good thing when you're giving a speech: it helps focus your attention. But in its extreme form, speech anxiety can prevent you from speaking clearly or keeping your train of thought while delivering your presentation. Although speech anxiety is quite common, you *can* learn to manage it. You may not be able to get rid of the butterflies, but you can at least get them flying in formation. You are already taking an important first step by participating in a public speaking course. Research indicates that students in classes like this one become more self-assured and experience less apprehension about speaking as the term progresses.[12]

The following strategies can help you combat speech anxiety and build confidence in your public speaking skills.

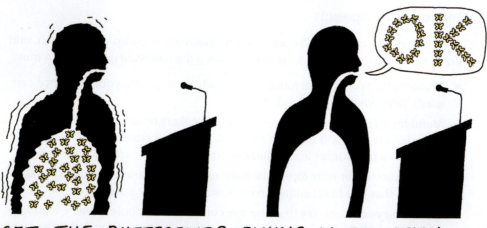

GET THE BUTTERFLIES FLYING IN FORMATION

## EARLY PREPARATION IS KEY

## Prepare Early and Follow a Plan

One of the best ways to build confidence in your ability to deliver a successful speech is to get to work soon after you receive an assignment and follow an organized plan to craft and practice your speech. Resist the temptation to procrastinate: speech apprehension is associated with inadequate preparation.[13] Conversely, high anxiety can be reduced by good preparation.[14] When speakers get down to business and make progress on a speech, they will feel less anxious.[15] The point is clear: select a topic as soon as possible, and draft an outline well in advance.

After you have an outline, you can take other steps to improve your speech and build confidence. One helpful suggestion is to get your instructor's feedback on your outline. This feedback—perhaps in the form of comments on your outline or a list of the standards used for grading—will help you improve your speech and reduce the stress of not knowing how it will be evaluated.[16]

## Deliver Your Speech to Others

You can also gain confidence by practicing your speech in front of other people. One study found that when students delivered their speech three times before a small group of classmates, they experienced a reduction in speech anxiety.[17] If it is not practical to practice with a group of classmates, you can present your speech to friends and family. When you speak in front of others, you gain experience speaking under pressure, and public speaking becomes less overwhelming.[18]

Earlier, we recommended that you practice your speech using the same format you will use to deliver it. One reason is that there are different sources of stress during a face-to-face speech, a speech delivered in real-time during a Zoom class, and a recorded speech. For example, during a Zoom presentation it is more difficult to decode nonverbal feedback (such as a nod in agreement, or a frown in disbelief) than it is when you are in the same room as your audience, and it can be stressful to see yourself on the screen as you speak.[19] Concerns about technological problems interfering with your speech can also lead to anxiety.[20] You want to be sure you are familiar with the format you will be using ahead of time, so you can get more comfortable speaking via that format.

▼ **Speech Practice with a Friendly Audience.** An American University student practices delivery with Dexter, the "audience dog." The Washington Post/Getty Images

## Try Imagined Interactions

**Imagined interaction** is another form of practice. During this process, a speaker mentally practices delivering a speech to the audience, presenting the content of the message, and picturing a positive interaction with the audience (such as applause).[21] Research has found that practice using imagined interaction reduces the number and length of silences during a presentation and strengthens the speaker's assessment of the performance.[22]

## Take Care of Yourself

Be sure to get a good night's sleep before a speech. Avoid excessive sugar and caffeinated beverages the morning of your presentation: these will make you more jittery. If you don't feel like eating much on the day of your speech, consume a light meal before you deliver your presentation. Then reward yourself with a favorite feast when it's all over.

Also, budget your time in the days leading up to your speech. It's hard to get sufficient sleep, prepare nutritious meals, and practice your presentation if you have to work six hours, study for a test, and write a ten-page paper the day before you deliver your speech. Having too much to do in too little time intensifies anxiety. To avoid this scenario, look at the syllabi for all your courses early in the term to see when major assignments are due. Consider other commitments as well, such as job, family, and community responsibilities. Then plan your time so that the days leading up to your speech are as relaxed as possible.

## Visualize Success

Researchers have found that a simple activity reduces anxiety for public speaking students—visualizing success.[23] With **visualization**, you imagine yourself scoring a resounding success, such as concluding your speech and winning enthusiastic applause from an appreciative audience. Make your visualization as specific as possible. For example, imagine yourself striding confidently to the front of the room. Contemplate speaking to the audience in the same way you would converse with a friend—natural and relaxed. Picture the audience nodding in agreement with a key point, smiling when an idea hits home, and laughing at your jokes. Listen to the thundering applause as you wrap up your speech. The power of positive thinking is no mere cliché; when you visualize success, you can ease your anxiety—if not eradicate it entirely.

## Use Relaxation Techniques

When you're suffering from speech anxiety, your muscles tense up and your mind swarms with negative thoughts. You know you should relax. But who can chill on command? **Relaxation strategies**—techniques that reduce muscle tension and negative thoughts—can help. Many people find exercise to be

a powerful relaxation strategy. It will help you expend nervous energy, and it will leave you feeling relaxed and limber on the day of your presentation. It's also renowned for clearing the mind. But exercising doesn't necessarily mean heading to the nearest gym to lift weights or take a Pilates class. All you have to do is practice tightening and releasing your muscles—wherever you are at the moment. Breathe in as you tighten a group of muscles, and then exhale as you release the tension. Consider progressing from your neck muscles down to your feet. You can use this and other relaxation techniques even while you're waiting to deliver your speech.

## Check Out Some Apps

You have probably heard multiple times that "there's an app for just about everything." Speech anxiety is no exception. If you are an inveterate app downloader, you may want to look at the free and low-cost options available. Apps such as Headspace help you practice general meditation and mindfulness techniques, which you can use to feel more at ease before you present your speech. There are also apps like Orai that allow you to practice your speech and analyze delivery skills such as vocal variety and pauses.[24]

## Volunteer to Speak First

Many public speakers experience more anxiety shortly before their presentation than during their actual speech.[25] While anxious speakers think about their upcoming presentation, it is also possible for them to exaggerate the risk that their speech will not succeed or that the audience will be critical when their nervousness shows.[26] If this describes you and you're going to be one of several speakers in a class or program, ask to speak first—or as early as possible in the lineup. That way, you'll have less time to work up a debilitating level of worry.

## Never Defeat Yourself

It is easy to become your own worst critic while giving a speech. If audience members are yawning or frowning, such feedback can increase your speech anxiety.[27] Don't fall into the trap of making negative judgments as you speak. There is a good chance that a frowning classmate is trying to remember where he left his keys or worrying about an upcoming math test.

Even if you do make a serious mistake during your speech, don't give up. Your classmates will be hoping you recover and finish strong. We have seen one student's outline disappear when her iPad crashed midspeech, another remain silent for two full minutes while putting a jumbled pile of note cards in the right order, and a third watch his dog (a visual aid) have an "accident" as the speech concluded. In these and similar situations, the first postspeech comment from an audience member has consistently been a supportive statement about the speaker's effort to recover.

## SPEECH CHOICES

### A CASE STUDY: *RAFAELA*

*Let's check in with Rafaela as she makes plans for a new speech assignment.*

Rafaela's second speech assignment was an informative speech. Students were required to submit an outline, include presentation aids, and cite at least four credible research sources. Rafaela was anxious about this speech and she had butterflies in her stomach when it was her turn to speak. She had left most of the work until the day before the speech was due, which gave her little time to practice—and it showed. Rafaela ended up reading most of her speech from her notes, and her speaking voice was tentative because she did not know her material well.

Rafaela wanted to step up her game for the third assignment, which was a persuasive speech. She would be presenting in four weeks, and there was much work to be done. To get started, Rafaela decided to review the steps for speech preparation—she wanted to be sure about what to do and when to do it—and then she drafted a schedule that would give her time to complete each step. She worked around days when she had tests in other classes and gave herself a couple of days off to relax. The instructor had told the class that it was important to select a topic early and stick to it, so she planned to do just that—maybe something about women running for office. Then she would finish her research and outlining early, leaving plenty of time to practice her delivery. Rafaela realized this practice would work best with an audience, so she planned to ask a couple of classmates to get together for a run-through before the big day. She still had some butterflies, but not so many as before—with a plan in place, she was already feeling more prepared.

### YOUR TURN:

Now that you've seen how Rafaela struggled when she didn't prepare for her informative speech and grew more confident when she planned for her persuasive, it's time to consider similar choices you'll need to make for your own speech assignments. Making speech choices involves asking and answering a series of questions related to your assignment or task. When it comes to speech preparation, those questions will likely include the following:

- What are the requirements for my speech, and what preparation work will I need to do?

- When is my speech due, and how should I schedule my time to complete these preparations?

- Once my speech is drafted, how will I plan to practice before presenting in class? Have I budgeted enough time for this practice in my schedule?

- What strategies will I use to minimize speech anxiety and "get the butterflies flying in formation"?

By thinking through your answers to questions like these and following the schedule you set up, you'll be well prepared to deliver your speech—successfully and with confidence!

> **Preparation and perseverance are the keys to a successful speech.**

The most successful presentations in history, such as Martin Luther King Jr.'s "I Have a Dream" speech, usually derive from careful thought, planning, and preparation. Both beginning and more experienced speakers should remember this lesson: even a first-time speaker can give a much stronger presentation by taking a bit of extra time and effort.

In this chapter, we emphasized the importance of preparing for public speaking. First, we introduced the five classical canons of rhetoric—a set of guidelines that continue to inform the way many speech instructors teach speech preparation today.

Next, we presented a step-by-step process for preparing your first speech. It's important to note that speech development is a craft comprising a set of specific skills that you can master. The nine main steps are analyzing your audience; selecting a topic; determining your speech's rhetorical purpose; creating a thesis statement; determining your main points; developing supporting materials; organizing and outlining the body, introduction, conclusion, and transitions; considering word choice and presentation aids; and practicing and delivering the speech. By making good choices at each step of the speech preparation process, you improve your chances of delivering a successful presentation.

In this chapter, we also outlined some basic techniques to help you overcome speech anxiety by emphasizing that you can channel your nervousness to help you become a better speaker. To help you "get the butterflies flying in formation," we suggest that you prepare early and follow a plan. Be sure to practice your speech, and use imagined interaction and meet-ups with small groups to gain confidence in your ability to deliver a successful presentation. Strive to take care of yourself by balancing responsibilities with personal needs. To build a positive outlook, try visualizing success, using relaxation techniques, checking out relevant apps, and volunteering to speak first. And when you are speaking, stay positive: don't be your own worst critic.

## Key Terms

classical canons of rhetoric *32*
invention *32*
arrangement *32*
style *32*
memory *32*
delivery *33*
audience analysis *35*
topic *35*

rhetorical purpose *37*
thesis statement *38*
main point *38*
supporting material *39*
brainstorming *39*
research *39*
citation *39*
outline *40*

## Review Questions

1. What are three common problems that inexperienced speakers make when preparing a speech?
2. Name and define each of the five classical canons of rhetoric.
3. What is audience analysis, and what are three questions you may want to answer about your audience?
4. Explain what is meant by rhetorical purpose. What are the three basic rhetorical purposes that speeches can serve?
5. What is a thesis statement, and how does it differ from a speech topic?
6. What are supporting materials, and how do they help a speaker develop main points?
7. Define *main points* and *subpoints*, and explain the principle of subordination.
8. What are presentation aids, and how can speakers make sure they support their message?
9. What is extemporaneous delivery, and why is it generally the best approach for speakers?
10. List three guidelines for effective delivery.
11. Name and explain five techniques that can help you overcome speech anxiety.

## Critical Thinking Questions

1. How would you analyze your public speaking classmates as an audience? Consider their backgrounds and interests. What are some of their shared experiences? How could you use this information to adapt a speech to your classmates?
2. How would the research and supporting materials you might use in a persuasive speech differ from those you might use in a special-occasion speech?
3. When you see a presenter who is obviously feeling nervous, how can you as an audience member help put the speaker at ease? How might your approach differ if the speeches were delivered during a Zoom class, rather than in the classroom? Can thinking about your experience as an audience member help you feel less nervous as a speaker?

## Activities

1. In small groups, look at each of the steps involved in preparing a speech (see "Preparing and Delivering Your First Speech"). Discuss which classical canons of rhetoric are applied during each step.
2. In small groups, prepare a skit in which a speaker uses at least three different techniques for reducing speech anxiety. Then present your skit to the entire class. Have other class members try to identify the techniques that each group is using.
3. Think back on any awards programs you like to watch (for example, the Oscars, Grammys, ESPYs, or Video Music Awards) and the ways in which different winners approach their acceptance speeches. Is it obvious when a winner has prepared a speech beforehand? Is it obvious when it is spontaneous? Have any speakers made comments that you thought were inappropriate for the type of event, or perhaps particularly impressive?
4. Watch a video of Kelly McGonigal's TED talk, "How to Make Stress Your Friend." Then discuss how a speaker experiencing speech anxiety can use the ideas McGonigal presents to better manage stress or even turn stress into a positive force.
5. Watch a video of Naomi Osaka's acceptance speech for receiving the Best Athlete, Women's Sports award at the 2021 ESPY Awards. How do you think the feedback from the audience early in her speech affected Osaka's confidence?
6. Find an app that can be used to minimize speech anxiety and try at least one of the suggestions. Did taking this particular action help you feel more confident about speaking in front of a group?

# SPEECH ETHICS

**❝Strive to be an ethical public speaker. ❞**

All of us face difficult choices throughout our lives. By way of example, consider Alex, a recent college graduate who works in the marketing division of a software company. He makes a good salary, but his hours are long, and his job is challenging. His boss travels a great deal for business and stays in touch with Alex and others in his division through Zoom. Because of conflicting calendars, the boss scheduled a meeting via Zoom with Alex early on a weekday morning and asked Alex to present a short oral report outlining any progress with a potential client. Because he knew that his boss would be out of town, Alex had planned to work from home that morning and then attend a Major League Baseball game in the afternoon.

When Alex set up his laptop to begin his Zoom session, he had on a dress shirt and tie (which were his usual work clothes). Beneath the laptop and the table, however, he was still in his pajama pants. After Alex gave his report, his boss complimented both the quality of the presentation and the fact that he was in the office and at work so early. Alex, who was at home, did not correct the boss's misperception and instead responded with a smile and a shrug: "Work, work, work!" While Alex did not overtly deceive his boss, he certainly misled and misdirected him with both his clothing and his non-answer. Alex rationalized

◀ **A Question of Ethics.** If you were working from home and your boss thought you were in the office instead, would you correct this misperception—or say nothing at all? SimonSkafar/Getty Images

this, believing that if the work got done, it wouldn't matter if he was in the office or not. Alex neglected to consider, however, how his boss would feel if he learned he had been deceived.

Alex's experience shows that ethical quandaries can arise when you *don't* speak up to correct a misperception, but they are also often related to what you *do* say. Consider Bob—a junior at a state university campus in California who decided to run for student-body president. Bob believed that having this position on his résumé would make him more marketable when he graduated and began to look for a full-time job. Over time, Bob got a good look at the different candidates who were running against him. Like him, they had good grades, and believed that being SB president would enhance their chances for opportunities after graduation. There were eight other candidates, which felt like a lot of competition. Feeling somewhat panicked that he needed to stand out to win, Bob responded to a question at the candidates' debate by overstating how much experience he had in student government: he said he had a great deal of experience when he actually had very little. When the school newspaper ran an article disproving Bob's claims, Bob grew convinced that he would lose the election to another candidate.

To no one's surprise, Bob did indeed lose to another candidate. In fact, six of the eight other candidates got more votes than Bob. Feeling humiliated by the loss but not wanting to admit it, Bob insisted on repeating his claim that he had been very involved in student government, leading those who had voted in the election to suspect he was now intentionally lying.

Both Bob's poorly handled campaign and Alex's response to his boss demonstrate the difficulty posed by ethical dilemmas—situations in which the right decision may be obvious, but at the same time may not serve the speaker's self-interest.

In public speaking, **ethics**—rules and values that a group defines to guide conduct and distinguish between right and wrong—come into play during every stage of creating and delivering a speech. For example, as you research and write your speech, you make decisions about what information you'll include and how that information will influence your audience. As you deliver your speech, you have to make choices about language, tone of voice, and the ways that those aspects of your presentation may affect your listeners. In this chapter, we examine the ethical responsibilities of both speakers and their audiences.

# CODES OF ETHICS: ABSOLUTE, SITUATIONAL, AND CULTURALLY RELATIVE

How do people make ethical choices? Some adopt a code of behavior that they commit to using consistently. These individuals are demonstrating **ethical absolutism**—the belief that people should exhibit the same behavior in all situations. For instance, you would be using ethical absolutism if you decided to tell your romantic partner how you really felt about their tendency to sing out of key. In this case, your code of ethics might contain a principle like this: "People should always tell the truth, even if doing so hurts loved ones."

Other people use **situational ethics**—a shifting code that suggests that ethics can vary depending on the situation at hand. For example, a student would be using situational ethics if she decided that under extenuating circumstances (say, a lack of time), it would be OK to stretch the truth "just this once" and tell her friends she was on her way to meet them downtown, when in fact she hadn't left campus yet.

Whether you see ethical decisions in absolute or situational terms, there are some generalizations that apply in most situations. For example, most societies believe that it's more ethical to tell the truth than to lie. In the context of public speaking, most people believe that lying is wrong. Audience members may see lying as an ethical violation and even, in some circumstances, a possible violation of the law.

Yet some of these same individuals might think little or nothing of intentionally exaggerating their qualifications during a job interview—especially if they believe that "everybody does it and gets away with it." Thus, many people use a blend of approaches when making ethics-related choices. In truth, most people are not strict absolutists. Even those who generally follow a strict ethical code may face dilemmas that compel them to engage in situational ethics at some point in their lives.

# LIES HAVE CONSEQUENCES

In this book, we do not presume to tell you what your ethical system must be; we do strongly encourage you, however, to always strive to make the most ethical choice. To help you with such choices, we expose you to the kinds of communication-related ethical dilemmas that speakers and audience members sometimes face, and we also explore behaviors most people consider unethical. As you'll discover, one guiding principle that can help you select ethical choices is that of respect for other people—the old adage of treating others the way you would want to be treated, as well as avoiding treating them in ways you would *not* want to be treated. For instance, if you would resent a public speaker who withheld important information in order to persuade you to take a particular action, you shouldn't exhibit that same behavior in delivering your own speeches.

Ethics can also vary across societies, making them **culturally relative**.[1] For example, in some cultures, people believe that knowledge is owned collectively rather than by individuals. In cultures with strong oral and narrative traditions, for example, stories are passed from one generation to another and are shared as general knowledge. Within such a system, people don't consider working together or paraphrasing without attribution to be cheating, or any other form of unethical behavior. By contrast, a Western cultural perspective holds that individuals *do* own the knowledge they create. This is the perspective we reflect in this book, which is why we require complete citations and source attribution for all speeches. This perspective also informs the academic guidelines and honor codes that are explicitly stated by most colleges and universities in the United States. Indeed, you will often find these guidelines cited in your instructors' syllabi.

As you read on, consider your own approach to making ethical decisions while developing and delivering presentations. What are your beliefs regarding proper behavior in general and in public speaking in particular? Do you always honor these beliefs strictly, or do you only do this in certain situations? To help you answer these questions, let's consider some of the ethical issues you may confront. These include communicating truthfully, crediting others' work, using sound reasoning, and behaving ethically when you're listening to someone else's speech. Although making ethical choices in public speaking situations can sometimes be difficult, this chapter helps you develop a responsible system for doing so. The key word here is *responsibility*. Whenever you give a speech, you wield power—over what your listeners think, how they feel, and what actions they end up taking—and are thus responsible for your audience's well-being. The following sections offer guidelines for shouldering that responsibility by exhibiting ethically responsible behavior in public speaking.

▼ **The Power of Speech.** Speakers wield power, and with that power comes a responsibility to communicate their messages truthfully and ethically. Climate activist Greta Thunberg took this responsibility seriously when addressing the United Nations, where she informed world leaders in very direct terms that young people demand action on climate change. Stephanie Keith/Getty Images

# LEGAL SPEECH VS. ETHICAL SPEECH

As we connect ethics and public speaking, it is worth observing that many people in the United States often confuse (sometimes intentionally) **ethical speech** with **legally protected speech**. Although these two concepts sometimes overlap—that is, what you say is both legal and ethically responsible to your audience—they are most definitely *not* the same. Ethical speech refers to incorporating ethical decision making into your public speaking process *and* into what you ultimately say. It means that you follow guidelines for telling the truth and avoid misleading an audience—because such actions are ethical and *the right thing to do*.

Focusing on legally protected speech, by contrast, refers to using the law as your boundary for what you may say *and* how you may say it. Thus, with this approach, you would make decisions about telling the truth or withholding information based on whether there is a legal requirement to take a certain action or a legal consequence for violating the rules. When you rely on legal guidelines for acceptable speech, your decision-making calculus has nothing to do with ethics: it is driven only by what is technically within the legal rules. Be mindful, however, that if you use legal protection as your guiding principle for speaking, you can technically stay within the bounds of what is lawful but still speak unethically.

It's vital to note that far more types of speech are technically legal than are strictly ethical. In the United States, the First Amendment to the U.S. Constitution mandates "freedom of speech," and this freedom allows for a vast range of legally protected statements. In fact, there are relatively few exceptions, and these typically fall under the categories of slander (also known as *defamation*, an intentional

falsehood about another person that may injure the reputation of that person when made public), fighting words (words meant to provoke a violent response), lewd speech (vulgar and crude language choice), obscenity (a hard-core, sexually explicit expression), and incitement (words that encourage unlawful activity).

Political speech—expression that relates to political discourse—is the most legally protected and privileged form of expression under the First Amendment, sometimes to a surprising degree. As an example, consider the modern-day politicizing of the COVID-19 global pandemic, a pandemic that has caused the deaths of hundreds of thousands of people, including more than 800,000 Americans and 5.5 million people globally (as of this writing). Sadly, the virus itself has in some respects been less controversial than the vaccines designed to eliminate, control, or at least limit it. Equally controversial have been the mandates in some parts of this country that people wear protective masks, which have led to violent altercations in enclosed areas, such as the interiors of large passenger planes. Lost in this violence-prone, polarized discourse is the fact that conspiracy theories, misstatements, and lies (some of them intentional) have encouraged many Americans to doubt the effectiveness of vaccines and masks—beliefs encouraged by popular and influential figures, including politicians, who sometimes argue that other more experimental remedies would work better. Today we know (because it can be proven with multiple examples of scientific evidence) that the vaccines do work in stopping the spread of COVID-19, as does wearing masks. But many who refuse to be vaccinated do so for political reasons connected to their fears of being harmed by the vaccines, which are prompted by the less-than-truthful conspiracy theories. To be clear, these beliefs are protected by the First Amendment—the speech is legal. But if this same speech also promotes misstatements or false claims, it can threaten the health of a sizable number of people. The question, then, becomes not whether that type of speech is legal, but whether it is ethical.

Make sure that you understand the distinction between ethical and legal speech when crafting your own presentations. When you consider ethics, you are doing more than just what is legally required: you are doing what is morally correct for your situation.

## COMMUNICATING TRUTHFULLY

The most basic ethical guideline for public speaking is this: *tell your audience the truth.* How do you feel when someone has lied to you or intentionally misled you? Audience members who discover that a speaker has deceived them seldom believe anything else that person says—and they rarely do what this person asks of them. They also remember being lied to. Speakers with a reputation for oversized exaggeration or outright lying often have trouble convincing future listeners of their credibility or trustworthiness.

That being said, the words *truth* and *truthfully* are fairly subjective and elude precise definition. It is easier to describe truth in public speaking by examining what is *not* truth.

## Lying

Public speakers who lie intentionally are usually seeking to deceive their audience. Why do people choose to lie? Some fear what their listeners would do if they knew the truth; they don't trust their audience to react in a supportive or an understanding way. Consider a student giving a speech on gun safety who fabricated his identity as a military veteran. Although he was an experienced hunter and certified in the safe handling of firearms, he lied because he thought it would give him more credibility. His audience might well have accepted his suggestions anyway; after all, hunting experience and a certification course are worthy credentials. But by lying about his background, he risked losing his listeners' trust if they ever learned of his deception.

## Half-Truths

When a speaker reveals only part of the truth and then mixes it with a lie, the speaker is telling a **half-truth**. In practice, a half-truth has the same damaging impact as a lie: it deceives the audience. For example, say a corporate manager has to explain to the board of directors why their company recently lost several top executives. In a presentation, the manager claims that many of the departing executives had accepted positions at other companies or simply elected to take early retirement—normal occurrences in business. Although the first part was true, the second part was a half-truth. The two executives who chose to retire early did so as part of a legal settlement related to accusations of accounting malpractice.

## False Inference

When a speaker presents information that leads listeners to an incorrect conclusion, that speaker has caused a **false inference**. Speakers who commit this ethical breach intentionally drop hints designed to make their audience believe something that isn't true. For example, in a presentation titled "UFOs, Extraterrestrials, and the Supernatural," a student described a series of events that occurred in a midwestern town—an increase in the number of babies with birth defects, a rise in the rate of kidnapping, and a jump in the amount of farmland seized by the federal government. This student did not say outright that there was a government conspiracy to conceal the presence of aliens and unidentified flying objects (UFOs), but he clearly intended his audience to draw this inference. In reality, the increase in birth defects amounted to exactly one—from six to seven. The rising kidnapping rate was actually a statewide statistic, caused by a change in the law regarding divorce and child custody. And the government seizure of land had indeed happened—but it was only for the construction of a highway overpass. The speaker had unethically arranged his facts in a way that could make his audience conclude that the government was trying to conceal the presence of aliens, *X-Files*–style.

---

▼ **False Inferences.** Does the fact that we often see fire trucks in the presence of fires mean that fire trucks *cause* fires? Of course not! Arctic-Images/Getty Images

False inferences can also occur accidentally, as when a speaker gathers insufficient data and therefore unknowingly presents an incomplete understanding of the speech topic to the audience. Creating accidental false inferences isn't unethical, but it prevents you from conveying accurate information to your audience, thus damaging the effectiveness of your speech. To avoid causing an accidental *or* a deliberate false inference, avoid overgeneralized claims based on statistical findings, and always explain to your audience what the statistics mean and how they were derived.

**Taking evidence out of context** is another form of false inference. Here, the speaker shares a source's data or statements without explaining how they relate to the original situation. The speaker uses these facts or words *selectively* to support an argument. For example, in a speech about the propensity of pit bulls to attack people, one student quoted an animal-behavior expert out of context to imply a genetic predisposition toward attack: "There is an observable tendency in the genetic makeup of pit bulls to viciously attack humans." The student did *not* explain to her audience that the quotation came from a longer statement that clearly defies this view:

> Some have argued that there is an observable tendency in the genetic makeup of pit bulls to viciously attack humans. But surely this is not the case. Although it is true that *some* pit bulls have attacked *some* humans, there is no research to definitively prove a genetic tendency to attack humans. More study of this is needed.

Philosophers—and cheating romantic partners—have long argued about whether keeping silent about something is the same thing as lying about it. Thus, **omission** is another source of false inference. Here, presenters mislead the audience not by what they say but by what they leave unsaid. For example, in a presentation about on-campus drug use, a student government representative was asked about the extent of drug use and abuse in her campus dormitory. In response, she merely smiled and moved on to another question. Her silence and body language implied that there was no drug problem in her dormitory, but in fact, her dorm had the worst record for on-campus substance abuse. Similarly, as you saw at the beginning of the chapter, Alex presenting a report on Zoom and not correcting his employer's perception about *where he was working* (at home, just before heading out to a baseball game) was also misleading. If silence about a topic will mislead your audience and you are aware of this likelihood but withhold information anyway, then you have acted unethically through omission. Such actions suggest that you view your listeners as consumers of information and take an unethical and cynical *caveat emptor* (let the buyer beware) approach to public speaking.

To communicate truthfully and therefore ethically, it is best not to lie, tell half-truths, or employ false inferences—regardless of whether you are taking evidence out of context or omitting pertinent information. There are almost always alternatives. For example, if you fear that the truth may weaken your argument, then you need to do further research and perhaps take a closer look

# OUT-OF-CONTEXT EVIDENCE

"~~... Some have argued that~~ there is an observable tendency in the genetic makeup of pit bulls to viciously attack humans. ~~But surely this is not the case. Although it is true that some pit bulls have attacked some humans, there is no case study to definitely prove a genetic tendency to attack humans. More study of this is needed...~~"

"... Some have argued that there is an observable tendency in the genetic makeup of pit bulls to viciously attack humans. But surely this is not the case. Although it is true that *some* pit bulls have attacked *some* humans, there is no research to definitively prove a genetic tendency to attack humans. More study of this is needed..."

at your own stance. There are at least two sides to every issue, as well as multiple solutions and perspectives to consider. If you fear what your audience might think if they knew the truth, consider the opposite: how will they react if they learn you have deceived them? In most situations, listeners will react to a lie much more negatively than they will to an unwelcome truth.

# ACKNOWLEDGING THE WORK OF OTHERS

Researching a speech topic exposes you to a wealth of interesting facts, information, and ideas—many of which you will want to include in your presentation. But finding these materials also raises some ethical questions: Should you include a particular piece of information in your presentation? If so, how should you use it? And how will you acknowledge its source?

Listeners—and especially speech instructors—want speakers to demonstrate their own ideas and thought process during a presentation. At the same time, all of us recognize that most speeches can be enhanced by research and examples from outside sources. The question is, how should you reconcile these objectives? To do so, you'll need to use materials that demonstrate your own ideas and also ethically incorporate and acknowledge the original ideas of others. This approach is both honest for you and fair to your listeners and sources.

Imagine coming across an article or a published essay addressing the same topic as your speech. Maybe you admire the way the author worded the prose. Would it be a problem to incorporate a few lines from the article word-for-word, without citing the quotations? What about taking a preponderance of the ideas from the publication, rewording them, but not attributing them to the author? Would that be unethical? The answer to these questions is an unequivocal yes.

Presenting another person's words or ideas as if they were your own is called **plagiarism**, and it is always unethical. Plagiarism can be both "the deliberate and knowing presentation of another person's original ideas or creative expressions as one's own,"[2] as well the accidental presentation of the same. If you plagiarize, you mislead your audience by misrepresenting the source of the material you've used. Unfortunately, plagiarism is increasingly common at colleges and universities—and much of that can be attributed to the Internet.[3] Students may feel that plagiarism is a lesser evil than other kinds of cheating and use rationales to excuse it ("I don't have time," "No will one find out").[4] However, these are still just excuses for unethical behavior. When you plagiarize, you are stealing the ideas and words of another person—either deliberately or through sloppiness and inattention—and that is a crime most colleges and universities consider worthy of expulsion.

Although plagiarism is wrong, people sometimes have difficulty discerning the line between plagiarism and the appropriate use of researched material. To illustrate why, let's consider plagiarism in two contexts—quoting from a source and paraphrasing the work of others. We'll also look at how to proceed if you are communicating what is considered common knowledge.

## Quoting from a Source

Suppose a student named Larissa was planning a speech about the history of drive-in movie theaters. She had drawn her inspiration from a magazine article she saw in an airport while traveling home from school for the holidays. She thought the topic was unusual enough to make an interesting presentation, and her instructor agreed and approved her choice.

When attempting to research the topic, however, Larissa could find little material beyond the magazine article she had found in the airport. Panic set in as the day for her in-class speech approached. In desperation, Larissa decided that no one in her class at the University of Michigan–Ann Arbor would know about the article because it had been published in *Nevada Horizons*, a magazine sold only in the greater Las Vegas area. Rationalizing her actions, she used nearly all the article verbatim in her speech.

It turned out that the article had appeared simultaneously in several different publications, including a large national newspaper, where Larissa's instructor had read it. Larissa earned an F in the class and was suspended from school.

---

▼ **Give Credit Where It's Due.** When you incorporate the words and ideas of others into a presentation, it's crucial to do so ethically. Say that you are writing a speech about the value of pursuing an education and you want to quote Nobel Prize laureate Malala Yousafzai (shown here). How should you proceed? Take care to limit the length of the direct quote you use and carefully cite the source of your information. That way, you'll reference her words in a way that's both appropriate and meaningful. James D. Morgan/Getty Images

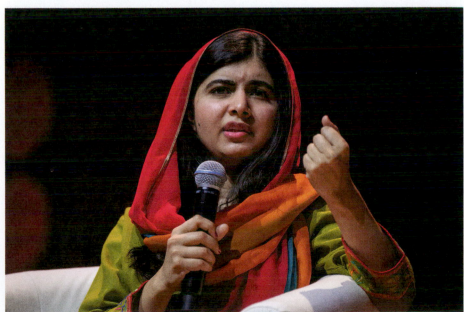

Clearly, what Larissa did constituted plagiarism. But what if she had taken only one-third, one-half, or even just a few lines of the story and represented the material as her own? Would any of these scenarios have constituted plagiarism? Yes. Whether she had lifted five pages, one page, or just a single sentence, she would still be stealing the original author's words and ideas. By analogy, a shop owner won't care whether you stole one egg or an entire dozen. Either way, you stole.

Plagiarism is particularly common among students who research their speech topics online. The temptation to lift and use text from a website can be overwhelming, but doing so without attribution is stealing. Students face the related danger of unintentional plagiarism when they copy a quotation from a source and paste it into their notes without writing down the citation information. When they return to their notes later, they may not remember that they copied and pasted the material as opposed to writing it themselves.

Most of the direct quotations you use in a speech will be short—a line or two or possibly a brief paragraph. To avoid plagiarism, you always need to attribute the quote to its source. How should you cite the source? If Larissa had just used several quotes from the magazine article, she might have attributed the material in the following way:

> As Roberta Gonzales wrote in the June 19 issue of *Nevada Horizons* (D4), "The growth and popularity of drive-in theaters tracked with the affordability of automobiles for a larger and younger population of drivers."

The first part of this sentence is the attribution, which includes the page number. In delivering your speech, it's OK not to cite the page numbers of all your sources. However, we strongly suggest that you document a complete citation on your speech outline or text. That way, anyone (including your instructor) who wants to check your facts can easily do so. Before preparing your speech, make sure to check with your instructor to find out if there are additional expectations for proper attribution.

## Paraphrasing the Work of Others

Suppose Larissa never lifted the text from the magazine article verbatim. Instead, suppose that she used **paraphrasing**—restating the original author's ideas in her own words. Would this constitute plagiarism?

This is where the rules defining plagiarism are a bit less clear. Is it stealing if you use your own words but not necessarily your own ideas? Your teachers will not expect you to be an authority on every speech topic you address; you *will* have to research your subject matter. This may cause you to wonder, "How could it be plagiarism if I'm paraphrasing someone else's words or ideas? After all, these are *my* words!"

Students at the college level regularly struggle with this challenge. To resolve the dilemma, consider this simple rule of thumb: if you're using

most or all of the original material, simply rearranged and restated in your own words, you're still taking another person's ideas and presenting them as your own. This isn't the same as directly copying without attribution, but it is wrong on several fronts. For one thing, you're not generating your own ideas and opinions about your topic—so you're not meeting your instructor's expectations. For another, you're being unfair to the person whose ideas you're presenting as your own.

The safest bet is always to acknowledge the original source of any material you use in your speech, whether you are directly quoting or paraphrasing. For example, if Larissa had paraphrased some ideas from the magazine article, she could have mentioned the author and source of this material in the following way:

> According to Roberta Gonzales, writing in the June 19 issue of *Nevada Horizons* on page D4, drive-in theaters tended to grow in popularity with Americans who were increasingly able to afford and enjoy the freedom of automobiles. This was especially true of younger drivers, who yearned for freedom of mobility and a common place to meet and socialize outside the scrutiny of Mom and Dad.

## Common Knowledge

There are limited situations—known as common knowledge—in which you can use information from a source without giving a direct citation. **Common knowledge** is information that is widely known and disseminated in many sources. For example, you may not need to cite the fact that France presented the Statue of Liberty to the United States in 1886, but you may need to cite a source if you wanted to give statistics, such as the statue's total weight (125 tons), the weight of the statue's concrete foundation (27,000 tons), or the distance the statue's torch sways in the wind (5 inches).[5] Be sure to check with your instructor on guidelines for common knowledge. But remember: when in doubt, include the citation.

# USING SOUND REASONING

All public speakers have a responsibility to provide well-reasoned support for their points. **Fallacious reasoning** is faulty (and thus unsound) reasoning, in which the link between a claim and its supporting material is weak. Unfortunately, fallacious reasoning is all too common in speeches, even if it's often unintentional. When public speakers *intentionally* misuse logic to deceive their audience, their actions are profoundly unethical. Four common ways in which a speaker might misuse logic include the following:

- **Hasty generalization:** Making a claim about all members of a group from information based on a limited part of the group
- ***Post hoc* fallacy:** Wrongly identifying the cause of one event as the event that immediately preceded it
- ***Ad hominem* (personal attack) fallacy:** Attempting to weaken someone's argument by making unsubstantiated claims about that person's character
- ***Ad populum* (bandwagon) fallacy:** Believing that an argument is true simply because other people believe it

We will discuss these and other logical fallacies in more depth in Chapter 18, Methods of Persuasion.

## SPEECH CHOICES

### A CASE STUDY: *RAFAELA*

*Let's check in with Rafaela as she makes ethical decisions about her speech assignment.*

Now that Rafaela had a preparation schedule for her persuasive speech, she decided to think more about topic ideas. After weighing several ideas that she was interested in (which you'll learn more about in Chapter 6), Rafaela narrowed her focus to one particular topic—young women who ran for student office in high school or college and the likelihood of their running for public office later on. As she began researching, Rafaela came across an article in an alumni magazine about a woman who had served as student-body president in college. The woman was now running for a seat in the California state assembly, and she credited her decision to run for public office with having run for office while in school.

Rafaela decided to contact the woman from the alumni magazine story to see if she might interview her for the presentation. She agreed, and Rafaela met with the candidate, who confirmed that her prior experience with school elections had been instrumental in leading her to run for office now. As a bonus, the candidate's daughter had run for president of her high school class. But though the daughter had been inspired by her mother's example, she had lost the race and seemed a bit discouraged about running again. She was also unsure about what impact running for class president would have on her later in life.

At first, Rafaela wasn't sure how to handle what she had learned from the candidate's daughter. Eventually, though, she decided she could use both the mother's and daughter's examples to illustrate how experience of (and exposure to) elections encouraged women to run for office—while also making it clear that additional factors influence women's choices about whether to run. By incorporating the real-life experiences of the candidate and her daughter, Rafaela was confident that she would be able to ethically and accurately prove her point—instead of overemphasizing the significance of running for office in school.

 **YOUR TURN:**

> Now that you've seen how Rafaela's ethical choices influenced her speech, consider similar choices you'll need to make for a speech of your own. Making speech choices involves asking and answering a series of questions related to your assignment. For speech ethics, your questions might include:
>
> - Am I comfortable with all of the ethical decisions that I've made in writing this speech?
>
> - Have I properly credited the sources that I referenced in my speech?
>
> - Is my paraphrasing sufficiently different from the original source?
>
> - Have I steered clear of all lies, half-truths, or false inferences?
>
> Making choices in response to questions like these will help you craft an ethical speech that meets class requirements—*and* respects your audience.

# BEING AN ETHICAL LISTENER

So far, we've focused our discussion of ethics on speakers' responsibilities. But audience members also have a responsibility to demonstrate ethical behavior. The qualities that characterize what we call an **ethical audience** include courtesy, open-mindedness, and a willingness to hold speakers accountable for their statements. When you're listening to someone who's giving a speech, consider the following guidelines for exhibiting ethical behavior.

## Show Courtesy

As previously noted, the old adage about treating others as you'd like to be treated applies just as much in public speaking as it does in any other area of life—and this includes audience members as well as speakers. When someone is delivering a presentation, extend the same courtesy you would appreciate if you were speaking. Courteous behavior includes focusing your attention on the speaker as soon as the speech begins, and stopping any activities that may distract you or the speaker (working on a class assignment, texting your friends, chatting with your neighbor). Show the speaker that you are actively paying attention.

Also, when a speech is being delivered online, keep in mind some specific tips regarding courtesy. First, if your video is activated, be aware that everyone else will be able to see what you're doing if you're not paying attention. As a good rule of thumb, behave as if everyone else in the class is watching. Likewise, if possible, avoid the temptation to turn off your video for long stretches—or find other ways to stay engaged without video, such as contributing a question to the chat or reacting to a particular point with an emoji. (For further discussion, see Chapter 15, Mediated Public Speaking.)

## Demonstrate an Open Mind

Avoid prejudging the speech or the speaker. Even if you have a strongly held belief on the topic or you dislike the speaker, look for parts of the message—or aspects of the speaker—that signal common ground. Consider the fact that you might actually hear something that changes your mind or that broadens your perspective on the speech topic.

## Hold the Speaker Accountable

Prejudging a speech or a speaker is clearly unethical. But mindlessly swallowing what the person says in a presentation can be equally damaging. To avoid this, you need to hold the presenter accountable for all claims that are made and offered as truth. How can you do this? If time is available at the end of the speech, ask questions that prompt the speaker to explain or defend statements you think require additional evidence. If your instructor allows time for a longer exchange, don't hesitate to honestly (and respectfully) express your response

to the speech. Convey questions and opinions politely, focus on the content of the speech itself, and scrupulously avoid attacking the speaker's character. For example, say, "Can you tell us more about how you arrived at those figures?" rather than, "You obviously didn't care enough to do a thorough job in your research." In offering feedback to the speaker on the presentation, frame your comments or suggestions constructively—that is, in ways that can help the person build their public speaking skills. Avoid destructive feedback, which diminishes the presenter and disparages the speech.

## CHAPTER REVIEW

❝Strive to be an ethical public speaker. ❞

As you saw with the scenarios about Alex's misleading Zoom appearance and Bob's campaign lies at the beginning of this chapter, public speaking can present numerous ethical challenges—dilemmas that make it difficult to determine what constitutes right and wrong behavior. In this chapter, we focused on those challenges from both speakers' and listeners' perspectives. First, we discussed the different codes of ethics, including ethical absolutism, situational ethics, and cultural relativity. We then examined the differences between legal and ethical speech. We showed how people can be unethical in public speaking, mainly through lying, telling half-truths, and causing false inferences. We also discussed the ethical ways to acknowledge the work of others (quoting from a source, paraphrasing the work of others, and using common knowledge). We touched on using sound reasoning, which we discuss in more depth in Chapter 18. Finally, we shared how to be an ethical listener: by showing courtesy, demonstrating an open mind, and holding the speaker accountable.

## Key Terms

ethics *58*
ethical absolutism *58*
situational ethics *59*
culturally relative *60*
ethical speech *62*
legally protected speech *62*
half-truth *64*
false inference *65*
taking evidence out of context *66*
omission *66*

plagiarism *68*
paraphrasing *70*
common knowledge *72*
fallacious reasoning *72*
hasty generalization *72*
*post hoc* fallacy *72*
*ad hominem* (personal attack)
   fallacy *72*
*ad populum* (bandwagon) fallacy *72*
ethical audience *74*

## Review Questions

1. Define *ethics*, and explain the difference between ethical absolutism and situational ethics.
2. What ethical responsibilities does the speaker have in a public speaking situation?
3. What rules govern legally protected speech? How do they differ from the rules governing ethical speech? Which category is broader, and why?
4. Describe three ways in which a speaker can present untruthful information.
5. Name and describe the different types of false inferences covered in this chapter.
6. Define *plagiarism*, and explain the importance of properly citing your sources.
7. How is a paraphrase different from a quote? How are they similar?
8. What are the ethical responsibilities of the audience in a public speaking situation?

## Critical Thinking Questions

1. As an audience member, have you ever felt that a speaker was intentionally misleading you? What gave you this feeling? How might you have verified this person's facts?
2. How does the failure to properly acknowledge a source in a speech affect the speaker's credibility?
3. The illustration on page 59 poses the ethical dilemma that arises when someone who loves or trusts you asks your opinion about something that may be personal to them, meaning that the truth may be uncomfortable for this person to hear. How would you handle an ethical dilemma like this? What is more important—keeping this person happy or telling the truth?
4. Name a practice on your campus that is legal but not necessarily ethical. Why do you think students engage in this practice, and what would you say to a friend who is considering it?

## Activities

1. As indicated earlier in the chapter, the approach to ethics can vary by individual and culture. Consider your family's cultural background; what examples might you provide that show some variance of opinion about ethics and communication? For example, how do members of your family feel about exaggerations or little white lies—as opposed to big lies? Do they tolerate the former and reject the latter? Do they think they are all unacceptable—or all unavoidable? Where do you stand on these questions?
2. Review your school's policies on plagiarism. How clear is the definition of *plagiarism*? Do you think the guidelines provide clear rules for citing the work of others? What is the punishment for stealing someone else's words or ideas? Based on this information and what you've learned in this chapter, where would you draw the line between plagiarizing material for a speech and using the material as inspiration for what you write?
3. Listen to a few of the twentieth century's greatest speeches (you can find most of them at AmericanRhetoric.com). Do they all stand up to ethical scrutiny? Does the Internet—which has multiple websites devoted to fact checking in real time—compel modern public figures to be more or less careful about what they say?

# LISTENING SKILLS

> **66** Listening is a vital skill in public speaking and beyond. **99**

Jason was excited. For an informative speech on the ways young people use the Internet, he had decided to focus on the popularity of Twitter. An active social media user, Jason found the topic fascinating and looked forward to developing the speech. To learn more about the habits of students using Twitter, he conducted six face-to-face interviews with classmates from his speech course. Jason felt pleased with the amount of information his classmates shared during the interviews, but when he later reviewed his interview notes, he realized they were a bit sparse.

With time running out, Jason finished developing his presentation using the few insights he could glean from his notes. On the day of the speech, Jason presented his claims about how young people use Twitter—basically, that they often repost content from other platforms (like news sites and blogs) instead of using it as an independent medium. Once he began speaking, he felt confident and comfortable talking in front of the class. All that changed, however, during the question-and-answer period following the speech. Judging from the questions his classmates asked, few of them—if any—agreed with Jason's observations and suppositions about student Twitter users. In fact, they argued that those who

---

◄ **Be a Speaker AND a Listener.** Are you hoping for an enthusiastic response like this one the next time you deliver a speech to an audience? It helps to listen. Paying attention to your audience's reaction can help you gauge whether your message is resonating—or whether you might need to make an adjustment. AJ_Watt/Getty Images

engaged in the kind of activity he had described were easy to recognize as being new to Twitter—and were often perceived as not having a lot to say. Confused and somewhat blindsided, Jason wondered where he'd gone wrong.

Jason's unpleasant experience reveals the importance of listening in public speaking. Unfortunately for him, he missed two major opportunities to listen:

1. When he was interviewing his classmates, Jason failed to pay enough attention to take comprehensive notes. This lack of attention was confirmed later, when he couldn't recall details from the interviews.

2. Jason failed to listen to his audience while delivering his speech. If he had focused on his classmates' reactions while he was talking, he might have detected both auditory and visual signs that they disagreed with his claims (eye rolls, head shakes, and muttered comments such as "Seriously?"). By not listening carefully while both researching and delivering his speech, Jason never connected with his audience members and thus lost credibility with them.

As Jason's story reveals, listening is a vital skill for public speakers at all stages of the speech preparation process. Yet many novice speakers find this idea surprising. After all, it's the *audience* who has to listen, right? To be sure, audiences can be good listeners by respectfully and carefully attending to the speaker's message, but speakers also have many opportunities to practice good

listening skills while preparing and delivering a presentation. Think about it: you interview people to research your speech. You practice your presentation in front of trusted friends or family members and listen to their feedback. And you deliver your speech, paying attention to your audience's responses to decide whether you need to adjust your voice, volume, pacing, or some other aspect of your delivery. By failing to listen at any of these stages, you risk ignoring information that will be necessary for presenting the most effective speech possible.

The above points are certainly true when you speak in front of a live audience, but interestingly enough, the necessity to be a good listener is even more critical when you are giving a presentation online (e.g., on Zoom). Some members of your online audience may be watching and listening to you, while others may have turned off their cameras and muted themselves, leaving you to wonder how much they are paying attention. In these more nuanced circumstances—as we discuss in Chapter 15—finding ways to connect with your audience, while staying engaged yourself, will help you speak successfully.

If you're not particularly skilled at listening (whether in person, online, or both), you're not alone: many people have a similar difficulty. Yet you *can* learn how to strengthen your listening skills, and this chapter offers helpful guidelines to achieve that outcome. In the following pages we explore the importance and process of listening in public speaking, and then consider the causes behind ineffective listening behaviors. We also offer suggestions for effective listening that you can put into practice as both a speaker and an audience member.

## THE LISTENING PROCESS

It's crucial for speakers *and* audience members to understand the listening process. How you listen as a speaker—while both preparing and delivering a speech—can have a powerful effect on the quality of your presentation and your ability to connect with your audience. How you listen as an audience member can strongly affect your ability to absorb the information the speaker is imparting to you. Equally important, improving your listening skills as both a speaker and an audience member will help you interpret and use more of what you hear from others in a wide variety of situations—not just in your public speaking course.

For example, consider the usefulness of listening within the field of civic engagement. Suppose that you marry and start a family—but just as your daughter is approaching the age of five, she is diagnosed with autism. There are a range of things that can be done to support her and your family, but in the meantime, you are disheartened to learn that your local school district has few special programs available for children with autism spectrum disorders. You realize you are not alone in dealing with this problem, so you decide to organize with other parents of children with similar needs. Good listening will help you identify which school board members are likely to be sympathetic to your demands for more services when you make a presentation at the school board meeting. It will also help you sense any confusion or disagreement among your audience members and adapt your delivery as needed to win their attention and support.

To understand the listening process, let's start with the specific differences between listening and hearing.

## Listening vs. Hearing

Listening and hearing are two different activities, and research affirms the importance of listening—versus merely hearing—for both public speakers and their audiences. Several studies have suggested that when people hear without actually listening, they can miss virtually all the content of oral messages (imagine the droning adult voices in Charles Schulz's *Peanuts* cartoons).[1] **Hearing** means merely receiving messages in a passive way. **Listening**, on the other hand, refers to actively paying attention to what you're hearing; it involves both processing the message to decide on its meaning and retaining what you've heard and understood.

To further explain this distinction, let's briefly consider how both science and communication researchers define listening and hearing. Cognitive scientists—those who study the mind—consider listening to be a conscious mental process that includes the following components:

- Selection (attention, perception)
- Organization (interpretation)
- Integration (storage, recall)[2]

Communication researchers define listening in a slightly different manner, using terms that describe listening as a step in the communication process. For them, listening involves:

- Sensing
- Interpreting
- Evaluating
- Responding[3]

Both cognitive scientists and communication researchers agree that hearing is a passive, physical activity—the act of sound waves reverberating against the eardrums, triggering messages that are sent to the brain.[4] Although listening is possible after hearing begins, listening is an altogether more complicated process.[5] Compare the act of watching television versus reading a book. Whereas watching TV is a passive activity (like hearing), reading is a learned activity that requires information processing (like listening).[6]

It is worth noting that hearing loss or deafness does not prevent a person from receiving and processing a message. Today, for example, people can use a variety of techniques that don't involve sound waves—from sign language to reading text on a screen behind a speaker—to follow what is being said. While

these methods may differ from the technical definitions noted above, they produce the same effect: people can both *hear* what is being said (that is, receive the message) and they can *listen* to what is being said (by actively paying attention to the message).

In the following section, we further discuss listening. For the purposes of this book, we focus on two main aspects of listening—processing (which inevitably draws from sensing, interpreting and evaluating) and retaining.

## Processing What You've Heard

When you engage in **processing**, you actively think about a message you're receiving from someone else—not only the words but also the nonverbal cues. For example, suppose you're a small-business owner who's meeting with Jeff—a salesperson for eLogic, a business-software developer. You want to decide whether eLogic's software for tracking and fulfilling orders is a good fit for your business. As Jeff describes the product, you consider the implications of what he is saying, how using the software will affect your bottom line, and whether Jeff represents a reputable company. You observe his attitude and body language (confident and knowledgeable or nervous and inept?). You may even jot down notes. You then mull over a series of questions: "Can my business afford this investment? Will I need to provide extensive training to help my workers learn the new software? Are there other programs that can deliver similar advantages while being cheaper and easier to use?" By weighing these matters—that is, by processing the information in your mind—you stand a better chance of making a smart decision for your business.

▲ **Process Actively.** As you listen, if you actively think about the message you're receiving—that is, you process it—there's a better chance you will remember that message. Here, an audience member listens carefully to the points being made by a U.S. presidential candidate in advance of the New Hampshire primary.
Win McNamee/Getty Images

## Retaining What You've Processed

The more carefully you process what you're hearing, the more you will engage your powers of **retention**—your ability to remember what you've heard. In fact, one of the authors of this textbook took part in a ten-year study of listening patterns and found that poor retention of a speech was directly related to audience attentiveness during the presentation.[7] This study also found that individuals with poor attention habits remembered only a fraction (25 percent or less) of what was said in a speech. Worse, what they *could* recall was often inaccurate or confused with something else they had in their heads at the time of the presentation. Among those who fail to process what they're hearing, the ability to accurately recall what they heard decays just three to six hours after the original communication.

The study also revealed a recurring pattern of attentiveness—called "the attentiveness curve"—in people who did not listen well. At the beginning of a presentation, poor listeners tended to pay little attention. Their attention quickly improved as the presentation continued (perhaps because they realized they *should* have been paying attention), but then it fell quickly again, before finally rebounding near the end of the speech. Clearly, their sporadic levels of attention made it much harder for these listeners to process messages; it is no wonder, then, that they retained very little of what was said.

## THE ATTENTIVENESS CURVE

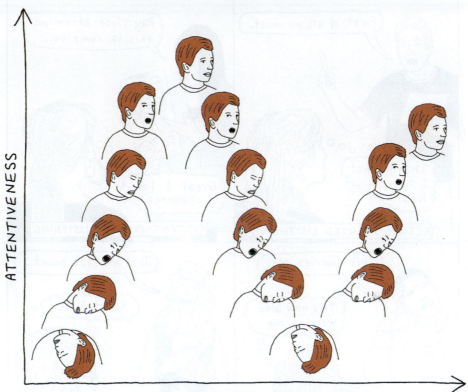

To further see the connection between processing and retention, consider your own listening behavior as a student. How much information do you retain if you pay little attention to your instructors in class? If you take notes during lectures, how accurate are they? How much do you remember from lectures in which you did not process what you were hearing? There's no doubt about it: the more carefully you process messages, the more likely you'll remember what you heard—and retain it accurately.

In the next section, we analyze listening behavior further by examining the different types of listening styles.

## Listening Styles

Research shows that the different ways people listen can be categorized into specific styles. In general, most people usually default to a specific style and are reluctant to switch from the style of listening they usually use, even if doing so might make them better at receiving and retaining information.[8] In fact, it appears that most people default to a traditional style of listening out of habit.[9] The best listeners, however, will often modify or alter their listening behavior

# LISTENING STYLES

depending on the context or situation.[10] Recognizing the different styles and adapting them to certain situations can help maximize your listening behavior as both a speaker and an audience member. As a speaker, you can recognize the style your audience might be using and adapt your message and delivery to best connect with them. As an audience member, you can change your listening style based on your situation in order to maximize your listening skills.

Learning about the different listening styles—*action-oriented listening, content-oriented listening, people-oriented listening,* and *time-oriented listening*[11]—is the first step to using them to your advantage. Let's consider each of these in turn.

- **Action-oriented listening.** People who use this style of listening usually focus on immediately getting to the meaning of a message and determining what response is required. These listeners indicate a preference for messages that are direct, concise, and error-free. Conversely, these listeners are easily frustrated by those who ramble or take a while to get to the point.

- **Content-oriented listening.** In contrast to action-oriented listeners, content-oriented listeners favor depth and complexity of information and messages. They are willing to spend more time listening, pay careful attention to what's being said, and enjoy discussing and thinking about the message afterwards.

- **People-oriented listening.** Like content-oriented listeners, people-oriented listeners are willing to invest time and attention in communications, yet they are differentiated by their interest in being supportive of friends and strengthening relationships. These listeners notice the mood and body language of speakers and express more empathy toward them.

- **Time-oriented listening.** The major identifying element of this listening style is time—or, more precisely, a concern with managing time. These listeners see time as a precious resource to be conserved and protected. Thus, they can exhibit impatience and rush interactions.[12]

Did you recognize any of these styles as your default? Using one or two of them more often doesn't mean you can't embrace other styles and use them in appropriate contexts. Do you have a friend with personal problems who needs someone to talk to? Most likely, a people-oriented approach is best. Did a fellow student ask you to critique an oral report she plans to deliver in class? You should consider a content-oriented approach. But what if she asks you to critique the report when you have your own looming deadline? In that case, you would probably take a time-oriented approach, explaining your time constraints and setting reasonable expectations about what you can listen to and deliver.

## THE CULPRITS BEHIND POOR LISTENING

Although recognizing and using the right listening style is a big step in the right direction, you will likely still face listening challenges—both as a speaker and as an audience member. Some of the causes behind poor listening include such behaviors as *unprocessed note taking, nonlistening, interruptive listening, agenda-driven listening, argumentative listening,* and *nervous listening.* Later in this chapter, we also discuss *defeated listening* and *superficial listening.* In the following sections, we cover the challenges and offer tips to help you overcome them.

### Unprocessed Note Taking

Ben is a former NBA center and is now working for a large national bank. As a business-development officer, he sells the bank's financial products to wealthy clients. This is his first job after a career in sports, and Ben is aware that a primary

▲ **Make Your Notes Count.** By staying focused on the speaker's message and thinking actively about what you're writing, you'll be more engaged in processing their most important points. FreshSplash/Getty Images

reason he was hired was his professional basketball experience. His manager thinks his background might open doors for him. Ben is very conscientious about keeping an accurate record of what he discusses with each prospective client. When prospects speak in these initial meetings, Ben takes copious notes—often without even looking up. Later, however, Ben finds that he recalls very little of these meetings and has a hard time distinguishing one prospective client from another. Why is this happening? Ben is taking in the information, but he is not processing it.

Note taking can be a useful tool at various stages of the speechmaking process—from writing notes while interviewing an expert during the research phase to jotting down key ideas when you're an audience member. However, note taking can become a problem if you engage in **unprocessed note taking**— copying the speaker's words verbatim without considering what you're writing down. Unprocessed note takers physically hear words, but they don't listen— that is to say, they fail to actively process and retain them. Instead, the words enter their consciousness and just as quickly exit, deposited in their notebooks or on their laptops—sometimes in an incomprehensible form. Unprocessed note takers usually have trouble remembering what was said in an interview, a lecture, or a speech. They also miss opportunities to ask clarifying questions or to comment in informed, thoughtful ways. When you're taking notes, be sure to focus fully on your interviewee or speaker, processing what this person is saying and writing down the most important points.

## Nonlistening

People who engage in **nonlistening** simply do not pay attention to what they're hearing. For example, if you're overly interested in asking your own questions during an interview, you won't be attuned to what the interviewee has to say in response. In a lecture, you are likely to engage in nonlistening if you are focused more on your own thoughts about the subject than on what the speaker has to say. Not surprisingly, nonlistening prevents you from processing another person's message—and therefore keeps you from retaining it. If you feel distracted when interviewing a source, listening to a presentation, or giving a speech, take a moment to calm your mind and redirect your energy to listening. Remind yourself of the importance of listening in this situation, whether it's to learn new information, to strengthen existing knowledge, or even to get a good grade.

## Interruptive Listening

With **interruptive listening**, one person consistently interrupts another. You may have seen or heard instances of interruptive audience members, voicing their opinions or blurting out questions before the speaker is ready to entertain them. Speakers, too, can be interruptive listeners. For example, a speaker might call on an audience member who raises his hand, but instead of listening to the question, the speaker cuts him off midsentence and finishes the question for

him. Speakers who do this are likely to miss certain aspects of the question or comment. Worse, they often come across as rude and arrogant, thus losing the respect of their audience.

Be sure not to interrupt when listening to others: let them get their thoughts out fully before responding (if you are asked to respond). If you are the speaker dealing with an interruptive listener, tell the audience you'll be happy to answer more questions at the end of the speech.

## Agenda-Driven Listening

Public speakers who focus solely on the mechanics of their presentation may demonstrate **agenda-driven listening**. This listening challenge applies primarily to a speaker who also has to accommodate questions and comments from audience members. For example, this speaker might ignore raised hands from the audience or "listen" to questions while scanning her notes. Or she might provide monosyllabic and overly brief responses, revealing that she's not really listening to her audience. Not surprisingly, this behavior can annoy audience members and damage the speaker's credibility. Agenda-driven listening is especially common with speakers who are anxious: they may be focusing so strongly on their task that they fail to notice their audience.

To avoid this problem, make sure to constantly analyze your audience in order to confirm that they are keeping up with and understanding your speech (see Chapter 5 for more on audience analysis). Happily, this may serve to quell

any nerves you may have because you'll be taking the focus off yourself and putting it on your audience.

## Argumentative Listening

People who feel in conflict with the individuals they are listening to may display **argumentative listening**, or selective listening—listening to only as much as they need to in order to fuel their own arguments. Argumentative listening can also afflict speakers who feel personally attacked by audience members during question-and-answer sessions. Because these speakers focus more on their irritation than on the actual question, they may listen to only part of what a questioner has asked and thus can't respond in a thoughtful, informed way. This hurts their credibility.

During an interview, speakers can fall victim to argumentative listening if they disagree with the interviewee's opinions or ideas. In this situation, they may again focus more on their own views and miss out on everything the other person has to say.

If you find yourself speaking to or interviewing people whose statements you disagree with, remind yourself to listen before making judgments. If you ever speak to an argumentative or a hostile group, you may need to address any potential disagreement—a process we discuss in Chapter 5. If you are the one who disagrees while listening to a speaker, try to keep an open mind—at least through the end of the speech!

ARGUMENTATIVE LISTENING

## Nervous Listening

People who fall victim to **nervous listening** feel compelled to talk through silences because they're uncomfortable with conversational lapses or pauses. If an interview subject takes a long time to answer a question, a nervous listener might blurt out more questions and comments, stopping the interview subject from answering fully and leading to incomplete research. As a speaker, imagine giving a speech introduction in which you ask a provocative question in an attempt to engage the audience. If no one in the room responds to your question, you might get thrown off and feel compelled to say something—anything—to get the speech moving again. You might fill in the silence with an awkward comment ("Tough crowd!"), only to see confused or annoyed looks on your listeners' faces.

Nervous listening—in any context—can damage your ability to gather and interpret the information you need to deliver an effective speech. If you feel twinges of nervousness, collect yourself and wait a few beats before continuing. Remember that pauses are normal and can even be used to stress the importance of what you're saying by demonstrating your thoughtful choice of words (see Chapter 13).

# BECOMING A BETTER LISTENER

Along with overcoming specific culprits of poor listening, you can improve your general listening skills by focusing on **interactive listening**, which includes *filtering out distractions*, *focusing on the speaker(s)*, and *showing that you are paying attention*. These behaviors help improve both processing and retaining, in turn making you a more effective listener.

## Filter Out Distractions

There are potentially countless distractions in any speaking situation, both external and internal. *External distractions*, or **external noise**, include street noise, a flashy visual aid left up during a presentation, or chattering audience members. Sadly, distractions very often occur as a result of our interaction with smartphones and other technology. Even though these things can make our lives better, we can limit or damage our interactions with one another when we improperly use them. Consider how often you see people on the street with earbuds inserted, listening to music, or with a cell phone pressed to their ear, loudly engaging in conversation. It may seem as though they are ignorant of or ambivalent to the external environment.

While some research indicates that cell phones can actually enhance listening skills to develop the learning of a new language (for example, teaching Russian speakers to learn the English language), there is also plenty of research indicating that addiction to and dependence on cell phones disconnects us from those around us and the people in our lives.[13] It can also negatively affect the tradition of face-to-face (F2F) interaction and conversation. In her book *Reclaiming Conversation*, MIT researcher Sherry Turkle suggests that continued dependence on cell phones decreases the amount and quality of our conversations.[14] In these circumstances, the ways we listen and process are affected as well. We may miss visual and aural cues that ordinary conversation could otherwise yield, such as eye contact and subtle nuances in vocal tone. We use these cues to develop empathy, which is necessary for being able to make connections and emotionally relate to what is being said. For this reason, Turkle and many others have urged people to put their phone away—not only when driving but also when sitting and talking with someone. Even a cell phone's presence on the table is a conversation buzzkill!

Of course, if you are actually using a smartphone or computer to connect to others—for example, in an online course—it's not possible to disengage from technology altogether. In this type of circumstance, do your best to stay focused on the task at hand by closing any other open apps or windows and disabling notifications, which might pull your attention elsewhere. (See more on this in Chapter 15.)

On the flip side of these external distractions are *internal distractions*, often referred to as **internal noise**. These are any thoughts that make it hard for you to concentrate, such as worrying about how well you're doing in class or pondering aspects of your personal life. If you are an audience member, filtering out distractions means avoiding nonlistening activities, such as gazing around the room or surfing online. As a speaker, filtering out distractions during presentations or question-and-answer sessions means focusing on reactions or questions from audience members rather than looking ahead to your next point. When conducting interview research, this means focusing on your current question and the interviewee's response rather than thinking about your next question or an unrelated topic.

ONE LISTENER EXPERIENCING INTERNAL NOISE

## Focus on the Speaker

In any listening situation, keep your mind on what the speaker is saying, not on what you may be about to hear or what you're going to say next. Ask yourself, "What does this statement that I've just heard mean? Do I agree or disagree with it? Do I have questions or comments of my own about it—or even a different point of view? How might other people think or feel about this comment or issue?"

## Show That You Are Paying Attention

As a responsible listener, you can use a combination of nonverbal and ver-bal cues to show that you are listening. Look at the other person while they are speaking *and* as you are responding. Indicate nonverbally—perhaps with alert posture and a smile or nod of your head—that you are paying attention. Research tells us that nonverbal encouragement from audience members can reduce a speaker's stress levels, whereas anxiety can increase if audience mem-bers appear bored or unresponsive.[15]

When the opportunity presents itself, you can also verbally communicate that you are listening. As an audience member, you can ask thoughtful ques-tions during a question-and-answer session or even applaud appropriately at a rousing portion of the speech. (If you're listening remotely and are muted, the

THE RIGHT WAY TO SHOW YOU ARE LISTENING TO AN AUDIENCE QUESTION

PARAPHRASE

Erm, didn't that woman who's on that court... Sonia something. Didn't she write something about all that?

You're asking if Sonia Sotomayor wrote a book about her journey to the Supreme Court?

Yes, that's right!

chat feature and the clapping emoji can serve similar purposes.) As a speaker, paraphrase questions asked by audience members to show that you understand and to allow them to correct any misinterpretation. And in interview situations, do your best to maintain eye contact and be ready to move into new lines of questioning based on your interviewee's responses.

## MAXIMIZING YOUR AUDIENCE'S LISTENING

Despite your best efforts, you may occasionally find yourself delivering a speech to audience members who do not listen well. Pay attention to your audience's nonverbal and verbal responses as you give your speech; you may notice some audience members who *act* as if they are listening but who you can tell (perhaps by their expression or lack of eye contact) are not listening at all. The good news is that there are strategies you can use to help your audience members listen more effectively to your speech. In this section, we outline several steps that you, as a speaker, can take to both anticipate and deal with audience listening challenges.

### Anticipate Ineffective Listening before Your Speech

Advance preparation is key to ensuring that your audience will truly listen to your message. Be sure to consider your audience's needs as well as outside factors, and plan your speech accordingly.

#### Consider Your Listeners' Attention and Energy Levels.

People listening to a speech at 8:30 on a Monday morning will likely have a limited attention span. Many may be tired from the weekend and may not have adjusted to the new week. Therefore, avoid delivering a long

▼ **Listening vs. Nonlistening.** Is it difficult or easy to tell when someone is paying attention? Consider the presentation shown here: Do all of these colleagues seem actively engaged? SolStock/Getty Images

speech with no audience interaction during times like this. Instead, give a concise presentation, and allot time for active listener participation.

### Assess Your Audience's Knowledge and Understanding.
If your audience members know little about the subject of your speech, they may become confused or start to tune out when faced with unknown jargon or many technical details. To avoid that, explain concepts and define key terms. Also, consider any barriers to understanding, such as whether everyone in your audience has a similar fluency in the English language or whether anyone has difficulty hearing. Then adjust your word choice or volume level as needed.

### Front- and Back-Load Your Main Message.
As you saw earlier in the chapter, listeners tend to pay the most attention just after the beginning of a speech and just before the end. For this reason, plan your speech ahead of time in the following way: front-load your main message (that is, present it early in your speech), and then use your conclusion to give listeners another opportunity to process and retain your message.

### Use Presentation Aids Strategically.
Presentation aids can help you capture audience attention and thereby encourage listening. Therefore, plan to space these aids throughout your speech to maintain interest. Also, don't incorporate a given presentation aid until you want your audience to see or hear it. When you are finished with it, put it away outside your listeners' view or hearing range.

## Encourage Active Listening during Your Speech

When you are ready to give your speech, be sure to pay attention to what you see among your audience. Practice **audience surveillance**, paying particular attention to if—and how—they are listening to you, and be prepared to make adjustments as you go.

### Tailor Your Delivery.
As you deliver your speech, pay attention to factors that affect your audience's ability to listen—voice, volume, fluency, projection, rate, and timing. Speaking too quietly can inhibit listening, as can

poor fluency, fast delivery, or excessive pausing. If you can, maintain eye contact with your audience and avoid making obtrusive gestures (such as pointing at the audience) or turning your back on the group while adjusting a visual aid.

**Watch Out for Argumentative Listeners.** As discussed earlier in the chapter, argumentative listeners will attend to only as much of your presentation as they need to build up their own case against it. To improve your chances of keeping their attention, acknowledge their viewpoints early in your speech (for example, "I know that some of you may not think that having tattoos will affect your careers"), and repeatedly press your main message throughout the presentation.

**Watch Out for Defeated Listeners.** **Defeated listening** occurs when listeners feel overwhelmed by your message and find it too difficult to follow. Speakers who deliver technical or detailed presentations may find this a particular challenge. Defeated listeners may avoid eye contact or work on something else while you speak.

You can prevent defeated listening by pausing occasionally during your speech to ask the audience questions—such as whether they understand your last point or if they can think of an example or an application of what you have just said. By doing so, you can test their comprehension while assessing whether they are really following along. If you cannot engage them here, back up and repeat your message, using simpler language and different examples.

**Watch Out for Superficial Listeners.** Audience members who pretend to pay attention but who are in fact distracted by internal or external noise

DEALING WITH DEFEATED LISTENERS

DEALING WITH SUPERFICIAL LISTENERS

(such as wandering thoughts, cell phones, or conversation) are engaged in **superficial listening**. To prevent it, request that people turn off cell phones and resist checking for messages on handheld devices or laptops during the presentation. (You can also encourage them to turn on their cameras, if you're delivering your speech virtually, though not everyone will feel comfortable doing so.) When possible, use direct eye contact with people who you sense are listening superficially (they will pay more attention if they see that you are watching them), and go ahead and ask them questions—or invite them to ask you some.

## LISTENING WHEN YOU ARE IN THE AUDIENCE

When you're an audience member, listening not only helps you retain the speaker's message but also enables you to provide the speaker with an informed **speech critique**—written or oral feedback offered after a presentation. Critiquing is an essential component of public speaking classes because it helps speakers learn from their experiences. Your instructor will likely specify what you should cover in a critique. The following can give you additional guidance:

- *Take notes.* While listening to a presentation, jot down your thoughts about the speaker's delivery and message. By recording your impressions as you form them, you'll be able to access your thoughts when it comes time to offer your critique.

- *Identify main points.* As you take notes, begin to distinguish the speaker's main points—the two or three most important ideas the speaker wants you to remember (often called "takeaways" or the "take-home message"). Most speakers preview their main points in the introduction, signal them in the body with transitions, and restate them during the conclusion.

- *Consider the speech's objectives.* To provide **constructive criticism**—feedback speakers can use to improve their skills—strive to understand what a presenter is trying to accomplish. Identify the speech's rhetorical purpose—to inform, persuade, or mark a special occasion. Next, evaluate how well the speaker achieves the main goal of the speech.

- *Support your feedback with examples.* Instead of offering overly general comments ("good eye contact" or "work on your organization"), be sure to provide specific details ("You made eye contact with people on every side of the room" or "You had a good preview, but I found the organization of your main points difficult to follow"). Specific comments help speakers know what they should do more of during their next speech and what they should avoid.

- *Be ethical.* Be courteous in your critique, and treat the speaker the same way you hope and expect to be treated when it's your turn to receive feedback. During the speech, avoid prejudging the speaker or topic, and think critically about the message you're hearing. Finally, make sure you hold speakers accountable for their words. If you are offended by or disagree with something in a speech, tell the speaker while providing your critique. Do so courteously, however, and avoid making your comment sound like a personal attack. Explain why you disagree, and offer examples.

# CHAPTER REVIEW

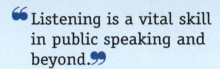

**Listening is a vital skill in public speaking and beyond.**

In this chapter, we discussed a major contrast—hearing noises, sounds, and words versus listening to them. *Hearing* refers to passively receiving these stimuli; *listening* refers to how one processes and understands them. This is particularly relevant to public speaking because both speakers and audience members must develop good listening skills to effectively convey and understand information. Good listening is not limited to words or even sound. By paying attention to an audience's responses, speakers can tell if they need to adjust tone of voice, rate of speech, or some other aspect of delivery.

We further explored how the listening process works, how information is retained, what the types of listening styles are, how individuals may listen differently in different contexts, what causes ineffective listening, and how to improve your listening skills both as a speaker and as an audience member. Listening is vital not only for developing and delivering a successful speech but also for observing and critiquing a presentation, and happily it is a skill that can be learned. To make the transition from hearing to listening, you must process the message, come to your own conclusions, and then retain or remember the message.

There are a host of culprits that lead to unsuccessful listening, including unprocessed note taking, nonlistening, interruptive listening, agenda-driven listening, argumentative listening, and nervous listening. Techniques for better listening include filtering out distractions, focusing on the speaker, and showing that you are paying attention. As a speaker, you can anticipate ineffective listening before your speech and plan accordingly, and you can maximize listening during your speech by tailoring your message and watching out for argumentative, defeated, and superficial listeners.

As an audience member, make sure to take notes and identify the speaker's main points. When giving feedback, offer constructive criticism by considering the speech's objectives, supporting your feedback with examples, and keeping appropriate ethical guidelines in mind.

## Key Terms

hearing *82*

listening *82*

processing *83*

retention *84*

action-oriented listening *86*

content-oriented listening *87*

people-oriented listening *87*

time-oriented listening *87*

unprocessed note taking *88*

nonlistening *89*

interruptive listening *89*

agenda-driven listening *90*

argumentative listening *91*

nervous listening *92*

interactive listening *92*

external noise *92*

internal noise *93*

audience surveillance *96*

defeated listening *97*

superficial listening *98*

speech critique *98*

constructive criticism *98*

## Review Questions

1. What is listening? How does it differ from hearing?
2. What are the various *styles of listening* identified in this chapter? How are they different from one another?
3. Identify and describe at least one internal and one external barrier to effective listening.
4. What two steps make up the listening process? Explain each one.
5. Detail four of the culprits behind poor listening.
6. What is interactive listening? Describe three methods for improving your listening skills through interactive listening.
7. Explain four ways you can prepare in advance to enhance the way your audience listens to your speech.
8. As a speaker, what do you need to look for to determine if your audience is listening? If audience members are not listening, how can you reengage them?
9. Explain three guidelines for listening when you are in the audience.

## Critical Thinking Questions

1. Reflect on your own listening skills. How well do you process information as you listen? How well do you retain a speaker's message? What are some techniques you can employ to improve each of these?

2. Give three reasons why our culture might negatively affect our ability to listen. How can we counteract each of these?

3. Consider the attentiveness curve presented earlier in the chapter. Do you recognize this pattern in your own behavior during lectures? How can you combat the pattern as both an audience member and a student? As a speaker, how might your knowledge of this pattern influence the way you choose to organize and deliver your speech?

4. How would you distinguish the ways you can anticipate ineffective listening before you speak from the techniques you might use to deal with ineffective listening once you are speaking?

5. How can good listening skills help you give a constructive critique to a classmate?

6. What are some tips you can use to enhance listening in an online setting, such as a Zoom meeting?

## Activities

1. Test your listening skills by going to either YouTube or Netflix and watching a monologue from a late-night talk show. After viewing it once, write down a summary of the monologue. Then watch it again with your summary in hand, and see how much you remembered. Try the same activity with a cooking program. Are the outcomes of the two tests any different? If so, what is different, and why?

2. For five or ten minutes in class, try viewing your public speaking instructor as a speaker trying to keep an audience (the class) engaged in effective listening. How does your instructor encourage good listening? How could your instructor be more effective in encouraging effective listening?

3. Look at the image "Dealing with Superficial Listeners" on page 97. Think of what the speaker might have said to encourage audience members to turn off their cell phones for the speech. In your opinion, would a direct approach work best, or is the promise of speech content worth their attention? Write your own speech bubble above the illustration.

# AUDIENCE ANALYSIS

**5**

> **Let the audience drive your message.**

Fresh out of college, newlyweds Helena and Matt decided to become organic farmers. In their search for *arable* land (meaning land where they could plough and grow crops), they were fortunate to find an agriculture park on rural land owned by the water district for a nearby city. For two years, they farmed their acres, growing more than eighty different varietals of organic vegetables and fruit. They sold their produce to restaurants and farmers' markets as well as to low-income families in a small town near their farm. One day they learned that the water district had plans to build an employee parking lot on land next to the agriculture park—a project that would wipe out most of Helena and Matt's farmland and threaten other farmers' land as well.

Representatives of the water district scheduled a public meeting to discuss the new parking lot. Helena and Matt encouraged other farmers to attend the meeting, hoping to convince the representatives of the district that the plan should be halted or altered. On the appointed day, Helena noticed that many local residents had come to observe the meeting; she also noted that reporters from the region's two largest newspapers were present. After a brief consultation, she and Matt took to the podium to address the water district officials, each

◄ **Consider Your Audience.** If, like Helena and Matt, your goal was to promote the continued importance of organic farming to your audience, what messages would you emphasize in your speech? Sascha Kilmer/Getty Images

using different messages intended for two separate audiences. Helena spoke at length about how important organic farming was to the local area—how local restaurants benefited and low-income families (including many in the audience) received healthy and affordable vegetables and fruit because of farms like theirs. Matt then spoke about how senseless it would be to destroy valuable and precious farmland (the soil at the ag park was unique and rich) and replace it with a parking lot—especially when other spaces for such a lot were available. When Matt spoke, he looked directly at the reporters, paraphrasing the lyrics to an old Joni Mitchell song: "Don't it always seem to go that you don't know what you got 'til it's gone? You pave paradise, to put up a parking lot!"

When they finished, many local residents stood in line to speak—and all echoed or repeated what Helena and Matt had said. No one spoke to support the parking lot idea. The next day, news stories in both papers reported the meeting and the controversy. Both led with headlines about "Paving Paradise to Put Up a Parking Lot." After local negative feedback and two stories that made the water district's plan appear foolish, the water district announced it would build a parking lot elsewhere.

This example illustrates that speakers who tailor their message to their listeners create enormous value for their audience *and* for themselves in the following ways:

- Listeners become much more interested in and attentive to the speech content.
- Listeners often experience positive feelings toward a speaker who tries to understand their concerns.
- Listeners open their minds to the speech message because it targets their specific needs, interests, and values.
- Listeners become more open to being persuaded by the message, since it is tailored to them and their specific interests.

Of all the things Helena and Matt did right, the most important was analyzing their audience—recognizing that the residents and the reporters were their real audiences and that, by motivating and persuading them, they could increase the likelihood of persuading the water district to change its plans. Audience analysis is used in more than just delivering a speech—for example, in everyday conversation, we continuously shape our message as we focus on the people we're addressing. But this skill is, of course, also highly significant in the context of public speaking.

To learn about your audience before developing your speech, you will need to gather various kinds of information about your listeners. In this chapter, we organize the types of information you will need to gather into the following categories: situational characteristics, demographics, common ground, prior exposure, and audience disposition. We also provide some tips for gathering these details, as well as suggestions for what to do if you discover halfway through a speech that you've misread your audience.

## TAILOR YOUR MESSAGE TO LISTENERS

# UNDERSTANDING SITUATIONAL CHARACTERISTICS

**Situational characteristics** are factors in a specific speech setting that you can observe or discover *before* you give your speech. They include audience *size*, *time*, *location* (*forum*), and *mobility*.

## Size

**Audience size** refers to the number of people who will witness your speech. In a classroom setting, the size of your audience will be obvious. But in the world beyond school, this information may not be so apparent. For example, if the leader of a charitable organization asks you to give a speech at an awards dinner, you would need to ask how many people will be attending: Seven to ten people? Twenty-five to thirty? Three hundred? A thousand?

When it comes to speech presentations and audiences, *size matters*. In other words, the number of audience members affects how you'll both craft and deliver your message. The smaller the group, the greater the opportunity for you to interact with your audience—for example, through question-and-answer

▼ **Audience Size Matters.** Depending upon what you decide to do for a living after graduation, you may find yourself invited to give presentations to differently sized audiences. Joseph Tuman, an author of this book, speaks about the current domestic political scene once every two years at the UC Berkeley campus. In the speech shown in this photo, he addressed an audience of approximately 800. Kirsten Weisser

sessions.[1] With small audiences, you can communicate a more detailed and specific message because you're tailoring it to the needs of just a few people. Conversely, the larger the audience, the less opportunity you have for interaction. You'll have to work harder to anticipate your listeners' questions and craft a more generally accessible message.

Consider the example of Jeanine, a marketing representative for a software company. Jeanine's boss asked her to visit several cities and deliver elaborate sales presentations—what the boss described as "dog and pony shows"—for a new software product designed to create striking visual online advertisements. Up to that point, Jeanine had presented the product only to groups of five to seven people in intimate boardroom settings. In contrast, the dog and pony shows would take place in large hotel ballrooms, and her audience would range from three hundred to five hundred prospective customers.

As she prepared for the first presentation, Jeanine realized that unlike in her previous experiences, answering every audience member's question as it cropped up might mean never getting through the presentation. Jeanine also realized there wouldn't be time for a lengthy question-and-answer period. With this in mind, Jeanine decided to anticipate and incorporate some of the more likely audience questions into the presentation itself.

Jeanine also realized that among the audience members, there would be a wide range of computer know-how. As a result, she decided to cover technical issues by *teaching to the middle*; rather than pitching the speech to the few listeners who would be extremely computer savvy or slowing things down for the few who would know very little about technology, Jeanine instead focused the speech content on the large group in the middle. That way Jeanine could feel confident that the talk would be accessible to the largest portion of her audience.

## Time

Time is an important aspect of any presentation you deliver, in terms of both the time allotted for the speech and your listeners' own time rhythms in the day. Thus, you will want to consider two aspects of timing—*presentation time* and *body clock*.

**Presentation time** is the length of time you have to deliver your speech. Is it one minute? Five minutes? Twenty minutes? As long as you wish? The answer should shape how you prepare and deliver your presentation.

For example, when your presentation time is short, you have to make tough choices about what to include and what to leave out. Remember, though, that television ads—some of the most powerful, persuasive messages we see—are just fifteen to thirty seconds long, yet they convey extensive information and can strongly influence an audience's beliefs and behavior. To exert the greatest effect in a very short speech, carefully reduce your message to something your audience can quickly digest and comprehend.

If your presentation time is relatively long, you'll have more opportunity to develop your main points, but you'll also be more at risk of digressing—or veering away from your central message. With long speeches, concentrate on sticking closely to your main message. That way, you'll keep your audience members (and yourself) focused.

**Body clock**—also known as **chronemics**—refers to the time of day or day of the week when your audience members will be listening to your presentation. If you have a choice about when to give your class presentation, which days and times would you select? Which would you avoid?

If you sought to avoid speaking early on a Monday morning, you'd be making a wise choice. Many students are still mentally rooted in the weekend and will have difficulty focusing on your speech. Similar distractions abound for people close to lunchtime, at the end of the day, or at the end of the week.

Nevertheless, you can still deliver an effective speech at such times. For example, you might include more humor or anecdotal references to engage your audience. Or with your instructor's approval, you might open by asking direct questions of some audience members, which would heighten their

## NOT CONSIDERING BODY CLOCK

OK, so just another 20 points to cover... Hey, what's that rumbling noise?

Rrrumble, rumble!

## CONSIDERING BODY CLOCK

OK, I can tell you guys are hungry, so just another two quick points...

Rrrumble, rumble!

attentiveness. Finally, you could simply shorten your speech to match your audience's attention span.

One of the authors of this book was once invited to give a presentation to a group of lawyers at 3 p.m. on a Tuesday. The twenty-five-minute speech about effective negotiating strategies was part of an all-day conference. Unfortunately, the conference schedule lagged, and the presenter realized that he would have to speak much later, at 4:30 that afternoon. Because his listeners' attention span would be minimal at that time, he quickly reframed the speech—five minutes of simple tips plus a quick question-and-answer period. Invigorated by the concise and lively presentation, the lawyers were fully engaged and asked spirited questions at the conclusion of the speech.

## Location

**Location**, also known as **forum**, is the setting where your audience will listen to your speech. Speech locations vary widely—from classrooms and auditoriums to conference rooms, outdoor venues, and even online. Each type strongly influences how you deliver your speech.

Consider the following story. Loren, a high school junior, was receiving a scholarship award, which required him to give an acceptance speech at an afternoon assembly. The location of the assembly was the recently completed high school quadrangle—a sunken plaza built about eight feet below the foundations of four surrounding brick buildings. This design produced some rather spectacular acoustics when sound within the plaza was projected against the brick buildings.

Loren received the first award at the assembly. Concerned that the crowd wouldn't be able to hear him deliver his acceptance speech, he had decided to speak with a microphone. What he hadn't realized was that the plaza design alone would amplify his voice. When he spoke into the microphone, the sound was so loud that his listeners grimaced and covered their ears. Because of his inattention to location, Loren's speech was literally too painful to hear!

Loren failed to consider the acoustics of his speech location. In addition to acoustical problems, locations can present other challenges, such as availability of audiovisual equipment (are there electrical outlets for your presentation aids, or should you bring handheld visuals?), lines of sight (will your listeners be able to see your visual aids?), and lighting (is it adequate?). And if you're delivering a speech online—perhaps from your own living space—that carries its own set of challenges, including noise interruptions and technology troubles. (For more on delivering speeches online, see Chapter 15).

How, exactly, can you anticipate and address location challenges like these? For starters, go to the place where you'll deliver your speech. Stand there and imagine yourself giving the presentation. Now position yourself where the audience will be, and imagine listening to the speech. Will all your listeners be able to see and hear you?

## NOT TAKING FORUM INTO ACCOUNT

## TAKING FORUM INTO ACCOUNT

If Loren had taken stock of the forum for his speech ahead of time, he probably wouldn't have elected to use a microphone. Given the size of the forum, he also might have decided to walk from behind the podium and make himself more accessible, so that those in the audience could both hear and see him better.

## Mobility

Different speech settings may have different implications for your audience's mobility—the degree to which listeners move around during a speech. For example, if you're giving a presentation in a classroom, lecture hall, or conference room, you will likely have a **stationary audience**, meaning that listeners will be relatively motionless (sitting or standing) and captive as you're talking. If you are delivering a presentation at an exhibitor's booth at a sales conference, on a town common, or on a city sidewalk, you'll probably have a **mobile audience**—listeners who will be strolling by, stopping for a moment to listen to you, or drifting off to get on with their day.

If you're giving a presentation in a college classroom (in person or online), you know that you will have a stationary audience because your listeners are captive; their grades depend in part on their class attendance and participation. Don't fall into the trap, though, of taking a stationary audience for granted. Surely you have encountered lecturers who do exactly that! Knowing that their audience must remain present, speakers may unwisely assume they don't have to work as hard to capture the audience's attention. But that assumption may be off-base. Veteran teachers know they need to work to maintain a lively, interested class.

Capturing the attention of a mobile audience is clearly more challenging than capturing a stationary audience. To do so, take a hint from the salespeople who make their livings at conventions and county fairs selling everything from rugs and hot tubs to organic produce and kitchenware. These vendors contend with an entirely mobile audience, so they must draw an audience's attention quickly and magnetically. For example, a seasoned vendor might try to sell a

▼ **Dynamic Speaking.** Iron Chef Masaharu Morimoto hosts a cooking demonstration at a wine and food festival in New York City. At events like this one, where audience members are often mobile, capturing their attention with a dynamic and interactive presentation is key. Dave Kotinsky/Getty Images

fruit and vegetable knife by arranging colorful, precut fruit in pleasing shapes, such as that of a flower or a windmill. She also might make the speech interactive by stopping passersby and encouraging them to "test-drive the knife, have some fruit, watch a little slice and dice!" You can adapt these effective techniques to your own presentations by offering fun (and perhaps edible!) visual aids and making your presentation interactive—either by inviting audience members to come over or by asking intriguing questions that fit with your overall message. (Just make sure the questions are appropriate to the speech setting and aren't personal or invasive.)

# INCORPORATING DEMOGRAPHICS

In addition to considering situational characteristics, you also need to take demographics into account. **Demographics**—a term that originated in the world of public relations and marketing—refers to certain characteristics of your listeners.[2] For example, demographics can include *age, gender identity, sexual orientation, race and ethnicity, disability status, religious orientation, socioeconomic background*, and *political affiliation*.[3] We should be clear that using demographics is very different from the fallacious practice of *stereotyping*—holding permanent mental impressions, which are often gross oversimplifications, of people in a particular group. By assessing your audience members' demographics, you can better anticipate their beliefs about your topic, their willingness to listen to your message, and their likely responses. In this section, we examine demographic characteristics you should consider while developing and delivering a presentation.

## Age

**Age** can affect how audience members respond to your message. For example, a presentation on safe snowboarding would not likely interest most retired persons. But it would probably hold great appeal for athletic students in their late teens and early twenties.

As a best practice, try tailoring your supporting materials (such as examples and quotations) to the needs of different age groups within your audience. For instance, older listeners may not always understand references to the popular musical groups or late-night comedy shows that younger people tend to appreciate. And younger listeners might not understand references to classic film stars, like Greta Garbo or Cary Grant, or even early rock and rollers, such as Elvis Presley. For younger listeners, you might avoid referring to events that took place before they were born unless you place the events in context for them.

Of course, when you're speaking to a large group of diverse listeners, their ages may vary considerably. With an audience of mixed ages, be sure to either add some context to your references so everyone can understand, or use references that would naturally appeal to a wide range of listeners.

## Gender Identity

Your audience's **gender identity**, which indicates "one's innermost concept of self as male, female, a blend of both or neither"[4] (see Chapter 1), also affects how your listeners will respond to your speech. Some stories, illustrations, or examples might resonate better with one gender grouping than another, and people who wish to be effective speakers understand this difference. At the same time, while consideration of gender is a valid component of audience analysis, it's important never to assume you know about an individual audience member's views based on gender—or even that you know their gender identity at all. The views of countless individuals cut against the grain of traditional ideas of **gender stereotypes**—oversimplified and often distorted views of what it means to be male, female, or any other gender. In addition, gender is more complex than a simple female or male binary—for example, someone's gender identity can be nonbinary (meaning they don't identify as exclusively male or female), agender (meaning they don't identify with any gender), or transgender (meaning their sex at birth isn't consistent with their gender identity).

Understanding these differences with respect to gender is the speaker's responsibility, and it is also incumbent upon speakers to consider ahead of time how to respectfully approach and address people's gender differences in ways that avoid making unevidenced or naïve assumptions. For example, when addressing a large group of people, it has been traditional to greet an audience with the words "Good evening, ladies and gentleman." This sounds polite, but it makes assumptions about the gender identities of audience members, which can be risky—and potentially insulting. Instead, it is likely appropriate to greet your audience with more general and potentially inclusive language-choice, such as: "Welcome distinguished guests and friends of the Music Conservatory! You honor us with your presence tonight!" Likewise, ethical speakers can respectfully approach gender differences by taking care not to resort to **sexist language**, or language with a bias against any gender identity.

## Sexual Orientation

Another demographic characteristic that has become increasingly important to consider and acknowledge is the **sexual orientation** of your audience members. This demographic includes people who are heterosexual and people who are members of the LGBTQ community, such as those who are lesbian, gay, bisexual, and queer or questioning. As the Gay and Lesbian Alliance Against Defamation (GLAAD) explains it, the difference between sexual orientation and gender identity is that "sexual orientation is about who you are attracted to and fall in love with; gender identity is about who you are."[5]

Acknowledging differences in sexual orientation can be accomplished both overtly and passively, depending on what is appropriate for your speech and your situation. Open and overt acknowledgment of these differences might be accomplished by including illustrations that reference both LGBTQ and heterosexual people. For instance, a speech on conflict in relationships might include examples of gay, lesbian, or bisexual couples alongside examples of heterosexual couples. Likewise, a speech on life as a working parent

might cite a recent documentary about Pete Buttigieg, the former Presidential candidate and current Secretary of the Department of Transportation, which explores his life in politics, his marriage to husband Chasten, and the couple's responsibilities as new parents. The film depicts two people juggling careers while trying to care for and raise children—an experience to which many working parents can relate! Examples like these demonstrate the importance of recognizing sexual orientation as a significant demographic characteristic, and also work to disrupt the idea of **heteronormativity**—a worldview promoting heterosexuality and heterosexual relationships as the norm and the only natural way of expressing sexuality.

In addition to more overt examples like these, it is also smart to offer passive acknowledgment of the LGBTQ community (and do so sensitively) through inclusive word choice. For example, instead of speaking only of "a man looking for a woman" (or vice versa), you might refer to "people seeking loving partners" or "individuals looking for a long-term commitment." Inclusive word choice invites everyone in the audience to share in the speech while avoiding language that privileges one form of sexual orientation over another.

## Race and Ethnicity

In the United States today, the population is far more racially and ethnically diverse than in previous eras. With this increased diversity, your audience is likely to encompass a wide variety of racial and ethnic origins. In preparing and delivering your speech, it's important to be sensitive to your listeners' diverse backgrounds and speak to their varied interests. At the same time, however, be careful to avoid generalizing about particular races or ethnicities. For example, all Americans of white European descent don't necessarily feel the same way about affirmative action, and neither do all Americans of African descent.

Still, **race**—common heritage based on genetically shared physical characteristics of people in a group—*can* affect how listeners respond to a speaker's message. This is especially true in situations in which racial issues are sensitive, affecting people throughout their lives.

**Ethnicity**—cultural background that is usually associated with shared religion, national origin, and language—is another important demographic aspect to consider because it can shape beliefs, attitudes, and values of audience members. A student named Gunther learned this lesson the hard way. Gunther gave a presentation to members of his campus's student-run Middle Eastern Society and spoke to an audience he was told consisted of students who had fled from Iraq shortly after the U.S. invasion in 2003. Attempting to show courtesy, Gunther addressed his listeners as "Iraqis."

Only later did Gunther learn that his audience had been made up of Assyrians who had been living in Iraq. Although Assyria no longer exists as an independent nation, there are millions of people who continue to identify themselves as Assyrian. They speak a common language, share religious beliefs, and have their own distinctive traditions and customs. Although many of the

Assyrians in Gunther's audience realized his mislabeling of them as Iraqis was unintentional, they still took offense at being categorized as part of a group with whom they did not identify. They (rightly) concluded that Gunther hadn't cared enough to look into their actual backgrounds. Offended and annoyed, many didn't bother to listen to much of Gunther's presentation.

## Disability Status

**Disability status** is another demographic category to consider in analyzing an audience. Recent data from the Centers for Disease Control and Prevention indicates that as many as 61 million American adults live with a disability of some kind; that is 26 percent of the adult population in the United States. Given these numbers, it is wise to anticipate that a definable number of audience members attending your speech will have disabilities of varying types. For example, there may be members of your audience who are deaf or hard of hearing. There may also be individuals in the audience who are blind or who have low vision, or those with developmental or mobilty-related disabilities. By anticipating and planning for the presence of audience members with disabilities ahead of time, you can take steps to better include all audience members. For example, many speakers now consider it a courteous and expected practice to have someone standing with the speaker signing for the deaf members of the audience, and, for those who are blind, designated individuals may record the presentation so audience members can listen again as needed.

## Religious Orientation

**Religious orientation**—a person's set of religious beliefs—can also influence how people respond to your speech. In the United States alone, there are as many as twenty-three hundred religious identifications—including Baha'is, Buddhists, Christians, Confucians, Hindus, Jews, Muslims, and Zoroastrians.

For some, religious orientation strongly shapes views on a wide range of issues—including but not limited to marriage equality, abortion, and gender roles in family life and society. Moreover, some of the larger religions have numerous subdivisions, whose adherents possess conflicting beliefs about specific issues. For example, Anglicans and Roman Catholics share common elements in the celebration of the Eucharist, but they are widely divided over such issues as allegiance to the papacy and the admission of women into the priesthood. Likewise, Reform and Orthodox Jews differ in their dietary laws and in their interpretations of the Torah. Thus, like any other demographic characteristic, religious orientation does not preordain (pardon the pun) an audience's reaction to a given message, yet it can still exert great influence. Presenters who craft their speeches accordingly stand a better chance of connecting with their listeners.

One particularly enduring example of this approach is the late Pope John Paul II's address to the state of Israel at the Yad Vashem Holocaust memorial

▲ **Speaking about Religion.** Often acknowledged as the face and leader of Buddhism, the Dalai Lama—a globally famous spiritual leader, hailing from Tibet— is shown here making a commencement address at UC San Diego. How might he best craft a speech for this audience, knowing that listeners are likely to have a variety of religious orientations? BILL WECHTER/Getty Images

in March 2000. The pope knew that many Jews believed that his predecessors had been indifferent to Jewish suffering during the Holocaust. Demonstrating his sensitivity to their feelings, the pope repeatedly used Old Testament passages to describe suffering and awareness of human evil. In addition, he condemned all the hatred, acts of persecution, and displays of anti-Semitism directed at Jews by Christians throughout time.

The current pope, Francis, has continued John Paul II's example and taken many steps toward further improving relations between Christians and the worldwide Jewish community. Welcoming a Jewish delegation to Rome in 2015, Francis declared in his address to the public at St. Peter's Square: "Yes to the rediscovery of the Jewish roots of Christianity. No to anti-Semitism."[6]

## Socioeconomic Background

Related to but distinct from questions surrounding demographic characteristics such as race and religion are those that concern the social and economic background of an audience member or group. **Socioeconomic status** is a measure of where individuals stand in relation to other people in terms of financial resources, education, and occupation. As a speaker, it's important to consider your audience's socioeconomic status and how it might influence their individual and collective concerns. For example, in 2012 both Barack Obama and Mitt Romney recognized that middle-class voters would largely decide the election and often tailored their messages specifically to them.[7] But four years later, the term *middle class* seemed to have disappeared from their speeches.[8] One explanation suggests that while the term *middle class* had earlier been associated with homeownership, a job, children's college funds, and money for retirement—accessible parts of the American dream—after the Great Recession (which began at the end of the first decade of the twenty-first century), the term came to be associated with a lower standard of living, difficulty in finding jobs without special technical training, and houses lost to bank repossessions. The number of people within this group had grown substantially, and the term began to remind people who identified as middle class of their (sometimes mistaken) sense of financial plight.

**Financial Resources.** It is likely that the experiences of people who come from wealth and privilege will be different from those with lower incomes who have fewer resources and options, as well as limited choices. For this reason, a person who has always been financially comfortable may have very different concerns than a person who is struggling financially. A speech extolling the benefits of using online coupon sites like Groupon, for example, might be of more interest to a lower-income group than to an affluent group. Conversely, a speech on stock market investing might fail to capture the attention of students worrying about how to repay college debt, with little or no extra money to invest of their own.

Negotiating your path through assumptions about socioeconomic status can be tricky business: labels like *high income*, *low income*, and *middle class* are relative terms that carry little real meaning. You can, however, analyze your audience to get an idea of their collective economic status. For example, for a speech focused on whether it was ethical and appropriate for regents of the state university system to increase student tuition, Eleanor considered

---

▼ **The Science of Effective Speaking.** Suppose that this speaker (the Director of Science for the Save the Redwoods League) is speaking before a group that includes both *dendrologists* (tree scientists) and *botanists* (scientists who focus on trees and plants). If the speaker is aware that both types of scientists are present, she would be smart to address each group within its own field, while also using both groups' shared interest in trees to bring them together. Al Seib/Getty Images

the following facts: many of her classmates had attended community colleges before transferring to the four-year state university; the majority worked to pay for all or part of their tuition; and due to work obligations, a large portion attended class part-time and would need five or six years to graduate. Eleanor concluded that these aspects of her audience's background would undoubtedly affect their attitudes about the cost of education and what they would be willing to spend.

**Education and Occupation.**  Your audience's level of education and occupation can also influence their reaction to your speech. For example, suppose many of your listeners are already familiar—through formal education or life experience—with the facts you plan to present in your speech. If you're aware of this familiarity beforehand, you'll know that you won't have to provide extensive background information in your speech. But if your audience is unlikely to have had exposure to your topic through formal schooling or life experience, you'll need to provide more explanation and examples to help them understand your presentation.

Listeners who lack background in your subject might also benefit from presentation aids that clarify the points you're making. In addition, carefully repeating your main points can help your audience members understand your presentation by giving them time to absorb and process the information.

## Political Affiliation

In some respects, **political affiliation**—a person's political beliefs and positions—is the most difficult of the demographic characteristics to pin down. Traditional labels like *liberal* or *conservative* and *Republican* or *Democrat* elude specific meaning and are so broad as to be relatively useless in predicting a person's views on every issue. *Conservative*, for example, may refer to *fiscal conservatism* (belief in balanced budgets and reduced taxes), *law-and-order conservatism* (belief in the need for a stronger criminal justice system), *defense conservatism* (belief in the necessity for a strong defense and military preparedness), or *social conservatism* (belief in the importance of preserving traditional values and established institutions, often informed by religious perspectives). Members of your audience who identify as conservative won't all necessarily hold the same beliefs about each of these dimensions of conservatism. Likewise, membership in a political party does not guarantee that someone will vote for a specific candidate or respond to a speaker's message in a predictable manner.

Nevertheless, knowing your listeners' political orientation—as well as their views on specific political issues—can help you determine how to craft your speech. In a highly polarized political climate, attention to your listeners' political orientation becomes especially crucial to making a successful presentation.

## Putting the Demographic Pieces Together

Great public speakers use knowledge of their listeners' demographic character-istics to understand the people they are addressing—and to make their messages more effective. Every audience is unique; by identifying characteristics that many of your listeners share, you gain insights into how they might respond to your message. You can then incorporate these insights as you develop your speech and frame your message for the audience.

For example, Jackie, a middle-aged doctor, was asked to give two speeches on safe-sex practices—one to a group of teens in a runaway shelter, and the other to a group of parents at a school. Jackie knew she would need to craft her message differently for each audience. Because she suspected the teens would be suspicious of authority figures, she avoided calling attention to the age differ-ence between herself and her listeners. In contrast, Jackie's speech to the group of parents included a reference to her own age and role as a mother.

Using demographics is also important in more complex situations—such as when you're trying to make a persuasive case to audiences with opposing views. For example, a city council member named Ignacio campaigned to fund a pension program for retired city workers while also scaling back benefits for younger, newly hired city employees. When speaking to an audience of retired workers, Ignacio acknowledged that the city had to honor its thirty-year-old promise to provide for their pensions—especially because he knew that many of these individuals grew up in a time when employers took care of their employees for life. In exchange for

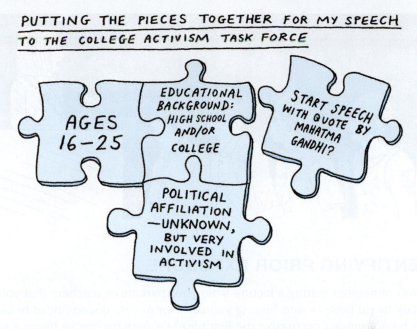

PUTTING THE PIECES TOGETHER FOR MY SPEECH TO THE COLLEGE ACTIVISM TASK FORCE

AGES 16–25

EDUCATIONAL BACKGROUND: HIGH SCHOOL AND/OR COLLEGE

START SPEECH WITH QUOTE BY MAHATMA GANDHI?

POLITICAL AFFILIATION —UNKNOWN, BUT VERY INVOLVED IN ACTIVISM

honoring the city's commitment, he asked them to consider increasing their financial contributions to their own health care. When Ignacio spoke to younger workers, he acknowledged that he, too, felt the burden of paying for retirees' pensions, but emphasized that in keeping this promise to older workers, the younger workers could trust him to keep his word regarding future policies as well.

## SEEKING COMMON GROUND

Another way to analyze your audience is to look for **common ground**—beliefs, values, and experiences that you share with your listeners.[9] Consider Jay, a student at a commuter school who gave a persuasive presentation to convince his listeners to use mass transit instead of driving to campus. Like many of his listeners, Jay had spent his first year of college driving to school every day, which involved getting caught in traffic, having difficulty finding parking, and arriving late for classes—none of which endeared him to his instructors. As he gave his presentation, Jay shared his personal experiences with driving because he knew that many of his listeners faced these same challenges. By establishing this common ground, Jay gained credibility with his listeners.

In some cases, you can communicate your perception of common ground nonverbally. For example, a candidate for national political office may don a cowboy hat while delivering a speech to voters in Texas or a sports cap from a local team. Of course, merely putting on a hat doesn't necessarily mean you share actual common ground with your audience. Use this technique only if you feel a genuine sense of shared identity with your listeners, and then reinforce that authenticity by referring to common ground during your speech.

# IDENTIFYING PRIOR EXPOSURE

Do you remember getting a lecture from your parents or teachers that you've already heard before—and finding yourself completely unconvinced because their points weren't persuasive the first time? Or perhaps you've heard a sales pitch or an ad slogan that seems dull initially, only to become even more so every subsequent time it plays? This type of thing can be a problem for public speakers, too—as a student named Henry discovered while giving a persuasive speech in an advanced speech class. Henry's speech critiqued the existence of climate change. In making this speech, he picked up where he had left off in an earlier informative speech, explaining how people uncritically accept what they hear from television news media. In the original speech, Henry had used climate change as an example of "stories that television media push on people," and then he'd added that climate change was a myth. At this point in the speech, people had begun to show that they were critical of his message (rolling their eyes and smirking), but Henry had failed to notice. When he received compliments for his speech delivery, he took that as a sign that his audience had agreed with his message. When Henry revisited the issue in his persuasive speech, he repeated the same criticisms of climate change—and was later surprised to learn that the audience disagreed with him. Henry's mistake was *not* in taking an unpopular position about climate change but in ignoring the audience's reaction to what he had said the first time and simply repeating those arguments for the same audience.

Analyzing your audience includes gauging listeners' **prior exposure**—the extent to which they have already heard your message.[10] The degree of this prior exposure should guide you either to include particular points in your speech or to craft something entirely new. How can you determine whether your audience has had prior exposure to your topic—and then use that information to shape your presentation? Ask yourself the questions included below (keeping in mind that prior exposure won't be particularly useful to either the speaker or audience members if the latter does not recall the content of that prior exposure).

## Has My Audience Heard This Message Before?

If your answer is no, your listeners have had zero prior exposure and will have no preconceived notions about or positions on your message. You can craft your message as you want, but you may have to explain all relevant issues and concepts in basic terms. If your answer is yes, your audience has had prior exposure. Move on to the second question.

## Has My Audience Responded Positively to the Message?

If the goal of an earlier speech on your same topic was persuasion, consider whether audience members actually engaged in the actions or adopted the beliefs the speaker advocated. If the purpose of that earlier speech was to inform, determine whether audience members became interested in the subject and understood the information the speaker shared.

If your answer is yes—meaning your audience responded positively to the message in the past—then use the new speech to reinforce the previous message, add any pertinent new information, and motivate your audience to take action (if you are giving a persuasive speech).

If your answer is no—meaning your audience did not respond positively to the message in the past—plan to avoid the approach used in the previous presentation. Then proceed to the third question.

## Why Did the Previous Message Fail?

Assess what went wrong the last time your audience heard the message. Then use the resulting insights to tailor a more successful approach. In the case of Henry's speech, he would have benefited from asking his classmates why they disagreed with his position in his first speech. Perhaps he would have discovered that some of them questioned his knowledge of science, some of them knew about climate change only from what they had heard on television, and some of them found him a bit arrogant. Knowing the answers to this question would have given Henry other options for his second speech.

▲ **Memory for the Message.** When prior exposure to a previously stated message is tough to recall—like how to tell alligators and crocodiles apart—a visual component (such as bringing an alligator into class) can add to your speech and better define the differences: that alligators have wide and short U-shaped faces, while crocodiles have slender, almost V-shaped muzzles. Mel Melcon/Getty Images

Additionally, if your audience has had a major change in perspective since the previous presentation, consider whether you need to adjust your message to accommodate listeners' new viewpoints. For example, if Henry's audience had initially been receptive to his message, only to watch their city experience severe flooding from a hurricane strengthened by global warming, he would need to consider how their opinions on the topic may have changed in crafting his second speech.

## IDENTIFYING AUDIENCE DISPOSITION

Finally, complete your audience analysis by assessing listeners' **disposition**— their likely attitude toward your message. In most situations, audiences can be divided into three groups—*sympathetic*, *hostile*, and *neutral*.

A **sympathetic audience** already agrees with your message or holds you in high personal esteem and will therefore respond favorably to your speech. For example, imagine that you are giving a speech advocating the controversial and hot-button issue of gun control to an audience made up of American Medical Association members—in this case, surgeons who work in emergency departments, often on victims of gun violence. More than likely, you will have found a sympathetic audience.

In contrast, a **hostile audience** opposes your message or you personally and will therefore resist listening to your speech. Imagine, for example, that you are giving the same speech advocating gun control, but this time you are a speaker at a convention of the National Rifle Association (NRA). The audience in this instance would likely be hostile to your message because the NRA strongly opposes restrictions on gun ownership.

A third type of audience is the **neutral audience**, which has neither negative nor positive opinions about you or your message. Listeners may be neutral for several reasons. Some may be apathetic and simply not interested in you or your ideas. Others may be very interested in hearing you talk but lack strong feelings about your topic. The key thing to remember about neutral audiences is that they can tip toward either supporting your message or opposing it. To extend the earlier example, imagine that you are now giving the same speech on gun control to the American Bar Association, an organization for lawyers. The membership of this association has mixed attitudes about gun control and would likely be considered a neutral audience.

As with the other elements of audience analysis, gauging your listeners' disposition can help you figure out how to craft your speech. For example, suppose you'll be facing a uniformly hostile audience. In this case, you should probably define realistic goals for your speech. Although you may not be able to persuade your listeners to follow a course of action you recommend, you might succeed in getting them to reevaluate their opposition to your message or to you personally. In other words, seek incremental or small changes, as opposed to a complete turnaround in attitudes.

An excellent example of this involves the late senator Edward (Ted) Kennedy, a Democrat from a storied family who was invited to speak in October 1983 at Liberty Baptist College (now Liberty University), a conservative Christian school established by the Reverend Jerry Falwell. Kennedy, a well-known liberal lawmaker, agreed to speak at the school, even though he knew he would face a hostile audience. For his speech, Kennedy addressed the emotionally charged subject of separating church and state. His speech, titled "Truth and Tolerance in America," focused on the appropriate place for religion in discourse about politics. In a speech that at times found common ground with Baptists and Falwell himself, Kennedy carefully but clearly encouraged religious groups to enter political

SYMPATHETIC          NEUTRAL          HOSTILE

discourse where moral and ethical questions were concerned. He also suggested they avoid name-calling or disparaging those who disagreed. It is unlikely Kennedy convinced many in the audience to change their minds about contentious issues like abortion, but he did gain the audience's respect for working to find some commonality with them.[11] Indeed, after Kennedy's speech, a bond of sorts was established between Kennedy and Falwell, and it remained so to the end of their lives.[12]

If you're addressing a sympathetic audience, you don't need to bother investing a lot of time and energy into trying to convince listeners that your ideas have merit or that you're a credible speaker. Instead, push for more commitment: rather than simply asking your audience members to agree with you, urge them to act on your message.

If you'll be facing a neutral audience, determine whether your listeners' neutrality stems from apathy, disinterest, or a lack of firm conviction about you or the issue at hand. Then figure out how to overcome these forces of neutrality and get your listeners to support you—not oppose you.

Note, though, that many audiences don't fit neatly into just one dispositional group. In most cases, some listeners in a particular audience will be hostile, others sympathetic, and still others neutral. You'll need to tread carefully to deliver the most effective speech possible. If most of the people in your audience are neutral, some are sympathetic, and the remaining few are hostile and very vocal, what should you do? Expend just enough effort to silence the hostile listeners, make an equally modest effort to motivate your sympathetic listeners to act on your message, and devote the lion's share of your energy to reaching your neutral listeners—and persuading them to take your side.

# GATHERING INFORMATION ABOUT YOUR AUDIENCE

Thus far, this chapter has reviewed the types of information you will need to analyze your audience. Here we examine three techniques you can use to obtain that information—*surveying*, *interviewing*, and *observing*.

## Surveying Your Audience

A **survey** is a set of written questions that you ask your audience to answer in advance of your speech. Surveys allow you to ask your future audience members direct questions about topics related to your speech. If the audience is small—let's say thirty or fewer—try to survey all of them. If it is larger, you may want to survey a small representative sample.

Three general types of questions typically appear in a survey—fixed response, scaled, and open ended.

A **fixed-response question**—such as a true/false, multiple-choice, or select-all-that-apply question—gives your respondents a set of specific answers to choose from. Fixed-response questions are useful for gaining concrete insights into an audience's experience with or views on a topic. For example, imagine that Megan, a student, is preparing to give an informative speech on why visiting the dentist is a good idea (partially to convince herself!). She could ask fixed-response questions to find out if audience members have any experience with dental care or even to see if there is any potential for common ground, as some audience members might also be nervous about dentist visits.

A **scaled question** measures the intensity of feelings on a given issue by offering a range of fixed responses. These ranges can take the form of a numerical scale (for example, from one to ten for lowest to highest) or a list of options (including "strongly agree," "agree," "neutral," "disagree," or "strongly disagree").

Determining the intensity of your audience's feelings about a topic can help you determine their prior exposure and disposition. For her speech, Megan sought to discover the extent to which pain influenced people's attitudes about visiting the dentist. If her classmates were very frightened by the prospect of pain, she could focus her points on advances in dental anesthesia and new teeth-cleaning technologies that lessen uncomfortable scraping.

An **open-ended question** invites respondents to write an answer of their choosing, rather than offering a limited set of responses. For such a question, Megan might ask respondents to describe any problems they have had when visiting the dentist.

▼ **Student Survey.** High school students in Los Angeles provide feedback about new food options for the school cafeteria. The chef for the school district enlisted students to help him plan a new menu by conducting a taste test for selections under consideration, including macaroni and cheese and enchiladas. Bob Chamberlin/Getty Images

Open-ended questions can help you identify issues you might not have otherwise considered or covered in your other questions. Thus, if Megan wanted to know the range of dentist-related problems her audience members had experienced, she could best find out through an open-ended question.

Open-ended questions also allow respondents to communicate in their own words. With fixed-response questions, it's possible that none of the options accurately describe the views of a specific audience member; open-ended questions allow each person to state an individual, nuanced answer.

## Interviewing Your Audience

In addition to distributing surveys, you may want to **interview** audience members. Ideally, you will do so in person, but you can also conduct interviews over the phone or even via email or instant message. Interviews allow you to interact through conversation, in which you learn facts and hear stories you couldn't have gotten through a survey. Interviews also allow you to get to know members of your audience before you deliver your speech. This can serve as a great icebreaker, especially if you don't know the people you will be addressing. Finally, you may find it more practical to interview a few audience members than to distribute a survey to a large group.

If you use interviews, carefully consider your interview subjects. Often, it's easiest to talk to audience members you already know. Also, if you are presenting to a professional group, it would be logical to interview the group's leader. And if your audience has diverse backgrounds and interests, be sure to interview a range of audience members.

When conducting interviews, ask the same sorts of fixed-response, scaled, and open-ended questions that are used in surveys. It is often a good idea to use fixed-response or scaled questions to get an overall impression of your interviewee's views on a topic and then ask open-ended questions to gain more insight. During your interview, make sure to put your listening skills into practice by paying attention and always being respectful. Make sure to observe the following: prepare your questions ahead of time, show up at the interview location

as scheduled, observe appropriate grooming habits, and be friendly. Also, make sure to thank each interviewee with a card or an email after the interview is over; after all, they are helping you out with your presentation!

## Considering and Observing Your Audience

Surveys and interviews are two effective methods of obtaining information about your audience. But you may not always have the chance to communicate with audience members before you speak. If this is the case, you will need to rely on less direct methods to learn about your audience. Ask yourself why your audience will be attending the speech. If your talk will occur during a class, you already know several things: you have a captive audience, your status as a student provides you with obvious common ground, and you share some background with your audience in the academic discipline of the course. If you are a member of the College Republicans and are asked to participate in a debate at the College Democrats club, you would likely find a hostile audience. Those attending would be there voluntarily and would thus be free to leave at any time. Nevertheless, politics would be a major interest to your audience, and the fact that both you and your audience participate in political clubs on campus would give you some common ground.

# SITUATIONAL AUDIENCE ANALYSIS

Occasionally in your speaking experience, you may find that you've done everything you're supposed to do in terms of tailoring your presentation to your expected audience, only to arrive at the venue to discover that the audience you're facing is not quite the audience you expected. At other times, you may notice that the audience does not seem to be following along while you are delivering a message or that listeners seem to disagree strongly with your main points. The following suggestions will help you analyze the audience *in the moment*—a skill known as **situational audience analysis**.

If the audience ends up being different from the one you expected, take a quick look at your outline and check whether the examples you've chosen make sense with this new audience. For example, if the audience is smaller than you expected, consider jettisoning a portion of your outline and making time for questions and answers. Also, quickly consider whether your assumptions about common ground, prior exposure, or disposition of audience still apply. If not, you may need to verbally include more (or less) background or explanation than you had expected. Finally, consider your presentation aids. Because it would be difficult to create new visual aids at this point, you may decide to get rid of some if the new audience is already informed about the topic. Or you may want to provide more explanation for certain aids if the new audience is less informed.

Because communication is a transaction between you and your audience, your audience will be sending you messages during your delivery as well. What if you are delivering your speech and your audience seems confused, lost, or hostile? Try to read the mood of your audience members, and adjust your delivery appropriately. If listeners seem confused, slow down, leave out some of the

## SPEECH CHOICES

### A CASE STUDY: *RAFAELA*

*Let's check in with Rafaela to see how she is integrating audience analysis into her speech preparation.*

As Rafaela continued to think about her idea for a speech about women running for office, she decided to interview several women in her class to get their perspective. She discovered that three women had been in student government before and two considered it a valuable experience. One student said it helped build her résumé when applying to college; the other said it gave her a helpful perspective of what it was like to be in charge. None of the women had received much encouragement, but they had run anyway because it was important to them personally.

Rafaela decided that women running for office was the perfect topic for her speech. However, it occurred to her that her speech was to be for the whole class, and only about half of her classmates were female. Rafaela wanted to inspire women in the class to run for office, but now she wondered, "How do I accomplish this if the speech is supposed to be for everyone?"

Rafaela decided to interview several of the men in her class to get a sense of their perspective, too. Seven of them had been in student government before, and five out of the seven said the experience had been positive—it gave them confidence about their public speaking ability and taught them to occasionally make concessions in order to reach agreements. Roughly half had been encouraged to run by friends and family, which had been motivating for them.

As she finished the interviews, Rafaela recognized one way to make the speech resonate with more students in the class: she would incorporate the perspectives of both groups she had interviewed into her speech, and then segue into how the benefits of running for office could extend to more women if more of them decided to run.

 **YOUR TURN**

> Now that you've seen how Rafaela's choices influenced her speech, it's time to consider similar choices you'll need to make for a speech of your own. Making speech choices involves asking and answering a series of questions related to your assignment. For audience analysis, your questions might include:
>
> - What situational characteristics do I need to consider?
> - What are the demographics of my audience members, and how should they influence my speech?
> - Do I have any common ground with my audience (aside from our shared status as students in a public speaking course)?
> - What is likely to be my listeners' prior exposure to my topic?
>
> Making thoughtful choices in response to questions like these will help you craft a speech that's meaningful—both for you *and* your audience.

## ADJUSTING TO THE AUDIENCE DURING A SPEECH

specifics or technical concepts, and instead explain a few of your points in more detail. Humor might also lighten the mood and get listeners on your side. If listeners seem bored or unengaged, consider inviting audience questions or spicing up your delivery by adding enthusiasm and varying your tone of voice.

You may notice from your listeners' body language, gestures, or even their voices that they are opposed to your position. In this situation, you can always flash a sincere smile or use a comforting tone of voice. You may want to reconsider common ground with the audience and your audience's prior exposure to your message. If you can see another element of common ground you share with audience members, you may wish to incorporate that into your speech. Likewise, if the new audience seems to have less prior exposure to your message than you anticipated, you may want to discard some of the points from your outline. If there is more prior exposure—coupled with a slightly more hostile disposition—emphasize points of common ground even more strongly.

## CHAPTER REVIEW

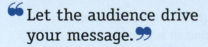

66 **Let the audience drive your message.** 99

In this chapter, we shared five ways to analyze your audience: assess situational characteristics, consider demographics, identify common ground, gauge prior exposure, and anticipate your audience's disposition. We suggested ways of gathering information on these elements of audience analysis, such as surveying, interviewing, and observing and considering your audience. Finally, we explained that exceptional speakers analyze their audience while they're preparing a speech *and* while they're delivering it to retain their audience's attention and support (situational audience analysis).

Given the fact that audience-driven presentations are consistently the most effective, we strongly encourage you to analyze your audience in advance of your presentation and to use that analysis as a tool to shape your main points, supporting material, and even delivery (including time and presentation aids). It is important to recognize, however, that audience analysis is an ongoing process—a process worth reexamining as you develop your topic and message and hone the final product into a speech. You may even be faced with a slightly different audience than you expected on the day of your delivery. Don't be afraid to alter your speech if assumptions you made about the audience are no longer accurate. Being flexible and open will help you craft and deliver a message that is targeted to the specific audience you address.

## Key Terms

situational characteristics *106*
audience size *106*
presentation time *107*
body clock (chronemics) *108*
location (forum) *109*
stationary audience *111*
mobile audience *111*
demographics *112*
age *112*
gender identity *114*
gender stereotype *114*
sexist language *114*
sexual orientation *115*
heteronormativity *116*
race *116*
ethnicity *116*

disability status *117*
religious orientation *117*
socioeconomic status *118*
political affiliation *121*
common ground *123*
prior exposure *124*
disposition *126*
sympathetic audience *126*
hostile audience *127*
neutral audience *127*
survey *128*
fixed-response question *128*
scaled question *129*
open-ended question *129*
interview *130*
situational audience analysis *131*

## Review Questions

1. Describe the following situational characteristics as they relate to audiences: size, time, location, and mobility.
2. Explain what demographics are, and note eight demographic characteristics that a speaker can consider when analyzing an audience.
3. Explain *stereotyping*.
4. Define *heteronormativity*.
5. What areas of common ground can a speaker focus on when addressing a diverse audience?
6. Define *prior exposure*, and explain why it is important.
7. Identify and describe three types of audiences in terms of audience disposition.

8. Name and describe three tools speakers can use to gather information about their audience.
9. Explain the nature of situational audience analysis.

## Critical Thinking Questions

1. After reading this chapter, answer this question: Is there ever an occasion when it may be better to make a general speech message you can apply identically in any audience situation?
2. Think back to speeches you have heard in your life (for example, a speech of a candidate running for student office): Are there any you recall in which the speaker was essentially repeating something they had said on earlier occasions—which also resonated with you? Have you had the opposite experience—someone repeating an earlier stated comment that did *not* resonate with you? Of the latter, is there any way this person could have repeated the nonresonating message in a way that would have been appropriate for you?
3. If your classmates are to be your primary audience for your speech, how can you use class time to perform informal audience analysis? How might the timing of your speeches (both day of the week and time of day) over the course of the semester affect your knowledge of your audience?
4. What kinds of situational adjustments do you make in everyday conversation? How can you apply these strategies to a speech?

## Activities

1. Make a list of the demographic groups to which you belong, including age, gender identity, sexual orientation, race and ethnicity, disability status, religious orientation, socioeconomic background, and political affiliation. If a speaker were to address you based on only one of these demographic characteristics, how would you react?
2. Take a good look at the other people in your public speaking class—they will be your audience for many if not all of your in-class presentations. Using some of the tools for audience analysis in this chapter, assess the ways that members of your audience are alike (what characteristics do they share?) and the ways that they are different. What do you think they may have in common with you and you with them?
3. President Joseph Biden is a practicing Catholic, and as president he has expressed support for abortion rights. Because of Biden's position—which is at odds with the position specified by the Vatican—very conservative American Catholic bishops have argued that he should be denied communion at church. Pretend that you are advising Biden. How would you suggest he address the Catholic bishops in America, and what would you have him communicate to the pope?

# SELECTING YOUR TOPIC

> **"Use your topic to focus the message."**

Early in the semester, Sara received the first major assignment for her public speaking class: "Prepare a speech on a topic of interest to you and your audience." Feeling panicked, Sara thought, "How on earth am I supposed to pick a topic?" While numerous ideas floated through her mind, she wondered how she could possibly make the best choice. The course had barely started, and already she felt overwhelmed.

But as Sara thought more about her situation, she realized that in a sense, she chose speech topics many times every day. When she wanted to start a conversation with a friend, a family member, or the student standing behind her in a long line at the bookstore, she needed to first figure out what to talk about. In these situations, she strove to select subjects that would interest both her and the other person. Usually this led to satisfying conversations.

With this in mind, Sara considered several topics for her speech. She knew what topics interested her, and most of them centered on emergency management—the process of preparing for and coping with disasters. (During the previous term, she'd interned for a state emergency management agency

◀ **Select a Meaningful Topic.** A speech on preparation to cope with a flood could be very useful for an audience in a region that experiences flooding. SAEED KHAN/ Getty Images

specializing in natural disasters.) Her first idea was a speech about the community hazard vulnerability analysis she had helped create, but this topic seemed technical and complex. Because Sara was planning on a career in emergency management, she considered speaking about potential jobs in this field (first responders, social service managers). But her classmates had diverse majors and career plans, so this topic wouldn't necessarily interest them.

Sara changed gears and tried to think of related topics that would interest both her and her audience. Because her school was located in a region that had recently sustained major flooding, she thought her classmates might wonder how they could best prepare for and deal with a future flood. Sara decided that this topic would be perfect: she knew it well, and it would be relevant and helpful to her audience. Plus, her experience presenting this topic in class would help her in the future when she was called on to discuss flood preparedness with government officials or community groups.

Sara's experience shows that even if you are initially unsure about what topic to choose for your speech, you can find something interesting if you put your mind to it. In this chapter, we present a process for selecting and refining your topic—including developing a list of possibilities, choosing the most promising one from the list, and narrowing that topic so that it meets your speech's objectives and can be covered in the allotted time. In addition, we discuss drafting a specific purpose and a thesis statement once you've selected your topic.

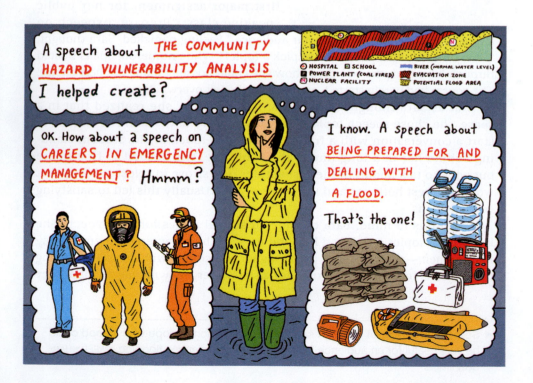

# DEVELOPING A SET OF POTENTIAL TOPICS

Possible speech topics are as varied as human experience. For example, your topic could be lighthearted or serious, address ancient history or current events, or relate to professional interests or a recreational activity—and that's just the beginning. Here are some topics we've seen students select over the past several years:

| | |
|---|---|
| 3D printed vaccines | life on other planets |
| artificial lung research | neonatal technology |
| college e-sports teams | Ozark trail |
| concussion prevention | Peruvian civilizations |
| food security on campus | preparing for the next pandemic |
| good bacteria | social music platforms |
| Great Wall of China | taking notes in longhand |
| Hmong weddings | using military experience in college |
| Iditarod dogsled race | volunteering in an election |
| lawnmower parents | zebras |

Often, it is the speaker's responsibility to select a topic, although in some instances you may be assigned a topic by your instructor, by your employer, or by those who have invited you to speak. When you are called upon to choose your own topic, there is a process you should follow to select the best topic for your speech. The first step is to develop a diverse set of possibilities using the following strategies—*research*, *brainstorming*, *word association*, and *mind mapping*. Each of these strategies encourages **divergent thinking**, meaning that your mind generates diverse and creative ideas.[1]

## Research

**Research** is often an effective way to begin your topic selection process. General newsmagazines, newspapers, and websites are great sources for subjects because they include articles on current events, science, geography and culture, famous people, and the arts. These resources can both provide ideas for topics that are new to most audience members or offer new perspectives on topic areas that may already be familiar to the audience. This can help you avoid repeating a message that many of your classmates have already heard. For example, you might read about new research suggesting that sleep enhances proficiency in gross motor skills (such as dancing, skateboarding, or playing an instrument).[2] This focus would provide a new twist on the more general topic of sleep or the overdone topic of sleep cycles.

Many libraries have an area where recent print periodicals and newspapers are available, often on the first floor. Check with a librarian at the reference desk if you are not sure how to locate them. You can also check online library portals

▲ **Conducting Research.** Library research is an excellent way to discover potential speech topics. Cavan Images/Getty Images

for these resources. Another option is to browse more broadly for topics online, but beware! As we note in Chapter 3, it is not ethical to plagiarize a speech. If online sites contain links to actual speeches, be sure not to copy all or part of what you find (or use it after changing some of the words) and represent it as your own work.

The ideas you generate through research serve not only as potential speech topics themselves but also as starting points for other topic selection strategies, including *brainstorming*, *word association*, and *mind mapping*.

## Brainstorming

When **brainstorming**, you list every idea that comes to mind without evaluating its merits. Your goal is to develop a sizable list of topics quickly; later, you will consider which one would be best. Don't censor any ideas at this point: just let your thoughts flow.

To brainstorm, consider your interests and experiences, issues you care about, organizations you belong to, people you admire, events you find significant, places you have been, and life lessons you have learned. Think about favorites in each of these categories. For example, what is your favorite use of spare time? The most interesting course you have ever taken? The best organization you've ever belonged to? By focusing on questions like these, you will soon build up a strong list of potential topics.

# BRAINSTORMING  (AKA: FISHING FOR IDEAS)

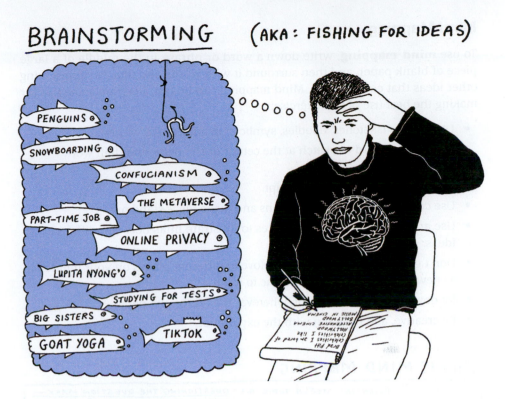

## Word Association

Another strategy for generating ideas is **word association**. Start by listing a potential topic (as you do when brainstorming). Then write whatever comes to mind when you think about that first idea. The second idea may suggest yet a third one, and so on. Write each new thought next to the previous idea. Word association (as well as mind mapping, which we discuss next) enables your mind to function somewhat like a search engine. Your brain is your database, and when you write down a word or phrase, your mind "searches" for other terms that you associate with the original idea. If you use word association for every topic idea you generated while brainstorming, your set of options will grow even more.

If you've done research for topic ideas, a current news story may also suggest a variety of topics through word association. For example, a story about wildfires could prompt you to come up with the following topic sequence— firefighters, fire prevention, smoke detectors, lie detectors. With this technique, even a topic that would not be a good choice may lead you to an appropriate one. Consider what Mike, a public speaking student, experienced. His assignment was to deliver a speech on "a tip for college success." One of Mike's starting-point ideas was "my football coach," an unlikely topic for this assignment. But he associated his coach with the coach's favorite saying: "Success comes when preparation meets opportunity." That quotation formed the basis for Mike's excellent speech on study habits.

## Mind Mapping

To use **mind mapping**, write down a word or phrase in the middle of a large piece of blank paper, and then surround it with words and images representing other ideas that come to you. Mind mapping can be fun; here are some tips for making the best use of this exercise:

- Use images (sketches, doodles, symbols) in addition to words.
- Start with a word or sketch at the center of the page, and then work outward.
- Print rather than writing in script.
- Use colors to indicate associations and make ideas stand out.
- Use arrows or other visual devices to illustrate links between different ideas.
- Don't get stuck on one concept. Move to different places on your mind map as new ideas or associations come to mind.
- Jot down ideas as they occur, wherever they fit on the paper.
- Be creative, and have fun with the experience.[3]

## THIS IS MIND MAPPING

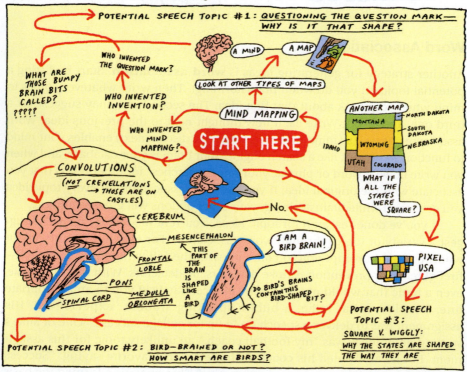

The use of multiple colors, pictures, and symbols to create a mind map stimulates your thinking process.[4] You use both sides of your brain and generate more—and more creative—topic ideas.

In addition to trying this technique by hand, you can also use mind mapping software.[5] A survey of both new and experienced mind mapping software users cited increased creativity as a benefit of this method.[6]

# SELECTING THE BEST TOPIC

You've generated a list of topics through one or more of the techniques described so far. Now you need to select the best one. To make your choice, *consider the assignment, your audience, your knowledge and interests*, and *the context of your speech*. And after you have selected a topic, stick with it. The following guidelines will help you pick the best topic from the list of possibilities you've generated.

## Consider the Assignment

As a student of public speaking, it's important that you select a topic that meets your instructor's criteria for the assignment. For most classroom speeches, your instructor will require that you include references to research. In such cases, you need to make sure that appropriate research sources are available for the topic you select. A humorous speech about your experiences as a food server, horror stories about your former roommates, or a demonstration of how you make your favorite fruit salad would probably fail to meet your instructor's criteria for the assignment.

In some cases, a specific topic might be assigned. For example, a history instructor may require an oral report on ancient China, or an agriculture professor may assign a debate on water policy. Say you are working as a promotions coordinator at a marketing firm. Your manager may ask you to speak to a group of potential customers about a client's product at a promotional event or on a videoconference. In life, you don't always get a choice of topics; nevertheless, it remains your responsibility to research the subject well and prepare an interesting presentation for your audience.

Even if you have some latitude in choosing a topic, your instructor may have a list of topics to avoid. These topics—which often include capital punishment, abortion, the drinking age, steroids in sports, and the legalization of marijuana—crop up in public speaking classes every semester and are obvious and overused. You would be much better off *getting ahead of the curve* when choosing a topic. For example, rather than talking about an existing social networking site, consider researching how first responders are using social media in emergency management situations.

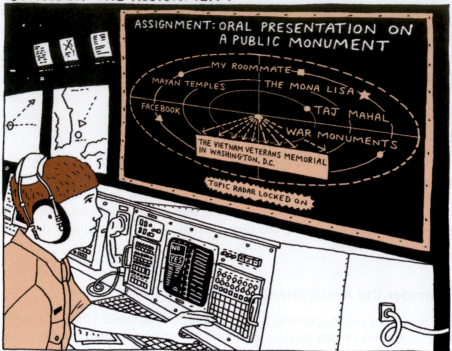

CONSIDER THE ASSIGNMENT

ASSIGNMENT: ORAL PRESENTATION ON A PUBLIC MONUMENT

MY ROOMMATE
MAYAN TEMPLES
THE MONA LISA
FACEBOOK
TAJ MAHAL
WAR MONUMENTS
THE VIETNAM VETERANS MEMORIAL IN WASHINGTON, D.C.
TOPIC RADAR LOCKED ON

## Consider Your Audience

Your audience members will devote valuable time to listening to your speech. In return, you owe them a presentation they will find interesting and important.

Based on your preliminary audience analysis (see Chapter 5), determine your listeners' priorities and backgrounds. The topic you select should meet one or more of the following criteria:

- It will interest your audience.
- It is something your listeners need to know about—for their own or society's benefit.
- It will inspire, entertain, or emotionally move your audience.

## Consider Your Knowledge and Interests

Among all the potential topics you've accumulated, which ones are you most interested in and knowledgeable about? When you choose a topic you're familiar with and passionate about, you'll give a more fluent and enthusiastic presentation. One of our students captivated his audience with a speech on Legos (even though his classmates had not played with toys for years) because his enthusiasm for the subject was so infectious. Conversely, a student who appeared totally

uninterested in her topic of job interviews failed to connect with her listeners, even though the subject was highly relevant to them.

Your listeners are also more likely to believe your claims if they know you have experience with the subject area. One student discovered firsthand the perils of selecting a topic she knew little about. Although she had no children or child-care experience, she chose child care as a topic and presented when the COVID-19 pandemic was at a peak. Because of her inexperience, she made some assumptions that didn't line up with the experiences of several parents in the class, and her research sources were all published before the pandemic began. As a result, she didn't realize that parents were having a more difficult time finding child care, that they were paying more for care if they did manage to find it, and that they were sometimes facing unique challenges—including their children getting exposed to COVID at the child-care facility. Because her claims were inconsistent with the experiences of class members with children, she had to defer to these more knowledgeable classmates during the question-and-answer session. By the time she sat down, she had lost most of her credibility on this topic.

Finally, by selecting a topic you're familiar with, you streamline the research process. You can focus on researching information that supplements the facts you already know rather than gathering general background information.

## Consider the Speech Context

The **context** of your speech is the occasion, surrounding environment, and situation in which you will deliver your presentation. These factors often make one topic choice better than another.

For example, if you are asked to speak at an awards banquet for a campus organization to which you belong, the audience will expect an upbeat speech on a topic related to that organization. A speech on a more serious idea, such as the need to restructure major requirements at your college, would be better saved for a less celebratory occasion.

Situational characteristics—such as the physical setting of your speech, the time of day, and audience size and mobility (see Chapter 5)—should influence your topic choice as well. For instance, suppose you need to play an audio snippet to effectively present a certain topic you care about. You should avoid that topic if you will be giving your speech in a large, noisy location, where listeners would have difficulty hearing the clip. Your choice may also differ if you are in a virtual class and your speech is going to be delivered using technology like Zoom or recorded and uploaded for independent viewing by your classmates. As we discuss in Chapter 15, there are special considerations to take into account when your audience won't be physically present.

Outside the classroom, speakers must also consider the context when selecting a speech topic. Consider the challenge faced by fashion designer and research fellow Suzanne Lee when she was asked to give "the talk of her life" at a TED (Technology, Entertainment, Design) conference. She selected a cutting-edge topic—growing your own clothes—but because she knew that few of the creative thinkers in her audience would be fashion or biology experts, she tailored her speech for a general audience. Rather than discussing the technical aspects of fabric farming from bacteria and microbes, she gave a basic step-by-step overview. She also supplemented her speech with compelling photos, animation, and videos. Her audience left with a new understanding of and appreciation for a topic that—until the speech—they hadn't known existed.

## Choose a Topic and Stick with It

After you've selected an appropriate topic from your list of possibilities, stick with it. In our experience, students who agonize over their topic selection for days or waver back and forth between several possibilities lose valuable speech preparation time.

An analysis of more than one thousand speech diaries kept by public speaking students revealed one consistent difference between strong speeches and weaker ones—the topic selection process. Speakers who delivered strong speeches carefully considered their topic choice but chose a topic promptly and then stayed with it, investing the bulk of their time in preparation. Less successful speakers spent days trying to settle on an acceptable topic.[7]

# REFINING YOUR TOPIC

After you have selected a topic, you must refine it by first *deciding on your rhetorical purpose*, or how you want your speech to affect your audience. Then you can *narrow your topic* to achieve that effect.

## Decide Your Rhetorical Purpose

Your primary goal for the audience constitutes your **rhetorical purpose**, as we discussed in Chapter 2. In a public speaking class, your purpose will often be assigned for each speech. Outside the classroom, your purpose may be assigned (for example, by your employer) or dictated by the context of a special occasion

---

▼ **Topics Refined by Rhetorical Purpose.** *Informative*: How to rescue a stranded sea mammal. *Persuasive*: You should join an organization that rescues sea mammals. *Special Occasion*: Today we honor the founder of the Sea Mammal Conservation Society. CHAIDEER MAHYUDDIN/Getty Images

(such as a wedding, memorial service, or roast). For other speeches, the choice of purpose will be left to you. The scenario that follows shows how one public speaking student went about deciding her rhetorical purpose.

Amber's instructor allowed students to select their own topic and purpose for their first speech. Amber chose to discuss her major, theater arts. She then considered a variety of purposes:

- *Informing.* When your purpose is **informative**, the message is educational, and your objective is to increase the audience's understanding or awareness of your subject. For her topic, Amber could tell her audience about the courses taken by theater arts majors and why they are important for the degree.

- *Persuading.* When your purpose is **persuasive**, you seek to convince audience members to consider or adopt a new position, strengthen an existing belief, or take a particular action. For a topic, Amber might try to persuade her audience to attend a play put on by the theater arts department.

- *Marking a special occasion.* When your purpose is **marking a special occasion**, you seek to honor that occasion by entertaining, inspiring, or emotionally moving your audience. For her topic, Amber could amuse her audience by roasting her favorite director or move listeners by presenting a tribute to a favorite drama professor who is retiring soon.

Each of these options could result in a speech that relates to theater arts on campus in some way. However, the rhetorical purpose of each would be different—to inform, to persuade, or to mark a special occasion. Therefore, each would have a different effect on Amber's audience.

## Narrow Your Topic

After you've determined your rhetorical purpose, think about which aspects of your topic you want to cover in your speech; in other words, how will you narrow your topic so that you fulfill your rhetorical purpose? You can't cover all aspects of the topic in a single speech, so you need to decide which aspects to focus on.

Narrowing your topic is vital for a couple of reasons. First, it allows you to fit your speech into the available time. Whether you are speaking in a classroom or in your community, it is inconsiderate to take more than the time allocated for your presentation. Audiences may stop listening if you exceed the time limit. Also, resist any urge to speak fast or to cover each idea at the surface level in order to say everything you had planned. Audiences don't respond well to those tactics.

Second, narrowing your topic helps you focus your speech. This is an especially important step for new speakers, who often select overly broad topics. When giving a speech on a specific sport, such as cricket, a novice speaker might try to cover the equipment required, the rules, the techniques for playing well, and maybe even the sport's history—way too much for the speaker to cover adequately or for listeners to remember.

Conversely, one of the best sports speeches we ever heard succeeded because the speaker effectively narrowed the topic of tennis. She focused her informative speech on four interesting professional tennis personalities. The points she covered—such as the classic 1973 "Battle of the Sexes" match between Billie Jean King and Bobby Riggs—truly captivated her audience. Even listeners who were not tennis fans or hadn't yet been born when that match took place enjoyed and remembered the speech.

How should you narrow your topic? Many of the techniques you used to select your topic can also help you narrow it.

## DON'T BITE OFF MORE TOPIC THAN YOUR AUDIENCE CAN CHEW

**Remember Your Audience.** Ask yourself whether the aspects of your topic will be interesting or important to your listeners. Kendra, a student who wanted to deliver a speech about figure skating, surveyed her classmates and found that few were interested in learning how to skate. However, most of the class planned to watch the Winter Olympics on television. Kendra narrowed her topic with the Olympics viewers in mind, choosing to explain in her speech how listeners could score the skating events while watching at home. Sara (introduced at the beginning of this chapter) kept this guideline in mind, too, deciding to emphasize how her classmates could protect themselves from nearby flooding.

SPEAKING ABOUT YOUR INTERESTS AND EXPERTISE

**Draw on Your Interests and Expertise.** Your special expertise or unique perspective on an aspect of your subject area can help you narrow your topic. Consider Cesar, a student who was passionate about the issue of food security on campus and regularly volunteered at his college's food pantry. The pantry had been operating with a limited staff during much of the COVID-19 pandemic, but now it was opening again for student volunteers. He delivered an excellent persuasive speech explaining the opportunities that were available for students and encouraging them to participate.

**Review Your Rhetorical Purpose.** Try to narrow your topic to an aspect appropriate for your rhetorical purpose. For example, suppose you want to give a speech about sleep. A focus on sleep disorders and sleep science could make an appropriate informative topic. A speech extolling the benefits of getting eight hours of sleep a night could be an emphasis for a persuasive speech. And a speech honoring the director of your university's sleep research center would make a great special-occasion speech.

**Evaluate the Situation.** You can also use situational characteristics to help narrow your topic. For example, one student, Michelle, was interested in entomology (the study of insects), so she chose bugs as her topic. Initially, she considered narrowing her topic to the use of insects to determine time of death of murder victims. But she rejected that idea when she remembered that she would be delivering her speech shortly after lunch—when listeners might be especially squeamish. Instead, she (wisely) narrowed her topic to interesting facts about bees, including how they make honey—a perfect after-lunch focus.

If your speech is going to be presented in a mediated context, the technology that you use can influence the direction of your speech. Consider an agricultural researcher who was used to relying on audience interactions when speaking in her local area about strategies for reducing pesticide use. Her employer asked her to record her presentation so that it could be viewed at remote locations, which would make interactions impossible. This required a change in her approach. In the weeks before she recorded the speech, she emailed customers in those locations to determine what agricultural pests were most problematic in their region so she could revise her message to focus on their concerns.

# DRAFTING YOUR SPECIFIC PURPOSE

After you've identified your rhetorical purpose and narrowed your topic, your next step is to determine your **specific purpose**—the objective of your particular speech—and express it in a concise phrase.

To write your specific purpose, start with a phrase expressing your rhetorical purpose ("to inform," "to persuade," or "to mark a special occasion"), and then add language indicating what you want to accomplish in your speech. Some good examples follow:

- "To inform my audience about the events at a Portuguese *festa*"
- "To persuade my audience to drink milk produced by our state's dairy farms"
- "To honor the organizers of our alternative spring break community development project"

You can use your specific purpose to guide which ideas you should develop in your speech. When selecting ideas, choose those that help you accomplish your specific purpose, and exclude those that aren't relevant. Thus, like the sideline on a football field, your specific purpose indicates which ideas are "out of bounds" given your speech's objective.

# DRAFTING YOUR THESIS STATEMENT

After you have determined your specific purpose, create your **thesis statement**—a single sentence that captures the overall message you want to convey in your speech. This statement conveys the "bottom line" of your speech—the ultimate message that all the points in your speech support. As long as your audience members can remember your thesis statement, they should be able to recall the essence of your speech.

In this book, we use the term *thesis* to mean the main position of any type of speech. Some speech instructors may prefer using the term *thesis statement* when a speaker is advocating a position in a persuasive speech and the term *topic statement* when a speaker intends to inform or mark a special occasion. Your instructor will let you know what usage they prefer.

Here are some examples of thesis statements:

- "Developments in robotics will change the job market in the next twenty years."
- "You should try healthy microwave mug recipes."
- "You should take class notes on paper in longhand."
- "Today we honor the Missouri Veterinary Medical Teaching Hospital's greyhound blood-donor program."

Here are some guidelines for ensuring that your thesis statement conveys your purpose and topic to the audience efficiently and accurately:

- *Keep it to one sentence.* Make sure that your thesis consists of a single sentence that states the bottom line of your speech.
- *Express your intentions.* Ensure that your thesis clearly conveys what you hope your audience will know, do, or feel after listening to your speech. Listeners can better follow your message if they know what to expect.

---

▼ **Thesis Statements Convey the Topic in a Sentence.** For example: "Prosthetic hand technology is making revolutionary advances." Yuri Smityuk/Getty Images

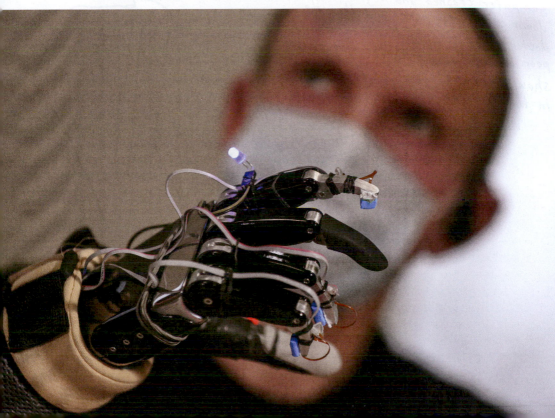

- *Be consistent with your specific purpose.* Because your specific purpose guides how you research and prepare your speech, make sure your thesis communicates the same idea as your specific purpose. That way, you'll avoid the all-too-common problem of presenting a thesis in your speech introduction that differs from the content of the body of your speech. For example, if your specific purpose (which explains the goal of your speech) is "to inform the audience about events at a Portuguese *festa*," your thesis (which explains the content of your speech) could be "A Portuguese *festa* features cultural events, dancing, music, and food."

## YOUR THESIS STATEMENT MUST BE ONE SENTENCE

**WRONG**

The dog ate my homework, then my special fella broke up with me, then my grandmother died and I had to go to the funeral. After that my computer crashed and my car broke down on the way here and then the doctor called and said I had iron-poor blood. For all these reasons, I should not be penalized for turning in this assignment late.

**CORRECT**

Due to unforeseen and serious circumstances, I should not be penalized for turning in this assignment late.

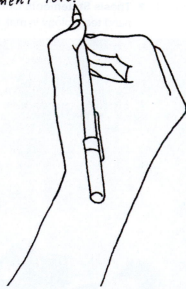

## SPEECH CHOICES

### A CASE STUDY: *RAFAELA*

*Let's check back in with Rafaela to see how she's handling topic selection.*

For Rafaela's persuasive speech assignment, she had been considering a speech encouraging women to run for office. She thought it had good potential, and it fit with her instructor's requirements: that students identify a problem, present a solution that included actions that audience members could take, and use multiple credible research sources to make their argument.

Even so, she decided to brainstorm a few more topic ideas to be sure she was satisfied with her choice. As she did so, one stood out: She had recently gone to a new tapas restaurant and the food was excellent. She checked out Yelp and discovered that the restaurant had already received multiple five-star reviews. She could use the reviewers as her research sources. Rafaela figured that this topic—persuading her classmates to eat at the new tapas restaurant—would be more fun.

Rafaela's instructor's response to the tapas restaurant speech was disappointing. She applauded Rafaela for thinking of a solution that involved the audience. However, she also told Rafaela that it would be hard to identify a problem in the community that could be solved by eating more tapas. And Yelp reviews were not the type of credible research sources she was looking for.

So Rafaela reconsidered her original idea—encouraging women to run for office. The more she thought it over, the better the topic seemed. The subject was important to her and it fit the assignment description well. From her preliminary research, she knew that there was credible evidence supporting the importance of more women running for office as well as evidence that student government experience provided good preparation. And she could advocate actions that her audience could take—for example, getting involved in elections on campus. Women in class could be encouraged to run themselves, and all classmates could be persuaded to encourage women to run. This topic looked like a winner, so Rafaela began her speech preparation.

 **YOUR TURN**

Now that you've seen how Rafaela's choices influenced her selection of a topic, consider how you'll choose a topic for your own speech. Making speech choices involves asking and answering questions related to your assignment. For topic selection, these questions might include:

- What method(s) will I use to generate potential topics?
- Of the topics I have in mind, which do I find most interesting? Which topics would be most interesting to my audience?
- Which topics seem to fit the assignment requirements the best?
- Will I research potential topics before making a final decision?

Making thoughtful choices in response to questions like these will help you select a topic that keeps everyone engaged—including yourself!

**Use your topic to focus the message.** As Sara's story revealed, selecting a topic for your speech can seem overwhelming at first. But the systematic approach described in this chapter can help you move past any feelings of frustration or confusion. First, develop a set of potential topics based on the results of research, brainstorming, word association, and mind mapping. Select the best topic based on an understanding of the assignment, your audience, your knowledge and interests, and the context of your speech, and stick with it. Then refine your topic by determining your rhetorical purpose and narrowing your topic to the most relevant aspects, given the time available for your speech. To draft your specific purpose, express your rhetorical purpose and decide what you'd like to accomplish in your speech. Finally, create your thesis statement—a single sentence that captures your overall message.

## Key Terms

divergent thinking *139*
research *139*
brainstorming *140*
word association *141*
mind mapping *142*
context *146*

rhetorical purpose *147*
informative purpose *148*
persuasive purpose *148*
marking a special occasion *148*
specific purpose *152*
thesis statement *152*

## Review Questions

1. Name and describe four techniques for generating speech topics.
2. Name four basic considerations speakers should keep in mind when choosing a topic.
3. Explain how you can narrow a speech topic by considering your rhetorical purpose.
4. Describe the specific purpose of a speech.
5. Describe the term *thesis*.
6. Name and explain three guidelines for drafting a thesis statement.

## Critical Thinking Questions

1. How do the topics you generate from an initial word in mind mapping or word association differ from the results you would get if you put that same term into a search engine? What are the benefits of writing possible topics on paper and drawing on your own thoughts, ideas, and knowledge? What

are the benefits of accessing the nearly endless topics available on the Internet?

2. How might your mind map differ if you used this technique to take notes during a lecture, rather than to select a speech topic?

3. Why is it ethical to search for speech topics on the Internet but unethical to use as your own all or part of a speech that you found on the Internet?

4. What role should audience analysis, discussed in Chapter 5, play in selecting a topic for a speech?

5. Based on what you know about students in your class, what would be a good specific purpose for an informative speech? For a persuasive speech?

6. How would your topic selection differ if you were delivering a speech to a club or team to which you belong rather than to students in a public speaking class?

## Activities

1. Working in small groups, brainstorm a list of potential speech topics. Then decide which topics would be most interesting to the group and which would be less interesting. Have group members explain why they decided that certain topics would be more interesting than others.

2. Divide into small groups. Have each group use one topic generation process (brainstorming, word association, or mind mapping) to create a list of potential topics. Have each group share with the class the topics they listed. Discuss how different processes can result in different topic ideas.

3. Discuss potential topics with other students in your public speaking class. Which topics are already familiar to students? Which topics are likely to be familiar to your instructor? For the topics that are familiar, discuss ways they could be narrowed to present new and original perspectives to the audience.

4. Check out articles in a national newspaper and articles in your college newspaper. How successful are the articles' topics at catching your interest? What do you think the topic selections in each newspaper suggest about how the writers view their audience?

5. Suppose that Rafaela (see the Speech Choices feature) was going to present her speech about encouraging women to run for office in front of members of a community organization, such as the League of Women Voters. Discuss how she might select a different thesis for this audience than the one she would select for a classroom speech.

# RESEARCHING
# YOUR SPEECH

**“It is not a fact until you prove it to the audience.”** One afternoon, Katie, Mandeep, and Sherri were strolling by their local courthouse after lunch when they noticed a police officer shooting at crows perched atop the building. They were appalled and immediately called the police department to complain. The police chief explained that this practice was warranted because the crows were a public nuisance: they were noisy and annoying, they left droppings that posed a health risk, and they made it impossible to keep the courthouse steps clean. The crows had to go, the chief said, and other solutions (such as catch and release) were just too expensive.

Unconvinced by this explanation, the three students decided to take action. They gathered dozens of signatures on petitions and presented them to city officials, who invited the students to speak about the subject at a city council meeting. The police chief would also attend to present her side of the issue.

The students knew that this was their one chance to make their case and that they had to be prepared to respond to the police chief's claims. To that end, they decided to find out whether the crows actually constituted a health hazard, whether other towns had found alternatives to shooting them, and how effective and costly these alternatives were.

---

◀ **Evidence Proves Your Point.** In your community and career, use evidence to support your claims if you want to make a difference—just as Katie, Mandeep, and Sherri did with the crows at the courthouse. Peter S. Turkin/EyeEm/Getty Images

In other words, these students set out to *research* their presentation so that they could convince the city council to end the practice of shooting crows. When you research well, your speeches can have a positive effect, whether you are participating in civic engagement like Katie, Mandeep, and Sherri, or using speaking skills on campus and in your career. In this chapter, we begin with a discussion of why research is a vital step in speech preparation, then cover how to go about setting up a research plan. Next, we consider how to evaluate the credibility of your research sources, followed by an explanation of how to best conduct research using library sources, online materials, and interviews. Finally, we discuss how to present the information you have researched in your speech.

# RESEARCH IS ESSENTIAL

Why should you learn how to research well and then use those skills to prepare your speech? The advantages are many. Research skills help you develop a quality speech, convince your audience, impress your instructor, and be effective in the workplace after you graduate. And they can be very helpful when you are active in civic engagement, as you saw in the opening example. Let's take a look at some of the benefits that can result when you invest time researching your speech:

- *You gain a broader understanding of your topic.* This knowledge will give you more choices when you decide which main ideas to include in your speech and how you can best develop them. Not only will you gain deeper knowledge, but you will likely discover new insights or determine that some of your existing beliefs on the topic are incorrect.

- *You gain audience agreement.* Research enables you to gather **evidence**—information from credible sources that you can use to support your claims. If audience members are uncertain about a point you are making (or if they outright disagree with you), evidence may convince them to accept that point.[1] For example, if they accept that the source of your evidence is trustworthy and better informed than they are, they will be more likely to agree with your claim, even if they would not accept your opinion alone. Some commentators have suggested that we live in a "post-truth" era, in which people disregard facts and evidence in favor of their personal opinions or fallacious reasoning.[2] However, recent research indicates that when people are presented with evidence, they tend to "update their views" to account for the new information.[3]

    Evidence also strengthens your own credibility with the audience. When you present evidence in your speech, it shows that you have prepared and learned about the topic. This makes audience members more likely to believe what you say.[4]

- *You demonstrate college-level skills to your instructor.* Instructors appreciate speeches that are backed by **academic research**, which means that any claims made are supported by experts who have education and experience in the topic area and whose work has been reviewed by other authorities in the field. Finding such sources requires more advanced research skills than might have been required earlier in your educational career. It won't suffice to go with the first three or four sources that you happen to come across. In academic speaking and writing, you are sharing *knowledge* with your audience. This means that you must research enough credible sources to be confident that the facts you present are accurate.

- *Research skills are increasingly important in the workplace.* In business, more and more decisions are being made based on "data-based analytics" rather than on "gut instinct."[5] Research shows that data-driven decisions improve productivity.[6] Thus, they are increasingly being used to resolve questions in such diverse fields as education, medicine, agriculture, and the military. They are also increasingly being used in the nonprofit sector.[7] In your career, if you are able to support the claims you make with evidence, you will be more convincing and contribute to your organization's success.

## YOU <u>ARE</u> DOING ACADEMIC RESEARCH WHEN...

### YOUR CLAIM IS SUPPORTED BY EXPERTS

### YOU USED SPECIALIZED LIBRARY INDEXES

### YOU ASKED A RESEARCH LIBRARIAN

## YOU ARE <u>NOT</u> DOING ACADEMIC RESEARCH WHEN...

### YOUR CLAIM IS SUPPORTED BY A RANDOM WEBSITE

### YOU GOOGLED YOUR TOPIC

### YOU ASKED YOUR ROOMMATE

# RESEARCH WORKS BEST WHEN YOU HAVE A PLAN

Skilled researchers develop a strategy for finding and keeping track of the information they need. Gaining experience, they improve on that strategy throughout their lifetime, particularly as new technologies change the nature of research. For example, libraries are increasingly placing content on social media and using social media to communicate with students.[8] College and university libraries also shifted reference options during the COVID-19 pandemic, providing more services that could be accessed online or by phone.[9] The following steps will help you formulate a **research plan**—a strategy for finding and keeping track of information to use in your speech. It's important to put this plan into action quickly, as almost three-fourths of college students report that procrastination harms their research efforts.[10]

## Inventory Your Research Needs

Begin by determining your **research objectives**—the goals you need to accomplish with your research. Your knowledge of the topic will influence your goals. If you don't know a lot about the subject, begin with general research to learn more about the basics. On the other hand, if you know your topic well (for example, you already have a good idea of your thesis and even some of your main points), you might want to use research to learn more about specific aspects of your topic. When determining which aspects of your topic to research further, consider your rhetorical purpose and your instructor's research requirements. Finally, before moving ahead with your research, make a list of the subject matter you need to research and the questions you need to answer. This will help you stay focused on your research objectives.

## Find the Sources You Need

After you've determined your research objectives, consider where you can find the information you need. The library is a great resource for researching your speech. You may also want to research Internet sources. Be aware, however, that although the Internet can be a useful source of information, there are risks in using online sources. Thus, it's always advisable to use general Internet research as a supplemental resource rather than the main focus of your efforts. You can also conduct research through personal interviews. If you have access to people with expertise on your topic, setting up an interview or two could be quite useful.

We strongly recommend that you discuss your topic with a **research librarian**. These librarians are career professionals who are hired to assist students and faculty with their research. They are experts at tracking down hard-to-find information, and can be amazingly knowledgeable about the resources available on your topic. Studies suggest that some students don't think librarians are there to help them or that their main job is to direct people to the correct location.[11] Nothing could be further from the truth! Their job is to help you find the best resources, and you can count on them to assist you in discovering the most useful and credible information sources. Research shows that library use increases both student performance in coursework and student retention in college.[12]

You will also need to consider what types of sources best meet your research needs. In the "Conducting Library Research" section later in the chapter, we discuss the benefits of different library resources, including books, journal articles, newspapers, reference works, and government documents.

Use library indexes (often available on the library's website) to develop a list of sources to research. Library indexes are usually organized by **keyword**—a word or term related to your topic, including a synonym. You enter one or more keywords and you get a list of sources that relate to the term(s) you used. If you don't find what you're looking for under the keywords you've chosen, be persistent. Try using broader, narrower, or related terms until you find useful sources.

---

▼ **Types of Keywords for Searches.** You can use different types of terms to conduct a keyword search. For example, you might select a broad term like *racial inequities* (left), or a narrower term like *environmental racism* (right). You could also search using a synonym for environmental racism, such as *environmental inequalities*. DANIEL LEAL/Getty Images; San Francisco Chronicle/Hearst Newspapers via Getty Images/Getty Images

## Keep Track of Your Sources

One of the most important (and unappreciated) steps in the speech preparation process is maintaining complete and accurate records of your research sources. When you prepare your speech outline (see Chapter 11), your instructor will expect you to properly cite the sources of all the research you'll use in your presentation. If you've lost track of the sources of your evidence or have incomplete citations, it will be very difficult to go back and find this information later. Furthermore, if you can't cite the source of a piece of information, you can't use that material in your speech.

For these reasons, it's essential that you find and keep full citations for all research sources you may use. The **citation** contains information about the author of the source and the location of your evidence; it's the academic equivalent of a map to your source. When a source is cited properly, it should be easy for another person to find the original material, whether in the library or online. Your instructor will have a particular citation format that you need to follow; be sure you know what information is required so you can make note of it immediately. Typically, the following information is needed:

- Name of the author and their credentials
- Title of the article or book chapter if the work appears in a newspaper, a periodical, an anthology, or online
- Source (name of the book, magazine, or newspaper)
- Date of the publication
- Volume number (for periodicals)
- Publisher and city of publication (for books)
- Page number where the evidence appears

## MAINTAIN ACCURATE RECORDS OF YOUR SOURCES

- URL for Internet sources
- DOI (Digital Object Identifier, a string of letters and numbers that identifies the source)

Many computer-based library indexes now allow you to **export** the citations for your research sources by copying and pasting the citation into a Word file. This is a very efficient way to keep track of source citations. If you aren't sure how to do this, check with a research librarian.

When researching Internet evidence, students sometimes mistakenly list the URL or the name of the database (for example, EBSCO or the Gale Group) as the evidence source. Beware! This information isn't sufficient. You also need to find and record the name of the authors of the information, their credentials, and the date of the information.

# EVALUATING A SOURCE'S CREDIBILITY

No matter where you gather evidence for your speech (library, Internet, or interviews), you must ensure that each source is a **credible source**—one that can be reasonably trusted to be accurate and objective. When you use the

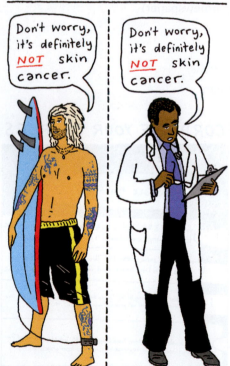

most credible sources possible, you can be confident that the facts you present are valid, and your audience will be more likely to accept your claims.[13]

To evaluate the credibility of a given source, examine four distinguishing characteristics— *expertise*, *objectivity*, *observational capacity*, and *recency*.

## Expertise

**Expertise** is the possession of knowledge necessary to offer reliable facts or opinions about the topic in question. An expert source has education, experience, and a solid reputation in their field. For example, a nutrition professor would likely have expertise on the topic of whether eating red meat is healthy, and a seasoned backpacker would have expertise on how to prepare for a long hiking trip. Likewise, you can look for expertise in printed or online sources by evaluating whether the authors or sponsoring organizations are established and well-informed in the areas about which they are writing.

## Objectivity

Sources who demonstrate **objectivity** have no bias—prejudice or partisanship—that would prevent them from making an impartial judgment on your topic. People can be biased for several reasons. Some have economic self-interest, or the desire to make money, so they may slant facts or explanations to make certain alternatives seem more attractive. Others may need to please superiors—for example, a government worker who defends poorly conceived government policies. Still others have what's called ego investment: they're so wrapped up in a pet theory or cause that they lose their ability to evaluate it with an open mind.

Needless to say, you should avoid evidence from biased sources. If you use it, audience members will be less likely to accept the point you are trying to prove.[14] Furthermore, you can't be confident that you have met your ethical duty to present truthful facts to the audience.

▲ **Observational Capacity Is Essential.** Reporters near the border of Poland and Belarus could better assess the humanitarian crisis facing Kurdish migrants in this location than could reporters in the studio back home. WOJTEK RADWANSKI/ Getty Images

## Observational Capacity

People who have **observational capacity** are able to witness a situation for themselves. For example, a person who was in Louisiana to analyze the recovery from Hurricane Ida or in Bangladesh to assess conditions at Rohingya refugees' camps would have more credibility than those who watched these events unfold on television. Sources with training and experience also make more credible observers. Thus, a person with expertise in child development would learn more by watching children respond to a violent video game than would a member of the general public.

## Recency

Credible sources are also characterized by **recency**, or timeliness. Generally, because many aspects of life change constantly, newer evidence is more reliable than older evidence. For example, whether you were attending high school or college at the time, chances are good that you experienced significant changes in the number of courses you took online between 2019 and 2021. In fall 2019, about 37% of all college students took at least one remote course.[15] Then many colleges and universities shifted to virtual courses in spring 2020 due to the coronavirus pandemic, causing this number to rise. By fall of 2021, more students began returning to campus and the numbers dropped again.[16] You would need very recent statistics to get an accurate picture of the number of students taking online classes. In general, if you have a choice between pieces of evidence from two equally credible sources and one is more current, you should select the more recent evidence.

Of course, some evidence is classic and endures to this day. For example, although the teachings of Confucius are ancient, they command more respect today than the precepts of many contemporary philosophers. And the ideas of Machiavelli are still pertinent to the subject of international relations, even though they are about five hundred years old. To decide whether evidence is outdated, ask yourself, "Has the claim made by my source become doubtful or false because of changing circumstances since the claim was made?"

With these criteria for source credibility in mind, let's now look closely at three major strategies for researching your speech—*using a library, searching the Internet*, and *interviewing experts in your topic*.

# CONDUCTING LIBRARY RESEARCH

Libraries remain one of the best resources for researching your speech. Despite the Internet's popularity as a research tool, the library offers convenient access to the broadest range of *credible* sources—including sources that aren't available on websites. In addition, no search engine can match the experience and expertise of professional librarians in guiding you to the best material on your topic.

Libraries house a wealth of information sources, including books, periodicals, newspapers, reference works, and government documents, along with powerful digital resources and databases that you might not be able to access otherwise. For students who are new to college, the sheer size of the library can be challenging. In one study, first-year college students encountered libraries with collections averaging nine times the size of their high school library. In addition, there were differences in how materials were arranged and the tools used for finding articles.[17] But as you gain experience and take advantage of the skills of the library staff, you can become a skilled library researcher.

## Books

Books are one of the best systems that humans have ever developed for storing and conveying information. They have important advantages as information sources and are often the best place to start your research. Because books have been a primary tool for sharing and storing ideas throughout human history (for example, a surviving part of the Egyptian *Book of the Dead* dates from the sixteenth century BCE), many of today's books contain thousands of years of accumulated human knowledge. In addition, many books are written by people with extensive expertise in their subject—although, of course, you should always check each author's credentials using the four criteria described earlier.

Books are longer than most other information resources and thus are likely to provide more in-depth information on your topic. Books typically offer *synthetic* thinking, which involves analyzing a variety of ideas on a topic to develop common themes. This is because authors combine information from diverse sources along with their own ideas and critical judgments. Additionally, most books—especially scholarly books—are vetted before publication. Both the publisher and other experts in the field may review and edit content to ensure a book's credibility.

To find books related to your topic, start by searching your library's electronic catalog by subject. After entering your search terms, you'll see a list of links specifying relevant book titles. By clicking on these links, you can find bibliographic information as well as details on where in the library the books are located. In addition to lending physical books, libraries increasingly offer books that can be accessed online or on a digital e-reader. And if the book you need isn't available, your library may be able to get it for you from another library through an interlibrary loan.

Finally, here's a tip from expert library users. After you find books on your topic in a library's catalog, go into the library stacks and locate the books you've identified. But don't just pull the books you found and leave; instead, browse through some of the books *nearby*. Because libraries organize nonfiction books by topic—typically using the Library of Congress or Dewey Decimal system—the books nearby are likely to have similar coverage and touch on some different but related areas. These nearby books might point you to aspects of your topic you haven't yet considered. If you're doing an online search, you can take a similar approach when you find a book that looks helpful. If you scroll down the page, there are often links to related subjects that you can click on to discover additional relevant library holdings.

## Periodicals

A **periodical** is a publication that appears at regular intervals—for example, weekly, monthly, quarterly, or annually. These publications include scholarly journals and newsmagazines. Often, the most credible information on your speech topic will come from articles in scholarly journals, which are generally written by people with expertise on a subject. Articles in such journals are subjected to **peer review**—that is, an editor decides to publish only those articles that are approved by other experts in the field and that meet the publication's other requirements. In contrast, newsmagazines (which are not peer reviewed) are particularly helpful for speeches on current events. The following strategies will help you locate appropriate periodicals.

**Consult General Periodical Indexes.** General periodical indexes list articles on a wide variety of topics. Traditionally, these resources were available in bound volumes, but today most college and public libraries have subscriptions to online indexes.

Online indexes are particularly helpful because they often include a **full-text source** for each entry—a link to the complete text of the article in question. In cases when they don't provide the full text, indexes often supply an **abstract**, or a summary of the article's contents. The abstract can help you assess whether the article would be useful for your speech. These indexes also provide other helpful utilities, such as the proper citation formats for the articles you find. Representative examples of online indexes that can be used to research a wide variety of speech topics include the following:

- *Academic Search Complete.* An index of over thirteen thousand journals, magazines, newspapers, and videos. Includes many full-text peer-reviewed journals and covers a wide variety of academic disciplines.

- *JSTOR* (journal storage). An archive of over twelve million articles, books, and primary sources (including artwork, manuscripts, and photos) representing the arts, humanities, social sciences, and science. Seventy-five

ONLINE INDEXES OFFER THE BEST OF BOTH WORLDS:
THE QUALITY OF LIBRARY MATERIALS AND THE SPEED OF THE INTERNET.

academic disciplines are covered. Allows full-text searches and provides scanned articles. Includes over one-hundred thousand e-books.

- *LexisNexis Academic.* Contains full-text documents from over fifteen thousand sources, including print, broadcast, and online media. Emphasizes news, business, and legal topics. New *NexisUni* research tool contains over seventeen thousand sources with more advanced search features.

**Use Specialized Periodical Indexes.**    Specialized periodical indexes focus on specific subject areas and are increasingly available online. Library websites often list available indexes and provide you with a link. These resources are available for a wide range of topics, as can be seen by the following sample list: *AGRICOLA* (agriculture), *Art Full Text, Chicano Database, Communication and Mass Media Complete, Criminal Justice Abstracts, Ethnic NewsWatch, Gender Watch, Historical Abstracts, MEDLINE* (medical journals), *PsycArticles*, and *Science Online.*

## Newspapers

Newspapers are another useful source, especially when you need very current information. Many college libraries have indexes for articles published in major national newspapers, such as the *Christian Science Monitor*, the *New York Times*, the *Wall Street Journal*, and the *Washington Post*. Most newspapers now have websites, and some are exclusively online (for example, the *Seattle Post Intelligencer,* the *Pittsburgh Tribune-Review,* and the *Christian Science Monitor*'s daily newspaper). Many newspaper websites allow you to search for articles, which can be particularly helpful if you want to focus on news from a specific region. For example, the *Texas Tribune* provided especially insightful coverage of Houston's vulnerability to hurricanes, thanks to journalists who "know their subjects and communities well and have covered these issues extensively."[18] And the *Maine Monitor* included detailed coverage of how the state's failure to provide a public defender's office to citizens affected the administration of justice.[19]

When trying to access news articles, you may run into a **paywall**—meaning that the article is available only to paid subscribers. Rather than paying for the article, check with your library to see if they have a subscription that allows students free access to the article.

General newspaper indexes include *America's News, Global Newsstream, LexisNexis Academic*, and the *National Newspaper Index*. Many such indexes provide links to full-text articles. More specialized indexes, such as *African American Newspapers, Alternative Press Index*, and *Hispanic American Newspapers*, cover a wide variety of newspapers with a particular focus.

## Reference Works

A **reference work** is a compilation of background information on major topic areas. Reference works are helpful for doing exploratory research on your subject area or for discovering a specific fact (such as the number of people with

Internet access worldwide or the capital of Kazakhstan), as opposed to gathering in-depth information. Reference works are increasingly available in both printed and online form in your library.

There are several major categories of reference works. Most include general works that cover a comprehensive range of topics as well as specialized works that focus on a single subject (for example, philosophy or art) in more detail. **Encyclopedias** offer relatively brief entries that provide background information on a wide range of alphabetized topics. **Dictionaries** offer definitions, pronunciation guides, and sometimes etymologies (the linguistic origins) of words, and **quotation books** offer famous or notable quotations on a variety of subjects. **Atlases** provide maps, charts, and tables relating to different geographic regions. Finally, **yearbooks**—such as *Statistical Abstract of the United States*—are updated annually and contain statistics and other facts about social, political, and economic topics.

## Government Documents

If your topic relates to government activities, laws, or regulations, government documents can provide useful information for your speech. Document authors may be experts, but beware of documents motivated by political objectives. To find government documents, use the following resources:

---

▼ **Government-funded Storm Chasing.** Scientists and meteorologists from the Center for Severe Weather Research get close to tornadoes to learn more about tornado prediction. For what type of speech might you find it helpful to access this kind of government information? Drew Angerer/Getty Images

- *Catalog of U.S. Government Publications* (catalog.gpo.gov) provides citations to federal print and electronic publications, congressional hearings, and committee reports. It includes records for over 500,000 publications, a number of which can be accessed online.

- *govinfo* (www.govinfo.gov) provides free access to information resources for all three federal government branches, including congressional hearings, the Congressional Record, and Supreme Court opinions.

- *CQ Electronic Library* (available through many college libraries) features information from *Congressional Quarterly*, which provides nonpartisan reporting on Congress and politics. *CQ Weekly* provides information about bills pending in Congress and articles about major issues confronting the federal government, whereas *CQ Researcher Online* provides extended reports on major news issues.

# USING THE INTERNET

The Internet has become the go-to research option for many college students, and the trend is for increased use of the Internet as a research source on assignments.[20] Unfortunately, while the convenience of the Internet is clearly appealing, a focus on general Internet searches—for example, typing search terms into Google and seeing what turns up—can be hazardous to the typical student's academic progress; in fact, multiple studies indicate that more frequent use of the library is associated with higher grades and the development of academic skills.[21]

Whereas libraries emphasize quality research sources (and it is fine to access library materials online), a general web search can be a bit like sending an untrained dog out to retrieve the morning newspaper. He might come back with the paper, but he could just as easily end up digging up your flower bed or eating a neighbor's chicken. In other words, you can't always be certain that your search will generate the most credible research for your speech. By understanding both the *benefits* and the *disadvantages* of Internet research (as well as the different methods you can use to find Internet resources), you can get the most from this type of information.

## Benefits of Internet Research

Internet research allows you convenient access to information on nearly any topic without leaving your desk. Even better, many libraries offer access to full-text periodical and newspaper indexes from remote locations. Such indexes are among the most useful available online, and we recommend that you focus on them when the convenience of researching from your own computer is important.

The Internet also offers speed—enabling you to track down a news report or a research finding almost instantly, from anywhere in the world. Finally,

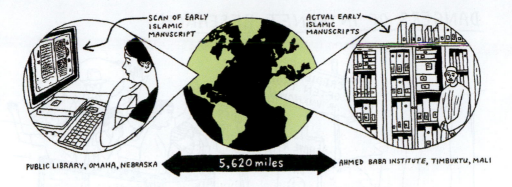

SCAN OF EARLY ISLAMIC MANUSCRIPT

ACTUAL EARLY ISLAMIC MANUSCRIPTS

PUBLIC LIBRARY, OMAHA, NEBRASKA    5,620 miles    AHMED BABA INSTITUTE, TIMBUKTU, MALI

this research tool puts an immense volume of information at your fingertips. A November 2021 estimate indicated that an individual would need 181 million years to download all the data that was currently available on the Internet.[22] With careful searching online, you may be able to find quality information that simply doesn't exist in your own library.

## Disadvantages of Internet Research

Despite the web's vastness, searches on academic databases (including online ones) are far more likely to lead you to credible evidence than would a general web-based search.[23] Authorities in many fields publish their works primarily in books and scholarly journals. Because many of these works are copyrighted, they won't likely be available on the websites that a typical online search engine will lead you to. And if they are available, you may need to pay a fee to access them.

Moreover, you can't assume that information you find online is credible, because most of it isn't vetted in the same way that books and periodicals are. There are literally millions of websites created by individuals, advocacy groups, clubs, and businesses that may contain incorrect or biased information.[24] As anyone who uses TikTok, Instagram, or Twitter knows, it's very easy to put information on the Internet without having to prove its accuracy. Although expert review is essential in academic research, Internet information is frequently posted without any professional review.[25]

As a consequence, many of the Internet sources found by students don't have the quality that is expected by their instructors. Professor Wendy Lerner Lym of Austin Community College compares Internet research to fast food: sources can be quickly obtained, but they aren't good for your academic health.[26] Studies have confirmed the low quality of many sources found on the web. For example, substantial research has concluded that online public health information is often inaccurate or incomplete.[27] Similar findings have been reported for information about vegan diets,[28] medical marijuana,[29] climate change, and genetically modified foods.[30]

# DANGERS OF INTERNET RESEARCH

## Evaluating the Credibility of Online Sources

Evaluating the credibility of websites can be particularly difficult. Many sites fail to identify authors or dates of publication, and even sites that indicate authorship may provide no information on authors' credentials. And, of course, many articles are posted online without expert reviewing or editing.

Thus, it's essential that you develop guidelines for evaluating the credibility of all sites you're considering using. For example, if a website provides the name but not the qualifications of an author, research that author further—either online or in periodical indexes such as *Academic Search Complete*—to see if they have published in scholarly journals. For online documents that don't indicate an author, try to determine what organization sponsored the site, and then assess that organization's credibility through further research.

Besides checking out the author(s), what are some other indicators that a website is credible? Nearly every college library has guidelines for making this assessment—here are some common elements:

- *Are there citations or links to credible evidence that supports claims?* The information on a website should be substantiated with citations or links to credible evidence; if this isn't the case, then the credibility of the information is doubtful (or at the very least uncertain).

- *Can you verify the information from other credible sources?* If your research uncovers evidence from other credible sources that supports the ideas expressed on a website, the website is more likely to be credible.

- *Is there advertising on the website?* If there is advertising, consider whether the website may focus on content that will attract advertising revenue, rather than information that is accurate.

- *Is the tone and word choice objective?* If the language on a website is loaded or biased (see Chapter 12) or it contains "over the top" attacks on persons with opposing viewpoints, it is less likely to be credible.

One additional note of caution: Be careful about determining the credibility of a website based on the **top-level domain** of its URL (uniform resource locator)—the designation at the end of a web address that indicates the site sponsor's affiliation. While *.com* was once assumed to designate a commercial business, *.org* an organization, and *.net* a network, this is no longer a reliable guideline for judging credibility. Websites may now choose to register as a .com, .org, or .net and many different kinds of entities use each suffix.[31] Today, top-level domains are not assigned based on objective criteria; rather, they are strategically chosen by the entity creating the website.[32]

And finally, as noted earlier, if it's not apparent that a website meets the criteria for credibility as an evidence source (expertise, objectivity, observational capacity, and recency), it's best to avoid that site.

## Credibility of Social Media

Online information is increasingly being found on **social media** sites, which people use to both create and access information. Social media has become a popular source of material about current events, for example, with a 2021 Pew Research survey finding that about half of all U.S. adults get their news this way often or sometimes.[33] However, the credibility of information on social media can be dubious, with sites containing substantial "content of questionable accuracy," including "clickbait, hyperpartisan content, pseudo science, and even fabricated 'fake news' reports."[34] In addition, inaccurate information tends to be shared more widely on this medium than factual information: According to MIT researchers, "false information is 70% more likely to be retweeted and it reaches other users six times faster than true information."[35]

*Wikipedia*, an online encyclopedia on which any user can modify the content, is a popular example of why information on social media requires careful cross-checking. While some studies have suggested that this site is a credible source of factual information, with similar error rates to other reference works,[36] another study found that *Wikipedia* can omit content due to "the limited expertise and interests of contributors."[37] An additional study concluded that *Wikipedia* isn't a neutral source of information; as a "socially produced" work, it "reflects the viewpoints, interests, and emphases of the people who use it."[38] Ironically, a *Wikipedia* entry actually admits the site's limitations, noting that "Wikipedia is not a reliable source for academic writing or research." The entry goes on to note that while *Wikipedia* and other reference works can be used to gain background information at the start of research, books, articles, and other sources will provide better academic research.[39]

For all of these reasons, it's best to proceed with caution before using evidence that comes from social media sources in your speech.

## Searching the World Wide Web

You've likely used **search engines**—specialized online programs that continually visit web pages and index what is found there. When you enter a search term, the engine searches billions of web pages to find the best matches for the term. The results are then sorted based on **algorithms**, which are formulas that attempt to provide you with links that are most useful to you. Each search engine has its own algorithm, so you'll receive different results depending on which one you use.[40]

Which search engine is best for you? Try several, then compare their features and functionality. You can also check online for reviews of search engines that highlight key features and provide updates as more features become available. The most frequently used search engine is Google by a landslide (86 percent market share in September 2021), followed by Bing, Yahoo!, and Baidu.[41]

How can you improve the quality of your search? Here are a few suggestions:

- *Use scholarly search features.* Search engines such as Google Scholar and Microsoft Academic limit their results to information from scholarly sources. Tip: If there is a fee to access an article, copy down the citation. Your college librarian can probably help you access the article for free.

- *Use quotation marks around key phrases.* If you're researching a proposed tax on soft drinks, searching for "soda tax" will focus your results on the proposed tax rather than sites dealing with soda or taxes more generally.

- *Use precise search terms.* For example, if you want to search for the health effects of a soda tax, search for "soda tax" and "health effects." Use the same process to focus your search on economic effects or the constitutionality of such a tax.

- *Use **advanced search** features.* These features allow you to limit your search by date, language, country, or file format. You can also prioritize your search terms based on where they occur on the web page (for example, in the title or in the text). The safe-search feature avoids sites with pornographic or explicit content.

# INTERVIEWING SOURCES

In addition to conducting research at the library and searching the web, you can also learn about your topic by interviewing people with expertise in a particular subject area. Here are some tips for getting the most out of your interviews.

## Prepare for Your Interview

First, determine what you want to find out through an interview. Are there any questions you're having difficulty answering through library and Internet research? Are there any individuals who, if interviewed, would add credibility to your speech?

Next, decide whom to interview. The person you talk with should be an expert on your subject. If your school has a department focused on your subject area, ask the chair or another knowledgeable person to recommend faculty members who would make good interview subjects for your speech.

Off-campus sources—such as high-ranking members of political organizations, government agencies, businesses, nonprofit entities, and community

▼ **Plan Your Interview in Advance.** You'll get more helpful information from your interview if you think carefully about the questions you plan to ask. SDI Productions/ Getty Images

groups or clubs—can also prove useful. Many of these individuals are "people persons," who will appreciate the opportunity to talk about their area of expertise. If the person whom you would like to interview is too busy, they may be able to give you a lead about another expert to interview.

Students who haven't researched their speech in advance sometimes rely on friends, family members, or neighbors for interviews because they can be found at the last minute. Although these sources may be able to provide some insight, they generally aren't the type of credible research sources that instructors will expect. Check with your instructor in advance before using this type of interview to obtain evidence.

## Set Up Your Interview

If possible, contact potential interview subjects in person. (It's far easier for busy people to say no to an interview request via email or over the telephone than face-to-face.) Identify yourself, explain that you're preparing a speech, and describe what you hope to learn from the interview. You'll need to be willing to accommodate the interviewee's schedule, since they'll be going out of their way to help you out.

## Plan Your Interview Questions

After you have set up the interview, decide what you want to ask the person you'll be interviewing. Prepare focused questions that your interviewee is in a unique position to answer, rather than general questions you could easily address through your own research.

In Chapter 5, we discussed fixed-response and open-ended questions. Frame each question based on the information you need. If you want your interview subject to elaborate or provide examples, use open-ended questions that require more than a yes or no response. For example, you might ask a journalist, "How does the growth of online media affect your profession?" You also might plan to ask the interviewee a candid question that you think they would prefer to avoid. If you do so, just be sure to phrase the question professionally. Coming across as needlessly confrontational will put your interviewee on the defensive and may cause them to stop talking.

## Conduct the Interview

Arrive on time for your interview, and dress professionally unless the occasion warrants different attire (for example, an interview on a farm). When you arrive, greet your interviewee, and introduce yourself if you haven't already met.

Keep the following considerations in mind during the interview:

- *Explain the purpose of your interview.* Be sure the subject understands that you are gathering information for use in a classroom speech, and ask for permission to use their responses in your speech.

- *Start with friendly, easy-to-answer questions.* Straightforward questions allow you to establish rapport before you pose more difficult questions. If the interviewee has a limited amount of time, however, move on to your most important questions quickly.

- *Take notes.* Be sure to jot down the words and phrases your interviewee uses.

- *Stay focused.* If the interviewee digresses, politely steer the discussion back to the topic.

- *Maintain eye contact.* Although you may occasionally need to look down to read your questions or to take notes, do your best to keep the interview conversational and relaxed through frequent eye contact.

- *Be open to new information.* If new and valuable ideas come up, don't feel forced to stick to your planned questions. Feel free to deviate from them to explore the new information.

- *Listen carefully.* To ensure you're hearing your subject's answers correctly, paraphrase key responses back to the person.

- *Record the interview if your subject gives permission.* Secretly recording an interview is a serious breach of ethics.

In addition to traditional face-to-face meetings, people are increasingly using remote technologies, such as Zoom or Google Meet, for interviews. These technologies may be a better option for you or your interviewee if you're not in the same location or you have other commitments that prevent you from meeting in person. For conducting virtual interviews, radio journalist Marie Naudascher offers several tips:

- If you're interviewing someone from home, do your best to find a quiet location before starting.

- Don't apologize for conducting a remote interview; instead, begin by showing your appreciation that they are available to talk.

- If you're recording the interview, let the participant know that the recording is only for your personal use (or obtain their consent if you intend to share it).

- Consider trying a phone interview instead if the video quality is poor.[42]

## Evaluate Your Notes

Immediately after the interview, check your notes to see whether you wrote down all the responses you may want to use in your speech. If you didn't get everything in your notes, write down the person's answers while the interview is still fresh in your mind. If you can't remember an answer accurately, contact the interviewee to clarify their response rather than guessing. You need to be sure you're quoting or paraphrasing accurately in your speech. And no matter what, send a thank-you note to the person to show that you appreciate their time and attention.

# PRESENTING EVIDENCE IN YOUR SPEECH

You've finished researching and have selected credible evidence to use in your speech. Good work! You're well on your way to earning the benefits of a well-researched speech, but another essential job remains. You need to cite your research correctly in your speech, while directly quoting or paraphrasing your sources' ideas. Let's take a look at how this is done in a manner that makes it clear to the instructor and audience that you're presenting evidence accurately.

## Clearly Cite Your Sources

As you saw in Chapter 3, when you use information in your speech that you have gained from your research, you have an ethical obligation to *attribute* that information to the author. This means that you state the author's name, their qualifications, the source where you found the information, and the date (see an example from a speech on thermal inequities below). The audience needs to understand that you are citing evidence. It is not enough that you have the citation on a works-cited page of an outline that you submit to your instructor. Audience members need to understand that you are citing evidence *at the time that you are presenting it* orally in your speech.

## Present the Information Accurately

After you cite your evidence, the next step is presenting the information. You have an ethical obligation to present the author's ideas accurately. This is accomplished either through direct quotation or paraphrasing.

When you use a **direct quotation**, you present the author's ideas word-for-word. Anytime you use the author's exact words (even a short phrase), you need to put them in quotation marks—both in your notes and in any written outline or copy of your speech that you submit to your instructor. If you leave out quotation marks when using information word-for-word, you are representing the wording choice as being your own rather than the actual author's. This is unethical and is likely to be a violation of your college's policy on cheating and plagiarism.

When you cite your source with a direct quotation, use the claim-source-support order. Begin by stating the point you are making. Next, fully cite your source, presenting the author, their credentials, the publication, and the date. Finally, quote or paraphrase the evidence. See the following example:

> Thermal inequities burden communities of color. [*claim*] As Fidel Martinez, Audience Engagement Editor, wrote in the *Los Angeles Times*, November 4, 2021 [*source*]: "Neighborhoods with large Latinx, Black and Asian populations are a lot hotter than their white counterparts and also get less shade from trees. According to a study conducted by UC Davis researchers, heavily Latinx neighborhoods in Los Angeles were 6.7 degrees hotter than neighborhoods with fewer Latinx residents during extreme heat days." [*evidence*]

When you **paraphrase**, you restate the author's information in your own words. To paraphrase ethically, be sure that the words you use are your own instead of the author's. A good technique for paraphrasing is to read the author's words and make sure you understand the idea. Then put the source aside and write down the idea without looking at the author's words. *Do not* use your word processor to cut and paste the author's words and then change a few terms. In our experience, this practice often gets students in trouble for plagiarism because they end up using words that are mostly the author's. If you discover that you're using sentences or even phrases that the author used, be sure to place those words in quotation marks.

It is also essential to paraphrase accurately. The words you use need to correctly represent the author's intent. For example, it is unethical to present evidence using **power wording**—that is, to reword evidence in a way that better supports your claim but misrepresents the source's point of view.

# PARAPHRASING AND QUOTING SOURCES

ORIGINAL QUOTATION:

"One factor that contributes to disparities in heat exposure is residential segregation. Historic housing policies, including redlining, resulted in residential segregation that pushed many low-income people and people of color into urban neighborhoods with fewer resources and more limited opportunities for development and advancement."[43]

DIRECT QUOTATION (QUOTE AUTHOR WORD-FOR-WORD AND USE QUOTATION MARKS):

"Historic housing policies, including redlining, resulted in residential segregation that pushed many low-income people and people of color into urban neighborhoods with fewer resources."

PARAPHRASE (REWRITE USING YOUR OWN WORDS):

Housing segregation, caused by years of government practices, forced economically marginalized and underrepresented people into areas with limited prospects.

APPROVED

PARAPHRASE PLUS QUOTATION MARKS WHEN USING AUTHOR'S PHRASE:

One cause of thermal inequities is housing policy. "Historic housing policies, including redlining" forced economically marginalized and underrepresented people into areas with limited prospects.

APPROVED

PLAGIARISM (USING TOO MANY OF THE AUTHOR'S WORDS WITHOUT QUOTATION MARKS):

One cause of disparities in heat exposure is housing segregation. Historic housing practices, not limited to redlining, resulted in residential segregation.

## SPEECH CHOICES

### A CASE STUDY: *RAFAELA*

*Let's find out how Rafaela researched her speech.*

Rafaela had her topic selected: persuading the audience to encourage women to run for office. The next step was finding evidence for her speech.

The assignment required speakers to cite multiple research sources, and Rafaela thought she was set. She had done an Internet search and saved the first three search results. The sources she found were InsideHigherEd.com, Yahoo.com/news, and StudyBreaks.com. "Since I already interviewed the state assembly candidate and her daughter, as well as some classmates," Rafaela thought, "I'll just read these three articles, select the best information, and be done."

Then she remembered that her instructor had cautioned students that the first search results are not necessarily the best ones for a speech. So Rafaela looked into the credibility of the sources she had found. The author of her first web article was an award-winning journalist with experience covering college topics—that was a source she could use. The author of the second article had no credentials listed, but Rafaela discovered that the writer's primary experience was in fashion reporting. She'd need to double-check the information in this one. The third source was a student publication. Her class would probably be interested in students' perspectives on the issue, but because she couldn't be sure of the author's credibility, she wouldn't make this source a central part of her speech.

Rafaela also decided to expand her search for sources and look at additional results. This was a good decision—the eighth result on the list was a scholarly report titled *Girls Just Wanna Not Run: The Gender Gap in Young Americans' Political Ambition*. Based on a survey of twenty-one hundred college students, researchers identified five reasons for the gender gap, including the fact that young women are less likely to receive encouragement to run for office.[44] This study would provide excellent support for her speech. Now Rafaela was on a roll. She topped off her research by finding more scholarly sources on her college library's website.

 **YOUR TURN**

Now that you've seen how Rafaela benefited from assessing her sources' credibility, it's time to think about your next speech. Making speech choices involves asking and answering a series of questions related to your assignment. When you conduct research, these questions might include:

- What will be my research plan?
- What library resources will be most helpful? Is there anyone I can interview?
- Have I evaluated the authors' credibility for all my sources?
- Are there any aspects of my topic that require more supporting evidence?
- Did I record all the citation information for each source?

Making thoughtful choices in response to questions like these will help you select and cite credible sources—two key pieces of a strong speech.

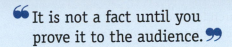 **It is not a fact until you prove it to the audience.** 〞 From the story about Katie, Mandeep, and Sherri's activism against police officers shooting at crows perched atop their local courthouse building, it's clear that providing evidence for the claims in your speech can help make your presentation more convincing and make you appear more credible as a speaker. To create your research plan, take the following steps: inventory your research needs, find the sources you need, and be sure to keep track of your sources. To evaluate a source's credibility, consider the author's expertise, objectivity, and observational capacity, as well as the source's recency. When conducting library research, vary your focus among books, periodicals, newspapers, reference works, and government documents. Although many students use the Internet for research, there are both advantages and disadvantages to this, and you need to carefully evaluate the credibility of online sources. You can also research your topic by interviewing experts. When you've gathered your research, be sure to present your evidence in claim-source-support order, cite your sources completely, and use direct quotes or accurate paraphrases every time you use evidence in your speech.

## Key Terms

evidence *161*
academic research *161*
research plan *163*
research objective *163*
research librarian *163*
keyword *164*
citation *165*
export (citations) *166*
credible source *166*
expertise *166*
objectivity *167*
observational capacity *168*
recency *168*
periodical *170*
peer review *170*
full-text source *171*

abstract *171*
paywall *172*
reference work *172*
encyclopedia *173*
dictionary *173*
quotation book *173*
atlas *173*
yearbook *173*
top-level domain *177*
social media *178*
search engine *178*
algorithm *178*
advanced search *179*
direct quotation *183*
paraphrase *184*
power wording *184*

## Review Questions

1. What are four key benefits of doing research for your speech?
2. Explain the three main steps involved in creating a research plan.
3. Why is it important to copy down complete citation information for a source at the time you obtain it?
4. What four key characteristics determine a source's credibility?
5. What advantages do libraries offer over the Internet?
6. Describe the advantages and disadvantages of Internet research.
7. Explain the steps involved in conducting a useful interview.
8. What is the proper way to present evidence in a speech?

## Critical Thinking Questions

1. How do peer review, vetting, and editing affect the quality of information presented in a book or journal? How can you determine whether information you find online has been through these processes?
2. How can you determine the credibility of information presented on a website? Are there any red flags that immediately make you question a site's integrity? What characteristics are likely to make you trust an Internet source?
3. Imagine you have been assigned to speak on a controversial topic. How would you go about choosing potential interviewees? What kinds of questions would you ask your interviewees? How would you use the information gleaned in interviews to bolster your thesis ethically?
4. Go to the *Wikipedia* entry for a subject you might like to discuss in a speech. Identify claims that are made without any supporting footnote or citation. How can you determine whether the author of these comments is credible? Next, identify claims that are supported by a footnote or citation. What would you need to do to determine whether the sources for these claims are credible?

## Activities

1. Divide into groups. Working individually, select a topic of interest, then jot down the steps you would follow in a research plan. Share your research plan with the group. After each plan is presented, have the other group members provide additional suggestions for how the topic might be researched effectively.
2. Working in groups, make a list of several potential speech topics. Then create a composite character for a person who would be a credible source on that topic. What is this source's educational background? Occupation? Reputation in the field? Observational capacity?

3. Working in groups, brainstorm potential speech topics. Then discuss search terms you might use when researching each topic. In your discussion, be sure to consider synonyms, broader terms, and narrower terms that could be used for each topic.

4. Suppose you are considering whether to purchase the next-generation iPhone and you are particularly interested in its features for playing music. In groups, discuss and rank the credibility of the following sources of information about this product: (a) a friend who has purchased the product, (b) a sales representative at the Apple Store, (c) an article by the technology editor of your local newspaper, (d) an instructor in the music department at your college, (e) a website that ranks portable media players.

5. Go to the campus library and locate a book on a topic you are considering for a speech. Then try the process discussed on page 170 to find other books on your topic. Did you find additional useful information in these books?

6. Use an index for scholarly sources, such as *Academic Search Premier* or *JSTOR*, to find three articles on a topic you are considering for a speech. Then find three websites that cover that topic. Compare the credibility of the authors of the scholarly sources with that of the authors of the online sources. Also compare the content of the information found on the scholarly and Internet sources.

7. Review the illustration that depicts how Katie, Mandeep, and Sherri used research to strengthen their presentation to local officials. Then consider a problem in your community that you might discuss at a public meeting, and decide how you could use evidence to strengthen your case. Create your own illustration of that scenario using the earlier illustration as a model. (Stick figures are fine if you are not a natural artist.)

40 Years
of Title IX
is
mighty fine

# USING SUPPORTING MATERIALS FOR YOUR SPEECH

**8**

> "The sum of the parts determines the success of the whole speech."

Graciela was a member of her college's varsity tennis team, so for her informative speech topic, she chose to focus on Title IX—the federal law prohibiting sex discrimination by educational institutions that receive federal aid. Title IX had greatly expanded women's opportunities in college sports. As she began her research, one of the first things she discovered was that there are three ways a school can demonstrate compliance with Title IX. Graciela's first feeling was relief: the assignment called for an eight- to ten-minute speech, and it would take at least six to explain the ways a college could comply. She was more than halfway done!

Then Graciela reconsidered. Of all the points she could make about this important and sometimes controversial law, would the details about compliance be the most interesting and noteworthy aspects to share with her audience? She decided to do more research about how Title IX issues were handled at her college. She found a tremendous amount of material—articles in the school newspaper about the effects of Title IX when it was first applied on campus, stories from athletes about their experiences on the college's first women's teams, and even a copy of the program from the first women's tennis

◀ **Title IX.** This legislation significantly increased participation in girls' and women's sports. David Sherman/Getty Images

tournament ever held on campus. She also interviewed two athletes from the college's first softball team.

Now Graciela had ideas and evidence that would be much more relevant and interesting to her classmates. By going the extra mile to find engaging support, she had the materials she needed to back up her main points soundly.

As we note in Chapter 2 and throughout the book, every speech includes a limited number of main points. **Supporting materials** are the different types of information you use to develop and support your main points. You discover these materials as you conduct research; they then become the building blocks you use to construct a successful speech.

Selecting the best supporting materials for your main points is a key step in the speech preparation process, similar to choosing the right mix of ingredients for a special meal you'll be preparing. In an outstanding speech, the supporting materials fit together to help your listeners better understand your message, to capture their interest, and to convince them that you've done your research and are informed about your topic.

Consider a class in which you learned a lot about a subject, a political argument you found persuasive, and a movie that kept you glued to your seat for hours. Chances are good that the instructor of the class used understandable language and examples that clarified the concepts and made the subject seem relevant. The person making the political argument likely offered convincing proof of their claims and touched your emotions in a way that you remembered at the voting booth. And the movie probably combined an interesting story with memorable characters and an exciting plot. With the right supporting materials, you can craft a speech that has an equally strong impact on your audience.

In this chapter, we show you why supporting materials are important, what supporting materials you can use, and how to present supporting materials effectively.

# WHY USE SUPPORTING MATERIALS?

Supporting materials strengthen your speech in many ways. They build audience interest in your topic, enhance audience understanding of your ideas, and help audience members remember your presentation. In addition, they convince the audience that your points have merit and breathe life into your speech.

## Building Audience Interest

If you want audience members to actively listen to your speech—and ignore everything else going on—you must motivate them to focus on what you're saying. By selecting supporting materials that appeal to your listeners' interests, you sweeten the odds that they will pay attention to you. For example, suppose

SELECT SUPPORTING MATERIALS THAT RELATE TO THE AUDIENCE

you are developing a speech on cooking with locally grown products. Your supporting materials should focus on ingredients that are available at farmers' markets in your region—citrus or tropical fruits in Florida, avocados in California, or summer squash in Michigan. It would also be important to choose foods your fellow college students can afford.

## Enhancing Audience Understanding

If you're presenting information that's new to your listeners, they may have difficulty understanding it. The key to strengthening understanding is to anticipate the reasons that an idea might be difficult for audience members to grasp and to select supporting materials that will help them comprehend it.[1]

For instance, let's say you're preparing a speech on string theory (a scientific theory that "string-like objects" are "the fundamental building blocks of the universe"[2]) for an audience of mostly liberal-arts students. In this case, definitions could help your audience members understand the meaning of technical terms such as *superstring*. In addition, brief comparisons or examples (e.g., comparing a superstring to a garden hose)[3] could help them grasp the basic concepts behind your topic and help them form mental images of a superstring. You might also show a brief video clip that shows a simplified model of how string theory works.

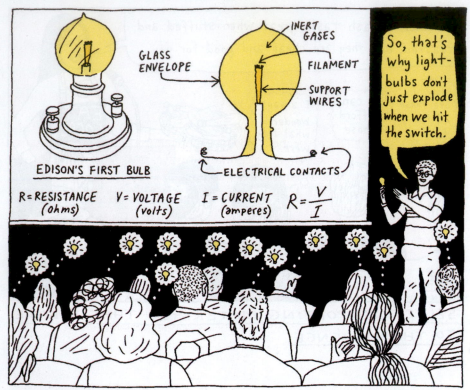

# ENHANCING AUDIENCE UNDERSTANDING

## Strengthening Audience Memory

An important goal of any speech is to make a lasting impression on your audience. If listeners applaud your presentation but can't remember much of what you said a week later, your speech had limited effect. To help audience members remember your presentation, you need to give them hooks that aid in the process. How does this work? A comparison to the fastener Velcro can demonstrate. Velcro contains tiny hooks on one side and loops on the other; when the sides are compressed, many of the hooks are caught in the loops, and they become attached.[4] Now imagine that a human brain has many millions of loops; the more hooks you can provide for an idea, the better the chance that an idea will stick in the minds of your audience members.[5]

Supporting materials provide hooks for the ideas you present. If you merely tell your audience that the Inca culture used groups of strings and knots called *khipu* (key-poo) to keep records, your listeners may quickly forget what *khipu* are and how they were used.[6] But suppose you follow up on that statement by showing the audience the word and having them pronounce it with you. Next, you explain that *khipu* means "knot" in the Inca language and that the strings are made from cotton or alpaca wool. Finally, you show a picture of a *khipu* and explain how the knots are positioned to store information. Now you have given the audience several hooks to help them remember what *khipu* are and how they were used.

## Winning Audience Agreement

You can't expect your listeners to unthinkingly embrace all the claims you make in your speech. Audience members may be skeptical of a point if they've never heard it before, if it strikes them as counterintuitive, or if it contradicts their worldview. To show that a claim is true, you need to provide supporting data that offer a good reason for accepting the claim. (This pattern of reasoning, first described by British logician Stephen Toulmin, is called the *Toulmin model of argument*.)[7] To do this, you might quote an expert, present a demonstration, or provide examples to illustrate the claim. For example, a speech asking for volunteers for a local Special Olympics competition might point out the benefits to participants. To support this point you might combine a study documenting the link between athlete participation and subsequent employment and the narrative of a former Special Olympics swimmer who is now in the workforce. If your audience accepts the link between the supporting materials and your claim, there is a good chance they will agree with your point.

▼ **Proving a Point.** In a trial, attorneys use supporting materials such as testimony, evidence, and videos to convince the jury. Pool/Getty Images

## Evoking Audience Emotion

Factual information greatly enhances any speech. However, you'll capture more of your audience members' attention and interest if you also touch their emotions. For example, effective speakers may use humor to warm up their listeners or give them a mental break from a slew of sobering statistics. The right supporting materials can also stimulate listeners' empathy, anger, or commitment. By including supporting materials that surprise audience members, make them laugh, or touch their emotions, you increase the chances that they will listen to what you are saying.

# TYPES OF SUPPORTING MATERIALS

There are many types of supporting materials from which to choose to develop your main points. Here, we take a closer look at some of the more common types—*examples*, *definitions*, *testimony*, *statistics*, *narratives*, and *analogies*.

## Examples

An **example** is a sample or an instance that supports or illustrates a general claim. In everyday conversation, you probably use examples frequently. To illustrate, suppose you tell a friend that parking is difficult on your campus, pointing out that you couldn't find a spot three times last week and your roommate drove around for thirty minutes the other day to find a space. In this case, you are using examples to support your claim that parking is difficult.

A **brief example** is a short instance (usually a single sentence) used to support or illustrate your claim. A set of three or four brief examples can often be used to great effect. The following excerpt shows how such examples can be used to support the claim that surveillance in the United States increased during the COVID-19 pandemic:

- During remote instruction, schools have expanded surveillance technology, including programs that "can collect many forms of data from students, including photos, video recordings of students at their computers, voice data, browsing history, keystroke data, and more."[8]

- Twenty-one states are using facial recognition software to check unemployment claims although the software is less accurate for identifying women and people whose skin tones are darker.[9]

- Companies have used programs to monitor people working from home, including software, sometimes called "tattleware," that "tracks everything employees are doing on their computers during the workday (including browser search terms and email text.)"[10]

You can also use an **extended example** to illustrate a point. An extended example provides many details about the instance being used, giving your

# EXAMPLES OF THREATS TO PRIVACY

audience a deeper and richer picture of your point. The following extended example provides an illustration of how surveillance of racial justice advocates has occurred:

> The Memphis Police Department made a Facebook profile and "friended" supporters of racial justice so they could glean information from activists' private and public posts. The profile of "Bob Smith" maintained that he was a person of color and a fellow protester. In reality, the profile was created by a white police detective. The police created dossiers on the activists and distributed them to other law enforcement agencies.[11]

## Definitions

When you introduce new information to audience members, you might use terms unfamiliar to them. If you don't take the time to define those terms, your listeners might have difficulty understanding your message, which can leave them feeling frustrated.

For example, suppose you're preparing an informative speech on the Persian empire, and you want to explain that the Persians practiced a religion called *Zoroastrianism*. This term will probably be new to your audience, so you'll need to define it. There are several different types of definitions you could use:

- A **dictionary definition** provides the meaning of a term as presented in a dictionary. You might use a general dictionary (such as *Merriam-Webster Collegiate Dictionary*) or, if available, a specialized dictionary for your topic. For example, "According to *Cambridge Dictionaries Online*, Zoroastrianism is 'a religion which developed in ancient Iran, and is based on the idea that there is a continuous fight between a god who represents good and one who represents evil.' "[12]

- An **expert definition** comes from a person who is a credible source of information on your topic. For example, "According to Mary Boyce, professor of Iranian studies at the University of London, Zoroastrians believe that 'there is a supreme God who is the creator; that an evil power exists which is opposed to him, and not under his control.' "[13]

- An **etymological definition** explains the linguistic origin of the term. This type of definition is appropriate when the origin is interesting or will help the audience understand the term. For example, "Zoroastrianism has been so named in the West because its prophet, Zarathustra, was known to the ancient Greeks as Zoroaster.[14] Zoroastrians believe that Ahura Mazda (God) revealed the truth through Zarathustra."

- A **functional definition** explains how something is used or what it does. For instance, a speaker might define *Zoroastrianism* in terms of how it is practiced by its followers: "According to the Ontario Consultants on Religious Tolerance, Zoroastrian worship 'includes prayers and symbolic ceremonies.' Rituals 'are conducted before a sacred fire. . . . [Practitioners] regard fire as a symbol of their God.' "[15]

## Testimony

**Testimony** consists of information provided by other people. Typically, you will gather testimony from the sources you research at the library and online or through interviews.

**Expert testimony** consists of statements made by credible sources who have professional or other in-depth knowledge of a topic. As with any source, you must carefully assess expert testimony to be sure that the sources have specialized knowledge of the topic, objectivity, and observational capacity (see Chapter 7). Testimony from expert sources is likely to increase audience members' acceptance of your claims. Thus, you should try to use expert testimony when you are asserting claims the audience may not accept.

A second type of testimony is **lay testimony**, which consists of statements made by persons with no special expertise in the subject they are discussing. Because they lack expertise, lay sources should generally not be used to prove factual claims in a speech. This type of testimony is *not* a substitute for evidence. For example, testimony from laypersons would not credibly prove that a low-carbohydrate diet improves people's health or predict the effect of expanded offshore oil drilling on the U.S. economy. However, lay testimony can help you show how a typical person has been affected by your topic. Thus, you could quote lay sources to explain their particular experiences with a low-carbohydrate diet or to discuss how they were affected by high gas prices.

## Statistics

A **statistic** is a piece of information presented in numerical form. Statistics can help you quantify points you're making in your speech and help your audience understand how often certain types of situations occur. Whereas supporting materials such as examples help the audience understand a single instance, statistics can help you show the big picture regarding multiple instances or instances over time of the situation you are discussing.

For example, in a speech on the rising costs of a college education, you might present an example of a single student who struggled to pay more than $1,400 for books and supplies in 2021. Then you could use statistics to argue that high costs are typical: "The College Board reports that the average cost of books and supplies at two-year colleges was $1,460 in 2021–22, and for four-year public colleges, the cost was $1,240."[16]

Although useful, statistics also have disadvantages. Specifically, as your use of statistics increases, so does the chance that your audience members will perceive your topic as overly complicated.[17] A long string of statistics may also bore or confuse your listeners if they're struggling to figure out what "all those numbers" mean. To present statistics in a way that helps your audience understand the information and remain interested in your speech, apply the following guidelines:

- *Limit the number of statistics you present.* Of all the possible statistics you could offer your audience, select three or four of the best ones.

- *Use visual aids to explain your statistics.* For example, you could use a bar graph to illustrate increases in textbook costs, tuition, and overall cost of living over the past decade.

- *Establish context.* Explain what the statistics imply for your listeners. For instance, "What does an 11 percent increase mean? The average cost for tuition, books, supplies, and room and board at a public four-year college in 2021–22 is $22,690.[18] At this rate of increase, the cost will rise to over $25,000 over the next decade after adjusting for inflation."

## Narratives

A **narrative** is an anecdote (a brief story) or a somewhat longer account that can be used to support your main points. Narratives stimulate your listeners' interest because humans (by nature) love a good story.[19]

Here is an example of a medium-length anecdote presented in a speech about two sisters seeking their stolen food truck:

> Karla and Eileen Enriquez were business majors at the University of Nevada, Las Vegas who managed the Amigo Taco food truck to gain business experience and earn money for school. Their food truck was stolen on a Friday at 3 in the morning and the sisters quickly put the word out on social media.[20] The good news is that their truck was found two days later.[21]

In a speech on the construction of the thousand-mile Alaska–Canadian highway during World War II, a presenter used the following longer narrative

THIS IS A NARRATIVE

Once upon a time, drawings of people having ideas in comic strips looked like this:—→

It's not really clear what I'm doing. Am I having an idea or just doing a funny little dance ?!?

But then, in 1879, Thomas Edison invented something:

I call it a LIGHT-BULB!

These "lightbulbs" made comic strip artists so happy. Now they could make it instantly obvious that someone in a drawing was having an idea:

However, the comic strip artists didn't just get to live happily ever after, as now, in the 21st century, people are beginning to have differently shaped ideas:

to show how the project not only built a highway but also contributed to civil rights:

> Three African American regiments were sent to the mountains of northern Canada to work on the highway. They faced hostile conditions as well as prejudice and doubts about their ability. Working nonstop for three days and using the headlights of trucks when it got dark, these soldiers cut down trees, built trestles, and worked chest-deep in the icy water to build a bridge across the Sikanni Chief River. The unit earned a reputation for its ability to rapidly build strong bridges in the worst of environments, helping "pave" the way for desegregation of the armed forces in 1948. The highway has been called "the road to civil rights."[22]

Stories like these are great for capturing audience attention or for illustrating a point. Consider incorporating such stories as attention-getters or when you want to show how concepts play out in the real world. And you can always use a quick anecdote—lasting no more than five or ten seconds—to reenergize an audience after tackling complex or technical material.

Narratives and anecdotes are like lay testimony in that they can effectively build audience interest or illustrate a concept; however, anecdotal evidence is no substitute for credible proof. Stories about a relative who smoked two packs of cigarettes a day and lived to ninety-eight or a roommate who partied every night and still maintained a 3.8 grade-point average do not prove that such behaviors are safe for the population as a whole.

## Analogies

An **analogy** is a comparison based on similarities between two phenomena—one that's familiar to the audience and one that is less familiar. Analogies can be **literal**, meaning that two entities in the same category are compared. For example, a speaker might help the audience understand the career of Diana Ross (lead singer of the Supremes in the 1960s and a solo star in the 1970s) by comparing her to Beyoncé, or explain the blockchain technology used to record Bitcoin transactions by comparing it to a bank vault full of glass deposit boxes—anyone can see what is in the boxes, but nobody can access the contents.[23] Analogies can also be **figurative**, which means that although the two entities are not in the same category, the characteristics of one (which is familiar to the audience) can help the audience understand the characteristics of the other (which is unfamiliar). This type of comparison helps listeners use their existing knowledge to absorb new information.[24]

Here's how Dr. Emily Conover, President of the D.C. Science Writers Association, explained the neutron drip line—"the boundary beyond which an atom's nucleus has more neutrons than it can contain"[25]—with a figurative analogy:

> "Imagine a greedy chipmunk with its cheeks so full of nuts that when it tries to shove in one more, another nut pops right back out."[26]

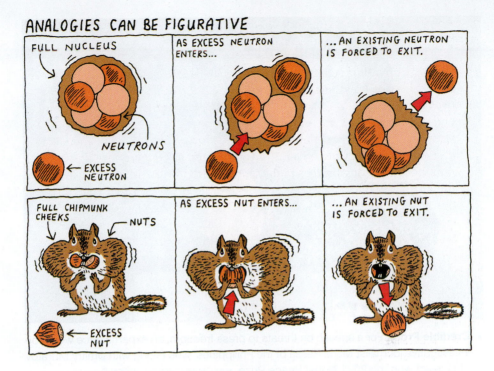

ANALOGIES CAN BE FIGURATIVE

When you are preparing a speech, one effective approach is to provide analogies that draw on concepts you've heard in your classmates' speeches. That way, you'll know that your audience members will understand the concepts you're using, and you'll demonstrate goodwill by showing that you have learned from your classmates' presentations. Additional good sources of analogies are familiar sights and traditions on your campus or aspects of college life that your listeners can all relate to. Everyday experiences may give you ideas, too—Dr. Conover thought of her analogy after watching a YouTube video of a chipmunk![27]

## GUIDELINES FOR USING SUPPORTING MATERIALS

Recall that supporting materials serve a variety of purposes in your speech—including building audience interest, helping the audience understand, and proving facts to the audience. As we noted in Chapter 7, in the Internet era, it is not difficult to find enormous quantities of information on your topic in a short amount of time. It is not as easy, however, to select the best supporting materials out of all the information you've found. How can you be sure to select the most effective supporting materials? The following guidelines can help.

### Choose the Most Credible Proof

Give priority to supporting materials that are backed by credible evidence. Whether you are relying on examples, testimony, statistics, or other types of support, these materials will be most effective when they are proven. For example,

▲ **Credible Proof.** For a speech on threats to press freedom, an expert source would be investigative journalist Maria Ressa of the Philippines, who (along with Dmitry Muratov of Russia) won the 2021 Nobel Peace Prize. HAKON MOSVOLD LARSEN/Getty Images

in a speech on the hazards of texting while driving, the statement that the average "eyes-off-road time" for sending a text message is equivalent to "traveling the length of a football field at 55 miles per hour without looking at the roadway" is a compelling analogy. But it will be a much more believable one if you identify the author of the study—the Virginia Tech Transportation Institute.[28] If you merely assert this fact without proof or attribute it to a website of uncertain authorship, the analogy will be much less convincing.

## Use a Variety of Supporting Materials

In the previous section, you learned about a number of different types of supporting materials. To get the best results, you should use a variety of these types of materials to support your main points. If you use the same type of supporting material over and over, your effectiveness will be reduced as fatigue sets in with your audience.

For instance, one funny personal example might pull listeners into your speech, a well-chosen analogy can help your audience understand a key point, and a startling statistic can convince audience members that a problem you're describing is serious. By contrast, a speech that uses mainly one type of support—whether personal examples, analogies, or statistics—will quickly lose listeners' interest.

How does employing a variety of supporting materials work in practice? Take the example of a speech about abstract art. To help audience members understand what abstract art is, you might begin with a *definition* of abstract art.

## REPETITIVE TYPE OF SUPPORT

## DIVERSE TYPES OF SUPPORT

Then you could follow that up with several *examples* of abstract art. Then you could present *expert testimony* on the topic—for example, noting that abstract artist Mary Heilmann uses the title of her artwork to suggest how the work is significant to her.[29]

Another option is to give your audience a chance to practice the concept you are explaining. For instance, after using a narrative to help her listeners understand how bees fly, one student invited audience members to manipulate their arms to simulate the motion of bees' wings.

### Avoid Long Lists

People usually find it difficult to understand and remember long strings of facts, examples, or statistics, especially when they aren't presented with any elaboration. Consider this excerpt from a speech titled "My Hometown":

There are great restaurants in my town. You can get Chinese food, Italian food, Mexican food, and Ethiopian food. There are lots of places to go. You can go to the lake, the amusement park, the movies, or the ballgame. If you like to exercise, try our running trails, swimming pools, and bicycling paths.

If this speaker followed this pattern for five minutes or more, his presentation would quickly become tedious and forgettable.

To avoid this scenario, select a smaller number of supporting materials (most should take between fifteen and thirty seconds to present), and focus on the materials that *best* develop your main points. The "My Hometown" speech could have been more effective if the speaker had concentrated on the most noteworthy aspects of the town and expanded on them. By focusing on a notable hometown restaurant, for instance, the speaker could use examples, testimony, and analogies to help audience members imagine themselves dining in that restaurant and tasting the food.

## Consider Your Audience

Your audience members' knowledge and interests can be useful in helping you choose the best possible supporting materials. For example, suppose you want to persuade your listeners to volunteer for community service. If your audience consists of future teachers, you might offer examples and narratives about service opportunities with young children. Or if many of your listeners enjoy outdoor activities, your supporting materials could relate more to environmental service.

## Respect the Available Time

Select supporting materials that you can comfortably fit into the time you have available for your speech. For a five- to ten-minute speech, for instance, you wouldn't have time to use supporting materials that each take one min-

ute or more to present— no matter how interesting and relevant they might be. To illustrate, suppose your employer asked you to prepare a ten-minute podcast about best practices in urban agriculture. You might be tempted to include a four-minute narrative about how you came to be involved in this field, but this would take up almost half of your speaking time and cut into the available time for explaining best practices. You would need to find a different, shorter narrative that would help viewers understand these methods.

## SPEECH CHOICES

### A CASE STUDY: *RAFAELA*

*Let's take a look at Rafaela's selection of supporting materials.*

After Rafaela finished her research, she felt well prepared to craft her speech. She had evidence from several scholarly sources and also lay testimony, based on her interviews with the classmates who had run for student government and the state assembly candidate's daughter. Rafaela selected her best evidence and timed herself as she read it. To her surprise, it took ten minutes—she literally had TMI! As she thought about what information to cut, Rafaela considered something else: that she might begin to lose the audience's interest if she focused only on presenting evidence, even if the evidence was credible.

Rafaela remembered that testimony was not the only type of supporting material she could use, and so she began considering other types of support that could pull the audience into her speech. One was using statistics to prove the claims she planned to make. For another type of supporting material, Rafaela considered including an example. After doing a little more research, a good candidate for that example emerged: she could talk about New Mexico's Deb Haaland, the first Native American woman elected to Congress. Haaland had first gotten into politics when she helped a friend challenge the Laguna Pueblo's ban on women running for tribal office. Plus, Ms. Haaland had run in marathons, and from her research, Rafaela had learned that sports participation was an important experience to prepare women for running for office. This example would work well.

Finally, Rafaela wanted to make sure she had supporting materials that would relate well to her audience, so she included a list of specific courses at her college that would be perfect for women interested in public office. She also looked up opportunities for participation in competitive clubs on her campus and found the debate and mock-trial teams, which would provide helpful experiences for women who ran for office.

### YOUR TURN

Now that you've seen how Rafaela's choices impacted the supporting materials she selected for her speech, it's time to think about how you'll use supporting materials in a speech of your own. Making speech choices involves asking and answering a series of questions related to your assignment. When you select supporting materials, these questions might include:

- What supporting materials are available to develop my ideas?
- Which of these supporting materials will be most interesting to my audience?
- Which of these supporting materials will best help my audience understand the ideas I'm presenting?
- Which of these supporting materials can be presented effectively in the available time?
- Have I selected a variety of different types of supporting materials?

Making thoughtful choices in response to questions like these will help you select just the right mix of materials to best support your speech.

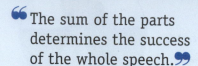

**The sum of the parts determines the success of the whole speech.**

As the story about Graciela's speech on Title IX illustrates at the beginning of this chapter, the right supporting materials can help you build listeners' interest in your presentation, enhance audience understanding of your topic, strengthen the likelihood that audience members will remember your speech, convince your audience that your claims have merit, and breathe life into your speech by touching on audience emotions. To choose the best supporting materials, you can start by understanding the many forms they take, such as examples, definitions, testimony, statistics, narratives, and analogies. You can then apply important guidelines, such as choosing the most credible proof, using a variety of supporting materials, avoiding long lists of information, considering your audience's knowledge and interests, and ensuring that your supporting materials don't consume too much of the time available for your presentation.

## Key Terms

supporting material *192*
example *196*
brief example *196*
extended example *196*
dictionary definition *197*
expert definition *197*
etymological definition *198*
functional definition *198*

testimony *199*
expert testimony *199*
lay testimony *199*
statistic *200*
narrative *201*
analogy *202*
literal analogy *202*
figurative analogy *202*

## Review Questions

1. Name five purposes for using supporting materials.
2. Name and define six types of supporting materials.
3. Explain why it is important to select supporting materials that are backed by credible evidence.
4. Identify four or more guidelines for using supporting materials in a speech.

## Critical Thinking Questions

1. What are a speaker's ethical obligations when presenting statistical information? How could failing to provide solid context for statistics mislead audiences?
2. Narratives and anecdotes are often used to evoke an emotional response. What other types of supporting materials might tap audience members' emotions? Could expert testimony support an emotional appeal? Could statistics generate an emotional response?
3. Think of a time when one of your instructors explained a subject effectively. What supporting materials did they use to help the class understand the topic? What supporting materials did they use to build interest in the subject?
4. Think of a topic that you understand well but that is likely to be new to many of your classmates. How could you use a figurative analogy to explain some aspect of that topic to your audience?

## Activities

1. Working in groups, select a speech topic, then have each group member select a different type of supporting material for that topic. Next, have each group member provide an example of their chosen supporting material that could be used in a speech on the selected topic.
2. Working in groups of up to five students, select a potential speech topic. Then have each group member choose a different purpose for supporting materials (such as building audience interest or strengthening audience memory) and select an example of a supporting material that would help achieve that purpose. Discuss whether each supporting material chosen would be likely to achieve its purpose.
3. Review the illustration on page 203 ("Analogies Can Be Figurative"). Select any speech topic of interest to you, and think of an analogy you could use as supporting material. Draw your own illustration of that analogy.
4. Review the evidence sources cited within this chapter, then look at the endnotes for this chapter. What types of sources did the authors use to back up the points they raised? What kinds of supporting materials are included in this chapter that do not require citations to research? Would the chapter work as well if only one or the other type of supporting material were presented?
5. Review an article or another source that presents statistics to support the points it makes. How well do the statistics support the author's thesis? Does the author provide appropriate context for the statistics?

# ORGANIZING YOUR SPEECH

**9**

❝Good organization makes the message clear.❞

Victoria stood in front of the class and began her speech. After trying to build audience interest with a joke ("What platform do vegans dread the most? Google meet!"), she stated that her speech would be about social media. Victoria made a number of different points. She began by comparing the features of TikTok, Instagram, and Facebook. Then she presented research about how much time people typically spend on social media each day and talked about how this time is often wasted. Using classroom technology, she displayed examples of posts that she thought were silly, along with posts presenting information that she considered false. Then Victoria criticized social media companies for censoring viewpoints that company management found objectionable. Finally, Victoria called for breaking up larger social media companies to "teach them a lesson."

When Victoria returned to her seat, she was confident that her speech had been interesting and convincing. However, when her instructor asked for student comments, many classmates indicated that they had been unable to follow her train of thought. They said that Victoria jumped from topic to topic and then ended with a call for action that she did not connect to the ideas she

◀ **Organization Is Essential.** To convince the audience, a speech on regulating social media networks needs to be well organized. Your speeches need good organization, too.   Bloomberg/Getty Images

had presented earlier. Disappointed with the audience feedback, Victoria didn't realize that she had made an all-too-common mistake—failing to organize her speech clearly.

Victoria's experience reveals the importance of organization in developing a successful speech. When you organize your ideas clearly, you help audience members see how the different ideas in your presentation fit together, which allows your listeners to better comprehend your message.[1] They know what to listen for because your organization provides cues to indicate the main ideas. And they don't have to devote their mental energy to figuring out what your main points are and how all the details in your speech relate to those points.

Good organization is particularly important in oral communication because listeners usually don't have the luxury of reviewing printed information to understand your message. By contrast, those who are reading a printed message—whether online or in a book or magazine—can go back and reread the text if they're confused. Thus, when giving a speech, you must take special care to help the audience follow your ideas.

When you organize your speech clearly, you also enhance your credibility. Effective organization shows that you have taken the time to prepare your talk.[2]

Organizing a speech is not merely a matter of applying an arbitrary set of rules. Rather, a well-organized presentation imposes order on the set of points you present in your speech by showing the relationship *between* ideas. Thus, the organizational pattern you select can communicate important information to the audience: What are the most important ideas? Why do you believe that each idea has merit? What evidence are you providing to back up your claims?

In this chapter, we focus on organizing the **body** of your speech—the part where you present your main points and support them with examples, narratives, testimony, and other materials. To organize a speech effectively, you must learn to group your ideas into a sequence your audience can easily follow. In the following pages, we explore ways to select your main points and structure your supporting materials. We also examine common patterns for arranging main points and present some organizing language you can use to make your speech structure clear to your audience.

ORGANIZING
THE BODY
OF YOUR

# SELECTING YOUR MAIN POINTS

The body of your speech should be structured around your **main points**—those few ideas that are most important for your listeners to remember. The body also contains **supporting points**—materials designed to prove or substantiate your main points. A speech body organized around main points and their corresponding supporting points helps listeners make sense out of the details of your presentation. By contrast, if you present randomly ordered ideas about your topic (as Victoria did), your audience will have trouble determining what is most important and understanding the information you're presenting. Even a five-minute speech requires careful organization because it can contain fifty or more sentences.

How should you select your main points? The following guidelines can help.

## Consider Your Purpose

Make sure that every main point you select relates to the specific purpose of your speech. For example, consider the following two sets of main points for a speech to the campus community with the following specific purpose—to persuade your college to adopt a plan to minimize food insecurity.

### FIRST SET OF MAIN POINTS

  I.   The elements of a healthy diet
 II.   Symptoms of malnutrition
III.   Our college should adopt a food insecurity plan.

### SECOND SET OF MAIN POINTS

  I.   Many students on our campus experience food insecurity.
 II.   Food insecurity has increased due to the COVID-19 pandemic.
III.   Our college should safely establish a food pantry and offer students emergency meal cards for campus food services that remain open.

Which set of main points would be a better option? In the first set, main points I and II do not relate to the speech's specific purpose but provide general background information about malnutrition and healthy diets. Only main point III relates to the specific purpose. Conversely, in the second set, each main point relates to the specific purpose: the first demonstrates the problem of food insecurity on campus, the second discusses one cause of the problem, and the third presents steps the college can take to reduce the problem. Given this contrast, the second set of main points would be a better alternative.

## Take Your Audience into Account

Out of the many relevant main points you might use to develop your topic, which ones will prove *most* interesting to your audience? Which ones will provide your listeners with the information that is most useful to *them*?

Consider the following two sets of main points for a speech on backpacking tips:

### FIRST SET OF MAIN POINTS

I. Choosing the right backpack
II. Remembering the essential equipment
III. Packing your backpack strategically

---

▼ **Selecting Main Points with the Audience in Mind.** A speech on techniques for playing the ukulele would have different main points if audience members were beginners or experienced musicians. Jesse Grant/Getty Images

**SECOND SET OF MAIN POINTS**

 I. Coping with extreme elevation changes
 II. Selecting light, nutritious food for weeklong trips
 III. Choosing optimal equipment for subzero temperatures

Both sets of main points contain information that fits the topic of "backpacking tips." Thus, they fit the first guideline for main points: they relate to the specific purpose of the speech. However, the question of which set is better depends on the audience. The first set contains basic information that would be appropriate for novice backpackers. The second set contains information that would be more useful for experienced backpackers who are contemplating challenging trips.

## Select an Appropriate Number of Main Points

In most situations, effective speeches present two to five main points. In our experience, student speeches typically contain three main points. However, there is no rule that you must have three. You can choose to have two, four, or five main points if that number gives you the most logical organization of ideas.

CHOOSING THE APPROPRIATE NUMBER OF MAIN POINTS

Most audiences have trouble remembering more than five points. Also, it is unlikely that you will have enough time to develop that many points in your speech. If you find yourself with too many main points, here are a few suggestions for whittling your list down to a manageable number:

- See whether any of your main points are related. Can two or more main points be combined into a single broader category?
- Review your audience analysis. Are there points that can be excluded because they are less likely to resonate with your audience?
- Evaluate which points are the most important to developing your topic or thesis. Exclude the point(s) that are less essential.

If you find that you have only one main point, consider making that point into the topic or thesis of your speech instead. Then organize the information you planned to use to support that point into two to five key ideas, which will become your main points.

## ORGANIZING YOUR SUPPORTING MATERIALS

After you select your main points, you need to develop (explain and prove) each one with supporting materials. Supporting materials enable your audience to understand your main points and help prove why you think those main points are valid. In Chapter 8, we discussed a number of different types of supporting materials that you can use, such as examples, definitions, and statistics. Now we consider how you can organize those supporting materials to help audience members follow your speech.

### Subordination and Coordination

The principle of subordination is the key to a well-organized speech. Using **subordination** means creating a hierarchy of points and their supporting materials in your speech. Thus, main points are the most important (or highest) level of subordination, and supporting materials used to develop a main point (called **subpoints**) are subordinate to—meaning they relate to—that main point. (There should be at least two subpoints to support each main point.) In the same way, materials that support subpoints are called **sub-subpoints**, and these sub-subpoints are subordinate to their corresponding subpoint. A well-organized speech also features **coordination**. Each main point is coordinate with other main points—that is, they are at the same level of significance—just as subpoints are coordinate with other subpoints, and sub–subpoints are coordinate with other sub-subpoints.

Sound confusing? It isn't, really. To see how subordination and coordination work, compare the main points (signaled by roman numerals) and the subpoints that support them (indicated by capital letters) in the following outline for an informative speech about taking notes in Zoom classes.

I. Zoom classes limit optimal note taking.
   A. Classroom whiteboards enable effective note taking. As instructors write notes on the board, students get an opportunity to process the content. Furthermore, the act of writing down notes helps students learn the material.[3]
   B. Zoom whiteboards provide more limited opportunities for instructors to create notes while teaching.
II. Note-taking apps are one alternative for Zoom classes.
   A. You can use a split screen with the Zoom window on one side and an app for note taking on the other.
   B. If your instructor records their Zoom classes, you can take notes while watching the recording.

A, B, AND C ARE SUBPOINTS

I. Leonardo da Vinci's art had many impacts.

A. Leonardo's artistic technique was unprecedented.

B. Leonardo's technique influenced future artists.

C. Leonardo's art has generated many controversies.

1, 2, AND 3 ARE SUB-SUBPOINTS

C. Leonardo's art has generated many controversies.

1. Who was the model for the *Mona Lisa*?

2. Who is to the right of Jesus in *The Last Supper*?

3. Is the *Vitruvian Man* a geometrical algorithm?

Notice that both subpoints for main point I relate to the subject of the main point—how Zoom classes make it difficult to take notes most effectively. These subpoints are *subordinate* to main point I. Next, consider main point II. Subpoint IIA supports the main point by discussing how note-taking apps can be used with Zoom. But subpoint IIB is not subordinate. Rather than providing additional information about note-taking apps, this subpoint focuses on watching a recording of a Zoom class and taking notes then. We will discuss options for your speech when a subpoint doesn't fit in the next section.

## When a Subpoint Doesn't Fit

In developing a speech, you may discover that some of the supporting materials you researched do not relate to any of the main points you selected. Nevertheless, you believe that these materials would improve your speech. What should you do?

One option is to reword one or more main points to encompass the additional information. In the first example that follows, the main point is that healthy eating is essential for college students. Note in this example how subpoint B focuses on getting exercise, not on healthy eating. Thus, it does not relate to the main point. In the second example, the speaker has rewritten the main point to make both subpoints subordinate.

**FIRST EXAMPLE**

 I. Healthy eating is essential for college students.
   A. Limiting fried foods, whole milk, and sweetened drinks helps you fuel your body effectively.
   B. Participating in intramural sports and walking to campus help you stay fit.

**SECOND EXAMPLE**

 I. A *healthy lifestyle* is essential for college students.
   A. Limiting fried foods, whole milk, and sweetened drinks helps you fuel your body effectively.
   B. Participating in intramural sports and walking to campus help you stay fit.

A second option is to create an additional main point to include the supporting material in question. If you use this option, be sure you have enough supporting materials to develop the new main point. Also, be sure the new main point relates to the specific purpose of your speech.

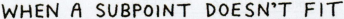

# WHEN A SUBPOINT DOESN'T FIT

## ARRANGING YOUR MAIN POINTS

After you have decided on your main points and supporting materials, you'll need to decide the best organizational format. To do so, first familiarize yourself with the common patterns of organization, and then select the pattern that best suits your speech. In this section, we take a closer look at these patterns: *spatial, chronological (temporal), causal, comparison,* and *categorical (topical)*.

### Spatial Pattern

In a **spatial pattern**, the main points represent important aspects of your topic that can be thought of as adjacent to one another in location or geography. This approach is effective with speech topics that can be broken down into specific parts that relate to each other spatially. When using this approach, you take the audience from one part to the next—much as a museum guide ushers a group from exhibit to exhibit or as an anatomy professor chooses to lecture about the parts of the human skeleton from head to toe.

For example, a geologist might use a spatial pattern to discuss seismic zones in the continental United States:

I. The Ramapo Fault goes through New York, New Jersey, and Pennsylvania.
II. The New Madrid earthquake region includes eight states in the central United States.
III. The Wasatch Fault runs just west of the Rockies.
IV. The West Coast has both the Cascadia subduction zone and the San Andreas Fault.

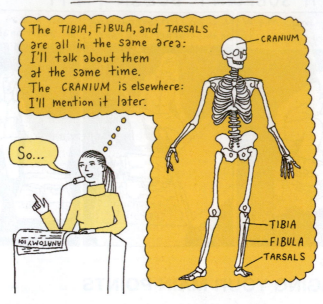

## Chronological (Temporal) Pattern

In a **chronological (temporal) pattern**, you present the information in a time-based sequence, from beginning to end. Each main point covers a particular point in the chronology. If you are discussing a subject that follows a sequence, such as a historical event or a process, this pattern can help your audience keep track of what you are saying. For instance, a speech discussing the decline and rebound of bald eagles in the lower forty-eight states could use a chronological pattern:

I. By 1963, the bald eagle had nearly disappeared from the lower forty-eight states.
II. In 1972, the harmful pesticide DDT was banned in the United States.

▼ **Chronological Pattern.** A speech about protest movements could have one main point discussing protests in the early 1900s and a second about contemporary protests. (left) PhotoQuest/Getty Images; (right) Richard Levine/Getty Images

   III. During the next twenty years, governments and individual citizens took steps to protect bald eagles.

   IV. In 2007, bald eagles were taken off the list of endangered species.

   V. In 2019, there were over 300,000 bald eagles in the lower forty-eight states.[4]

## Causal Pattern

If your speech is explaining a cause-and-effect relationship, a **causal pattern** will help your audience understand the link between particular events and their outcomes. There are two ways to organize main points when you use this pattern. First, if several major causes exist for the situation or phenomenon you are discussing, each main point can cover one of the causes. For example, in a speech about causes of fashion trends, a speaker could use the following main points:

   I. Major news events influence fashion choices.

   II. Styles displayed in popular culture become fashionable.

   III. Economic conditions affect clothing trends.

   IV. Technological innovation creates new fashion options.[5]

Second, if there is a chain of events between cause and effect, each main point can become one link in the chain from cause to effect. For example, when consumers shop online, they can spend more time looking at products because they can shop when it fits their schedule in an environment that is comfortable to them. To explain why businesses have changed to adapt to this trend, you could use the following chain of causation:

   I. The pandemic caused consumers to significantly increase online shopping.

   II. Businesses responded by increasing their digital presence.

   III. In this digital environment, businesses needed to redesign the shopping experience to better account for how people shop at home.[6]

THIS IS A CAUSAL PATTERN

THE REASONS WHY FLARES ARE A FASHION TREND

## Comparison Pattern

A **comparison pattern** organizes the speech around major similarities and differences between two events, objects, or situations. Each main point discusses an important similarity or difference. This pattern can help your audience learn

THIS IS A COMPARISON PATTERN

FIXED ORBITS

SUN
MERCURY
VENUS
EARTH
MARS
JUPITER
SATURN
URANUS
NEPTUNE

OUR LOCAL PLANETS:

I. Our sun (a star) has planets orbiting it.

II. Our planets orbit ONE star (the Sun).

III. Our planets have stayed in fixed orbits.

IV. Our planets are smaller than many recently discovered planets.

EXOPLANETS:

I. Other stars (suns) have planets orbiting them.

II. Many exoplanets orbit TWO suns (stars).

III. Exoplanets have changed their orbits.

IV. Exoplanets tend to be bigger than our local planets.

CHANGEABLE ORBITS

X-STAR 1
X-PLANET B
X-PLANET E
X-PLANET G
X-STAR 2
X-PLANET A
X-PLANET C
X-PLANET D
X-PLANET F

about a new subject by comparing or contrasting it to a subject with which they are familiar. To illustrate, an informative speech about two exoplanets (planets outside our solar system) recently discovered by NASA's Transiting Exoplanet Survey Satellite might compare these planets with Earth:

I. The exoplanets' size is similar to that of Earth.
II. The exoplanets' orbit takes much less time than does Earth's.
III. The exoplanets are far too hot to support life, unlike Earth.[7]

## Categorical (Topical) Pattern

Another option for organization is a **categorical (topical) pattern**. This pattern is effective when you have a diverse set of main points to support the thesis of your speech. Each main point emphasizes an important aspect of your topic that you want the audience to understand.

For example, Jodie was presenting an after-dinner speech (a humorous speech that also makes a serious point) poking fun at the practice of holiday gift giving. She used a categorical pattern as follows:

I. Gift wrap and gift bags generate four million tons of waste.
II. Holiday shopping is a major source of anxiety.
III. Half of all Americans admit to regifting.
IV. Charitable donations are a worthwhile alternative to gift buying.

### Persuasive Speech Patterns

When your rhetorical purpose is persuasion, there are a number of organizational patterns that can help you convince your audience. We elaborate on these formats in Chapter 17, Persuasive Speaking.

# USING ORGANIZING WORDS, PHRASES, AND SENTENCES

As the person who has developed your speech, you will know what your main points are, when you are moving from one point to the next, and what part of the speech you are delivering at any point in time. However, without assistance from you, your audience members will have difficulty keeping track of your organization. To see how challenging this task can be, watch a speech with two or three classmates, and have each person try to outline the speaker's main points. Unless the speech is very well organized, chances are good that you will each have a different perception of what the main points were.

To make the structure of your speech easy for audience members to follow, you need to insert organizing words, phrases, and sentences throughout your presentation. These words, phrases, and sentences offer the audience clear signals that will help them identify your main points and navigate your supporting information. The primary types of organizing language include *transitions*, *signposts*, *internal previews*, and *internal summaries*.

## Transitions

A **transition** is a sentence that indicates you are moving from one part of your speech to the next. The words in a transition should indicate that one thought is finished and a new idea is coming. The following are examples of transitions from an informative speech on Joan of Arc:

- Now that *we have seen* how Joan of Arc prevailed at Orléans, *let's take a look* at her efforts to free Paris.
- *You have learned* about Joan of Arc's military strategies; *next* we will consider the effects of her spiritual beliefs.

Note how these transitions both signal the end of the previous point and introduce the start of a new point. Students often have trouble creating transitions that achieve both of these tasks, as shown by the following failed attempts:

- What happened when Joan of Arc attempted to free Paris?
- Joan of Arc's military strategies were influenced by her spiritual beliefs.

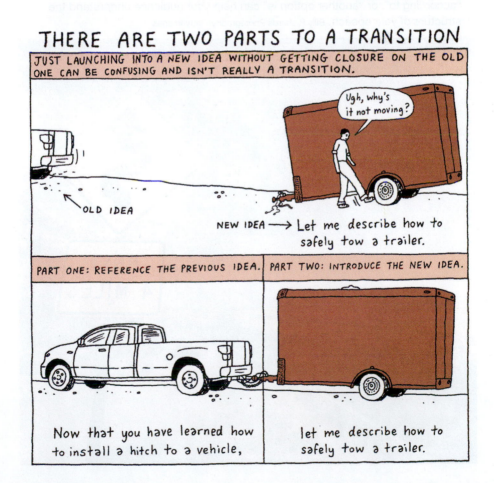

THERE ARE TWO PARTS TO A TRANSITION

JUST LAUNCHING INTO A NEW IDEA WITHOUT GETTING CLOSURE ON THE OLD ONE CAN BE CONFUSING AND ISN'T REALLY A TRANSITION.

Ugh, why's it not moving?

OLD IDEA

NEW IDEA → Let me describe how to safely tow a trailer.

PART ONE: REFERENCE THE PREVIOUS IDEA. | PART TWO: INTRODUCE THE NEW IDEA.

Now that you have learned how to install a hitch to a vehicle, | let me describe how to safely tow a trailer.

Neither of these sentences would make a good transition. The first one asks a question pertaining to the main point to follow (the campaign to retake Paris), but it does not help the audience see that the speaker has finished discussing Joan's efforts at Orléans. The second sentence includes two different ideas, but it does not use any words to signal that one idea is finished and a new main point is about to begin.

## Signposts

A **signpost** is a word or phrase within a sentence that helps your audience understand your speech's structure. Signposts in a speech serve the same function as their counterparts on a road. Highway signs tell drivers what

▼ **Signposts Help Audiences Understand the Message.** Just as road signs help drivers understand the characteristics of roadways, terms such as "in summary", "according to", or "another option is" can help your audience understand the structure of your speech. Billy Richards Photography/Getty Images

direction they're traveling in and how the roads are organized. In a similar vein, speech signposts inform audiences about the direction and organization of a presentation.

You can use signposts to show that you are at a specific place in your speech (for example, "to preview my main ideas," "my third point is," or "in summary"). You can also use signposts to indicate that you are about to cite research ("according to") or to indicate that a key point is coming ("if you remember one idea from this speech, I hope it's that . . ."). In addition, signposts help your audience understand the structure of your subpoints. For example, in a speech about how the pandemic affected elementary and high school student learning, you might have a main point on the causes of decreased student achievement. You could then write your subpoints with signposts, as follows:

- *One cause* of decreased achievement is the loss of students' instructional time with their teachers.
- *Another cause* is the challenges faced by students, teachers, and parents as schools shifted to a virtual learning environment.
- *An additional cause* is that students lost access to school support services such as counseling and tutoring.

## Internal Previews and Internal Summaries

In crafting your speech, you may have selected a main point or subpoint that needs several different points of support or requires considerable detail to develop. To help the audience follow your explanation of a complex point, you may want to use an **internal preview**—a short list of the ideas that will follow. Or to help the audience remember a particularly detailed point, you might use an **internal summary**—a quick review of what you just said in your point.

INTERNAL PREVIEW

Coming up in the next half hour...

INTERNAL SUMMARY

Here, again, are the headlines...

## SPEECH CHOICES

### A CASE STUDY: *RAFAELA*

*Now that Rafaela has chosen her supporting materials,
let's see how she organizes them into main points.*

Rafaela had worked hard to compile supporting materials for
her speech, and the next item on her schedule was planning her
main points. She wrote a brief description of each of her supporting
materials on an index card and sorted them into categories. Rafaela was
amazed to discover that she had seven different categories of supporting materials she could include in her speech! There would only be time to present three
of these ideas, so she selected her favorites: the history of women running for
higher office, the successes of women in recent elections, and her plan of action
to encourage even more women to run. To organize her main points, Rafaela
thought she could use a chronological pattern—past, present, and future.

During a workshop day in her speech class, students shared their ideas for main
points and provided feedback to one another. Rafaela's classmates thought her third main
point was a great idea, but they noted that her first two main points were not *subordinate*
to her thesis: they didn't provide reasons why more women should run for office.

So Rafaela reconsidered her main points. She did some research on what main
point patterns would be best for a persuasive speech (these are in Chapter 17 of
this book) and revised her plan. Main point I would discuss the problem—despite
recent electoral successes, women are still less likely to run for office than men.
Main point II would discuss the causes of the problem—reasons why women are
less likely to run. Finally, in main point III, she would present her solution to the
problem—women in the class should carefully consider running for office, and
everyone else should encourage and support women who are open to running.

 **YOUR TURN**

> Now that you've seen how Rafaela's choices impacted the organization of
> her speech, it's time to think about how you'll organize a speech of your own.
> Making speech choices involves asking and answering a series of questions
> related to your assignment. For speech organization, these questions might
> include:
>
> - What main points am I planning to develop in my speech? Do I have two to
>   five of these main points, or will I need to pare back—or add more?
>
> - What organizational pattern will best present my main ideas?
>
> - Do I have subordinate supporting materials to develop each main point?
>
> - What organizing words and sentences can I use to make the structure of
>   my speech clear to the audience? Consider transitions, signposts, and
>   internal previews and summaries.
>
> Making thoughtful choices in response to questions like these will help
> you organize the body of your speech so it clearly communicates your
> message—and confirms your credibility.

For example, in an informative speech on test-taking strategies, suppose that one of your main points covers test preparation. You might state your main point followed by an *internal preview*, as shown here:

> Test taking requires good planning and healthy living. *The four steps for test preparation that I will cover are as follows: plan your study time in advance, follow your study schedule, get a good night's sleep, and eat a healthy breakfast.*

In a speech on reducing student loan debt, you might follow a main point on potential solutions to this problem with an *internal summary*:

> *To review my proposed solutions: First, all student loan payments should be deferred until the economy is on a sounder footing. Second, all persons with student loan balances should have up to $50,000 of their loan debt cancelled. Finally, the interest rate on all federal student loans should be reduced to zero.*

# CHAPTER REVIEW

> ❝ Good organization makes the message clear. ❞

In this chapter, we focused on the importance of a well-organized speech and presented strategies for organizing the body of your speech. Good organization helps your audience understand your message and enhances your credibility as a speaker. Remember the following principles when you organize the body of your speech: With your purpose and audience in mind, select an appropriate number of main points. Organize your supporting materials to back up each main point. Arrange your main points in a pattern that will best convey your ideas to the audience. Finally, use organizing words, phrases, and sentences to help the audience keep track of where you are in a speech.

## 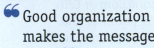 Key Terms

body *212*
main point *213*
supporting point *213*
subordination *216*
subpoint *216*
sub-subpoint *216*

coordination *216*
spatial pattern *219*
chronological (temporal)
    pattern *220*
causal pattern *221*
comparison pattern *222*

categorical (topical)
    pattern *223*
transition *225*
signpost *226*
internal preview *227*
internal summary *227*

## Review Questions

1. What three main factors should speakers consider when selecting their main points?
2. Explain the importance of subordination and coordination when organizing supporting materials.
3. Name and describe five organizational patterns that you can use to arrange the main points of your speech.
4. Describe transitions, signposts, and internal previews and summaries, and explain how these types of organizing language help speakers indicate the structure of their speech to the audience.

## Critical Thinking Questions

1. In what ways does organizing a speech resemble organizing a piece of written work? How does it differ? Are there any organizational tools that a writer can use that a speaker cannot? Does a speaker have any options that a writer does not?
2. Which kinds of organizational patterns do you think are most common in public speaking? Is there one kind of pattern that you think can work for almost any speech?
3. Select a speech from a website such as AmericanRhetoric.com or Gifts of Speech (gos.sbc.edu). How could you revise the main points or add organizing language to make the speech's structure more apparent to the audience?
4. In the illustration on page 224, the speaker dons a large hat whenever he makes a main point. Although this is clearly an exaggeration, might a speaker use nonverbal cues or presentation aids to help the audience navigate a speech? Would such tools work if the speech itself did not make proper use of organizing language?

## Activities

1. Consider Victoria's speech about social media, described at the beginning of the chapter. If you were to reorganize her speech, how would you do it?
2. Divide into groups. Each group should select three organizational patterns, and choose a topic area. For each pattern you have chosen, come up with a topic, a specific purpose title, and three to five main points on your topic that fit that pattern.
3. Page 217 includes illustrations of the Mona Lisa and provides examples of subpoints and sub-subpoints. Select a different famous painting and briefly research its history. Then create your own example of a main

point with subpoints and sub-subpoints for a speech about the painting you selected.

4. Review the comparison pattern illustration on page 222. Then think of three points of comparison between being a student in college and being a student in high school. Illustrate each point of comparison (stick figures are fine).

5. Consider the newscaster illustration on page 227. With that image in mind, watch a broadcast of a nightly newscast, and jot down the different types of transitions, internal previews, and internal summaries that are used by the news anchor. What purpose do they serve? Would you use the same tools in a speech? Why or why not?

# INTRODUCTIONS AND CONCLUSIONS

# 10

> 66 Strong introductions create audience interest; strong conclusions create lasting impressions. 99

You've finally had time to break away from your schoolwork to see your favorite actor playing the title role in the latest James Bond movie. You're sitting in the theater, munching popcorn as the curtains open, the lights dim, and the film's opening sequence starts to roll. Every element of that sequence—the music, the visuals, the credits for the movie's title and cast—conveys information about the film and heightens your desire to see more.

For the next two hours, you're transported into an exciting world. And at the end of the movie, you're left with the lasting sense that you've had a great time. The final close-ups of Bond's face, the swelling of the classic James Bond theme, and the sweeping views of gorgeous scenery as the camera pans back: all these elements combine to conclude your experience on a satisfying note.

Just as a movie's opening and closing elements powerfully influence the quality of your theater experience, your speech's introduction and conclusion play crucial roles in your audience's reception of your message. An effective introduction builds audience interest, orients audience members to the speech,

◄ **Introductions Set the Stage for Your Speech.** The beginning of a movie gets the audience's attention and builds their interest. You want to accomplish these goals with the introduction of your speech, too. Klaus Vedfelt/Getty Images

**233**

and establishes your credibility as a speaker, and a strong conclusion leaves audience members with an enduring impression of your speech.

After planning the body of your speech, your next step is to prepare the introduction and conclusion. Although these elements are shorter than the body, they're just as crucial. After all, you won't get your message across unless your audience is eager to listen. You also want audience members to remember your presentation long after it ends—so they can put the information you've imparted to them into action. In this chapter, we show you how to craft memorable beginnings and endings to your presentations.

# INTRODUCING YOUR SPEECH

In public speaking, as in many other situations in life, first impressions are vital. Your introduction creates a first impression of you as a speaker *and* of your message. For as long as people have discussed speechmaking, scholars have recognized the importance of the introduction: Cicero included the introduction as one of six essential parts of a speech, and contemporary scholars note that the introduction is a key opportunity for the speaker to build a bond with the audience.[1]

A good introduction thus accomplishes a number of important purposes:

- Gains your audience's attention
- Signals your thesis
- Shows your audience what's in it for them
- Establishes your credibility
- Previews your main points

Your introduction must accomplish all of this in a brief period of time. For example, in a five- to ten-minute speech, the introduction should take no more than one minute. With these kinds of time constraints, there's no doubt about it: your introduction needs to be efficient *and* effective. Let's look more closely at each of the objectives your introduction must achieve.

## Gain Your Audience's Attention

Begin your speech with an **attention-getter**—material intended to capture the audience's interest at the start of a speech. People listening to a presentation may have other things on their minds (for example, a problem at home, a distracting sound coming from the next room, or worries about an upcoming test or paper). You need to help your listeners redirect their focus from these other matters to you and your message. Otherwise, they won't absorb or remember the information you convey in your speech.

How do you craft an effective attention-getter? These guidelines can help.

**Tell a Story or an Anecdote.** Most people love a good story, so opening with one can be a compelling yet comfortable way to begin your speech. If you start your speech with a story, be sure it relates to your message, takes up an appropriate amount of time, and comes across as believable. Avoid opening your speech with a made-up story unless you disclose that you are offering a hypothetical example.

Here is how one student began a speech calling for policies to assist unhoused persons burdened by debts:

> Lori lost her business and her home in 2014. While she was unhoused, she accumulated over $50,000 in hospital bills and other debts and then she was incarcerated for six months when she could not pay a fine for the "crime" of bathing in a river.[2] Lori's story provides an example of the challenges unhoused persons experience due to debts incurred while coping with the loss of their homes.

▼ **Telling Your Story.** Tatenda Ngwaru, founder of True Identity, an organization that builds public awareness of Intersex issues, shares her story in a live-streamed show. Michael Loccisano/Getty Images

**Offer a Striking or Provocative Statement.** A compelling fact or idea pertaining to your topic can immediately pull the audience into your speech. For example, you might present a surprising statistic or make an ironic statement to defy your listeners' expectations about what they'll hear during your speech. This approach works only if you present a fact or an idea that's new, ironic, or counterintuitive to your audience. You are also likely to be more effective if you incorporate dynamic language into your striking or provocative statement.

Consider the example of Aparna Mehta, a global solutions director for UPS. She, like many online shoppers, often ordered clothes in multiple sizes and colors, tried them on, and then returned those that she didn't want. One day, an experience with a client caused her to reconsider this practice and look for a better way to manage returns. Here is how she used striking facts and statistics in the introduction to her speech, "Where Do Your Online Returns Go?"

> Just this past holiday season alone, [this client] had 7.5 million pieces of clothing returned to them. I could not stop thinking about it. What happens to all these returned clothes? So I came home and researched. And I learned that every year, four billion pounds of returned clothing ends up in the landfill. That's like every resident in the US did a load of laundry last night and decided to throw it in the trash today.[3]

**Build Suspense.** Consider increasing audience curiosity and anticipation before you reveal your topic. For example, "What will be the next virus to threaten the world?" or "One of the best movies to be released last year is a film that few people have seen." Here's how one student built curiosity in the introduction of their speech:

> Researchers have identified a strategy that can help you reduce stress in college. It is not improving your study skills, getting more sleep, or exercising regularly, although these practices can help. It involves something fun, and some students can even earn money while pursuing this strategy. What is it? Spending time on one of your favorite hobbies.

This student then proceeded to document the benefits of spending time on hobbies while in college and offered tips for incorporating hobbies into students' schedules.

**Let Listeners Know You're One of Them.** Consider highlighting similarities or shared interests between you and your audience. When listeners believe that a speaker is like them, they tend to see that speaker as more credible—something that encourages them to pay close attention to the speech. However, to make this type of attention-getter effective, be sure to assert *genuine* common ground. Otherwise, you won't win your audience's confidence.

Here's how one student highlighted common ground in a speech about the resources available on the U.S. Department of Agriculture's MyPlate website:

> When I surveyed our class, I discovered that over 70 percent of you agreed with this statement: "I try to eat a healthy diet." Like many of you, I have tried several different food programs, and I do my best to eat my fruits and vegetables. I would like to share one of the best resources that I have

found—the U.S. Department of Agriculture's MyPlate website. This site includes tips for healthy eating, healthy recipes, and a QR code you can scan to find good deals on nutritious foods in your area.

**Use Humor.** Most people enjoy jokes, amusing stories, or other humorous references. Opening your speech with a funny or playful attention-getter can be a great way to gain audience interest, break the ice, and enhance your credibility. However, not all humor is created equal. If you begin a speech with humor, the material should relate to your topic. Also, consider your audience members, and choose material they will find funny. Don't tell jokes or stories that may offend some or all of your listeners.

Also note that using humor as your attention-getter can be a high-risk, high-reward approach. If the audience appreciates a joke, your credibility is liable to increase, you'll feel especially confident, and your speech will be off to a great start. For example, here is how an informative speaker began her speech about scientific skepticism regarding extrasensory perception (ESP):

> If you have ESP, raise your hand and tell the audience what this speech will be about.

If you have trouble telling jokes or remembering punch lines, you may find that a relevant anecdote from your own life is a better source of humor. At one time or another, most people have told a funny story about something that

has happened to them. This more personal approach may help you feel more relaxed and conversational.

**Ask a Rhetorical Question.** A **rhetorical question**—one that you want listeners to answer in their heads—can capture audience members' attention because it gets them thinking about your speech topic. For example, to introduce a speech about the Winter Olympics, you could ask, "What's the first sport that comes to mind when you think about the Winter Olympics?" Make sure your rhetorical question addresses something of interest to your audience. And avoid asking overly general questions ("What would you like to learn about winter sports?"). Your listeners won't find them as interesting as more focused queries.

Here is how a speaker could use a rhetorical question to gain audience attention in a speech about digilantism, or vigilante behaviors on the Internet:

> Imagine that a photo of the back of your car (showing the license plate number, your bumper stickers, and a rather large dent) driving past a visible street sign appeared on a social media forum in your community. Below it was this caption—"40 mph in a school zone." You are confident that you have never gone over the speed limit on that street. How would you feel?

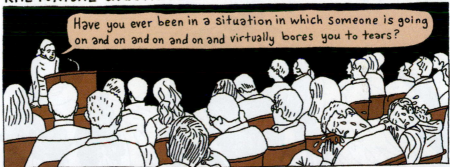

**Provide a Quotation.** A stimulating quotation that illuminates your topic can make an effective attention-getter—especially if you're quoting someone your audience likes and respects or if the quotation is thought provoking or counterintuitive. For example, in a speech about the credibility of *Wikipedia*, you might quote a related joke from Stephen Colbert about the site: "It's the first place I go when I'm looking for knowledge, or when I want to create some."[4]

You can also quote an expert in the field as an attention-getter. Consider this attention getter for a speech advocating that college students take more breaks from sitting:

> In the *Journal of American College Health*, Burton Cowgill and Vanessa Perez from the UCLA Healthy Campus Initiative Center and their colleagues noted the following: "According to a study conducted at a large Midwestern university, students spend close to 30 hours a week engaging in sedentary activities, nearly a third of which involves studying. [In addition, a] study of college professors revealed even though most faculty members understood the importance of reducing prolonged sitting, less than half of them were actually utilizing practices to address the issue."[5]

As Black Panther's father said: "You're a good man with a good heart. It's hard for a good man to be king."

## Signal Your Thesis

Recall from Chapter 6 that your thesis statement is the single sentence that expresses the aspect of the topic you will be emphasizing in your speech—that is, your speech's "bottom line." Providing this statement early in the speech answers a question that is in the minds of many audience members—"What will this speech be about?" It also allows listeners to focus on your message rather than having to use their mental energy to try to identify your speech topic.

Your thesis statement should clearly convey your topic and purpose in delivering the presentation, further preparing your audience members to listen. It should also be specific and include a signpost that makes it clear that your attention-getter is finished and you are now revealing your topic.

Consider the following example:

### ATTENTION-GETTER

I.   The tallest mountain in North America. Grizzly bears eating berries just ten feet from the road. Clean, fresh air that you will not find in "the lower forty-eight."

---

▼ **Make Your Thesis Clear in the Introduction.** Whether your thesis is that audience members should visit Denali National Park (shown here) or something entirely different, be sure to present it in your introduction. Johnny Johnson/Getty Images

### TWO POSSIBLE THESIS STATEMENTS

    II.  *Vague thesis statement:* All these features can be found in a pristine wilderness environment.

    III.  *Specific thesis statement:* You can find all these features in Denali National Park and Preserve, Alaska, and I hope to convince you to visit there.

Notice that the specific thesis statement clarifies that the subject of the speech is Denali National Park and Preserve and that the presenter's purpose is to persuade his audience to go there.

## Show Your Audience What's in It for Them

After you have revealed your thesis, you need to generate audience interest and motivate active listening. Our former colleague Dr. Gail Sorenson referred to this as "What's in it for me?" or WIIFM ("whiff-em"). Through WIIFM, you clarify why your message is relevant to and important for your listeners.

    To accomplish this goal, provide one sentence or a short paragraph that indicates why the audience should take an interest in your topic. Instead of going on and on, give listeners just enough to whet their appetite. You'll go into more detail in the body of your speech, where you'll show how the ideas or suggestions in your presentation will benefit listeners.

Following are some examples of effective WIIFM statements:

- The dangerous practice of drunkorexia—or eating little food during the day to offset calories consumed by drinking in the evening—is not just a problem on somebody else's campus. The director of our health center reports that this is a growing concern at our college.

- We need to take technology addiction seriously, as it is a common problem for college students. Today, we'll consider studies that show how brain scans of people who have Internet addiction disorder resemble those of persons addicted to substances.

- Today we will consider the history of the 1846 war between the United States and Mexico from a Mexican perspective. This will provide an alternative to the romanticized version many of us were taught in our high school history classes.

- The creator economy is not just a term you might find in an economics class. It is a $100 billion market and in the next few minutes, we'll discuss how you can be part of the action.

## Establish Your Credibility

Your audience members now know what they'll get out of listening to your speech. Next, you need to answer the question in many of their minds, "Why should we listen to *you*? What makes you a credible source on this topic?"

How do you build credibility? You do it the same way that your sources of evidence do—by showing that you have relevant experience and education and that you've thoroughly researched the subject area of your speech. You gain even more credibility when your listeners see you as trustworthy and perceive that you have their best interests at heart.

To establish credibility, explain how you have gained knowledge about your topic. In one or two sentences, emphasize your most relevant credentials (resist the urge to recite your entire résumé or life history!), making sure to adopt a modest tone.

A student speaker named Alexandra established her credibility in an informative speech about judging competitive ice skating by emphasizing her own relevant experience. Alexandra was especially qualified to speak on the subject because she had won nearly one hundred awards during her skating career and had also served as a judge at several prestigious skating events in her home state. She could have chosen to discuss her many accomplishments in the sport, but she chose to establish her credibility in this clear, concise, and unpretentious way:

I have been active in the sport of ice skating since I was six years old and have won my fair share of events. I still love skating, so after retiring from competition, I became certified as a judge and have judged at many competitions during the past two years.

With this information, Alexandra left no doubt in her listeners' minds that she was a good source of information on ice skating. She also held their interest by summarizing her experience without providing excessive detail about specific awards or competitions, which would have meant little to them.

## Preview Your Main Points

A **preview** is a brief statement of the main points you will be developing in the body of your speech. It lets your audience members know what main ideas to expect and helps them visualize the structure of your speech—the sequence of ideas you'll present. Your preview should consist of no more than one sentence per main point.

To differentiate the main points in your preview, include *signposts* (for example, *first*, *next*, and *finally*) to help your audience grasp the structure of your speech. Also, avoid the use of *and* or other connecting words while previewing a single main point.

Consider the following two previews, which Alexandra might use in her speech about judging competitive ice skating.

### WEAKER PREVIEW

The rules of judging and the ways you can judge, along with the many controversies about Olympic judges, are all interesting aspects of judging competitive skating.

### STRONGER PREVIEW

Today we'll look at *three major topics* about judging competitive ice skating: *first*, we'll look at the rules for judging a skating event; *next* I'll share

some tips you can use to score the performances yourself; and *finally*, I'll discuss some of the judging controversies that have occurred at past Olympics.

Both of these previews offer information about the main points to be developed. However, the first preview is much less explicit than the second. It mentions the three points Alexandra plans to cover but runs them together in a single clause. This won't help the audience understand the structure of the speech. It also contains no hints indicating that Alexandra is previewing her main points; it could just as easily be an attempt to connect with the audience. By contrast, the strong second preview clearly signals the speech structure, which will make it easy for Alexandra's audience to recognize the main points and the sequence in which she will cover them.

## CONCLUDING YOUR SPEECH

Your introduction helps you set the stage for your speech, and your conclusion serves another equally important purpose: it helps you sum up the message you developed in the body of your speech and leave a memorable impression with your audience. Don't use the conclusion to develop new ideas about your topic or further expand on points you've just made. Instead, use it to highlight content you have already presented. A good conclusion generally takes one minute or less (few sins of a speaker are worse than saying "in conclusion" and then continuing to speak for several more minutes). Your conclusion should start with a *transition*, *summarize your main points*, and *finish with a memorable clincher*. We examine each of these elements in this section.

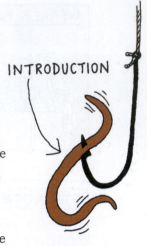

INTRODUCTION

## Transition to Your Conclusion

After presenting your final main point, insert some transitional language that signals you're ready to wrap up your presentation. For example, a persuasive speech encouraging students to take advantage of opportunities to help at the campus vegetable garden might offer this transition to the conclusion:

CONCLUSION

> Today *we have seen* how you can volunteer at our new campus vegetable garden.

In this example, the use of the phrase *we have seen* signals that you're finished with the main part of your speech and ready to move on to the next part. Here's another example of a transition into the conclusion:

> I hope *you have learned more* about the first cultures to inhabit the Americas.

## Summarize Your Main Points

The first part of your conclusion is a **summary**, a brief review of your main points. The summary is similar to the preview of your main points that you offered in your introduction, except that here you are reminding the audience of what you already said instead of telling them what ideas you'll be presenting. You may summarize in a single compound sentence that covers each main point, or you may restate each main point in a complete sentence. In either case, your goal is to efficiently remind the audience of your main ideas one last time. An effective summary helps listeners remember your message by enabling them to put your speech together in their own minds.

Be sure that your summary includes each main point from your speech. That way, you'll break the speech down into manageable sections for your audience members and remind them of the presentation's structure.

# DON'T REGURGITATE YOUR WHOLE SPEECH... SUMMARIZE IT WITH QUICK BULLET POINTS

Here is how Alexandra might summarize her main points during the conclusion of her speech about judging competitive ice skating:

> This afternoon *we have covered* three major topics about judging competitive ice skating. First, we considered the rules for judging ice skating. Then, we considered some tips for you to use if you want to score at home. Finally, we considered controversies in the judging at past Olympics.

Note how Alexandra made a clear reference to each main point and used the past tense to help the audience recognize that she was reviewing her points rather than developing new material.

## Finish with a Memorable Clincher

Finish your conclusion with a **clincher**—something that leaves a lasting impression of your speech in your listeners' minds. After your speech ends, audience members will have countless demands on their time and attention. To make your presentation memorable, select and word your clincher carefully.

The clincher should take only about thirty seconds in a five- to ten-minute speech. Rock musicians have been known to smash their guitars at the end of a show to leave a lasting impression. We would not recommend such mayhem in a speech, but there are a number of less destructive strategies you can use to make your speech memorable. Following are several ways to craft a good clincher.

**Tie Your Clincher to the Introduction.** If you began your speech with a compelling anecdote or example, consider extending it in your clincher. One speech encouraging classmates to volunteer their services for a campus tutoring program began with the story of Albert, a middle school student who was struggling to cope with the shift to online instruction. The presenter effectively touched again on this narrative in their clincher:

> This speech began with the story of Albert, who was struggling with online instruction. Raj, a student at this university, became his tutor. The university trained her in online tutoring and she helped him master pre-Algebra and provided encouragement and support. Albert graduated from middle school and now he is taking college prep classes in high school. There are many more Alberts in our local schools, and your help as a tutor will make sure that there is a happy ending to their stories, too.

▼ **Tying a Clincher to the Introduction.** If you begin a speech with a narrative describing a challenging situation (for example, a student struggling in school) and you show how the audience can make a difference (say, by providing tutoring, as shown in this photo), consider including a clincher that shows how their help can lead to a happy ending. EMS-FORSTER-PRODUCTIONS/Getty Images

## End with a Striking Sentence or Phrase.

There may be a single sentence or phrase that effectively sums up your speech. Advertisers and political campaign managers often use this technique because the words are easy to remember. For example, an advertiser refers to a product as "the one," or a campaign manager describes his candidate as possessing "the right stuff for the job." We do not recommend ending your speech with a trivial phrase or a catchy tune. However, do consider using memorable, relevant phrasing to conclude your speech.

A speech about Hmong history effectively concluded with a theme that had been evident in each main point:

> The word *Hmong* means "free." And no matter what continent we are living on, that is what we will always be—a free people.

Also, consider Manal al-Sharif, a Saudi women's rights activist who was jailed in 2011 after posting a YouTube video showing her driving a car. (Women were forbidden to drive in Saudi Arabia until the law changed in June 2018.) She used the following clincher in a speech to the Oslo Freedom Forum:

> The struggle is not about driving a car. It is about being in the driver's seat of our destiny.[6]

## Highlight Your Thesis.

Rather than summing up your speech with a single key sentence, you may decide to use a few lines to reinforce the heart of your message. Consider an example from Sally Ride, the first American woman in space (she was awarded a posthumous Presidential Medal of Freedom in 2013). After ending her career as an astronaut, Dr. Ride became a dedicated advocate for improving math and science education for kids. Here is how she concluded her speech "Shoot for the Stars":

> When I was a little girl, I always dreamed of flying in space. And amazingly enough (I still cannot believe it to this day), that dream came true for me. Now it is up to all of us to ensure that this generation of students in school today has access to a high-quality education so the boys and the girls

# FINISH WITH A MEMORABLE CLINCHER

can build the foundation that will enable them to reach for the stars and achieve their dreams too.[7]

**Conclude with an Emotional Message.** Recall a speech or presentation that ended by appealing to your emotions. If you're like most people, that speech affected you more than a speech that used only cold hard facts. Often, a clincher that delivers an emotional charge makes a speech particularly memorable—especially in a persuasive or commemorative presentation. For example, one student concluded a tribute to a beloved pet in the following way:

> My mind flooded with memories—finding him as a tiny kitten and nursing him to health with my own hands. He became my best friend. I let him go lovingly, with the same arms that held him fast as a baby. Good-bye, my friend. I'll never forget you.

**End with a Story or an Anecdote.** A story that illustrates the message of your speech can make an effective clincher. Consider the following anecdote about Albert Einstein that a student used as her clincher in a speech

## SPEECH CHOICES

### A CASE STUDY: *RAFAELA*

*With her main points organized, it was time for Rafaela to plan her introduction and conclusion.*

Once Rafaela organized the body of her speech with main points and supporting materials, she budgeted some time to draft her introduction and conclusion.

Rafaela began by writing down the first words she planned to say—"Hi, I'm Rafaela, and my topic is women in politics." She would then present current statistics that she had researched on the percentage of women in various state, federal, and local offices.

Rafaela tried her introduction out on her best friend and was a bit surprised when her BFF called it "BOR-RING!" Surprised or not, she decided to review her notes and her textbook. This was a good decision, as she was reminded that a speech should begin with an attention-getter that really captures the audience's interest. The string of statistics Rafaela had presented had caused her friend to lose interest.

So Rafaela reconsidered how to begin her speech. She had written down several different options for gaining audience attention. One stood out to her, "Tell a story or an anecdote." She enjoyed telling stories, and a good example immediately came to mind. Rafaela had recently spoken with her college's student-body president, a woman who had run for that office twice. After she lost the first election, her big brother told her that he was proud of her for running and encouraged her to give it another try. The importance of providing encouragement was a key point that Rafaela would be emphasizing in her speech. This narrative would set up that theme perfectly. Now Rafaela was ready to draft the rest of her introduction, and then move on to her conclusion.

 **YOUR TURN**

Now that you've seen how Rafaela's choices impacted her introduction, it's time to think about how you'll begin and conclude a speech of your own. Making speech choices involves asking and answering a series of questions related to your assignment. Here are some questions to consider as you prepare your introduction and conclusion:

- What type of attention-getter would be the best way to gain my audience's interest?

- How will I establish credibility? Will I focus on my experiences? My education? My research?

- What will I say about my topic to show the audience "what's in it for them"?

- How will I use my thesis statement, preview, and summary to make the main takeaways from my speech stand out?

- What type of clincher will help end my speech in a memorable way?

Making thoughtful choices in response to questions like these will help you craft an introduction that intrigues your audience and a conclusion that makes a lasting impression.

advocating greater efforts to raise students' self-esteem and prevent them from dropping out:

> Over one hundred years ago, there was a boy who was considered "backward" by his teachers. They said the boy was mentally slow and adrift forever in his foolish dreams. His father said that when he asked the headmaster what profession his son should adopt, he was told, "It doesn't matter; he'll never make a success of anything."[8]
>
> Who was that hopeless student? Believe it or not, his name was Albert Einstein.
>
> We must never give up on the mind of a child. Educators must convince all students that they are valued and capable of learning. Even one dropout is unacceptable.

# CHAPTER REVIEW

**❝ Strong introductions create audience interest; strong conclusions create lasting impressions. ❞**

In this chapter, we provided ideas for crafting effective introductions and conclusions for your speeches. We noted that a good introduction has several purposes—including capturing your audience's attention, indicating your thesis, conveying the importance of your topic for audience members, establishing your credibility, and previewing your main points. We also showed that an effective conclusion transitions smoothly from the body of your speech, helps your audience remember your main points, and enables you to leave a lasting impression on listeners. There are many strategies to choose from in developing your introduction and conclusion, so you have room to be creative. By tailoring these elements of your speech to your audience and allotting the right amount of time to each, you stand an excellent chance of delivering an effective presentation.

## Key Terms

attention-getter *234*        preview *244*        clincher *247*
rhetorical question *239*     summary *246*

## Review Questions

1. Briefly explain the five major functions of a good introduction.
2. Describe seven specific strategies you can use to create an attention-getting introduction.
3. What three steps must you take to develop a solid conclusion?
4. Offer five types of memorable clinchers.

## Critical Thinking Questions

1. Why is it important to offer an attention-getting introduction in a speech? In what kinds of public speaking situations do you think it might be preferable to present a less dramatic or entertaining opener?
2. How can you effectively use audience analysis to determine whether humor would be a good attention-getting strategy and whether a particular joke will work or fall flat?
3. What happens if you fail to present a solid conclusion to your speech?

## Activities

1. Working in groups, select a potential speech topic. Then have each group member select a different attention-gaining strategy and use that strategy to develop an attention-getter. Share your attention-getter with other group members.
2. Imagine that you are about to give a speech to a group of total strangers you know little about. How would you use your introduction to establish credibility? How would this differ from the way you would establish credibility for a group you had something in common with—for example, students at your college, members of your religious faith, or people who participate in the same sport or activity that you do?
3. Working in groups, select a potential speech topic that is relevant at your campus. Then discuss how you could show each of the following audiences "what's in it for them": students who work while attending school, student athletes, students who are active in extracurricular activities, and students with children.
4. Review the illustration "Finish with a Memorable Clincher" and the accompanying text on page 250. Imagine that you are presenting a speech on a problem of concern in your community. Indicate what your topic would be, and develop your own memorable clincher, using astronaut Sally Ride's speech as an example.
5. Watch a TED Talk on a subject of interest to you. How does the speaker gain the audience's attention? How does the speaker conclude their speech? Do you think that the speaker's choices were effective? Why or why not?

# OUTLINING YOUR SPEECH

> **A good outline strengthens organization and preparation.**

Carmelita, the mother of two elementary school–aged children, had taken an active role in her kids' education. She served on the School Site Council and volunteered in their classrooms when her work schedule permitted. Before the COVID-19 pandemic hit, her kids had thrived in school, both academically and socially. But when her school district changed to remote learning, that change had a negative impact on her children. They struggled with online courses and Carmelita found it difficult to balance her own work responsibilities and her kids' learning needs. They also missed spending time with their friends.

When the school board held meetings to decide when kids should return to in-person classes and whether the schools should take any COVID precautions once students returned to school, Carmelita attended. She was appalled by the some of the parents' behavior at the meetings. A number of parents delivered angry rants that focused more on insulting other parents and board members who disagreed with them than on giving reasons to support their stance on the issues. The atmosphere at one meeting became so hostile that the board had to adjourn.

◄ **Getting Organized with an Outline.** A speech outline helps ensure that a speech on safely reopening schools will be successful. A good outline will also assist you in presenting the most effective speech possible. Scott Olson/Getty Images

Carmelita wanted to express her viewpoint that in-person schooling was needed for students, but that schools should reopen safely. She didn't want to be another one of those parents who just vented their anger without contributing something constructive to the discussion. So she did her research and decided to focus on three main points at the next school board meeting: the importance of reopening schools, the need to reopen safely, and finally, a call for parents to calm down and be kind to each other at these meetings, even when they disagreed.

Carmelita wrote down those main points and under each, listed the ideas she could use to support that point. She practiced her speech to become familiar with the material and make sure it would fit the allotted time. When she felt confident about her speech, she wrote briefer notes on her tablet which she could reference during her presentation if needed.

Carmelita's speech was a rousing success. Many audience members cheered when she called for parents to be kinder to one another. Other speakers agreed with Carmelita's ideas and the school board committed to finding a way for schools to resume face-to-face instruction safely.

Carmelita's use of **outlining**—organizing the content of her speech into a structured form—played a big role in her success. And just as it did for her, outlining can help you plan and organize a successful speech. Outlines allow you to lay out the sequence of your ideas so that you can see if your speech flows logically and covers the subject matter adequately. They can also be used to practice your delivery, so that you can present your speech with confidence and flair. In most speech situations, an outline can help you polish your skills. Even seasoned presenters find outlining highly useful!

The key function of *all* outlines is to show the hierarchy of the ideas in your speech—your main points and the material that supports each main point. By using indentation and alphanumeric headings—beginning with Roman numerals for main points (I, II, III, etc.) and moving through capital letters (A, B, C, etc.), Arabic numerals (1, 2, 3, etc.), and so on—you can present all your points and show how each is supported by evidence. This system makes outlines different from manuscripts and essays, which are organized paragraph by paragraph. In this chapter, we discuss the creation of two types of outlines—detailed outlines and speaking outlines.

## TWO STAGES OF OUTLINING

Imagine that you're about to set off on a road trip to a place you've never been before. Unless you prefer to use a GPS or an app like Waze to call out directions as you go, there are two steps you would probably take before you begin. First, you'd likely consult a website like Google Maps to pinpoint where you need to go, how you might get there, and how long it would take. You'd study the route, commit the general picture to memory, and figure out any tricky portions. Second, you might print out a brief set of directions that summarize the information from the map ("Take this highway to that exit, turn right at this street") for quick reference as you go.

In much the same way as you'd take these two steps to ensure a safe journey, many speech instructors suggest taking two steps when outlining your speech. In fact, many instructors require two versions of your outline for each presentation. The first is a *detailed outline*, which functions as a road map to help you prepare your speech. The second is a *speaking outline*, which, like a brief set of directions, provides you with quick and easy-to-follow notes you can refer to without "taking your eyes off the road"—or, in this case, your audience.

## THIS IS AN OUTLINE

I. How an outline helps speakers organize their thinking

    A. Shows relationships between ideas

        1. SHOWS IDEAS IN THE ORDER OF PRESENTATION

        2. SHOWS WHICH IDEAS ARE MOST IMPORTANT

II. How outlines can improve presentations

## THIS IS A MANUSCRIPT, NOT AN OUTLINE

Today I will discuss the major ways that outlines are especially important tools for public speakers. First, outlines show relationships between ideas by showing ideas in their presentation order and showing which ideas are the most important.

▲ **Reference Materials.** To ensure a well-organized speech, outline your speech in advance and have it available for reference if needed during your speech. This speaker has her notes on a smartphone; other speakers may prefer note cards or a tablet. Alex Wong/Getty Images

In this section, we take a look at these two types of outlines, each of which represents an important step in the development of your presentation. It's essential, however, for you to make sure you know the requirements for outlining in your speech course. Individual instructors have different philosophies about creating outlines, so be sure to follow your instructor's requirements.

## The Detailed Outline

A **detailed outline** (also referred to as a *working, full-sentence,* or *preparation outline*) is a complete outline that you use to craft your speech. A detailed outline includes all the elements of your speech—from attention-getter to clincher—with each idea written down in full sentences or detailed phrases (depending on your instructor's preference). And because it is an *outline*, it is structured in outline form, rather than written as an essay or a manuscript (see the illustration on p. 257). If you were to wake up with laryngitis on the day of your presentation, another classmate should be able to use your detailed outline to deliver your speech.

A detailed outline offers many benefits, both for you and for your instructor. Because it is detailed and formatted in a way that shows the hierarchy of ideas, it helps you assess the content and organization of your speech, ensure that your thesis and main points are well supported, and create smooth transitions between (and connections among) all the points and evidence you present. Because your instructor might wish to review your detailed outline to evaluate your preparation effort, it should show that you have included all required components, cited research sources properly, developed your ideas in sufficient detail, and organized all your information thoughtfully. Finally, your detailed outline can serve as a reference when you *begin* to practice your speech, helping you become familiar with the content. After you've become more comfortable with the material, you're ready to transition to a speaking outline.

## The Speaking Outline

A **speaking outline** is a short outline that expresses your ideas in brief phrases, key words, or abbreviations rather than in complete sentences or detailed phrases. You will use this outline when you actually deliver your speech. Like the brief set of driving directions we discussed earlier, this brief outline (which may be displayed on a tablet or smartphone or written on note cards, rather than manuscript paper) provides quick notes that you reference, rather than read, as you deliver your speech.

The purpose of a speaking outline is to facilitate **extemporaneous delivery**. As we discuss in both Chapter 2 and Chapter 13, extemporaneous delivery involves speaking with limited notes—not reciting from memory or reading word-for-word from your manuscript. Your limited notes serve as a reminder of what idea comes next, but when you trust yourself to deliver the details more spontaneously, your speech feels fresh and conversational. In other words, if you were to deliver a speech two times using the same speaking outline, both versions of the speech would share the same structure and points, but they would not be identical, word for word.

FULL SENTENCE:

The study showed that even a large spider, on a good day, makes only 1.5mg of silk.

DETAILED PHRASE:

Study — large spider on good day makes 1.5mg silk

BRIEF PHRASE / KEY WORD:

Study: Best = 1.5mg silk

## CREATING YOUR DETAILED OUTLINE

A detailed outline consists of three main sections—the introduction, the body, and the conclusion of your speech. (Most instructors will recommend that you outline the body of your speech first and then go back to outline the introduction and conclusion.) As you create your detailed outline, label each of these three parts ("Introduction," "Body," and "Conclusion") in bold so that you can more easily see the speech's structure. You will also label your reference list and potentially the title, specific purpose, and thesis of your speech.

## Outlining the Body of Your Speech

You can think of the **body** of your speech as the heart of your presentation. As you saw in Chapter 9, in the body, you'll present your main points and supporting materials (such as examples, stories, statistics, and testimony from experts). The body thus contains most of the content of your speech. Follow the practices listed in this section to outline the body of your speech effectively.

**Use Proper Labeling and Indentation.** Start each main point at the left margin of your detailed outline, and indicate each new main point with a Roman numeral. Indent each of your subpoints, and label them with capital letters. If you develop a subpoint further with two or more supporting ideas, indicate each of these sub-subpoints with Arabic numerals, and indent the sub–subpoints another step beneath the subpoint they support. Typically, you'll want to include between two and four subpoints for each main point and the same number of sub-subpoints for each subpoint. (In a proper outline, support can never stand alone. You must *always* include a minimum of two subpoints supporting each main point and, if you use sub-subpoints to develop a subpoint, you need at least two of them.)

**Use Full Sentences or Detailed Phrases.** In your detailed outline, you should express your main ideas, subpoints, and sub-subpoints in complete

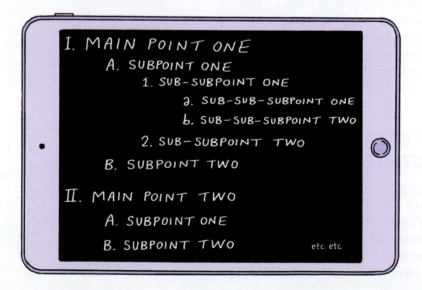

I. MAIN POINT ONE
  A. SUBPOINT ONE
      1. SUB-SUBPOINT ONE
          a. SUB-SUB-SUBPOINT ONE
          b. SUB-SUB-SUBPOINT TWO
      2. SUB-SUBPOINT TWO
  B. SUBPOINT TWO

II. MAIN POINT TWO
  A. SUBPOINT ONE
  B. SUBPOINT TWO        etc. etc.

## IN A DETAILED OUTLINE, NEVER LEAVE THE READER GUESSING

sentences or detailed phrases (instructors will have their own preference for the level of detail required). As noted earlier, your detailed outline should cover your ideas completely, such that another person could deliver your speech from it. Furthermore, you will likely be required to turn in a copy of your detailed outline. If it is too brief, your instructor may misinterpret the points you want to make or, even worse, conclude that you haven't put enough effort into preparing your speech.

**Check for Subordination.** As we note in Chapter 9, supporting materials must show **subordination** to the point being made. This means that each subpoint must be relevant to the main point it is designed to support, and each sub-subpoint must relate to its corresponding subpoint.

To see how this works, consider the following examples from a speech about honeybees.

*Subpoints ARE Subordinate to the Main Point:*
    I. Honeybee alternatives can capably pollinate crops.
       A. Bumblebees pollinate watermelons and blueberries well.
       B. Blue orchard bees pollinate almond and cherry trees effectively.
       C. Ground-nesting alkali bees pollinate alfalfa successfully.

*Subpoints ARE NOT Subordinate to the Main Point:*
    II. Honeybee populations are threatened.
       A. Pesticides are a serious threat to honeybee colonies.
       B. Honeybees are effective at pollinating crops.
       C. Without sufficient honeybees for pollination, U.S. crop production will suffer.

In the first main point, each subpoint is relevant to the claim that alternatives to honeybees pollinate crops effectively—the speaker notes three different species of bees as alternatives. However, in the second main point, only the first subpoint is relevant to the claim that honeybee populations are threatened.

# SUBORDINATION

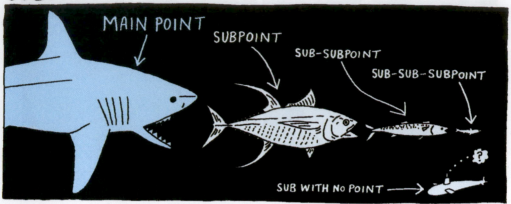

The next two subpoints do not provide any explanation of how the populations are threatened. Rather, one subpoint states a fact about honeybees' usefulness, while the other focuses on the harmful consequences of honeybees' becoming scarce. For that second main point, the speaker's second and third subpoints should have focused on other threats to the bees, for example, parasites or malnutrition.

How can you tell whether your supporting materials are subordinate to their corresponding main point? Complete the following sentence for each of your supporting materials:

"This supports the point I am making because . . ."

If you can't come up with a logical way to complete this sentence, either use different supporting materials that *do* support that point or reorganize your speech. For example, you might want to move a subpoint to a place in your outline where the idea fits better. Or you may decide to reword a main point or subpoint so that your supporting materials do apply or keep the main point and select more relevant supporting materials. Finally, you could consider developing an idea that does not fit your existing main points into a new main point. Here is how this could be done with the second main point on honeybees:

- *Move the supporting materials.* If the speaker had a main point about the impact of honeybees on crop production, the second and third subpoints could be moved there.
- *Reword the title of the main point.* The speaker could title the main point "Pesticides threaten crop production by killing honeybees."
- *Create a new main point.* If the speaker did not yet have a main point about the importance of honeybees to crop production, the speaker could add that main point and place the last two subpoints there.

**Include Full Information for Citations, Quotations, and Other Evidence.** When you use *evidence* to support a claim, you need to include in your detailed outline all the information about the source of that **evidence**—the author, their qualifications, the source publication or web page, and the date of publication. And if you are quoting a source, be sure to present the information word-for-word and enclose it in quotation marks to indicate that you are using someone else's words.

For example, here's how you would outline evidence for a commemorative speech about Cammi Granato, one of the first two women elected to the Hockey Hall of Fame and a two-time U.S. team captain at the Winter Olympics:

I. Cammi Granato is a trailblazer.
   A. She captained the first U.S. Olympic Women's Hockey Team. In *Positive Power*, 2014, National Hockey League skating coach Barbara Ann Williams noted that when the U.S. women's team defeated Canada in the 1998 gold medal game, "little girls were now able to turn on their TVs and see Cammi Granato, captain of the U.S. team, on Nike commercials with other famous athletes."
   B. She is the first woman hired to be a scout for the National Hockey League. According to sports journalist Marisa Ingemi in *The Seattle Times,* October 27, 2021, Cammi Granato, "the first woman hired as an NHL scout, has been a builder of this first [Seattle] Kraken team. From the time she was hired in 2019, she has been a leader in the effort to fill the roster."

**Insert Transitions.** As we discuss in Chapter 9, a **transition** is a sentence that indicates you are moving from one part of your speech to the next. For example, when moving from one main point to the next, a good transition sums up the point you have just made in a few key words and then introduces the next point, also in a few key words. Using transitions helps you keep on track and makes it easier for listeners to follow along. At a minimum, include transitions

- between the introduction and the body,
- when you move from one main point to the next, and
- between the body and the conclusion.

In your outline, indicate a transition by labeling it and placing it in brackets, as shown in the following example:

> [TRANSITION     We have considered the physical skills needed to become a
>                          Navy Seal; next, let's turn our attention to mental abilities.]

Note that this example includes both necessary elements of a transition between main points. First, it expresses the previous point in a few words ("the physical skills needed to become a Navy Seal"). Second, it uses a *signpost* ("let's turn our attention to") to show movement to the next point, which is also expressed efficiently ("mental abilities"). When drafting your transitions between main points, be sure to follow the same format.

## Outlining Your Introduction

After you've outlined the body of your speech, it's time to outline the *introduction*. In Chapter 10, we identify the five purposes of an introduction—gaining your audience's attention, signaling your thesis, showing the relevance of the topic for your audience, establishing your credibility, and previewing your main points. Each of these purposes provides the basis for one part of your introduction. As you prepare each part, insert it into your detailed outline using the following structure:

**INTRODUCTION**
    I.  Attention-getter
   II.  Thesis statement
  III.  Relevance of topic for audience
  IV.  Speaker's credibility
   V.  Preview of main points

In your detailed outline, each of these five elements should be expressed in complete sentences or detailed phrases so that a reader would know what you were planning to say for each part.

## Outlining Your Conclusion

After you've outlined your introduction, do the same for your speech's *conclusion*. Just as the introduction should grab your listeners' attention, your conclusion should end your speech on a strong note. Start by outlining the transition to your conclusion and then move on to the summary of your main points and your clincher. In your detailed outline, the summary and clincher will be indicated as shown here:

> **CONCLUSION**
> I. Summary of main points
> II. Clincher

## Creating a List of References

Your instructor may require you to include your **references** at the end of your outline. Your references list (which may also be referred to as *works cited* or a *bibliography*) is a record of all the sources you cited in your speech. Your list should *not* include sources you discovered during your research but did not quote or otherwise use in your speech. Some colleges consider including unused sources in a reference list to be academic dishonesty and will take strict disciplinary action against students who commit this kind of wrongdoing.

If a list of references is required, include a full citation for each source you used in your speech. Your instructor will probably require you to use a particular style for documenting sources. The three most common documentation styles are those recommended by the American Psychological Association (APA), the Modern Language Association (MLA), and the *Chicago Manual of Style* (CMS). Regardless of which style you use, make sure to follow your instructor's requirements for the list.

Finally, note that a reference list is *not* a substitute for the proper citation and quotation of evidence in your outline or speech. Even if you include this list at the end of your detailed outline, it remains your ethical obligation to attribute all information that comes from research sources. Each time such information is used in your outline or speech, you must identify the source.

## Inserting the Title, Specific Purpose, and Thesis

Some instructors may ask you to write the title, specific purpose, and thesis of your speech at the top of your detailed outline to guide the development of your main and supporting points. If your instructor has requested this information, type or write out the title of your speech in relatively large or bold type. Indicate

▲ **Phantom Energy Speech.** Audience members might be surprised to see how much phantom energy common electronic devices (like televisions) waste. By developing a detailed outline, you can confirm that this and other key points from your speech are clearly explained. Donald Iain Smith/Getty Images

your speech's specific purpose and thesis, too, as shown in the following example from a speech on phantom energy.

### THE HIDDEN COSTS OF PHANTOM ENERGY

| | |
|---|---|
| SPECIFIC PURPOSE | To inform my audience about the nature and effects of phantom energy |
| THESIS | Many household devices consume phantom energy, wasting power and costing you money. |

## A SAMPLE DETAILED OUTLINE

How do all these guidelines for creating a detailed outline come together? Consider the following example of a detailed outline for a speech about reducing distractions for students.

## A CHALLENGING SOLUTION TO DISTRACTIONS

SPECIFIC PURPOSE    To persuade my audience to reduce distractions by taking on more challenging work

THESIS    You should reduce distractions by taking on more challenging work.

## INTRODUCTION

I. You don't need to raise your hand, but are any of you on Instagram right now? Have you been on social media during any class this week? How about when you were trying to study? If you answered yes to any of these questions, you are not alone. But what I am about to tell you may be surprising. •  — • Rhetorical questions for the attention-getter

II. You can reduce distractions by taking on more challenging work.

III. Over three-fourths of the students in our class who responded to my online survey indicated that they have attempted to cut down on distractions when trying to study, so many of us are looking for some strategies.

IV. Like many in this class, I have attempted to cut down on distractions when trying to study. My research on possible solutions revealed that experts on time management and productivity support the idea of getting focused by taking on challenges. •  — • Introduction includes all five components: attention-getter (I), thesis (II), connect with audience (III), credibility (IV), and preview (V)

V. To understand why you should give this unexpected solution a try, it is necessary to first understand how widespread distractions are in the typical student's life, then take a look at how distractions affect our ability to do well in college, and finally analyze how we can become more focused by taking on more challenging work. •  — • *First*, *then*, and *finally* are signposts

[TRANSITION    Let's begin by taking a look at how distracted many of us are.] •  — • Transition from introduction to body

## BODY

I. College students are distracted.

   A. Distractions are common for students in our class.

      1. On my online survey, over three-fourths of our class members reported that they checked their phones or browsed the Internet in class five or more times during the past week. •  — • Subpoints and sub-subpoints are indented properly

2.  Furthermore, nearly 90 percent of our class reported that when studying at home, they find it difficult to focus on a reading assignment or paper for one hour without taking a break.

3.  Smartphones and computers are not the only culprits; classmates also report other distractions, such as talking with roommates, getting a snack, watching a television show, or just zoning out. •

• Sub-subpoints are subordinate to the subpoint they support

B.  Distractions are common for college students in general.

1.  According to the Derek Bok Center for Teaching and Learning at Harvard University, in "Technology and Student Distraction," 2018, "in one survey at six different universities, college students reported using their phones an average of 11 times per day in class," and "in another study, 92 % of college students reported using their phones to send text messages during class." •

• Full citation of research sources

2.  Bernard McCoy, Professor of Broadcasting at the University of Nebraska, in the *Journal of Media Education*, July 2021, wrote that according to a survey of 500 students at thirty U.S. colleges, almost 80 % of the students "described online/remote learning as 'a lot more' or 'a little more' distracting than classroom learning."

• Transition indicates that first main point is done and introduces next main point

[TRANSITION    Now that we've seen how common distractions are, let's turn our attention to how distractions harm our ability to study and learn.] •

II.  Distractions are hazardous to student success.

A.  Distractions take time away from learning. Professor McCoy, previously cited, was quoted in the January 15, 2016, issue of *Nebraska Today* saying that "during the typical four years they're in college classrooms, the average student may be distracted for two-thirds of a school year."

B.  Distractions cause students to study inefficiently. According to Sharita Forrest, Education Editor, in the *Illinois News Bureau Research News*, October 13, 2020, "Researchers in psychology, cognitive science and neuroscience found that media multitasking during schoolwork interferes with students' attention and working memory. Students' learning is shallower and spottier; they understand less and have difficulty recalling what they have learned and applying it in new contexts." •

> • Use quotation marks when quoting a source word for word

C. Distractions hurt our academic performance in another surprising way.

1. In *Sleep Health*, 2016, Psychology Professor Larry Rosen of California State University San Bernardino and his colleagues reported a study finding that "three-quarters of students slept with their phones on (or set to vibrate)," and about "half of them checked their phones in the middle of the night (for reasons other than to check the time; social media was the main culprit)."

2. Professor Rosen, in *Phi Delta Kappan*, 2017, states that "this is a huge problem, given that sleep plays an absolutely critical role in learning, allowing us to consolidate important information, rid ourselves of unwanted information, and dispose of stray toxic molecules left in the brain during the day."

[TRANSITION     We have seen how distractions limit our ability to do well in school, so let's turn our attention to a surprising strategy for dealing with distractions.]

III. You can reduce distractions by taking on more challenges.

A. There are many options for making your education more challenging.

1. Add a class that is not required but that you have always wanted to take.

2. Take a course from a professor who is very interesting but also demanding.

3. Sign up for an internship in a field of interest.

4. Get more involved in campus activities.

B. You might think, "Wait a minute, if I add a new challenge to my overbooked schedule, my life will be even more stressful."

C.   Actually, we are less likely to be distracted when faced with a challenge.

1. Chris Bailey, author of two best-selling books on productivity, writes in the *New York Times*, August 26, 2018, that "our workload tends to expand to fit the time available" and that due to distractions, "small tasks that should take two hours to complete will take an entire workday if we have that time available."

2. In the *New York Times*, September 6, 2018, digital staff writer Concepción de León notes that "our brain's scratchpad is pretty small and can only hold a handful of tasks at a time," but "when one of those tasks is complex—like putting together a business proposal or taking care of a toddler—that number dwindles down to one or two."

3. Chris Bailey, in the previously cited article, explains why. "You may need to take on more work, and work on stuff that's a little harder," because "complex tasks demand more of our working memory and attention, meaning we have less mental capacity remaining to wander to the nearest stimulating distraction."

**• Transition from body to conclusion**

[TRANSITION    Today, we took a look at a surprising way for students to resist distractions.] •

## CONCLUSION

I.   First, we considered the many ways that college students are distracted. Second, we saw how these distractions limit student success. Finally, we looked at the idea of reducing challenges by taking on more challenging work. •

**• Summary of main points. *First*, *second*, and *finally* signpost these main points.**

II.   So the next time you reach for your phone to go on social media in class or in the library, don't check Instagram. Instead, remind yourself to add a challenge to your educational game plan. •

**• Clincher tied back to introduction**

**• This reference list is in APA format. Check with your instructor to see which citation style they require.**

### References •

Bailey, C. (2018, August 26). Distracted? Work harder! *The New York Times*, SR10.

De León, C. (2018, September 6). May I have my attention, please? *The New York Times*, C17.

Derek Bok Center for Teaching and Learning. (2018). Technology and student distraction. Retrieved from https://bokcenter .harvard.edu/technology-and-student-distraction

Forrest, S. (2020, October 13). Distracted learning a big problem, golden opportunity for educators, students. *Illinois News Bureau Research News*. https://news.illinois.edu/view/6367/

McCoy, B. (2021, July). In the trenches: college student online/ remote learning experiences during the COVID pandemic. *Journal of Media Education, 12*(3), 18–41.

Reed, L. (2016, January 15). Study: Digital distraction in class is on the rise. *Nebraska Today*. Retrieved from https://news.unl. edu/newsrooms/today/article/study-digital-distraction-in-class-is-on-the-rise

Rosen, L. D. (2017). The distracted student mind—enhancing its focus and attention. *Phi Delta Kappan*, 99(2), 8–14. https:// doi.org/10.1177/0031721717734183

Rosen, L. D., Carrier, L. M., Miller, A., Rokkum, J., & Ruiz, A. (2016). Sleeping with technology: Cognitive affective, and technology usage predictors of sleep problems among college students. *Sleep Health* 2(1), 49–56. https://doi. org/10.1016/j.sleh.2015.11.003

# CREATING YOUR SPEAKING OUTLINE

As noted earlier, your speaking outline is a brief version of your detailed outline. Essentially, it is a set of notes that helps you deliver your speech extemporaneously. By limiting these notes to brief phrases, key words, and abbreviations, you prevent yourself from reading the speech word-for-word and allow yourself to improvise by choosing fresh words as you speak. The speaking outline provides useful reminders of your main and supporting points.

To deliver the most effective extemporaneous presentation possible, you'll need to transform your detailed outline into a speaking outline. You may want to prepare the speaking outline *after* you've practiced your speech several times with your detailed outline and become thoroughly familiar with the ideas in your presentation. Then you can use the speaking outline for your final practice sessions and for delivering your speech.

## Elements of Your Speaking Outline

In a speaking outline, you create a similar structure to a detailed outline by using Roman numerals, capital letters, and Arabic numerals and by indenting subordinate points. However, a speaking outline is significantly shorter than a detailed outline. In a speaking outline, you express your ideas in key words and phrases,

▲ **Fresh Delivery.** This speaker demonstrates extemporaneous delivery, looking at the audience while presenting but having notes available for reference if needed. NurPhoto/Getty Images

trusting yourself to develop these ideas conversationally while delivering your speech. Include the following elements in your speaking outline:

- *Main points.* Be sure to record each of your main points. Stating your main points using similar words or parallel structure will signal to your listeners that these points are important.

- *Subpoints and sub-subpoints.* Write just enough to remind yourself of the key idea.

- *Abbreviations.* To condense your outline, use abbreviations whenever possible. However, as you have probably realized when going back to study notes you took in class, the abbreviations need to be easily recognized.

- *Evidence.* Because you are presenting others' ideas, evidence will be more detailed than other parts of your speaking outline. Include necessary citation information and word-for-word quotations where they are used. If you are paraphrasing, you can just use key words, but be sure they accurately reflect the author's ideas.

- *Difficult words.* If you'll be using words that are difficult to pronounce or remember, include them in your speaking outline. It helps to spell difficult words phonetically, so they are written out to look how they sound.

- *Transitions.* Include a brief reminder of each transition in your speech. These reminders don't need to be word-for-word, but make them detailed enough to indicate to your audience that you're done with one idea *and* you're moving on to the next. Consider using brackets to set your transitions apart from your points.

- *Delivery notes.* Consider putting down a **delivery reminder** to handle any speaking challenges effectively. For example, place "SLOW DOWN!" in places where you tend to rush, or "LOOK UP!" if you often read from your notes rather than making eye contact while presenting. Consider noting "KEY POINT" or "EMPHASIS!" to remind yourself to use inflections or gestures to highlight an important idea. Use "COVER WHEN DONE!" as a reminder for what to do after you've finished presenting a visual aid. To make reminders stand out, circle them, bold them, write them in capital letters, use a different color, or highlight them.

## The Medium for Your Speaking Outline

The choice of what medium you will use to display your speaking outline while you are presenting is important. Some instructors have specific requirements for what you should use. If not, you might choose a traditional method, such as note cards or 8½ in. × 11 in. paper, or a digital format, such as a tablet. When you have a choice, think carefully about what you will use. There are advantages and disadvantages to these different options. When you need to refer to your notes, it is essential that you be able to quickly locate the right place on your outline so that you can prompt yourself and return your focus to the audience. Some mediums are smaller than others, placing less of a barrier between you and your listeners. Credibility is another factor; some audiences may find a speaker who uses the latest technology to be more credible, while others may be fine with an old-school approach. Before you decide, it can be helpful to practice speaking with different mediums to see which works best for you. Here are some additional points about a number of popular options.

- *Note cards or paper.* If you decide to use note cards or 8½ in. × 11 in. paper for your speaking outline, make sure that what you've chosen is easy on the eyes, so you can find your place quickly. If you write your notes by hand, be sure to write neatly and leave space between each line. If you print out notes on paper, double space and select a font size that will be easy for you to read. To make it easy to find your place when you refer to your notes, you may wish to use one note card or page for the introduction, one for each main point, and one for the conclusion. If you are going to use fewer cards or pages, you can use bold type or a larger font size to make the title of each main point stand out, allowing you to navigate your notes quickly. When using multiple cards or notes, be sure to flip each one as you finish it, so that the one on top matches your place in the speech.

- *Tablets.* Tablets are an alternative to paper or note cards. Again, you want to use a font size that is easy to read. If you have your notes on your tablet, it might be a challenge to swipe precisely so that the correct part of your notes is always displayed (and an even greater challenge to find your place if you haven't looked at your notes in a while). A tablet will therefore work best when you have a briefer outline. There are also a variety of apps available for creating and viewing speech notes. If you decide to use one of these apps, be sure to practice with it in advance so that you can feel confident using it while you are speaking.

- *Laptops.* Some speakers put their notes on a laptop, which gives them the benefit of a larger screen. However, it is difficult to speak while holding a laptop in one hand, and its larger size makes it a distraction and a barrier between you and your audience. Conversely, if there is a place to rest your laptop during your speech, such as a podium, doing so will limit your

IF YOU NEED TO CHECK YOUR NOTES DURING YOUR SPEECH...      ...WHICH OUTLINE WOULD YOU PREFER TO READ?

ability to move while you are speaking. (We cover the benefits of controlled movement in Chapter 13.)

- *Smartphones.* An additional option is to keep your notes on a smartphone. Their small size makes them easy to hold in one hand. However, the small screen size limits how much of your outline you can see at one time during the presentation, making it more difficult to navigate your notes during the course of your speech. Smartphones will work best when your outline contains only a few key ideas that you need for reference. And make sure your sound notifications are not on!

If you do use technology for your notes, don't forget that tech can be temperamental. Be sure that your battery is charged in advance, and if you need Internet access, be sure that you can connect where you'll be speaking. It is always a good idea to bring printed notes as a backup, just in case your technology fails.

We conclude this section with two important reminders. The first is that instructors may have specific requirements about the form, length, or medium for your speaking outline. Be sure to follow their instructions. The second is that no matter what medium you use, do your best to be sure that you can access your notes if needed while speaking and ensure that notes or devices do not block your face.

## A SAMPLE SPEAKING OUTLINE

After you have practiced and become familiar with your speech, it is time to prepare the more limited speaking outline that you will use to present your speech. Check out this example of a speaking outline for the speech on reducing distractions for college students. Compare this outline to the detailed outline included earlier to see how the two are similar and how they differ.

## INTRODUCTION

• Delivery reminder

Look Up—eye contact •

I. Instagram, social media, studying? Surprising information to tell

• Include all five parts of intro, use key words

II. Reduce distractions, challenging work •

III. Survey, ¾-plus try to cut down distractions

IV. Researched time management and productivity experts

V. Distractions widespread, affect college success, challenging work

• Delivery reminder: pause before transition

Pause •

[Begin with how distracted many of us are.]

## BODY

I. College stu. are distr.

• Abbreviate common terms, like *distractions*

A. Distr. common for our class •

1. Online survey, over ¾ of class on tech in class 5+ per week

2. Almost 90% difficult to focus for one hour without a break

3. Other distr. = roommates, snack, TV, zoning out

B. Distr. common students in general

1. Bok Center at Harvard, "Technology and Student Distraction," 2018, "in one survey at six different universities, college students reported using their phones an average of 11 times per day in class," and "in another study, 92% of college students reported using their phones to send text messages during class." •

• Include citations for all sources

2. Bernard McCoy, Broadcasting Prof, Nebraska, *Journal of Media Education,* July 2021, survey of 500 students, almost 80% of the students "described online/remote learning as 'a lot more' or 'a little more' distracting than classroom learning."

[Seen how common distr. are, turn attention to how distr. harm studying, learning]

II. Distr. haz. stu. success

A. Take time away. Prof. McCoy, *Nebraska Today,* January 2016, "during the typical four years they're in college classrooms, the average student may be distracted for two-thirds of a school year."

B. Study inefficiently. Sharita Forrest, Educ Editor, Ill News Bureau, October 2020, "Researchers in psychology, cognitive science and neuroscience found that media multitasking during schoolwork interferes with students' attention and working memory. Students' learning is shallower and spottier; they understand less and have difficulty recalling what they have learned and applying it in new contexts." •

> • Use quotation marks for word-for-word quotations

C. Distr. hurt acad. perf. another way
  1. *Sleep Health*, 2016, Larry Rosen, CSU San Bernardino: "three-quarters of students slept with their phones on (or set to vibrate)," and about "half of them checked their phones in the middle of the night (for reasons other than to check the time; social media was the main culprit)."
  2. Rosen, *Phi Delta Kappan*, 2017, "huge problem, given that sleep plays an absolutely critical role in learning, allowing us to consolidate important information, rid ourselves of unwanted information, and dispose of stray toxic molecules left in the brain during the day."

[Seen how distr. limit stu. success, turn atten. to surprising strat.]

III. Reduce distr. take on more chall.
  A. Many options
    1. Add non-required class
    2. Interesting, demanding prof.
    3. Internship
    4. Campus activities •

> • Sub-subpoint notes can be brief

  B. Might think "more stressful"
  C. Less likely to be distr. if challenged
    1. Chris Bailey, productivity author, *New York Times*, August 26, 2018: "workload tends to expand to fit the time available," and due to distractions, "small tasks that should take two hours to complete will take an entire workday if we have that time available."
    2. *New York Times*, September 6, 2018, digital staff writer Concepción de León: "our brain's scratchpad is pretty small and can

only hold a handful of tasks at a time," but "when one of those tasks is complex—like putting together a business proposal or taking care of a toddler—that number dwindles down to one or two."

3. Chris Bailey: "you may need to take on more work, and work on stuff that's a little harder," because "complex tasks demand more of our working memory and attention, meaning we have less mental capacity remaining to wander to the nearest stimulating distraction."

[Surprising way to resist distr.]

• Briefly note summary of main pts. and clincher

### CONCLUSION •

I. How stu. are distr., how stu. success limited, how more chall. work reduces distr.

II. Next time reach for phone, remind self to add chall. to educ. game plan

---

▼ **Benefits of a Challenging Task.** As the sample speech points out, you are less vulnerable to distractions when you work on a challenging task. Tom Werner/Getty Images

## SPEECH CHOICES

### A CASE STUDY: *RAFAELA*

*Let's check Rafaela's plan for outlining her speech.*

Countdown: There was one week to go before Rafaela was scheduled to deliver her speech. Her preparation work was done, and she was ready to create her detailed outline and then condense her notes into a speaking outline.

Rafaela began to draft the body of her speech. She had plenty of supporting materials for each of the main points she had selected: problem (women are less likely to run for office), cause (the reasons women are less likely to run), and solution (more women should run for office).

Rafaela set out to select and organize the supporting materials for each main point. When she had finished that process, she remembered that it would be important to check for subordination. Her first two main points were fine, but the third main point was more problematic. She had titled this third main point "More women should run for office." However, her supporting materials did not match this title well. To relate her speech to everyone in the audience, she wanted to call on all classmates to support and encourage the women in their lives to run. In addition, although the main point's title referred to women in general, her supporting materials focused on why women *in her class* should run.

Rafaela reviewed her options for what to do when subpoints don't relate to a main point. She could keep that main point and change the subpoints to focus her solution on women running for office across the nation. Another option was to change the title of the main point to make it better reflect the supporting materials. Because she was passionate about the subpoints she had chosen and wanted to relate the speech to her classmates as much as possible, she chose the second option. She changed the title to "Women in this class: run for office; classmates: support us."

 **YOUR TURN**

Now that you've seen how Rafaela's choices impacted her outlining, it's time to think about how you'll construct detailed and speaking outlines in a speech of your own. Making speech choices involves asking and answering a series of questions related to your assignment. Here are some important questions to ask as you draft your outlines:

- Does my detailed outline include all required elements (introduction, body, conclusion, transitions, and properly cited evidence)?
- Are all main points subordinate to the thesis and all subpoints subordinate to the main point they support?
- Have I condensed my detailed outline into a speaking outline in a way that makes the outline briefer but also helpful for me when I am speaking?
- Have I included delivery reminders and other useful notes in my speaking outline?
- Have I practiced with my speaking outline to make sure I am able to use it effectively in my speech?

By making thoughtful choices in response to questions like these, you'll craft strong outlines that help you structure your speech.

> " A good outline strengthens organization and preparation. "

In this chapter, we explained the importance of outlining. We showed you how to develop and use both detailed and speaking outlines to organize your ideas, practice your presentation, and ultimately deliver an effective speech. A detailed outline consists of complete sentences or detailed phrases that show the structure of your speech and the hierarchy of your ideas, and includes full quotations for any evidence you'll provide in your speech. This long outline also includes notes for transitions and presentation aids (if you are using them). Use your detailed outline to practice your speech until you're thoroughly familiar with it.

Your speaking outline is shorter and condenses your ideas into brief phrases, key words, and abbreviations. However, it should retain word-for-word quotations from your evidence sources. Speaking outlines are typically prepared on numbered note cards or on pieces of 8 ½ in. × 11 in. paper, but they may be viewed on a variety of electronic devices as well, including a tablet, laptop, or smartphone. Either way, the writing on these outlines must be clear and easy to read. You may want to develop your speaking outline after you've practiced your speech several times with your detailed outline. The speaking outline helps you present your speech conversationally—by conveying your ideas in your own words, maintaining eye contact with the audience, and not reading a word-for-word script or reciting your presentation from memory. The speaking outline also serves as a handy reminder if you lose your place while delivering your speech, if you need to quote evidence during your talk, or if you want to remember certain delivery tips (such as emphasizing a particular point while presenting your speech).

## Key Terms

outlining 256
detailed outline 258
speaking outline 259
extemporaneous delivery 259
body 260

subordination 261
evidence 263
transition 264
references 265
delivery reminder 273

## Review Questions

1. Explain the differences between a detailed outline and a speaking outline.
2. How does creating an outline help ensure that your ideas are well supported?
3. Describe the most important guidelines for creating a detailed outline for a speech's body, introduction, and conclusion.

4. What are the benefits of delivering a speech from a relatively brief speaking outline?
5. Describe the most important guidelines for creating an effective speaking outline.

## Critical Thinking Questions

1. If you were to give a speech on the nature of detailed outlines, what would your main points be? How would they compare to the main points of a speech about the nature of speaking outlines?
2. How can the process of developing a detailed outline help you be more confident when delivering your final speech?
3. Can you think of a situation in everyday life in which you use subordination? How might you use subordination in a conversation with a friend? In a writing assignment? What does this lead you to believe about the importance of subordination in communication?
4. What are the advantages and disadvantages of each of the primary formats of your speaking outline—note cards, paper, tablet, laptop, and smartphone?

## Activities

1. Select any of the sample speeches in this textbook. Working individually or in groups, condense the speech into a speaking outline.
2. Take a look at both the detailed outline (pp. 267–271) and the speaking outline (pp. 276–278) for the sample speech on reducing distractions. Could you deliver the speech yourself using the detailed outline? Why would it be difficult to deliver the speech yourself, right now, using only the speaking outline? What type of preparation could help you deliver the speech from the speaking outline?
3. Locate a speech of interest to you (e.g., a TED Talk or YouTube video). Watch the introduction and prepare a brief speaking outline of the speaker's introduction. Use that outline to deliver that excerpt from their speech. Then watch the video clip again. How closely did your speech match the presentation?
4. Open one of your textbooks from another course, and outline a chapter based on the headings, subheadings, and key terms that appear in boldface or colored text. Do these elements show a clear hierarchy of ideas? How clear is the picture of the chapter that the outline creates? Could you summarize the chapter using only the outline?

# LANGUAGE AND STYLE

**12**

> **66** Choose your words carefully. **99**

On January 31, 2022, President Joe Biden delivered a proclamation speech—a public, and often official, announcement regarding a topic of significance. The speech coincided with the beginning of National Black History Month, a month-long event celebrating Black history and culture. A passage of Biden's proclamation included these sentiments:

> Our Nation was founded on an idea: that all of us are created equal and deserve to be treated with equal dignity throughout our lives. It is a promise we have never fully lived up to but one that we have never, ever walked away from. The long shadows of slavery, Jim Crow, and redlining—and the blight of systemic racism that still diminishes our Nation today—hold America back from reaching our full promise and potential. But by facing those tragedies openly and honestly and working together as one people to deliver on America's promise of equity and dignity for all, we become a stronger Nation—a more perfect version of ourselves.[1]

◄ **Word Choice Is Important.** Whether a speech is a formal presidential address or a classroom presentation, a speaker's language should be carefully chosen.
Brandon Bell/Getty Images

Presidential proclamations have a long history, dating back to George Washington's Thanksgiving Proclamation in 1789.[2] They provide chief executives with an opportunity to commemorate a significant event or highlight a policy decision. The words for these declarations are carefully chosen so that presidents can most effectively communicate their ideas and inspire their audiences. In this proclamation, President Biden did not just say "racism is bad and we need to do better." Powerful phrases such as "the blight of systemic racism" allowed the President to express the magnitude of the problem. With equal impact, the phrase "a more perfect version of ourselves" echoes language from the preamble to the U.S. Constitution, challenging the nation to live up to its highest ideals.

Similarly, word choice factored heavily in Martin Luther King Jr.'s "I Have a Dream" speech, which we discuss in Chapter 2. When Dr. King presented this address on August 28, 1963, at the March on Washington, he didn't give it an official title. Only later did people start calling it the "I Have a Dream" speech. Why has this phrase endured in people's memories? It was an exceptionally powerful expression that encapsulated King's vision of a time and place that would be free from prejudice and discrimination. Now, decades after his death, people still experience profound emotions when they recall this expression. If King had calmly used the words "I hope" instead of "I have a dream," he would have made less of an impact on his listeners.

These examples show that word choice is an important consideration for all speakers, whether they are national leaders or students in the classroom. **Word choice**, or **diction** (the choice of words and phrases for a speech, as well a style of enunciation in speaking), requires you to consider your audience, the occasion, and the nature of your message when choosing language for a speech.

While it is true that an average speech may contain hundreds or even thousands of words, it is also true that every one of those words matters. Selected carefully, your words can help you connect with your audience and get your message across clearly. Used thoughtlessly, they may confuse, offend, bore, or annoy listeners, preventing them from absorbing your message. In this chapter, we examine the importance of choosing the right words for your speeches, the differences between oral and written language, and the two kinds of meaning that words can have. Then we explain how to use language to present your message clearly, express your ideas effectively, and demonstrate respect for your audience.

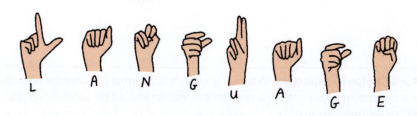

L  A  N  G  U  A  G  E

# THE IMPORTANCE OF LANGUAGE AND WORD CHOICE

You make word choices every day when you talk with friends and family, take notes in class, write emails, make phone calls, and send text messages. Most of us try to choose our words carefully in each of these situations. After all, our words have a lot of power: they can inform, inspire, and uplift others. But they can also confuse people (for example, if you've used jargon or slang that others might not understand), and they can hurt others (for instance, if you've used biased language).

A speaker's personal credibility can influence an audience's perception of the presenter's message. Your words and phrases convey this credibility to your listeners because they say something about you as a person. In this way, your word choice defines you as a speaker.

How do you use words in ways that clarify your message and enhance your credibility? Along with using appropriate and considerate language, you can explain technical terms and use presentation aids to further demonstrate their meaning (for clarity), thus effectively incorporating such terms into your speech (to enhance credibility).

A student speaker named Gillian applied these practices while delivering an informative presentation about armor plating used during the Ottoman empire. Gillian showed photographs depicting the armor worn by soldiers and their horses. She also used technical terms in a way the audience would understand. For instance, at one point she discussed "a gilded copper *chanfrein*," which she immediately explained was "forehead armor for the horse—like the helmet a soldier might wear." By using the correct technical terminology, she showed authority and gained credibility in the eyes of the audience. And by explaining these terms through devices such as analogy ("like the helmet a soldier might wear"), she made her message accessible without coming across as condescending to her listeners.

## EXPLAIN TECHNICAL TERMS

# DIFFERENCES BETWEEN ORAL AND WRITTEN LANGUAGE

You may have noticed that words and sentences that are spoken aloud can come across quite differently from words that you read to yourself. In a public speaking context, the difference between spoken and written language can be even more pronounced. To help you craft better language for your speeches, consider these three key differences between oral and written language:

- *Oral language is more adaptive.* Writers seldom know exactly who will read their words or in what context. The best they can do is to take educated guesses and make language choices accordingly. When you speak before a live audience, however, you can get immediate feedback, which is virtually impossible for a writer. Thus, you can observe your audience members during your presentation, interact with them, and *respond* to the way they are receiving your message. Because a speech is often delivered live with physical interaction that generates instantaneous audience feedback, you can adapt to the situation, such as by extending an explanation if listeners seem confused or by choosing clearer or simpler language.

- *Oral language tends to be less formal.* Because writers have the luxury of getting their words down on paper (or on screen) and then going back to make

▼ **Oral Language Is Adaptive.** During a speech at a march for Hurricane Maria relief, Lin-Manuel Miranda and Rita Moreno used language that appealed to audience members, resulting in immediate feedback. Paul Morigi/Getty Images

changes, they typically use precise word choice and follow the formal rules of syntax and grammar. This careful use of language aligns well with most readers' expectations. In most speech situations, however, language choice tends toward a somewhat less formal style. Because listeners lack the chance to go back and reread your words, you will want to use shorter and less complicated sentences. (Of course, certain speech situations—such as political settings— require elevated sentence structure and word choice.) In addition, effective oral language is often simpler and less technically precise than written language. Thus, consider incorporating appropriate colloquialisms (informal phrases), a conversational tone, and even sentence fragments into your speeches.

- *Oral language incorporates repetition.* Most writing teachers and coaches advise their students to avoid repeating themselves or being *redundant* by covering the same ground more than once. But in speaking situations, repetition can be an especially effective tool because your listeners usually can't go back and revisit your points: unless your speech is being recorded, your words are there and then are suddenly gone. Because most audience members don't take notes (especially outside a classroom setting), there is nothing for listeners to rely on except their own memory of your words. You can help your listeners remember your message by intentionally repeating key words and phrases throughout your presentation. If they hear certain words often enough, they will remember them.

## ORAL vs. WRITTEN LANGUAGE

# DENOTATIVE AND CONNOTATIVE MEANING

In addition to selecting words that express your message clearly and enhance your credibility, you need to be aware that words can have two very different kinds of meanings. By understanding these differences, you can select your language more strategically to create the effect you want. In the sections that follow, we look at this notion of two meanings—*denotative meaning* and *connotative meaning*.

## Denotative Meaning

The **denotative meaning** of a word is its exact, literal dictionary definition. When you use a word that has one dictionary definition (and is not overly technical), you can usually expect that your audience will understand what you mean. But many words have several dictionary definitions. In these cases, you may need to take steps to avoid confusion.

Consider the word *run*. According to *Merriam-Webster's Collegiate Dictionary*, *run* has numerous definitions. For example, it can be a verb meaning "to go faster than walking" ("He runs 6.2 miles every morning"), or "to dissolve or spread when wet" ("The rain made the ink on the paper run"), or "being in a melted state" ("runs like butter"). It can also be a noun meaning "an unbroken course of performance" ("The company had a good run of profits this year"). Suppose you wanted to use the word *run* in a speech to refer to a successful series of victories by your school's track team. If you said, "We had a great run this season," your listeners may wonder if you're referring to a specific race or to a string of victories scored by the team during the season. In this case, you may want to avoid the risk of confusing your audience by saying instead, "We consistently trounced the competition this season."

## Connotative Meaning

Many words also have at least one **connotative meaning**—an association that comes to mind when people hear or read the word. A word's connotative meanings may bear little or no resemblance to its denotative meanings. For example, when used as a noun in a statement about stocks, the word *dog* may connote a poor investment opportunity—yet the literal meaning of the noun *dog* is a canine animal.

DOG

"DOG"

By using words in your speeches deliberately for their connotative meanings, you can make a powerful impression on your audience. For example, a student named Betty made the following statement in her presentation on the history of hairstyles in the twentieth century: "In the roaring twenties, the short 'bob' or 'flapper' haircut blew up onto the scene through the rise of silent film star Louise Brooks." When Betty used the verb *blew up*, she triggered the strong, fiery association that most people have with the words. This savvy use of the connotations of *blew up* helped Betty make her point far more forcefully than if she had merely said that the bob "became very popular."

On the other hand, carelessly using a word that has very different denotative and connotative meanings can backfire and confuse your audience. Consider Albert, a student who made the following statement in an impromptu speech about a school district's refusal to lower the student-to-teacher ratio for class size in elementary schools: "That kind of decision really demonstrates some bigotry by the school board." The word *bigotry* literally means the state of mind of a person who is intolerantly devoted to their personal opinions or prejudices and not open to alternatives—the meaning that Albert intended in his comment. At the same time, many people have come to associate the word *bigotry* with racial prejudice. Albert did not intend a racial connotation; he just wanted to say that he thought the school district was unreasonably committed to its decision about class size. But because many students in Albert's class had experienced the pain of racial prejudice firsthand, they inferred from Albert's use of *bigotry* that issues of race underlay the school board's decision, which wasn't true. If Albert had analyzed his audience more carefully, he might have known to avoid using the word due to its potentially misleading connotative meaning. Instead, he could have said that the school board stubbornly refused to change its view about reducing class sizes.

---

▼ **Connotative Meaning.** The word *jam* was used as a term for a fruit preserve beginning in the 1700s. Two hundred years later, in the context of jazz, *jam* was used to refer to a brief, improvised musical passage. The jazz usage may have been adopted because the music was "something sweet, something excellent."[3]
(left) MassanPH/Getty Images; (right) Taiyou Nomachi/Getty Images

# PRESENTING YOUR MESSAGE CLEARLY

You can't get your message across to your audience unless you present it clearly. To make your message as clear as possible, use language that's *understandable*, *concrete*, *accurate*, and *concise*.

## Understandable Language

Understandable language consists of words your listeners find *recognizable*. In most situations, the best way to ensure that you're using understandable language is to choose words that reflect your audience's language skills, avoiding technical terms that they may not know. For example, if a cell biologist gave a talk to a roomful of English majors, she would quickly confuse her listeners with terms such as *ribosomal DNA* and *anaerobic cellular metabolism*. Yet those terms could be appropriate in a speech delivered to a group of experts or insiders—for example, when presenting a paper to scientists at a biology conference.

Thus, you need to analyze your audience to determine what language your listeners will recognize. Audience members' educational background can suggest their general vocabulary level. Meanwhile, demographic information and stories about listeners' life experiences can help you predict what specific language the audience will understand.

Be sure to take care in using **jargon**—specialized or technical words or phrases that are familiar only to people in a specific field or group. Jargon includes technical terms as well as abbreviations, acronyms, slang, and other esoteric expressions. For example, people in the field of telecommunications use jargon extensively—including expressions such as *7G* (seventh-generation telecom networks), *CapEx* (capital expenditures), *first-tier ops* (telecom operators with the largest market share), and *the cloud* (servers available over the Internet). The jargon can be even trickier to use if its definition is still in a state of evolution. The word *pivot* is one such case. Originally, the word simply referred to a physical action—turning around and going in a different direction. But in the last seven years, political commentators on channels like MSNBC, CNN, and FOX have used the word *pivot* in a different way, making it synonymous with shifting away from an old political position to a new one that will be more accepted by a population of voters.

Here are two simple guidelines for deciding whether to include a particular instance of jargon in a speech:

- *If you can say something in plain language, do so.* Unless you see a pressing reason to use jargon—such as to clarify an important point or to bolster your credibility—use widely accessible words.

- *If you do use jargon, explain it.* By clarifying your use of jargon, you can gain whatever advantages it offers and still ensure that your audience understands you.

*Jargon Can Be Confusing

For example, a student named Patrick made a presentation in his public speaking class about safe horseback-riding practices. Most of his fellow students had grown up in the city and had little experience with horses. In explaining the steps required to prepare a horse for a trail ride, Patrick said, "Be very careful about how you tack up your horse—that is, how you put the bridle and saddle on." He guessed (correctly) that many of his listeners wouldn't understand the phrase *tack up*. By using the term—which is common among people who ride horses—he gained credibility as someone familiar with his topic, and by explaining it, he helped his audience understand the information.

## Concrete Words

Whenever possible, strive to use concrete words instead of abstract ones. What's the difference? A **concrete word** is specific and suggests exactly what you mean. An **abstract word** is general and can be confusing and ambiguous for your audience. Consider the following four sentences, which range from abstract to concrete:

- This past week, Jane arrived in a vehicle. *(abstract)*
- Four days ago, Jane arrived in a car. *(less abstract)*
- Last Tuesday at noon, Jane arrived in a blue Toyota. *(more concrete)*
- Last Tuesday at noon, Jane arrived in a blue 2022 Toyota Corolla. *(most concrete)*

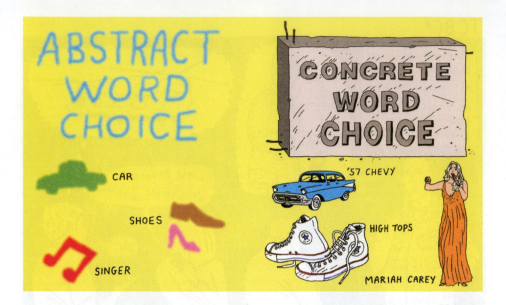

Only the third and fourth sentences convey in specific terms how and when Jane arrived. If this information is relevant to the presentation, either of these sentences would help the speaker convey more information than would the first and second sentences.

This does not mean that you should never use general language. In fact, some situations call for a general language style. In the language of speechwriters, this is the difference between speaking from "five thousand feet, as opposed to fifty feet." When you want to describe a concept or theory from a broad perspective and give the audience the *big picture* or the *grand vision*, you will invariably use general language. For example, here is how the Reverend Dr. Dennis Wiley, pastor emeritus of the Covenant Baptist United Church of Christ provided a grand vision of his support for equality in his testimony before the House Judiciary Committee Hearing on the Equality Act (a proposed law to ban discrimination based on "sex, sexual orientation, and gender identity in a wide variety of areas"[4]):

> This is why, in our tenure as pastors of Covenant Church, my wife and I have unashamedly and unapologetically strived to build a "Beloved Community" where Blacks and whites, men and women, gay, lesbian, bisexual, transgender, and "queer" persons are not rejected but welcomed, not tolerated but celebrated, not excluded but included, not denigrated but elevated, and not discouraged but encouraged to be their true selves as they seek to realize their full, God-given potential. So when any of these precious human beings joined our church, we opened our doors, our arms, and our hearts so that they might become members with all the rights, responsibilities, and privileges that any other member enjoyed.[5]

## LANGUAGE FLYING AT 5,000 FEET

Speaking as a swallow, I think it's well worth making the long, long journey to California every summer...

## LANGUAGE FLYING AT 50 FEET

As a member of the species of *Petrochelidon pyrrhonota*, I always look forward to flying over 12,000 miles from Goya, Corrientes, Argentina to San Juan Capistrano, California, USA...

Still, sometimes specificity can help you make your point. At the same hearings, Kenji Yoshino, professor of constitutional law at New York University, provided specific, grounded examples to support his argument that ongoing discrimination created a need for this legislation:

> Since the Stonewall Riots inaugurated the modern LGBT-rights movement fifty years ago, our society has seen significant gains in recognizing the dignity and humanity of the LGBT community—including the 2015 Supreme Court decision allowing same-sex couples the constitutional right to marry. Nevertheless, the LGBT community continues to face serious discrimination in many areas of life, including in employment, in housing, by businesses, in credit lending, in the criminal justice system, and in education. In some twenty-nine states, no state laws explicitly prohibit discrimination in employment and housing on the basis of sexual orientation and/or gender identity.[6]

## Accurate Use of Words

The audience's understanding of your message will improve if you use words that correctly express the point you want to make. Incorrect word choice can confuse listeners or undermine your credibility. For example, if you used the words *recession* and *depression* interchangeably in a speech on the economy, you would most likely lose credibility with any audience members who know the difference between these two economic terms. At the same time, you might confuse or mislead audience members who do not understand the distinction.

▲ **Inaccurate Word Choice.** Representative Marjorie Taylor Greene probably did not intend to say that the Speaker of the House was aggressively monitoring soup options in the Congressional Dining Room when she referred to Nancy Pelosi's "gazpacho police." Taylor Greene is hardly the only politician to make this type of mistake. For example, during a speech to world leaders, President Joe Biden mixed up Syria and Libya several times, although these nations are over 1400 miles apart and on different continents. Bloomberg/Getty Images

You should also watch out for words that are commonly misused (such as *literally* and *effect*).

It's also easy to fall into the trap of mixing up words that sound alike. For example, one student delivering a speech on the Seattle music scene of the 1990s accused the late Kurt Cobain of "immortal behavior." The audience laughed, knowing that musicians clearly don't live forever and that the speaker probably meant "immoral behavior." Although the speaker's listeners were amused, the joke was on him: many of his audience members lost some respect for him.

## Concise Language

Because audience members usually cannot reread or rehear portions of your speech, they have only one chance to grasp your ideas. For this reason, make sure that each of your sentences expresses just one thought. Although long sentences linking different ideas may be understandable in print, they're hard to follow in a speech.

As a rule of thumb, aim to be *concise*—that is, use the fewest words necessary to express an idea. If you are one of the millions of Twitter users, you may already be used to being succinct because tweets are limited to 280 characters; this restriction forces you to think and express yourself concisely. Giving a speech needn't be as restrictive as writing a tweet, but a similar philosophy can be used. When you outline your speech, focus on making your points in the fewest words possible. You may occasionally want to add words or phrases to incorporate color, eloquence, wit, or humor into your presentation; just make sure you have a good reason to insert those extra words.

Keep it simple!

AMOEBA

The term for unnecessary words in a presentation is **verbal clutter**—extraneous words that make it hard for the audience to follow your message. Here are three examples:

- "The death penalty cannot deter crime *for the reason that* murderers do not consider the consequences of their actions."
- "*Regardless of the fact that* you disagree with the government's position, you cannot dispute the FCC's ruling."
- "If we are to *make contact* with our bargaining opponents, we have to find a mutually acceptable schedule."

You could easily revise those sentences to eliminate verbal clutter:

- "The death penalty cannot deter crime *because* murderers do not consider the consequences of their actions."
- "*Although* you disagree with the government's position, you cannot dispute the FCC's ruling."
- "If we are to *meet* with our bargaining opponents, we have to find a mutually acceptable schedule."

# EXPRESSING YOUR IDEAS EFFECTIVELY

Words have great power to move an audience, especially when they are used compellingly. Empower your own language through the use of *repetition*, *hypothetical examples*, *personal anecdotes*, *vivid language*, and *figurative language*.

## Repetition

*Repetition*—saying a specific word, phrase, or statement more than once—helps you grab your audience's attention and leave listeners with enduring memories of your speech:

At the end of the battle, every soldier was killed. Every soldier.

This use of repetition draws listeners' attention to the fact that all the soldiers *on both sides of the conflict* died at the end of the battle, driving home a sobering point that the speaker wants to make.

To get the most from repetition, use it sparingly. If you repeat too many statements during your speech, your listeners won't be able to discern the truly important points.

You can also use repetition by returning to a point later in your speech to provide a gentle reminder to your audience. In the following example, a student named Allyson employs this technique in a speech about trekking across Russia:

> When most people think about mountains in Russia, they think about the Urals. These are old mountains, stretching some twelve hundred miles from north to south. The mountains themselves are covered with taigas—large forests that blanket the area. . . .

---

▼ **"It Is Time."** Just before the 2022 Super Bowl kickoff, Dwayne "The Rock" Johnson repeated the phrase "it is time" at several key points in his hype speech to fire up the crowd. Ronald Martinez/Getty Images

As I mentioned a few minutes back, these twelve hundred miles of Ural Mountains are an impressive sight, with all sorts of wildlife, including wolves, bears, and many different game birds.

Later in her speech, Allyson again repeats the north-to-south distance ("twelve hundred miles") to emphasize the challenges of backpacking through the vast range of the Ural Mountains.

Finally, you may want to repeat a point through *rewording* it—making the point again but in different words. When your original point might be confusing, rewording gives your audience another option for grasping what you mean. Rewording is similar to the technique you use to explain jargon. Here's one example:

> According to the engineering report, the shuttle booster rockets had systems failure with the cooling system, not to mention serious problems with the outer hatch doors and the manually operated crane. Put another way, there were at least three mechanical problems we know of with this last shuttle mission.

Rewording works particularly well in those parts of your speech where you enumerate a list or make a technical statement that might be difficult for your audience to follow.

## Hypothetical Examples

Consider using hypothetical examples with technical information, complicated messages, policy statements, and points in a speech where you want to focus your audience's attention. A **hypothetical example** is an imagined example or scenario you invite your listeners to consider in order to help them follow a complicated point that will be presented immediately afterwards.

For instance, a student named Blake wanted to inform his audience about the legal test for defamation of character. He introduced his presentation with the following hypothetical example:

> Suppose that a television news crew is shadowing a paramedic team to record its average day, and the paramedics are called out to a highway accident. Now suppose that the camera crew tapes the whole rescue, and the reporter talks to a badly injured victim who is sedated with painkillers. Under the influence of the painkillers, the victim says many foolish things, including some unkind words about their employer. Would the news station be justified in broadcasting the whole story—including everything the victim said to the reporter? What are the victim's rights here, if any? This scenario suggests the difficulty of determining whether defamation of character has taken place.

## Personal Anecdotes

Illustrating a concept with *personal anecdotes* (brief stories) can help you further build credibility and reassure your listeners that you're not judging them. Kimberley, a student in a speech class, used the following personal anecdote in a speech about phobias:

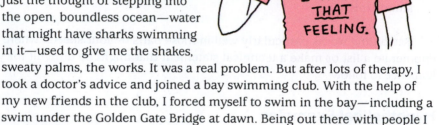

> Phobias come in many different forms—and most, if not all, can be cured with therapy, medication, or a combination of the two. I know this because I've lived with one of these myself. Although you would not know it to look at me today, I once had a horrible fear of swimming in the ocean. Just the thought of stepping into the open, boundless ocean—water that might have sharks swimming in it—used to give me the shakes, sweaty palms, the works. It was a real problem. But after lots of therapy, I took a doctor's advice and joined a bay swimming club. With the help of my new friends in the club, I forced myself to swim in the bay—including a swim under the Golden Gate Bridge at dawn. Being out there with people I really trusted cured me of the fear.

Kimberley illustrates one type of phobia in a way that gives her credibility (she speaks from experience). Her personal anecdote also demonstrates that she takes her subject seriously. Finally, it enables her to encourage her audience members who may have struggled with similar fears.

You can achieve similar effects with anecdotes about events your listeners may have experienced personally. In a speech on credit card debt, a first-year student named Jackson sought common ground with the audience through the following anecdote:

> You really have to be careful about credit cards. You usually get on somebody's mailing list right out of high school. Suddenly your mailbox is filled with offers for free credit cards. And they don't have a service charge for the first three months. You can get credit up to five thousand dollars and pay just

a minimum payment each month. Hasn't that happened to most of you in this room? It happened to me, too. And we all know how fast that credit card debt can pile up!

## Vivid Language

**Vivid language** grabs the attention of your audience with words and phrases that appeal to all the senses—sight, smell, touch, hearing, and taste. The following examples from an autobiographical presentation illustrate the differences between ordinary and vivid word choices. In the first example, Jaime describes his childhood years with his family in relatively uninspiring language:

> I remember those mornings at home only too well. Mom would call us if we overslept. She was downstairs making breakfast every morning at eight o'clock sharp. My brothers and I would fight to be the first into the bathroom.

Now consider this more vivid version of Jaime's story:

> Mornings were memorable in my house. It was always cold in the room I shared with my brothers. With no curtains on our windows, light streamed in, poking us in the eyes before Mom called us down for breakfast. The smell of bacon wafting upstairs did the rest. Routinely, we shoved one another, forming a line outside the bathroom, knowing Mom would demand to know if we had washed up before coming to the table.

The second version conveys the same basic information as the first. However, it paints a more graphic picture of the scene, with stronger **imagery**—mental pictures or impressions—for the audience. We can *see* the bright light. We can also smell the bacon and hear Mom's voice.

To use vivid language, select descriptive words that evoke pictures, smells, textures, sounds, and flavors in your listeners' minds. But use such language sparingly. If you overuse it, it may lose its effect.

## Figurative Language

**Figurative language**, or *figures of speech*, refers to the specific techniques or forms of expression that speakers use to convey ideas or meaning. Although there are literally hundreds of kinds of figures of speech, we focus on four of the most commonly used—*anaphora*, *antithesis*, *simile*, and *metaphor*.[7]

**Anaphora.** **Anaphora**—the repetition of a word or phrase at the beginning of successive phrases, clauses, or sentences—is used to achieve emphasis and clarity, as well as a rhetorical sense of style. For example, in a special-occasion speech known as a *eulogy*, a surviving relative of someone who was recently deceased said the following:

> *Allen is watching over us* now, listening to me give a speech I wish I never had to give. And so it will go for everyone. *Allen is watching over us* as we drive his youngest daughter to school every morning. *Allen is watching over us* as we face the uncertainty of continuing to run the business he built.

Here, the repetition of "Allen is watching over us" allows the speaker to imply that the deceased is not really gone and that those who grieve for his loss can be consoled by the suggestion of his continued presence.

**Antithesis.** Speakers may occasionally wish to compare or contrast topics in a speech, even if they know in advance how they would like their audience to resolve the points in conflict. When speakers do this, they are employing **antithesis**—clauses set in opposition to one another, usually to distinguish between choices, concepts, and ideas.[8]

For example, a student named Stephen employed antithesis to persuade people to invest in solar power:

> Do we want to go forward or backward? Live in the future or be stuck in the past? Continue to be dependent on oil from other countries or invest in safe, free sunshine right here to meet many of our electricity and power needs?

Here, Stephen contrasts "forward" and "future" with "backward" and "stuck in the past." He wants his audience to choose "safe, free sunshine" over being "dependent on oil from other countries."

**Similes and Metaphors.** Similes and metaphors suggest similarities between objects that are not alike. A **simile** makes explicit comparisons and contains the words *like* or *as*. Examples include "His mind works *like an adding machine*" and "The baby's crying was *as sweet as music* to their ears."

A **metaphor** makes implicit comparisons of unlike objects by identifying one object with the other. The comparisons, however, are not meant to be taken literally.[9] For example, the phrase "innovation is the engine that drives our economy" doesn't mean that innovation is an actual engine.

Similes and metaphors can add color, vividness, and imagery to your speech and they can help your audience understand one idea through its reference to another. Metaphors can also help listeners experience a new idea "in terms that resonate with their past experience."[10]

When you use these devices, be sure to use clear and consistent terms so that the images make sense. Mixed metaphors—such as "it's not rocket surgery" or "he nailed that one out of the park"—can conjure images that either don't make sense or are unintentionally funny. Further, overly complicated metaphors can become tiresome in a speech.

# CHOOSING RESPECTFUL AND UNBIASED LANGUAGE

When you use respectful language in your speeches—words, phrases, and expressions that are courteous and don't reflect bias against other cultures or individuals—you deliver far more effective presentations. Why? Your audience members remain open to your ideas and view you as trustworthy and fair. In this way, you gain immense personal credibility.

By contrast, using **biased language**—word choices that suggest prejudice or preconceptions about other people—erodes your credibility and
distracts your audience from listening to your message. For these reasons,
avoid language that suggests you're making judgments about your listeners'
or someone else's personal characteristics, including race, ethnicity, gender,
sexuality, religion, or mental or physical ability. In the rest of this section, we
present ideas for respecting the audience and keeping biased language out of
your speech.

## Use Respectful Language

As a speaker, consider whether are you speaking to your audience (or audiences
plural) in ways that acknowledge their heritage, as well their presence and contributions in a diverse society. Similarly, is your choice of words inclusive? Does
the language you use make connections with most or all of your individual audience members and make them feel like they are part of the greater audience as
a whole?

Here is an example of how civil rights activist Angela Davis used language
to connect with the diverse groups in her audience at the Women's March on
Washington, D.C. in 2017:

> [W]e the hundreds of thousands, the millions of women, trans-people, men
> and youth who are here at the Women's March, we represent the power-
> ful forces of change that are determined to prevent the dying cultures of
> racism, hetero-patriarchy from rising again. . . . [W]e follow the lead of
> the first peoples who despite massive genocidal violence have never relin-
> quished the struggle for land, water, culture, their people.[11]

## Avoid Stereotypes

A **stereotype** is a generalization based on the false assumption that characteristics displayed by some members of a group are shared by all members of that
group. Stereotypes are often based on ethnicity, race, gender, religious beliefs,
or sexual orientation. But stereotypes can also be based on people's economic
backgrounds, the schools they attended, the regions they come from—even
their appearance or musical taste. Stereotypes are a form of biased language that
put a speaker's credibility at risk.

Stereotyping can come into play when speakers make claims beyond the
facts that their evidence proves—that is, by generalizing about their topic.
Suppose a presenter claims that people who received jobs through affirmative action policies didn't have the skills or experience required for those
jobs, but includes no credible evidence to support this claim. The presenter
would be making a claim without proof and thus perpetuating a negative
and false stereotype about persons who have received affirmative action
opportunities.

## Use Gender-Neutral References

Experts in grammar recommended using the generic *he* as early as 1553, and by 1850, this preference was legally supported (*he* was said to stand for *he* and *she*).[12] By the 1970s, however, modern linguists began questioning whether the generic use of masculine pronouns was reinforcing gender-based stereotypes. As a result, it became increasingly common to use "he or she" when referring to the holder of a job or title as a way to acknowledge that the position was not limited to men. For example, a speaker could say "after finishing medical school, a new doctor should be ready to work long hours while he or she completes a residency." For the first five editions of this textbook, the authors used "he or she" in exactly this way.

But language is a dynamic, evolving system of communication, which means that the meaning and usage of words changes over time—including how society approaches gendered terminology. Today, the word *they* (along with *their* and *them*) is increasingly being used as a *singular* way to refer to an individual person, not just a *plural* way to reference multiple persons.[13] (Interestingly, this is not exclusively a twenty-first century trend; authors such as Shakespeare and Jane Austen used *they* to refer to a singular person too![14]) As a result, a speaker could now say "after finishing medical school, a new doctor should be ready to work long hours while *they* complete a residency."

▼ **Respecting Gender Identity.** Standing in line at the DMV is not usually an experience to be treasured. However, Nic Sakurai wore this pin when they left home at 4:24 a.m. so they could be the first person in line to obtain Washington, D.C.'s new gender-neutral driver's license. The Washington Post/Getty Images

Why the change? As we discussed in Chapter 1, persons who identify as nonbinary do not identify exclusively as male or female, so the phrase "he or she" excludes them, just as the generic "he" excluded all who were not male. Using a more inclusive word like "they" is important because the choice of terms that a speaker uses when referring to gender is not just a matter of complying with pesky grammar rules: The words speakers use have real consequences. A study by professors Margit Tavits and Efrén Pérez found that the use of nonbinary pronouns "is associated with individuals expressing less bias in favor of traditional gender roles and categories, as reflected in more favorable attitudes toward women and LGBT individuals in public life."[15]

Using "they" as a singular word is becoming more common, but it is not the only way to avoid gendered terminology. Another way of dealing with gender specific language is to replace a gendered word with a **gender-neutral term**—a word that does not suggest a particular gender. For example, you could swap out *woman* for *person* or *husband* for *partner*.[16] You could also replace gender-specific nouns or noun phrases such as *poetess*, *chairman*, *congressman*, *cleaning lady*, and *fireman* with comparable gender-neutral terms such as *poet*, *chair*, *representative*, *cleaner*, and *firefighter*. Using plurals where appropriate can also help: "Good *presidents* keep *their* meetings organized, listen to *their* employees, and put *their* company's needs first."

## Make Appropriate References to Ethnic Groups

To show respect for your audience, use the noun or phrase that people in a particular ethnic group prefer when you refer to that group. Also keep in mind that sometimes people from a group may use more than one name to refer to themselves—for example, *Latino/Latina/Latinx* and *Chicano/Chicana* or a name derived from their country of origin—and that people in the same group don't always use the same name. If you are uncertain about which term to use in a particular case, ask the person you will be referring to how they identify; or, if referring to a public figure, try to research the term they prefer.

When ethnicity is relevant to your speech, be sure to refer to ethnic groups correctly. Not all people from Laos are Hmong, a visiting professor from Nigeria is not African American, and people from Puerto Rico or Spain are not Mexican Americans. Moreover, when a word comes from a language that uses different masculine and feminine forms, you'll want to pay attention to those forms (keeping in mind that, as with English, there are initiatives to employ gender-neutral words in these languages as well). For example, author Ana Castillo is a *Chicana*, not a *Chicano*. Attentiveness to such distinctions during a speech will pay big dividends in the form of appreciation from your listeners.

## Steer Clear of Unnecessary References to Ethnicity, Religion, Gender, or Sexuality

When a personal characteristic such as someone's ethnicity, religion, gender, or sexuality is not relevant to a point you are making, there's no need to mention it in your speech—in fact, doing so can hurt your credibility, because it makes people wonder why you are calling attention to this characteristic if there is no clear reason to do so. For instance, if you say "the *male* first-grade teacher," listeners may believe that you find it odd for a man to be a first-grade teacher. Of course, that doesn't mean that you can never reference personal characteristics in a speech. If you are delivering an informative speech about baseball great Jackie Robinson, for example, you would probably want to refer to his heritage. Why? Robinson was subjected to many forms of racism and broke the "color barrier" in Major League Baseball when he joined the Brooklyn Dodgers in 1947. His enduring legacy stems just as much from his experiences as a Black American as it does from his talent as a ballplayer. Thus, it would be appropriate and even necessary to acknowledge his race during that speech.

UNNECESSARY REFERENCE

Hank Greenberg, the Jewish first baseman, played on the Tigers from 1930 to 1946.

NEUTRAL REFERENCE

Hank Greenberg, the big-hitting first baseman, played on the Tigers from 1930 to 1946.

USEFUL REFERENCE

Hank Greenberg was a principled man who took his Judaism seriously. In 1934, he refused to play on Yom Kippur, even though the Tigers were fighting for the American League Pennant.

## SPEECH CHOICES

### A CASE STUDY: *RAFAELA*

*Let's see what choices Rafaela is making about language and style.*

As Rafaela worked on her speech, she focused on how to tell . the stories of women who had run for political office. She wondered if these stories might be best characterized as personal journeys—she could outline the women's experiences and identify ways that elections had impacted them. Rafaela planned to incorporate vivid language, in order to bring the stories to life.

She wrote out several stories in her own words, using specific words and phrases that would engage the senses. One of the stories she focused on was a description of Khemarey Khoeun, a young Cambodian woman who had come to the United States in 1981, after her family fled the Khmer Rouge genocide. With illustrative language and careful word choice, Rafaela described the conditions in Cambodia that Khemarey's family had been fortunate to escape. She described a society in which ethnic and religious minorities were targeted for displacement and eventually for murder. Using words like "brutal" and "inhuman," she described what have been called "the killing fields"—plots of land in which more than a million bodies of victims had been buried. With chilling frankness, Rafaela acknowledged that Khemarey would likely have perished if she had stayed in Cambodia during this period of genocide. Rafaela then contrasted that beginning to Khemarey's life in suburban Chicago, where many different and distinct immigrant populations lived and were welcomed. She described how Khemarey found her political voice thirty-six years after coming to this country and became park district commissioner for Skokie, Illinois. Rafaela decided to add that she was certain Khemarey would seek further public service in the future.

In these ways, Rafaela hoped to paint a strong and moving image of Khemarey, her family's harrowing journey, and her continuing journey as an elected official. She wasn't sure every detail she wrote down would make it into her final speech, but she was pleased with the result of her work.

 **YOUR TURN**

Now that you've seen how Rafaela's language and style choices influenced her speech, consider choices you'll make for a speech of your own. Making speech choices involves asking and answering a series of questions related to your assignment. For language and style, your questions might include:

- Am I using words that the audience will understand or defining any unfamiliar terms?

- Have I included a variety of strategies (e.g., repetition, vivid language, and figurative language) to express my ideas in a compelling manner?

- Am I using gender neutral references and making appropriate references to ethnic groups?

Making thoughtful choices in response to questions like these will help you select language that makes your speech come alive.

# CHAPTER REVIEW

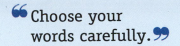 **Choose your words carefully.** Word choice can make or break the effectiveness of your speech. In this chapter, we explained how to use language to clarify your message, captivate your audience, and enhance your credibility. Key concepts included understanding the differences between written and oral language, as well as understanding denotative and connotative meanings of words and evoking those meanings strategically. We also offered ideas for presenting your message clearly—such as using understandable language and concrete words, employing words accurately, and adopting concise language. In addition, we suggested several devices you can use to infuse your speech with color and evocative imagery: repetition, hypothetical examples, personal anecdotes, vivid language, and various forms of figurative language. Finally, we addressed the importance of using unbiased language to show respect for your listeners. Suggestions on this front include avoiding stereotypes; using gender-neutral references; referring to ethnic groups appropriately; and avoiding references to personal characteristics such as ethnicity, religion, gender, or sexuality that are irrelevant to a point you're making.

## Key Terms

word choice (diction) *284*

denotative meaning *288*

connotative meaning *288*

jargon *290*

concrete word *291*

abstract word *291*

verbal clutter *295*

hypothetical example *297*

vivid language *299*

imagery *300*

figurative language *300*

anaphora *300*

antithesis *300*

simile *301*

metaphor *301*

biased language *302*

stereotype *302*

gender-neutral term *304*

## Review Questions

1. How does a speaker's choice of words affect credibility?
2. Describe three ways in which oral language differs from written language.
3. Define *denotative meaning* and *connotative meaning*, and describe the differences between the two.
4. What four qualities ensure clear language?
5. Describe five tools you can use to express your ideas more effectively.

6. Explain four steps you can take to ensure that the language you use is unbiased and respectful.

## Critical Thinking Questions

1. Think of a topic you might describe at fifty feet. How might you describe or explain the same topic at five thousand feet?
2. Is the dictionary your only tool for checking that you understand a word's meaning and have used it properly? How else can you assess connotative meanings that might be associated with a particular word?
3. When is it appropriate to use the rhetorical figure of speech known as antithesis? What advantages does it offer a speaker? How would you use it?
4. When people discuss political issues or candidates on social media, the language they use is often misleading or biased, and they often use harsh words criticizing people whose views differ from their own. Does the format for interaction on social media encourage this intense word choice? Why or why not?
5. Are words like *fireman* and *cleaning lady* merely offensive to some people, or are they inaccurate? Are there any words that would offend you if they came up in a speech? How would you make sure that the language you use is not offensive to audience members?

## Activities

1. Consider three examples of current political jargon: astroturfing, dark horse, and gaslighting. Try explaining these terms in ways that make them understandable to other people.
2. Open a dictionary at random, and try to find a particularly long entry. How many different meanings are listed for the word you found? How do the meanings vary? Can you think of any connotative meanings not listed in the definition?
3. Find a news article that references a relatively complicated study, a piece of legislation, or a reputable survey. Compare the news article with the original item (which you can usually find through a web link or search). How different is the language presented in each? What choices has the news writer made in deciphering the study, legislation, or survey for a more general audience?
4. Find a news article that discusses the language that Vladimir Putin of Russia used in an attempt to justify his invasion of Ukraine. Identify any words and phrases that were used in a misleading or biased way.

5. Select a political issue such as immigration, abortion rights, or climate change. Find a news article that discusses the issue, as well as a social media post that discusses the same issue. Compare the use of language in these two different channels of communication.

6. Think about a funny and engaging story that you enjoy telling about yourself or your family. How might you use such a story (or anecdote) to illustrate a point in a speech? What kinds of topics might your story lend itself to?

# DELIVERING YOUR SPEECH

> " How you say something is often as important as what you say. "

Roberta, an expert on finding ways to develop more affordable housing, delivered a presentation at the invitation of a local city council; it was a speech based upon an opinion column she had written for a local newspaper regarding ways to improve the city's inadequate housing supply. Roberta had researched and outlined her speech carefully and delivered it using visual aids—slides with charts and data indicating how much city government spending had been used to address homelessness. She also displayed emotionally compelling pictures of substandard housing in the city and places where unhoused people had constructed shelters.

Despite Roberta's preparation, the speech did not go well. Audience members fidgeted, yawned, and checked their phones. Few people were paying attention even though she had many important facts to share. The reason that Roberta's speech was unsuccessful was because of her **delivery**—the combination of verbal and nonverbal communication skills used to present her speech. She had spoken too fast and used a monotone voice. She also read her speech, rarely looking at the audience. Thus, she was unaware that people were tuning out her presentation.

---

◄ **Delivery Is Important.** When speaking in public, excellent delivery skills are a key to a successful presentation. filadendron/Getty Images

Roberta's experience reveals a major lesson for all public speakers: how you say something can be as important as what you say. Why is effective delivery crucial in public speaking? It helps make your speech compelling and memorable. In an age when audience  members may be easily distracted by their many responsibilities, even the most carefully researched and clearly organized talk may not be enough to hold their attention. Speakers today need every advantage they can get to capture—and hold onto—their listeners' interest. Skillful delivery gives you that edge. Think about it: in your lifetime, you may have listened to dozens or even hundreds of speeches. Of these, how many did you find truly memorable? And what made them outstanding? If you're like most people, the best speech you've ever heard not only contained valuable ideas but was also delivered in a way that held your attention and had you remembering the speech long after it was over.

In fact, delivery is what comes to mind for most people when they think about speechmaking. Although audience analysis, research, preparation, and practice play vital roles in public speaking, *how* you deliver your speech also determines whether you'll be effective with your audience members. In this chapter, we discuss speech delivery—focusing on the various ways you can present a speech as well as the verbal and nonverbal skills you need to deliver a powerful, evocative, and exciting presentation.

## SELECTING THE RIGHT MODE OF DELIVERY

Imagine yourself standing before an audience as you prepare to make an address. How will you actually deliver your speech? Will you read from a manuscript? Recite from text you've memorized? Speak while referencing an outline?

In most classroom settings, as well as many settings outside class, speaking *extemporaneously* from an outline (meaning you write a detailed outline ahead of time, learn the material in the outline, and then speak spontaneously in the presentation with only your speaking outline available for reference) will allow you to achieve the best possible results. This delivery mode enables you to adopt an authentic, conversational style that audiences appreciate. Yet there are also certain situations in which you may want to read from a manuscript or recite your speech word-for-word, from memory. We examine each of these three delivery modes in turn, beginning with reading from a manuscript.

### Reading from a Manuscript

In this delivery mode, you give your speech by reading directly from a **script**—a typed or handwritten document containing the entire text of your speech. If you follow this approach, you typically do not deviate from your script or improvise as you read.

Although most people using this delivery mode read from a printed script, it has become increasingly popular for speakers to use teleprompter devices when addressing large audiences. From the audience's perspective, teleprompters are clear, appearing as small glass screens around the speaker; from the speaker's perspective, however, they display lines of text, which advance in time with the speech. Having more than one teleprompter allows a speaker to appear to shift their gaze toward different parts of the audience while continuing to read the text from the teleprompter. Although these devices might seem ubiquitous—they are used by television news anchors, politicians, presenters at award ceremonies, and so on—the necessary technology is not available in most public speaking situations. Thus, for the purposes of our discussion, reading from a script means reading from a printed or handwritten manuscript that the speaker holds in their hands.

Delivery from a script is most appropriate when speakers (or speechwriters) want or need to choose their words very carefully. The word-for-word manuscript delivery method ensures that listeners hear *exactly* what you want them to hear. For example, public speakers often use this mode of delivery

ONLY SPECIFIC, FORMAL SITUATIONS CALL FOR MANUSCRIPT DELIVERY

Dear valued customers,
As a father of two, I know nothing is more important than the safety of children.
Quality and safety have always taken highest priority at ACME PLASTIC ANIMALS INCORPORATED. It is therefore with great regret that I must announce the total recall of our GREAT WHITE SHARK, model number 884A. During the manufacturing process an error was made...

CEO

#884A
LACERATION HAZARD

in press conferences. Imagine a lawyer approaching the microphone to "make a statement" to the press about their client, a professional athlete accused of wrongdoing. The lawyer reads directly from a carefully prepared manuscript to ensure that their exact words are heard and reported in the news, with no deviations and no surprises. By closely controlling the message, they stand a better chance of controlling what journalists say about them or their client and therefore influencing public perception.

Still, reading from a script can have its disadvantages. To begin with, the script itself becomes a prop—something you can hide behind as you read. And as with other props, it can limit your eye contact with the audience.

In addition, when speakers use a script, they tend to speak with less vocal variety and may speed up their rate of delivery, rather than using their regular speaking voice. This can cause them to lose connection with the audience.

## Memorizing from a Manuscript

To recite a speech memorized from a script, you learn your script word-for-word and deliver it without looking at any text, notes, or outline. You behave like an actor on the stage, who memorizes dialogue and recites the words as part of a *performance*. When would you want to deliver a speech by memorizing from a script? Memorization is advisable only if you are called upon to deliver a precise message and are already trained to memorize a great deal of text and deliver it flawlessly.

This delivery mode does offer some advantages over reading from a script. There's no barrier between you and your audience, so you can be more attentive to the audience throughout the speech. It will be easier to make expressive gestures and present your visual aids. And, as when reading from a manuscript, you can control your word choice by repeating precisely what you've memorized. Memorization was a key feature of classical rhetorical training, but it is no longer considered the best form of speech preparation and delivery in most situations.

This mode of delivery has several distinct disadvantages. For one thing, memorized presentations often come across as slick and prepackaged, or "canned." Listeners may view the speech as a stale performance delivered the same way every time, regardless of the audience. As a result, they may take offense or lose interest.

...but then, the most famous line, one of the most famous lines in all of Shakespeare's plays, comes when Brutus...er... I mean Mark Antony addresses the, er... ...citizens... in the, er... Forum! He takes the pulpit and says: "Friends, Romans, countrymen, lend me your eyes..." Aaagh! I mean <u>ears!</u> Sorry!

This leads me to my next point which is... er.............. Um.......Aaaagh! Well... er..... ............................................. ...................Sorry!

ONE DOWNSIDE OF MEMORIZATION

Memorizing is also very challenging, especially with a long speech. And people who speak from memory are typically wedded to their text, which means the presentation can grind to a halt if the speaker forgets even a single word or sentence. This happens more times than one would expect.

Because this delivery mode's disadvantages outweigh its advantages, we recommend avoiding it unless you have a specific background in memorizing large bodies of text (as a trained actor, for example) *and* your speech situation requires it.

## Speaking from an Outline

In this mode of delivery—which is the preferred mode in most speech situations—you deliver your speech by referring to a brief outline you prepared in advance. Typically, you will want to prepare and practice first with a full-sentence detailed outline. Next, you'll want to condense the detailed outline into a briefer speaking outline (complete with delivery cues), recorded on sheets of paper, note cards, or an electronic device (for more information on outlines, see Chapter 11).

▼ **Benefits of an Outline.** When using an outline, speakers can look at the audience for most of the speech, but still have notes available for quick reference. alvarez/ Getty Images

You should be able to glance at this brief outline and instantly remember what you want to say. If you've made your notes easy to read (for example, by using large print and sufficient space between lines), you can maintain eye contact with your audience. Using this brief outline to deliver your speech will enable you to speak extemporaneously.

Speaking from an outline offers the best aspects of reading from a script and memorizing your speech while avoiding the previously mentioned disadvantages. You can glance at the outline just long enough to spur your memory, so there's no barrier between you and your audience, and your eye contact does not suffer. Also, you don't have to worry about forgetting your place because the outline is at hand to remind you.

Equally important, when you speak from an outline, your delivery becomes more *conversational*. You sound as if you are talking with your listeners instead of reading a speech *to* and *at* them. Finally, with this delivery mode, you choose your words flexibly, so you can adapt your message as needed to the audience at hand. For instance, if you notice that a listener looks confused, you can backtrack and provide further explanation for the point you're discussing.

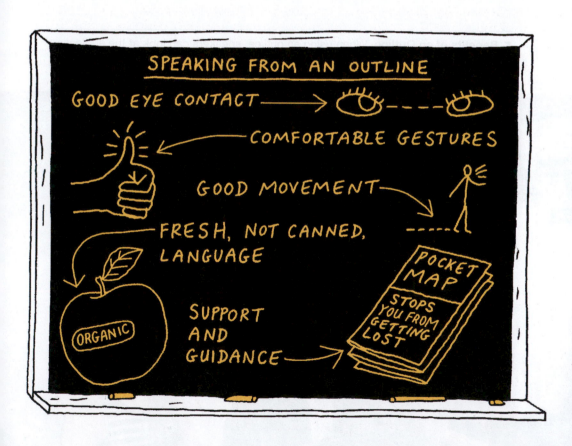

Of course, speakers need to practice delivering from their outlines to give the best possible presentation. This practice is also beneficial in another way: research indicates that practice and preparation can lessen the anxiety that speakers feel when it's time to present.[1]

## Impromptu Speaking

In some situations, you may be called on to speak unexpectedly. **Impromptu delivery** means that you are generating your speech content in the moment, without time to prepare in advance. These kinds of speeches are both quite common and very challenging for inexperienced speakers. They occur regularly in a variety of situations: for example, you might be called upon to speak at a meeting at the last minute, to comment in a class, or to offer a spur-of-the-moment toast at a wedding or party. You also use impromptu delivery when fielding unexpected questions after a presentation.

Although such situations can seem terrifying for new speakers, it is possible to handle them effectively as long as you follow a few simple guidelines for impromptu delivery. One key is to remember that even in a spontaneous speaking situation, you can still present from a mental outline that you draft quickly and keep in your mind, just as you would with a physical outline in an extemporaneous situation. (Or if you have a few moments to collect yourself, you might try to jot down your main points.) You can pull together a mental outline by quickly asking yourself the following questions:

- *What is the question or topic?* Begin by thinking carefully about the precise nature of the question or topic you have been asked to address. In speech parlance, this is sometimes referred to as *thinking about the call of the question/topic*. Ask yourself, "What is the specific topic to speak about? What is the specific question to answer?" Be precise here.

- *What is my answer or view?* As you are developing a mental outline, consider what you think about the topic or what you think the answer to the question might be.

- *How do I support my position?* Consider the reasons or facts that support your view or your answer.

Your answers to these questions should quickly yield a precise thesis or topic statement that also serves as a preview of the organization and body of the speech. This entire process can occur in a matter of seconds.

Because this is an impromptu speech, people will not expect a carefully prepared introduction; thus, a direct one will suffice (for example, "I'm delighted to tell you what our division has been developing this year"). Your conclusion need only summarize your points and restate your position (for example, "So that's what we've been working on this year. I hope you're all as excited about these new products as we are").

IMPROMPTU SPEAKING

## USING VERBAL DELIVERY SKILLS

To deliver a successful speech, you need to consider more than just your mode of delivery; you also need to draw on a variety of speaking skills, both verbal and nonverbal. In this section, we examine the importance of **verbal delivery skills**—all the ways you effectively use your voice when delivering a speech. Developing verbal delivery skills involves careful consideration of the use of *volume*, *tone*, *rate of delivery*, *projection*, *articulation*, *pronunciation*, and *pausing*.

### Volume

**Volume** refers to how loud or soft your voice is as you deliver a speech. Some speakers are not audible enough and others are too audible. A guiding rule for volume is to be loud enough that everyone in your audience can hear you but not so loud as to drive away the listeners positioned closest to you.

The biggest challenge for many presenters is speaking loudly enough to be heard. Because audience members don't have the option of "turning up the volume" if you're delivering your speech in person, you will need to provide that volume yourself when no microphone is available. If you speak too softly and don't project enough, your listeners will have trouble hearing you. They may even see you as timid or uncertain—which could damage your credibility.

Yet speaking too loudly is also problematic. For example, a student named Samuel once gave an informative presentation in one of our classes. During his speech, many listeners in the front row began leaning back in their chairs. For the students sitting in the first two rows, Samuel was speaking so loudly that they were trying to put some distance between themselves and him.

When you begin preparing your delivery, think about your volume level. How loud is your regular speaking voice? If you aren't certain, ask some friends or relatives to give you an assessment. Then consider your audience for the speech presentation, as well as your speaking forum. How will the size of the audience or the room affect you? Will you be using any audio aids, like a microphone? What if you are delivering your speech online? Finally, focus on visual

▼ **Presenting the Message with Volume.** When Robert Walley, a Navajo World War II Code Talker, couldn't speak loudly to the troops he was addressing, he found a creative way to produce volume: He would whisper to his grandson, a member of the company, who would then project the message. Steven Clevenger/Getty Images

cues from your audience while delivering your speech to help you determine whether your volume level is appropriate, and adjust your volume as needed.

## Tone

The **tone** of your delivery refers to sound of your speaking voice. This includes **pitch**—how high or low your voice is. If you can mix high and low tones and achieve some tonal variety, you'll add warmth and color to your presentation. By contrast, if you speak without vocal variety (speaking in a **monotone**), audience members may have a more difficult time focusing on your speech. Tone also includes the use of your voice to express emotions, such as happiness, determination, or uncertainty.

How much tonal variety should you aim for to make your voice interesting and enticing? Follow this guiding rule: use enough tonal variety to add warmth, intensity, and enthusiasm to your voice but not so much that you sound like an adolescent whose voice is cracking. As you practice your speech, try dropping your pitch in some places and raising it in others. If you're not sure whether you're achieving enough tonal variety, practice in front of a trusted friend, family member, classmate, or colleague, and solicit their feedback.

Additionally, consider using *inflection*—raising or lowering your pitch—to emphasize certain words or expressions. For instance, try a lower pitch to convey the seriousness of an idea, or end on a higher pitch if you are posing a question. Like italics on a printed page, inflection draws attention to the words or expressions you want your audience to notice and remember.

TONAL VARIETY ADDS WARMTH AND COLOR

HIGH  MEDIUM  LOW

## Rate of Delivery

Your **rate of delivery** refers to how quickly or slowly you speak during a presentation. As with other verbal delivery skills, going to one extreme or another (in this case, speaking too quickly or too slowly) can hurt your delivery.

Consider the example of Lou, a college student who had a very slow rate of delivery. While giving a presentation during a seminar on music theory, he noticed that many students (as well as the teacher) seemed inattentive. In addition, those listeners who *were* paying attention began interrupting him— not with questions about the content of his speech but with queries about his next point. Clearly, they were trying to move him along, which probably meant they were irritated and distracted by Lou's slowness in expressing his main ideas.

Do you fall into the "slow speaker" category? Do people tend to finish your sentences for you—either during conversations or while you're delivering a public address? Although people who try to finish your statements may seem rude, their behavior sends an important signal that you can learn from: you likely

need to increase your rate of delivery. Fail to catch that signal and you risk losing your audience's interest and appreciation.

Swinging to the other extreme—talking too fast—presents the opposite problem. Overly fast talkers tend to run their words together, particularly at the ends of sentences, which prevents their audiences from tracking what they're saying. Listeners often have a difficult time in this situation—not because they are disinterested or impatient but simply because they cannot comprehend what is being said. In the worst-case scenario, potentially interested audience members may transform into defeated listeners because of a fast talker's verbal onslaught (see Chapter 4, Listening Skills).

The guiding rule for achieving an appropriate rate of delivery is this: speak fast enough to keep your presentation lively and interesting but not so fast that you become inarticulate. You can also practice your speech in front of a friend or relative and ask for feedback about your rate of delivery. Finally, resist any temptation to speed up your delivery to fit an overly long speech into the allocated time. Instead, shorten the content of the presentation.

▼ **Posture Aids Projection.** Take a tip from performers. When you have a good speaking posture, it is easier to project your voice to the audience. Bruce Glikas/ Getty Images

## Projection

Have you ever observed someone singing without a microphone and wondered how the person's voice managed to reach people near *and* far? What about actors on a stage who speak their lines quietly yet can still be heard by everyone in the theater? These individuals use **projection**—"booming" their voices across a forum to reach all audience members.

To project, use the air you exhale from your lungs to carry the sound of your voice across the room or auditorium. Projection is all about the mechanics of breathing. To send your voice clearly across a large space, first maintain good posture: sit or stand up straight if you're able to do so, with your shoulders back and your head at a neutral position (not too far forward or back). Also, exhale from your diaphragm—that sheet of muscle just below your rib cage—to push your breath away from you.

## Articulation

**Articulation** refers to the crispness or clarity of your spoken words. When you articulate, your vowels and consonants sound clear and distinct, and your listeners can distinguish each of your words as well as the syllables in your words. The result? Your audience can easily understand what you're saying.

Articulation problems are most common when nervousness increases a speaker's rate of delivery or when a speaker is being inattentive. Whatever the cause of your articulation issues, focus on this rule to get better results: when you deliver a speech, do your best to clearly and distinctly express all parts of the words in your presentation, and make sure not to round off the ends of words or lower your voice at the ends of sentences.

ARTICULATION

## Pronunciation

**Pronunciation** refers to saying words as they typically sound in the language or dialect of your speech. Are you saying them in a way that your audience will understand? If you pronounce unfamiliar words or technical terms incorrectly, your listeners may have difficulty grasping your meaning. Equally troublesome, they may question your credibility.

Elizabeth, a banking professional, related the following story about the problems that can arise when a speaker mispronounces words:

> In my job, I was required to work with lawyers because they drew up the trust documents for their clients. I worked with lawyers, but I was no lawyer myself. Sometimes they can be a little arrogant about their position, thinking that if you didn't go to law school, you shouldn't be working in a law-related field. I worked hard to earn their respect. But I noticed that when I used some legal terms in front of them, they occasionally looked at one another and smiled, as though they were sharing a private joke. One such word was *testator*. That's the person who creates a testament like a trust or a will. Whenever I used that word, I always said "TES-tah-tore," so that it sounded like it would rhyme with *matador*. And the lawyers would smirk—but nobody ever corrected me. Eventually, I was embarrassed to learn that the word is pronounced "tes-TAY-ter."

USE CARE PRONOUNCING UNFAMILIAR WORDS OR TECHNICAL TERMS

How can you ensure that your pronunciation is accurate? The guideline here is simple: if you're not certain how to pronounce a word or a name you want to use in your speech, find out how to say it *before* you deliver your presentation. For names of public figures, search for radio or television interviews with the subject to find out the preferred pronunciation. For other words, you can ask for guidance from instructors, classmates, coworkers, or friends who might be familiar with the term. Better still, refer to a reputable dictionary, which will provide phonetic spellings for each word as well as a general guide to pronunciation. Many online dictionaries and other resources provide useful audio clips that demonstrate pronunciation.[2]

## Pausing

Used skillfully, **pausing**—leaving gaps between words or sentences in a speech—provides you with some significant advantages. Besides enabling you to collect your thoughts, it reinforces the seriousness of your subject because it shows that you're choosing your words carefully. Pausing can help you create a sense of importance as well. If you make a statement and then pause for the audience to weigh your words, your listeners may conclude that you've just said something especially important.

To get the most from pausing, use it judiciously, pausing every so often rather than after every sentence. Otherwise, your listeners may wonder if you're having repeated difficulty collecting your thoughts, or they may think you're being melodramatic. In either case, your audience could begin to take you less seriously.

When pausing during a speech, it's best to fill those pauses with silence rather than with verbal fillers or verbal tics. A **verbal filler** is a word or phrase, such as *like* or *you know*, that speakers use to fill uncomfortable silences. Here's an example of what verbal fillers do to a speaker's delivery:

> *And so*, the library was closed . . . *you know*. But I had to study somewhere. *But* . . . I didn't get to study there, *and* . . . *but* . . . I had to go somewhere . . . *but* . . . *and* . . . I tried the dorm reading room. *And, like* . . . it was so quiet there, *you know*?

In the context of public speaking, a **verbal tic** is a sound, such as *um* or *ah*, that speakers use when searching for a correct word or when they have lost their train of thought:

> *Um* . . . the purpose of my speech is . . . *ah*, to . . . *um* . . . make you see how . . . *um* . . . dangerous this action . . . *ah* . . . really is.

Everyone uses verbal fillers or tics at some point while giving speeches: it's hard *not* to. But using them too often can distract your listeners or make them wonder if you're tentative or ill-prepared. The best way to avoid overusing fillers and tics is by learning to be more aware of when you use them.

How? Try speaking in front of a friend who is holding a clicker or some other low-level noisemaker; have your friend use the noisemaker every time you use a verbal filler or tic. If you want to hear yourself speak, ask a friend to record you or record yourself with your smartphone—so you can hear the fillers and tics for yourself. At first you may be surprised by how often you use them, but with some practice, you will develop better awareness and better habits.

## USING NONVERBAL DELIVERY SKILLS

In addition to verbal delivery, you will need to consider your nonverbal behavior as part of the delivery of your speech. **Nonverbal delivery skills** involve the

▲ **Nonverbal Delivery Skills.** Nonverbal behaviors enhance the presentation. Here, X González remains silent for six minutes and twenty seconds to symbolize the time it took for their seventeen classmates to be slain at Marjory Stoneman Douglas High School. And Jury President Spike Lee gestures to emphasize a point at the opening ceremony of the 2021 Cannes Film Festival. His suit drew raves from GQ and by using a portable mic, he was able to move around the stage.
(left) Chip Somodevilla/Getty Images; (right) VALERY HACHE/Getty Images

use of physical behaviors to deliver a speech. In this section, we discuss how specific elements of nonverbal delivery—*eye contact*, *gestures*, *physical movement*, *proxemics*, and *personal appearance*—can help you connect with your audience and leave a lasting impression.

One note to consider as you read: the suggestions included in this section are guidelines that speakers should ordinarily follow if they are able. At the same time, it may not be possible for every person to follow every guideline—for example, there may be speakers or audience members who refrain from making eye contact because they are on the autism spectrum (more on this below), or speakers with physical disabilities that affect their movement or gestures. A good rule of thumb: as a speaker, recognize that it's all right if there are principles of nonverbal delivery that you aren't able to follow, and as an audience member, do your best to understand that not every speaker will be able to implement every principle.

## Eye Contact

To understand what **eye contact** is, you may find it helpful to think first about what it is *not*. Eye contact is not you looking at your audience members while they look at something else. Nor is it audience members looking directly at you while you stare at your notes or gaze nervously at the ceiling for some divine guidance on what to say next. Rather, with true eye contact, you look directly into the eyes of your audience members, and they look directly into yours.

Eye contact enables you to gauge the audience's interest in your speech. By looking into your listeners' eyes, you can discern how they're feeling about the speech (fascinated? confused? upset?). Armed with these impressions, you can adapt your delivery if needed. For example, you could provide more details about a particular point if your listeners look fascinated and hungry for more, or you may want to reexplain a key point if your listeners look confused or overwhelmed.

Eye contact also helps you interact with your audience. By noticing, for example, that a particular listener seems eager to ask a question, you might be prompted to stop and take queries from the audience.

In addition, eye contact helps you compel your audience's attention. Father Paul, a wise Episcopalian priest, once shared the secret of his effective sermonizing technique: "When I speak, I look right at my congregation. And when I do that, I make them look at me, too. And it is harder not to listen to me when I do that . . . precisely because of that!"[3] When you and your audience establish eye contact, it becomes more difficult for listeners to look away or mentally drift as you're talking.

Finally, eye contact may also influence credibility. In Western cultures, many people consider a willingness to make eye contact evidence of a speaker's credibility—especially truthfulness. An old saying holds that "the eyes are the windows of the soul," meaning that our eyes can betray who we really are or what we really think or believe. Of course, just because someone makes eye contact does not mean that they are telling the truth, or vice versa. Nevertheless, as long as audience members believe that the eyes are the windows of the soul, it can help to make eye contact if you are able.

At the same time, however, be careful not to make assumptions about speakers or audience members who aren't making eye contact. In a number of world cultures, for example, eye contact isn't always a desired behavior during

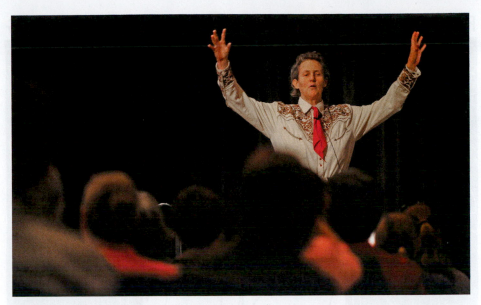

▲ **Advocating for People on the Spectrum.** Dr. Temple Grandin, a professor of animal sciences, is also a renowned advocate for the rights of people with autism. Here, she is giving the keynote speech at a conference on meeting the needs of students who are autistic. RJ Sangosti/Getty Images

communication interactions.[4] In addition, some people with Autism Spectrum Disorder indicate that when they look at others' eyes, it causes great stress—and may even burn.[5] Whether you are a speaker or an audience member, then, remember that someone who is not making eye contact could have a good reason not to do so.

As a speaker, how you use eye contact depends on the size of your audience. With small audiences, try to establish and sustain direct eye contact with each listener at various points in your speech. With large audiences, this may not be practical. Therefore, you'll need to use a technique called **panning**. To pan your audience, think of your body as a tripod and your head as a movie camera that sits atop the tripod. Imagine yourself "filming" everyone in the group by moving your "camera" slowly from one side of your audience to the other. With this technique, you gradually survey all audience members—pausing and establishing extended eye contact with an individual listener for a few moments before moving on to do the same with another listener.

Panning with extended eye contact gives your audience the sense that you're looking at each listener, even if you aren't. And it still enables you to gauge your audience members' interest, hold their attention, and interact with individual listeners if needed.

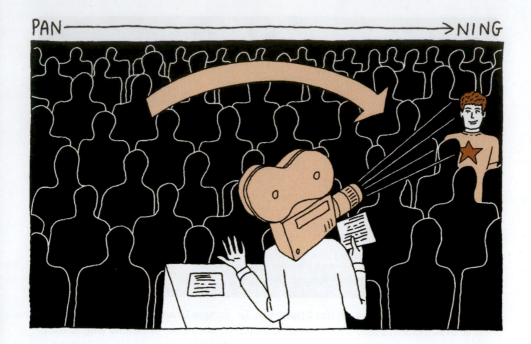

## Gestures

A **gesture** is a hand, head, or facial movement that emphasizes, pantomimes, demonstrates, or calls attention to something.[6] Gestures can add flair to your speech delivery, especially when they seem authentic rather than overly practiced.[7] Research also indicates that gestures can benefit a listener's ability to understand a speech's message.[8] The effectiveness of a gesture depends on how it links with the speech topic; gestures depicting physical actions communicate more than those depicting abstract topics. Hand gestures that link with speech content are called co-speech gestures (CSGs). CSGs communicate thoughts and ideas in two different ways—linguistically (through the words that are heard) and visually (through the gesture that is seen). Neuroimaging of the brain shows that when CSGs are used with speech, there is more activity in the parts of the brain involved with language processing, meaning that listeners understand and retain more.[9]

But gestures can also backfire. For one thing, not all your listeners will interpret the same gesture—be it a clenched fist, an open palm, a raised forefinger—in the same way.[10] For example, some people see a fist as a symbol of violence, whereas others consider it a show of forcefulness or determination. If an audience member interprets a particular gesture differently from what you intended, you may inadvertently send the wrong message to that person.

You should also be aware that gestures may communicate a message that is inconsistent with your verbal message. For example, some people criticized then-President Obama for wagging his index finger back and forth when he spoke. This gesture can work if the intention is to criticize or dismiss an individual or a group, but it risks making the speaker seem arrogant, overly pious, or condescending. Gestures like this can also reinforce negative perceptions that a particular audience may already have. For example, many of the former president's critics in Congress had felt that he was book smart but not experienced in the political realities of Washington, D.C., because he had served only four years in the U.S. Senate before being elected president. For them, the president's wagging finger may have reinforced the image of a professor lecturing them as if they were his students and not his political peers.

In addition to ensuring that your gestures reinforce your spoken message, it is good general practice to avoid using distracting gestures born of nervousness, such as stuffing your hands in your pockets; jingling keys or change in your pockets; or fiddling with a watch, ring, or pen. These behaviors can distract audience members to the point that they'll start focusing more on your gestures than on your speech. At the same time, however, some speakers use repetitive gestures and movements for specific reasons—for example, because they are on the autism spectrum and these acts help them cope with stressful situations.[11]

▼ **Using Gestures to Reinforce Your Message.** Tara Houska of the Couchiching First Nation uses expressive gestures during a speech about a pipeline route that would threaten food and water resources. Stephen Maturen/Getty Images

Speakers who need to use these behaviors should be accommodated and supported, rather than criticized.

To get the most from gestures, follow these guidelines if you are able:

- Use gestures deliberately to emphasize or illustrate points in your speech.
- Be aware that not all audience members may interpret your gestures in the same way.
- Make sure your gestures reinforce your spoken message.
- Avoid nervous, distracting gestures.

## Physical Movement

**Physical movement** describes how much or how little you move around while delivering a speech. Not surprisingly, standing still (sometimes referred to as the "tree trunk" approach) and shifting or walking restlessly from side to side or back and forth (pacing) in front of your audience are not usually effective. A motionless speaker may come across as tense or distant from the audience, and a restless one may take attention away from their message.

Instead of going to either of these extremes, strive to incorporate a reasonable amount and variety of physical movement as you give your presentation. Skillful use of physical movement injects energy into your delivery *and* signals transitions between parts of your speech. For example, when making an

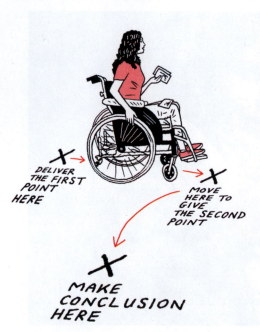

MOVEMENT EMPHASIZES TRANSITIONS AND ENGAGES LISTENERS

DELIVER THE FIRST POINT HERE

MOVE HERE TO GIVE THE SECOND POINT

MAKE CONCLUSION HERE

important point in your presentation, you can move a bit to the left, casually returning to your original spot when you shift to the next major idea. One useful tip is to combine moderate movement with the panning approach to eye contact, discussed earlier in this section.

How much physical movement is right for you? Move as much as is necessary to invigorate your speech but not so much that you confuse or distract your audience. You might feel more comfortable speaking from behind a lectern or podium, but it can act as a barrier between you and your listeners. Unless you need to stay at the lectern—for example, due to a physical disability or a fixed microphone—we recommend that you come out from behind it at least part of the time.

## Proxemics

**Proxemics**—the use of space and distance between yourself and your audience—is related to physical movement. Through proxemics, you control how close you are to your audience while delivering your speech.

The size and setup of the speech setting can help you determine how best to use proxemics. For example, in a large forum, you may want to come out from behind the podium and move closer to your audience so that listeners can see and hear you more easily. Moving toward your audience can also help you communicate intimacy; it suggests you're about to convey something personal, which many audience members will find compelling.[12] Research has shown that audiences not only perceive a strong association between closeness and intimacy but between closeness and attraction; they also perceive closeness as an indication of the immediacy/nonimmediacy of the speech message.[13] That is to say, audience members will be more likely to feel that the message enhances the connection between themselves and the speaker.

Of course, people have different feelings about physical proximity. Whereas some welcome a speaker's nearness, others consider it a violation of their personal space or even a threat. Culture can influence a person's response to a

# THE POETICS OF SPACE (AKA PROXEMICS)

speaker's proximity. In some cultures, physical closeness is considered essential to positive relationships; in others, it is considered offensive or invasive.[14]

To determine how much space to put between you and your listeners, consider your audience's background, the size and setup of your forum, and your ability to move around the forum. When speaking, move close enough to your listeners to interact with them and allow them to see and hear you but not so close that you violate anyone's sense of private space.

## Personal Appearance

By **personal appearance**, we refer to the impression you make on your audience through your clothing, jewelry, hairstyle, grooming, and other elements influencing how you look.[15] Personal appearance in a public speech matters for two reasons. First, many people in your audience will form their initial impression of you *before* you say anything—just by looking at you. Be sure your appearance communicates the right message. Second, studies show that this initial impression can be long lasting and very significant.[16]

The rule for personal appearance is to do what is appropriate for the audience you are addressing, given the occasion, the forum, and perhaps the topic of your speech. If you're eulogizing a friend and the audience is likely to be somber, you would strive for a more formal look. Conversely, if you're delivering a presentation to a potential client in an industry known for its relaxed and playful corporate culture, you may want to wear casual business attire.

▼ **Matching Attire to Topic.** NASA flight engineer Bobak Ferdowsi wears his NASA gear when speaking at a "Science of the Expanse" panel. Albert L. Ortega/Getty Images

## SPEECH CHOICES

### A CASE STUDY: *RAFAELA*

*Let's check back in with Rafaela to see what adjustments she made for her delivery.*

Rafaela had two speaking habits that she wanted to work on. For one thing, her tone of voice often rose at the end of a sentence, as though she were asking a question instead of making a declarative statement. This made Rafaela sound as if she were asking the audience whether she was right rather than telling them what she really thought or believed. She mentioned this to her instructor, who advised her to be confident in her own voice by being more assertive and ending her sentences in a lower tone. In addition, Rafaela knew that anxiety made her speak quietly, which in turn made it difficult for people to hear her.

To work on her tone and volume, Rafaela asked a friend to be her audience. At this point, Rafaela had already practiced her speech using her speaking outline, knew the material and the structure very well, and only occasionally had to glance at the outline for reference. When presenting the speech to her friend, Rafaela focused on using an extemporaneous delivery style. Because she knew the speech, she could also engage with her audience through sweeping (panning) eye contact (even though she had only one audience member for this practice run). Finally, she tried hard to speak at just the right volume: loudly enough to be heard easily, but not so loudly that it seemed like she was shouting. Afterward, her friend congratulated her on her interesting speech and warm delivery, which gave her confidence a nice boost.

 **YOUR TURN**

Now that you've seen how Rafaela's choices impacted her speech delivery practice, it's time to think about optimal delivery in a speech of your own. Making speech choices involves asking and answering a series of questions related to your assignment. Here are some important questions to ask as you work on delivering your speech:

- Which mode of delivery will I use for my speech?
- How will I use my speaking voice to connect with the audience?
- How will I use nonverbal delivery skills to enhance my message?
- How will I practice my speech to be sure that I am in command of my material and ready to speak effectively?

By making thoughtful choices in response to questions like these, you'll be sure to sharpen your speech delivery skills.

# CHAPTER REVIEW

> ❝ How you say something is often as important as what you say. ❞

As Roberta's story shows, how you deliver your speech and the verbal and nonverbal skills you use while making your presentation can spell the difference between success and failure. In this chapter, we shared the pros and cons of three modes of prepared delivery—reading from a manuscript, reciting from a memorized text, and speaking extemporaneously from an outline—and noted that extemporaneous delivery is preferred in most contemporary settings. For unprepared delivery, or impromptu speaking, we offered guidelines for coming up with a presentation on the spot. We also discussed the many different elements of verbal delivery—volume, tone, rate of delivery, projection, articulation, pronunciation, and pausing—and the ways that you can use them to create more effective speeches. Employing elements of nonverbal delivery—eye contact, gestures, physical movement, proxemics, and personal appearance—can further captivate and engage your audience. By applying the right delivery mode and the right blend of verbal and nonverbal skills, you can get your message across to your listeners—and leave them wanting more.

## Key Terms

delivery *311*
script *312*
impromptu delivery *317*
verbal delivery skills *318*
volume *318*
tone *320*
pitch *320*
monotone *320*
rate of delivery *321*
projection *323*
articulation *323*

pronunciation *324*
pausing *325*
verbal filler *325*
verbal tic *325*
nonverbal delivery skills *326*
eye contact *327*
panning *329*
gesture *330*
physical movement *332*
proxemics *333*
personal appearance *334*

## Review Questions

1. Describe four methods of speech delivery.
2. What are verbal delivery skills? Describe seven elements of verbal delivery discussed in the chapter.
3. Explain what is meant by nonverbal delivery. Describe five elements of nonverbal delivery discussed in the chapter.

## Critical Thinking Questions

1. What is the advantage of memorized delivery over other forms of delivery? What is its chief disadvantage? In what public speaking situations might memorization be appropriate for you?
2. What kinds of audience considerations should you take into account when making decisions about your nonverbal delivery? For example, how might gender, culture, age, and other factors affect the way particular gestures are perceived?
3. What hand gestures would you use in an informative speech that describes kitchen knives and techniques for chopping vegetables or making thin slices of tender meat? How would you use the visual imagery of co-speech gestures (CSGs) to enhance the literal meaning of your speech's words?

## Activities

1. Think back to the example of former President Obama's finger wagging in the section on gestures in this chapter. Come up with two speech topics for which this gesture would be appropriate. Now think of two speech topics for which this gesture would not be appropriate.
2. Without practicing, make a brief recording of yourself explaining a simple and familiar task—for example, providing directions for traveling from your home to campus. Then make another recording of yourself describing a less concrete concept, such as the musical qualities of a favorite song. Take note of how often you use verbal fillers and verbal tics in each case. Do you think you would have used them as often if you had prepared an outline and rehearsed? Try it, then compare your results.
3. Check out a few stand-up comedy performances on YouTube, Netflix, or some other streaming TV service. Take note of how the comics use nonverbal delivery skills—such as eye contact, panning techniques, and movement—to engage with their audience. Which comics are most effective at using nonverbal delivery skills? Why?

# USING
# PRESENTATION
# AIDS

# 14

❝Listening can lead to understanding; seeing can lead to believing.❞

Phil couldn't wait to deliver his speech about Harley-Davidson motorcycles to his class. The purpose of the speech was to inform his audience of the differences in quality between American motorcycles and those made in Japan and Germany. A longtime Harley owner, Phil felt that if audience members could *see* a Harley up close and *hear* the distinctive rumble of its engine, they would understand his point in a visceral way. But how could he provide this experience without driving his Harley into the classroom?

Phil considered other possibilities, such as playing a recording of a Harley engine being revved, showing enlarged photos of different Harley models, or playing some video footage from a recent motorcycle convention he'd attended. He knew that any of these presentation aids would help him convey the unique character and quality of Harley-Davidson bikes. But for him, they still weren't as potent as showing his listeners an actual motorcycle.

That night, Phil shared his concerns with his wife, Claire. She came up with a solution: she would park the family Harley outside the classroom's windows during Phil's talk. When the day of the speech arrived, Phil opened the window shades and invited his classmates to stand near him as he extolled the virtues of

◀ **You Have Many Options for Presentation Aids.** Sometimes, the actual object is the presentation aid that will best help the audience understand your message.

Europa Press News/Getty Images

Harley motorcycles. Outside, Claire pointed to various parts of the bike as he mentioned them. Phil's audience immediately grasped his passion for Harleys (not to mention his wife's love for him!). Through creative use of presentation aids—in this case, an actual bike and an assistant who focused his listeners' attention on various aspects of the machine—Phil was able to deliver an exceptionally engaging and interesting speech.

In this chapter, we take a close look at presentation aids, examining their advantages, the many different forms they can take, and strategies for using them effectively.

## WHY USE PRESENTATION AIDS?

Speech communication experts have long believed that listeners are much more likely to grasp spoken facts and concepts if presenters also provide visual and other nonverbal cues.[1] As early as the 1950s, studies showed that the use of audio and visual aids in a speech could increase learning by as much as 55 percent.[2] Today, teachers recognize that aids help students learn the course material.[3] Studies show that aids enhance learning for both inexperienced audience members and those who are experienced and knowledgeable about the subject matter.[4] Recent studies also indicate that picture-based teaching is useful for enhancing the student learning experience.[5]

A **presentation aid** is anything beyond your spoken words that you employ to help your audience members understand and remember your message. Also known as *audiovisual aids*, presentation aids include any materials you might use to support and convey the points and subpoints in your speech. Consider your own learning experiences over the years. For example, how did you come to understand difficult math concepts? Did your teacher expect you to know how to solve complex problems after merely lecturing to you about algebra or geometry? Or did she *illustrate* the problems and concepts on the chalkboard—with plenty of examples? Most likely, you found the illustrations helpful and even essential for grasping the concepts. Likewise, if you studied a language not native to you, did your teacher merely lecture to you about the language in your native tongue? Or did the teacher model the language for you, demonstrating correct pronunciation and perhaps playing recordings of native speakers using the language? Again, you probably found the demonstrations and recordings crucial for mastering the basics of the new language.

Savvy use of presentation aids can help you gain several important advantages as you deliver a speech.

## Presentation Aids Can Make Your Speech More Interesting

A colorful and attractive presentation aid can help you spice up any presentation, especially one on a slightly dry topic. For instance, a financial-services salesperson giving a talk on retirement savings might display a photo of an older couple looking relaxed, happy, and healthy. The salesperson could also provide graphs that show the makeup of sensible investments. Or, to extend this example, suppose you are recently retired and you have the opportunity to do things you always wanted to do but never had time for. Say you had always dreamed about qualifying for and competing in a triathlon (a race in which you swim, bike, and run). To share your excitement about such a race with family members, perhaps you would elect to show them a brief slide presentation of a triathlon in Hawaii called the Ironman World Championship—a race that involves swimming 2.4 miles, cycling 112 miles, and then running a marathon (26.2 miles). Perhaps you would include photos of all three legs of the race in your presentation to make the experience really come alive.

▼ **Adding Interest with a Visual Aid.** Mars Science Lab Mission Manager Jennifer Trosper uses a model of the Mars rover Curiosity to build interest in her presentation. REUTERS/Alamy

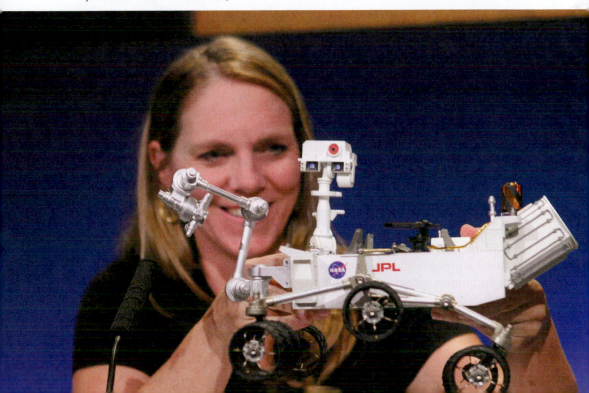

## Presentation Aids Can Simplify a Complex Topic

If you are giving a speech on a technical or an otherwise complicated topic, a presentation aid can help you simplify your message so that your listeners can better understand you. For example, a student giving a presentation on how to skydive could show a drawing of a simplified parachute, with labels highlighting each part of the equipment.

As another example, consider an August 2021 TED (Technology, Entertainment, and Design) talk delivered by Freeman H. Shen, Chairman and CEO of WM Motor. In Shen's speech, he forecasts the impact of shifting from gas-powered vehicles to electric vehicles and describes how he and his colleagues developed the technology to make cars autonomous—effectively allowing a car to drive, pay for parking, and then park itself. Shen uses a full-screen animation to make the idea of an autonomous electric vehicle accessible to all.[6]

## Presentation Aids Can Help Your Audience Remember Your Speech

Many individuals find visual information much easier to recall than spoken information.[7] Thus, the right presentation aids can help ensure that you leave a lasting impression on your listeners. For example, a speaker sharing a long list of reasons for changing the entrance requirements at a community college might hammer home his message by displaying a bulleted list of his main points at the end of his speech.

# TYPES OF PRESENTATION AIDS

A presentation aid may provide only audio assistance (such as a recording of a Harley-Davidson motorcycle engine), only visual assistance (such as a photograph of a person on a surfboard), or both audio and visual assistance simultaneously (as in a digital video recording of an exotic bird singing). Traditional aids include *the speaker*, *assistants*, *objects*, *animals and people*, *visual images* (maps, photographs and drawings, diagrams), *graphs* (line, bar, pie), *text-based visuals*, and *audio and video*. Here, we take a closer look at each type of presentation aid.

## The Speaker

You yourself can be an effective visual aid, particularly if your topic calls for an explanation of an action. Consider Zoya, a student who loved rock climbing and gave a presentation on the sport's basics. During her speech, she covered some common climbing moves and provided tips for taking lessons and finding the best beginner climbing spots. To illustrate her points, Zoya wore the clothes, special shoes, and equipment (harness, belay device, carabiners) that she used while climbing. Through her attire, she served as a visual aid.

YOU CAN BE YOUR OWN PRESENTATION AID

In addition to wearing cloth-ing or other apparel or equipment related to your topic, you can be a visual aid by demonstrating or acting out an aspect of your speech topic. Shenille, a college sophomore in a speech class, prepared an informa-tive presentation about three styles  of African dance. She described them and then demonstrated each one by dancing briefly before the audience.

## Assistants

If serving as a presentation aid yourself would complicate things too much or prevent you from interacting with your audience, consider asking someone to help you reinforce points from your speech or to demonstrate something. For example, in speeches about lifesaving techniques and the use of cardiopulmo-nary resuscitation (CPR), lifeguards teaching new recruits often ask an assistant

to play the role of a victim of a drowning accident, concussion, heart attack, or stroke. The lifeguard then demonstrates techniques and procedures on the assistant while the class watches. As we saw in the chapter opener, using an assistant can help you surmount unique challenges involving presentation aids—such as how to show a motorcycle to a classroom of students.

## Objects

Any object can be a visual aid. For example, in a speech about James Bond movies, one student presented a collection of posters depicting all the actors who ever played 007.

Objects can vary in size, which is something to consider when selecting your presentation aid(s). If you are using a small object as a presentation aid in a speech to your classmates, consider walking closer to them and holding up the object for them to see. And if you have the opposite problem and your object is too large or unwieldy to present in its entirety to your audience, the situation may call for equally creative problem solving.

Consider Riely, a student who gave a speech on the physics of bowling. He explained everything about bowling—including the science behind the holes drilled into the balls, the effect of the rotation and angle of the bowler's arm on the ball's momentum, and the ball's effect on the pins. Riely couldn't bring an entire bowling alley into the classroom, so he came up with an ingenious alternative. He showed his audience three bowling balls—all with different kinds

▲ **Using an Object as a Presentation Aid.** Andrés Better uses the actual object to help explain pink oyster mushrooms to his customers. Hyoung Chang/MediaNews Group/ The Denver Post via Getty Images/Getty Images

of holes. Then he rolled each ball down a slanted table and into the hands of a waiting assistant. With each roll, he pointed out to the audience how the ball's particular speed and path was determined by the ball's design and his technique.

## Animals and People

When giving a speech about animals or people, you'll want to think carefully about your choice of presentation aids. An old Hollywood adage, often attributed to comedian W. C. Fields, is "Never work with children or animals." While this sentiment originally referred to filmmaking and the risk of being upstaged by an adorable child or a cute animal, the advice is not all that different for presentations, at least in the case of animals. Here, the suggestion is to show photos or video of animals—material you have carefully selected and edited— simply because you may not always be able to control a live animal during a speech. Animals can be unpredictable, which makes photos or video the safer and more reliable choice.

The same can sometimes be true for children, although a different TED talk, delivered in 2021, turned that old adage on its head. In an impressive presentation addressing the topic "How every child can thrive by five," a seven-year-old speaker named Molly Wright worked admirably with a new

# ANIMALS AS VISUAL AIDS (CAUTION)

baby named Ari and the baby boy's father, Amarjot. Molly brought both Ari and Amarjot on stage as she spoke, and she also showed video of Ari's interactions with his father. Much of her presentation focused on these interactions and the level of interest the father had for his son, and vice versa. Including these individuals in her presentation made Molly's points especially persuasive.[8]

## Visual Images

As the old saying goes, "A picture is worth a thousand words." When giving a speech, you can sometimes save time and improve clarity by presenting a simple visual representation rather than describing something. If you are explaining the layout of a room, for example, showing audience members a scale drawing will provide them with a clearer image than verbally describing the room's dimensions. Several types of visual aids can give your audience a clearer image of what you are talking about, including *maps*, *photographs and drawings*, and *diagrams*.

**Maps.** A map is a visual representation of geography and can contain as much or as little information as you wish. In addition to the map itself, you can add highlighting or labels to make the map more useful to your audience. For example, if you're giving a talk on the architecture of a particular city, you could show a map with labels for the city's most important buildings. For a presentation about competing in the Ironman triathlon in France at Lake Gérardmer, you could use a map to show the route of the race—an exceptionally steep former Tour de France bike course that requires three revolutions to accomplish the 112 mile cycling distance!

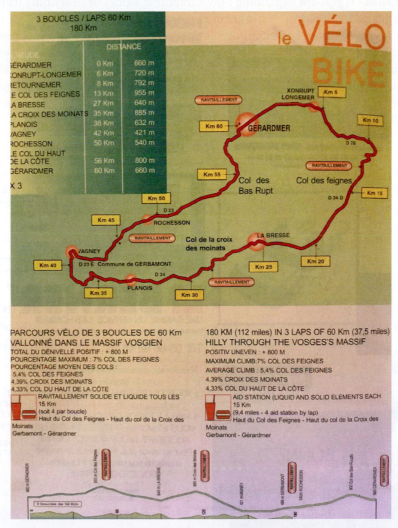

▲ **The Gérardmer Bike Course.** A map can help the audience visualize the route or area you are discussing. Kirsten Weisser

**Photographs and Drawings.** Photographs can help you provide an exact depiction. For example, if you're giving a speech about the Mona Lisa, you could display a photograph of the painting and point out certain aspects of Leonardo da Vinci's technique. Drawings enable you to emphasize certain details about your topic. For instance, in a speech about how mosquitoes spread malaria, you could display a drawing of the insect that shows how its proboscis is the tool for spreading disease. As with maps, you can add labels or other types of highlighting to a photograph or drawing to focus your audience's attention on specific details.

**Diagrams.** If you are explaining how something works or describing its parts, a diagram can be helpful. A **diagram** is a drawing that details an object or an action and the relationships among its parts. Coaches, for example, routinely diagram plays to convey strategy to their players. Diagrams can be drawn by hand or rendered on computers or tablets, and they typically include visual images, labels, and other important information. You might use an annotated diagram during a speech to provide instructions or point out the elements of something, such as bicycle equipment.

---

▼ **Photos and Diagrams.** A photo shows the audience an exact depiction, here of a top triathlete. An annotated diagram shows the audience the different features of a triathlete on the bike. AFP/Getty Images

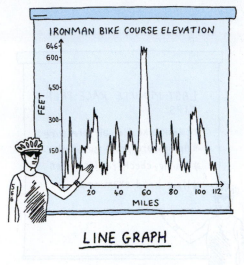

LINE GRAPH

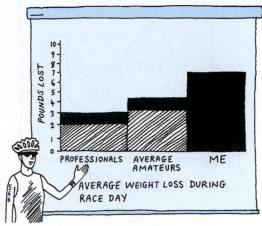

BAR GRAPH

## Graphs

A **graph** is a visual representation of the relationship among different numbers, measurements, or quantities. Graphs are especially useful when presenting a great deal of statistical evidence. Some common types of graphs are *line graphs*, *bar graphs*, and *pie charts*.

**Line Graphs.** A **line graph** uses lines plotted on vertical and horizontal axes to show relationships between two elements. For example, you could use a line graph to show the various elevations of the Ironman triathlon or the profits that a company made over a ten-year period.

**Bar Graphs.** A **bar graph** consists of parallel bars of varying height or length that compare several pieces of information. For instance, you could use a bar graph to compare the weight loss of three categories of triathletes in a series of races.

**Pie Charts.** A **pie chart** (also known as a **circle graph**) is used to show how percentages and proportions relate to one another and add up to a whole. A pie chart resembles a pie that has been divided into slices, with each slice representing a percentage of the total sum. You could use a pie chart to show the percentages of different types of foods in a recommended diet for triathletes or the amount of money your town spent in a given year on various services, such as education or road repair.

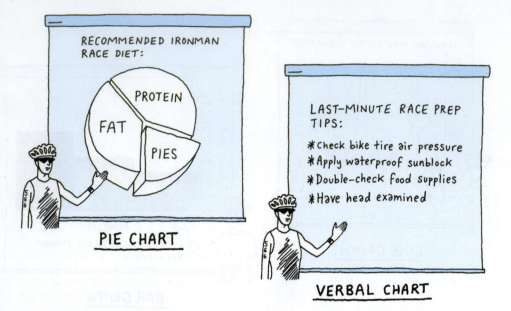

PIE CHART

VERBAL CHART

## Text-Based Visuals

In some cases, presenting text graphically can help your audience organize and understand information. For example, to highlight key ideas or important take-aways from your speech, you could use a **verbal chart**, which arranges words in a certain format, such as bullet points or columns. You might use a verbal chart to list tips for last-minute preparations for the Ironman competition, to show the parts of a motorcycle engine, or to compare the pros and cons of a particular issue.

Text and graphics can be combined to convey both information and action. A **flowchart** is a text-based visual that demonstrates the direction of informa-tion, processes, and ideas. You might use a flowchart to show the steps that someone takes to prepare for the Ironman competition or the process that a bank uses to decide whether to lend money to a mortgage applicant. It is import-ant to use text-based visuals sparingly; you do not want to present your entire speech outline as a visual aid.

## Audio and Video

In many speech situations, it can be useful to demonstrate an action that cannot eas-ily be described in words or presented in a still image. In such cases, you may incor-porate audio selections or video clips into your presentation to explain, demonstrate, or illustrate a key point. We discuss several means of sharing audio and video, as well as practical considerations for doing so, in the next section on technology. But first, let's consider the circumstances in which this type of content is most useful.

**Audio.** Presenting sound recordings or effects can greatly enhance a presen-tation if it is done well. In a speech about a particular musician or composer, for example, it makes sense to play a recording of their work for the audience.

Audio can also make abstract concepts easier to understand. For example, Monica prepared a speech about the effects of loud music on hearing. Because *loud* is a relative term, Monica decided to play audio recordings of different sounds (the engine of a compact car, a radio turned up all the way, a jet engine during takeoff) at different volumes. Although Monica couldn't subject her audience to a roar as loud as a real jet engine, she arranged the *relative* loudness of the sounds to demonstrate noise levels by decibel and to help her audience understand the nature of sound and the ways it is measured.

**Video.** A video is useful to your presentation whenever showing the subject in action or motion would enhance the audience's understanding more than showing a still photo or describing the subject verbally would. For example, a photograph depicting Erin Jackson crossing the finish line to win a 500-meter speedskating gold medal at the 2022 Olympics would identify her as a world-class athlete. But a video showing her skill during a race would be more useful if the speech focused on racing techniques.

Video may be a better choice for your presentation aid if a moving image can better capture the scene or setting. For example, a photograph of a redwood tree on fire might be useful in a speech about forest fires, but a digital video of a burning tree could better demonstrate how quickly a fire can spread.

Not all video clips are useful. Video works best when it is clear, compelling, and easy to see. For example, Meg is a bird-watcher, and she wants to give a speech about a type of seabird that nests near her home. Showing a grainy video clip of the fast-moving bird in flight would probably not add much to her presentation, as it would not provide a clear image of the bird or a real sense of how it moves. However, a color illustration or photo of the bird, along with an audio clip of its call, would greatly enhance her presentation.

# USING TECHNOLOGY WISELY

You've prepared your speech, and you've collected audio and visual aids that will support your points in an interesting way. Now you need to decide how to present them. Should you create a digital slide show on your laptop, complete with audio and video, or will a cell phone and a portable speaker do the job just as effectively? In this section, we look at various ways you can use technology with your presentation aids.

## Using Presentation Software

**Presentation software** (sometimes referred to as *slideware*) enables users to create, edit, and present information, usually in a slide-show format. You can use presentation software to create tables, charts, graphs, and illustrations. In addition, smartphones have transformed the world of presentation aids by enabling you to capture, download, and share photos, audio, and video cheaply and easily. If you have access to a computer as well as a digital projector and audio speakers, this software makes it relatively easy to incorporate all of your aids into a digital slide show and present it to your audience. Such digital presentations have become widespread in business settings, in communities across the world, and on college campuses; indeed, some instructors may require a digital presentation for a public speaking course.

According to a 2021 review of presentation software, five top options are Powtoon, Prezi, RenderForest Presentation Maker, Mentimeter, and Libre Office Impress.[9] Microsoft PowerPoint is another well-known tool. You may want to do some online research about available options to decide which will be best for your presentations. (We will elaborate on using presentation aids during virtual speeches in Chapter 15.) Instructions for using each of these programs vary and change with each new version, so refer to a particular program's user guide for technical guidance.

▼ **Using Presentation Software.** Presentation software can display a wide range of content, including lists and pictures. Compare the green background and the white background on the slides used in these two presentations. Which makes the content easiest for the audience to process?

Along with the general guidelines for any presentation aid, there are certain things you should keep in mind when developing a digital slide-show presentation.

### Use It to Unify a Mixed-Media Presentation.
If you have many different types of aids (pictures, data graphs, lists, video, and audio), presenting them in a unified way helps keep the audience focused on your message. Digital slide shows allow you to incorporate a variety of presentation aids and present them in one consistent frame. They also make it easy to print out parts of your slide show for audience members to take home. Such handouts are especially useful in informational presentations.

### Remember, Content Is King.
Don't let your speech be eclipsed by technological bells and whistles. As with any presentation aid, you should use presentation software to share material that supports your points. A slick digital presentation that lacks substance might look good, but it is unlikely to impress your audience (or your instructor). Your speech should be solid enough to deliver without any aids at all.

### Don't Let the Software Steal the Show.
Presentation software should be used to assist you in delivering your speech; it shouldn't deliver your speech for you. Remember that *you* need to be the center of attention—not your slides. Help your listeners focus on you and your message: do your best to avoid reading from your slides, move around as you speak, maintain eye contact with listeners, and limit the amount of text in your slides. Use your slides to show material; use your speech to talk about the material you show.

## Using Other Technology

Although integrating audio and video into presentations using computer software and a digital projector is very common, you can also present audio and video examples by themselves— without first incorporating them into a presentation—using devices like a laptop or smartphone.

In addition, when you incorporate audio and visual aids into a presentation, you can consider a mixed approach that makes use of both digital technology tools and more traditional presentation aids. A student named Justine did this when she gave an informative

speech to her classmates on the history of jazz. During her presentation, she showed actual instruments—a tenor saxophone and an electronic keyboard—and demonstrated a few riffs on each. She later used a record player to play a vintage recording of a rare Charlie Parker selection. Finally, she shared a digital recording of saxophonist Sadao Watanabe by using a smartphone and a Bluetooth speaker.

# GUIDELINES FOR DEVELOPING PRESENTATION AIDS

Effectively developing your presentation aids—that is, figuring out exactly what aids to use and how they should appear and be organized—can make your speech more interesting, simplify your topic, and help your audience remember your speech. Even if you have a general idea of what you want your aids to achieve—for example, to show audience members paintings from Pablo Picasso's Blue Period or to help them remember the most important aspects of the job–interview process— you still have many factors to consider to achieve maximum impact. As you develop your presentation aids, *consider the forum, consider your audience, make sure your aids support your points, keep your aids simple and clear,* and *rehearse with your presentation aids.* Let's address each of these important factors in turn.

## Consider the Forum

As we discuss in Chapter 5, consider the location, or **forum**, as you're mulling over which presentation aids to use. Where will the audience hear your speech? Are you presenting in person or online? Is the forum equipped to handle

MAKE SURE YOU CHECK OUT THE FORUM BEFORE YOUR SPEECH

presentation aids? For example, is a large screen available? Are outlets available for a laptop computer, or even a simple computer projector? If you want to visit a website during your presentation and show it to your audience, is wireless access available? If you need to play audio during an online speech, will your audience be able to hear the audio over Zoom? If you plan to use printed visual aids, do you have access to poster boards, flip charts, marker boards, or chalkboards?

## Consider Your Audience

Because presentation aids become part of the message you are sharing with listeners, your analysis of your audience should drive your aid selection. When choosing appropriate aids, be sure to consider audience demographics and listeners' prior exposure to the presentation subject matter. Ask yourself, "Of all the possible aids for this speech and its content, which one or which combination would work best with this audience?"

**Demographics.** Think about the *demographics* of your audience. Demographics—such as listeners' age, gender, or occupation—can easily predetermine how audience members respond to a particular audio or visual aid.

For example, a student named Anna is giving a presentation on costume design in film. The main point of her speech is that clothing plays an important role in defining film characters. As she speaks, she clicks through a variety of film images to show how costume designers carefully choose appropriate clothing in order to offer insights into characters' personalities and experiences. In presenting this speech to a class of traditional-aged college students, Anna might include images of Alana Haim and Cooper Hoffman in the 2021 film

▼ **Selecting Presentation Aids Based on Demographics.** If giving examples from a movie, an image from *Spiderman: No Way Home* could be best for a younger audience, whereas a photo from *Do the Right Thing* could better illustrate a particular point if audience members were more middle aged. (left) © Sony Pictures Releasing/© Marvel Entertainment/Courtesy Everett Collection; (right) ©MCA/Courtesy Everett Collection

*Licorice Pizza*, directed by the visually creative Paul Thomas Anderson. But if Anna is presenting her speech to people in their fifties and sixties, she might make the same points and present the same evidence, but choose images of characters from an earlier film, such as *Annie Hall* (1977).

### Prior Exposure.

As noted in Chapter 5, **prior exposure** to certain elements of your speech may positively or negatively influence how your audience responds to those elements. This can be true of presentation aids as well. Consider Crystal, a student who gave a persuasive speech opposing abortion. She knew from interviews that many of her listen-

▲ **Building Audience Interest.** When you choose presentation aids that the audience has not seen before, they will be especially attentive. For example, a photo of the rare blanket octopus will show the audience a species that they have probably never seen. Stephen Frink/Getty Images

ers identified themselves as pro-choice. Therefore, she avoided using graphic photos or images of abortion procedures, which these audience members had probably seen many times before. (These graphic images may not be a good choice in any event.) Instead, Crystal chose visual aids to make her argument that all life has value, including pictures of healthy infants and the children and young adults they grew up to be. Although she may not have persuaded all her listeners to change their viewpoint on abortion, her speech was thought provoking and held her audience's attention.

How can you determine whether your audience has had prior exposure to the presentation aids you're considering—and what that exposure implies? Ask the same kinds of questions we introduced in Chapter 5:

1. *Has my audience seen or heard this aid before?* If so, proceed to the next question.
2. *Has my audience responded positively to the message?* Were listeners persuaded to take the action the speaker advocated? If not, proceed to the next question.
3. *Why did the previous message fail?* Ask yourself how you can avoid repeating the mistakes made by the previous presenter, who failed to persuade the audience through those particular aids.

## Make Sure Your Aids Support Your Points

Can your points be enhanced by specific images or sounds? For example, if you're giving a speech about a particular city's architecture, a map would strongly support your message. A recording of a song about that same city would be less relevant to your speech.

## Keep Your Aids Simple and Clear

Consider the following suggestions for making your presentation aids clear and easy to understand:

- *Keep your aids simple.* A presentation aid works best when audience members can simply glance at it or hear it once and quickly grasp what you're trying to communicate. If they have to stare at it, see it more than once, or listen to it several times, the aid is likely too complex or detailed.

- *Test the size of visual aids.* Make sure each visual aid is large enough to be seen by everyone in your audience. The bigger your audience is, and the farther they are from you and your visual aid, the larger the aid should be.

- *Create contrast.* On visual aids, contrast increases readability. To create contrast, place dark colors against a light background or light colors against a dark background. On a poster, for example, dark text will stand out and be easier to read against a light background.

- *Test the legibility of visual aids.* Be sure to check whether all the numbers, letters, words, sentences, and graphics in your visual aids are legible—that is, easily distinguished at a distance. For instance, ask a classmate, friend, or roommate to view a poster or projected slide from a distance and tell you whether they can see everything on it. If not, continue refining your aid—for example, by increasing font size and adding white space between elements.

- *Test the volume and clarity of audio aids.* Be certain that your audio aids will be loud enough *and* clear enough (that is, free of static or other "noise") for all your listeners to hear. If you are presenting a speech virtually, be sure you are able to share audio and video so audience members can see and hear your presentation aids.

## Rehearse with Your Presentation Aids

We strongly advise that you create your aids while developing your speech—and then practice using them as you rehearse your presentation. Don't put yourself in the risky position of needing to create aids on the fly while delivering your speech because you were not prepared. At the same time, we suggest that you prepare for the unexpected—including power failures and technology glitches (frozen programs, system crashes, or a failed Internet

connection). As many public speakers have discovered, technology can fail just when you need it most. Imagine how you'd feel if, at a key point in your speech, you turned on your computer to project an important photo and the device didn't work. To avoid this scenario, always prepare a hard copy of any presentation aids you plan to present using computers or other technology or equipment. You can always pass the hard copy around the room as a last resort.

When delivering PowerPoint or other sorts of digital presentations, make sure to practice a number of times with your slides, just as you would with a speech outline. To guard against any surprises, check that your media will work with the computers in the speech setting before it's time to speak. When incorporating a computer into your presentation consider taping power cables to the floor (to avoid tripping over them during your speech), and make sure you have the video cued to the right scene before beginning your speech.

Additionally, you may find that a presentation that contains visual aids requires you to physically direct your audience's attention to specific points in an aid. One way of doing this is to approach the wall or screen where the visual is being displayed and use your hand or a pointing device to indicate content that you want the audience to make note of. Another way is to use a laser pointer; a laser pointer produces a red dot on the screen, which can be flicked around the visual aid content, directing the audience's focus. The advantage of using this device is that it allows you to stay at the podium, where you may be operating the equipment that's controlling the visual aid. If you are delivering a virtual presentation, check to see if your app has a feature that allows you to point to a specific place on your screen. You can experiment with any of these strategies during your practice sessions.

## USING PRESENTATION AIDS DURING YOUR SPEECH

Skillful development of your presentation aids isn't enough to ensure a successful speech. You also need to use the aids correctly during your presentation. Otherwise, you risk making all-too-common mistakes, such as distracting your audience by keeping aids displayed after you're finished with them or losing eye contact with your listeners while discussing an aid. The following strategies can help you use your presentation aids successfully.

### Make Sure Everyone Can See and Hear Your Aids

Position stereo speakers so that all listeners can hear the audio recordings you're playing. In the same vein, position a computer screen so that everyone can see it. Place a printed graph, chart, or picture prominently on the wall or flip chart so that your entire audience can view it.

## Control Audience Interaction with Your Aids

To avoid distracting your audience unnecessarily, do not show or play an aid until you are ready for listeners to see or hear it. When you're finished presenting the aid, put it away or shut it off. This strategy keeps your audience's attention focused on you instead of your aids—and helps ensure that listeners don't miss important parts of your speech.

You can control audience interaction with your aids in several ways. For example, if you are using an audio recording, cue up the desired track ahead of

▼ **Using a Flip Chart.** A flip chart can be a good way to present a diagram or list. When using a flip chart, be sure to include a blank page between each image. Also be sure to look at the audience while explaining the material, as the speaker is doing here. wavebreakmedia/Shutterstock

time so that you can play it promptly when you're ready. Avoid playing background music (e.g., from a cell phone) during your speech. If you are presenting a segment of a video, you can pause it at the place where your segment begins. If you plan to tape or pin a chart to the wall, do so in advance, but fold half of the display over the other half and tape or pin it down. That way, you'll block the audience's view until you are ready to refer to the chart in your speech, at which point you'll undo the tape or pin.

Use a similar technique when displaying a series of images on successive sheets of a flip chart. Insert blank sheets between each sheet containing an image. When you finish with one image, flip the page so that your audience sees a blank page. This technique also works well with slide shows, document cameras, and computer images in a PowerPoint presentation. Remove each image from view after you've discussed it, leaving a blank screen, or turn off the equipment and refocus the audience on you—the speaker!

What about handouts? To ensure that they're informative rather than distracting, issue clear instructions about how to use them. For example, pass out handouts facedown, and tell the audience not to look at them until you say so. Explain that you don't want listeners to get ahead of you. Of course, there will always be someone who ignores this instruction and takes a peek. To keep audience members focused on your speech, watch them during your presentation. Look for listeners who are flipping through the handouts. Then adjust your delivery by increasing your volume or moving closer to those audience members to draw their attention back to you. Additionally, if your handouts are identical to your slides, make sure to tell the audience as much, and promise to give them copies at the end of the speech; this will allow audience members to relax and listen, since note taking in this context will be unnecessary.

MAINTAIN EYE CONTACT WITH YOUR AUDIENCE, NOT YOUR VISUAL AID

## Maintain Eye Contact

Many inexperienced speakers look at their visual aids during their presentation instead of maintaining eye contact with their audience. Of course, you need to glance at visual aids as you present them—especially if you're referring to something specific on an aid. But this should be *only* a quick glance—not a lengthy gaze.

## Remember the Purpose of Your Aids

As we've mentioned, you should treat your presentation aids as tools that supplement your speech—not as the main vehicle for delivering your speech. Your presentation contains your message, and you are the messenger. If you forget this, your audience might focus on your aids instead of you. For instance, many inexperienced salespeople rely too heavily on brochures and handouts during a presentation. They assume—mistakenly—that good marketing materials are all they need to sell a product or a service. But a brochure can't answer listeners' questions or interact spontaneously with them. Only a human being can connect with audiences in these crucial ways. The best speakers understand that presentation aids support a speech—not the other way around.

## SPEECH CHOICES

### A CASE STUDY: *RAFAELA*

*Let's look in on Rafaela to learn which presentation aids she decided to include.*

Rafaela had a variety of options for presentation aids that she might use in her speech, and she made a list of some possibilities to consider. For example, there were photos and videos available to complement her anecdotes about women who had successfully run for office. She had found a photo of Khemarey Khoeun, the first Cambodian American to be elected to public office in the United States, conducting her campaign. And she had located a video of Interior Secretary Deb Haaland (a former member of Congress) running in the Boston Marathon.

Rafaela also considered creating charts to depict some of the statistics that she would present in her speech—for example, a bar graph showing that a higher percentage of men in the class had been encouraged to run for office. In addition, she thought she might make a graph comparing the percentage of women in national legislatures around the world, to show how the United States was lagging behind.

To support her point that men and women hold different priorities, Rafaela thought about creating a chart that showed the differences between the top five issues for men in the United States and the top five issues for women in the United States, according to a recent poll.

She also considered using photos showing women in action on college sports teams and college academic teams such as debate and mock trial. This would go well with her idea that there are many college activities where women could gain experience that would be helpful in the political world.

Now that Rafaela had a number of good ideas for presentation aids, it was time for the next step: developing these aids and making sure they expressed her points both clearly and effectively.

 **YOUR TURN**

Now that you've seen how Rafaela's decisions about presentation aids influenced her speech, consider similar choices you'll make for a speech of your own. Making speech choices involves asking and answering a series of questions related to your assignment. When it comes to presentation aids, here are some questions to consider:

- What types of presentation aids would be a good fit with my speech topic?
- Which of the available presentation aids would best help me gain audience interest and build understanding?
- Would it help my speech if I used technology to display presentation aids?
- As I prepare my presentation aids, am I following the guidelines for developing these aids introduced in this chapter?
- Have I practiced my speech while presenting my visual aids so I'm sure that I can display them smoothly?

Making thoughtful choices in response to questions like these will help you include presentation aids that communicate your message effectively and make your speech even more engaging.

# CHAPTER REVIEW

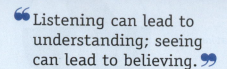**Listening can lead to understanding; seeing can lead to believing.** In this chapter, we examined how the right selection and strategic use of presentation aids enhance your audience's interest in, comprehension of, and retention of your speech. Aids can take many forms, including the speaker, assistants, objects, animals and people, visual images, graphs, text-based visuals, and audio and video. You can display presentation aids in a variety of ways—such as in printed form or through presentation software and other technology. To get the most impact from your aids, you need to develop them with the following points in mind: consider the forum, consider your audience, make sure your aids support your points, keep your aids simple and clear, and rehearse with your presentation aids. Then use your aids judiciously during your presentation to support your points—not to deliver your message for you. A key point to remember is that presentation aids supplement your message, but they can never replace you. *You* are the messenger!

## Key Terms

presentation aid *340*
diagram *348*
graph *349*
line graph *349*
bar graph *349*
pie chart (circle graph) *349*

verbal chart *350*
flowchart *350*
presentation software *352*
forum *354*
prior exposure *356*

## Review Questions

1. What are three key reasons for using presentation aids in a speech?
2. Describe at least eight types of presentation aids you might use in a speech.
3. According to the chapter, when is presentation software most useful?
4. What factors should you consider when developing your presentation aids?
5. What four things does a speaker need to keep in mind when delivering a speech with presentation aids?

## Critical Thinking Questions

1. Are all presentation aids visual aids? What other senses might a good presentation aid engage?
2. What advantages does presentation software offer over more traditional ways of presenting visual and audio aids?

3. Do some types of speeches work better with presentation aids, and if so, which types of aids work best with which types of speeches?

## Activities

1. Take a look at the illustration on page 358, which shows a speaker using a visual aid that's the wrong size. If you were to redraw this illustration to correct the speaker's mistake, what would that illustration look like?
2. Television commercials are persuasive appeals created from video and audio elements. With this in mind, consider a few television commercials you have found especially memorable. How do they use presentation aids (such as music and images) to grab your attention? How do these aids relate to the commercials' main points? How could you apply lessons from these effective commercials to your own presentations?
3. Think of ways that you, as the speaker, are a visual aid. How can you tailor your nonverbal delivery—things like your posture or your appearance—to reinforce your main point?

# MEDIATED PUBLIC SPEAKING

# 15

> **" Effective mediated public speaking offers a world of challenges and opportunities. "**

Marshawn signed up to take his required public speaking course in an online format. His work schedule was unpredictable, and he appreciated the flexible hours that an online course would provide. Because the class would never meet face-to-face, he figured he wouldn't be required to deliver any speeches. Besides quelling his nerves, this idea made him think the course would be easier to manage.

However, when Marshawn logged on to the course website for the first time, he received a surprise. Four speeches were required for the course, and although they would not be presented live in a classroom, students were responsible for recording their presentations and submitting them to the instructor electronically. This was not good news. Not only would Marshawn have to do all the work required to prepare and present his speeches, but he would also have to worry about recording them. "Who does my instructor think I am?" he wondered. "Jordan Peele?"

After the first week of classes, Marshawn began to reconsider. He had been involved in making videos for most of his life. He had recorded special events with

---

◀ **Mediated Communication in Action.** For a 2021 ceremony in which 1,250 Buddhist monks were ordained in Thailand during the third lunar month, thousands of participants accessed the ceremony using Zoom. Examples of mediated communication—from virtual ordination ceremonies to online public speaking courses—are all around us every day. Anadolu Agency/Getty Images

**367**

friends and family members on his smartphone and posted them on YouTube. His church choir had made a DVD of its best work, which featured Marshawn singing a solo. And whenever he brought a new romantic interest home to meet his parents, Marshawn's mom could not resist showing a video of his campaign speech for sixth-grade class president. Maybe he had more video experience than he'd originally thought.

Marshawn's experience is not unique. Twenty-first-century technology has increased the ways that we can communicate with one another, and one consequence of the COVID-19 pandemic has been a major increase in online presentations delivered from remote locations and a significant decrease in face-to-face communication. You have likely experienced this directly in high school or college classes, as well as your personal life. For example, you may have logged into class via Zoom, livestreamed on Twitch, or shared a video you created on a site like Twitter. When you send a message through digital media, you are participating in **mediated communication**. This means that you use technology to deliver your message, rather than speaking to the audience face-to-face. You will likely have opportunities to take part in mediated communication in all facets of your life, including your college courses and activities, your career, your community, and social interactions.

Fortunately, when it comes to public speaking, preparing a mediated presentation is not hugely different from preparing a face-to-face presentation. Just as you follow a set of manageable steps to prepare and deliver successful speeches in a face-to-face (F2F) environment, you can use a similar approach when called on to deliver a mediated presentation. This chapter will help you learn how to adapt when you speak to a remote audience and also how to feel more comfortable when presenting remotely or recording a presentation. We begin by discussing the rise of mediated communication and the advantages and challenges of both real-time and prerecorded presentations. Then we move on to strategies for optimizing delivery of effective messages in a mediated environment. Finally, we discuss how to make a prerecorded video of your presentation successfully.

# THE RISE OF MEDIATED COMMUNICATION

Even before the pandemic, rapidly evolving communication technology was changing how we live and interact with one another. For example, for many of us, texts, emails, and social media have replaced handwritten letters and landline telephones as channels for staying in touch with friends and family members. And rather than visiting the library to begin a research project, most students can access quality library resources online. Trends like these have affected the workplace, too. In 2019, a survey found that about one-third of employees in the United States reported that they had used the Internet to telecommute or work from a different location.[1]

Then, these trends accelerated: in spring 2020, the COVID-19 pandemic forced a sudden, massive increase in mediated communication as schools and businesses shut down in-person sites and transitioned to remote operations. As just one measure of how intensely mediated communication increased as a result of COVID, consider these numbers: in December 2019, Zoom averaged 10 million meeting participants per day; five months later, the average had skyrocketed to 300 million participants.[2] Interestingly, even as COVID cases and hospitalizations have dropped, communication practices have not returned to pre-COVID patterns. Rather, a new mix of face-to-face and remote communication in education and the workplace has emerged, with a greater increase in mediated communication than in times past. For example, more hybrid and online college course offerings are available now than they were before the pandemic.[3] And many employers are

## MEDIATED PRESENTATIONS CAN BE FUN...

*Actually, just find your pants.

not fully reverting to pre-pandemic work patterns, meaning there are increased opportunities for employees to work remotely.[4]

These trends will continue to affect many aspects of our lives, and public speaking is no exception. As a student, for example, you will likely use technology like Zoom to give more **real-time (synchronous) presentations**—presentations that are delivered directly to the audience as you speak from a remote location. You will likely also prepare **prerecorded (asynchronous) presentations**—those created by the speaker for later viewing by one or more live audiences—that you then upload to online learning management systems such as Blackboard or Canvas. In the workplace and in community forums, you are likely to present both synchronously and asynchronously, using video-conferencing technology to present remotely in real time and creating digital recordings such as podcasts that can be accessed any time.

Change is constant, and the day will undoubtedly come when our current technologies are replaced by newer mediated communication options that are even more beneficial for speakers and audiences. Nevertheless, as is the case now, there will also be situations where F2F speeches remain the best option, with personal presence offering the best chance for speaker and audience to interact and build community. For this reason, the best public speakers today—and in the future—will need to be at the top of their game when it comes to both F2F *and* mediated speeches.

## ADVANTAGES AND CHALLENGES OF MEDIATED PRESENTATIONS

Mediated presentations offer both opportunities and challenges for speakers. Why—and when—might a mediated presentation be a good choice? Let's consider the main benefits to presenting a mediated speech to a remote audience and the types of situations in which you may want to deliver a mediated speech, as well as the challenges that come with delivering mediated presentations.

## Advantages of Mediated Presentations

There are a number of advantages to mediated presentations. Some advantages apply to all mediated speeches, while others are specific to either prerecorded or real-time settings.

**General Advantages.** This first group of advantages applies to both prerecorded and real-time presentations.

- *Flexibility.* With either type of mediated presentation, audience members can access your speech from multiple—and presumably more convenient—locations. With prerecorded speeches in particular, audience members can also view the content at different times.

- *Savings.* It can be expensive for an organization to bring everyone who should hear a message to a common location, and the travel involved in an event like that also places demands on participants' time. Mediated technology can more efficiently bring the speech to the audience.

---

▼ **Mediated Communication Can Reach Mass Audiences.** South Korean boy band BTS spoke to the UN General Assembly about the importance of sustainable development. Over one million people watched the speech on the UN's YouTube channel and many fans used live chat to provide positive feedback. Pool/Getty Images

- *Audience size.* Attendance at a F2F presentation is limited to the number of people who can fit in the available space and attend at the designated time. With mediated presentations, there are no such limitations on space or (in the case of prerecorded speeches) limitations on time, giving you an opportunity to address a greater number of people. If a speech video goes viral, for example, it may attract millions of viewers.

**Advantages of Prerecorded Speeches.** Prerecorded presentations come with several specific advantages—do-overs, pause and rewind buttons, and access to a saved copy.

- *Do-overs.* In a real-time speech, if you make a mistake or your technology fails, you need to adapt to the problem as best you can and continue. If you are prerecording, you can do another take if your speech does not go well the first time.

- *Pause and rewind buttons.* Prerecorded speeches can provide audience members with additional opportunities to process and reflect on your message by going back and reviewing a section of the presentation, pausing the speech to discuss it, or watching the entire speech again.

- *Access to a saved copy.* Prerecording creates a permanent record of your speech for future audiences to view. In addition, if you have a recording of a classroom speech, you can use it to provide prospective employers with a sample of your public speaking skills, much as you might provide them with a writing sample.

**Advantages of Real-Time Technologies.** In a real-time mediated presentation, remote technology cannot create the same sense of presence that comes when a speaker and an audience share the same physical space. However, real-time presentations do allow for some of the benefits of a F2F speech, including audience feedback and audience interaction, and they offer the option to save.

- *Audience feedback.* Depending on the type of technology available, you might be able to experience audience feedback and adapt your speech in the moment. If you have the advantage of top-flight technology and large screens, you will be able to observe more of your audience's nonverbal responses.[5]

- *Audience interaction.* Real-time technology allows audience members to interact with the speaker during or immediately after the speech. For example, there can be a question-and-answer session. Or audience members may put questions in chat during the presentation.

- *Option to save.* As is the case with prerecorded speeches, real-time presentations can often be saved and made available for future viewing, provided someone remembers to record the session. That way, audience members can review your speech whenever they'd like to, and you can also share it with wider audiences in the future.

---

▼ **Advantages of Presenting in Real Time.** While teaching an online class, this teacher can interact with her students—in this case, the other teachers she is training to use Zoom—and observe their feedback. OLIVIER DOULIERY/Getty Images

## Challenges of Mediated Presentations

Now that we have considered some of the potential advantages to mediated presentations, let's turn our attention to the main challenges. Think of an in-person political rally, commencement speech, or technology conference—in any of these situations, even with a large crowd, the speaker has the opportunity to connect personally with the audience. A major concern with mediated communication is that the in-person connection is missing. This section explores specific challenges that are created by mediated presentations, including difficulties related to a loss of naturalness and technological difficulties not found in F2F communication. Later in this chapter, we discuss strategies for minimizing these challenges.

**Loss of Naturalness.** Our brains are hardwired for F2F interaction. Since the Stone Age, humans have used facial expressions and sound as primary means of communication, and the **naturalness** of a communication medium is determined by the extent to which it matches the features of F2F interaction.[6] Key factors that contribute to feelings of naturalness include sharing the same space, sending and receiving messages quickly, and being able to send and receive both verbal and nonverbal expressions.[7]

The human brain enables us to send and receive messages in our natural F2F mode with a minimum of effort. However, when we use a less natural medium, we face greater barriers to effective communication. In this way, video interactions can be seen as more natural than text-based media because they have the ability

to convey vocal and visual cues (such as tone and body posture) synchronously, not unlike F2F communication. By contrast, emails provide mostly text-based cues and are typically asynchronous. Emoticons can be added to email messages, but they lack the richness and variety of cues found in F2F communication.[8]

Listed here are some of the specific challenges caused by mediated presentations in terms of the naturalness we often take for granted in F2F communication. Unless otherwise noted, these challenges apply to both prerecorded and real-time communication.

- *Loss of immediacy.* In a F2F presentation, audience members are physically close to you. They can observe your eye contact and sense your movement, creating "interest and warmth between communicators."[9] Conversely, when you and your audience are in different locations, you both feel less of a psychological link.[10] In a less natural environment, speakers face greater challenges establishing credibility and building common ground.[11] You may also feel less of a bond with your audience when presenting to a camera, which can feel like "presenting into the void."[12]

- *Decreased nonverbal communication.* In a F2F speech, audience members can observe the full range of your nonverbal behaviors.[13] In a mediated presentation, however, it may be difficult to capture the full range of your nonverbal expression, especially when you are presenting via a laptop camera. When audience members can only see facial gestures, they miss other nonverbal cues that would help them decode a message accurately.[14] For example, it is difficult for the speaker to move around. Furthermore, the flat images of facial gestures that appear on a screen are not the same as the ones that would be perceived in a three-dimensional F2F environment.[15]

- *Diminished feedback.* Feedback is central to effective speaker-audience interaction, but even with real-time technology, it's difficult for listeners to provide the same quality of feedback that they can in a F2F enviroment.[16] For example, if you don't have a clear view of your entire audience, you cannot determine if they are losing interest and thus add some energy to your presentation to compensate.[17] Feedback also provides positive

---

▼ **Challenges of Mediated Presentations.** Typical challenges include managing distractions (such as your cat) and videoconferencing burnout. (left) Kanawa_Studio/ Getty Images; (right) Andia/Getty Images

reactions—such as attentive listening, a smile, or a nod—that show that you are on the right track, and these types of reactions aren't always as clear to the speaker in a mediated setting. And when a speech is prerecorded, your audience has no chance to provide real-time feedback at all, which can be challenging: you won't receive feedback if audience members don't understand an idea, for example, so you won't know that you need to expand on your explanation to provide clarification.[18]

- *Difficulty managing distractions.* Remote audience members are more likely to be **multitasking** while they watch your speech—that is, "juggling multiple tasks with and without technological devices."[19] When you are delivering a speech F2F, common courtesy should discourage listeners from multitasking, but when audience members are watching you on a screen, it is easier for them to give in to distractions around them. If you are not speaking on location, you also lose the opportunity to use nonverbal strategies to reengage audience members (such as moving closer to a person who is multitasking to gain attention).

- *Videoconferencing fatigue.* When communicators interact through videoconferencing technology, the lack of naturalness requires increased mental energy in order to receive and process messages.[20] In F2F settings, nonverbal communication occurs naturally. But in virtual contexts, participants must work harder to encode and decode these behaviors.[21] For example, it takes more effort to give a "thumbs up" on Zoom than to smile or nod when you are in person. This problem, often called "Zoom Fatigue" in popular culture, results from "long and repeated use of videoconferencing tools." Users experience a variety of symptoms, such as "tiredness, worry, anxiety, burnout, discomfort, and exhaustion."[22] These conditions are particularly likely when students take several remote classes in the same day or if a workplace requires frequent virtual meetings.

**Technological Difficulties.** In addition to issues related to naturalness, mediated presentations are subject to unique technological difficulties. Internet connections may be weak—you have probably seen this in Zoom classes when an instructor or student's image suddenly freezes as they are speaking—or the Internet connection may cut out altogether. This is especially likely if multiple people in a living space or workspace are accessing the Internet at once—for example, if your roommate is streaming Netflix. If you have Internet connectivity problems, you may want to consider reserving a room at your college library or other spot on campus for your mediated presentation. You could also record your speech on your smartphone and then upload it when you are at a location with a better connection.

You may also find that you experience technical difficulties when using videoconferencing features that you are less familiar with, such as screen sharing or playing a video. The audio on mediated presentations may also not always be clear for technical reasons, and human error is not uncommon here either—you have probably seen a speaker begin to talk many times during classes or work meetings, only to discover that their audio is on mute and no one has heard a word they've said!

▲ **Technological Difficulties.** Pastor Sarah Scherschligt may have needed divine intervention to resolve technological difficulties before starting a virtual mass.
ANDREW CABALLERO-REYNOLDS/Getty Images

# OPTIMIZING DELIVERY AND MESSAGES IN MEDIATED PRESENTATIONS

The key principles of speech delivery, content, and practice discussed in this book apply to both mediated and F2F speeches. However, there are a few unique considerations to keep in mind when your presentation is mediated. In this section, we discuss *delivery considerations*, *message adaptations*, and *practicing delivery and recording*.

## Delivery Considerations

First, let's discuss some considerations for delivery. These points apply to both prerecorded and real-time speeches unless otherwise noted.

**Voice.** To make sure your speaking voice is effective in a mediated presentation, a good general rule is to speak at about the same volume you would use to address people seated in a conference room. Because remote audience members are more likely to be distracted, you will also want to be sure you are speaking with vocal variety. A study comparing video mediated and F2F communication found that video mediated speakers had less tonal variety in their speech and greater volume than F2F presenters.[23] Consider doing a quick voice check if you get the chance to practice with the technology you will be using. Record yourself delivering a part of your speech and play it back to ensure that you are speaking with enough vocal variety and at an appropriate volume.

Maintaining an effective rate of delivery can be another vocal challenge. There is a natural tendency to speed up your presentation if no audience is present, and the absence of an audience means you will not receive feedback alerting you if you speak too fast. To keep your rate under control, be sure to pause at natural stopping points in your speech.[24] For example, you might pause before you transition to the next main point, after you display a visual aid, or after you present evidence.

Finally, recall that speaking to a camera rather than a roomful of people can make it seem as though you are communicating with a vast empty space, which can cause you to lose energy. Imagine that you are speaking to a live audience, and consciously try to maintain an energetic delivery. Include some reminders on your extemporaneous notes, such as "Energy!" or "Enthusiasm!"

**Eye Contact.** Eye contact is a helpful nonverbal behavior that enables a speaker to show interest in audience members and builds a social connection between speaker and audience in F2F interactions.[25] However, eye contact can be a challenge in a virtual environment. In virtual meeting apps, the "Hollywood Squares" layout of the participants creates the perception that (unless someone is looking down) everyone is looking directly into the eyes of the other participants for the entire meeting. As a result, participants can feel "smother[ed] with

▼ **Maintaining Eye Contact.** Li Sanping, a village elder in rural China, uses livestreaming sessions to promote the village's tourism opportunities and agricultural specialties. Here, he uses eye contact to connect with his growing audience. Xinhua News Agency/Getty Images

eye gaze."[26] In speeches, meetings, or conversation, communicators do not typi-cally make eye contact 100 percent of the time.

To make effective virtual eye contact, look at the camera (not the audience members) regularly if you can, so you don't appear to be staring off into space or looking down while speaking. Then, just as you would rotate eye contact in a F2F speech, occasionally shift your focus a bit to the left or to the right. Look down at your notes when needed, too, just as you would do in a live presenta-tion. This way, your eye focus will seem more varied as you speak.

What if you have two different audiences to consider? For example, you may be taking a virtual course where the instructor requires that you record your speech while speaking to a live, in-person audience. Or you may be participating in a F2F meeting at work or in your community that is also being streamed to a virtual audience. When you have dual audiences, make sure to make eye contact with audience members in the room and also to look at the camera during your presentation. That way both audiences will feel included.

**Movement and Gestures.**  Elements of nonverbal delivery such as move-ment and gestures are also affected in a mediated presentation. On a screen, your gestures will appear more prominent because you are being displayed in a smaller area. Expansive gestures may also move out of the frame of your video. (Even a skilled cameraperson can't anticipate your spontaneous conversational gestures.) It is important to gesture when you are recording a speech, but do your best not to gesture too expansively.[27]

Movement also needs to be controlled. Ensure that all movement remains within the range of the camera so that you do not move in and out of view. If your smartphone camera is stationary because you are recording your own speech or you are participating in a videoconference on your laptop, you will need to speak from a fixed location. This may limit your use of nonverbal cues (such as pointing to an item on a visual aid or moving to indicate a transition), so be sure to provide clear verbal cues to help audience members understand your point. During a videoconference, you will likely be seated while speaking, so, when possible, sit up straight and avoid slouching in your chair.

## Message Adaptations

A speaker and audience are more likely to experience "psychological closeness" and feel a sense of "similarity, solidarity, openness, and understanding" when the participants are in the same room than when they are distant.[28] When you as a speaker are distant, your connection with your audience will be diminished, espe-cially if you are not communicating in real time. You will have a greater challenge *building common ground* and *keeping audience members engaged*, and you'll need to focus on *selecting presentation aids* that are easily viewable on camera. Thus, you must plan your message carefully when your presentation is mediated.

**Building Common Ground.**  To compensate for diminished presence, you'll want to emphasize common ground even more than you would in a classroom setting. If you are taking an online public speaking course, try to make brief references to other classmates' speeches during your presentation. If the class includes virtual discussions, you can note points that have been made during these sessions. For example, in a speech on nuclear energy, you might say, "Jesse showed us how to save money by cutting back on meat in our diets, and now I would like to show how we can all save money on our utility bills." You also might be able to relate common experiences of students in virtual classes to concepts in your speech. In an informative speech on the use of smoke signals, you might note how this ancient system of communication was used to warn soldiers up and down the Great Wall of China when the enemy was near.[29] Thus, students can see how methods for communicating over great distances have evolved, with technology now enabling them to interact with one another online.

You also want to emphasize common ground during mediated workplace or community presentations. If you have interacted with audience members in the past, use relevant ideas from your previous discussions. If you do not know your audience, you might emphasize goals or principles that are familiar to everyone in the group. For example, you might refer to a company's logo or the mission of a nonprofit organization.

▼ **Building Common Ground.** In Ukrainian President Volodymyr Zelensky's March 2022 speech to the U.S. Congress from his capital city, Kyiv, delivered after Russia invaded Ukraine, he emphasized common ground such as dreams for freedom and democracy. Zelensky also compared the Russian invasion to attacks on the United States, such as Pearl Harbor and 9/11. Xinhua News Agency/Getty Images

**Keeping Audience Members Engaged.** It is more difficult for listeners to remain attentive when staring at a screen than when watching a live human being.[30] As discussed earlier, remote listeners are more likely to multitask, and a speaker may not be able to see the nonverbal cues that could indicate lack of interest. This is especially true if viewers' cameras are turned off and you can only see a person's blank square or avatar. Thus, you will need to make it easier for them to stay focused on what you are saying. There are several strategies you can use to maintain audience interest when speaking in a mediated setting. Many of these approaches are helpful in a F2F context, but they are especially important when your speech is virtual.

- *Use interactive features.* If your videoconferencing technology allows for polling, this is one good way to keep audience members engaged during a real-time presentation. For example, if you are informing the audience about a new social media platform, you could present response options like (a) never heard of it, (b) heard of it but haven't used it, (c) used it for gaming, and (d) used it to hang out and chat. Depending on the responses you receive, you can explain the platform in more basic terms or explain how more experienced users can get the most out of the platform. You can also ask audience members to put questions into chat and respond to them as you are speaking, or address them after your presentation concludes.

- *Ask rhetorical questions.* Even if your technology does not have interactive features or your presentation is prerecorded, you can make greater use of rhetorical questions and other strategies that encourage active participation. In a speech on the need to get more sleep, a speaker might ask, "How many hours do you think the average college student sleeps?" Even if you are not physically present, this type of question invites the audience to think about the answer and wait with anticipation for you to provide the correct response.

- *Increase the variety of supporting materials.* Another way to maintain interest is to increase the variety of materials you present. A remote audience is more likely to lose interest if a speaker seems to be talking on and on. Conversely, a switch to another mode of presentation can keep an audience's interest. For instance, a speaker who participates in rodeos might discuss rodeo equipment, focusing on the proper saddle in one of her main points. Her first subpoint could be an explanation of why a proper saddle is needed—and what went wrong the time she brought the wrong saddle to a barrel-racing event. Next, the speaker could display an actual saddle as a visual aid. Finally, the speaker could show a video clip of a rider in action while explaining how this rider used the saddle effectively. (For more on selecting presentation aids, see the next section.)

- *Keep it simple and relevant.* A fourth strategy for maintaining engagement is to reduce complexity when explaining a main point or subpoint. Instead of discussing five ways for college students to decrease stress, pick the three that will be most relevant to the audience. If two credible research sources make the same basic point, choose the shorter quotation. Rather than presenting a long list of statistics, choose the most important one or two, and invest more time in helping the audience understand and remember them. If you must go into more detail on a particular main point, use signposts along with an internal preview or summary to help the audience keep track of your train of thought (see Chapter 9).

If you have options for how long to speak, plan a virtual message that comes in at the shorter end of the range. For example, if you are asked to speak for five to ten minutes, plan a five- or six-minute speech. If audience members have been sitting in front of the screen for a long time, they will appreciate that you kept your message brief and to the point, and you can use the extra time to let audience members ask questions that are most interesting to them. Of course, in a classroom speech, you always want to meet any minimum time requirement while making your message as interesting as possible.

- *Highlight takeaways.* Finally, emphasize key takeaways for your audience to remember. A **takeaway** is a memorable phrase or sentence that captures

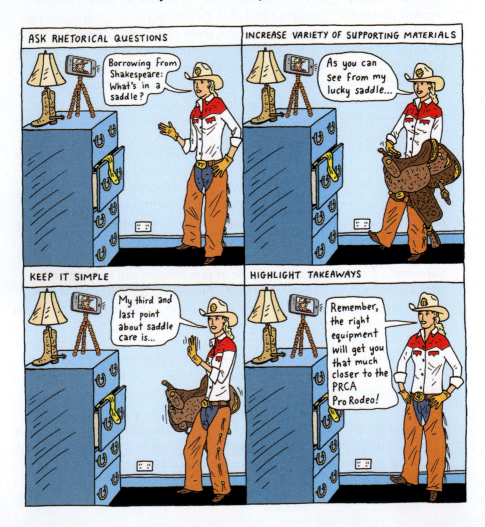

the essence of your speech and can be repeated at key points in the speech. For example, in her speech on cardiovascular disease, Aubrey focused on three risk factors in her main points: stress, poor nutrition, and lack of exercise. Her subpoints explained the importance of minimizing these risks and the many feasible steps students could take. At the end of each main point, Aubrey used repetition, noting, "If you focus on this preventive measure now, your heart will thank you later." She also closed with this key sentence in her clincher.

**Selecting Presentation Aids.** The best presentation aids for a mediated speech need to be easy to see and understand when viewed on a screen, so some presentation aids that would work on campus would not work well in a virtual setting. For example, it would be very difficult to demonstrate a sequence of self-defense moves or display a large object (such as the motorcycle referenced in Chapter 14) when you are using your laptop camera in a Zoom meeting. As another potential challenge, if you hold up a chart for the camera, it can block your face. Here are some ideas for selecting presentation aids in a virtual setting.

- *Use the screensharing feature for videoconferencing.* With many video-conferencing apps, you can share your screen with other participants. This means that presentation aids on your device can be displayed to your audience. For example, you could present photos, videos, graphs, or charts. So rather than demonstrating self-defense moves during your speech, you could show a video of yourself (or another person) performing these moves. You can also incorporate many different types of presentation aids into a presentation using Prezi, PowerPoint, or other similar software.

- *Use an assistant when recording your speech.* If you have a friend or family member who can record your speech, have that person shift the camera shot from you to a presentation aid or widen the angle so that you and your aid are both visible. They should return the camera shot to you when you have finished discussing your presentation aid.

- *Record yourself with presentation aids.* If you need to record your own speech, you can set the camera angle so that both you and your presenta-tion aids are visible. Thus, you might have your aids on a flip chart, or place a model or object on a table next to you.

In Chapter 14, we presented guidelines for developing and presenting your aids, such as making sure they are clear and easy to see, and covering or remov-ing aids when they are not in use. Whether your speech is mediated or F2F, these guidelines are essential.

## Practicing Delivery and Recording

Now that you've considered strategies to combat the challenges of mediated presen-tations, it's time to move to the next stage: practice. Whether you are giving a prere-corded or a real-time speech, you should allocate time to practice your presentation, just as you would if you were addressing your audience F2F. If you have a friend or family member who will be recording your speech, have them practice recording you, too. If your camera is not fixed and there are points in your speech where the operator should zoom in on a visual aid, take a closer shot of you, or pan a live audience (if you have one), this can be practiced to ensure that it is handled smoothly.

After you record yourself practicing (or someone else records you), play back the recording to see how your speech will appear to your audience. As you watch, note areas for possible change by considering the following questions:

- Are your rate and volume appropriate?
- Do you appear to be looking at the audience?
- Are all your movements and gestures within view?
- Can your presentation aids be clearly seen? Does the audience have sufficient time to process the content of each of them?
- Does the setting of your speech look professional?
- Do the lighting and background work to create a clear picture of you?

# RECORDING YOUR PRESENTATION

After preparation and lots of practice, it's time to turn to the nitty-gritty of recording. In this section, we discuss how to set up and record your speech effectively. These suggestions will help you record both in-class and out-of-class presentations, such as a video for a scholarship application or a virtual presentation in the workplace.

Finally, although this section focuses primarily on prerecorded speeches, keep in mind that many of the tips about the *video technology*, *setting and background*, *attire*, and *camera positioning* can also be applied to real-time presentations. In the case of prerecorded speeches, *reviewing your speech before you submit* it will be an additional important step.

## Video Technology

There is no need to buy an expensive camcorder to record your speech when you can make a very good recording with an iPad or a smartphone camera. In our experience, most students use smartphones to record their speeches. When using a smartphone to shoot video, remember these tips:

1. Use a tripod to steady your shot or place your phone on a surface where it will be level and not move. Small tripods for smartphones can cost under $10.
2. Shoot your video horizontally (wide screen) instead of vertically (narrow screen) because it will help you capture more in the shot.
3. Shoot a ten-second sample video, then replay it to make sure the lighting and sound quality are acceptable.

For best results, do any editing on your computer, where a larger screen will allow you to see everything in more detail.

## Setting and Background

The background for your prerecorded presentation should look as professional as possible. You don't need a setting that would get top marks on Twitter's Room Rater, just make sure your surroundings are neat and orderly. Think about what appears behind you on the screen as well, because even an appropriate item may create a distraction. For example, be sure that the plant or lamp you're standing in front of doesn't appear to be growing out of your head.[31] If you'd prefer to try something different, another option is to use a virtual background when recording your speech; many colleges have a set of campus-themed backgrounds available that can set the scene. You may also choose to deliver your speech in a conference room at your college or in a neighborhood library.

Be sure to avoid background noises that might compete with your speech, like an episode of *RuPaul's Drag Race* blaring in the background or a boisterous friend barging into the room to celebrate because they got off work early. If it is difficult to find a time where it is quiet at home, that is another reason you might want to reserve a room at your college library.

The primary light source should be behind the camera and directed toward you. Avoid standing in front of a sunny window or a bright light; otherwise, you will be in shadow. It is generally better to have more light than less, so be sure to select a well-lit room. You can also bring in additional light if the room seems too dark.[32] However, if you're blond, beware of standing directly beneath a bright light (it might make your head appear to glow).

---

▼ **Virtual Speech Backgrounds.** Stacey Abrams and N.K. Jemisin hold their Keynote Conversation on the power of storytelling for SXSW Online 2021. Abrams has a cityscape virtual background, Jemisin—a science fiction author—has a fictional character in the background, and the ASL interpreter uses a plain background. SXSW/Getty Images

## Attire

In addition to selecting clothing that is appropriate for public speaking (see Chapter 13), you need to choose clothing that will make a good impression on camera. Solid neutral colors are generally better than plaids or stripes.[33] Striped clothing can result in a "strobing effect" that will distract the audience.[34] Checked clothing may blur, and the brightness of pure white may make it difficult to see your face clearly.[35] When you practice your speech, you will be able to see how you and your speech setting will appear to the audience, so be sure to wear the clothes you will wear for the actual speech. A special note about jewelry: avoid wearing bangles or anything that can make noise, as it will be an audible distraction during your presentation.

## Camera Positioning

You or your carefully chosen camera operator should check that the camera is trained on the correct shot. Your instructor may have specific visual requirements (such as having the video show your full body or show you from the waist up). If you are required to speak to an audience, your instructor may also

DO NOT ASK ANY OF THESE PEOPLE TO BE YOUR CAMERA OPERATOR

THE SLEEPY OPERATOR

THE CLUMSY OPERATOR

THE DISTRACTED OPERATOR

ask you to record the comments of listeners both before and after your speech. You'll need to plan for these types of shots.

When recording your speech, be sure the camera view is wide enough to capture your movements and gestures. If no specific shot is required, avoid using "talking head" shots, in which the audience can see only your head and upper body. These tend to be perceived as boring by the audience, and they limit much of your nonverbal communication. Also, if you are recording yourself without a tripod, be sure your device is on a flat surface to avoid camera shakiness.

Take care to position the camera at the level of your eyes. This will make you appear to be having conversational eye contact with audience members rather than looking down on them.[36] Changing the camera shot while recording presents challenges, but it can help enliven your speech.[37] If you have an assistant recording your speech, coordinate with them so these changes look seamless and they are done at the correct points in your speech. Assuming your microphone is in the camera, it should remain about the same distance from you for the entire speech. If that distance becomes greater, you will sound farther away: a microphone can't zoom in or out the way a lens can.[38]

## Reviewing Your Speech Before You Submit

Practicing in advance should minimize problems when you do a final take for a prerecorded presentation. However, allow sufficient time for a do-over if you experience any issues during recording. As with your practice takes, watch the finished product to make sure you have a quality recording before you submit your speech. Also, remember to save your final speech in more than one place (such as the cloud, a USB drive, or an external hard drive), as you would for any important school materials.

> **Effective mediated public speaking offers a world of challenges and opportunities.**

In this chapter, we examined mediated public speaking, in which a message is transmitted using technology. We contrasted mediated communication with F2F communication. Although mediated communications do not have the immediacy of F2F communications, they offer several advantages and, even post-pandemic, are sure to be used increasingly in schools and the workplace. Mediated speeches fall into one of two categories—prerecorded presentations and real-time presentations.

Some of the general advantages of all mediated presentations are flexibility, savings, and audience size. The advantages of prerecorded presentations include do-overs, pause and rewind buttons, and the access to a saved copy. The advantages of real-time presentations include audience feedback, audience interaction, and the option to save. The loss of naturalness that comes with mediated presentations brings about some challenges as well, including loss of immediacy, decreased nonverbal communication, diminished feedback, difficulty managing distractions, and videoconferencing fatigue. In addition, mediated presentations are subject to unique technological difficulties. Still, there are ways to combat these challenges effectively—by optimizing delivery methods (voice, eye contact, and movement and gestures) and adapting your message appropriately (focusing on building common ground, keeping audience members engaged, and selecting helpful presentation aids). It's also important to practice a mediated speech beforehand.

When recording a presentation, carefully consider your video technology, the setting and background, your attire, and the camera positioning. Also be sure to review your recording before you submit it and save a copy.

## Key Terms

mediated communication *368*

real-time (synchronous) presentation *370*

prerecorded (asynchronous) presentation *370*

naturalness *374*

multitasking *376*

takeaway *382*

## Review Questions

1. Define *mediated communication* and provide three examples of situations in which a mediated presentation might be used.
2. Name and define the two major categories of mediated presentations.
3. Identify three advantages of mediated presentations.

4. Define *naturalness*, and explain the challenges speakers face when not presenting in a F2F situation.
5. Identify three things to keep in mind for effective delivery of mediated presentations.
6. Name five ways of keeping your audience engaged during a mediated presentation.
7. Name three suggestions for practicing the delivery of a mediated speech.
8. Explain how the background for a prerecorded speech should look.

## Critical Thinking Questions

1. Will mediated public speaking ever replace F2F speeches as the preferred format for presentations? Explain your answer.
2. Most schools changed from F2F to mediated classes during the pandemic. What were the advantages to remote instruction? The disadvantages?
3. Say you have been assigned to record a presentation for your class, and you have three choices for locations—the campus study lounge, your apartment, or the campus bar. The campus study lounge may be occupied by students who are prepping for final exams, your apartment has stains on the carpet and the sofa, and the campus pub (where you work) will be mostly empty when it opens a little before lunchtime. Which location would you choose, and why?
4. Instead of trying to replicate the features of F2F communication to the greatest extent possible, as often happens now, Professor Yulia Shkorko suggests that we embrace video–mediated communication's uniqueness and develop a separate set of best practices optimized for users interacting in mediated contexts.[39] Consider your own experiences with mediated communication. Are there ways that your communication differs from how you interact in F2F settings? If so, do you think that these different communication practices work better in a virtual environment? Explain your response.

## Activities

1. Working individually or in groups, prepare a plan to prerecord a speech. Include the type of camera you will use, as well as the setting and background, speaker's attire, and camera positioning.
2. Look at the illustration on page 387. How would you redraw this picture to correct the three camera operators? What should each person do differently?
3. Working individually, think of a face to face speech that you have given in the past. How would you change your message or delivery if you were presenting that speech in a mediated environment?

# INFORMATIVE
# SPEAKING

# 16

66Effective informative speakers share accessible, understandable information in a compelling way.99

Suppose that many of your class-mates are interested in voting in the next election. But as you talk with them about the candidates and issues, you discover that few students are registered to vote and many are not sure how to go about registering. To complicate matters, there were changes in voter registration procedures for your state during the COVID-19 pandemic, and then some of those procedures were changed again by the state legislature in advance of the upcoming election. Given all of this information, you decide that for your next speech topic—an informative speech—you will explain how to register to vote.

An informative presentation would teach the audience about this topic, increasing listeners' understanding of key elements of the registration pro-cess: who can register, where and how to register, when to register, and what to expect after submitting a registration application. If some of the students you'll be speaking to intend to live in their home state when not at school, you might also explain the mechanics of registering in only one location, including how to sign up for an absentee ballot. And for a generation accus-tomed to using smartphones in all aspects of life, you might direct audience

---

◄ **Registering to Vote.** An informative speech about registering to vote needs to clearly let the audience know their options. Shana Novak/Getty Images

members to accessible websites where they can begin the registration process online.[1] Your goal should be to provide all the information eligible students need to decide whether they want to register to vote, and explain how to do so.

In this chapter, we take a close look at informative speaking and explore how best to craft an informative speech. First, we examine specific techniques for informing. Next, we consider the common types of informative speeches. Finally, we address how to develop an informative speech and how to simplify complex information in your presentation.

# TECHNIQUES FOR INFORMING

Most informative speeches rely on one of the following techniques for conveying information—*definition*, *explanation*, *description*, *demonstration*, or *narrative*. Although some topics may lend themselves to one or another of these techniques, you will typically use a blend of techniques in your informative presentation.

## Definition

Through **definition**, you break down something by its parts and explain how they add up to identify the topic. In short, you explain the essence, meaning, purpose, or identity of something. That "something" could be any of the following:

- An object—for example, "What is an E-V?"
- A person or a group—for instance, "What are progressives?"
- An event—such as, "What was 'the shot heard round the world?'"
- A process—for instance, "What is hacking?"
- An idea or a concept—for example, "What is obscenity?"

As we discuss in Chapter 8, there are four types of definitions. An example of each is shown in the table on page 393, which demonstrates how you might use each of the four types to define the word *obscenity*.

## Explanation

Through **explanation**, you analyze something clearly and specifically by tracing a line of reasoning or a series of causal connections between events. While you do this, you might also offer examples to illustrate the information you're sharing. Explanation works well when you're giving a speech about a process, tracing the history of an important event, or describing how an interesting object

## TYPES OF DEFINITIONS

| Type | Explanation | Example |
|------|-------------|---------|
| Dictionary | The meaning of a term as it appears in a dictionary | *Merriam-Webster's Collegiate Dictionary*, Eleventh Edition, defines *obscenity* as "something that is obscene"—that is, "disgusting to the senses." |
| Expert | The meaning of a term that comes from a person or an organization that is a credible source of information on the topic | According to Chief Justice Warren Burger of the U.S. Supreme Court in the 1973 case *Miller v. California*, obscenity is expression that appeals to a "prurient" (sick or unhealthy) interest in sex or sexual matters; depicts sexual conduct in a "patently offensive way"; and, when taken as a whole, "lacks serious literary, artistic, political, or scientific value." |
| Etymological | The understanding of a word or concept that is obtained by tracing its roots in the same or other languages | The word *obscenity* may derive from the Latin word *obscaenus*, combining the prefix *ob* (meaning "to") and the word *caenum* (meaning "dirt," "filth," "mire," and "excrement"). |
| Functional | The meaning of a term that comes from examining how it is applied or how it functions | In practice, American law recognizes *obscenity* as hard-core pornography (and not as violence, disease, or other social ills). |

*JUSTICE POTTER STEWART, CONCURRING OPINION ON *JACOBELLIS V. OHIO* (1964)

works. For instance, you could use explanation to help your audience understand any one of the following:

- The most common causes of running injuries
- The events and decisions that led to the demise of the Soviet Union
- How the engine in a hybrid car works
- The stages that a person usually goes through when grieving
- How cell mitosis works
- How to participate at city council meetings—virtually or in person

Let's assume you are giving a speech that explains how to take part in civic engagement with local government. Your speech might begin by explaining how audience members can participate if they want to attend a city council meeting. You might talk about how this effort shows a commitment to democracy, but acknowledge that it may not be feasible for people who have family and work-related obligations. You could then explain the process for virtual participation if you cannot be there in person.

Alternatively, you might use explanation to introduce the audience to an element of cultural diversity. For example, your presentation may explain key elements of the Bahá'í religion, which celebrates and honors the life of Bahá' u'lláh

▼ **Explaining the Bahá'í Faith.** Bahá'í Gardens, a UNESCO World Heritage Site in Haifa, Israel, is one of the most holy places in the Bahá'í faith. IAISI/Getty Images

(also called the Báb). Being monotheistic, the Bahá'í faith generally acknowledges all of the world's religions, including Judaism, Christianity and Islam, and the religion celebrates several holidays, beginning with Naw-Rúz, the first day on the Bahá'í calendar (on or near March 21). Bahá'ís also celebrate the birth of their leader, as well his ascension to heaven. You could address all of these facts in your explanation.

## Description

When you use **description**, you use words to paint a mental picture for your listeners, so that they can close their eyes and imagine what you are saying. If you provide sufficient information and detail, audience members should be able to experience vividly what you describe—and through multiple senses. For example, you might decide to use description to help your audience understand one of the following:

- What the aurora borealis looks like
- What's involved in working on a presidential campaign
- What the people you see each morning on public transportation look like
- How you felt when you drove a car alone for the first time
- What the crow's caw sounds like early in the morning
- How your city would look if people stopped littering
- What it's like to attend the Burning Man festival in Nevada
- What it looks like when humpback whales breach
- What a freshly applied tattoo feels like

Your descriptions can have maximum effect when you use vivid language, presentation aids, and details that evoke the senses of sight, sound, smell, touch, and taste. This can be especially effective if you use a description as a subpoint to engage listeners' imaginations and place it in the middle of what you're defining, explaining, demonstrating, or telling a story about. (See Chapter 12 for more on effective description.)

## Demonstration

You might choose to provide a **demonstration** of a topic if your goal is to teach your audience how a process or a set of guidelines works. Demonstrations often call for both physical modeling and verbal elements, which you employ as you lead your audience through the parts or steps of whatever you are demonstrating. Your audience learns by watching your modeling and by listening to your words. Because physical modeling often requires the use of props and visual aids, be sure to practice with your aids before giving your speech. And because the purpose of your speech is to teach your audience, you need to be confident that you know your topic thoroughly.

Demonstrations could be helpful for a wide range of informative speeches. For example, you might use a demonstration to show your listeners how to do one of the following:

- Fix a flat tire on a bicycle in five minutes or less
- Care for an orchid in inclement weather
- Create a Zen garden sandbox
- Sell something on Facebook Marketplace
- Milk a goat without assistance
- Perform a praise dance, incorporating music and movement as worship
- Practice self-defense using only your hands
- Properly display and store an American flag

For some of these demonstrations, you could bring the needed props to your speech forum. For instance, to demonstrate how to fold an American flag, you could easily bring in a large flag and—with an assistant—show the proper way to fold it for storage according to military custom.[2] You could also improvise by asking members of your audience about the flags that they've seen in advertising, used as decoration in dorm rooms, or printed on T-shirts and other clothing—before noting that such seemingly patriotic displays are actually violations of the U.S. Flag Code.[3]

Demonstration coupled with repetition of the speech message has proven especially effective as a learning and memory-enhancement tool. A good example of this can be seen in the practices of an organization called Per Scholas, which provides job training to people with low incomes. This program has been spectacularly effective with helping to train computer-repair technicians who

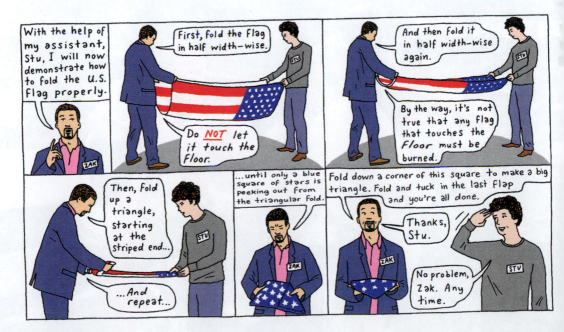

have little or no previous formal education. The practice of demonstrating the repair process and repeating the message has been key to the program's success.[4]

## Narrative

A **narrative** is a story (see Chapter 8). When you use a narrative in an informative speech, the story enables you to share information and capture the audience's attention. The story itself can take the form of a personal remembrance, a humorous anecdote, or a serious account of an event that happened in someone else's life—all told in a way that informs the audience about your topic. Used skillfully, narratives make a speaker more relatable to listeners and thus enhance the speaker's credibility.

Using narrative in an informative speech is a good way to get your point across in an engaging, memorable way. For example, you could use narrative to do one of the following:

- *Open a speech on the risks and dangers associated with playing tackle football.* A poignant introductory story—perhaps about Chris Borland, the star rookie player for the San Francisco 49ers who retired after only one season because he was concerned that repetitive head trauma could cause him

---

▼ **Narratives Tell a Story.** A narrative would be a good technique for telling the story of Chris Borland, who retired from a promising professional football career at age 24 after weighing the risks of head injuries. Michael Zagaris/Getty Images

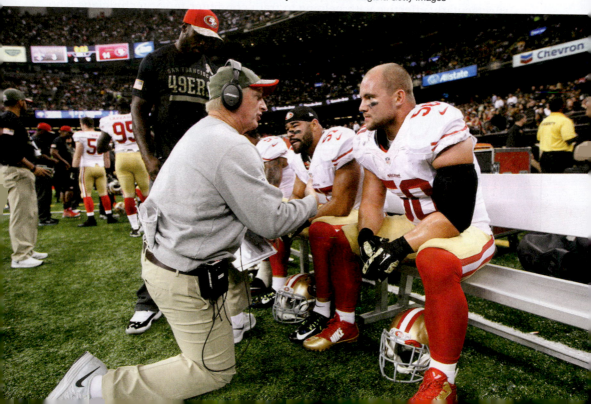

permanent brain damage—could help win your listeners' attention and stir up their emotions right from the start.

- *Emphasize the importance of communication in sustaining intimate relationships.* An entertaining narrative about a misunderstanding that you and your romantic partner ultimately cleared up through skillful communication could help you make your point in a lighthearted but meaningful way.

- *Help your listeners appreciate the need for careful preparation before a job interview.* A story about a friend who failed to research the dress code of a company she was interviewing with and felt embarrassed when she showed up wearing overly casual attire could leave a lasting impression on your listeners.

- *Reveal the difficulty of getting a job after serving time in prison.* A story about the hardships that people who have been to prison face when trying to find jobs and rebuild their lives could raise audience awareness.

Using narrative effectively takes careful thought and preparation. For starters, choose a story that supports your message and avoid throwing in a narrative simply to entertain or captivate your audience. The stories that you select—and the details that go into them—should be based on audience analysis. If you are giving a speech about the risks and dangers of playing tackle football to an audience made up of people who know little about football, you might want to explain who Chris Borland is and why he was important to the San Francisco 49ers team and fans. You might also want to explain how he came upon a study that found degenerative brain disease in posthumous examinations of seventy-six out of seventy-nine former National Football League players.[5] You would probably want to describe how Borland believed that he should walk away from the game before he suffered serious damage from head injuries. Even if you know the elements of the narrative well, you might want to research background information and specific details of the story and weave that information into your speech.

Finally, remember that telling a compelling story in a way that also informs and educates your audience is in itself an art form. You want to come across as casual (rather than over-rehearsed) but also authoritative, which requires extensive preparation and practice. It's as if you need to practice acting unrehearsed. In truth, using narrative in a speech can be risky, but if you do it well, it offers you and your audience real rewards.

# TYPES OF INFORMATIVE SPEECHES

Informative speeches seek to share information, explanations, or even ideas with an audience. Unlike persuasive speeches, which seek to make an argument and therefore confirm or alter an audience's beliefs or actions, informative speeches are meant to give audience members knowledge they might not have possessed before the speech. As suggested earlier in this chapter, informative speeches can be about a wide range of topics—*objects, individuals or groups, events, processes,* or *ideas.* In this section, we take a closer look at each of these types of informative speeches.

## Objects

If you're giving an informative speech about an object, you have a virtually unlimited range of possibilities to choose from. The one thing all objects have in common, though, is that they're not human. The following table shows a small sampling of the large universe of possible objects your speech could address.

### TYPES OF OBJECTS SUITABLE FOR AN INFORMATIVE SPEECH

| Type | Examples |
| --- | --- |
| Mechanical or technological | motorcycle<br>blender<br>smartphone<br>weapons system |
| Natural | flowering plant<br>river<br>elephant<br>planet |
| Cultural | clothing<br>art<br>religious item<br>gourmet dish |
| Personal | jacket<br>credit card<br>ice skates<br>necklace |

In giving an informative speech about a particular object, you could use a number of techniques. For example, suppose you're preparing a presentation about the benefits of chocolate—which is a food and therefore an object. In this case, you could easily use description to inform your audience. You might describe the smooth, creamy texture and sumptuous flavor of a high-quality chocolate truffle and the feeling of well-being that can come from eating it.

Depending on the purpose of your speech, you could also use one or more of the other techniques. For example, you might use

- *definition* to clarify what chocolate is and how it differs from other consumable products derived from cacao beans
- *explanation* to trace the process by which chocolate bars are made
- *demonstration* to show how you might bake a chocolate cake, or how you might enjoy it with red wine
- *narrative* to convey chocolate's popularity as a romantic gift

Finally, note that an informative speech about an object may also contain elements of process—especially if that object has moving parts. For instance, to deliver a presentation on how a motorcycle operates, you might explain how the bike's fuel and transmission systems work together to create the process of acceleration.

## Individuals or Groups

Giving an informative speech about an individual or a group offers an equally wide range of possibilities. People are fascinated by others, as can be seen from the popularity of celebrity-focused magazines, reality-based television shows, and personal memoirs. Human subjects with extraordinary physical or emotional characteristics or compelling life stories can provide engaging and informative material for speeches. Groups, likewise, are collections of people with whom your audience can identify; these can include famous politicians in the same party or musical performers who capture tremendous amounts of attention. To illustrate, you could focus your talk on one of the following:

- *A famous politician, entertainer, sports star, explorer, or artist.* For example, you might give a speech about Shirley Chisholm, the first Black woman elected to the U.S. Congress (in 1968) and a candidate for president in the 1972 Democratic primary, nearly four decades before Barack Obama or Hillary Clinton.

- *An unidentified hero* (a person or a group that did something great but never won personal recognition for the accomplishment). For instance, you could tell your audience about the so-called "Ghost of Kyiv"—said to be an unnamed pilot (or perhaps even a legend representing all Ukrainian pilots) who shot down multiple Russian fighter planes in February 2022, once Russia had invaded Ukraine in an attempt to reconstruct the former Soviet Union.

- *A tragic figure whose life provides a cautionary tale.* For example, you might discuss a fictional tragic figure by highlighting Daniel Craig's performance as James Bond in Craig's final 007 film ("No Time to Die"), in which he sacrifices his own life to insure others around the planet will be spared.

- *An influential political party, artistic movement, sports team, or musical group.* For instance, you might discuss the rise of women in comedy—including those writing and starring in their own television shows and those helping to diversify existing shows. Alternatively, you might discuss how the influence of the Republican party changed when Donald Trump became president and many of his

▼ **Informing the Audience about a Trailblazer.** Shirley Chisholm won the fourth highest number of delegate votes at the 1972 Democratic convention, finishing ahead of former Vice President Hubert Humphrey and future Vice President Walter Mondale. Throughout her career, she was a powerful advocate for the rights of women and people of color. PhotoQuest/Getty Images

supporters felt more loyalty to him and the policies he supported than to the traditional Republican platform.

As with objects, you could easily use description to deliver your informative speech about an individual or a group. For example, if your speech focused on aviator Amelia Earhart, you could describe her youth and personal qualities along with her famed accomplishments. You also might use narrative to tell a story about the defining experience that led her to become a pilot (namely, attending a stunt-flying exhibition in her late teens). Or you could use explanation to trace the events that led her to attempt her biggest challenge—flying around the world.

Remember that although you will not be able to describe all of a person's life experiences in a single speech, you can use life events to make a larger point about a person's character—what kind of person they are. You could support such claims by using narratives supplied by the person's family, friends, and associates, or even critics and enemies.

A presentation on a person or a group might effectively incorporate information about an object or a process as well. For example, consider a talk on Lucid Motors'

▲ **Women in Comedy.** Comedians Tiffany Haddish and Ali Wong, who provide the voices for Tuca and Bertie in the animated comedy of the same name, at the 2019 Tribeca Film Festival. Astrid Stawiarz/Getty Images

Chief Executive Officer Peter Rawlinson (a former Tesla engineer), who not only helped develop and create the Lucid E-V (electric vehicle), but also built it so well that it outperformed Tesla, with the Lucid E-V going 520 miles on a single charge. To convey Rawlinson's innovative spirit, you could discuss his experiences at Tesla and how they led to his great achievements with Lucid. You could also describe the process by which his Lucid "Air" model was named Motor Trend's Car of the Year for 2022.[6]

**EARHART, Amelia**

BORN IN ATCHISON, KANSAS (1897)

SHE FELL IN LOVE WITH FLYING IN HER LATE TEENS AT A STUNT-FLYING EXHIBITION.

SHE NAMED HER FIRST PLANE "CANARY."

IN 1928, SHE BECAME THE FIRST WOMAN TO FLY ACROSS THE ATLANTIC. THE TRIP TOOK 21 HOURS.

DURING THE LAST LEG OF HER 1937 FLIGHT AROUND THE WORLD, SHE DISAPPEARED OVER THE PACIFIC OCEAN.

## Events

An event is a notable or exceptional occurrence, either from the present time or from some point in the past. Here are just a few examples of events on which you could focus an informative speech:

- The signing into law of the Twenty-Sixth Amendment, which lowered the voting age to eighteen
- The discovery of a new planet or species
- The outcome of a high-profile murder trial
- The publication of an important new book
- An underdog's surprising victory over the favorite in a sporting event
- The emergence in the business world of a new and different kind of company
- The unearthing of new evidence suggesting the origins of humankind
- A wedding, funeral, or religious ritual in your family
- The Stonewall Uprising
- The deaths of multiple, unarmed Black men at the hands of the police
- The Billabong Pipe Masters at Banzai Pipeline
- A commemoration at the Tomb of the Unknowns
- Fashion Week in New York City
- The January 6, 2021, insurrection attempt to overturn the presidential election of Joe Biden

How do you decide what event would make a good topic for an informative speech? Look for events that your audience will consider exciting, newsworthy, historically important, or interesting because they are unfamiliar or surprising.

# BLENDING NARRATIVE AND DESCRIPTION

In delivering an informative speech about an event, you could easily use narrative to tell the story of how the event unfolded. You also could use description to explain how the event affected a group of people. Or you could employ a blend of both narrative and description. For instance, suppose you were presenting a speech about the day you became an American citizen. You might begin with a narrative about your experiences as an immigrant, including anecdotes about your travels from your home country and your family's struggle to establish itself in America. You might then detail the process of applying for citizenship. Finally, you might describe what happened at your naturalization ceremony and how it felt for you to take the citizenship pledge.

## Processes

Imagine that you're filing a tax return, changing a tire, planting a vegetable garden, or giving a haircut to a friend. Or maybe you're thinking about how two countries resolve a border dispute, how Major League Baseball owners and the players' union negotiate the baseball salary cap for each team, or how marriages are arranged in a particular culture.

Each of these is a process—a series of steps or stages that lead to a particular outcome. You can detect processes at the level of something localized and simple (such as how to change a tire) and at a much broader level (such as how changes in labor and immigration laws and trade policies affect the cost of automobiles, including tires, in different countries and markets). Thus, we sometimes suggest

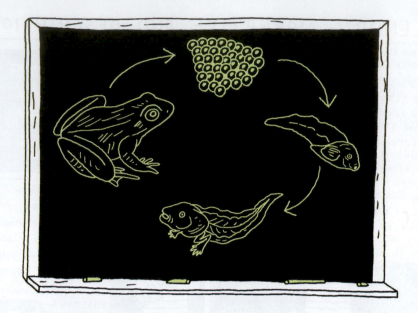

that processes can be seen at both the micro level (the view of a process from fifty feet) and the macro level (the view from five thousand feet). Many of the informative presentations in a speech class will involve the micro level (which is easier to explain and grasp), but that shouldn't discourage you from trying a macro-level topic (such as the ways in which global warming occurs). When presented as a process, even large topics can be digestible for most audiences.

Remember that some topics (such as how changes in the tax code will affect the alternative minimum tax) do not lend themselves well to a discussion of process because they are highly technical. Does this mean you should avoid a technical topic? No, but it does mean that if you select a topic because it *is* process oriented, you should focus on subject matter that is within your audience's level of understanding, break down the topic into smaller parts, and only then show how those parts work together as part of a larger process.

▼ **Speeches about a Process.** A speech about a process could inform listeners about how dogs donate blood (left) or how to launch a hashtag (right). (left) The Sydney Morning Herald/Getty Images; (right) SAUL LOEB/Getty Images

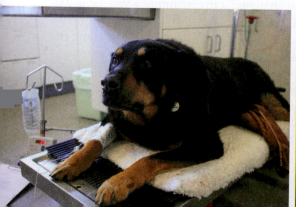 

When you deliver an informative speech about a process, you will probably want to walk your listeners through the steps that make up that process, explaining how each is carried out and in what order.

Depending on your goal, use a variety of techniques to inform your audience about a particular process. For example, if you want listeners to understand how a specific object is made or how it works, you might use explanation to clarify what each step is and how it leads to the creation of the object.

By contrast, if your goal is to teach audience members how to perform the process themselves, combine both explanation and demonstration—that is, verbally and physically model the steps of the process.

To illustrate, suppose you're giving a presentation on cake decorating. You'd probably want to explain what tools are needed and what kinds of icings are appropriate for particular styles of decoration. You also might demonstrate by showing the actual techniques used to produce a certain decoration—for example, a basket-weave design—through enlarged photographs or a video. If you are in a relatively intimate environment, you might even decorate an actual cake as part of your presentation.

In deciding which process to focus on in an informative speech, take care to avoid overused topics (such as how to make the perfect peanut butter and jelly sandwich) and topics related to alcohol (such as how to make Jell-O shots or brew beer at home). Instead, think about processes that would be interesting and fresh for your listeners. Also, consider how you might discuss the effects of an important process. For instance, suppose you're informing your audience about how the baseball farm system works. In this case, you could add interest to the topic by using a narrative to convey how the process changes young players' lives by giving them a shot at the big leagues.

## Ideas

An idea is a theory, principle, belief, or value. Ideas are relatively abstract compared to other informative speech topics, such as an object, a person, or a process. For example, it's easier to explain what the aurora borealis looks like or how a motorcycle engine works than it is to describe the notion of freedom of speech. Freedom of speech is more difficult to explain for two reasons: first, it's an idea and not a physical object or process, and second, there are limits to freedom of speech. Indeed, this concept has several subtleties that restrict its application in many situations (for example, it is illegal to incite certain kinds of violence or to threaten to kill another person).[7]

Some ideas are emotionally loaded because people have difficulty agreeing on their meaning. Consider the notion of terrorism. Its meaning seems obvious to many after the September 11, 2001, attacks in New York; Washington, D.C.; and Pennsylvania and their repercussions. But are all violent acts against civilians or noncombatants terrorism? Are nation-states guilty of terrorism when their troops accidentally kill civilians? Why do people say things like "One man's terrorist is another man's freedom fighter?" Like freedom of expression, terrorism is a more complex and abstract notion than it may initially appear.

Here are some additional ideas that could be topics for an informative speech about an idea:

- Family values
- Income inequality
- The economic effects of globalization
- Generational theft
- The disadvantages of technology
- The saying "It's better to give than to receive"
- The separation of church and state
- The advantages of working for employers who contribute to social or ethical causes
- Critical race theory

Because ideas are abstract, it's important to make a careful selection when considering topics for an informative speech. Otherwise, you might fail to connect with your audience during your presentation. Be sure to consider your audience's interests and level of education when you weigh potential ideas to discuss in your speech. For example, if you want to inform your listeners about the economic effects of globalization, think about how much your audience already knows about the topic. If audience members' knowledge is scanty, you'll need to provide more background on globalization during your speech; alternatively, you might decide to select another topic with which your listeners are more familiar.

Also ask yourself whether audience members have had prior exposure to the idea you want to discuss in your presentation. If they have—and did not find the idea compelling—you may want to consider selecting a different topic.

Finally, consider how you might make a particularly abstract idea more understandable to your listeners during your presentation. In a talk on the effects of globalization, for example, you could draw the following analogy: "Globalization is like agriculture. In agriculture, the more evenly you spread seeds across a large field, the more certain you can be that crops will grow in every corner of the field. Likewise, the more you allow commercial activity to flourish across many countries, the more you'll encourage economic well-being among the world's populations."

Most informative speeches about ideas require the use of definition or explanation, both of which enable you to clarify the meaning of the idea you're discussing and to examine its various ramifications. For instance, although the meaning of the word *terrorism* is hotly debated in academic and political circles, most people define it as a form of calculated violence (or the threat thereof) against civilians or noncombatants for the purpose of creating mass anxiety and panic while publicizing a political or social agenda.[8] An informative speech on terrorism might begin with that definition, but to further clarify the idea of terrorism, you could separate each part of the definition and explain it individually. For instance, to clarify what "publicizing a political or social agenda" means, you could offer several examples of groups that have committed violent acts and used the resulting publicity to advance their cause.

# DEVELOPING YOUR INFORMATIVE SPEECH

To develop an informative speech, you use the same strategies described in earlier chapters, such as analyzing your audience's background and needs, deciding which supporting materials to include, and determining how to organize your content. In this section, we examine several specific strategies in the context of informative speaking: *analyzing your audience, selecting a technique* for your speech, *selecting an organizational pattern, focusing on your goal to inform,* and *clarifying and simplifying your message.* Taking these steps enables you to prepare a solid foundation and structure for your speech.

## Analyzing Your Audience

As with any type of public presentation, audience analysis is essential for developing a successful informative speech. As you would in any speech, focus on situational characteristics, demographics, and common ground. These topics are covered in depth in Chapter 5.

In addition, it is important to understand that analyzing your audience for an informative presentation raises unique challenges. Prior exposure is a significant concern when analyzing your audience for an informative speech. To make your speech as useful as possible for them, you will want to analyze what your audience already knows about the topic and what they do not. That way, you can focus on aspects of your topic that will be new to your listeners. Building audience interest is also very important. Try to anticipate which elements of the topic will be most interesting to the people you will be addressing. Finally, anticipate which elements of the topic may be the most difficult to understand and be sure to devote enough time and diverse supporting materials to develop those parts of your speech.

## Selecting a Technique for Informing

Your audience analysis also informs which technique(s) you choose for delivering your informative speech. Which technique(s) would *most* help you inform your audience about your topic—definition, explanation, description, demonstration, narrative, or a combination of these? Your choice of technique is crucial because it helps you decide how you'll develop and organize the main points and supporting materials in your presentation.

For example, suppose you were considering using demonstration to present your informative speech. In this case, you would want to ask yourself the following questions:

- *Forum:* "Where will the audience be situated—and will there be ample space for me to move around as I give my demonstration?"
- *Audience size:* "How many people will be in my audience—and will they all be able to see and hear my demonstration?"

## SELECTING A TECHNIQUE TO INFORM

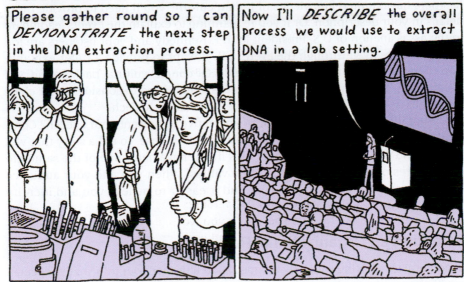

As another example, let's say you were considering using explanation or description to deliver your speech. In this case, you would focus more on demographics to analyze your audience. Look for anything in your listeners' backgrounds and characteristics that may make it difficult for them to understand the explanation or description you're planning to offer in your speech. For instance,

if you're planning to describe how the New Year is celebrated in India and your listeners have limited knowledge of Indian culture, you'll need to provide more details in your description. Or if you're planning to explain the events leading up to the assassination of U.S. President John F. Kennedy and your listeners are too young to have lived through the event, you'll want to provide a fuller explanation than you would for an older audience. Of course, cultural background and age are only two examples of demographics. You'll need to consider other characteristics in order to develop an effective informative speech.

What if you're thinking about using narrative to present your speech? Common ground becomes particularly important in this case. To tell a story that will interest and move your listeners, it helps if you have had some of the same life experiences or share some of the same values. When you and your audience have common ground, listeners will find it easier to believe you and identify with the narrative you're presenting.

## Selecting an Organizational Pattern

In addition to selecting which technique(s) you'll use for your informative speech, you'll also need to make another significant decision: selecting an organizational pattern for your speech. For more on organizational patterns, see the discussion in Chapter 9, as well as the examples included in the table below.

### ORGANIZING YOUR INFORMATIVE SPEECH

| Organizational Pattern | Pattern Description | Example |
|---|---|---|
| Spatial | Describes or explains elements or events as they occur in space | A speech that explains the trajectory of a meteor that may come dangerously close to Earth |
| Chronological (temporal) | Moves from the beginning to the end by referencing points in time | A speech that describes a negotiation process, breaking down each bargaining step as it occurs |
| Causal | Explains the roots of a phenomenon or process | A speech that explains how plate tectonics cause earthquakes and tsunamis |
| Comparison | Presents major similarities and differences between two items | A speech that compares the global reach and power of the twenty-first-century United States with that of ancient Rome |
| Categorical (topical) | Main points constitute separate topics, each of which supports the thesis | A speech that explains running a marathon, breaking it down into separate categories for training, nutrition, technique and style, and mental preparation |

## Focusing on Your Goal to Inform

When developing an informative speech, it's particularly important to remain focused on your rhetorical purpose: to inform. If you know your subject well, be sure to establish your credentials—noting, for example, "As someone who's played in poolrooms all over this state for more than two decades, I am fairly well schooled in the rules of the game." You should also remember that it's your responsibility to remain objective. If you find yourself choosing evidence that supports a particular point of view, you are going beyond informing. Some topics make it easy to remain objective (such as knitting or explaining how an engine works), whereas other topics (such as defining terrorism or freedom of speech) invariably wander into more persuasive territory. We discuss persuasion further in Chapters 17 and 18.

## Clarifying and Simplifying Your Message

As you prepare your informative speech, focus on clarifying and simplifying your message as much as possible. It will help your audience understand and thus retain your message.

Clarity is something you'll want to strive for in every informative speech, no matter what your topic is or who your listeners are. If you present a message that's confusing or use words that have vague meanings, it will be hard to connect with your audience.

In addition to clarifying your message, your audience analysis will help you decide how much to simplify your informative speech. For example, if listeners have little knowledge of your topic and the topic is complex, simplicity will be vital. A student named Jean once gave an informative presentation on a complex

COMPLEX                    SIMPLE

experimental genetic treatment that doctors and research scientists could use to fight cancer. Her audience was made up of students in her speech class, few of whom had more than a general knowledge of the subject matter. Jean wisely simplified things by first narrowing the broad topic of "treatment" to the more specific area of "gene therapy." She then simplified the topic further by describing a simple three-step process for introducing genes into cells to prevent disease.

To clarify and simplify complex messages, consider the techniques that follow.

### Move from General to Specific. Ask yourself, "At a minimum, what do I want my audience to take away from my speech? What basic message should they carry away with them?" Your answer can help you narrow a general or broad topic to a specific, simpler one—as in Jean's speech on gene therapy.

▲ **General to Specific.** An informative speech about ants could begin with a general idea about ants, such as that many types of ants can sting. Then the speech could move to a specific example, such as bullet ants, which have especially painful and venomous stings. Their venom has been researched for use as a natural pesticide.
(left) Elizaveta Galitckaia/Shutterstock; (right) Dr Morley Read/Getty Images

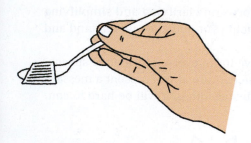

REDUCE THE QUANTITY
OF INFORMATION YOU
PRESENT

**Reduce the Quantity of Information You Present.** An informative speech may contain a tremendous amount of information for the audience to hear, process, and remember. An old adage still rings true here: "Less is more." Look for ways to reduce the number of details you present. A speech about gene therapy could contain huge volumes of information, but Jean pared back the quantity of information she presented by reducing the details to a three-step process.

**Make Complex Information Seem Familiar.** You can further clarify a complex message by using definition to explain difficult-to-follow terms and ideas. You can also avoid **jargon**—technical or insider terminology not easily understood by people outside a certain group or field (see Chapter 12). In addition, you can draw analogies between complex ideas and things your listeners

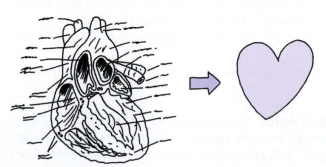

are already familiar with.[9] For example, Jean could have made an analogy between gene therapy (a new concept for her audience) and a vaccine against polio (something that is probably familiar to her audience).

▲ **Presentation Aids Clarify the Message.** You probably couldn't bring goats into the classroom to demonstrate goat yoga, but photos would help the audience understand what this experience is like. picture alliance/Getty Images

**Use Presentation Aids.** Presentation aids can help you clarify and simplify your message. For instance, a diagram of the three-step gene-therapy process that Jean described could have helped her listeners envision the process and thus remember it. Likewise, if you are giving a speech on various bird calls, you could play a recording of a particular call instead of relying only on lengthy descriptions or demonstrations of what the call sounds like.

**Reiterate Your Message.** Through *reiteration*, you clarify a complex message by referring to it several times, using different words each time. For example, in an informative presentation about training for a biathlon, a speaker referred three times to the importance of using a heart-rate monitor. The first time he made the point, he said, "It's vital to use a heart-rate monitor to regulate intensity while you're training." The second time, he said, "Using a heart-rate monitor can really help you regulate your intensity." The third time, he

REITERATE YOUR MESSAGE

**REPEAT YOUR MESSAGE**

said, "The more you use the monitor, the more information you'll have on whether you are maintaining the right intensity." By reiterating key points, you help your audience remember your message.

**Repeat Your Message.** Conveying a key point several times using the same words can also help ensure that your audience understands your message. For example, while introducing the gene-therapy process, Jean could have said something like, "This three-step process offers the best hope for treating cancer in the future." Then, in the conclusion of her speech, she could have said, "Let me repeat: this three-step process offers the best hope for treating cancer in the future."

## SAMPLE INFORMATIVE SPEECH

### SPIDER SILK: A MIRACLE MATERIAL DERIVED FROM . . . GOATS?

**Rachel Parish**
*Southeastern Illinois College*

*Student Rachel Parish gave this informative speech in the 2007 finals of an annual national tournament hosted by Phi Rho Pi, a group that fosters public speaking and debate for junior and community college students throughout the United States. In this speech about an object, Rachel explains the astonishing strength and versatility of a material that may surprise her listeners— spider silk. Rachel's speech is organized categorically, or by topic, with the main points describing spider silk's properties, the means of producing it, and a number of its applications.*

In the classic book *Charlotte's Web*, we find the story of a loving spider saving pitiful Wilbur from becoming bacon through messages spun in her webs. However, this is not the first time that such power has come from such a seemingly delicate medium.

In ancient Greece, spiderwebs were used to stop bleeding in open wounds. Aboriginal people use spider silk in small fishing lines. And how could we not mention Peter Parker's amazing ability to swing from buildings and catch the bad guys, all through the power of the web?

Now, that last example may be fictional, but Spider-Man's formidable weapon, the web, is no less amazing in real life. Spider silk is one of the strongest fibers known. It is incredibly fine and tough, and as the November 9, 2006, *London Daily Mail* tells us, "When woven into a fiber, it is weight-for-weight five times stronger than steel." •

So we know that the spiderweb, or spider silk, is tough, and over the past decade we found it to have both practical and medicinal benefits for us. However, to date, we've never actually seen any of the benefits. Why? Well, gathering large quantities of spider silk has been relatively impossible—until now. You see, while we may not have a real-life Spider-Man, we do have Spider*goats*. These are transgenic goats that are producing spider silk on a much larger scale than Charlotte ever could. •

Today we'll learn about the value of spider silk and how these scientifically altered goats are allowing its once unavailable advantages to become a reality. First, we'll look at the background of spider silk; second, the goats' role in its production; and finally, its current and future uses. •

Let's first learn about the value of spider silk and how these goats are allowing its once unobtainable potential to be a reality. According to BBCNews.com, July 12, 2006, "Spider silk has been admired by scientists for decades due to its unique combination of strength, toughness, flexibility, and light weight; its thickness is less than one-tenth the size of a human hair, but it has 400,000 pounds per square inch of strength." To put this in perspective, if you built a massive spiderweb in which each strand was the width of a pencil, you could catch a 747 jumbo jet in full flight.

So if spider silk is indeed the strongest fiber on earth, why haven't we taken advantage of this miracle material before? The June 16, 2006, *Science and Technology* tells us that "spiders are incredibly hard to farm so silk can be harvested, mainly due to a spider's nature." • Basically, if you put two spiders together in a confined space, due to their cannibalistic nature you'll suddenly find yourself with only one spider.

In addition, even when they are contained properly, you can harvest only so much silk from a spider. A study this past November by Randy Lewis of the University of Wyoming showed that even when dealing with large spiders, on a good day you can gather only 1.5 mg of silk. Thus, even if you could get the cannibals to get along, a spider farm capable of raising enough useful silk would simply be impossible. •

However, all that has now changed. Last year, Nexia Biotechnologies—a Canadian research firm—began looking

• Rachel's attention-getter includes stories and compelling facts.

• "What's in it for them?": Here she provides an interesting fact about goats and spider silk.

• Rachel quickly gives her thesis and previews her three main points, organized topically.

• Rachel establishes her source's credibility here by citing publication title and date. She could add more credibility by consistently including the author's name and credentials.

• Here and throughout, Rachel offers a variety of supporting materials—mainly examples, expert testimony, and statistics.

at normal farm goats as the key to bringing spider silk to the masses. According to Christopher Helman at Forbes.com, February 19, 2001, Jeffrey Turner, a geneticist at Nexia, discovered that the silk gland of spiders and the milk gland of goats were almost identical, but the goat's is obviously much bigger. At the turn of the millennium, Nexia began implanting spider genes into goats in order to breed "spider goats" capable of producing spider silk in large enough quantities for commercial use. The end result was Webster and Pete, the first two goats born with the spiderweb gene.

Now that we've looked past the roadblocks to cultivating spider silk by showing the creation of a feasible silk resource thanks to Webster and Pete here, let's examine the process by which the spider gene was passed on to the goats. ● According to the January 15, 2006, issue of the journal *Nature*, "Spider silk starts out as a substance called scleroprotein, which shoots out from the spider's web spinnerets. . . . It dries into a thread, and when this thread hardens we end up with something that looks a little more familiar to us."

When Nexia discovered that the silk glands of spiders were similar to goats' mammary glands, Nexia applied this discovery to dairy goats. Taking a goat embryo, Nexia injected the spider gene controlling the creation of silk into the goat's mammary cells. These cells then took effect and activated the female goats when they started lactating, or creating milk for their young. When the lactation period in the goat is over, these cells stop functioning and stop producing silk until the goat starts lactating again. According to *Materials Today*, December 2002, Jeffrey Turner reports that each transgenic goat is "capable of making 'literally miles' of this spider silk–based material." Fifteen thousand goats could produce enough silk to meet projected medical and industrial demands. Plus, because they're not cannibalistic, we're able to farm goats on a large scale. ●

However, the spiders do have one advantage: the goats can't spin the silk they produce, so then there's a weaving process. As explained in the October 10, 2006, airing of *Modern Marvels* on the History Channel, "The goats are milked as they normally would be, then the milk is put into a centrifuge that spins rapidly. This causes the silk fibers to separate from the milk so they can be extracted. Salts are then added to the silk fibers to help them harden. Once this step is completed, you have what researchers have dubbed 'bio-steel.'" According to the June 3, 2006, *Journal of Biological Chemistry*, this new silk made from spider-enhanced goats is the same strength and composition as normal spider silk. The method is environmentally safe, and the goats are not harmed in any way during the milking process. ●

So we've examined the background of spider silk, its genetic switch to goats, and how it has evolved into bio-steel.

**Margin notes:**

● An effective transition signals the end of a previous point and introduces the next one.

● Rachel offers this explanation of a process within her larger topical organization.

● Rachel shows solid audience analysis by anticipating listener concerns: the process is environmentally safe and doesn't harm the goats.

But what benefits can we anticipate from this evolution? Will the use of goat silk bring us from the research lab to the battlefield and the operating room? •

*Biotech Week*, December 13, 2006, reports that bio-steel is now being used to construct bulletproof clothing for soldiers and police. Dr. Randolph Lewis, a biologist at the University of Wyoming, stated in the same issue of *Biotech Week* that Kevlar, the most popular fiber used in bulletproof vests, is very difficult to make and requires a chemical process that is highly damaging to the environment. Unlike Kevlar, spider silk bio-steel is made in water-based conditions, and it's completely biodegradable. • In addition, in tests performed in early 2006 at the University of Wyoming, it was proven that when woven into a bulletproof vest, spider silk was stronger and more durable than the now-outdated Kevlar.

Yet bio-steel's most promising benefits are medicinal rather than military. According to the Royal College of Surgeons of England in "Secrets of the Spider Web," March 9, 2007, "The demand for spider silk in the medical profession is high, with a myriad of potential uses, such as scaffolds, bone grafts, or ligament repair." The real strength of bio-steel as an internal support is its great wall strength and its ability to naturally dissolve over time, without the need of additional surgeries. In addition, the spider silk bio-steel can be used as wonderful, durable, and biodegradable stitches, which can be used in the most delicate of areas due to the material's thinness and strength. What's more, as *Science*, June 23, 2006, reports, spider silk bio-steel provokes a very low immune response when introduced into the body. What does that mean for us? Well, heavy immune responses cause rejection of artificial medical implants, thus making bio-steel a much more successful option than any previous materials. •

The main challenge for researchers is breeding enough goats to meet the demand for bio-steel. However, according to an October 31, 2006, *CBC News* report, "If breeding continues as is, then the University of Wyoming's herd of goats alone will be bountiful enough to meet commercial demands by the end of 2008." In 2006, they produced over 5,200 pounds of spider silk, and just this past August, the UW researchers received a quarter-million-dollar grant from the Department of Defense to expand their output, so the future of goat bio-steel looks very promising.

Today we looked at the background of spider silk, the goat's role in its production, and finally its current and future applications. We can see the value of goat bio-steel for both military and medicinal uses, and in time, perhaps we could imagine America's favorite web slinger changing from Peter Parker to Pete and Webster. •

• Questions act as a transition and keep listeners involved.

• Rachel returns to the theme of environmental safety.

• By outlining bio-steel's medical uses, Rachel again shows what's in it for listeners.

• The conclusion brings the speech full circle with a reference to Spider-Man.

> **Effective informative speakers share accessible, understandable information in a compelling way.**

As the chapter's opening example suggests, informative speaking is about teaching your listeners something and increasing their awareness of your topic. You probably use informative speaking many times during a typical day—whenever you're defining, explaining, describing, demonstrating, or telling a story about something. Whether you're speaking informatively in everyday situations or delivering a formal presentation to a class or another type of audience, you can greatly enhance your effectiveness by applying the key practices presented in this chapter.

First, know how and when to use the five techniques for informative speaking—definition, explanation, description, demonstration, and narrative. Second, decide on the type of informative speech you want to give—whether it will be about an object, an individual or a group, an event, a process, or an idea. Third, employ key strategies to develop your informative speech. Use audience analysis to determine your audience's background and needs and to help you decide which technique you should use to organize your speech. In addition, select an organizational pattern for your speech and stay focused on your goal to inform, which includes maintaining an objective viewpoint. And finally, focus on clarifying and simplifying your message as much as possible.

When you apply these practices, you improve the odds of achieving your purpose in giving an informative speech. You enable your audience members to learn something new and important, and you hone their understanding, awareness, or sensitivity to your topic.

## Key Terms

definition *392*

explanation *392*

description *396*

demonstration *396*

narrative *398*

jargon *414*

## Review Questions

1. Name and explain five techniques for informing.
2. What five types of topics for informative speeches are offered in the chapter?
3. What basic steps must be considered as you develop your informative speech?
4. Name the six basic techniques you can use to clarify and simplify your informative message.

## Critical Thinking Questions

1. What are some potential informative speech topic areas where you have experience or expertise? How would you establish credibility in these areas in your introduction?
2. Have you ever felt that someone who claimed to be informing you was in fact trying to persuade you? What was it about the speaker's presentation that tipped you off? Did this feeling make you more or less receptive to the information the speaker was presenting?
3. Is it possible to define and describe a controversial idea, such as assisted suicide for terminally ill patients, without becoming emotional? Can an informative speech be emotional without becoming persuasive?
4. If you had to give a speech explaining that your fellow college students are at risk by not getting flu shots and providing some options for them, what would you choose to say? Also, how would your audience analysis of your listeners (especially with respect to their age and generation) inform your choices?

## Activities

1. Take a look at any persuasive speech (you can find one at the end of Chapter 18 and another in the Appendix, or search at the library or online for any political campaign speech). Edit it so that the focus of the speech is only on informing. How much of the speech is left?
2. Do you know a topic well enough to prepare a fifteen-minute informative presentation on it? Create a quick outline showing how you would do it.
3. Look up a "how-to" topic (such as how to make compost, play blackjack, or file your taxes) at the library or online. What kinds of sources do you find? Which ones do you find most helpful—and credible—and why?

# PERSUASIVE SPEAKING

# 17

> " Good persuaders make strategic choices in an ethical manner. "

Kaliya was excited about a community service opportunity she'd discovered. The local public television station was going to hold a membership drive, and the station manager was looking for volunteers who could spend four hours on the phones or online helping people set up their memberships. She couldn't wait for the next meeting of ACTION, her service club on campus, so that she could ask club members to volunteer to participate virtually or in person in support of the station, which broadcasted several of her favorite programs.

At the next club meeting, Kaliya stood up and presented her idea. She talked about the mission of public television and listed the programs that were scheduled that day on the station. She then suggested that the club volunteer as a group to participate in the membership drive the following Sunday from 3 to 7 p.m. Finally, she passed out a sign-up sheet. Much to her disappointment, the other club members had little enthusiasm for her idea, and only two people volunteered.

Kaliya had made a common error that frustrates the best intentions of those attempting to persuade others to adopt their ideas. Although she loved her local public television station, she had not considered how other club members might respond to her plan. For one thing, she failed to explain how volunteering would benefit the participants—an important consideration in any persuasive

---

◄ **Persuading Your Audience.** To succeed as a persuasive speaker, you need a message that is both strategic and ethical. izusek/Getty Images

speech. Furthermore, she lost her audience's attention when she began listing the station's programs, so by the time she suggested that club members should get involved, many were only half listening. Some club members thought that they would have to make cold calls to ask for money, and they were uncomfortable with telemarketing. In addition, Kaliya had not considered the fact that final exams would be starting that same week, and many students were already stressed out about studying. No wonder she was unsuccessful.

Kaliya should have done more to tailor her message to her audience. She might have drawn club members into her speech by talking about popular public television shows that they probably watched as children. Because she knew many of the club members well, she might have focused on programs she knew they would like rather than listing every show on the schedule. She might have told listeners that this service opportunity would be helpful for their future job search because many local businesses supported this station. If she had interested her listeners, then they would have been more attentive when she explained that they would be talking with people who wanted to be members—not cold calling. She also could have selected a better time to participate rather than the afternoon before finals started.

As Kaliya discovered firsthand, knowing how to speak persuasively is a vital skill in all areas of life. Consider your own situation: Do you want to get a new policy adopted on campus? Advance in your career? Influence members of your community to support an important cause? Convince your roommate to listen to the music you want to hear? Win a major contract for your company from a new customer? Get an extension on the deadline of a paper? In these and many other cases, you'll need to master the art of persuasive speaking if you hope to generate the outcomes you want.

In this chapter, we introduce the topic of persuasive speaking. We start by explaining the nature of a persuasive speech, followed by the process of persuasion. Then we show you how to select your thesis, main points, and supporting materials based on your audience analysis. We also consider the ethical obligations of a persuasive speaker and present several strategies for organizing your persuasive message. In Chapter 18, we go into more detail about specific methods of persuasion.

# THE NATURE OF A PERSUASIVE SPEECH

In a **persuasive speech**, your goal is to *influence audience members' beliefs, attitudes, or actions* and to *advocate fact, value, or policy claims*. Let's take a closer look at these characteristics.

## Persuasive Speeches Attempt to Influence Audience Members

Depending on your goal, influencing audience members might mean trying to *strengthen audience commitment*, *weaken audience commitment*, or *promote audience action*.

## THREE GOALS OF PERSUASION

**Strengthen Audience Commitment.** If audience members already agree with your perspective, you might try to strengthen their commitment. For instance, your classmates may be aware that they should try to select healthy foods when eating on campus. If you provide them with convincing evidence that further solidifies this belief, you may persuade them that this is an important factor to consider the next time they have a meal or snack at school.

**Weaken Audience Commitment.** If many audience members disagree with your perspective on an issue, you might try to weaken their commitment to their viewpoint. For example, suppose that you support the removal of all fast-food outlets on campus but your audience survey reveals that most of your classmates like to eat at those establishments. Your speech is unlikely to succeed if you advocate a ban on campus fast food. Instead, you might try to weaken your listeners' commitment to fast food; for example, you could attempt to persuade them that eating fast food less frequently has many benefits.

**Promote Audience Action.** You might also seek to persuade audience members to take a specific action. Asking students to drink less caffeine, serve on the college's Library Improvement Committee, or vote for an activity-fee increase would be examples of this type of speech. You might also advocate taking action in the community, such as volunteering to help assemble bags of food for a local food bank.

## Persuasive Speeches Advocate Fact, Value, or Policy Claims

In any persuasive speech, you will make one of three types of claims—a *fact claim*, a *value claim*, or a *policy claim*.

**Fact Claim.** A **fact claim** asserts that something is true or false. Fact claims that are debatable make for especially strong persuasive speech topics. For example, your thesis might be that energy drinks cause more health problems than coffee does, that a deepfake (a fake video of an actual person created through an artificial-intelligence-based technique) can mislead significant numbers of people, or that first-person-shooter video games cause players to commit violent crimes.

**Value Claim.** A **value claim** attaches a judgment (such as good, bad, moral, or immoral) to a subject. Examples of persuasive speech topics making value claims include "student loan forgiveness is fair," "it is unethical to let artificial intelligence select targets for drone strikes," and "mask mandates are an unjustifiable burden on liberty."

Many people can reach agreement on fact claims when presented with enough evidence, but value claims often provide greater challenges. Audience members' ideas of right and wrong may be deeply held and may stem from religious or philosophical beliefs—and thus be difficult to change. If you decide to make a value claim in a persuasive speech, select one that your audience is at least open to considering.

**Policy Claim.** A **policy claim** advocates that action should be taken by organizations, institutions, or members of your audience. Examples include advocating that the federal government should increase natural gas exports to Europe, that immigration authorities should not separate minor children from their parents, or that listeners should adopt a "grandfriend" and regularly visit or help a senior citizen in need.

Now that you know the typical objectives of persuasive speeches, let's turn our attention to how persuasion works.

# HOW PERSUASION WORKS

How do audience members make a decision to accept or reject a speaker's persuasive message? Richard Petty and John Cacioppo's **elaboration likelihood model**[1] provides a well-respected explanation.[2] This model presents two ways that audience members may evaluate a persuasive speaker's message: the central and peripheral routes. The **central route** denotes a high level of *elaboration*—a mental process that involves actively processing a speaker's argument. Audience members reflect on the message and consider it in light of their preexisting ideas about the issue.[3] After considering the speaker's points, they may view the argument favorably or unfavorably. Central route listeners are more likely to develop a positive attitude when the argument is strong; in other words, if the speaker argues well enough, audience members will be more likely to agree with the message.[4] We provide a detailed discussion of how to develop strong arguments in Chapter 18.

Audience members who follow the **peripheral route** do not actively process the message (low elaboration). Instead, they're more easily influenced by cues that are peripheral (less directly related) to the message's content.[5] Such cues may include the likability or attractiveness of the speaker, flashy presentation aids that add little to the message, or aspects of the speaker's delivery. These peripheral factors allow receivers to take an easier path to agreement or disagreement without carefully considering the speaker's arguments.

## The Importance of Central Route Processing

The positive effects of central route processing continue even after the speech concludes. When audience members seriously evaluate the content of a persuasive message, they form attitudes that are longer lasting and less likely to change

## TWO PATHS TO PERSUASION

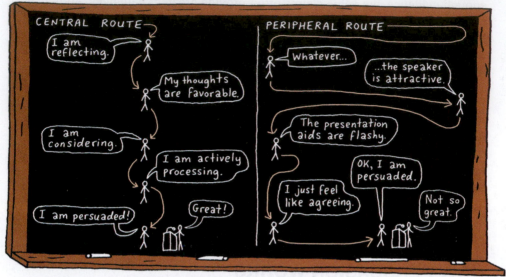

in response to future counterarguments. They are also more likely to take action based on those attitudes.[6]

Conversely, the effects of the peripheral route are more likely to fade quickly. Furthermore, trying to convince an audience with peripheral factors can raise major ethical concerns. You can probably think of commercials that use celebrities or trendy music to sell their product, rather than offering factual evidence to prove a product's benefits. These marketing schemes may be successful, but they often miss the ethical mark by relying on fallacious instead of rational appeals. Similarly, if a speaker manages to persuade audience members by playing a catchy song during transitions or by quoting a pop-culture celebrity (who has no expertise on the topic), the speaker has not persuaded ethically because they failed to help audience members make a rational decision. (See Chapter 3 for more on ethical standards.)

## Which Route Will Audience Members Follow?

Audience members will most likely take the central route when your topic is relevant or important to them and they are able to follow your argument.[7] Thus, you should explain how your topic is directly related to their lives.[8] Audience-involving strategies, such as the use of rhetorical questions, can also increase message processing.[9] Also remember that to help your audience understand your presentation, you need to present a well-organized message (see Chapter 9) and make effective use of language (see Chapter 12). These practices are also important if you are countering an argument for a different point of view. A 2022 study on messages to counter fake news about COVID-19 found evidence that when the message is more understandable, audience members are more likely to accept the rebuttal.[10]

▲ **Countering Misinformation.** When rebutting misinformation in a persuasive speech, it is essential to make your message clear and understandable. Here, the U.S. Surgeon General, Vivek Murthy, addresses misinformation related to COVID-19. Chip Somodevilla/Getty Images

# TAILORING YOUR PERSUASIVE MESSAGE TO THE AUDIENCE

Effective persuasive speakers use **strategic discourse**—the process of selecting supporting arguments that will best persuade the audience in an ethical manner. There are many supporting ideas that you could present, typically far more than can fit into the available time. Your job is to make strategic choices by selecting the ethical arguments that are *most* likely to persuade your particular listeners.

## Adapting to Audience Disposition

Your listeners' disposition—their attitude toward your topic—should affect your approach to persuading them. As we discuss in Chapter 5, your audience may be sympathetic, hostile, or neutral toward the topic of your speech, and you should adjust your thesis depending on which audience type you are addressing.

The starting point is to determine where your audience stands on the issue. (Strategies for learning about your audience are covered in Chapter 5.) For example, suppose your speech is in favor of de-extinction, a process that uses DNA from an extinct species to change the DNA of a similar living species. The end result of the process would be a human-created creature that is genetically similar

## AUDIENCE DISPOSITION

to a creature that had gone extinct, such as a woolly mammoth or a passenger pigeon. Audience members might have very different attitudes about this process:

- Audience members might be excited about seeing extinct species recreated and confident that they would be reintroduced in an ethical way.
- Audience members might be concerned about the species that would be recreated (think *Jurassic World*'s Indominus Rex) or worried that the new species would be exploited by humans.
- Audience members might not be interested in the topic at all, finding it irrelevant to their daily lives.

After you know where your audience stands, you can tailor your thesis appropriately. **Social judgment theory** explains that audience members make a decision about your thesis by comparing it with their own perspectives on the issue. Listeners have a **latitude of acceptance**, which is the range of positions on a given issue that are acceptable to them. Likewise, they have a range of positions that are unacceptable, constituting their **latitude of rejection**.[11] Listeners who are very concerned about your issue tend to have a narrower latitude of acceptance. If the issue is not important to them, they will be open to a broader range of positions.[12]

Therefore, you're most likely to persuade your listeners to change their minds if the position you take on your topic falls within their latitude of acceptance. Conversely, you probably won't persuade audience members if your position falls within their latitude of rejection—especially if they have very strong viewpoints that differ from yours. Under these conditions, your speech may even produce a **boomerang effect**—the act of pushing your listeners to oppose your idea even more vigorously than they did before they heard your speech.[13]

How does all of this work in practice? Let's return to the de-extinction speech. If your audience is sympathetic, their latitude of acceptance would likely include support for your idea and they would be open to taking action.

# THE LAND OF AUDIENCE DISPOSITION

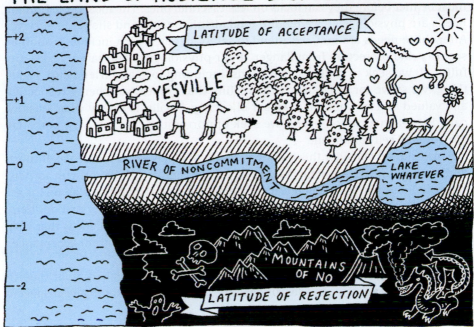

They could be persuaded to support on-campus research or take a science class related to the topic.

However, if your audience is hostile, a speech calling for support and action is likely to be counterproductive because it would fall within their latitude of rejection. Instead, you could attempt to weaken their commitment to opposition by addressing some of their concerns. For example, you might make the case that recreated species could be introduced into ecosystems where they would benefit the natural environment.

Finally, you would take yet another approach for a neutral audience. Calling for action could be outside their latitude of acceptance, but you could strengthen their commitment to the thesis that de-extinction is good. For example, you could make the case for the benefits of de-extinction research and the reintroduction of species.

## Appealing to Your Audience's Needs

Audience members have **needs**—objects they desire and feelings that must be satisfied. Human needs powerfully affect how we behave and how we respond to one another's ideas. As we note in Chapter 5, your message is more likely to succeed when it is relevant to the audience—that is, when it answers their question, "What's in it for me?"[14] Experts from previous eras, such as psychologist Abraham Maslow and social critic Vance Packard, have identified specific sets of needs, which continue to be emphasized in many persuasive appeals.[15]

According to Maslow's **hierarchy of needs**, people's most basic needs must be met before they can focus on less essential ones. The most basic human needs are physiological: we require food, drink, health, and shelter to survive. After these needs are met, we attend to safety needs, which include economic security and protection from danger. If our physiological and safety needs are fulfilled, we seek to satisfy social needs, including love and friendship. From there, we strive for self-esteem, the feeling that comes from being respected and valued as a contributing member of society. Finally, to satisfy what Maslow called self-actualization needs, we seek opportunities for creativity, personal growth, and self-fulfillment.

You should consider this hierarchy when analyzing your audience. If most audience members are struggling to pay their rent, it will be difficult to persuade them to donate to a political campaign, eat organic food, or sign up for an elective class in pottery. These activities may be worthy, but they will not help students who are dealing with late fees or the threat of eviction. Ideas that cost money are likely to fall outside these audience members' latitude of acceptance, potentially resulting in a boomerang effect.

By focusing on needs that are of concern to audience members, your speech will be more likely to persuade. For example, let's say you want to give a speech

---

▼ **Saying the Wrong Thing Can Push Your Audience Away.** If audience members do not trust virtual currency or have little extra money to spend, a speech calling for them to invest in Bitcoin would be outside their latitude of acceptance. Joe Raedle/Getty Images

that will convince your classmates to exercise more often. Exercise fulfills a number of different needs: it can improve people's health, help them perform better at work and in school, increase their self-esteem, and (if done in a social setting) provide opportunities to forge friendships and meet romantic partners. You should determine which of these needs are most important to your audience and then emphasize them in your main points and subpoints.

## Connecting to Your Listeners' Values

**Values** are "core conceptions" of what is desirable for our own life and for society.[16] They guide people's judgments and actions.[17] Each of us has values that guide how we live—for example, being helpful, honest, logical, imaginative, or responsible. We also have ideas about what kind of society we want to live in, such as one that offers equality, freedom, happiness, peace, or security.[18] All of these are values. Because values play a central role in guiding our lives, adapting an argument to audience values is one of the most important considerations for ensuring that your argument will be persuasive.[19]

A speech about increased oil drilling in the United States provides one example of how a message can be tailored to audience values. If reducing the cost of living is an important value for your listeners and your speech emphasized how more drilling would reduce the cost of gas, you would have a persuasive argument. If national security was a more important value to audience members, then you could focus on how oil drilling would promote U.S. energy independence. Conversely, if protecting the environment was more important to your

▲ **Connecting to Audience Values.** In planning a persuasive speech on increased oil drilling, audience values such as saving money, promoting national security, and protecting the environment would need to be taken into account. Tom Paiva Photography/Getty Images

audience, then you would need to be able to show how oil drilling could expand without increasing pollution and destroying natural habitats. If pro-environment audience members also value human rights and world peace, you might make the case that *at this time*, more drilling is essential. You could argue that, due to Russia's 2022 invasion of Ukraine, it is important for the United States to produce more energy so that other countries do not need to finance the invasion by purchasing Russian oil.

## Accounting for Audience Beliefs

Your audience's **beliefs** (the facts about your topic that they consider to be true) will have a significant effect on their **attitude** (their favorable or unfavorable feeling) toward your thesis. For example, suppose you want to convince the students in your speech class to get a flu shot. Audience members might believe that the flu affects mostly senior citizens and that the effects of the flu are not serious for younger people. If listeners do not believe that their risk from the flu is serious, their attitude toward your proposal is likely to be negative. To persuade audience members that they need to act, you could present credible evidence to show that the risk from the flu is significant for college students and that the flu can seriously affect their ability to study and work.[20] You could also provide

COLLEGE STUDENTS ARE AT RISK OF INFLUENZA; VACCINATION RATES ARE LOW, HURTING ACADEMIC SUCCESS AND ATTENDANCE*

*Stephanie Benjamin and Kaitlin Bahr, "Barriers Associated with Seasonal Influenza Vaccination Among College Students," Influenza Research and Treatment, 2016

evidence that, although the number of flu cases declined while COVID-19 prevention policies were in effect, the number will return to pre-pandemic levels as these policies are lifted.[21]

You may find that certain arguments are more effective than others depending on the beliefs of your target audience. For example, if you are proposing a policy to improve public health, you might demonstrate how the policy will improve health outcomes overall. However, if you know that many audience members believe there are serious inequities in public health, demonstrating how this policy would improve health equity would likely be more convincing.[22]

## Focusing on Peripheral Beliefs

In addition to considering audience members' specific beliefs, you need to take the intensity of their beliefs into account. You'll be more likely to persuade your audience members if you avoid threatening their core beliefs. A **core belief** is a viewpoint that is held closely, often for many years. Such beliefs are particularly immune to persuasion—especially as a result of a single speech.[23]

A **peripheral belief** is a viewpoint that is not held quite as closely or as long as a core belief. People may form peripheral beliefs from hearing a news report, reading a book or magazine, or listening to a statement made by a political or religious leader. These beliefs are more open to change by a persuasive message than are core beliefs. Thus, you can boost your chances of success if you focus your appeal on your listeners' peripheral beliefs.

▲ **Focus on Peripheral Beliefs.** You would not be likely to convince devoted parkour practitioners that they should abandon the sport. But you might be able to persuade them to give up one Saturday morning of parkour to volunteer on campus. Westend61/Getty Images

For example, suppose you want to persuade various groups of people at your college to spend one Saturday morning working on a campus beautification project. You first address the Parkour Club, whose members usually practice their sport on Saturday mornings. (Parkour is a physical activity that involves getting past obstacles efficiently using skills like running, climbing, and jumping rather than walking around them.) If you argue that parkour is a pointless activity, you probably won't gain volunteers because you'd be attacking a core belief. On the other hand, the tradition of practicing on Saturday morning is more peripheral. You would have a better chance of winning these listeners' support if you said that devoting one Saturday morning to doing something to benefit the campus community would be a worthy cause—and that club members could practice afterward.

## Demonstrating How Your Audience Benefits

Audience members weigh the costs and benefits whenever they are deciding whether to take action in response to a persuasive appeal.[24] They are most likely to support your proposal when you show how they will benefit from doing so and when they feel that the costs involved are minimal—or at least worth the benefits.

For example, suppose you want to persuade your classmates to change their study strategies for exams. You could explain how evidence does not support the effectiveness of traditional practices such as highlighting in the textbook or rereading notes. Then you could provide evidence to support alternative study strategies that are more likely to prepare students to succeed—for example, spaced practice (reviewing the material for briefer spaced-out sessions rather than waiting until the exam is imminent) and practice testing.[25] This argument would be especially strong because the cost of this action is low—students are not being asked to change the time they devote to studying; instead, they are being asked to use their time more effectively.

## Acknowledging Listeners' Reservations

In analyzing your audience, you may discover the reasons that your listeners are opposed to your thesis, or at least uncommitted or neutral toward it. To address these reservations, consider using a two-sided argument. This does not mean that you simply present two different perspectives to audience members and leave it for them to decide. Rather, in a **two-sided argument**, you briefly note an argument *against* your thesis and then use evidence and reasoning to refute that argument.

For example, suppose you are trying to persuade members of your class to purchase a password manager for their online accounts. You anticipate that many classmates will be reluctant to spend $20 or more each year on this software. In a two-sided argument, you would first acknowledge that money is often an important concern for college students. Then you would present evidence to show that the risk of having accounts hacked is serious and that it can be a long and difficult process to recover any funds stolen as a result of identity theft.

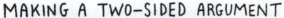

## MAKING A TWO-SIDED ARGUMENT

**STEP 1: ACKNOWLEDGE THE OPPOSING VIEWPOINT**

"I know many of you think that you don't need to wear a seat belt if you've got an air bag, and indeed, an air bag can help protect you in a head-on collision."

**STEP 2: REFUTE THE OPPOSING ARGUMENT USING REASONING AND EVIDENCE**

"However, research shows that air bags don't help you in a side or rear crash; only your seat belt can do that—so be safe and buckle up."

A well-presented two-sided argument can help you change audience members' attitudes in favor of your thesis and strengthen your credibility.[26] This is because people are more likely to support an idea if they know that its proponent is sensitive to their concerns and understands their views.

# ETHICAL PERSUASION

As we note in Chapter 3, a public speaker must be ethical as well as effective. You want your audience members to accept your thesis, but you should earn their support with honest—not deceptive—persuasion. In this section, we highlight important ethical considerations for persuasive speakers.

## Helping Your Audience Make an Informed Decision

Ethical speakers help their listeners reach well-informed decisions rather than manipulating them into agreement. Unfortunately, some persuaders use unethical tactics. For example, one study found that a detailed description of a single individual who had been received TANF (temporary assistance for needy families) benefits for sixteen years exerted a greater influence on an audience's perception of TANF recipients than did statewide statistics showing that 90 percent of TANF recipients go off the rolls within four years.[27] Using vivid evidence that depicts an atypical situation is an unethical half-truth unless the speaker informs the audience that the situation described is not the norm.

To persuade ethically, present solid, truthful claims that support your thesis. Scrupulously avoid arguments based on faulty reasoning, and include all the key facts that would help your audience carefully weigh what you're proposing. Remember, you can address counterarguments to your position by using a two-sided argument.

## Researching Your Facts

As a public speaker, you have an ethical duty to research your topic so that you can be sure the facts you present to your audience are accurate. If your research reveals that a fact is supported by a consensus of credible sources, you can confidently use that fact in your speech. Conversely, if you find that the jury is still out on a claim you wish to make, don't present that point as an established fact. Instead, acknowledge that the point is being debated. Then use a two-sided argument to show why you believe the support for your side outweighs the support for the other side. If you find that few credible sources support your claim and that most sources disagree, do not include the point in your speech. Research other arguments for your position instead.

## Noting Any Biases

Some communicators stand to benefit personally if they succeed in persuading their audience. For example, a former homeland security official who advocated

## FIND THE DIFFERENCE

full-body scanners at airports was a consultant for a company that made these devices, and a health economist who discussed government health care policies had a contract with the government.[28] Audience members will understandably feel cheated if such potential conflicts of interest are not disclosed because such facts are relevant to their decision of whether to believe a speaker. Therefore, you should practice **full disclosure** to your audience. This means that you acknowledge any vested interest you may have in your topic. For example, if you'd receive extra credit for persuading students to participate in an instructor's study, your audience members deserve to know that information. They will also be more likely to respect you if you're honest enough to reveal such biases.

## Attributing Your Research Properly

Include citations *every* time you present ideas that you got from other sources. Make sure that quotations and paraphrases are accurate and that they represent the original author's point of view. For more information on presenting evidence ethically and accurately, see Chapter 7.

# ORGANIZING YOUR PERSUASIVE SPEECH

Audience members must be able to follow your message in order to process it carefully. Thus, you need to choose an organizational pattern that clearly conveys your message *and* maximizes your persuasive impact. There are different patterns to consider, depending on whether your thesis advances a fact, value, or policy claim. Typical patterns for each type of claim are discussed here, and organizational patterns are also covered in Chapter 9.

## Organizing Fact Claims

If you're planning to make a fact claim, you will be seeking to prove that something is true or false. In this type of persuasive speech, consider using a *causal pattern* or a *categorical pattern*, depending on the main points you'll be presenting.

**Causal Pattern.** Many fact claims argue that one thing causes another. If this describes your fact claim, a **causal pattern** is ideal. To illustrate, here is how a presenter might organize a speech claiming that food prices are likely to climb higher.

---

▼ **Causal Organization Pattern.** Rising food prices are affecting both consumers and organizations such as food banks. A causal organization pattern would be a good way to structure a speech about the reasons food prices are going up.
Michael Loccisano/Getty Images

THESIS    Food prices will increase.

**MAIN POINTS**

   I.  Problems in the food supply chain will continue to cause shortages.

  II.  Increased demand for food products as the economy recovers from the pandemic will push up prices.

 III.  The Russian invasion of Ukraine will limit that nation's productivity and compound shortages.

**Categorical Pattern.** Sometimes each main point in your speech will reflect a different reason that you believe your fact claim to be true. In this case, you can use a **categorical pattern** to organize your presentation. Consider the following example from a speech intended to convince listeners that climate change is actually happening:

THESIS    The earth is experiencing climate change.

**MAIN POINTS**

   I.  Droughts are lasting longer, and their effects are more critical.

  II.  Extreme weather is on the rise.

 III.  Greenland's ice sheet and glaciers are melting at an accelerating rate.

 IV.  Coral reefs are disintegrating.

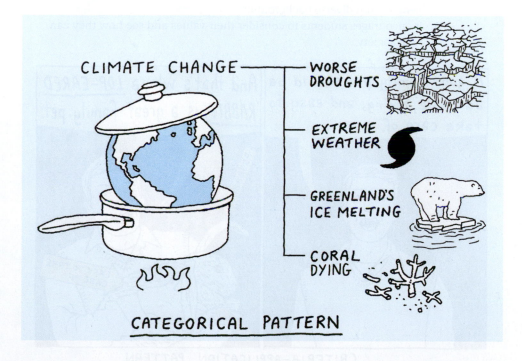

## Organizing Value Claims

In making a value claim in a persuasive speech, you attach a judgment to your subject and then try to get the audience to agree with your evaluation. Three organizing patterns—*criteria-application*, *comparison*, and *categorical*—can help you.

### Criteria-Application Pattern.

A **criteria-application pattern** has two main points. One establishes standards for the value judgment you are making; the other applies those standards to the subject of your thesis. Here is how you could use this pattern in a persuasive speech on the value of community service in college:

THESIS      Community service is a valuable part of the college experience.

**MAIN POINTS**

I. A college education should provide students with several benefits.
   A. New knowledge and skills
   B. Preparation for the workforce
   C. Participation in new experiences
   D. Clarification of students' values and their place in the world
II. Community service provides college students with the opportunity to gain all these benefits.
   A. It leads to higher grade-point averages and stronger communication skills.
   B. It provides valuable work experience and a chance to discover career interests.
   C. It offers an opportunity to experience new situations and work with people from diverse backgrounds.
   D. It encourages students to consider their values and see how they can help society.

CRITERIA—APPLICATION PATTERN

## COMPARISON PATTERN

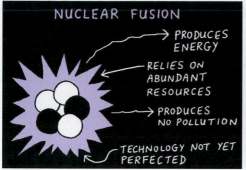
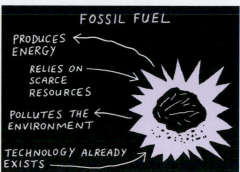

**Comparison Pattern.** When you want to claim that two situations are similar or different, a **comparison pattern** can help you support that claim. Here is how this pattern could be used in a speech about the benefits of nuclear fusion (producing energy by colliding atomic nuclei together) as compared to current sources of energy.[29]

> **THESIS**    Nuclear fusion is a more beneficial power source than present energy sources.

**MAIN POINTS**

  I.  Fusion relies on abundant resources, unlike fossil fuels, which are scarce.
 II.  Fusion produces no pollution, unlike fossil fuels, which harm the environment.
III.  Fusion reactors do not risk meltdowns, unlike nuclear fission plants.

**Categorical Pattern.** In some persuasive speeches, you may decide that it isn't necessary to explain how each main point supports the value judgment you are making because your audience already understands each point's relevance. In this case, you can use a categorical pattern.

To illustrate, suppose you want to convince your audience that advanced driver-training courses are beneficial. Your listeners probably know that they could judge the value of a driver-training course by considering such factors as reduced accident risk and lower insurance premiums. Therefore, you could organize your main points in a categorical pattern, such as the following:

> **THESIS**    Advanced driver-training courses are beneficial.

**MAIN POINTS**

  I.  They reduce the risk of accidents.
 II.  They lower drivers' insurance premiums.
III.  They lower drivers' maintenance and gas costs.
 IV.  The savings gained from these courses exceed their cost.

## Organizing Policy Claims

When you advance a policy claim, you call for action. You might want audience members to do something in particular, or you might want to convince them that an organization or institution (such as a state or local government) should take a particular action. For this type of persuasive speech, you can use a *motivated sequence* or *problem-cause-solution pattern*.

**Monroe's Motivated Sequence.** Developed by Alan Monroe nearly eighty years ago, this organizational pattern remains popular.[30] Monroe's motivated sequence follows the stages of thinking that people often go through while solving a problem or considering new ideas.[31] A **motivated sequence** aims to establish five main points—attention, need, satisfaction, visualization, and action—as shown in the following example from a persuasive speech encouraging students to study abroad:

   MAIN POINTS
   I. *Attention* (creating a willingness to listen to your message). Few members of our class are looking forward to final exams next month. Do you think it

▼ **Example of a Motivated Sequence.** For a speech related to the problematic nature of social media algorithms, as explained by Facebook whistleblower Frances Haugen,[32] a motivated sequence might present these main points: *Attention*: Social media algorithms are not your friend. *Need*: These algorithms can steer you to content that is bad for your mental health. *Satisfaction*: Our college's resiliency network is a group for people who find social media stressful and would like to make their social media participation more productive. *Visualization*: See yourself taking control of your social media use to make it a good experience. *Action*: Join our resiliency network; there's free pizza at the next meeting. Kimberly White/Getty Images

would be more exciting if your finals were happening in Rome, Seoul, Sydney, or Buenos Aires?

II.  *Need* (identifying a need relevant to your audience). Every member of this class plans to get a job after graduation. The job market is highly competitive.

III.  *Satisfaction* (showing how your proposal will fulfill the need you identified). Participating in our college's Study Abroad Program will strengthen your credentials in the job market. Employers report that they are more likely to hire a candidate with international experience.

IV.  *Visualization* (helping listeners form a mental picture of the benefits of your proposal). Imagine that you have returned to the United States after an amazing semester in Spain or Japan. At an interview for a job you really want, the interviewer asks if you have experience with other cultures. You answer yes, and you see the interviewer's interest perk up. The next day, the company makes you an offer.

V.  *Action* (clarifying what you want listeners to do). Attend an informational session on next year's Study Abroad Program in the Student Union next Wednesday. You can learn more about the exciting options open to you, hear from past participants, and ask questions. After that, I hope you will decide to make Montreal, Mumbai, or Madrid your home for next fall.

**Problem-Cause-Solution Pattern.**  With a **problem-cause-solution pattern**, the first main point describes a problem that needs to be addressed, the second explains the cause of the problem, and the third presents a solution that

## SPEECH CHOICES

### A CASE STUDY: RAFAELA

*Let's see whether Rafaela used audience-centered persuasive strategies.*

Rafaela was passionate about her topic, and she was very confident that she had a good message—that it was vital for more women to run for office. She had plenty of credible research sources, compelling narratives, and examples to support her thesis. All she had to do was finalize her outline and practice her speech a few more times to make sure she was familiar with the content.

As the date of the speech got close, Rafaela and some other students were talking about their upcoming persuasive speeches. Several students gave her encouraging feedback, but one woman took a different tack, playing devil's advocate and asking, "What if a guy wants to run for office? Are you telling him no?"

This classmate's questions made Rafaela think. It was not enough to simply present ideas that *she* found persuasive. Rafaela recalled that the audience should drive the message, and she did not want to present ideas that were outside audience members' latitude of acceptance and risk a boomerang effect. She really wanted her speech to make a difference.

So Rafaela reconsidered the details of her third main point, her solution. To address the concern of excluding some of her classmates, Rafaela would clarify that she was not telling anyone *not* to run but rather encouraging women to run in addition to others; she also could ask all classmates who wanted to be politically active to encourage the women in their lives to do the same.

Once Rafaela had made revisions, she was ready to practice for the big day. She now felt confident that all her audience members could relate to her speech.

 **YOUR TURN**

Now that you've seen how Rafaela's choices impacted her persuasive speech, consider how you'll use persuasive strategies in a speech of your own. Making speech choices involves asking and answering a series of questions related to your assignment. As you work to persuade your listeners, your questions might include:

- Am I trying to influence audience members by strengthening their commitment, weakening it, or promoting action?

- Is my speech advocating a fact, value, or policy claim? Have I selected an organizational pattern that makes sense based on this type of claim?

- Which strategies for tailoring my persuasive message would work best for my audience?

- How will I attempt to assess audience members' latitude of acceptance?

- How will I evaluate my persuasive speech to make sure my message is ethical?

Making thoughtful choices in response to questions like these will help you persuade your listeners effectively, and do so with honesty and integrity.

can minimize the problem. This pattern can be especially helpful if you are asking the audience to support a policy change by an organization or institution. Because your ultimate goal is new behavior on the part of the organization or institution, the problem-cause-solution pattern builds to the action you are advocating.

Here is an example of how a speaker might use this pattern in a persuasive speech advocating changes in the criteria used to award financial aid to college students:

THESIS     The federal government should change its financial aid criteria to accurately reflect what parents can afford to contribute.

**MAIN POINTS**

    I. *Problem*. Limited financial aid forces students to work excessive hours.
   II. *Cause*. Financial aid formulas are based on inaccurate assumptions about what students' parents can afford to contribute.
 III. *Solution*. Financial aid formulas should be changed to accurately match students' financial circumstances.

## CHAPTER REVIEW

> 66 Good persuaders make strategic choices in an ethical manner. 99

In this chapter, we explored how persuasive speakers strengthen or weaken their audience's commitment to a particular topic or motivate their listeners to take a particular action. In doing so, persuasive speakers make one of three types of claims—fact, value, or policy. In evaluating a message, audience members may take the central route and carefully process the message or take the peripheral route and be influenced by cues that have little to do with speech content. If they are interested in the topic, they will most likely follow the central route, resulting in more effective and longer-lasting attitude change.

We also shared strategies for relating a persuasive message to your audience, including choosing a thesis based on your listeners' disposition, linking your message to your audience's needs and values, focusing on your listeners' peripheral beliefs, demonstrating how the costs of your proposal are worth the benefits, and addressing audience reservations about your thesis.

Additionally, we covered how you can develop your message in an ethical manner by helping your listeners make an informed decision, researching your facts thoroughly, disclosing any biases, and properly attributing your research sources. Finally, we offered strategies for organizing your message, depending on whether you are making a fact, value, or policy claim.

## Key Terms

## Review Questions

1. Describe three goals of persuasive speeches.
2. What are the three types of claims used in a persuasive speech?
3. Describe the elaboration likelihood model. What are the differences between central route processing and peripheral route processing of a message?
4. Describe six ways in which a speaker may adapt a message for an audience.
5. What four steps can you take to ensure that your persuasive speech is ethical?
6. Describe two ways to organize a persuasive speech for each of the following—a fact claim, a value claim, and a policy claim.

## Critical Thinking Questions

1. Why do you think that persuasion that is created when audience members follow central route processing is more effective than persuasion created through peripheral route processing?
2. How does using strategic discourse to craft a persuasive speech differ from preparing a speech in which you explain how you feel about a particular issue?
3. How would understanding Maslow's hierarchy of needs help you deliver more effective persuasive speeches? How could it hurt your effectiveness if you do *not* consider it?
4. Consider the way that talking heads and audiences for twenty-four-hour news channels tend to break along ideological and party lines. Also, think

about how presentation of political ideas on social media pages tends to break the same way. What does this tell you about latitudes of acceptance and rejection? How would you characterize the latitudes of acceptance and rejection for people who prefer not to listen to messages limited to one end of the political spectrum or the other?

## Activities

1. Working individually or in groups, select a persuasive speech topic. Identify three possible audiences for that speech—sympathetic, hostile, and neutral. Select a thesis and at least three main points for each audience. Discuss how your thesis and main points should differ for each audience type.
2. Select any thesis for a persuasive speech that advocates action by the audience. How could you use each of the strategies for adapting your argument to the audience in a speech on the topic you have chosen?
3. Review Anna Martinez's persuasive speech in the Appendix. How does Martinez tailor her thesis to fall within audience members' latitude of acceptance? Identify other strategies she uses to adjust her speech to the audience.
4. Review the editorial page in several newspapers, and consider their attempts to persuade you. How many editorials make fact claims? Value claims? Policy claims? Can you tell what organizational pattern the writers are using?
5. Visit Factcheck.org, the website of a nonpartisan group that investigates claims made by politicians, news organizations, and interest groups. Are you surprised by any of the information presented there? What examples of unethical speech did you come across?

# METHODS OF PERSUASION

# 18

> **Persuasive speakers are credible, logical, and emotionally affecting.**

For an upcoming persuasive speech, Maya picked a unique topic that hit particularly close to home. Three years earlier, her uncle was released from a twenty-two-year imprisonment after DNA tests revealed that he hadn't committed the murder for which he'd been incarcerated. During her presentation, she planned to ask the audience to lobby for states to provide compensation to innocent people who are exonerated by new DNA evidence.

Maya knew she would face a challenge in persuading her listeners. After all, not many people are wrongly imprisoned, so why should her audience members take time out of their busy lives to lobby state governments for a new policy? In short, why should they care?

To build the most persuasive case possible, Maya decided to use three powerful tools—*ethos* (demonstrating her credibility), *logos* (presenting sound reasoning for her claims), and *pathos* (evoking intense emotion in her audience). She established her credibility by citing trusted researchers' findings on the accuracy of DNA testing and the inaccuracy of eyewitness accounts (which typically lead to wrongful convictions). She demonstrated solid reasoning for her

---

◄ **Advocating for Justice.** When speaking up for justice or other societal issues, a good speech incorporates ethos, pathos, and logos. grandbrothers/Shutterstock

**451**

proposal by presenting statistics about the difficulties that people who are exon-erated face in finding paid work after their innocence is proven. And she evoked her listeners' compassion and empathy for exonerees by describing the harsh realities that her uncle had endured since his release from prison—including long stretches of unemployment.

Maya's presentation proved a resounding success. By skillfully blending ethos, logos, and pathos, she not only captured her listeners' attention but also convinced them that exonerees deserve to be compensated for the ordeals they suffer as a result of errors made in the justice system. By the time Maya wrapped up her speech, some students were jotting down the tips she'd shared for lob-bying state governments to introduce an exoneree compensation law. Her audi-ence embraced her proposal, and some listeners intended to take the actions she recommended—solid evidence that she had given an effective persuasive speech.

You can use these strategies as successfully as Maya did. In this chapter, we discuss the use of ethos, logos, and pathos to create an effective speech.

## ETHOS: YOUR CREDIBILITY AS A SPEAKER

Since ancient times, people have recognized that a speaker with **ethos (credibility)** has far more persuasive power than one without. Credible speak-ers are seen as knowledgeable, honest, and genuinely interested in doing the right thing for their audience. Ethos can help you win audience members' trust and persuade them to embrace your viewpoint. But what is credibility, exactly? By taking a closer look at what it consists of, we can get a deeper understanding of this crucial persuasive tool.

## Understanding the Elements of Credibility

The ancient Greek philosopher Aristotle believed that practical wisdom and virtue are major components of ethos. Modern communication scholars use the term **competence** to refer to practical wisdom and the word **trustworthiness** instead of virtue. When audience members perceive a speaker to be both competent (knowledgeable and experienced) about a subject and trustworthy (honest and fair), they find it easier to believe that speaker's claims.[1]

Aristotle also urged public speakers to exhibit **goodwill** toward their audiences—by wanting what is best for their listeners rather than what would most benefit themselves.[2] According to contemporary researchers, speakers who demonstrate goodwill do the following:

- Understand their listeners' needs and feelings
- Empathize with their audiences' views (even if they don't share them)
- Respond quickly to others' communication[3]

## Building Your Credibility

When you're just starting out as a public speaker, your audience members may not immediately recognize your credibility. You'll need to build your ethos through what you say during your speech—and how you say it. Here are some helpful strategies:

- *Share your qualifications to speak on the topic.* If you have some expertise in the subject, outline your credentials for your audience. In some cases, this might involve listing your educational qualifications and work experience ("I have a degree in finance and have worked in banking for six years"). In others, it might mean telling the audience about your personal stake in the subject, just as Maya did when she spoke about her uncle's having been exonerated of murder by DNA evidence. If your knowledge is based mostly on your research, that should be indicated, too.

- *Present strong evidence from reputable sources.* When you provide evidence for your claims, you indicate that you have carefully researched your topic, which communicates your competence. Citing a number of well-balanced and credible sources shows the audience the extent of your research and helps establish your credibility in the process.

- *Highlight common ground with the audience.* Reminding the audience of your shared experiences can make your message—and you—more credible. A teacher speaking to parents of preschoolers, for example, might mention the anxiety he felt the first time he dropped off his own young son at preschool before attempting to persuade them that their nervous child will have fun when school activities start.

- *Choose your words carefully.* The words you select for your speech can demonstrate your understanding of your listeners and thus your goodwill toward them. Be careful to use any technical terminology appropriately to

▲ **Establishing Credibility.** Chris Smalls, leader of the movement to unionize a Staten Island, N.Y., Amazon warehouse, established credibility with workers by understanding their lives (he had worked at the facility himself) and understanding their needs. ANDREA RENAULT/Getty Images

show that you understand the subject matter, and make sure to use respectful and unbiased language when presenting your message.

- *Show respect for conflicting opinions.* Throughout your speech, use respectful language to refer to people who disagree with you. For example, "Some of you may not share my thinking on this, and that's OK. There are lots of ways to look at this issue."

- *Practice your speech until your delivery is fluent.* When you demonstrate effective delivery skills during your presentation—for example, by interacting comfortably with the audience—you are more likely to come across as trustworthy.

## Avoiding Loss of Your Credibility

You have many strategies available for enhancing your credibility during a speech. But there are just as many ways to make a misstep and erode your ethos while giving a talk. Anytime you say something that shows a lack of competence, trustworthiness, or goodwill, you damage your credibility.

Such errors are common during political campaigns, and you can probably think of examples of gaffes that dimmed the election chances of a candidate for

## KNOW YOUR FACTS OR RISK LOSING CREDIBILITY

office. But we have also seen such errors hurt the credibility of student speakers. In your speeches, careful preparation can help you avoid credibility-draining mistakes. Here are some common sources of this type of error:

- *Getting your facts wrong.* Your competence and preparation will be questioned if you present factual information that is just plain inaccurate. Mushers and dog-show enthusiasts would immediately recognize the error of calling the Alaskan husky a purebred dog because these sled dogs are crossbred from diverse bloodlines. Likewise, a speaker who mixed up the Brontë sisters would alienate fans of Victorian literature, and scientists in the audience would question the credibility of a speaker who said that artificial intelligence would replace doctors in the near future. One benefit of selecting a topic you know well is that you are less likely to present factual errors on a familiar subject.

- *Pronouncing words incorrectly.* Your experience in a topic area will be questioned if you mispronounce the names of key persons or concepts related to the topic. For example, a student who referred to hip-hop pioneer Afrika Bambaataa (pronounced *"bam-BAH-tah"*) as Afrika *"BOM-bait-a"* would not be credible to audience members who know that genre of music well, and a charitable organization seeking volunteers in the southern part of the Bay Area of California would quickly lose credibility by referring to the region as *"SIL-i-cone"* Valley (as opposed to *"SIL-i-con"*).

- *Failing to acknowledge potential conflicts of interest.* In Chapter 17, we note the importance of disclosing your biases. If you fail to acknowledge any personal interest in your topic, it will hurt your credibility when it is revealed. For example, suppose that one of your classmates' persuasive speeches advocated increased funding for the arts As part of the solution, he asked the class to sign his petition to get an arts funding measure on the ballot for the next election. If you later found out that your classmate was a paid for each signature that he obtained, you would view the message suspiciously and wonder whether he really cared about arts funding at all. You would be more skeptical of his future speeches, wondering if the message was authentic.

- *Stretching to find a connection with the audience.* Have you ever seen speakers attempt to speak a language they do not know well, try to use local or professional slang, or act interested in the audience's favorite sports team? They often end up mangling words or using terms incorrectly, getting distracted from their message, and worrying about possible mistakes. These errors end up highlighting just how disconnected a speaker is. Local dialect can also be a challenge. For example, when speakers address a Missouri audience, they must decide whether to refer to the state as "*Mi-SSOUR-ee*" or "*Mi-SSOUR-uh.*"[4] You should always show respect to your audience, but the best choice is to be your authentic self. If a change in your typical pronunciation seems forced rather than sincere, you will lose credibility. On the other hand, it is fine to use a pronunciation that is specific to your dialect, as long as it is authentic.

After a speaker's credibility has come into question, it's very difficult to repair the damage. Thus, before giving a speech, examine the language you intend to use, and make sure that it communicates competence, trustworthiness, and goodwill.

But even bulletproof ethos isn't enough to deliver an effective speech by itself. As we discuss in the next section, you also need to deliver a solid set of facts to prove the claims you're making.

## LOGOS: THE EVIDENCE AND REASONING BEHIND YOUR MESSAGE

Reliable facts can further strengthen your credibility and help your audience members make well-informed decisions—key effects of ethical public speaking. Sound reasoning that supports your claims is also essential if you hope to persuade audience members to change their beliefs or behaviors. When you present trustworthy facts to back your claims and clearly show how those facts have led you to those claims, you use **logos (evidence and reasoning)** effectively.

▲ **Evidence and Reasoning Convince Audiences.** Engineer Christian Olivares needed to use strong evidence and reasoning to show that this biodegradable material would be an effective alternative to plastic bags. CLAUDIO REYES/Getty Images

For example, suppose you want to deliver a persuasive speech arguing that mindfulness practices can help reduce student stress. To convince the audience that you know what you're talking about, you'll need to supply proof, or **evidence**, of your claim. To further strengthen your logos, you'll need to show that the conclusions you've drawn from the evidence make sense. Is your train of thought logical, or are you using **fallacious (faulty) reasoning** to twist or distort the facts in your favor?

In the following sections, we discuss how *using evidence, using reasoning,* and *avoiding logical fallacies* can help you build a persuasive message.

## Using Evidence

When your audience analysis suggests that listeners may not accept a claim you want to make, you'll need to supply proof. One of the best ways to do so is to research evidence from credible sources (see Chapter 7) and then present that evidence in your speech. Furthermore, policies that are not based on evidence are less likely to be able to solve the problems you cite in your speech.[5] To use evidence effectively, apply the following principles.

**Identify your sources and their qualifications.** Indicate who your source is for each piece of evidence you present, along with their qualifications, before

providing the evidence during your speech. Concrete documentation strengthens your credibility.[6] It shows audience members that you have done your research and learned about your topic by looking at ideas from experts in the field. To ensure your sources' credibility, use facts provided by unbiased experts.[7]

**Give listeners new evidence.**  Use audience analysis to determine what evidence is likely to be new to your listeners. Facts that they're not yet familiar with are more likely to increase their perception of your credibility.[8]

**Provide precise evidence. Precise evidence** consists of specific dates, places, numbers, and other facts. Here's an example of this kind of precision:

> According to Doctors Naveed Sattar and Nita Forouhi, in *Circulation,* April 27, 2021, adults who eat five servings of fruits and vegetables daily have a 35 percent lower risk of death from respiratory diseases compared to adults who eat two servings.[9]

This evidence provides a specific percentage to indicate the decreased mortality rate, along with the specific number of daily fruit and vegetable servings used in the study.

**Look for compelling evidence.**  Audiences are more likely to be persuaded by compelling evidence that includes concrete or detailed examples. Such evi-

dence engages listeners' senses, helps them visualize the point you're present-ing, and increases the likelihood that they will remember the information.[10] For example, in your speech about the benefits of mindfulness, you could include a compelling anecdote about a student who used this practice to manage stress during final exams.

Credible evidence documenting the significance of a problem to the audi-ence can also be compelling. A study of public health messages found that evidence documenting the severity of a health condition to which audience members are susceptible made the message more persuasive.[11]

**Characterize your evidence accurately.** Carefully word your claim so that it accurately reflects what your evidence proves. For example, if all the facts you've gathered strongly support the idea that mindfulness practices can reduce student stress, then use those very words to state your claim about mindfulness, rather than saying something like "Mindfulness practices are good for you."

## Using Reasoning

Reasoning is the line of thought that connects the facts you present and the con-clusions you draw from those facts. Persuasive speakers typically use **inductive reasoning**—generalizing from facts, instances, or examples and then making a claim based on that generalization. The table that follows shows several exam-ples of inductive reasoning from everyday life.

▲ **Inductive Reasoning.** If you are good at playing the trombone, you could probably learn to be a good trumpet player, too. Leonardo Macedo/500px/ Getty Images

## EXAMPLES OF INDUCTIVE REASONING

| Fact | Claim |
|---|---|
| At three different locations at this university, food service was slow. | All food-service outlets at this school are probably slow. |
| Lonyae is good at football. | It's plausible that Lonyae would be good at soccer. |
| Two students in the back row just fell asleep. | This is a boring class. |
| Brisa sets aside time each day to study in a quiet place. | Brisa is likely to do well on the exam. |

There are four types of inductive reasoning—*example, comparison, sign,* and *causal reasoning.* Let's explore each type in detail and consider how to use them effectively.

**Example Reasoning.** When you use **example reasoning**, you present specific instances to support a general claim. Your goal is to persuade the audience that your examples supply sufficient proof of your claim.

For instance, here's how you could use example reasoning to argue that plastic bag restrictions reduce litter:

In California, a ban on plastic bags reduced litter on the coast by 72 percent.[12] After Ireland placed a tax on plastic bags, the bags dropped from 5 percent of total litter to 0.14 percent.[13] And in Israel, a tax on bags cut the amount of bags found in the ocean by 50 percent.[14]

To use example reasoning skillfully, be sure to provide enough instances to persuade your audience that your general claim is reasonable. The more examples you can find, the more confident you can be that your claim is correct.

Of course, in a short speech, you may have time to present only three or four examples to back up your argument. In this situation, you'll need to choose the most representative examples. A **representative example** is an instance typical of the class it represents. In this example, the use of plastic bag restrictions in three different countries would be more representative than presenting examples from only cities in California.

If you're planning to use example reasoning in a speech you're researching, think about counterexamples your audience might consider. For instance, in your research you may find that plastic bag restrictions have not been effective everywhere throughout the world. In that case, you could revise your claim to "plastic bag restrictions *generally* reduce litter."

REPRESENTATIVE EXAMPLES

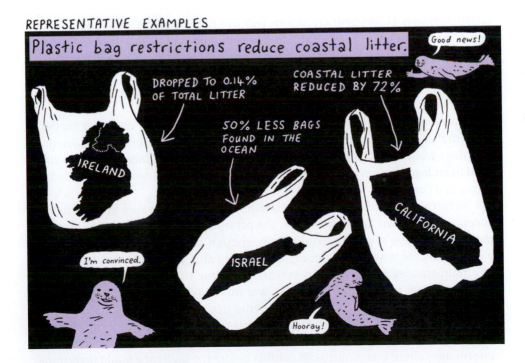

NONREPRESENTATIVE EXAMPLE

**Comparison Reasoning.** When you use **comparison reasoning**, you argue that two instances are similar, and that what you know is true for one instance is likely to be true for the other. For example, Columbia University Professor John McWhorter contends that "just as some kids at 16 are ready for a college education, just as many kids at that age are ready to take their places in the working world."[15]

For comparison reasoning to work, your audience must agree (or be persuaded) that the two instances are in fact comparable. In this example, audience members would need to agree that the kinds of skills and habits required to succeed in college courses at age 16 are similar to the ones that would be needed to thrive in a career position at the same age.

To further strengthen your comparison reasoning, make sure your audience accepts the "known facts" as true. In the previous example, you could assume that most college students would know enough about college and the work world to decide whether the comparison was valid. But consider another set of circumstances, where a speaker wants to argue that because Russia failed to defeat Japan in the Russo-Japanese war in 1904–05, Russia will also fail to defeat Ukraine in its 2022 war.[16] It is doubtful that most audience members will know enough about the Russo-Japanese war to be able to determine whether the Russian invasion of Ukraine is comparable. You would need to provide more information about the century-old conflict before the audience could determine how similar the two conflicts are.

▲ **Comparison Reasoning.** If a speaker compares the Russo-Japanese war of 1904–05 to the Russian invasion of Ukraine, the audience would need to understand how the two wars are comparable. DEA/BIBLIOTECA AMBROSIANA/Getty Images; SOPA Images/Getty Images

**Sign Reasoning.** When you use **sign reasoning**, you claim that a fact is true because indirect indicators (signs) are consistent with that fact. For example, you might claim that college students are facing serious financial challenges, as evidenced by students working longer hours.

This type of reasoning is most effective if you can cite multiple consistent signs of the fact you are claiming. For instance, you could strengthen your claim that students' financial challenges are rising by noting an increase in student loans and a higher rate of students dropping out of school. However, as you're researching your speech, also be sure to look for signs that are *inconsistent* with your argument. If you discover that students are spending more money on entertainment and clothes, you may find it difficult to convince your audience that the signs prove that financial struggles are on the rise.

You might use sign reasoning to decide whether you should take a particular class. For example, you might note that on the first day of the semester, the classroom is so full that students are sitting on the floor. Furthermore, there is a long waiting list for the class, and the book for the course is sold out at the bookstore. Each of these facts would be an indirect indicator that the course and the instructor are very good.

## SIGNS OF RISING TUITION

**Causal Reasoning.** When you use **causal reasoning**, you argue that one event has caused another. For instance, you would be using causal reasoning if you claimed that playing violent video games leads children to get involved in destructive and illegal activities.

You can strengthen your causal reasoning in several ways.

- *Explain the link between cause and effect.* For example, you might contend that when children play violent games, some may empathize with the violent character they control in the games. Thus, they are more likely to emulate that character in their everyday lives.

- *Support the cause-and-effect link with evidence from credible sources.* For instance, you could use quotations from the American Academy of

# SUPPORTING CAUSAL REASONING

1. EXPLAIN THE LINK BETWEEN CAUSE AND EFFECT

Ouch! POW! Ouch! SMACK!

Kids may empathize with violent video game characters and then emulate those characters in real life.

2. PROVIDE CREDIBLE EVIDENCE

BLAM! BLAM! BLAM! Die! Die! Die!

University researchers conclude that youths who play video games may be prone to delinquency and violence.*

3. DEMONSTRATE A CORRELATION

BEFORE PLAYING VIOLENT VIDEO GAMES:

AFTER PLAYING VIOLENT VIDEO GAMES:

Grrrr! Grrr!

A recent study shows a correlation between video games... ...and juvenile delinquency and violence.*

* M. DE LISI ET AL, "VIOLENT VIDEO GAMES, DELINQUENCY, AND YOUTH VIOLENCE: NEW EVIDENCE," YOUTH VIOLENCE AND JUVENILE JUSTICE 11, no. 2 (2013): 132–42, 138.

Pediatrics or a Senate Judiciary Committee report to bolster your argument about the effects of violent video games on children's behavior.

- *Show a correlation between cause and effect*—for example, by presenting a study indicating that "playing violent video games is correlated with delinquency and violence," even after controlling for other factors associated with juvenile delinquency.[17]

Causal reasoning can be tricky because it is easy to misinterpret the evidence or come to the wrong conclusion. We take a look at errors in causal reasoning and other common reasoning errors in the following section.

## Avoiding Logical Fallacies

Reasoning is fallacious (faulty) when the link between your claim and supporting material is weak. We briefly mention several fallacies in Chapter 3 in the context of unethical persuasion—*hasty generalization*, post hoc *fallacy*, ad populum *(bandwagon) fallacy,* and ad hominem *(personal attack) fallacy.* Here we explain the logical error in these four fallacies and highlight five other common fallacies—*causal reasoning errors* (including *reversed causality*), *straw person fallacy*, *slippery slope fallacy*, *false dilemma fallacy*, and *appeal to tradition fallacy*—that you'll want to avoid in your speeches.

**Hasty Generalization.**  When using example reasoning, be sure to avoid **hasty generalization**. This fallacy occurs when a speaker bases a conclusion on limited or unrepresentative examples. For example, it would be fallacious to reason that jobs could be created in any city whose leaders put their minds to

---

▼ **Hasty Generalization.**  It would be a reasoning error to assume that just because a city such as Austin could create many jobs, all cities could ensure robust job creation. Some cities have advantages that others do not. dszc/Getty Images

## POST HOC FALLACY

it based on the example of Austin, Texas. Austin has a number of unique job-creation advantages that other cities may not be able to match: it is the home of a first-rate university, a highly educated population, the state capitol, and a robust venture-capital scene.[18]

**Causal Reasoning Errors.**   One common error in causal reasoning is the ***post hoc* fallacy**. This fallacy lies in the assumption that because one event followed another, the first event caused the second. But this sequence of events, in itself, does not prove causality. For example, suppose a college expands the size of its library, and students' grades subsequently increase. It might be tempting to conclude that the expansion of the library caused the improvement in grades. However, other factors could have led to the higher grades—rising admission standards, increased student motivation to achieve, or grade inflation. Before you can confidently claim that library expansion was the cause of the higher grades, other likely factors would have to be ruled out.

It's also important to watch out for **reversed causality**, in which speakers miss the fact that the effect is actually the cause. For example, an improvement in students' academic performance may have led the college to expand the library to accommodate the study habits of these highly motivated students.

**Ad Populum (Bandwagon) Fallacy.**   You've committed the ***ad populum* (bandwagon) fallacy** if you assume that a statement (for example, "The police are adequately trained to avoid excessive force," "Millennials and members of Generation Z will receive no social security benefits when they retire," or "Free public college tuition for all qualified students would bankrupt the United States") is true or false simply because a large number of people say it is. (*Ad populum* is Latin for "to the people.")

# AD POPULUM FALLACY

The problem with basing the truth of a statement on the number of people who believe it is that most people have neither the expertise nor the time to conduct the research needed to arrive at an informed opinion about the big questions of the day. For this reason, it's best to avoid using public-opinion polls to prove facts.

***Ad Hominem* (Personal Attack) Fallacy.** Some speakers try to compensate for weak arguments by making personal attacks against an opponent rather than addressing the issue in question. These speakers have

committed the ***ad hominem* (personal attack) fallacy**. (*Ad hominem* is Latin for "to the person.") For example, in a campaign speech for student body president, one candidate referred to her opponent as a a an "arugula eating, fair-trade loving snowflake." Her goal was to stir up listeners' biases against outspoken environmental and labor activists on campus and persuade them to reject her opponent as an extremist. This tactic was unethical because she supplied no evidence to support her claims, and provided no reasons why environmental or labor activism should disqualify a candidate from serving as president.

### Straw Person Fallacy.

You commit the **straw person fallacy** if you replace your opponent's real claim with a weaker claim that you can more easily rebut. This weaker claim may sound relevant to the issue, but it is not; you're presenting it just because it's easy to knock down, like a person made of straw.

For example, suppose a speaker was opposed to a policy prohibiting federal government surveillance of social media communications without a warrant. If that speaker claimed that "the government must be able to conduct surveillance of terrorists' communications or the risk of an attack will increase," that claim would be fallacious. The policy would not prohibit surveillance of terrorist communications; it would only require that the government obtain a warrant to do so.

## SLIPPERY SLOPE FALLACY

**Slippery Slope Fallacy.** You've fallen victim to the **slippery slope fallacy** if you argue against a policy because you assume (without proof) that it will lead to a second policy that is undesirable. Like the straw person fallacy, this type of argument distracts the audience from the real issue at hand. Here's one example of a slippery slope argument during a televised community forum on gun control:

> We cannot expand background checks on gun purchases. That would lead us down the road to allowing the federal government to confiscate the guns of law-abiding citizens.

In this example, the speaker had no evidence or reasoning to explain how the first policy (background checks on gun purchases) would lead to the second (confiscation of guns from persons who have a legal right to own them).

**False Dilemma Fallacy.** You fall prey to the **false dilemma fallacy** if you claim that there are only two possible choices to address a problem, that one of those choices is wrong or infeasible, and that your listeners must therefore embrace the other choice. For example:

> Our college is at a crossroads. Either we return to face-to-face instruction as it was before the pandemic or we become a distance education program.

The weakness in a false dilemma argument is that most problems have more than just two possible solutions. To illustrate, in the previous example the two options expressed (either return to pre-pandemic instruction modes or become a distance education school) are certainly not the only possibilities. Schools could offer a mix of instruction modes for students, providing face-to-face instruction in courses where it is especially beneficial and offering other courses virtually.

▲ **A False Dilemma.** Colleges don't need to select between *only* a virtual format or *only* a face-to-face format; another option would be to offer a mix of online and on-campus courses. Drazen_/Getty Images; skynesher/E+/Getty Images

**Appeal to Tradition Fallacy.** You've committed the **appeal to tradition fallacy** if you argue that an idea or a policy is good simply because people have accepted or followed it for a long time. For example:

> We must continue to require general education courses at this college. For the past fifty-three years, the students at State U have taken general education courses.

This argument is weak because it offers no explanation for why the tradition of general education courses is a good thing in the first place. The fallacy lies in presenting history and tradition as proof that a policy is good. A speaker defending something historic or traditional must show why it is worth preserving. In the previous example, a speaker might support the point by noting the benefits that students gain from taking general education courses (versus taking more classes of their choice or in their major) or the increased career options that students with broad general education backgrounds have after college.

# APPEAL TO TRADITION

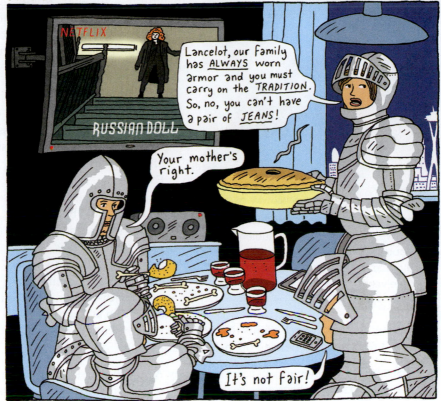

## PATHOS: EVOKING YOUR LISTENERS' EMOTIONS

When used with ethos and logos, emotional appeals—known as **pathos**—help you put a human face on a problem you're addressing. When you stir your listeners' emotions, you enhance your persuasive power. Indeed, some experts have referred to human emotions as "the primary motivating system of all activity."[19] Thus, by providing a heartwarming example of someone who benefited from an action you're recommending in your speech, you could complement statistical evidence of all those who could benefit. An emotional appeal can be an effective ethical component of a strong persuasive speech; however, this kind of appeal can also be abused, so it needs to be used responsibly.

### Using Emotional Appeals

Humans have the capacity to experience a wide range of emotions—including empathy, anger, shame, fear, and pity—and each of these feelings can be used to enhance pathos when you prepare a persuasive speech.

▲ **Appealing to Audience Emotions.** In a persuasive speech asking the audience to contribute to panda conservation projects, a photo and narrative about this little cub could be very convincing. Alatom/Getty Images

For example, in a presentation in which a speaker advocated greater freedom in doctor selection for health maintenance organization (HMO) patients, she used this emotional appeal:

> Trey McPherson was born with half of his heart shrunken and nearly useless, a condition that causes most children to die in infancy. Fortunately, Trey was not one of these victims because he was treated by a leading pediatric heart surgeon. After two surgeries, Trey's parents were able to experience the joy of seeing their ten-month-old son climb out of his crib at the hospital.
>
> Except for a bandage on his tiny chest, it was difficult to tell that Trey had recently experienced open-heart surgery.
>
> Sadly, many babies are not as lucky as Trey. Although this skillful surgeon's patients have far-above-average survival rates, many pediatric cardiologists in the New York area find that their "favorite [pediatric] surgeon frequently is off-limits because of price if a child belongs to an HMO."[20]

This example evokes a variety of emotions. It stimulates listeners' *anger* and *pity* at the thought that small children are being denied the best available care. It prompts them to *empathize* by imagining how they would feel if a loved one with a serious disease were forced to accept low-quality medical care. It also causes *joy* at the thought of how Trey's parents must have felt when their child recovered from surgery.

Notice that this emotional appeal is accompanied by sound reasoning. The speaker provides evidence that Trey's access to excellent care is atypical, which justifies the anger she evokes.

**Fear Appeals.** A **fear appeal**—an argument that arouses fear in the minds of audience members—can be a particularly powerful form of pathos.[21] However, to be effective, a fear appeal must demonstrate a serious threat to listeners' well-being.[22] To be ethical, it must be based on accurate information and not exaggerated to make your argument sound more persuasive.

A fear appeal is also more likely to succeed if your audience members believe that they have the power to remedy the problem you're describing.[23] Consider messages by National Park Service rangers advocating safe storage of food in national parks. The rangers provide statistics showing how often bears have broken into cars or tents when people have left food out. They augment these statistics with videos that show bears smashing car windows and climbing inside the vehicles to get food. These images usually strike fear into viewers' hearts. The rangers then show how easy it is to store food safely in lockers or bear-proof canisters. Because audience members realize they *can* readily adopt these practices, they *do* adopt them.

# HOW A FEAR APPEAL SUCCEEDS

Fear appeals can often be effective when audience members experience two different feelings as the message is developed. First, the appeal needs to create a feeling of apprehension in receivers. But then, if audience members perceive that the proposed action will be effective, they experience a feeling of calm.[24]

**Word Choice.**  Effective word choice (see Chapter 12) can also strengthen the power of an emotional appeal. When a speaker's language connects with the values and passions of audience members, the persuasive effectiveness of a message is enhanced.[25] Political consultants on both the right and the left carefully consider the exact words that are used to express an idea to voters. Emory University psychology and psychiatry professor Drew Westen notes that "every word we utter activates what neuroscientists call networks of association— interconnected sets of thoughts and emotions."[26] The selection of metaphors, for instance, has a significant influence in framing how audience members perceive an issue. For example, the use of the term *global warming* makes audiences more likely to express concern about rising earth temperatures than the term *climate change.*[27] A policy on student loans could be framed as *student loan relief* or, alternatively, *cancelling student debts.* The term *loan relief* would cast the policy in a more favorable light, suggesting the elimination of an unjust burden. On the other hand, the term *cancelling debts* suggests that borrowers would be allowed to get out of an obligation they agreed to.

Although effective word choice can make a message more compelling, be aware that persuasive language can also be too intense. When a speaker's goal is to persuade, their natural tendency is to use language that is more emotional. This approach can create a boomerang effect when the audience is using central route processing (see Chapter 17) or the speech context calls for a more measured approach.[28] For example, suppose a student was adversely affected by a change in their school's scheduling policy. This student could use very harsh

▲ **Word Choice Matters.** When advocating for climate justice, the use of the term *global warming* will be more compelling than *climate change.* SOPA Images/Getty Images

words to describe the policy and express their frustrations with it. This language could be counterproductive if audience members were trying to understand how the change affected them but felt that the speaker was overemphasizing personal frustration at the expense of explaining how the policy worked.

Unlike politicians, you probably won't hire a high-priced consultant to help you choose the words that will be most compelling to your classmates; nevertheless, you can use your audience analysis to inform the language you select. If you express the key points of your message with words that relate to the values, needs, and aspirations of your audience members, your ideas are more likely to resonate. For example, in a classroom speech that took a stance on a campus issue, Taja spoke in favor of competency-based education (a system where students earn credit when they show they've learned course material and can apply it, rather than obtaining a passing grade by the end of a fixed term). Because the term "competency-based education" was very general and not very compelling, Taja explained this as "showing professors what you've learned, not how long you've sat in your seat." She also noted that the system was "student-centered" rather than a "one size fits all" approach to college, because individual students can complete a course early in the term or take a few extra weeks if that is what they needed to master the material. Just as Taja's word choice helped her relate the message to her audience members, the words you choose to express your message can strengthen your persuasive appeal. However, they must also be used in an accurate and ethical manner.

## Ensuring Ethical Use of Pathos

As we've discussed, emotional appeals, when combined with ethos and logos, can be very effective. But emotional appeals can have a dark side, too. You may be able to persuade some of your audience members even if you don't establish a sound connection between your point and the emotion you are invoking, but your appeal will not be logical and certainly will not be ethical. This is unacceptable. History is replete with persuaders (including Adolf Hitler) who used pathos to achieve unethical and even horrific ends. Recall the old adage "With great power comes great responsibility," and don't use emotional appeals to manipulate your audience.

Let's take the HMO example previously discussed. The key to that appeal to pathos was that the speaker used sound reasoning to connect a relatively rare health emergency (a baby born with a damaged heart) with a broader challenge facing many potential patients (access to a wide selection of qualified physicians). If the speaker had failed to make the logical connection between the points, however, she would have been acting unethically. How might that happen? Suppose she could not provide evidence that access to a wide range of doctors would actually help families faced with Trey's situation and other health crises as well. In that case, her speech would merely be an emotional ploy to manipulate the audience into accepting her argument.

Numerous examples of fear appeals are premised on "facts" that are blatantly untrue. One instance involves politicians who offer "misbeliefs about the alleged risks of autism and other injuries from childhood vaccines" despite detailed analyses of vaccine safety that "disprove completely claims of vaccine-linked

## UNETHICAL USE OF AN EMOTIONAL APPEAL

autism."[29] Certain climate scientists lost credibility after inaccurately stating that the Himalayan glaciers, which feed many rivers in Asia, could melt by 2035.[30] Fear appeals that exaggerate the health consequences of drug use (such as claims that using marijuana is similar to playing Russian roulette) have rarely succeeded.[31] Indeed, poorly substantiated claims can have a boomerang effect.[32] To present a convincing fear appeal and preserve your own ethos, you must use credible evidence to substantiate the harmful consequences that you predict.

Ethical speakers must also ensure that they select language that accurately describes the ideas they are discussing. Although compelling word choice can be used as an ethical persuasive tool, it can cross the line into manipulation, exaggeration, or untruth. The **loaded language fallacy** is committed when emotionally charged words convey a meaning that cannot be supported by the facts presented by the speaker. For example, a speaker arguing that students should be allowed to choose their own speech topics referred to instructors who place some limits on topics as "the thought police." This wording was not ethical because the instructors were only setting limits on the available topics for a single speech assignment, not telling their students what to think. Students were free to advocate for any stance on their particular topic when developing their speech.

# SAMPLE PERSUASIVE SPEECH

## ADDRESS TO THE U.S. CONGRESS

### Volodymyr Zelensky
*President of Ukraine*

*On March 16, 2022, Ukrainian President Volodymyr Zelensky addressed the U.S. Congress. He spoke from the capital city, Kyiv, as his nation was under assault by Russian forces. It was the first time a national leader spoke to Congress virtually and it was the first speech delivered to Congress from a war zone by a national leader. President Zelensky called for Congress to provide additional military aid for Ukraine and for President Biden to be the world leader for peace.*

*President Zelensky's speech was exceptional. As you read the transcript, note how he uses a variety of persuasive strategies in the content and word choice of his presentation. He connects with his audience—the political leaders and people of the United States—by establishing common ground, referring to important events in U.S. history, and highlighting the shared core values of Ukraine and the United States. When he delivered this speech, President Zelensky wore an olive-green T-shirt with the Ukrainian armed forces insignia rather than the type of expensive suit typically worn by political leaders (including Russian President Vladimir Putin), symbolizing his role as president of a nation at war. He also showed a video that provides a graphic depiction of the war's impact on the Ukrainian people.*

*Note: This material has been lightly edited for clarity. See www.president.gov.ua.*

Mrs. Speaker,
Members of Congress,
Ladies and Gentlemen,
Americans! Friends!

• Striking statement in the introduction

I am proud to greet you from Ukraine, from our capital— Kyiv. From a city that is under missile and air strikes by Russian troops daily. • But it does not give up. And it doesn't even think to give up for a single minute! This is true for dozens of other cities and communities in our country, which have found themselves in the worst war since World War II.

I have the honor to greet you on behalf of the Ukrainian people, brave and freedom-loving people. For eight years they have been resisting the aggression of the Russian Federation. They sacrifice the best children—sons and daughters— to stop the full-scale Russian invasion.

Now the fate of our state is being decided. The fate of our people. It is being decided whether Ukrainians will be free. Whether they will preserve their democracy. Russia has attacked more than just our land and our cities. It went on a brutal offensive against our values. Basic human values. It threw tanks and planes against our freedom. Against our right to live freely in our country, choosing our own future. Against our desire for happiness. Against our national dreams. Just like yours, ordinary people of America. Just like those of everyone in the United States. •

• Establishing common ground

I remember your Rushmore National Memorial, the faces of your prominent presidents, those who laid the foundations of America as it is today: democracy, independence, freedom, and care for everyone. Everyone who works diligently. Who lives honestly. Who respects the law. We in Ukraine want the same for ourselves. All that is a normal part of life for you.

• Zelensky uses these salutations as transitions to new ideas.

Ladies and Gentlemen! Americans! •

In your great history you have pages that will allow you to understand Ukrainians. Understand us now, when it is needed most. Remember Pearl Harbor, that terrible morning of December 7, 1941. When your sky was black from the planes attacking you. Just remember that. Remember September 11th. A terrible day in 2001, when evil tried to turn your cities into a battlefield. When innocent people were attacked. Attacked from the air. In a way no one expected. In a way you could not stop it. •

• Analogy of attacks on Ukraine to infamous attacks in U.S. history

Our state experiences this every day! Every night! For three weeks now! Different Ukrainian cities . . . Odesa and Kharkiv, Chernihiv and Sumy, Zhytomyr and Lviv, Mariupol and Dnipro. Russia has turned the Ukrainian sky into a source of death for thousands of people. • Russian troops have already fired nearly a thousand missiles at Ukraine.

• Appeal to pathos

Countless bombs. They use drones to kill more precisely. This is a terror Europe has not seen for 80 years!

And we ask for a response. For a response from the world. For a response to terror. Is this too much of a request? To establish a no-fly zone over Ukraine is to save people. • A humanitarian no-fly zone. Conditions under which Russia will no longer be able to terrorize our peaceful cities every day and night. If that's too much, we offer an alternative. You know what defense systems we need: C-300 and other similar systems.

You know how much on the battlefield depends on the ability to use aircraft. Powerful, strong aircraft. To protect your people. Your freedom. Your land. Aircraft that can help Ukraine. That can help Europe. And you also know that they are available. But on land. Not in the Ukrainian sky. They do not protect our people.

"I have a dream"—these words are known to each of you. • Today I can say: I have a necessity. The necessity to protect our sky. The necessity for your decision. Your help. And it will mean exactly the same thing. The same thing you feel when you hear: I have a dream.

Ladies and Gentlemen! Friends!

Ukraine is grateful to the United States for its overwhelming support. For all that your state and your people have already done for our freedom. For weapons and ammunition, for training and funding, for leadership in the free world, which helps put pressure on the aggressor economically. I am grateful to President Biden for his personal involvement, for his sincere commitment to the defense of Ukraine and democracy around the world. I am grateful to you [the Congress] for the resolution, which recognizes all those who commit crimes against the Ukrainian people as war criminals. •

However, now, in the darkest time for our country, for the whole of Europe, I urge you to do more! New packages of sanctions are needed every week until the Russian military machine stops. Restrictions are needed as regards everyone on whom this unjust regime is based. We ask the United States to impose sanctions against all politicians in the Russian Federation who remain in office and do not sever ties with those responsible for the aggression against Ukraine, from State Duma deputies to the last official who lacks the morale to sever ties with state terror. All American companies must leave Russia, their market. Leave this market flooded with our blood.

Ladies and Gentlemen. Members of Congress!

Take the lead! If you have companies in your constituencies that sponsor the Russian military machine, keeping their business in Russia, you have to apply pressure so that the Russian state does not receive a single dollar to spend on

• Zelensky makes a request that the United States had denied before and would likely deny again. After saying no, the United States is more likely to agree to the smaller requests coming later—like an antiaircraft weapons system.

• Zelensky quotes Dr. Martin Luther King's "I Have a Dream" speech, one of the most inspirational speeches in U.S. history.

• Zelensky shows gratitude for U.S. efforts and explains why more is needed.

**• Actions that people in the United States can take**

**• Effective use of style to make a value argument**

the destruction of Ukraine. On the destruction of Europe. •
All American ports must be closed to Russian goods and
ships. Peace is more important than profit. • And we must
defend this principle throughout the world together.

We have already become part of the anti-war coalition.
The great anti-war coalition, which unites many states, dozens of states—those who reacted in a principled manner to
President Putin's decision, to Russia's invasion of our state.

But we have to move on. We have to create new tools
to respond quickly and stop the war. The full-scale Russian
invasion of Ukraine began on February 24. And it would be
fair if it ended in a day, in 24 hours, so that evil is punished
immediately. Today the world does not have such tools. The
wars of the past have prompted our predecessors to create
institutions that were supposed to protect us from war. But
they don't work. We see it. You see it. So, we need new ones.
New institutions. New alliances.

And we offer them.

**• New proposal to promote peace**

We offer to create an association—U-24. United for peace. •
A union of responsible states that have the strength and conscience to stop conflicts. Immediately. Provide all necessary
assistance in 24 hours. If necessary—weapons. If necessary—
sanctions. Humanitarian support. Political support. Funding.
Everything necessary to preserve peace quickly. To save lives.

In addition, such an association could provide assistance
to those who are experiencing natural disasters, man-made
disasters, and those who fall victim to a humanitarian crisis
or epidemic. Remember how difficult it was for the world to
do the simplest thing—to give everyone vaccines. Vaccines
against COVID. To save lives. To prevent new strains. The world
spent months and years doing things that could have been
done much faster so that there were no human losses. •

**• Analogy. Just as faster action would have limited COVID deaths, faster action in Ukraine would save lives by preserving peace.**

Ladies and Gentlemen! Americans!

If such an alliance, the U-24, had already been formed, I
believe it would have saved thousands of lives. In our country and in many other countries that need peace so crucially,
that have suffered inhuman destruction. . . . I ask you to
watch one video now, video of what Russian troops did on
our land. We have to stop this. We must prevent such things.
Preventively destroy every aggressor who seeks to conquer
another nation. Please watch. . . . •

**• As a presentation aid, Zelensky provides video evidence of destruction caused by Russian attacks, juxtaposed with examples of life in Ukraine.**

And in the end to sum it up: Today it is not enough to be
the leader of the nation. Today it takes being the leader of the
world. Being the leader of the world means being the leader
of peace. Peace in your country does not depend anymore
only on you and your people. It depends on those next to
you, on those who are strong.

Strong does not mean big. Strong is brave and ready to fight for the life of one's citizens and citizens of the world. • • Effective use of style to advocate for human rights
For human rights, for freedom, for the right to live decently and to die when your time comes, not when it is wanted by someone else, by your neighbor.

Today the Ukrainian people are defending not only Ukraine, we are fighting for the values of Europe and the world, sacrificing our lives in the name of the future. That's why today the American people are helping not just Ukraine but also Europe and the world, to keep the planet alive, to keep justice in history. Now I am almost 45 years old. Today my age stopped when the hearts of more than 100 children stopped beating. • • Appeal to pathos
I see no sense in life if it cannot stop death. And this is my main mission as the leader of my people—great Ukrainians.

And as the leader of my nation I am addressing President Biden. You are the leader of the nation, of your great nation. I wish you to be the leader of the world. Being the leader of the world means to be the leader of peace. • • Conclusion reiterates key point of the speech

Thank you.
Glory to Ukraine!

# CHAPTER REVIEW

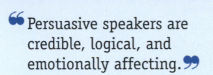
**" Persuasive speakers are credible, logical, and emotionally affecting. "**

After you have selected a topic for your persuasive speech, analyzed your audience, and chosen an effective thesis, you need to develop a message that compels listeners to accept your thesis and thus allows you to reach your ultimate goal of changing or strengthening their beliefs, attitudes, or actions. You can do this by combining ethos, logos, and pathos.

Through ethos, you establish your credibility as a speaker. The audience must perceive that you are competent and trustworthy and have their best interests at heart. You can avoid losing credibility by avoiding statements that raise doubts about your knowledge, honesty, or goodwill.

Through logos, you use credible evidence to support your claims. You also present sound reasoning to establish these claims by using examples, comparisons, signs, and cause-effect relationships. When reasoning, it is essential to avoid logical fallacies.

Through pathos, you further strengthen your persuasive power by evoking your audience members' emotions—not to manipulate your listeners but to move them in an ethical and responsible manner to take the action you're proposing or adopt the belief you're advocating.

Together, ethos, logos, and pathos can help you win your listeners' heads (their reason), hearts (their emotions), and hands (their commitment to action). Master these three tools, and you'll greatly enhance your prowess as a persuasive speaker.

## Key Terms

ethos (credibility) *452*
competence *453*
trustworthiness *453*
goodwill *453*
logos (evidence and reasoning) *456*
evidence *457*
fallacious (faulty) reasoning *457*
precise evidence *458*
inductive reasoning *459*
example reasoning *460*
representative example *461*
comparison reasoning *462*
sign reasoning *463*
causal reasoning *464*

hasty generalization *465*
*post hoc* fallacy *466*
reversed causality *466*
*ad populum* (bandwagon) fallacy *466*
*ad hominem* (personal attack) fallacy *468*
straw person fallacy *468*
slippery slope fallacy *469*
false dilemma fallacy *469*
appeal to tradition fallacy *470*
pathos *471*
fear appeal *473*
loaded language fallacy *477*

## Review Questions

1. Explain the three primary elements of credibility.
2. Indicate six steps you can take to enhance your own credibility.
3. What are four mistakes you can make that may harm your credibility?
4. What are three fundamental components of a logical message?
5. Identify and explain nine logical fallacies.
6. What factors come into play when making an emotional appeal?
7. What kinds of practices can harm an emotional appeal?

## Critical Thinking Questions

1. What role does audience analysis play in establishing your credibility? Is the speaker's responsibility to back up claims with solid evidence the same for a sympathetic audience as it is for a hostile or a neutral audience?
2. As an audience member, how can you identify logical fallacies during a speech? How can you identify weak or misleading evidence? How do you react when a speaker's claims are based on unsound evidence or reasoning?

3. How should a speaker who favors a particular tradition develop a logical argument in favor of that tradition that avoids committing an appeal to tradition fallacy? For example, how might a speaker build a case for the general education requirement described in the text on page 470? In a broader sense, how can you build a strong and ethical argument for maintaining a tradition that you support?
4. What types of presentation aids can you use to build your credibility?
5. Reflect on your position on a controversial issue in society. What evidence could persuade you to change your mind or adopt a neutral position? Who or what would be a credible source that might induce you to rethink your position? How can the answers to these questions help you in your own efforts as a persuasive speaker?

## Activities

1. Working in a group, select a thesis for a persuasive speech. Then prepare four supporting arguments for that thesis, using a different type of inductive reasoning (example, comparison, sign, and causal) for each supporting argument.
2. Select an issue that would be appropriate for a persuasive speech. Construct three different arguments for that issue using powerful language. Break into groups, then share your arguments. After each person shares, have the others rate the effectiveness of the argument on a scale of 1 (not convincing) to 10 (highly convincing). After providing ratings, group members should explain why they found some words and phrases more powerful than others.
3. Create a credibility checklist based on the bulleted list on pages 453–54. Review a persuasive speech in this text or one that you find on the Internet, and see how many of the criteria the speaker fulfills.
4. Find a college graduation speech that you can watch online. Identify how the speaker uses ethos, pathos, and logos to develop the message. Were there any ideas presented that you believe would be helpful to you after you graduate? Why were these ideas convincing to you? (If none were convincing to you, how could the speaker have improved the presentation?)
5. Review the illustration "Supporting Causal Reasoning" on page 464. Working individually or in groups, select a claim based on causal reasoning that you could make in a persuasive speech. Then think of one argument in support of that claim that explains the link between cause and effect, explain the types of credentials that would make an author credible on this claim, and identify a correlation that would help show a link between cause and effect.
6. Watch a few episodes of a program such as *The Daily Show*, *The Late Show*, or *Last Week Tonight*. For one episode, assess each comedic bit or segment, and identify those that focus on pundits' and politicians' use of loaded language and fear appeals. Characterize a few of the fallacies being exposed.

# SPECIAL-OCCASION SPEAKING

# 19

> **Whether to mark a celebration, a milestone, or a passing, we all participate in special-occasion speaking as speakers or listeners.** 

Speeches that praise, celebrate, memorialize, or otherwise commemorate special occasions have a long history. A Sumerian tablet dating back to about 2000 BCE records the funeral utterances of Ludingirra, a teacher and poet, as he laments the loss of his father and his wife by eulogizing (or memorializing) their achievements and personal qualities. Indeed, **epideictic** rhetoric—speaking that praises or blames—was one of the three genres of oratory identified by the fourth-century BCE Greek philosopher Aristotle.[1] Speakers typically used this form of address to celebrate timeless virtues during occasions such as funerals or holidays.[2] And ever since Aristotle's time, people around the world have continued to use public speaking to help themselves and others celebrate joyous occasions, mourn the passing of loved ones, honor friends' or colleagues' achievements, and observe other milestones such as retirement in their communities.

Think about the times you've been moved by a speech marking a special occasion. Perhaps on a Labor Day, you heard a speaker praising workers who helped build

◀ **Special-Occasion Speeches Mark Important Events.** When speaking to commemorate a special occasion, such as a wedding, you want to meet audience expectations, evoke shared values, and fit the mood of the occasion. Gary John Norman/Getty Images

some of the great bridges and highways in your area. Or maybe you've attended a gathering to observe the passing of another September 11th on the calendar, and the speaker's words helped you reflect once again on the magnitude of the terrorist attacks in 2001. You also might have attended a wedding, clapping and cheering along with the other guests as friends and relatives of the newlyweds offered toasts to the couple. And if you've excelled at your job, perhaps you've been presented with an award, along with words of praise from your boss, during a department meeting or party. If you've attended a formal dinner for your company or a community organization, you may have listened to an after-dinner speech—a traditional presentation designed to entertain an audience after a meal. And you'll certainly have the opportunity to listen to many speeches of congratulation and advice if you take part in graduation ceremonies after completing your college degree.

Special-occasion speeches mark some of the most important events in our lives—those that bring us together with others in our community and those that unite us in our humanity. As you go through life, you'll hear many such speeches and will probably be called upon to give one or more yourself. Even if you never have to deliver a formal presentation in an official capacity (such as at work or in a community setting), you will almost certainly be invited to "say a few words" at various points in your life. For example, your grandmother might ask you to say good-bye to your deceased grandfather during an intimate graveside service. Or you might host a large gathering of family at your home for Thanksgiving, and your guests will expect you to start things off by sharing some inspiring words about the meaning of the holiday. Or perhaps you've arranged for your friend's band to play for the first time at a local pub, and he asks you to introduce the performers to the crowd.

Whatever your special speaking occasion, you'll have to face that ever-daunting question: "What am I going to say?" This chapter will help you answer that question. We start by introducing six types of special-occasion speeches and discussing the purposes each type serves. Next, we offer some general guidelines for speaking at a special occasion. After that, we go into detail about each of the six types of special-occasion speeches, providing tips tailored to each type.

# TYPES OF SPECIAL-OCCASION SPEECHES

Although there are various types of special-occasion speeches, the six most common are as follows:

- *Speech of introduction.* Sometimes referred to as "the speech before the speech," this is a brief presentation designed to prepare an audience for the *main event*—a speaker, a performance, or an activity that will follow. A speech of introduction provides context and gives credentials for the main speaker or performer.

- *Speech of presentation.* Awards, honors, and special designations often require speeches before they are conferred. A presentation speech explains the background and significance of the award and the reasons that the recipient is deserving of it.

- *Speech of acceptance.* Recipients of honors, awards, or designations are often expected to give a short presentation of their own—something beyond a simple thank-you, but succinct enough to make a relatively brief statement. Recipients typically express gratitude for the award, extol the award's significance to them, and acknowledge others' support and contributions.

- *Speech to memorialize or eulogize.* A **eulogy** comments on the passing of an individual, celebrates that person's life, and often shares personal reflections and stories about the deceased. It offers an appropriate method for recovering from grief, helps people feel consolation, and pays tribute to their sense of loss.[3] A speech to memorialize uses the same approach but is expanded to honor the sacrifice and heroism of a group of individuals—often on a significant anniversary, such as Veterans Day or September 11.

- *Speech to celebrate.* Events that represent rites of passage—such as christenings and circumcisions, bar and bat mitzvahs, graduations, weddings, reunions, and retirements—often demand celebration speeches. These may take the form of a toast or special observance that focuses the audience's attention on the milestone achieved and recognizes the joy and pride the participants feel.

- *After-dinner speech.* At times, a speaker needs to use humor and good storytelling to lighten the mood of an occasion or soften up an audience. Although these presentations are called "after-dinner speeches" (in the tradition of author Mark Twain, who gave over 150 such speeches during his career[4]), they can follow or precede a meal. Light in tone, they can help a speaker entertain listeners or set the stage for an event that follows the meal, such as a fund-raising effort for a charitable cause.

▲ **Speech of Acceptance.** Tim McGraw speaking after receiving a star on the Music City Walk of Fame. While speaking to a crowd of family and fans an emotional McGraw said "I can't look at my mom right now." Raymond Boyd/Getty Images

At some events, you'll hear more than one type of special-occasion speech being delivered. Consider the Academy Awards (or Oscars) ceremony hosted in Los Angeles by the Academy of Motion Picture Arts and Sciences. This star-studded annual event begins with a *speech of introduction*. Typically, a master of ceremonies—perhaps Jimmy Kimmel, Chris Rock, or Ellen DeGeneres—prepares the audience for the main event, often acknowledging the honored tradition of the Oscars, while also telling jokes to loosen up the crowd. At some point during the evening, a well-known actor gives a *presentation speech* before announcing a lifetime achievement award for a long-famous director or producer. Recipients of Oscars and lifetime achievement awards deliver *acceptance speeches* thanking the academy, exclaiming how much the award means to them, and acknowledging (sometimes seemingly endlessly) the support they've received from their families and colleagues. Later in the evening, a presenter might *eulogize* a recently departed luminary from the motion-picture industry.

Each of the six types of special-occasion speeches serves a unique purpose and evokes a different mood, but they all have something in common: to deliver them effectively, you must apply certain common skills (such as evoking your listeners' emotions and being mindful of their expectations). We present the following guidelines to give you a basic foundation of knowledge and then explore strategies tailored to each of the six types of speeches.

# GENERAL GUIDELINES FOR SPECIAL-OCCASION SPEECHES

A handful of general guidelines can boost your chances of delivering an effective special-occasion speech, no matter what type you'll be giving. These guidelines include *appealing to your audience's emotions, matching your delivery to the mood of the occasion, adapting to your audience's expectations, evoking shared values*, and *respecting time constraints for the speech*.

## Appealing to Your Audience's Emotions

Successful special-occasion speeches often evoke emotional responses, such as laughter, tears, joy, and pride. Because many special occasions are intimately connected with important human events, your audience will likely be predisposed to experiencing a particular feeling during the occasion. Your job in giving the speech will be to signal when it's time for that emotion to come to the surface.

For example, suppose you're about to deliver a eulogy at a graveside service for your grandmother. Although generally designed to comment on a loved one's passing, a eulogy can be presented in several formats—to celebrate, to mourn, to commemorate, or to honor.[5] Let's imagine that in this case, your grandmother was a loving family woman, an accomplished artist, and a dedicated supporter of important causes. Family members and friends are gathered around the gravesite under a canopy of maple and oak trees. Everyone present is reflecting on your grandmother's life, and the sorrow of saying good-bye begins to settle into their thoughts. The moment arrives for you to deliver the eulogy. You begin speaking. As you recall your grandmother's special qualities and achievements and talk about how much she meant to you, your eyes fill with tears and your voice cracks at times. The combination of your words and the expression of your grief gives those gathered around the gravesite permission to let their own feelings well up. By enabling your family and friends to begin experiencing and expressing their grief, you help them embark on the mourning process—something we all must do when we have lost a loved one.

## Matching Your Delivery to the Mood of the Occasion

Whether joyous or solemn, lighthearted or serious, your demeanor and words should match the overall mood of the special occasion for which you're giving

the speech. As the saying goes, there's a time and a place for everything—a time to tell funny stories, a time to show respect, and a time to share your own sadness. By ensuring that what you say and how you say it are appropriate for the occasion, you will enhance your effectiveness.

For example, a eulogy calls primarily for a somber, sad tone, although a lovingly humorous recollection about the deceased may also be appropriate and appreciated. At the graveside service for your grandmother, for instance, family members and friends might smile through their tears and nod their heads knowingly when you help them recall her famous midnight excursions into the kitchen for chocolate ice cream.

If you're the best man at your older brother's wedding and you're giving a toast at the reception, you'll evoke a different overall mood. You'll want to express your happiness that your brother has found a loving spouse as well as give voice to everyone's wish that the new couple will share a long and joyous life together. Depending on the traditions of your culture, you may also introduce a bit of humor by hinting at the escapades your brother had in his younger years and expressing your satisfaction that he's finally settling down with a wonderful partner. You certainly would not go on and on about any hard or painful times the couple experienced while dating. Nor would you be in any way critical of their relationship.

## Adapting to Your Audience's Expectations

Listeners' cultural background, age, values, and other characteristics affect how they perceive a special occasion and what they expect from a speech delivered during that occasion. For example, a community of Christian Arab immigrants living in Chicago would likely want to attend a church funeral service after one of their community members died. Moreover, they would probably expect a mostly religious service, with only a brief discussion of the deceased, focused on how the person cared about the community and shared its traditions. At a community dinner in honor of the deceased later in the day, speakers might share more personal stories.

On the other hand, an audience of amateur comedians might expect a fun and lighthearted presentation at a roast for a fellow entertainer, with speakers revealing funny stories about the individual being roasted. At this kind of event, it would run against audience expectations to bring up painful events from the person's childhood and thus bring an overly serious turn to the proceedings.

The lesson? Before giving any special-occasion speech, make sure you're aware of your audience's expectations regarding what should be said during the speech and how it should be expressed.

▲ **Matching Audience Expectations.** At the 2022 White House Correspondents Dinner, Trevor Noah poked fun at President Joe Biden, Democrats, and Republicans, and ended on a serious note, calling for the press to live up to their responsibility of informing the public about the important issues in society.
Bloomberg/Getty Images

## Evoking Shared Values

Oftentimes, effective special-occasion speeches appeal to values shared by members of the audience and the speaker. For instance, imagine that you're a member of PeopleAid, an organization that helps people who are homeless in your community, and you're presenting a plaque to Olivia, a fellow member, for her steady dedication to PeopleAid's mission. Olivia has recruited an unusually large number of volunteers to serve boxed lunches at shelters throughout the community and has taken the lead on other valuable projects for the organization. Before handing the plaque to Olivia, you deliver a speech extolling her ability to embody PeopleAid's values, which include compassion for those in need and a strong work ethic. Your speech about Olivia reaffirms your listeners' own dedication to these values and inspires them to strive for the same high standards she has set.

Other special-occasion speeches may touch on such values as patriotism, fairness, shared sacrifice, and religious belief. To illustrate, suppose you're giving a speech at a ceremony recognizing the fifth anniversary of the death of Frank, a close friend who lost his life while serving in the U.S. Army in Afghanistan. The ceremony is held at the town hall near where you and Frank grew up. Neighbors and family members have gathered to remember Frank and honor the five-year anniversary of his death. In your speech, you note that "Frank felt the same love for his country that everyone in this room feels. We have all made sacrifices for that love. Frank lost his life, and we lost him all too soon. We will never forget our lost friend, brother, son, and neighbor." Through these words, you tap into the patriotism in your listeners' hearts and their sense of shared sacrifice—reminding them that you are all connected in a close community.

## Respecting Time Constraints

Most special occasions are carefully planned affairs. Recall a wedding or retirement dinner you've recently attended. The occasion likely had a program that listed specific times for certain events. The program for a retirement dinner, for example, might look something like this: "Cocktails at 4:00. Award ceremony at 5:00. Dinner at 6:00." The occasion also may feature several speeches. Whenever refreshments, meal service, and multiple speakers are involved, skillful management of the overall program schedule becomes important. If an event listed in the program starts late or if one speaker uses up more time than the program has allotted, then the entire event can quickly go off the rails. If you're giving a speech at such an occasion, make sure you know beforehand when you're scheduled to speak and what your time allotment is. Then be certain to stick to those logistics while delivering your presentation. As a courtesy, be willing to modify the time for your own presentation if a previous speaker has gone overtime.

# STRATEGIES FOR EACH TYPE OF SPECIAL-OCCASION SPEECH

Although the general guidelines described in the preceding section can help you deliver an effective special-occasion speech, you'll also want to master strategies tailored to each of the six types of speeches. By pairing these specific practices with the general suggestions, you'll increase the odds of delivering a top-notch speech—no matter what the occasion.

## Strategies for Speeches of Introduction

When you're giving a speech to introduce another speaker, a performer, or an event, you will likely have three goals:

- Shifting your listeners' focus from interacting with one another to paying attention to the upcoming event

- Building anticipation and excitement for the upcoming topic and speaker or presentation
- Introducing the person, performance, or event that's coming next

When making an introduction, remember that as a speaker, you are not the main entertainment or focus. Your primary goal is to facilitate what's coming next, and there is nothing more disastrous than an introductory speaker who goes on too long or tries too hard. Thus, take care not to upstage the speaker or event you're introducing. In particular, resist any urge to talk at length about yourself. Also, be sure to express some of your own appreciation for and anticipation of the upcoming event. The following tips can help you keep your audience focused on the main event, and effectively achieve your three-part goal in giving a speech of introduction.

**Be Patient.** If you're delivering your speech in person, when the time comes for you to start your introduction, many listeners may still be settling into their seats, finishing a meal, or simply chatting with one another. To help them gradually shift their attention to you, stand up and begin talking above the background noise and voices in the room. But be patient: it takes time for people to transition away from what they're doing at the moment. If you are speaking at a virtual ceremony, pause for a moment to give audience members a chance to get focused.

**Use Attention-Getters.** To help focus your listeners on the upcoming speaker or event, use attention-getters to cut through any noise or conversation in the room, making sure that you remain appropriate for the setting. Consider the attention-getters mentioned in Chapter 10, particularly one of the following: incorporate a striking statement, use a little bit of humor, or take the opportunity to let listeners know you're one of them.

**Modulate Your Volume.** Even if you are working with a microphone during an in-person speech, you may need to speak loudly at first to overcome the prevailing noise in the room and grab listeners' attention. After your speech is underway, be sure to lower your voice as the room quiets down. If conversation stirs again later during your speech, you can always raise your voice once more to an appropriate level.

**Be Focused and Brief.** Remember that your job is to prepare the audience to pay attention to the speaker or performance that will follow. To that end, keep your comments focused on that event. Also, make sure your introduction is concise. Otherwise, audience members may start seeing you as the main entertainment, or they may lose interest in the next part of the program.

# THE ART OF INTRODUCTION

## Strategies for Speeches of Presentation

Like a speech of introduction, the presentation of an award or a commendation precedes and facilitates what comes next for the audience. But unlike a speech of introduction, a presentation speech usually *celebrates* the person, organization, or cause being honored—whether it's a service commendation for a teacher at a local PTA meeting, an award for team members at a sports banquet, or even an Emmy Award for lifetime achievement in television.

Thus, in a presentation speech, your role will be more fundamental than in a speech of introduction; you must provide your listeners with background and context for the honor to follow. This might seem unnecessary because listeners probably already know what the honor is and why they are there to observe it. Yet your job is to highlight the significance of the award and to build excitement and even reverence for it. You can do this by describing in detail the importance of the award itself and the background and contributions of the recipient.

Handled skillfully, a presentation speech can inspire intense emotion in listeners and even move them to dedicate themselves to the award recipient's work. Strong and enthusiastic applause after you've presented the award or commendation is another sure sign that you've nailed the speech. The following tips can help you achieve this kind of effect.

**Adopt the Persona of a Presenter.** In this type of speech, you're not just announcing the conferring of an award or honor; you're also presenting it. To demonstrate your authority as a presenter, be sure to speak respectfully and knowledgeably about your subject.

**Explain the Significance and Background of the Award or Honor.** Most people in your audience will understand that they are there for the presentation of an award. But they may not know why the honor or award really matters. What is its significance? Does it have an interesting history you could share? In a nutshell, a major goal of your presentation speech is to make clear why your listeners should care about the award about to be bestowed.

**Connect the Recipient's Background to the Award's Criteria.** Every award has qualifications or criteria that a potential recipient must meet and perhaps exceed. But these may not be obvious to the audience. In your speech, be sure to explain the criteria—and then point out how and why the recipient has met or surpassed them. Consider using stories and examples of the recipient's achievements to show dramatically (and perhaps humorously) why this person deserves the honor.

**Use Appropriate Presentation Aids.** A video or a slide presentation, perhaps with a light music or audio accompaniment, can complement your speech. Consider using presentation aids to explain both the criteria for the award and the ways that the recipient fulfilled the criteria. For example, if you're presenting

# THE ART OF PRESENTING

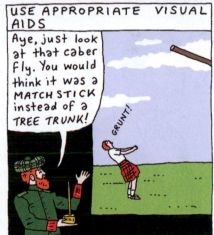

an award for a person who has helped teach literacy to children in need, you could provide a short slide show depicting the recipient performing this work and some audio snippets of children who benefited from the person's efforts.

## Strategies for Speeches of Acceptance

Imagine this: you're the beneficiary of a prestigious award, and the presenter has just handed it to you. What do you say now?

A high-quality acceptance speech is less about what you're saying ("Thank you. I couldn't have done this without the rest of the team") and more about how you're behaving while accepting the honor. By being there, you transform the presentation into a kind of public spectacle. The audience will expect you to show both humility and responsibility. You can fulfill those expectations by

> Your Majesty, Your Royal Highnesses, Ladies, and Gentlemen. The work I have done has, already, been greatly rewarded and recognized. Imagination reaches out, repeatedly trying to achieve some higher level of understanding, until suddenly I find myself momentarily alone before one corner of nature's pattern of beauty and true majesty revealed. That was my reward.

**RICHARD FEYNMAN**
**1965 NOBEL PRIZE IN PHYSICS**

giving a brief, gracious, and heartfelt speech that expresses your gratitude while also recognizing the efforts of others who contributed to your achievement. The following tips can help you attain this blend of important qualities.

### Use Appropriate Volume and Articulation.

Accepting an award can stir intense emotions within you, causing your voice to drop or crack, as noted before—and if you are using a microphone, such lapses will be amplified. To overcome this challenge, anticipate the effects of strong feelings, and feel free to gather yourself for a moment or two before you start talking. Strive to speak with sufficient volume and clarity throughout, especially when thanking others during your acceptance.

### Show Genuine Humility.

Listeners can easily spot the difference between someone who's genuinely modest and humbled by an honor and someone who's just acting humble. Think about it: you've probably seen people stand at a podium, gush about how this award has caught them off guard and left them speechless, but then pull out a sheet of paper and give a canned speech. Irritating, isn't it? To avoid making this mistake, don't act surprised if you knew you would be receiving the award. But definitely express your genuine gratitude for the honor and for the people who helped you achieve it. Most important, be yourself and be genuine. In 2019, Lady Gaga won the Academy Award for Best Original Song for "Shallow," from *A Star Is Born*, offering the following emotional and humble words:

> I've worked hard for a long time, and it's not about, you know . . . it's not about winning. But what it's about is not giving up. If you have a dream, fight for it. There's a discipline for passion. And it's not about how many times you get rejected or you fall down or you're beaten up. It's about how many times you stand up and are brave and you keep on going. Thank you!

▲ **Effective Acceptance Speech.** Lady Gaga won an Oscar for Best Original Song in 2019. Although some Oscar acceptance speeches are far too long, she completed hers in just over a minute. Lady Gaga displayed emotion and humility, telling the audience to fight for their dreams. VALERIE MACON/Getty Images

**Remember That Less Is More.** Going on too long while accepting an award can give the impression that you always talk about yourself and rarely exhibit interest in others. To avoid conveying this impression, aim for brevity in your acceptance speech. Say enough to demonstrate your humility (perhaps through a bit of self-deprecating humor) and to acknowledge your deep appreciation for the award or honor. Briefly thank those to whom you are indebted, and then sit down. Otherwise, the music may start playing, and your presenter may take you by the elbow and start ushering you offstage.

## Strategies for Speeches to Memorialize or Eulogize

Because death is a part of life, at some point you will inevitably lose a beloved family member or friend. You may be asked to deliver a eulogy about the person at a memorial service after their passing. As noted earlier, your purpose during this type of speech is to review and celebrate the life of your loved one and to console your listeners while helping them grieve publicly. It may seem that the two goals (consoling and facilitating grief) are in conflict, but consolation actually supports grieving—primarily because you can express these strong emotions as you encourage your audience to do the same. Witnessing a eulogist publicly expressing grief gives the audience license to do so as well.

▲ **Celebration of Life.** At the celebration of life ceremony for Hall of Fame Football Coach John Madden at the Oakland Coliseum, speakers talked about Madden's qualities as an accomplished coach and a generous human being. Lachlan Cunningham/Getty Images

Delivering an effective eulogy is about helping the living by showing your own emotion as well as extolling the departed loved one's virtues and achievements. The following tips can help you provide this assistance when giving this kind of speech.

**Focus on Celebrating the Person's Life.** Each person's life has both high and low points, good experiences and bad. Instead of focusing on negative memories in your eulogy, highlight the deceased's accomplishments, important relationships, and unique qualities, citing examples and stories familiar to your listeners. You'll establish common ground with your audience members and help them collectively celebrate the best of the person they've lost.

**Use Humor Judiciously.** At most memorial services, several people will stand up and say something about the deceased. If each person in a series of speakers focuses unrelentingly on the profound sorrow of the occasion, the collective heaviness may become too much for the audience to bear. For this reason, consider providing a humorous (but appropriate) anecdote about the deceased at some point during your remarks to relieve the tension. Listeners may feel profound relief when they can laugh through their tears.

**Don't Be Afraid to Show Your Emotions.** The best way to give the audience permission to grieve openly during a memorial service is to show your

## IT'S OK TO HELP LISTENERS LAUGH THROUGH THEIR TEARS

*Central Intelligence Agency    **Culinary Institute of America

own emotions. A display of feeling can set loose a flood of feelings in your listeners, which can provide a healthy emotional release.

## Strategies for Speeches to Celebrate

Life is as much about joy and celebration as it is about tragedy and loss. The birth of a child, a couple's decision to spend their lives together, a graduation, a rite of passage from youth to adulthood: these and other major milestones in our lives are all causes for happiness. And they're all marked by special occasions at which people deliver speeches to help celebrate the joyous event.

If you're delivering a speech of celebration at such an occasion, your role is to explain the significance of the occasion, acknowledge the joy everyone is feeling, and inspire the audience to take part in the celebration. The following tips can help you achieve this goal.

**Aim for Brevity.** Take enough time to remind your audience why the gathering is important and joyful—but not so much time that you drift off-topic, or tire, bore, or distract the audience from the subject of the celebration.

**Share Your Insights.** During a celebration, it is not unusual for several different people to speak. Your speech will be especially interesting and effective if you provide information you know about the person(s) being celebrated that others at the event may not know.

**Use Humor Appropriately.** Different cultures define "appropriate" humor in different ways. Use audience analysis to determine whether humor is OK for

▲ **Adapting to the Context of the Celebration.** Pictured is the annual Valentine's Mountaintop Matrimony Ceremony at Colorado's Loveland Ski Area. Minister Harry Heilmann jokes to the couples that "you never thought you'd be getting married in safety helmets" and reminds them that "sometimes you have to put it in four wheel drive." JASON CONNOLLY/Getty Images

the particular celebration or whether listeners would find it distracting or offensive. Never use humor to hurt; instead, use it to highlight endearing qualities of the people being celebrated. Tell stories that the celebrant will find funny, and avoid making jokes about matters the person is embarrassed about or considers sensitive. Consider using humor in a self-deprecating way, so that the story you're sharing is funny rather than hurtful.

## Strategies for After-Dinner Speeches

After-dinner speeches have a long and storied tradition in the United States. They emerged in an age before television and other mass media were on the scene and when speaking was a major form of entertainment. This tradition produced such literary giants as Mark Twain, who gave several hundred of these kinds of addresses, always after a meal.[6] Like others who delivered these types of presentations, Twain usually salted his after-dinner speeches with entertaining stories, personal references, and a great deal of wit.

After-dinner speeches in the United States have developed their own unique flavor, but other cultures have their own after-dinner speaking traditions. For

# MARK TWAIN (1835 TO 1910)

It usually takes me more than three weeks to prepare a good impromptu speech.

To cease smoking is the easiest thing I ever did. I ought to know, I've done it a thousand times.

Always acknowledge a fault. This will throw those in authority off their guard and give you an opportunity to commit more.

It is my custom to keep on talking until I get the audience cowed.

example, some scholars argue that the North American style of toasting arose from a long-standing tradition in Great Britain, centered around formal affairs and traditional British men's clubs.

Effective after-dinner speakers assume the role of entertainers and have a talent for amusing and delighting their audiences while occasionally making a more serious point. Indeed, many after-dinner speeches are given at gatherings designed to raise funds for a particular cause, such as a charitable organization or a politician's election campaign. These speeches are longer and more involved than simple toasts, and they require the ability to thrill and captivate an audience, often after listeners have consumed a full meal and perhaps a few glasses of wine. To overcome these challenges, apply the following strategies for delivering an effective after-dinner speech.

**Focus on Humorous Anecdotes and Narrative Delivery, Not Jokes.** In after-dinner speeches, the tradition has always been to employ witty stories and anecdotes as opposed to a series of one-liners or jokes with punch lines. Remember that your after-dinner speech should be a combination of anecdotal references and storytelling wrapped around a larger theme, not a stand-up comedy routine.

ADAPT YOUR DELIVERY TO YOUR AUDIENCE AND THE OCCASION

**Practice Your Storytelling and Narrative Delivery.** The success of your after-dinner speech depends as much on *how* you tell a story as it does on what you say in the story itself. Sufficiently rehearse your narrative so that you will feel comfortable and relaxed sharing it during the actual speech. Think of your after-dinner speech as a kind of performance, and understand that—like all performances—this one will benefit from lots of practice and polish.

**Link Your Speech to the Occasion's Theme.** If the dinner gathering has a serious theme—for example, the importance of raising funds to support cancer research—consider linking a lighter narrative to that weightier theme. You'll help the audience adopt a relaxed and receptive frame of mind while still accepting the urgency of the topic.

**Adapt Your Delivery to Your Audience and the Occasion.** Be prepared to make spontaneous adjustments to your structure and content based on what's happening around you. Look for opportunities to focus your wit or good-natured satire on something that another speaker or a member of the audience has said. By commenting on a point that a previous speaker made or a question that an audience member asked, you show that you're delivering an original rather than a canned or prepackaged speech. Thus, you let your audience know that you consider them worthy of a fresh presentation tailored specifically to them. You're also conveying in this moment that you have listened to what others had to say.

# SAMPLE SPECIAL-OCCASION SPEECH

### SWEARING-IN CEREMONY FOR NEW U.S. CITIZENS

**Joseph Tuman**
*San Francisco State University*

*In addition to being one of the authors of this book, Joseph S. Tuman has worked in broadcast news media as a political analyst for various news services, including ABC News and CBS News. In 2009, Tuman—who was born in Texas to parents who immigrated to the United States—was invited by the U.S. Immigration and Naturalization Service to give the keynote address at a swearing-in ceremony in San Francisco for people from all over the world who were about to become U.S. citizens. What follows is the text of his speech to this large and diverse audience.*

Good morning! I didn't quite hear you. Let's try that again: good morning! I still can't quite hear you. Don't be polite! This is a special day. This is *your* day! Come on, say it like you mean it. Scream it. One more time: good morning! •

    That's better.

    This *is* a special day. And I want to tell you how honored I am to be here to share it with you. I'm not going to say congratulations just yet because I have a few words I would like to share with you first. You may have noticed that I have someone sitting up here with me on the stage as I'm speaking. This is my mother. Her name is Turan. Turan Tuman! • When the people putting on the ceremony asked the folks I work with at CBS5 if I would be willing to speak today, I immediately thought about my mom and this particular year.

    It's a significant year for her, because fifty years ago the woman you see sitting with me up on the stage was out in the audience with *you*. In that year, she was being sworn in as a new citizen of the United States of America, just like all

• The call and response with the audience is an attention-getting device that focuses everyone and generates excitement for what is to come.

• Tuman is using his mother as a visual aid because she was sworn in as a citizen fifty years earlier. Her experience allows Tuman to share common ground with his audience.

of you. And so I asked their permission for her to join me today, as I speak. Mostly because I wanted her to be more proud of me than my brothers. . . . But also because some of what I'm going to say to you also hopefully will have some meaning for her. So I'm looking at her now, and she's blushing. Either that means I've embarrassed her, or she's annoyed with me. Well, we'll see. The person who is not up on the stage with me today, sadly, is my father. We lost him two years ago. But he's with me here today in spirit. •

• Tuman invokes the memory of his father, who also was an immigrant to America, to find more common ground.

My father's name was Vladimir. Vladimir S. Tuman. In this country, it was a hard name for people to pronounce, so his colleagues and friends just called him Bill. As an accommodation, my mom called him Villa. He was born, like some of you, on the other side of the world, in a country called Iran and in a place called Kermanshah. At a young age, because he was gifted at math and science, my father won a scholarship. The scholarship allowed him to travel to England, where he earned degrees in engineering and physics and geology. After many years, he returned to the place where he had grown up. And there he faced the dilemma that many people who become immigrants face.

He had developed a worldview outside of Iran. A larger worldview. He was Westernized. He wore different clothes, and he spoke more and different languages. He had seen other parts of the world. And, sadly, he realized it would be difficult for him to fit in, back in the place he had once called home. He worked for a time in the petroleum industry as an engineer. At some point, his boss took him aside and said to him, "Tuman, you're a good man, and a good employee. But this is a Muslim country, and you are a Christian. You will never go further in this company than you already have."

My father was somewhat devastated at this news. "What should I do?" he asked.

The man said with a straight face, "You should go to America!"

"America?" my father asked. "Why?"

And the man responded, "Because in America they don't mind if you are a Christian!" •

• This anecdote injects some humor into a serious subject. The audience laughed, which means they understood the joke even if English was not their first language.

Yes, my father thought that was funny later, too. Little did he realize how close to correct the man was.

When my father came to this country, he landed in Texas, and my mother and my older brother soon joined him. Texas is where I was born and where I entered the picture. My father eventually became a professor. We moved from Texas to Illinois and eventually to California. He was at Stanford University for a time, before moving our family to Turlock, a place that seemed very different from Palo Alto.

I spent my younger years there, up through high school. My brothers—I have two of them—always wondered why my father moved us there. It wasn't until he died a few years ago and I went to speak at his funeral that it occurred to me why he moved us to Turlock. Turlock was a small agricultural town, with the anomaly of having a new liberal arts college in its midst. My father started the first physics department there. But he would've been just as happy to stay in Palo Alto at Stanford. For years we wondered: Why had he left Palo Alto for Turlock? That day as I spoke at his funeral, it finally occurred to me.

As I stared out into the hundreds of people who had come to the tiny Assyrian church for his funeral, I realized that most of them also came from the town he grew up in, in Iran. You see, all his life, my father wanted to go back to the place he called home. But he realized when he went home, he no longer belonged there. America became his new home—but he never stopped missing the place of his birth. And so at a later stage in life, he decided he would bring home to him here. With my father's assistance, many of those people in the church that day had already become citizens like you . . . and like my father. ●

• The description of his father's funeral and the many people from his father's hometown is dramatic and poignant. It also provides some ethos for the advice to come, which Tuman borrowed from his father.

As a new citizen of this country, my father immediately embraced the culture here, especially the politics of this place. He loved it. Most of all, he loved the fact that he could express himself openly without fear of retaliation or punishment. He adored this country. It is in his memory today that I offer you these three small pieces of advice that my father often shared with others who wanted to become citizens here.

First, he always said that everyone who came to this country should be educated. If they were uneducated when they came, he insisted that they become educated once they were here. And more important, he always insisted that they made sure that their children and their grandchildren would not only finish high school but go to college and graduate. In our family, all of my brothers and myself earned not only undergraduate degrees but graduate degrees as well. And all of us, incidentally, became professors and teachers. My mother, who sits up here with me, was in the PhD program at UC Berkeley as well, and taught for many years in Turlock.

My father understood that education was not just an end unto itself, but really for all immigrants to this country, it was the great equalizer. It is not a cliché to say that America is the land of opportunity. And what all of us get when we come here is a chance to *do better*. The thing that equalizes everything for everyone in the end is education.

That's what makes the American dream possible. So to paraphrase my father, make sure you are educated. Make sure that your children go to college. And if you really want to follow his advice, make sure they go to graduate school after college, too! •

• This message about education is bolstered by and reinforces Tuman's ethos as a professor.

The second thing my father would always say to people who wanted to become citizens of this country was this: once you are a citizen, make sure that you always exercise your right to vote. Our country graciously allows all citizens the right to vote, but sadly in America today, too many of the people who can vote, don't vote. I can't tell you how important it is that you not only register to vote but also become what is known as a *likely voter*—meaning that you establish a pattern and history of voting regularly in elections.

In this country, voters choose our leaders. Voters provide input about policy and decision making by exercising their choices at the ballot box. If you never vote, you shouldn't complain about things you don't like. Also, by not voting you are ignoring your responsibility as a citizen. Take this responsibility seriously. Make sure that you vote. Make sure that everyone in your family votes. And make sure that your children are ingrained with the same sense of responsibility. It is an awesome responsibility and *also one of the greatest gifts of this country.* •

• The point about voting is bolstered by and reinforces Tuman's other ethos as a television political analyst.

I'm getting near the end of my speech now. And I want to share one last piece of wisdom with you. This was something I once heard my father say in slightly different words to a man who was very timid about becoming a citizen here. It wasn't that he didn't want to be a citizen but rather that he feared people would still see him as a foreigner. So let me say to you in my words the equivalent of what my father said that day. Now that you have been sworn in and you are citizens of this country, *don't ever let someone tell you that you aren't a real American.* Let me repeat that: *don't ever let someone tell you that because you came from somewhere else and you had to get sworn in as a citizen here, somehow that makes you less of an American. Or not a real American at all.* Nothing could be further from the truth.

Anyone can be born here. And when you're born here, it's not as if you had to exercise your choice to be born in America. That was a decision that your parents made for you. But when you are a person who has to fight to come to this country, who has to suffer, who has to work hard, who has to endure many hardships and challenges to get to this place—well, at that moment, the very moment you're at today, you know exactly what it is to not only be a citizen of this country but also to be a real American. *You weren't born here. You chose this country. You took affirmative steps to become a citizen here. And you are as much, if not more, an American as any other citizen here today. Never, ever let someone speak down to you or tell you otherwise.* •

So now, say it with me, say it out loud: *I am an American!* Geez, this is as bad as when I said good morning. Come on, say it louder: *I am an American!* Again! *I am an American!* •

And this last part is also for you, Mom. This year you celebrate fifty years of citizenship in this country. And for nearly fifty years, I have listened to you make jokes about how you will always be seen as a foreigner. Well, Mom, you're not a foreigner. You are a citizen of this country. And I guess I need to remind you that you've lived in this country longer than you've lived anywhere else, by several times over. *Mom, you are an American, too.* And you are as much an American in this country as anyone. •

Oh, she's blushing again; I guess I am going to hear about this after the speech. So let me wrap this up by saying once again: my hearty congratulations to all of you. Welcome to your new country. Welcome, fellow Americans! Thank you and good day!

> • Tuman's advice is an inspirational call to action.
>
> • Another call and response, which brings the audience vocally back into the speech.
>
> • Tuman gives another message to his mother, who has become an additional audience member. She now serves as an example of what people in the audience can become in time.

# CHAPTER REVIEW

**❝Whether to mark a celebration, a milestone, or a passing, we all participate in special-occasion speaking as speakers or listeners.❞**

At some point in your life, you almost certainly will be asked to deliver a special-occasion speech, whether it's to mark a joyous or sorrowful event, present or accept an award, introduce another speaker or performer, or give a witty but evocative talk after a formal dinner. By applying the general guidelines described in this chapter as well as the strategies tailored specifically to each of the six types of special-occasion speeches, you can lay the groundwork for a successful presentation that will make your listeners remember the event for many years to come. If you are asked to deliver a speech on such an occasion, be aware of the type of speech your audience will expect, and follow the specific strategies designed to tailor your special-occasion speech for both the occasion and the audience.

## Key Terms

epideictic *485*                                    eulogy *487*

## Review Questions

1. Name and describe six types of special-occasion speeches identified in the chapter.
2. What five general guidelines should be adhered to when delivering a special-occasion speech?
3. What four strategies for speeches of introduction are offered in the chapter?
4. Describe four strategies for speeches of presentation.
5. What three strategies should you use when delivering a speech of acceptance?
6. What three strategies should you use when speaking to memorialize or eulogize?
7. Describe three strategies that can help you deliver a celebratory speech.
8. Offer four strategies for effective after-dinner speeches.

## Critical Thinking Questions

1. What characteristics do television hosts like Jimmy Fallon and Stephen Colbert share with famous speakers like Mark Twain? In what ways are after-dinner speeches and late-night monologues similar? Which one do you think would be more difficult to prepare and deliver, and why?
2. How does a eulogy differ from a celebratory speech? How are they the same?
3. Are there occasions when you might need to deliver a celebratory speech in front of a somewhat hostile audience? How might you change your speech in those circumstances?

## Activities

1. Imagine that you have been tasked with delivering a speech of introduction for a controversial figure (such as Andrew Cuomo, Rudy Giuliani, Novak Djokovic, or Johnny Depp). How would you handle introducing someone whom you dislike or do not respect or whom the audience might view negatively? Craft an attention-getter for this type of speech.

2.  Suppose that a close friend or a sibling has asked you to give a toast at their wedding. What would you say? How would you use humor?
3.  Imagine that you have to give a special-occasion speech honoring someone important to you. Prepare three outlines—one for a speech that introduces the person, another for a speech that presents an imaginary award, and the third for a speech that toasts the person for a life event (such as a wedding, graduation, or retirement). How do your three outlines differ?

# GROUP COMMUNICATION 20

> **"Several heads are better than one."**

A local community college was offering a course called Community Service 101, which gave students class credit for performing volunteer work. On the first day, the instructor organized the class into five groups. Each group was tasked with choosing a volunteer project, to which each group member would have to contribute at least thirty hours of service. At the end of the term, each group would then deliver a thirty-minute presentation informing the rest of the class about its project. Five students—Jenny, Sam, Juan, Ashley, and Yolanda—were placed together as a group.

Throughout the term, these students experienced firsthand the challenges and benefits of working in a group. For example, they argued over what to call themselves and, after an intense and uncomfortable debate, eventually settled on HELP (Hands-on, Empowering, Loving People). In their first few meetings, Sam and Yolanda kept interrupting each other, and Ashley tried to dominate the discussion. Eventually, Juan reminded the others that to fulfill the requirements of the course, they needed to select a volunteer project and work out a plan for implementing it. Jenny realized that smoother cooperation would help them achieve this goal, so she suggested that group members agree on rules

---

◄ **Collaboration Creates Great Ideas.** When participating in a service project, discussing everyone's ideas can help determine the best approach. SDI Productions/ Getty Images

for communicating and making decisions. They settled on several rules, including these: first, no one would be allowed to interrupt when someone else was speaking; second, everyone would have an opportunity to contribute ideas; and third, all group decisions had to be unanimous.

As the project unfolded, the group's attention to effective leadership and productive participation enabled its members to select and carry out a worthy project—supporting a program at a nearby food bank. Through spirited but respectful discussions, each member was able to offer unique and valuable ideas for carrying out the project.

Despite the rocky start, the group's commitment to the mission—and to one another—paid big dividends. By the time HELP was scheduled to deliver its presentation on the project to the rest of the class, Jenny, Sam, Juan, Ashley, and Yolanda had mastered the challenges of managing group dynamics. Each group member described a different aspect of how HELP had carried out its project and what results the group achieved, and the presentation was a success.

Through their project, these students encountered both the difficulties and the advantages of working within a **small group**—a limited number of people (three or more) gathered for a specific purpose. This classroom experience showed them that **group dynamics**—the ways in which members relate to one another and view their roles and functions—can determine whether a group achieves its mission.

Learning how to manage group dynamics, work well with others in pursuit of a common goal, and communicate your group's achievements to others are valuable life skills. Although group interactions can sometimes be frustrating, you will inevitably participate in a group at some point in your educational and professional lives—whether in the classroom, in your community, or at work.[1]

Why is working effectively in a group important? Small groups offer important advantages over individual efforts. Often people can achieve a better outcome by collaborating on a task rather than working alone. Each group member has unique experiences and perspectives to offer. By sharing ideas, each member has the chance to spot potential problems or improvements in a plan that a lone individual might miss. Additionally, each person in a group has different strengths and interests. The group can divide up a project so that individual members take responsibility for the portions of the job they are best suited for.

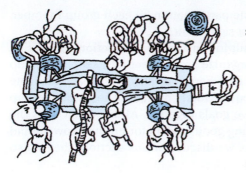

But as we've seen with HELP's story, to gain the benefits of collaboration, group members must interact productively. This chapter provides suggestions for managing key elements of group dynamics—including how to lead a group, how to participate in a group, how to make decisions as a group, and how to present the group's findings or decisions to an audience.

## EFFECTIVE GROUP LEADERSHIP

When the coach of a gold medal–winning Olympic team, the leader of a Nobel Prize–winning medical research team, or the director of a successful play is interviewed, that person is usually recognized as a successful leader. While

▼ **Effective Leaders Make the Whole Group Better.** Haley Jones, the Final Four Most Outstanding Player when Stanford won the 2021 National Championship, is a great team leader. She wants her teammates to thrive and knows how to get everyone to work together.[2] C. Morgan Engel/Getty Images

successful groups depend upon capable participation by each group member, the leader's actions are critical and most significant.

This is the case because it's difficult for any group to function without an effective leader. Somebody needs to organize group meetings, keep the group focused, encourage participation by all members, mediate conflict, and facilitate decision making. A leader does not require total control but must help group members reach a decision and achieve goals together. All of which begs the question: given the importance of having good leaders for groups, how should groups go about acquiring leaders? As we discuss in this section, they do so through several means.

## Selecting a Leader

Groups gain leaders in various ways. Sometimes an external authority selects a **designated leader** to help the group move forward with its mission in a timely manner. For example, a president may assign a cabinet secretary or other

administration official to personally lobby members of Congress for their support on legislation the president is keen to sign; a mayor may appoint a blue-ribbon committee to investigate ways to improve mass transit, designating a leader to guide the inquiry; or an army lieutenant who is sending soldiers on a reconnaissance mission may designate a leader from the group of troops selected.

In other situations, there may be an **implied leader**, someone with preexisting authority or skills who is well suited to the task at hand but not formally assigned the role. For instance, a marketing manager may decide to form a task force to evaluate her company's advertising strategies. At the task force's first meeting, she's the implied leader because she formed the group.

In still other situations, a group may have an **emergent leader**, one who comes to be recognized as a leader by the group's members over time. Although not officially elected or even named as such, emergent leaders usually come to assume the role because they have the most time to commit to the group, demonstrate exceptional competence and goodwill, or simply take the initiative and start leading. For example, Juan and Jenny did this for HELP.

## Leading Meetings

Effective group leaders conduct meetings in ways that enable members to work together productively, contribute their ideas, and make well-informed decisions. If you're the leader of a group, consider these tips for facilitating group meetings.

**Address Procedural Needs.** Consider the following questions: Where and when will meetings take place? Who will start meetings and record notes? How will notes be circulated to members who cannot attend a particular meeting?

**Model the Behavior You Expect.** Avoid interrupting others or dismissing their questions or comments. Make group members feel they can interact comfortably with you, and resist any urge to dominate discussions or decisions.

**Facilitate Discussion.** Ensure that all members of your group have an equal opportunity to participate in each discussion. If some group members are not speaking during a meeting, strive to bring them into the discussion. ("Anil, what do you think?" or "That's a good point, Sarah. You've clearly researched this carefully. But let's also give Tyler a chance to share his ideas.") Although it's important to contribute when you have an idea that nobody else has raised, try to let other members speak first. If you make your position known early, members may feel intimidated and hesitate to challenge or contradict you.

**Keep Members on Task.** If the discussion begins to stray from the item under consideration, keep members on task in a friendly manner. For example, "I agree with Harry that our department's holiday party should be fun for all and give us more opportunities to get to know one another, but I think it would be wise to talk about how we're going to reserve the space for the event."

**Help Members Avoid Groupthink.** The term **groupthink** refers to the tendency of group members to accept ideas and information uncritically because of strong feelings of loyalty or single-mindedness within the group.[3] Left unchallenged, groupthink can erode lively and open exchange of ideas necessary for informed decisions; worse, groupthink can eliminate independent, critical thinking.[4] If one person advocates a course of action in your group and everybody else nods in agreement, try to broaden the discussion before moving the group toward making a final decision. For instance, ask a particularly insightful participant if they can think of any potential risks to the proposed course of action. If nobody is willing to offer any reservations, consider raising some concerns yourself: "I like Sangeeta's idea, but let me play devil's advocate for a minute. . . ." Be sure that the group has considered the pros *and* cons of the proposed options before selecting one. One former American president—Franklin Delano Roosevelt—believed in assigning the same task to different staff members without their knowing they were duplicating one another's efforts. Roosevelt wanted to see if they would come back with identical recommendations or different ones. If the latter, it made for more diverse discussions; if they came back with similar recommendations, Roosevelt felt more confident in the group's ability to reach consensus without encountering groupthink.

▼ **Groupthink Leads to Bad Decisions.** The Challenger tragedy, in which seven astronauts died, is often blamed on groupthink. Pressure to launch the space shuttle on schedule caused the decision makers to act without taking the time to discuss why a launch could be dangerous. Museum of Flight Foundation/Getty Images

FACILITATE A DECISION

**Facilitate Decisions.** If it seems that members of your group have thoroughly discussed the issue at hand, help them come to a decision. As leader, you will participate in the final decision, but your leadership role does not entitle you to make the decision for the group. In other words, never use your power to manipulate the group. After the decision has been made, ensure that it is recorded, and then move the group on to the next issue. Revisit decisions only when new circumstances make the original decision unfeasible.

**Help Organize the Group's Presentation.** Does your group need to present its conclusions? If so, who will serve as the speaker or speakers? How will the presentation be framed to best meet the audience's needs? As leader, you don't necessarily need to make all the decisions yourself, but you do need to coordinate the decisions on these topics.

HELP ORGANIZE THE GROUP'S PRESENTATION

## Managing Conflict

Whatever the situation or setting, disagreements can inevitably crop up when group members work together on a project. Sometimes conflict can be useful. For example, when members express honest disagreement about proposed plans of action, they help minimize the risk of groupthink. But interpersonal conflicts that have nothing to do with the group's mission can often create distractions. Whenever conflict arises in your group, strive to minimize it or channel it in a productive direction. The following guidelines can help.

**Refer to Ideas by Topic, Not by Person.** Focus on the content of specific suggestions rather than attributing those suggestions to individual members. For example, suppose you're part of a group that's trying to get a candidate elected as head of the town council. Monique advocates sending a mass email to build support for the candidate, but Tim thinks that leafleting would be better. Refer to these ideas as "the email plan" and "the leafleting plan" rather than "Monique's idea" and "Tim's suggestion." When ideas get associated with an individual, the person may develop a feeling of personal investment in that option. Thus, the person may become defensive if the proposal is criticized—even if it has real shortcomings.

**Resolve Conflicts Quickly.** If a conflict between group members becomes distracting, try to resolve it rather than allowing it to continue or repressing it. Give the members who disagree an equal opportunity to explain their perspective; let each person speak without interruption, and then ask other members for their views. If both people's ideas have merit, attempt to assist and help the group

▼ **Manage Conflicts Effectively.** When group members are upset with one another, show respect for each person's perspective and get the discussion back on track.
skynesher/Getty Images

find a solution that draws the best from each perspective. As leader, you may ultimately need to offer your opinion or vote to break a deadlock on an issue, but try to give group members an opportunity to speak before injecting your opinion.

**Focus on Tasks, Not Disagreements.** Help members concentrate on the task at hand rather than on interpersonal tensions that may be simmering. Rather than criticizing individuals (by saying things like "Sally, your answers to Noah's questions are always sarcastic"), articulate desired changes in behavior (by saying things like "Let's get back to discussing our project").

A personality clash may be best resolved by discussing the problem in private with the members who disagree rather than airing the conflict in front of the entire group. If a group member gets along well with the people experiencing the conflict, that member may also be able to help them find a way to manage their disagreement.

**Manage Disruptive Emotions.** Conflicts can spark intense and disruptive emotions within a group. Even after a conflict has been resolved, members may still feel angry, upset, or embarrassed and may withdraw from the discussion. If this happens, bring reluctant members back into the discussion by inviting their input on important issues.

**Seek to Create a Diverse Group Atmosphere.** Working with others allows us to draw on everyone's unique experiences and perspectives. Group members with different ideas can tackle complex problems by offering up, weighing, and trying out multiple solutions. Greater group **heterogeneity**, or member difference (as compared to **homogeneity**, or member similarity), is not without its challenges. In groups that are highly heterogeneous, members may have to provide more background information for their ideas and may be more likely to disagree with one another. Nevertheless, although homogeneous groups may run more smoothly, heterogeneous groups find ways to coordinate multiple perspectives more productively.[5] In other words, a group with diverse perspectives that values all those perspectives and is able to use them effectively has the best chance of reaching their goals.

# EFFECTIVE GROUP MEMBERSHIP

Although strong leadership is essential to effective group communication, productive participation by members is equally vital. To contribute your best to a group as a member, start by understanding the types of roles you can take on to support your group's success.

## Three Types of Member Roles

There are three types of roles that group members can fill.[6] Two of them—*task-oriented roles* and *maintenance-oriented roles*—are helpful. The third type—*self-oriented roles*—is not productive and should be avoided. People can take on different types of roles, even during the course of a single meeting, although most members of a group have the tendency to gravitate toward one or two. If you're able to note which roles you often take on, you can consider whether they are the most helpful for the situation you're in and adapt accordingly.

**Task-Oriented Roles.**  Task-oriented roles contribute to a group's ability to accomplish its goals through enhancing members' participation and the free flow of information within the group. In a group made up of members who are fulfilling these roles, you'll likely see people asking helpful questions and making constructive comments. There are eight task-oriented roles:

- *Initiators* suggest the group's goals and offer new ideas or propose new solutions.
- *Information providers* offer facts relevant to the issue under discussion. These facts might include researched evidence or examples based on personal experience.
- *Information gatherers* ask other members to share facts they know, or they seek out needed information from other sources.
- *Elaborators* add supporting facts, examples, or ideas to a point that someone else has made during a discussion.
- *Clarifiers* attempt to make the meaning of another member's statement more precise.
- *Evaluators* offer their own judgments about the ideas put forward during a discussion.
- *Synthesizers* identify emerging agreements and disagreements among the group as a whole.

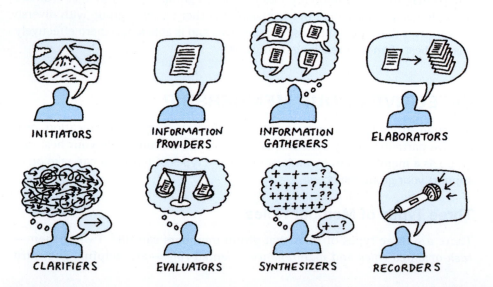

INITIATORS     INFORMATION PROVIDERS     INFORMATION GATHERERS     ELABORATORS

CLARIFIERS     EVALUATORS     SYNTHESIZERS     RECORDERS

▲ **Task-Oriented Roles.**  Everyone has a job to do in order to create oyster beds at a marine reserve. MediaNews Group/Long Beach Press-Telegram via Getty Images/Getty Images

---

- *Recorders* take notes during a meeting, tracking major decisions and plans made by the group. They may send memos or emails to group members summarizing previous meetings, providing agendas for future meetings, or reminding people of tasks they agreed to work on between meetings.

**Maintenance-Oriented Roles.**  Used effectively, maintenance-oriented roles help sustain and strengthen efficient and effective interpersonal relations in a group. When members perform maintenance roles effectively, they are more likely to work together comfortably as a team, support one another, and present findings or recommendations that reflect group consensus. There are five maintenance-oriented roles:

- *Harmonizers* decrease tension in the group, perhaps by infusing humor at just the right moment or by making positive and optimistic comments.

▲ **Encouraging the Group.** One important maintenance-oriented role is to encourage group members when they share a good idea. heshphoto/Getty Images

- *Compromisers* attempt to find common ground between adversaries within the group and offer solutions that may be palatable to people on both sides of a conflict.
- *Encouragers* inspire other group members by complimenting their ideas and work.
- *Gatekeepers* facilitate the exchange of information among group members.
- *Norm facilitators* reinforce healthy group norms and discourage the use of unproductive norms.

**Self-Oriented Roles.** Self-oriented roles accomplish little for a group and are motivated by the selfish ends of individual members. Groups with a heavy emphasis on these roles may experience incomplete findings, infighting, and dissension. There are four self-oriented roles:

- *Blockers* stop the group from moving toward its objective—by refusing to accept decisions the group has made or by arbitrarily rejecting other members' ideas or opinions.
- *Withdrawers* refuse to make any contribution or to participate in the discussion. They may feel out of their element in the group or may be having difficulty following other members' comments and ideas.
- *Dominators* monopolize group interactions by interrupting others and arguing for the sake of arguing, and they often insist upon having the last word.

This behavior may stem from feelings of insecurity, an aggressive personality, or some other factor.

- *Distracters*—the opposite of *harmonizers*—send the group in irrelevant directions with off-topic comments or extraneous conversation, perhaps because they have trouble concentrating on a topic or focusing on the completion of a process.

When you're participating in a group, focus on how you can fulfill task-oriented and maintenance-oriented roles (and/or encourage others to do so). Also, avoid playing self-oriented roles, and discourage others from adopting them.

## Tips for Participating in a Small Group

In addition to fulfilling task- and maintenance-oriented roles, you can improve your effectiveness at group participation by applying the following practices.

**Prepare for Group Meetings.** If an agenda has been distributed for an upcoming meeting, think about the topics under consideration *before* you gather with other group members. Keep track of any commitments you made for the meeting (such as researching the answer to a question or bringing your laptop), and be sure to fulfill them. If you are planning to disseminate information to group members, be sure to iron out any wrinkles in your presentation beforehand.

PREPARE FOR GROUP MEETINGS

**Treat Other Members Courteously.** Courtesy begins with arriving at a group meeting on time, or at least informing the group if you will be late. Turn off your phone unless you are expecting a call that will help the group conduct its business (or you are using the phone to attend your meeting virtually). During the discussion, treat other members with respect, even when you disagree

TREAT OTHER MEMBERS COURTEOUSLY

with their views. If you do disagree with other members, be sure to focus on the issue at hand rather than on personalities or personal capabilities. For example, if someone proposes an idea you find questionable, don't say "I'm not sure you have the patience to carry out this idea." Instead, try to learn more about it, perhaps by asking, "What's your experience in doing this sort of thing? Can you tell us more about the kinds of challenges we should expect?"

In the same vein, avoid overreacting if others disagree with an idea you have presented. Instead, let others explain their position. If you disagree with what you're hearing, explain your position calmly and rationally. If you listen to their criticism and find it to be valid, then be honest and acknowledge that you agree.

**Listen Interactively.** Inattention between members can cause tension in a group. Someone who doesn't feel heard may, in turn, not listen to other people's comments. To avoid this problem, practice interactive listening (see Chapter 4). As other members of your group share their ideas and comments, try to understand their viewpoints and show that you are listening. Ask for clarification if you need it, and make sure you understand a point before challenging it.

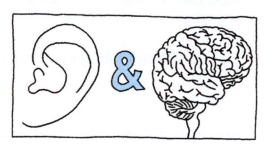

**Participate, Don't Dominate.** To gain the benefit of diverse perspectives, a group needs contributions from each member. When you have a relevant point to make, share your idea. Your participation is particularly important when you have experience with a topic or a unique viewpoint that hasn't been expressed.

At the same time, avoid monopolizing the discussion. If you find yourself speaking a disproportionate amount of the time, take a break and let other members contribute. You may even ask other members to chime in—especially if it seems that they have an idea but are reluctant to speak.

**Participate Authentically.** A group functions at its best when members put diverse ideas and perspectives on the table. Therefore, be guided by honesty, not popularity, when considering problems and solutions. If you have an idea that you believe is important, don't be afraid to mention it, even if you're worried about how it may be received and perceived by others. If you have concerns about another member's suggestion, explain your reservations to the group.

PARTICIPATE AUTHENTICALLY

Be sure to balance candor with tact when questioning or challenging a colleague's idea. Critique the idea, not the person, in a manner that makes your concerns clear. By way of example, you might say "I'm not sure our group can afford to rent that facility for our project," instead of "Where in the world do you think we're going to get the money for that?"

### Fulfill Your Commitments.
For a group to achieve its goals, members must accept responsibility for performing certain tasks—both the ones assigned to them individually and the ones required of all participating members. For example, you may have promised to research the cost of an item that your group needs to purchase, or perhaps you've agreed to distribute notes from the last meeting to the group.

When group members make commitments, the rest of the group will rely on them to fulfill those commitments. If people consistently fail to meet their commitments, the group as a whole will find it more and more difficult to carry out

its work. Moreover, in most situations, because work assigned to another group member will depend on work that's been assigned to you, failing to follow up on your commitments will hurt not just you but the other member as well.

### Use Technology to Your Advantage.
Sometimes you will need to use technology during a face-to-face group meeting, or the entire meeting may be held virtually. All forms of technology have benefits and limitations to consider. For example, during an in-person meeting, members may be able to use laptops or smartphones to quickly look up and share information the group needs. Of course, if group members are using those same devices to text a friend or check out a new game, this use can prevent them from participating effectively.

When it comes to meeting virtually, speaking with one another on the phone can work for simple information sharing. However, if your meeting requires thorough discussions of group issues, you may want to consider

▲ **Effective Group Participation.** An engineering project requires each group member to share their ideas and listen carefully to the other members' perspectives. MediaNews Group/Boulder Daily Camera via Getty Images/Getty Images

videoconferencing so that you can see and hear one another in real time and better connect with your fellow group members. Be sure that all the group members have access to and feel comfortable using the technology you have selected and that the technology is serving a helpful purpose (rather than acting largely as a distraction). Tips for communicating effectively using technology are covered in more detail in Chapter 15.

## GROUP DECISION MAKING AND THE REFLECTIVE-THINKING PROCESS

Although there is no single method that a group must use to make decisions, research has shown that the **reflective-thinking process** is a particularly effective approach.[7] The reflective-thinking process has five steps:

1. Define the problem.
2. Analyze the problem.
3. Establish criteria for solving the problem.
4. Generate possible solutions.
5. Select the best solution.

In this section, we take a closer look at each of these steps.

# THE REFLECTIVE—THINKING PROCESS

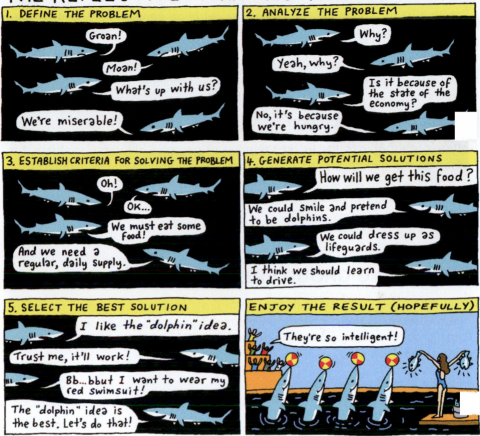

## Define the Problem

Before your group can select a course of action, you must know exactly what problem (or objective) you will address. As a group, work to define the problem (or objective) as precisely as possible.

## Analyze the Problem

After your group has defined the problem, analyze its nature. What are the primary aspects of the problem? Which of these are most important for the group to focus on?

## Establish Criteria for Solving the Problem

Decide which factors will be most important when weighing possible solutions to the problem your group will be addressing. Each proposed solution will have strengths and weaknesses; therefore, establishing criteria will help you select the best overall solution.

## Generate Possible Solutions

Create a list of potential solutions to the problem your group is addressing. Brainstorming (see Chapter 6) is an effective technique for building this list. Remember that in brainstorming, the goal is to generate as many ideas as possible—without judging them. Research can also be a good way to learn how other individuals or groups may have handled similar problems.

## Select the Best Solution

After your group has developed a number of potential solutions, evaluate the advantages and disadvantages of each based on the criteria you've defined.

After a group has reached a consensus, it often needs to communicate its findings to others. In the following section, we explain how to plan and deliver effective group presentations.

# DELIVERING GROUP PRESENTATIONS

To share its ideas with an audience, a group may select from several common approaches, including a *symposium*, a *panel discussion*, or a presentation by a *single group representative*. In this section, we offer tips for using each of these three approaches.

## Symposium

During a **symposium**, in which several or all group members speak to the audience in turn, each group member takes responsibility for delivering a different part of the presentation, depending on their expertise, their interest, or the needs of the group. For example, suppose that a product team at a computer company wants to propose a design for a new handheld device to its R&D (research and development) department. One member might describe the competing handheld designs the team used as reference points for its own design.

Another member might then present the technical resources that will be required to manufacture the device. And a third member might conclude the presentation by sharing the group's thoughts about how to minimize the costs of producing the design.

If your group has decided to use this presentation format, plan your symposium carefully. Make sure everyone in the group agrees on the portion that each speaker will address and the time they will take. Be certain that all members know what will go into each presentation so that no one unwittingly repeats points made by someone else (or forgets to mention important ideas).

When you participate in a symposium, avoid speaking longer than your allotted time. Otherwise, subsequent speakers may have insufficient time to deliver their parts of the presentation. Also, treat other speakers' ideas with respect. If you need to mention points on which group members disagree, present others' ideas in a professional manner, without judging the individuals who advocate those ideas.

As you close your part of the presentation, make sure to introduce the next speaker briefly and note any connections between topics in your transition. As a courtesy to both the next speaker and the audience, introduce the speaker by name.

Like a speech by an individual, an effective symposium has an introduction, a body, and a conclusion. In addition to presenting their ideas, the first speaker should begin with an introduction that gains the audience's attention, reveals the topic of the presentation, connects with the audience, establishes credibility, and previews the main idea that each subsequent speaker will develop. The final speaker should conclude by summarizing each presenter's main idea and leaving the audience with memorable concluding remarks.

## Panel Discussion

In a **panel discussion**, members engage in discourse with one another while being observed by the audience. While group members sit at a table and speak as if they were conversing among themselves, the audience watches and listens. There may be time for audience questions after the discussion, but the panel members' primary role is to speak, and the audience's primary role is to listen. For example, a professor might ask a team of students to come back the next semester and conduct a panel discussion for a new class about a research project they successfully conducted.

A panel discussion usually requires a **moderator**, who introduces each **panelist** (participant) and facilitates the discussion. The moderator's role is similar to that of a leader in a group discussion. In addition to monitoring the time, the moderator asks questions that keep the discussion moving, and ensures that each panel member has an opportunity to participate. Moderators may also participate in the discussion, although they should not dominate the presentation.

Panel participants, too, should contribute to the discussion without monopolizing the presentation. As a panel member, it is important to participate if you have special experience or expertise with the point being made. If you have less information on a given issue or you have been speaking more than

▲ **Panel Discussion.** In this panel, four student activists share their perspectives on the issue of gun violence. Bryan Bedder/Getty Images

other members, give other panelists an opportunity to talk. Also, be tactful and professional when disagreeing with another member's point.

The atmosphere in a panel discussion is usually more casual than that in a symposium, and panelists may interact with one other spontaneously, making comments or asking questions. Talk about the panel discussion in advance with your group so that you all know which questions or topics you want to use and discuss. That way, the group will be well prepared and able to prioritize the most important issues to be covered.

## Single Group Representative

Sometimes one person will be responsible for presenting on behalf of the entire group. If your group has selected this format, keep the following considerations in mind.

First, check that your group has discussed and decided on the best approach for the presentation. Which person is most qualified to present the group's opinions? Who would have the most effective delivery? Is this a topic that requires the ethos or authority of a group

PRESENTATION BY
ONE MEMBER
REPRESENTING THE GROUP

leader or a group member with particular expertise? Select the member who best meets these criteria.

Second, if you're chosen to give the presentation, be sure your group has carefully thought through all aspects of the speech. There's an important difference between a speech that you prepare, research, and deliver yourself and one that emerges from a group: in the latter instance, the group contributes substantially to the speech-creation process. Get input from all group members before you start preparing the presentation, and solicit their feedback after you outline your speech.

Third, as you are delivering the presentation, take care to distinguish whether you are representing your own views, the views of some members of the group, or a consensus of all group members. Be fair and accurate when summarizing other members' viewpoints. In addition, if another member came up with a good idea, be sure to give them credit when presenting it.

# CHAPTER REVIEW

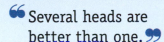

**❝Several heads are better than one.❞**

An effective group discussion requires skillful leadership and constructive participation. The leader must manage key elements of group dynamics, including the flow of the discussion. In addition, a group leader needs to lead a productive discussion—by keeping the group on task and encouraging all persons to contribute and listen—and then help the members reach a decision after the issue has been sufficiently discussed. When conflict comes up, they need to work to resolve it and get the discussion back on track.

Group members can play several different types of roles. Task-oriented roles contribute to the group's ability to reach a good decision, with members sharing their knowledge and opinions about the topic. Maintenance-oriented roles help the group work well together and promote group cohesion. Self-oriented roles, such as monopolizing the conversation or getting the discussion off track, should be avoided. The most effective group members actively share their ideas, consider one another's viewpoints, constructively participate, and help the group reach a sound decision—perhaps through the five-step reflective-thinking process.

Groups may present their findings in a symposium, during which each member presents part of the group's message. At other times, the group may use a panel discussion format, in which there is less formal structure and more give-and-take among members. In either case, thorough preparation will allow each member to know who will present which topics.

If you're called upon to deliver a presentation for your entire group, preparation will again help ensure that you're accurately reflecting the group's decisions, opinions, or findings. Be sure to get input from other group members while preparing the presentation, and acknowledge other members' viewpoints as you're giving the speech.

## Key Terms

small group *514*

group dynamics *514*

designated leader *516*

implied leader *517*

emergent leader *517*

groupthink *520*

heterogeneity *523*

homogeneity *523*

reflective-thinking process *530*

symposium *532*

panel discussion *533*

moderator *533*

panelist *533*

## Review Questions

1. Name and describe three types of leaders and the ways they are selected.
2. What are the two main jobs of the group leader?
3. What are the three main types of member roles in a group?
4. What seven strategies should group members employ to participate in a small group effectively?
5. Explain the five steps of the reflective-thinking process.
6. Describe the three common approaches to group presentations identified in the chapter.

## Critical Thinking Questions

1. In what ways do the public speaking skills you have developed in this course increase your ability to participate effectively in groups? Offer specific examples.
2. If you are participating in a group for this speech course, are you performing task-oriented roles, maintenance-oriented roles, or self-oriented roles? Do your roles change depending on the nature and circumstances of the group you are in?
3. How might the reflective-thinking process for groups help you make better decisions on an individual basis?

## Activities

1. In your own words, write an answer to this question: What positive gains for helping to avoid groupthink can be achieved by assigning the same task to different individuals in your group without their knowledge that the assignments are duplicating one another?

2. Make a list of individuals with whom you share a group identity—for example, your classmates in a study group. Is there a leader among you? How did this person come to be the leader? In different circumstances (for example, if all of you volunteered to help with a grassroots political campaign), do you think the leader and group member roles would be the same?
3. Have you ever been part of a group that came to a bad decision? Having read this chapter, explain how you would modify your past behavior to produce a better outcome if you were given the chance.

# CIVIC ENGAGEMENT

# 21

**❝Use your public speaking skills to make a difference.❞** Esmeralda had never thought of herself as an activist. Then she signed up for a general education course titled "Sustainable Communities." A presentation was required in that class and one of the suggested topics was the rise of community solar gardens. Esmeralda wasn't sure what a solar garden was, but she knew her parents had installed solar panels on their home and their utility bills had gone down significantly. She did a little research and found out that a community solar garden places solar panels on land that is not currently being used. Then community members can pay to get power from the solar garden, which helps people save money and reduces pollution. Esmeralda had family members and friends who rented apartments and homes, meaning they couldn't install their own solar panels. A community solar garden could be just what they needed.

At a family gathering, when her aunt asked how college was going, Esmeralda talked about the presentation she was working on. She was surprised to learn that her aunt had seen a flyer on a community bulletin board advertising an upcoming meeting on a possible community solar project. Her aunt had heard Esmeralda's parents talk about the benefits of solar and she wanted to get in on the action, too. She asked Esmeralda to go to the meeting with her.

---

◀ **Civic Engagement for Social Change.** Giving speeches to support community improvements such as solar gardens, and talking to neighbors about projects like these, are examples of civic engagement. Mike Harrington/Getty Images

At the meeting, Esmeralda heard community members talk about pros and cons of the project. Because she had been researching the topic for her presentation, she thought of several points she could add to the discussion and she quietly told her aunt about them. Her aunt was encouraging and whispered back, "You should go up there and share your ideas!"

With a little more prodding, Esmeralda decided to join the line of people waiting for a turn to speak. Esmeralda had taken a public speaking course the previous semester, so she reminded herself that she was prepared to express her thoughts aloud: "I can do this," she thought. When handed the mic, Esmeralda provided examples of community solar gardens in other locations that had been successful. She received a nice round of applause when she finished and afterward, the meeting chair asked if she would be willing to visit other people in the community and talk to them about the project. Esmeralda's aunt gave her a smile: "Come on, we can do it together." And they agreed to visit the residents in her aunt's apartment building.

By speaking at a public meeting and volunteering to go door to door and explain the solar project to others, Esmeralda was practicing **civic engagement**. As we noted in Chapter 1, civic engagement involves active public participation in political affairs and social and community organizations. Civic engagement can take different forms. For example, you can participate in civic engagement related to a very local issue, such as advocating to install a speed bump on a dangerous stretch of road, or on an issue of national or international significance, like racial justice or the right to privacy. With civic engagement you can make a difference, but achieving what you are fighting for requires effort—and communication skills.

This chapter is designed to provide a bridge between using your public speaking skills in the classroom and using these skills to make a difference in your community. It is our aspiration that you will use what you've learned this term to take an active role in supporting a cause or issue that has personal meaning—just as we, your authors, have done in our own lives. For example, one of us learned about civic engagement at an early age when his community banned bicycles on downtown sidewalks, meaning cyclists were forced to ride in the streets. Upset that this decision was made without input from people who actually rode bicycles, he collected signatures on a petition and spoke at a city council meeting. In the end, after a lot of hard work, the city installed bike lanes.

With examples like this as our guide, this chapter takes an in-depth look at how civic engagement works and how it relates to public speaking. We begin by discussing how civic engagement is important to society and exploring how it benefits participants. Then we take a look at different forums where you can participate in civic engagement, and finally, we discuss how to apply the skills you have learned in this class to take an active role in society.

# CIVIC ENGAGEMENT AND ITS IMPORTANCE TO SOCIETY

Civic engagement encompasses a wide range of activities, from voting, engaging in voter registration efforts, circulating petitions, and taking part in community or political organizations, to attending government meetings, participating in demonstrations, and discussing issues.[1] Civic engagement is not limited to any particular ideology or political perspective. The #BlackLivesMatter movement, libertarians, Occupy protesters, and Tea Party advocates, among many other groups, have used civic engagement in an effort to express their message and achieve social change.[2] What is the current state of civic engagement in the United States? Let's take a look at a snapshot of where we've come from, where we are, where we might be going—and why that matters.

## Civic Engagement Trends

Although civic engagement is vital for a healthy society, until recently, participation in public affairs had been decreasing in the United States. Harvard professor Robert Putnam triggered a discussion about the decline in civic engagement in 1995 with his article "Bowling Alone: America's Declining Social Capital."[3] In the article, Putnam observed that voting, attending public meetings, attending political rallies and speeches, and serving on local communities had declined since the 1960s.[4] He found that in regions where there was a higher level of public participation and connection, there were also better schools, greater economic development, reduced crime rates, and successful local government.[5]

Declining rates of civic engagement continued even after "Bowling Alone" was published. For example, a 2018 study by the Public Religion Research Institute

found that during the twelve months previous, few people had contacted an elected official (19 percent), attended a community meeting (12 percent), or attended a rally or demonstration (8 percent). Despite the popularity of social media, less than one-fourth of all Americans (23 percent) had posted on an issue that mattered to them.[6]

Fortunately, in the last handful of years, the news about civic engagement in the United States has become more positive. There is evidence that civic engagement rebounded during the COVID-19 pandemic—especially for members of Gen Z (born between 1997 and 2012). For example, during summer 2020, between fifteen and twenty-five million people participated in Black Lives Matter demonstrations following the murder of George Floyd. These protests were, thus far, the largest social movement in U.S. history.[7] And in May 2022, there were demonstrations in 380 cities across the United States following the leak of a draft Supreme Court opinion that would overrule the *Roe v. Wade* abortion rights decision,[8] as people on both sides of the issue passionately expressed their viewpoints.[9]

According to a 2020 survey of people's participation in civic engagement and plans for the future in light of the pandemic, people in the United States were especially interested in taking action on issues related to COVID-19, such as health care, food insecurity, and children's well-being. They were also looking for opportunities to aid their communities directly.[10] The survey further indicated that members of Gen Z had been the most engaged (compared to other age cohorts) in a number of activities, including more traditional forms of action such as participating in demonstrations, signing petitions, and volunteering, as well as newer forms, such as making purchase decisions based on how they rated a business's social responsibility and posting on social media.[11] If this trend continues, it will be a step in the right direction.

## Quality of Public Discourse

While the news about levels of civic engagement may be getting less gloomy, another important measure to examine is the quality of the public discourse—and it is currently low. The news is loaded with stories about members of Congress making racist comments, a candidate for governor threatening to "stomp on his opponent's face with golf spikes," news show panelists shouting over each other, and family members who no longer speak to one another due to political disagreements.[12] A 2021 Pew Research survey found that the number of people who believe that it is "stressful and frustrating" to have a discussion about politics with someone who disagrees with them has risen to 59 percent, up from 50 percent two years earlier.[13] Former Supreme Court justice Anthony Kennedy noted that although "civil discourse is critical to democracy's survival," we are seeing "the death and decline of democracy" in the twenty-first century.[14] It comes as no surprise that an American Psychological Association survey found that almost 60 percent of Americans were stressed out by divisions in society.[15]

Online public discourse can be particularly hostile and there are features of social media that enable angry and unproductive interactions. For example, the ability to remain anonymous encourages users to express rage and anger.[16] Research also shows that when people receive likes and shares for expressing moral outrage, it encourages them to express more and greater outrage in future posts.[17] An engineer who worked on Twitter's "Retweet" button later expressed remorse for this feature, thinking, "We might have just handed a 4-year-old a loaded weapon."[18] Women and Black people are particularly susceptible to harassment on social media and people who would like to participate in reasonable online discussions are turned off from participating.[19]

Low levels of civil public discourse like this are unhealthy for democratic self-government, as are low levels of civic engagement. So what can we do to encourage civil discourse and keep levels of civic engagement moving in the right direction? It's up to all of us to take action to protect our democracy.

## Protecting Democracy by Taking Action

If government is to be "by the people and for the people," then those people must be actively involved and interact respectfully. The public needs to make its goals and desires known and put pressure on its leaders when they are not serving in the public interest. Hollie Russon Gilman, a lecturer at Columbia University's School of International and Public Affairs, notes that members of the public can take many different steps in order to serve as watchdogs. From recording the actions of law enforcement, to using Freedom of Information laws to demand documents, to providing testimony that may be more credible than sources linked to special interests, there are many ways to hold elected officials accountable.[20] To successfully address major problems, members of the public need to deliberate and collaborate, interacting with others who come from different backgrounds and experiences.[21]

While civic engagement is essential for democratic self-government, the levels of public participation and the quality of discourse must improve. The good

▼ **Benefits of Civic Engagement.**  Democracy works better when concerned people work together to express their views. Octavio Jones/Getty Images

news is that when you choose to participate in public affairs and use your voice to share perspectives on important issues with well-reasoned messages, your efforts benefit society. There are also benefits to you that come from that participation, as we'll see next.

## HOW CIVIC ENGAGEMENT BENEFITS PARTICIPANTS

As a participant, civic engagement provides you with a chance to make your voice heard on issues that you care about. For example, suppose your campus is considering a plan to increase tuition, change graduation requirements, or move some classes to Saturdays. There will likely be a decision-making process that includes opportunities for student input where you can express your views, or you may take part in protests if students' voices seem to be excluded from the process. Or suppose you encounter a policy in your community about which you have a strong opinion; for example, your city council may try to prohibit people from giving food or money to those on street corners who are homeless, or you may feel very passionately about issues at your child's school if you are a parent (or if you become one). In cases like these, and many others, there is power in taking action on behalf of something that has personal meaning.

Civic engagement benefits all participants, but when you participate in civic engagement as a college student, it has particular benefits—both for you and for your community. As a student, civic engagement gives you a chance to apply the skills you have learned in a variety of courses—in public speaking certainly (more on this in the chapter's last section) but also in group communication, political science, and classes that relate specifically to the issue you are addressing (perhaps environmental science, engineering, criminology, or philosophy). While traditional courses are focused on a single subject, with civic engagement you get the chance to see how your different coursework fits together. In addition, while you may understandably be focused on how your coursework can provide you with job skills to use after graduation, civic engagement helps you view coursework through a new lens: it gives you the chance to see issues from the perspectives of others and contribute to social change.[22]

When you participate in civic engagement as a student, you gain skills and experiences that will help you take an active role in public affairs throughout your life and successfully resolve problems with the government or other power structures you may encounter.[23] College students who actively participate in public discussion or political activities tend to be more confident in their ability to make a difference in their communities.[24] There is also evidence that college students who participate in civic engagement experience gains in well-being.[25] And on top of these personal gains, there are gains at the community level: the community benefits from the participation of college students, who can contribute unique perspectives and their passion for making a difference.[26]

# FORUMS AND VENUES FOR CIVIC ENGAGEMENT

If you are looking to participate in civic engagement while you attend college, one option is to join with existing organizations that advocate on campus. Most campuses have political clubs and organizations (e.g., College Republicans, Democrats, Greens, or Libertarians). Student government meetings generally include opportunities for students to express their ideas. There may also be groups that advocate on issues that directly relate to college students, such as tuition or student debt, or those that focus on public issues, such as abortion, gun policy, or the environment. Most of these groups will have a social media presence, so you can find out when and where they meet. By doing so, you can learn when these groups will be active in advocacy, whether it's speaking to the college community, organizing a rally or protest, or sponsoring a forum.

Another option is to take a campus leadership role on an issue that is important to you by starting a club or an organization focused on that issue and encouraging like-minded students to join. There are typically bulletin boards located throughout college campuses where students can post messages. Be sure that yours stands out in order to attract students' attention and inform them of the issues your group will be addressing. There is typically a process to gain recognition as a student club or organization. Once recognized, campus groups can often gain the use of meeting rooms on campus and even receive funding for events.

Many colleges and other public spaces offer designated locations for students to express their message. College **free speech zones** are specific spaces on campus that are set aside for the expression of students' opinions, individually or as a group, and some schools require that students get permission before speaking.[27]

---

▼ **A Forum for Civic Engagement.** Free speech zones, which are areas specifically set aside for people to express their viewpoints, are one type of site you may use for civic engagement. This one is located in a national park. Ramin Talaie/Getty Images

This may seem like the best location for you to express your opinion, but it may not always be the case. In reality, your right to express yourself at a public college or university campus is not limited to a specific location. Colleges may place limited restrictions on the time, place, or manner of expression (for example, not allowing loud demonstrations near classrooms or blocking the entrance to the library), but they may not place broad restrictions on student expression. When free speech zones have been challenged in court, they have been found to be unconstitutional.[28] If you have any questions about the exercise of free speech on campus, advocacy groups such as the Foundation for Individual Rights in Education and the American Civil Liberties Union are valuable resources.

You can also take civic engagement out into the community. If there is an issue in your town of importance to you, this is your chance to make a difference. Determine the government organization that is responsible for your issue (school board, city council, county board of supervisors, water resources board). Members of the community typically have the chance to speak at these organizations' public meetings. Contact the agency or check its website to see what the process is for community involvement; then get ready to present. There will often be a time limit, so you will need to practice to make sure your presentation will fit within the allotted time. Be sure your speaking material is well organized, so that your main ideas stand out (remember the example in Chapter 11 of Carmelita, who successfully advocated to safely reopen schools during the pandemic). If you are addressing elected officials, one of their main concerns will be how many of their constituents are concerned about an issue because that translates into votes. You may want to bring a petition that has been signed by others who share your concern, or you may choose to have them be part of the audience, so you can point to a larger group of people who are looking for action from their government.

Rather than participating in forums established by college officials or governments, you may decide to work outside the system. Many of the movements that have been able to change society, from the U.S. civil rights movement to the movement for Indian independence, have succeeded because people worked together against governmental power structures.[29] Civic engagement outside the system offers another option for making your voice heard and working with others to achieve social change.[30]

You may also choose to participate in rallies, demonstrations, forums, and other public events, which at times may fall within the system (for example, if you get a permit for a demonstration or parade) and at times may occur outside the system (as with spontaneous events that happen without official permission). Some issues are very localized—for example, a city ordinance about homelessness—but in recent years, there have been multiple examples of issues that have inspired participation across the nation:

- Black Lives Matter
- The Women's March
- The March for Life (abortion)
- The March for Our Lives (gun violence)
- Solidarity with Ukraine

# CIVIC ENGAGEMENT

INSIDE THE SYSTEM

OUTSIDE THE SYSTEM

Many movements make active use of social media to get the word out about upcoming events, to encourage others to get involved, and to put pressure on elected officials. These sites can help you find out how to get involved.[31] When a big event is taking place in a large city, organizers have often arranged for experienced speakers to make presentations, and you may need to start by being a supporter in the audience. In smaller towns, there may be greater opportunities for you to participate as a public speaker. In either case, another great way to start is to volunteer to help with the setup, the running, or the takedown of the event. This will give you a chance to network with others in the organization, and as you get to know them, you may get the opportunity to be more involved.

Now that we have discussed how you can begin to participate in civic engagement, let's turn our attention to how you can use the skills you have learned in public speaking to deliver a successful presentation related to a personally meaningful topic.

# APPLYING PUBLIC SPEAKING SKILLS TO CIVIC ENGAGEMENT

Using your public speaking skills to join a public conversation on issues that matter to you is not very different from presenting classroom speeches. The same principles that you have been learning and practicing all term can help you share your ideas and influence audience members. In this section, we will show you how the advice offered throughout this book can be applied to civic engagement.

## Developing Your Message

When you are planning to speak in a public forum, such as a rally or a meeting, your need to plan your message carefully. It is important to consider your topic, analyze your audience, research the issue, and develop supporting materials. And although you may feel very passionate about your issue, you need to express that passion in an ethical manner.

**Topic Selection.** When you are participating in civic engagement, your general topic is likely to be apparent. Whether it is on-campus parking, the #MeToo movement, a change in the local bus schedule, or any other issue, civic engagement often starts because there is a cause or a policy that really matters to you. You are determined to make a difference.

With your general topic in mind, it will be important to narrow it down in order to fit the available time. If you are part of a program at a rally or speaking before a government agency, there will likely be a time limit that you need to follow. Even if there is no formal time limit, it is difficult to keep the listeners focused on every word you say, especially if you are one of several speakers. Here are some ideas to consider as you narrow your topic:

- Is there a personal experience or example related to your issue that you can share?

- Is there an aspect of your issue on which you have new or unique ideas to contribute?

- Is there an aspect of your issue that you feel especially passionate about discussing?

- Is there an aspect of your issue that you need the audience or decision makers to focus on?

For example, when college student and activist Sophia Bautista had the opportunity to speak at the 2018 Women's March in Fresno, California, there

▼ **Narrowing the Topic.** Graduate student employees focus on the reasons they believe they need a union at the University of Indiana. SOPA Images/Getty Images

was a wide variety of topics that she could have addressed. Ms. Bautista decided to focus on preserving the DACA (Deferred Action for Childhood Arrivals) program. This issue was especially important to her, and she had taken a leadership role on this issue in her community.[32]

**Audience Analysis.** It will be important to analyze your audience in advance of your speech in order to find ways of relating your message to them and to be sure that your ideas fit within their latitude of acceptance. Conducting a *situational audience analysis* (looking at factors in the speech setting, such as audience size and location) before beginning to speak is also useful because at many public events the audience will be mobile, and it will be important to keep them engaged.

Civic engagement can be especially effective when you can focus on issues that directly affect your audience. For example, Derrick Palmer and Christian Smalls led a successful effort to unionize an Amazon warehouse in Staten Island, New York. Mr. Palmer worked at the warehouse and Mr. Smalls had worked there until he was fired because he protested safety conditions. They knew the concerns of warehouse workers firsthand and tailored their strategies to these workers. As a result, they won the vote to unionize, whereas campaigns conducted by national organizers had failed at another facility.[33]

It is also important to consider audience disposition, which is likely to differ depending on the forum you are addressing. For example, at a rally or demonstration you will probably have a sympathetic audience that agrees with your perspective on the issue. This will make it easy to identify common ground. Prior exposure is another important consideration. If previous speakers have already made a point that you were planning to make, you want to be flexible enough to bring in different ideas and avoid repeating what has already been said.

There are also times when you may encounter hostile audience members. For example, if you are addressing a controversial topic at a city council or school board meeting, a majority of the officials may disagree with your perspective. Our nation is passionately divided on many issues, and if you address an issue such as sanctuary cities, gun rights, or marijuana policy, it may be a challenge to persuade leaders who feel differently than you do. When speaking to a hostile audience, you may need to ask them to reconsider their position or seek a small or incremental change rather than calling for a total reversal of policy. You will also need to support your claims with credible evidence and present your ideas in a reasoned manner.

Finally, you may have a neutral audience. If the audience does not know much about your topic, you will need to inform them and show how the issue connects to their lives. The audience may also be neutral because they have heard about the issue many times but don't find it important. In this case, providing new information or new examples that directly relate to them may spark interest. If you are addressing elected leaders, for example, you can demonstrate widespread support for your idea by presenting a petition that has been signed by other community members.

## USE EVIDENCE TO PROVE FACTS

**Evidence.** Any time you advocate in public, you have an ethical responsibility to present truthful information. Thus, it is very important that you do careful research for your speech so that your facts are accurate. In addition, as we noted in Chapter 7, the use of evidence adds to your credibility as a speaker, which is essential if audience members are uncertain about a point you are making (or if they disagree with you).

*Atlantic* staff writer James Fallows was fed up with the noise and pollution caused by gas-powered leaf blowers in his neighborhood, so he and his wife joined a small group that advocated before the city council to phase out these yard tools. After a successful campaign, Fallows noted the importance of evidence:

> Having facts also matters—yes, even in today's America. At the beginning of the process, it felt as if 99 percent of the press coverage and online commentary was in the sneering "First World problem!" vein. That has changed. . . . Reflexive sneering is down to about 5 percent among people who have made time to hear the facts. Noise, they have come to understand, is the secondhand smoke of this era.[34]

**Supporting Materials.** Supporting materials play an essential role in the success of public advocacy. These materials can help you build audience interest if your topic is new to them, convince them that your claims are true, and help them remember your presentation (especially important if you are at a rally or government meeting where multiple people are speaking!).

X González gained national acclaim for their powerful emotional appeal at the Washington, D.C., March for Our Lives rally, where they remained silent for six minutes and twenty seconds to represent the length of the mass shooting that took the lives of seventeen of their classmates at Marjory Stoneman Douglas High School. They also wove a variety of effective supporting materials into their presentation. For example, they used an *analogy* to argue that students would succeed in changing the laws, comparing their movement's impact to the students who won the right to wear black armbands to school to protest the Vietnam War in *Tinker v. Des Moines School District*.[35] They used the *examples* of Australia, Japan, Canada, and the United Kingdom to show that government policies can successfully limit mass shootings.[36] Moreover, they used *anecdotes* to personalize endearing traits of the seventeen friends whose lives had been taken.[37]

## Organization

Good organization is very important in public advocacy. You want to make your main ideas stand out so that the audience can recognize and remember them. As we noted in Chapter 9, the audience cannot usually review your speech as they might reread a book or magazine. In addition, it is easy to lose the audience's attention (especially in an outdoor, mobile environment) when your speech appears to be rambling.

Structure your main points in an appropriate format. Here is an example of how Sandy Rivera—a junior at Indiana University–Purdue University Indianapolis, studying to be a teacher—structured her speech about DACA in a *chronological* format at the 2018 Indianapolis Women's March:

- Migrating to the United States with her mother and brother
- Staying in the shadows in her early years of school
- Realizing how her immigration status held her back in high school
- Benefiting from the DACA program, which created a pathway to college[38]

An effective introduction is also very important when you participate in public advocacy. Kelsey Juliana, now a University of Oregon student, has been active in environmental issues since she was ten years old. In 2018, she marched from Nebraska to Washington, D.C., as a participant in the Great March for Climate Action.[39] She began her speech calling for other millennials to take an active role on the issue of climate change with a striking statement:

> When I was fifteen, before I could vote, drive, or even have my first kiss, I sued the governor of Oregon. Now I'm twenty and I've gone to court six times. By choice. Yes, by choice, I have sat in front of a judge and filed cases against my state and federal government with the help of local nonprofit Our Children's Trust. Because by choice, my government has been funding and permitting excessive amounts of fossil fuel projects that are polluting our land, air, water, and contributing to climate destabilization.[40]

Be sure to include the other elements of an effective introduction—state your thesis, connect with the audience, establish credibility, and preview your main points. These elements are important for building audience interest and orienting audience members to the direction your speech will take.

A strong and memorable conclusion is equally important because you want to leave a lasting impression. In 2014, LeeAnne Walters—a Flint, Michigan,

▲ **Ending with an Inspiring Conclusion.** LeeAnne Walters (shown here speaking at a congressional hearing) ended her Goldman Prize acceptance speech with a memorable statement on the power of community action. Bill Clark/Getty Images

mother of four—found that her whole family was becoming progressively sicker. When her water began coming out of the tap brown, she suspected the cause of the health problems. She tested the water in her home and then worked with neighbors to collect over eight hundred water samples, proving that the city's water contained toxic levels of lead.[41]

Ms. Walters was awarded the Goldman Prize for grassroots environmental activism, and the conclusion of her acceptance speech captured the spirit of that activism:

> Even the smallest action can make a difference. When someone tells you to stop, ignore them and keep on your path. I am the catalyst for Flint, but this was a community effort. I personally can make a difference, but a community is unstoppable.[42]

## Language and Style

The words that you use to express your ideas are another key aspect of civic engagement. When you are trying to influence an audience on an issue that really matters to you, your language is what will convey your passion to the people you are addressing. In Chapter 12, we highlighted several strategies for using words that have the power to move your audience.

As one example of such words, at the 2022 Academy Awards, Ukrainian-born actress Mila Kunis used *figurative language* during her introduction of a performance by Reba McEntire:

> Recent global events have left many of us feeling gutted. Yet when we witness the strength and dignity of those facing such devastation, it's impossible not to be moved by their resilience. One cannot help but be in awe of those who find strength to keep fighting through unimaginable darkness.[43]

Another example of powerful style is Natalie Warne, who was determined to make a difference after watching the film *Invisible Children*. This documentary called attention to children who were being abducted and forced to kill for a rebel army in Uganda led by Joseph Kony. Ms. Warne joined ninety-nine other college-age students to serve as interns with Invisible Children, a nonprofit organization committed to helping vulnerable communities defend themselves from threats of violence.

In her speech, "Being Young and Making an Impact," Ms. Warne told the story of her experience with Invisible Children and its campaign to "rescue" one hundred U.S. cities by holding a rally until a public figure spoke out on behalf of the child soldiers. (Ms. Warne played the lead role in the Chicago rally, gaining recognition by Oprah!) In her speech, she acknowledged how important it is to have people who support the leaders of social movements. She used a personal anecdote about the time she met Dr. Vincent Harding, a professor who supported Martin Luther King Jr. during the civil rights movement. She also used a

memorable expression, coining the term "anonymous extraordinaries" to characterize people who worked for social justice based on personal conviction and not the need for recognition.[44]

Your advocacy can also make use of **symbolic expression**—the use of nonverbal symbols to express a message. These have included establishing tent cities to bring awareness to the issue of homelessness;[45] conducting "die-ins," in which students lie down on campus to protest violence; wearing a ball and chain to symbolize the burden of student debt; and using a road sign pointing sharply higher to symbolize the problem of rising gas prices. The use of nonverbal symbols can draw attention to a cause and make the message more memorable than would words alone.

## Preparation

When you participate in civic engagement, you want to have command of your material. The confidence and sincerity that you project will be important in persuading your audience and making an impact. This means that you should practice your speech until the content is familiar.

It is understandable if you are nervous before a public presentation, especially if it is your first time speaking to a community audience. If you are feeling apprehensive, use some of the strategies from Chapter 2 for managing speech anxiety as part of your preparation. Leave yourself plenty of time to prepare, and follow a plan to make sure you are not putting your speech together at the last minute. Imagined interactions and visualization can help you feel optimistic about your performance. In addition, practicing for friends and family will give you an opportunity to speak in front of a supportive audience. If you are one of a group of presenters at a rally or public meeting, try to practice together.

PRACTICE BUILDS CONFIDENCE

## Delivery

As we noted in Chapter 13, effective delivery helps make your message compelling and memorable, and the mode you use is an important choice that affects your delivery. Unless there is some reason you must read from a manuscript, *extemporaneous delivery* is the best format. If you want to connect with your audience, make eye contact if you're able to do so and engage them directly. You will lose your connection and, along with it, audience interest if you read your presentation. When you are participating in civic engagement, you are speaking out on an issue that matters to you. Therefore, you can trust yourself to explain ideas in your own words.

When speaking extemporaneously, you have limited notes for reference. Practice speaking with your notes so that you are comfortable finding your place if you need to use them. Carefully consider the medium for your notes. If you will be speaking outside on a windy day, you don't want pages of notes flapping around while you are speaking. If there is no access to an electrical outlet and you are using a tablet, take care that it is fully charged in advance. If you are using your phone, be sure you can quickly access the parts of your speech you need to reference without having to scroll extensively.

The forum for your presentation must also be considered. If you are speaking in person and you will be using a microphone, it can be helpful to practice in advance so that you are comfortable with it and can decide on an appropriate volume. If you do not have amplification, it is important to practice your projection so that everyone in the audience can hear you.

As another important note, be mindful of your tone in delivery. Stacey Park Milbern was one of the leaders who established the disability justice movement to advocate for disabled LGBTQ people and people of color. She was recognized with the Google Doodle for May 19, 2022, the day that would have been her thirty-fifth birthday. Her father described the power of her advocacy this way: "As a visionary speaker, Stacey captivated audiences in the largest auditoriums, not by the strength of her voice but through the wisdom of her words and the power of her convictions."[46]

Finally, during public advocacy, keep in mind that you can allow your emotions to surface gently, in a way that allows the audience to understand that you mean business. In 2019, comedian and 9/11 first responders advocate Jon Stewart testified before a congressional committee, sharing his anger that the federal government had dragged its feet in passing legislation to pay for health care of surviving 9/11 first responders. Here is an example of his emotion, reflected not only in the tone of his voice, but also his word choice, delivered extemporaneously. Stewart says in closing:

> Al Qaeda didn't shout "Death to Tribeca." They attacked America, and these men and women and their response to it is what brought our country back. It's what gave a reeling nation a solid foundation to stand back upon. To remind us of why this country is great, of why this country is worth

fighting for. . . . Thank God for people like John Feal, thank God for people like Ray Pfeifer, thank God for all these people who will not let it happen. They responded in five seconds. They did their jobs with courage, grace, tenacity, humility. Eighteen years later, do yours![47]

# SAMPLE CIVIC ENGAGEMENT SPEECH

## SCHOOL LIBRARIES ARE NO PLACE FOR CENSORSHIP

### Tariq Jackson

*As one of the speech assignments in Tariq Jackson's public speaking class, students were required to develop a persuasive speech on a policy issue that could be presented in a public forum. For this assignment, Tariq decided to speak against school library censorship. The context for his speech is a public meeting addressing whether the local school board should create a commission to review and remove books they find objectionable from school libraries.*

Author Stephen Chbosky once said "banning books gives us silence when we need speech. It closes our ears when we need to listen." That is one of the reasons I am here today, speaking against the proposal to establish a committee that will remove "objectionable" books from our schools' libraries. As school board members and members of our community, we all have an interest in adopting policies that encourage students to read, learn, and grow. I am a parent of school aged kids who love their library time, and I have also conducted research on this topic.

• Tariq includes each element of a speech introduction, concluding with a preview.

To see why creating the proposed committee is not a good policy for our students, first, let's take a look at the books that are most likely to be removed, then consider why book removal is harmful for our students, and finally, focus on why our district's current book selection policy is a better alternative. •

Let's begin by considering which books are most likely to be removed from our school libraries.

Many quality books are at risk. Among the books that have been proposed for elimination from our school library are Toni Morrison's Pulitzer Prize-winning *Beloved,* Newbery Award Medal Winner *Roll of Thunder, Hear My Cry* by Mildred Taylor, and Leah Johnson's *You Should See Me in a Crown,* which made *Good Housekeeping*'s Ten Best List of LGBTQ+ Inclusive Children's Books. •

• Example reasoning shows quality books are at risk.

There are common themes in the books most often selected for removal. In *Education Week,* January 18, 2022, the National Coalition Against Censorship (NCAC) writes that removed books often discuss "the lived experiences of racism or of growing up LGBTQIA and experiencing bias, discrimination, hate and even violence."

Now that we have seen which books are at risk, let's consider how removing these books would hurt our students. •

There are many harms that result when we ban books from our school libraries. First, students benefit from books that relate to their life experiences. For example, Kate Messner's *The Seventh Wish* is controversial because it discusses a twelve-year-old girl's struggles due to her older sister's addiction. Yet, as Ms. Messner points out in an interview on the *NCAC's Banned Books Week*, 2021, "I know from talking with kids that books can act as a mirror of their lives. [Through books] a child can feel that even though we're not talking about [a difficult issue they are going through] in the classroom, that even though my teachers aren't talking about these things, I am still not alone."

In the *Education Week* article previously cited, George Johnson, author of *All Boys Aren't Blue,* notes that they wrote that book because, in their words, it is "the book that I wish that I could have read when I was a young adult, struggling with my identity, struggling with trying to figure out why I was feeling the way I was feeling." •

Sometimes removing materials that relate to students' lives can have severe consequences. A Trevor Project *Research Brief,* August 2021, stated that when LGBTQ students learn about LGBTQ people or issues in school, they have 23 percent lower odds of attempting suicide.

Some parents claim that controversial books will cause students to lose their innocence. But for students whose lives mirror what is portrayed in these books, the situations are very real and books let them know they are not the only ones going through these experiences. •

Second, student achievement and reading habits improve when they can select books that interest them. Professors Hall, Hedrick, and Williams note in *Childhood Education*, March 2014, that "research in the field of literacy has identified choice as a key component affecting students' reading habits and their resulting literacy growth." They go on to say that "for many students, school is the only place with access to high-quality, appropriate, and interesting books."

Buffalo State Education Professor Sherri Weber indicates in *The Language and Literacy Spectrum,* June 2018, that independent reading programs are "vital to encourage lifelong reading habits." She further notes that the "essence" of these programs is to provide students with regular times to silently read "books of their own selection."•

*Marginal notes:*

• Tariq consistently uses transitions to make his organization clear.

• Appeal to pathos

• Two-sided argument

• Tariq regularly uses evidence to demonstrate the benefits of books that relate to students' lives.

Third, students need to learn about challenging issues and topics. If students cannot read about topics such as racism, sexual assault, divorce, or addiction, these issues will not cease to exist. Students should have the chance to read age appropriate literature that helps them understand the problems we face in society. Our students are the future generation of voters and leaders and they need to be well • Causal reasoning prepared to address social problems. • Removing books will not shield students from these issues. They will hear about them from friends or they may experience them in their own lives. It is better to let students learn about social problems by reading quality materials selected by a professional librarian, than to have them figure out these issues on their own.

Whereas book removal would limit student learning, we already have a good book selection policy in our district.

Current policies are a better alternative to book removal. Our district policy requires that librarians consider the age and social development of students when selecting books, in addition to promoting a love of learning and reading. Librarians have the expertise to make good book choices. They have the education and training needed to choose quality books that will appeal to all the diverse students in our district.

Some advocates for creating a book removal committee say that book banning is an issue of parents' rights, but this is a false claim. The committee will serve the goals of parents who make the most noise and are the most involved. • Other parents have work or family responsibilities that would make it difficult to serve on such a committee to speak up for their children's interests. The committee will deny the rights of parents who want their kids to have access to books that interest them and relate to their lives. This is especially harmful for families who cannot afford to stock their own homes with books. I hope that our school board will decide not to create a book removal committee.

We have considered the types of books that are most likely to be removed, the reasons why book removal would limit student learning and love for reading, and the rationale for maintaining our current book selection process. Let's make sure that our district libraries continue to provide students with quality books that will increase their reading achievement and make them lifelong readers. As my second-grade teacher Ms. Broughton always told our class, "readers are leaders." •

**Margin notes:**

• Causal reasoning

• Tariq appeals to the value of equity. The policy should be fair to all the students' parents.

• Tariq concludes with a summary and clincher.

## SPEECH CHOICES

### A CASE STUDY: *RAFAELA*

*Let's see what civic engagement activities are right for Rafaela.*

As the end of the term grew near, it was Rafaela's turn to present her persuasive speech—which she did successfully, thanks to all her preparation and hard work. After her speech, a classmate asked Rafaela if she herself would like to run for office. Then, in one of the last classes of the term, her instructor talked about civic engagement and its relationship to public speaking and encouraged students to take action to support an issue or a cause. This got Rafaela thinking about how she might get involved on campus.

Rafaela considered running for a student government position, but she wasn't sure that holding an office at that point in time was the best option for her. She would be carrying a heavy course load in the fall and it would be difficult to add more meetings and other commitments to her schedule. Although she was passionate about issues relating to women, she did not have the same passion about many of the issues that would be emphasized in student government.

As Rafaela thought about her speech, she considered other ways that she could get involved. She remembered the She Should Run website that she had presented as part of her solution (see Rafaela's full speech in the Appendix), and considered women who had stood out in her classes as strong advocates who supported their ideas convincingly. She nominated three women on the website and made it a point to tell each one why she thought they would make excellent candidates.

Rafaela's friend, the student body president, also asked her when she was going to start getting involved. Rafaela noted that she did not have time to serve in a student government office. Her friend suggested that they find a rally in town or on campus on an issue that they both felt passionate about and attend together. Rafaela thought it was a great way to get involved; she decided she might even volunteer to speak for a cause now that she had experience addressing an audience in her class.

### 💬 YOUR TURN

> Now that you've seen how Rafaela's choices impacted her involvement in civic engagement, consider how you might take action on behalf of a cause that is important to you. To help you get started, consider your answers to these questions:
>
> - What are some issues or causes that are important to me?
>
> - What are some ways that I could participate in civic engagement on those issues?
>
> - If I decide to speak out on these issues, what are some ways I could apply the skills I've learned in this public speaking class?
>
> By considering your responses to these questions, you can reflect on how best to incorporate civic engagement and community involvement into your own life.

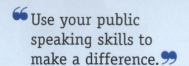

**Use your public speaking skills to make a difference.**

In this chapter, we explained how to use your public speaking skills in service of civic engagement—defined as active public participation in political affairs and social and community organizations. We showed you how and why civic engagement can be a benefit to you as well as to society as a whole, whether performed from inside or outside the system. These engagements can take place in a variety of forums, including on campus, in your community, at demonstrations, and at other public events. A variety of public speaking skills are applicable in these situations, including developing your message, organization, language and style, preparation, and delivery. In civic engagement, for example, it's particularly important to narrow your topic so that it will fit an achievable goal. Organization also becomes important, to help your ideas better stand out to an audience that may be interacting with a great number or variety of people. You must also choose your words carefully and practice your speech until the content is familiar. Finally, in most civic engagement opportunities, it is best to speak extemporaneously, rather than from a manuscript, to better connect with your audience about the importance of the issue at hand.

## Key Terms

civic engagement *540*
free speech zones *546*

symbolic expression *556*

## Review Questions

1. Define civic engagement and provide three examples of how people can participate in civic engagement.
2. Explain why civic engagement is important for self-government.
3. Explain how you can benefit by participating in civic engagement.
4. What are four questions you can ask when narrowing the topic you plan to address during civic engagement?

## Critical Thinking Questions

1. How is preparing to speak in a public setting different from preparing to speak in your public speaking class? In what ways would your preparation be similar?
2. If you are speaking at a city council or school board meeting, what non-verbal feedback can help you determine whether the elected officials are paying attention to your speech? How can you draw their attention to your

presentation if they are multitasking (for example, checking their phones or laptops)?

3. If you are speaking at a public event where speakers are offering different perspectives on an issue, how could you differentiate your position from them while still leaving room for common ground between speakers?

## Activities

1. Working in groups, brainstorm different issues on campus that need to be addressed. For each issue, discuss how to best use civic engagement to generate action on the part of your college.
2. Watch a video of a speaker addressing an audience on a public issue. Identify times when the speaker generates an audience response. What kind of messages or nonverbal behaviors pull the audience into the speech?
3. Working in groups, select an issue on your campus or in your community. Discuss how you could use social media to draw interest in your event and to remain connected to audience members.
4. Watch an excerpt of an online video of a U.S. Presidential Debate that happened before 2016 and another from 2016 or 2020. (As one option, PBS.org has a video library called "Watch All the Presidential Debates Since 1960.") Compare the candidates' verbal and nonverbal behavior. Do you think the more recent debate is an example of a decline in the quality of public discourse?

# Speech Choices Outline and Full-Length Speech

## WHY WOMEN SHOULD RUN FOR OFFICE: SPEECH CHOICES OUTLINE

*As you have progressed through the chapters in* Speak Up!, *you have followed the story of Rafaela's preparation for her persuasive speech. Here is a full-sentence outline of her presentation. Rafaela's hard work at each stage of the process has paid off. She has a well-organized outline that displays her audience adaptation, research, planning of main points, selection of supporting materials, and choice of presentation aids.*

### INTRODUCTION

I. Sometimes, all it takes is a little encouragement. A woman I know ran for student-body president two years ago. She received almost no encouragement or support during the campaign and she finished fourth—out of four candidates. She dreaded telling her brother that she had come in last place, expecting him to call her a loser. However, she was pleasantly surprised when he told her how proud he was that she had run. • He said that she would be a great president and encouraged her to learn from the experience and run again. The next day, she started planning her campaign, and the following spring she won the election. Today she is our student-body president. Hopefully some of you will follow her example by running for or encouraging the women in your life to run for office.

• Use of narrative for attention-getter

II. I am calling on women to run for office and all classmates to provide support.

III. It is very important that we have more women in office on campus and in our community. Women make up over half of the population but hold far less than half of all offices.

• Rafaela includes all five components of a good introduction— attention-getter, thesis, relevance to audience, credibility, and preview.

IV. My research on this topic includes interviews with women who have run for office, along with studies and news articles that discuss this issue. •

V. We will focus on three topics: first, why it is important for women to run for office; second, why women are less likely to run than men; and finally, how all of us can take steps to reduce this imbalance.

## BODY

• Transition to main point I, noted in brackets.

[TRANSITION Let's begin by considering how women are underrepresented.] •

I. Despite recent successes, women remain less likely to run for office.
   A. Women are underrepresented in public office.
      1. NPR Political Reporter Danielle Kurtzleben noted in *A Record Number of Women Will Serve in Congress* on November 7, 2018, that in the 2018 election, the number of women in Congress reached 23 percent, "a new high, but far from parity."
      2. As Mary Jordan, national political correspondent, noted in the *Washington Post*, November 8, 2018, "Even with the gains, women were still underrepresented. The United States trails behind many other countries, from Mexico to Britain, in the legislative representation of women." •

• Rafaela fully cites each source and uses quotation marks for direct quotations.

      3. The situation is the same at the state and local level. Saskia Brechenmacher of the Carnegie Endowment reported in *Tackling Women's Underrepresentation in U.S. Politics*, February 2018, that "women remain underrepresented at the federal, state, and local levels. The current uptick in women running for office, while encouraging, is unlikely to close this gender gap." •

• Subpoints and sub-subpoints are properly indented.

[TRANSITION This lack of representation is problematic.]

   B. Women's equal participation in public office is essential.
      1. One reason is equity. Women represent over 50 percent of the population, and it is only fair that women have the same level of representation.

2. Republican representative Diane Black of Tennessee, in *Representation Matters: Women in the U.S. Congress*, 2017, provides a second reason, noting that "women look at issues differently than men do, and that's just the way we are. We come at things in a different way, and since 52% of the population is female, it behooves us to make sure that we have a voice, a woman's voice in the discussions." •

3. Amanda Ripley, contributing writer to the *Atlantic* and senior fellow at the Emerson Collective, offered yet another reason in Politico, June 12, 2017, writing that "to be blunt, women may actually be better at politics," especially "the kind that Americans say they want to see more often." Women "are more likely to say they entered politics because of a specific policy concern," whereas "men are more likely to say they were looking to fulfill a lifelong dream." In addition, "Women are also more likely to sponsor bills—and, when they're in the minority party, women tend to keep their proposals alive longer, partly by reaching across the aisle."

4. Finally, when women are elected to office, they serve as role models.
   a. One of the students I interviewed while researching this speech was inspired by Khemarey Khoeun, the first Cambodian American elected to public office. •
   b. Soksreinith Ten, a VOA reporter, shared Khemarey's story on *Voice of America News*, May 9, 2017, noting that she and her family had escaped the brutal Khmer Rouge genocide in Cambodia and came to Chicago from a refugee camp in Thailand. That traumatic experience has made Cambodian Americans less likely to participate in politics, but Khemarey is determined to "help Cambodians see there is little risk in taking an active role in their new home."

• Sub-subpoints show subordination. Each one provides a reason why equal participation is essential.

• Narrative supports Rafaela's claim.

[TRANSITION    Now that we have seen why it is important to increase women's representation in public office, let's turn our attention to some of the reasons representation is lower.]

II.  Three barriers to increased participation are encouragement, experience, and confidence.

    A.  One cause is a lack of encouragement.

        1.  When interviewing our class, I discovered that women were rarely encouraged to run for any office by friends, family members, or teachers. However, about half the men were encouraged to run for office while in school and after graduation. •

        2.  Our class members' experiences are consistent with research from Professors Jennifer Lawless (American University) and Richard Fox (Loyola Marymount) in *Girls Just Wanna Not Run*, March 2013, who found that "the effects of encouragement to run for office are substantial. Sixty-six percent of women who received any encouragement to run for office reported interest in a future candidacy, compared to 21 percent who never received encouragement to run."

    B.  A second • cause is lower rates of participation in experiences that build political skills.

        1.  In *Why Our Student Council Presidents Are Women, but Our Politicians Are Not*, August 24, 2017, Sydney Nelson, George Washington University executive vice president, provides the example of debate, noting that in college student government, "when you're presenting a proposal, you're debating it and you're trying to get votes for it by lobbying and advocating for what you want. In high school, it's more of a collaborative effort."

        2.  Professors Lawless and Fox, previously cited, discuss another example: sports.

            a.  They state that "even though sports participation might seem somewhat removed from political ambition, the competitiveness associated with sports appears to serve as a significant predictor of interest in running for office."

            b.  Lawless and Fox go on to note that "women who played sports were

• Rafaela relates her message to the audience.

• "Second" is a *signpost*.

          approximately 25 percent more likely than those who did not to express political ambition."

    c.  For example, associate editor Cody Hooks reported in the *Taos News*, December 3, 2018, that Deb Haaland, one of the first two Native American women elected to Congress, runs marathons.

  C.  A third cause is lack of confidence, despite their considerable abilities. Although Stefanie Johnson, associate professor of organizational leadership at the University of Colorado, noted in *Why Don't Women Run for Office*, October 31, 2018, that women's college graduation rates exceed men's and that women "are also more likely to study in fields that provide great skill sets for political offices and leadership, such as law, business and management," women "tend to rate themselves as less effective leaders."

[TRANSITION  Although there are barriers to women's political participation now, you can all take an active role in changing that trend.]

III.  Women in this class: run for office; classmates: support us.

  A.  Women in the audience, I am talking to you. In your speeches, you have spoken with passion about many issues facing our community, the nation, and the world. I am calling on you to use those voices to take a leadership role on campus and in the community.

  B.  There are many classes and activities on campus that can help you get in touch with your political side and gain helpful experience and skills.

    1.  Our Political Science Department offers several options, including a Women in Politics course and an internship class in which students can work in the office of local and state political leaders. •

> • Rafaela uses *examples* as supporting materials.

    2.  In addition, both our debate and moot court teams are open to any interested student, with no experience required. These activities give you a chance to learn how to advocate and respond to the arguments of others and to match your skills against those of students from other colleges.

3. Another option is sports. Our college has women's club teams that are open to any interested student. You don't need to run marathons like Representative Haaland; our cross-country team's races are just five kilometers!

4. Finally, when you are ready to run for office, remember that student government elections take place every year.

• Rafaela notes where presentation aids will be used.

[SHOW VISUAL AID ABOUT CAMPUS ELECTIONS] •

C. Classmates, I'm calling on all of you to provide support for the women in your classes and in your lives to run for office.

1. Your support can make a difference. The previously cited study by Professors Lawless and Fox found that "although young women are less likely than young men ever to have considered running for office, they are just as likely as men to respond positively to encouragement to run." •

• Rafaela explains how men in the audience can provide encouragement.

2. When you hear a woman give a great speech in class or show leadership skills in a group, tell her she would make a good student-body officer, city council member, or even president! And if you have sisters, don't forget to encourage them, too.

3. There are organizations that are ready to help you recruit. For example, She Should Run is a nonprofit organization that offers resources for women who are interested in running for public office.

[SHOW VISUAL AID OF GROUP'S WEBSITE]

There is a link for you to recommend a promising candidate, and the site will offer support.

## CONCLUSION

[TRANSITION     Today, we have looked at the importance of having women run for office.]

I. First, we took a look at how women are underrepresented in public office. Next, we considered three reasons why this is true—encouragement, experience, and confidence. Finally, I appealed for women in this class to run for office and for all classmates to provide support. •

• Efficient summary of main points

II. Professors Lawless and Fox note that when women run for political office, "they are just as likely as men to win their races." What it takes to get women to run is encouragement, and I am calling on the women in this class to run and all classmates to provide support. When I look at the students in this room, I see future school board members, mayors, and legislators. Perhaps the first woman president of the United States— or, better yet, the fourth or fifth woman president!

## References •

Brechenmacher, S. (2018). *Tackling women's underrepresentation in U.S. Politics.* Carnegie Endowment for International Peace.

Dittmar, K., Sanbonmatsu, S., Carroll, S. J., Walsh, D., & Wineinger, C. (2017). *Representation matters: Women in the U.S. Congress.* Center for American Women and Politics, Eagleton Institute of Politics, Rutgers, The State University of New Jersey.

Hooks, C. (2018, December 3). These women rule: New Mexico voters put more women in power. *Taos News.* https://taosnews.com/stories/these-women-rule,53464

Jordan, M. (2018, November 8). Record number of women heading to Congress. *Washington Post.* https://www.washingtonpost.com/politics/record-number-of-women-appear-headed-for-congress/2018/11/06/76a9e60a-e1eb-11e8-8f5f-a55347f48762_story.html?utm_term=.36658997dc70

Kurtzleben, D. (2018, November 7). *A record number of women will serve in Congress (with potentially still more to come).* NPR. https://www.npr.org/2018/11/07/665019211 /a-record-number-of-women-will-serve-in-congress-with-potentially-more-to-come

Lawless, J. L., & Fox, R. L. (2013). *Girls just wanna not run: The gender gap in young Americans' political ambition.* Women & Politics Institute. •

Leeds School of Business (2018, October 31). *Why women don't run for office. And how business schools can help.* https://www.colorado.edu/business/news/business-education /2018/10/31/why-women-dont-run-office-and-how-business -schools-can-help

Ripley, A. (2017, June 12). *What it will take for women to win.* Politico. https://www.politico.com/interactives/2017/women -rule-politics/

Ten, S. (2017, May 9). *Victor in Illinois is first Cambodian-American woman elected to US Public Office.* VOA. https://www.voanews.com/a/victor-illinois-first-cambodian -american-woman-elected-united-states/3845181.html

Wang, C. (2017, August 24). *Why our student council presidents are women, but our politicians are not.* Yahoo. https://www.yahoo.com/news/why-student-council-presidents-women -175000243.html

• Rafaela includes full citations of all sources in her references.

• Rafaela uses APA format. Check with your instructor to see which style manual is preferred.

# WHY WOMEN SHOULD RUN FOR OFFICE: FULL-LENGTH SPEECH

Sometimes, all it takes is a little encouragement. A woman I know ran for student-body president two years ago. She received almost no encouragement or support during the campaign and she finished fourth—out of four candidates. She dreaded telling her brother that she came in last place, expecting him to call her a loser. However, she was pleasantly surprised when he told her how proud he was that she had run. He said that she would be a great president and encouraged her to learn from the experience and run again. The next day, she started planning her campaign, and the following spring she won the election. Today, she is our student-body president. Hopefully some of you will follow her example by running for or encouraging the women in your life to run for office.

I am calling on women to run for office and all classmates to provide support. It is very important that we have more women in office on campus and in our community. Women make up over half of the population but hold far less than half of all offices. My research on this topic includes interviews with women who have run for office, along with studies and news articles that discuss this issue.

We will focus on three topics: first, why it is important for women to run for office; second, why women are less likely to run than men; and finally, how all of us can take steps to reduce this imbalance.

Let's begin by considering how women are underrepresented. Despite recent successes, women remain less likely to run for office. NPR Political Reporter Danielle Kurtzleben noted in *A Record Number of Women Will Serve in Congress*, on November 7, 2018, that in the 2018 election, the number of women in Congress reached 23 percent, "a new high, but far from parity." As Mary Jordan, National Political Correspondent, noted in the *Washington Post*, November 8, 2018, "even with the gains, women were still underrepresented. The United States trails behind many other countries, from Mexico to Britain, in the legislative representation of women."

The situation is the same at the state and local level. Saskia Brechenmacher of the Carnegie Endowment reported in *Tackling Women's Underrepresentation in U.S. Politics*, February 2018, that "women remain underrepresented at the federal, state, and local levels. The current uptick in women running for office, while encouraging, is unlikely to close this gender gap."

Women's equal participation in public office is essential. One reason is equity. Women represent over 50 percent of the population and it is only fair that women have the same level of representation. Republican Representative Diane Black of Tennessee, in *Representation Matters: Women in the U.S. Congress*, 2017, provides a second reason, noting that "women look at issues differently than men do, and that's just the way we are. We come at things in a different way, and since 52% of the population is female, it behooves us to make sure that we have a voice, a woman's voice in the discussions."

Amanda Ripley, contributing writer to the *Atlantic* and Senior Fellow at the Emerson Collective, offered another reason in Politico, June 12, 2017, writing that "to be blunt, women may actually be better at politics," especially "the kind that Americans say they want to see more often." Women "are more likely to say they entered politics because of a specific policy concern," whereas "men are more likely to say they were looking to fulfill a lifelong dream." In addition, "women are also more likely to sponsor bills—and, when they're in the minority party, women tend to keep their proposals alive longer, partly by reaching across the aisle."

Finally, when women are elected to office, they serve as role models. One of the students I interviewed while researching for this speech was inspired by Khemarey Khoeun, the first Cambodian-American elected to public office. Soksreinith Ten, a VOA reporter, shared Khemarey's story on Voice of America News, May 9, 2017, noting that she and her family had escaped the brutal Khmer Rouge genocide in Cambodia and came to Chicago from a refugee camp in Thailand. That traumatic experience has made Cambodian Americans less likely to participate in politics, but Khemarey is determined to "help Cambodians see there is little risk in taking an active role in their new home."

Now that we have seen why it is important to increase women's representation in public office, let's turn our attention to some of the reasons representation is lower. One cause is a lack of encouragement. When interviewing our class, I discovered that women were rarely encouraged to run for any office by friends, family members, or teachers. However, about half the men were encouraged to run for office while in school and after graduation.

Our class members' experiences are consistent with research from Professors Jennifer Lawless (American University) and Richard Fox (Loyola Marymount), in *Girls Just Wanna Not Run*, March 2013, who found that "the effects of encouragement to run for office are substantial. Sixty-six percent of women who received any encouragement to run for office reported interest in a future candidacy, compared to 21 percent who never received encouragement to run."

A second cause is lower rates of participation in experiences that build political skills. In *Why Our Student Council Presidents Are Women, but Our Politicians Are Not*, August 24, 2017, Sydney Nelson, George Washington University Executive Vice President provides the example of debate, noting that in college student government, "when you're presenting a proposal, you're debating it and you're trying to get votes for it by lobbying and advocating for what you want. In high school, it's more of a collaborative effort."

Professors Lawless and Fox, previously cited, discuss another example: sports. They state that "even though sports participation might seem somewhat removed from political ambition, the competitiveness associated with sports appears to serve as a significant predictor of interest in running for office." Lawless and Fox go on to note "women who played sports were approximately 25 percent more likely than those who did not to express political ambition." For example, Associate Editor Cody Hooks reported in the *Taos News*, December 3, 2018, that Deb Haaland, one of the first two Native American women elected to Congress, runs marathons.

A third cause is lack of confidence, despite their considerable abilities. Although Stefanie Johnson, associate professor of Organizational Leadership at the University of Colorado noted in *Why Don't Women Run for Office*, October 31, 2018, that women's college graduation rates exceed men's and that women "are also more likely to study in fields that provide great skill sets for political offices and leadership, such as law, business and management," women "tend to rate themselves as less effective leaders."

Although there are barriers to women's political participation now, you can all take an active role in changing that trend.

Women in this class: run for office; classmates: support us.

Women in the audience, I am talking to you. In your speeches, you have spoken with passion about many issues facing our community, the nation, and the world. I am calling on you to use those voices to take a leadership role on campus and in the community.

There are many classes and activities on campus that can help you get in touch with your political side and gain helpful experience and skills. Our Political Science department offers several options, including a Women in Politics course and an internship class where students can work in the office of local and state political leaders.

In addition, both our debate and moot court teams are open to any interested student with no experience required. These activities give you a chance to learn how to advocate and respond to the arguments of others and to match your skills against those of students from other colleges.

Another option is sports. Our college has women's club teams that are open to any interested student. You don't need to run marathons like Representative Haaland; our cross-country team's races are just five kilometers!

Finally, when you are ready to run for office, our student government elections take place each year.

Classmates, I'm calling on all of you to provide support for the women in your classes and in your lives to run for office. Your support can make a difference. The previously cited study by Professors Lawless and Fox found that "although young women are less likely than young men ever to have considered running for office, they are just as likely as men to respond positively to encouragement to run." When you hear a woman give a great speech in class or show leadership skills in a group, tell them they would make a good student-body officer, city council member, or even president! And if you have sisters, don't forget to encourage them, too. There are organizations that are ready to help you recruit. For example, She Should Run is a nonprofit organization that offers resources for women who are interested in running for public office. There is a link for you to recommend a promising candidate, and the site will offer support.

Today, we have looked at the importance of having women run for office. First, we took a look at how women are underrepresented in public office. Next we considered three reasons why this is true—encouragement, experience, and confidence. Finally, I appealed for women in this class to run for office and for all classmates to provide support.

Professors Lawless and Fox note that when women run for political office, "they are just as likely as men to win their races." What it takes to get women to run is encouragement, and I am calling on the women in this class to run and all classmates to provide support. When I look at the students in this room, I see future school board members, mayors, and legislators. Perhaps the first woman president of the United States. Better yet, the fourth or fifth woman president!

# Additional Sample Speeches

## SAMPLE SPECIAL-OCCASION SPEECH

### John McCain
*at Liberty Medal Ceremony*

*The Liberty Medal is presented by the National Constitution Center to a person who has demonstrated a devotion to liberty and service. Award winners have included George W. and Laura Bush, Bill and Hillary Clinton, Rep. John Lewis, Muhammad Ali, Malala Yousafzai, and the Dalai Lama.*

*The 2017 award winner was Senator John McCain. On October 16, 2017, his award was presented by then–Vice President Joe Biden. The speech that follows is Senator McCain's acceptance of this award.*

Thank you, Joe, my old, dear friend, for those mostly undeserved kind words. Vice President Biden and I have known each other for a lot of years now, more than forty, if you're counting. • We knew each other back when we were young and handsome and smarter than everyone else but were too modest to say so.

*• Thanking presenter in introduction*

Joe was already a senator, and I was the navy's liaison to the Senate. My duties included escorting senate delegations on overseas trips, and in that capacity, I supervised the disposition of the delegation's luggage, which could require, now and again—when no one of lower rank was available for the job—that I carry someone worthy's bag. Once or twice that worthy turned out to be the young senator from Delaware. I've resented it ever since.

Joe has heard me joke about that before. I hope he has heard, too, my profession of gratitude for his friendship these many years. It has meant a lot to me. We served in the Senate together for over twenty years, during some eventful times, as we passed from young men to the fossils who appear before you this evening. •

*• Using self-deprecating humor*

We didn't always agree on the issues. We often argued—sometimes passionately. But we believed in each other's patriotism and the sincerity of each other's convictions. We believed in the institution we were privileged to serve in. We believed in our mutual responsibility to help make the place work and to cooperate in finding solutions to our country's problems. We believed in our country and in our country's indispensability to international peace and

• Evoking shared values

stability and to the progress of humanity. • And through it all, whether we argued or agreed, Joe was good company. Thank you, old friend, for your company and your service to America.

Thank you, too, to the National Constitution Center, and everyone associated with it for this award. Thank you for that video, and for the all too generous compliments paid to me this evening. I'm aware of the prestigious company the Liberty Medal places me in. I'm humbled by it, and I'll try my

• Expressing gratitude for the award

best not to prove too unworthy of it. •

Some years ago, I was present at an event where an earlier Liberty Medal recipient spoke about America's values and the sacrifices made for them. It was 1991, and I was attending the ceremony commemorating the fiftieth anniversary of the attack on Pearl Harbor. The World War II veteran, estimable patriot and good man, President George H. W. Bush, gave a moving speech at the USS *Arizona* memorial. I remember it very well. His voice was thick with emotion as he neared the end of his address. I imagine he was thinking not only of the brave Americans who lost their lives on December 7, 1941, but of the friends he had served with and lost in the Pacific, where he had been the navy's youngest aviator.

"Look at the water here, clear and quiet," he directed. "One day, in what now seems another lifetime, it wrapped its arms around the finest sons any nation could ever have, and

• Evoking audience emotions

it carried them to a better world." •

He could barely get out the last line, "May God bless them, and may God bless America, the most wondrous land on earth."

The most wondrous land on earth, indeed. I've had the good fortune to spend sixty years in service to this wondrous land. It has not been perfect service, to be sure, and there were probably times when the country might have benefited from a little less of my help. But I've tried to deserve the privilege as best I can, and I've been repaid a thousand times over with adventures, with good company, and with the satisfaction of serving something more important than myself, of being a bit player in the extraordinary story of America. And I am so very grateful.

What a privilege it is to serve this big, boisterous, brawling, intemperate, striving, daring, beautiful, bountiful, brave, magnificent country. • With all our flaws, all our mistakes, with all the frailties of human nature as much on display as our virtues, with all the rancor and anger of our politics, we are blessed.

• Using style: Sen. McCain uses multiple adjectives to describe his vision of the United States.

We are living in the land of the free, the land where anything is possible, the land of the immigrant's dream, the land with the storied past forgotten in the rush to the imagined future, the land that repairs and reinvents itself, the land where a person can escape the consequences of a self-centered youth and know the satisfaction of sacrificing for an ideal, the land where you can go from aimless rebellion to a noble cause, and from the bottom of your class to your party's nomination for president.

We are blessed, and we have been a blessing to humanity in turn. The international order we helped build from the ashes of world war, and that we defend to this day, has liberated more people from tyranny and poverty than ever before in history. This wondrous land has shared its treasures and ideals and shed the blood of its finest patriots to help make another, better world. • And as we did so, we made our own civilization more just, freer, more accomplished and prosperous than the America that existed when I watched my father go off to war on December 7, 1941.

• Adapting to audience expectations by providing an optimistic, nonpartisan tribute to the country's role in the world

To fear the world we have organized and led for three-quarters of a century, to abandon the ideals we have advanced around the globe, to refuse the obligations of international leadership and our duty to remain "the last best hope of earth" for the sake of some half-baked, spurious nationalism cooked up by people who would rather find scapegoats than solve problems is as unpatriotic as an attachment to any other tired dogma of the past that Americans consigned to the ash heap of history.

We live in a land made of ideals, not blood and soil. We are the custodians of those ideals at home, and their champion abroad. We have done great good in the world. That leadership has had its costs, but we have become incomparably powerful and wealthy as we did. We have a moral obligation to continue in our just cause, and we would bring more than shame on ourselves if we don't. We will not thrive in a world where our leadership and ideals are absent. We wouldn't deserve to.

I am the luckiest guy on earth. I have served America's cause—the cause of our security and the security of our friends, the cause of freedom and equal justice—all my

• Showing humility

adult life. I haven't always served it well. • I haven't even always appreciated what I was serving. But among the few compensations of old age is the acuity of hindsight. I see now that I was part of something important that drew me along in its wake even when I was diverted by other interests. I was, knowingly or not, along for the ride as America made the future better than the past.

And I have enjoyed it, every single day of it, the good ones and the not so good ones. I've been inspired by the service of better patriots than me. I've seen Americans make sacrifices for our country and her causes and for people who were strangers to them but for our common humanity, sacrifices that were much harder than the service asked of me. And I've seen the good they have done, the lives they freed from tyranny and injustice, the hope they encouraged, the dreams they made achievable.

May God bless them. May God bless America, and give us the strength and wisdom, the generosity and compassion, to do our duty for this wondrous land, and for the world that counts on us. With all its suffering and dangers, the world still looks to the example and leadership of America to become another, better place. What greater cause could anyone ever serve.

• Thanking the National Constitution Center and showing appreciation in conclusion

Thank you again for this honor. I'll treasure it. •

## SAMPLE PERSUASIVE SPEECH

### CHILD SLAVERY AND THE PRODUCTION OF CHOCOLATE

### David Kruckenberg
*Santiago Canyon College*

*Student David Kruckenberg presented this speech in the finals of the Phi Rho Pi National Tournament in 2007. David uses a problem-cause-solution format to address the compelling issue of child labor in the production of chocolate. He uses diverse reasoning strategies and consistently documents his claims with evidence. David's speech is well organized, with a clear preview and transitions between each main point. His audience-centered solution demonstrates how each of us can be personally involved in addressing the problem.*

I was forced to stay in a large room with other children from a neighboring plantation. I tried to run away, but I was caught. As punishment they cut my feet; I had to work for weeks while my wounds healed.

This moving testimony may sound like past history, when slavery was prevalent. But these words are not a reminder of the past. They're found in the April 24, 2006, issue of *Forbes* magazine. These are the words of an enslaved boy working in the cocoa fields of the country of Côte d'Ivoire, also known as the Ivory Coast. And he is not alone. UNICEF reports in February 2006 that child trafficking is on the rise in this African region. •

It may surprise you to learn that the last chocolate you ate may well have been tainted with child slavery. Despite the promises and agreements made in recent years by chocolate companies, they continue to use child labor in the production of their chocolate. We as consumers must communicate that this is unacceptable. •

To do so, we will first reveal the connection between chocolate and child slavery, second examine why the problem continues, and finally discover just how much power we have in bringing child slavery to an end.

How are chocolate and child slavery connected? •

Cocoa bean production is limited to areas near the equator, such as Central America, Indonesia, and the Ivory Coast. The International Cocoa Initiative website, last updated on February 8, 2007, explains that with almost a million acres devoted to growing cocoa, the Ivory Coast accounts for more than 40 percent of world cocoa production. According to a November 10, 2006, report by the *Vancouver Sun*, because growing cocoa is labor intensive and labor is a significant part of the cost of production, many farmers in the Ivory Coast have turned to using forced child labor to cut costs.

The conditions of these children are beyond comprehension. The International Cocoa Initiative details the hazards they face each day. They must work long hours in the fields in brutal conditions. They clear fields with machetes and apply pesticides without protective gear. After harvesting the cocoa pods, they must split them open with heavy knives. Once the beans are dried and bagged, they must carry these large loads long distances on their young backs.

Even more alarming is just how many children are forced to live this life. The *New York Times* of October 26, 2006, reports that more than 200,000 children in the Ivory Coast are forced to work in the cocoa fields. The *Chicago Tribune* of May 5, 2006, reports that in contrast to the rest of the world, this region of Africa has the highest rate of child laborers of all children five to fourteen years old; more than one in four are forced to work. Earth Save International, last updated February 14, 2007, says that these children are either enticed with promises of good wages and easy work or outright kidnapped. One example is a boy named Molique, who came to the Ivory

**•** Attention-getter: A shocking first-person quotation plus evidence that the problem is growing

**•** David connects with the audience and presents his thesis.

**•** Preview statement and transition to first main point

Coast at the age of fourteen. Despite the promises, he was never paid. When he asked to be paid, he was beaten. He had to scavenge for food and at night was locked up with the other kids. The *New York Times* of October 29, 2006, says that almost twelve thousand children in the Ivory Coast have been trafficked far from their families' homes and into slavery. •

• Combination of examples to build pathos and statistics to document the extent of the problem

The growing use of child slavery is reprehensible, but why is it allowed to continue? The answer is our widespread and growing demand for chocolate. •

• Transition to main point II

Unfortunately, child slavery continues because our demand for chocolate continues, enabling the Ivory Coast and the chocolate companies to ignore the problem. Farmers in the Ivory Coast invest in cocoa for its large profits. In order to maximize their gain, they cut costs by using the forced labor of children. These 600,000 farmers then turn to large export companies in the Ivory Coast to buy their cocoa. The *New York Times* of October 26, 2006, reports that these export companies are able to keep the price that they pay for cocoa low because they have so many farmers to choose from. The exporters then sell their cocoa to large chocolate companies, such as Hershey's, Nestle, M&M/Mars, and Cadbury. •

• Causal reasoning

The *Calgary Herald* of November 17, 2006, tells us that in 2001, almost all of the big chocolate companies signed the Harkin-Engel Protocol, agreeing that by 2005 they would certify that their chocolate was not tainted with child slavery; however, this deadline passed two years ago, with the companies making excuses and saying they need more time. But the September 20, 2006, *Seattle Post-Intelligencer* suggests that they're more concerned about the civil war in the Ivory Coast interfering with their supply of cocoa. Clearly, the civil war is also the top priority with the Ivory Coast government. The Associated Press on June 15, 2006, explains that the government doesn't want to interfere with the supply of cocoa because export taxes are its primary source of revenue. The government uses this money to buy military arms and equipment. The Ivory Coast may not have blood diamonds, but the nation certainly possesses blood chocolate. •

• Blood chocolate: a compelling analogy to blood diamonds

Ultimately, the blame rests on us because consumer demand for chocolate keeps the industry insulated from pressure. The World Cocoa Foundation website, last updated February 14, 2007, tells us that North America and Europe consume nearly two-thirds of all cocoa products and that demand for confectionary products containing chocolate rises 4 to 5 percent each year. The sad truth is that most consumers are not aware of chocolate's connection to child slavery. Because we continue to buy its chocolate, the industry feels no urgency to change. •

• Evidence shows that the speaker and audience members are part of the problem.

Now that we understand the problem and why it continues, we must ask what we can do, and the answer is simple. We must stop buying chocolate produced by forced labor.

But don't worry, I'm not suggesting that we stop buying chocolate altogether. There is an alternative, and it's called fair-trade chocolate. TransFair USA, a nonprofit organization, is the only independent third-party certifier of fair-trade products in the U.S. It allows companies to display the fair trade–certified label on products that meet strict standards. Some of these standards found on the organization's website, last updated November 16, 2006, include a prohibition on forced child labor, safe working conditions, living wages, environmentally safe farming methods, a guaranteed minimum price, and direct trade between the farmers and chocolate companies, thus eliminating the manipulative exporters. ●

> ● How the audience can be personally involved in the solution

If we as consumers change how we buy chocolate, the industry will have to respond. Currently, companies are trying to distance themselves from the bad press associated with forced labor, and as a result the Ontario *Guelph Mercury*, February 3, 2007, reports that some have begun to buy into the fair-trade market. For example, *Business Wire*, October 11, 2006, reports that Ben and Jerry's is expanding its fair trade–certified ice cream flavors. *Forbes* magazine, previously cited, says that fair trade has even made inroads into the Ivory Coast but still accounts for only about 1 percent of cocoa exports. ●

> ● David explains how one solution can reduce the problem.

Economics teaches us that demand controls supply; they can only sell what we buy. A perfect example of this is the industry's response to the rise in demand for organic food products. The *Boston Herald* on October 16, 2006, reports that organic food sales have risen more than 15 percent in the last two years. According to the September 20, 2006, *Sacramento Bee*, with a multibillion-dollar market, big companies like Walmart and Frito-Lay have made organic food mainstream. If we demand more fair-trade chocolate, the industry will have to supply it, and when the chocolate companies start buying more ethically produced cocoa, farmers in the Ivory Coast will have to abandon slavery to keep their buyers. ●

> ● Analogy to consumer-generated demand for organic products

Today we have exposed the connection between chocolate and child slavery, examined why the problem continues, and finally discovered how we can bring it to an end. The next time you go to buy chocolate, remember the words of a child, quoted in the November 10, 2006, *Toronto Star*: "When the rest of the world eats chocolate, they're eating my flesh." The Ivory Coast may be seven thousand miles away, but we have a responsibility to protect all children. Fair-trade chocolate may cost us a little more money, but that's a small price to pay to free thousands of children from slavery. ●

> ● The clincher includes another compelling quotation that connects to the introduction.

# SAMPLE PERSUASIVE SPEECH

## EXTRA CREDIT YOU CAN LIVE WITHOUT

### Anna Martinez
*California State University–Fresno*

*Student Anna Martinez selected student credit card debt as the topic of her persuasive speech. Based on her survey of the audience, she determined that it would not be feasible to argue that students should not use credit cards. She selected a different thesis that was within their latitude of acceptance—encouraging students to be more careful credit card consumers.*

*Anna's speech is targeted to an audience of college students, and she refers to information gleaned from a survey she conducted to support her points. Anna consistently uses evidence to support her claims, and she has organized her speech in the problem-cause-solution format.*

There is a dangerous product on our campus. It is marketed on tables outside the student union and advertised on the bulletin board in this classroom. Based on my audience survey, it is likely that most of you have this product in your possession right now. By the end of my speech, this product may be costing you more than it is right now. This dangerous product is credit cards. •

• Suspense-building attention-getter

Today I would like to discuss the problems created by college students' credit cards and hopefully persuade you to be a careful credit card consumer. If your credit card situation is anything like mine—and over two-thirds of this class indicated that they are currently carrying a balance on one or more cards—take note: you can save money.

My husband and I paid for our own wedding. More accurately, we used our credit cards to charge many of our wedding expenses. And thanks to Visa, we are still paying for our wedding every month! We have saved money with some of the suggestions I will present today, and you can do the same.

To that end, let's cover some of the problems created by students' credit card debt, then analyze the causes of the problem, and finally consider steps you can take to be a careful credit card consumer. •

• Anna includes her thesis, connects with the audience, establishes credibility, and previews her main points.

We'll start with a look at the problems created by these "hazardous products."

Credit card debt on campus is a significant and growing problem. Many students have credit card debt. According to Matthew Scott, in *Black Collegian*, April 2007, "College financial aid provider Nellie Mae reported that 76 percent of undergraduate students had credit cards in 2005, with an average balance of $2,169. An alarming 25 percent of undergraduates had credit card balances totaling $3,000 or more." In *Business Week*, September 5, 2007, Jessica Silver-Greenberg notes that "the freshman 15, a fleshy souvenir of beer and late-night pizza, is now taking on a new meaning, with some freshmen racking up more than $15,000 in credit card debt before they can legally drink." If you are not sure how your own balances compare, you are not alone. The previously mentioned Nellie Mae study found that the average balance reported by students was 47 percent lower than the average balance computed from data provided by credit bureaus. •

High credit card use can change our lives for the worse. According to the April 2007 *Black Collegian* article, Rhonda Reynolds of Bernard Baruch College built up $8,000 worth of debt and was unable to make even the minimum payment. Her account went into collections. *Business Week*, March 15, 1999, provided another example: Jason Britton, a senior at Georgetown University, accumulated $21,000 in debt over four years on sixteen cards! Jason reports, "When I first started, my attitude was 'I'll get a job after college to pay off all my debt.'" Then he realized that he was in a hole because he could not meet his minimum monthly payments. He had to obtain financial assistance from his parents and now works three part-time jobs. •

You probably do not owe $20,000 on your credit cards, but even smaller balances take their toll. Robert Frick, associate editor for *Kiplinger's Personal Finance* magazine, March 1997, states that if you make the minimum payments on a $500 balance at an 18 percent interest rate, it will take over seven years to pay off the loan and cost $365 in interest.

High credit card debt can also haunt your finances after you graduate. Matthew Scott, previously cited, notes that credit bureaus assign you a credit score, which is "your economic report card to the rest of the world." That score will "determine the interest rates you pay for many forms of credit and insurance." He also notes that prospective employers will check your credit score and use that number to decide whether or not you are responsible.

Many people in this class are carrying student loans, which will need to be paid back upon graduation. When you add credit card debt to student loan payments, rent, utilities, food, the payment on the new car you want to buy, family expenses, and so on, the toll can be heavy. Alan Blair, director of credit management for the New England Educational Loan Marketing Corporation, in a 1998 report on the corporation's website, notes serious consequences for students who cannot balance monthly expenses and debts, including

• Anna consistently uses research sources to support her points.

• Supporting material: examples

• Relating the problem
to a college audience

"poor credit ratings, inability to apply for car loans or a mortgage, collection activity, and at worst, a bankruptcy filing." •

Don't let this happen to you. After all that hard work earning a degree and finally landing a job where you don't have to wear a plastic name tag and induce people to get "fries with that," the last thing any of us needs is to be spending our hard-earned money paying off debt, being turned down for loans, or, worse yet, being harassed by collection agencies.

Credit card debt is hazardous to students' financial health, so why are these debts piling up? Let's move on to the causes of this problem. •

• Transition to main
point II

The reality is that credit card issuers want and aggressively seek the business of students like us. As Jessica Silver-Greenberg writes in her previously cited September 2007 article, "Over the next month, as 17 million college students flood the nation's campuses, they will be greeted by swarms of credit-card marketers. Frisbees, T-shirts, and even iPods will be used as enticements to sign up, and marketing on the Web will reinforce the message."

Card issuers actually troll for customers on campus because student business is profitable. Daniel Eisenberg, writer of the Your Money column for *Time* magazine, September 28, 1998, notes that "college students are suckers for free stuff, and many are collecting extra credit cards and heavier debts as a result." Eisenberg refers to a U.S. Public Interest Research Group survey, which found that students who sign up for cards at campus tables in return for "gifts" typically carry higher unpaid balances than do other students. Jessica Silver-Greenberg, in an October 15, 2007, *Business Week* article, writes that "college kids are a potential gold mine—one of the few growing customer segments in the saturated credit-card market. And they're loyal, eventually taking three additional loans, on average, with the bank that gives them their first card." •

• Supporting material:
explanation of why
card issuers market to
students

Companies use "sucker rates" to induce students to apply for credit. *Business Week*, March 15, 1999, writes that "credit card marketers may advertise a low annual percentage rate, but it often jumps substantially after three to nine months. First USA's student Visa has a 9.9% introductory rate that soars to 17.99% after five months. Teaser rates aren't unique to student cards, but a 1998 study by the Washington-based U.S. Public Interest Research Group found that 26% of college students found them misleading."

So it appears that credit card companies will not stop demanding student business anytime soon. What can we do about it?

My proposed solution is to be a careful credit card consumer.

Why not get rid of your credit cards before it's too late? All right, maybe you won't go for that solution. My survey indicated that most of you enjoy the flexibility in spending that credit cards provide. •

So here are some other ways you should be credit card smart. One practice is to shop carefully for the best credit card deals. The companies that are not spending their money giving away pizzas and iPods on campus may be able to offer you a better deal. In her September 5, 2007, *Business Week* article, Silver-Greenberg recommends that you beware of offers from South Dakota or Delaware corporations. Those states are "considered 'safe harbors' for credit card companies because they have no cap on interest rates or late payment [fees]."

A second solution is to read the fine print on credit card applications to learn what your actual interest rate will be. Alison Barros, a staff writer for the Lane Community College *Torch*, October 29, 1998, quotes Jonathan Woolworth, consumer protection director for the Oregon Public Interest Research Group, who wrote that "students need to read the fine print and find out how long those low interest rates last. Rates that are as low as 3% can jump to 18% within three months, and the credit card company doesn't want the student to know that."

Here is an example of the fine print on an ad that begins at 1.9 percent and soon rises. If you read the fine print, you note that the rate can rise to more than 20 percent. •

Third, even if you can only make the minimum payment on your cards, pay your bills on time. • Silver-Greenberg's September 5 article indicates that students' "credit scores can plunge particularly quickly, with one or two missed payments, because their track records are so short." She further cautions students to be aware of "universal default" provisions in their credit agreements. These provide that if you miss a payment on one card, other credit card companies can also raise your interest rate (even if you have paid those cards on time), perhaps to 30 percent. *Business Week*, March 15, 1999, cautions that "because students move often and may not get their mail forwarded quickly, bills can get lost. Then the students fall prey to late fees." •

Finally, you can keep money in your pocket and out of the credit card company's by paying attention to your credit report. If any agencies are "talking trash" about you with inaccurate information, be sure to have it corrected.

• Anna notes that her listeners are likely to reject her strongest suggestion. She then advocates a solution within her audience's latitude of acceptance.

• Anna shows a visual aid here.

• *Second* and *third* are examples of signposts.

• Adapting the solution to a college audience

• Internal summary of main point III

To sum up these solutions, even if you do not want to stop using credit cards, there are many ways to be a careful credit card consumer. Shop for a good rate, and be careful to read the fine print so you know what the rate really is. Know what you owe, and take the responsibility to make payments on time. •

• Summary of main points

This morning, we have learned about a hazardous product on campus—credit cards. We have noted the problem of high student credit card debt, analyzed some of the causes of this problem, and considered several methods for being a careful credit card consumer. •

• The clincher sums up Anna's speech with irony.

If your instructor offers you a chance for extra credit in their class, take advantage of the opportunity. But when a credit card issuer offers you a free T-shirt or phone card if you will sign up for their extra credit, just say no. When you pay off a credit card with a 19.9 percent interest rate, that "free" T-shirt could turn out to be the most expensive clothing you will ever buy. •

## Chapter 1

1. Testimony of Simone Biles, Senate Judiciary Committee Hearing, "Dereliction of Duty: Examining the Inspector General's Report on the FBI's Handling of the Larry Nassar Investigation," September 15, 2021, https://www.judiciary.senate.gov/meetings/dereliction-of-duty-examining-the-inspector-generals-report-on-the-fbis-handling-of-the-larry-nassar-investigation.

2. RAINN, "The Criminal Justice System: Statistics," 2022, https://www.rainn.org/statistics/criminal-justice-system. See also Testimony of Simone Biles.

3. National Association of Colleges and Employers (NACE), "Career Readiness for the New College Graduate: A Definition and Competences," 2017, https://www.naceweb.org/uploadedfiles/pages/knowledge/articles/career-readiness-fact-sheet.pdf.

4. R. H. Whitworth and C. Cochran, "Evaluation of Integrated versus Unitary Treatments for Reducing Public Speaking Anxiety," *Communication Education* 45 (1996): 306; D. J. DeNoon, "Help for Public-Speaking Anxiety," *CBS News Healthwatch*, April 20, 2006, http://www.cbsnews.com/stories/2006/04/20/health/webmd/main1523045.shtml.

5. M. Layton Turner, "Higher Ed's Digital Showcase: How Colleges and Universities Use ePortfolios to Promote the Work of Students and Institutions," *University Business*, May 25, 2016, https://www.universitybusiness.com/article/higher-eds-digital-showcase.

6. K. Gray, "The Attributes Employers Seek on Students' Resumes," NACE, April 19, 2021, https://www.naceweb.org/talent-acquisition/candidate-selection/the-attributes-employers-seek-on-students-resumes.

7. Heldrich Center for Workforce Development and Center for Survey Research and Analysis, *Making the Grade? What American Workers Think Should Be Done to Improve Education*, June 2000, http://www.heldrich.rutgers.edu/sites/default/files/products/uploads/Making_the_Grade.pdf, 14.

8. M. Feliú-Mójer, "Effective Communication, Better Science," *Scientific American*, February 24, 2015, https://blogs.scientificamerican.com/guest-blog/effective-communication-better-science/.

9. L. Gehrig, "C250 Celebrates Columbians ahead of Their Time," *Columbia 250*, 2004, http://c250.columbia.edu/c250_celebrates/remarkable_columbians/lou_gehrig.html.

10. J. Calfas, "This Is the Moment Sen. Tammy Duckworth and Her Baby Made History on the Senate Floor," TIME, April 19, 2018, https://time.com/5247060/tammy-duckworth-vote-baby-senate-floor.

11. L. S. O'Leary, "Civic Engagement in College Students: Connections between Involvement and Attitudes," *New Directions for Institutional Research* 162 (2014): 55, 61.

12. M. I. Finley, *Politics in the Ancient World* (New York: Cambridge University Press, 1983), 59, 73.

13. D. Bodde, *China's First Unifier* (Hong Kong: Hong Kong University Press, 1967), 181.

14. A. A. Boahen, "Kingdoms of West Africa," in *From Freedom to Freedom*, ed. M. Bain and E. Lewis (New York: Random House, 1977), 69.

15. G. Welch, "The Authors Who Talked," in Bain and Lewis, *From Freedom to Freedom*, 39.

16. R. T. Oliver, *Culture and Communication: The Problem of Penetrating National and Cultural Boundaries* (Springfield, IL: Charles C. Thomas, 1962), 141.

17. C. Brooks, R. W. B. Lewis, and R. P. Warren, *American Literature: The Makers and the Making*, vol. 1, *Beginnings to 1861* (New York: St. Martin's Press, 1973), 1179.

18. "Lincoln-Douglas Debates of 1858," *Illinois in the Civil War*, 2000, http://www.illinoiscivilwar.org/debates.html.

19. E. C. DuBois, *The Elizabeth Cady Stanton–Susan B. Anthony Reader* (Boston: Northeastern University Press, 1992), 8.

20. A. Ayres, ed., *The Wisdom of Martin Luther King, Jr.* (New York: Penguin Books, 1993).

21. H. Yang, "'We Need to Help Them': Asian Americans Demand Justice for George Floyd," MPRNews, June 11, 2020, https://www.mprnews.org/story/2020/06/09/we-need-to-help-them-asian-americans-demand-justice-for-george-floyd.

22. Pew Research Center, "Experts Say the 'New Normal' in 2025 Will Be Far More Tech–Driven, Presenting More Big Challenges," February 18, 2021, https://www.pewresearch.org/internet/2021/02/18/experts-say-the-new-normal-in-2025-will-be-far-more-tech-driven-presenting-more-big-challenges.

23. R. M. Berko, A. D. Wolvin, and D. R. Wolvin, *Communicating: A Social and Career Focus*, 3rd ed. (Boston: Houghton Mifflin, 1985), 42.

24. J. Stewart, *Bridges, Not Walls*, 7th ed. (New York: McGraw-Hill, 1999), 16.

25. M. W. Lustig and J. Koester, *Intercultural Competence: Interpersonal Communication across Cultures* (New York: HarperCollins, 1993), 31.

26. E. Bowman, "After Data Breach Exposes 530 Million, Facebook Says It Will Not Notify Users," NPR, April 9, 2021, https://www.npr.org/2021/04/09/986005820/after-data-breach-exposes-530-million-facebook-says-it-will-not-notify-users.

27. "Calvin Coolidge Delivers First Presidential Address on Radio," *New York Times*, December 6, 2011, http://learning.blogs.nytimes.com/2011/12/06/dec-6-1923-calvin-coolidge-delivers-first-presidential-address-on-radio; "First Presidential Speech on TV," http://www.history.com/this-day-in-history/first-presidential-speech-on-tv (accessed May 23, 2012).

28. N. Schwartz, "Zoom-Alternative Engageli Raises $33M to Grow its Digital Learning Platform," Higher Ed Dive, May 11, 2021, https://www.highereddive.com/news/zoom-alternative-engageli-raises-33m-to-grow-its-digital-learning-platform/599901.

29. M. Chang, "Why Face-to-Face Meetings Are So Important," *Forbes*, February 20, 2015, https://www.forbes.com/sites/ellevate/2015/02/20/why-face-to-face-meetings-are-so-important/#1fbbb53faee9.

30. J. H. Bodley, "An Anthropological Perspective," *What Is Culture?*, 1994, http://www.wsu.edu/gened/learn-modules/top_culture/culture-definitions/bodley-text.html.

31. U.S. Census Bureau, "Racial and Ethnic Diversity in the U.S.: 2010 Census and 2020 Census," August 12, 2021, https://www.census.gov/library/visualizations/interactive/race-and-ethnicity-in-the-united-state-2010-and-2020-census.html.

32. Pew Research Center, "Key Findings About U.S. Immigrants," August 20, 2020, https://www.pewresearch.org/fact-tank/2020/08/20/key-findings-about-u-s-immigrants/.

33. Human Rights Campaign, "Sexual Orientation and Gender Identity Definitions," https://www.hrc.org/resources/sexual-orientation-and-gender-identity-terminology-and-definitions, last visited October 9, 2021.

34. R. Picheta, "Demi Lovato Says They are Nonbinary and Changing Their Pronouns," CNN, May 19, 2021, https://www.cnn.com/2021/05/19/entertainment/demi-lovato-nonbinary-intl-scli/index.html.

35. J. Bell, *Evaluating Psychological Information: Sharpening Your Critical Thinking Skills*, 2nd ed. (Boston: Allyn and Bacon, 1995), 72, cited in J. Bell, *Critical Thinking as Described by Psychologists*, December 15, 1996, http://academic.pg.cc.md.us/~wpeirce/MCCCTR/bell1.html (accessed June 12, 2006).

36. Whitney v. California, 274 U.S. 357, 375 (1927).

37. National Communication Association, *What Should a Graduate with a Communication Degree Know, Understand, and Be Able to Do?* (Washington, DC: National Communication Association, 2015), https://www.natcom.org/sites/default/files/publications/LOC_1_What_Should_a_Graduate_with_a_Communication_Degree.pdf.

38. National Communication Association, "Credo for Ethical Communication," 2017, https://www.natcom.org/sites/default/files/Public_Statement_Credo_for_Ethical_Communication_2017.pdf.

39. P. Bizzell and B. Herzberg, *The Rhetorical Tradition* (Boston: Bedford/St. Martin's, 1990), 35.

40. M. Brenan, "Americans' Confidence in Major U.S. Institutions Dips," GALLUP, July 14, 2021, https://news.gallup.com/poll/352316/americans-confidence-major-institutions-dips.aspx.

41. Penn State University Libraries, "What Is Fake News," July 9, 2018, http://guides.libraries.psu.edu/fakenews.

## Chapter 2

1. L. G. Davis, *I Have a Dream: The Life and Times of Martin Luther King, Jr.* (Westport, CT: Greenwood Press, 1973).

2. A. Ayres, ed., *The Wisdom of Martin Luther King, Jr.* (New York: Penguin Books, 1993).

3. Davis, *I Have a Dream*, 137.

4. K. D. Miller and E. M. Lewis, "Touchstones, Authorities, and Marian Anderson: The Making of 'I Have a Dream,'" in *The Making of Martin Luther King and the Civil Rights Movement*, ed. B. Ward and T. Badger (New York: New York University Press, 1996), 151.

5. Ayres, *Wisdom of Martin Luther King, Jr.*, 62–63.

6. E. Rothstein, "A Resonance That Shaped a Vision of Freedom," *New York Times*, June 29, 2006, B7.

7. J. F. Wilson and C. C. Arnold, *Public Speaking as a Liberal Art*, 3rd ed. (Boston: Allyn and Bacon, 1974), 337.

8. P. Bizzell and B. Herzberg, *The Rhetorical Tradition* (Boston: Bedford/St. Martin's, 1990), 32, 310.

9. J. B. Taylor, "My Stroke of Insight," TED 2008, https://www.ted.com/talks/jill_bolte _taylor_s_powerful_stroke_of_insight.

10. C. Gallo, "The Best Ted Speakers Practice This 1 Habit before Taking the Stage," *Inc.*, March 7, 2017, https://www.inc.com/carmine-gallo/the-best-ted-speakers -practice-this-1-habit-before-taking-the-stage.html.

11. K. K. Dwyer and M. M. Davidson, "Is Public Speaking Really More Feared Than Death?," *Communication Research Reports* 29, no. 2 (2012): 106.

12. H. Liao, "Examining the Role of Collaborative Learning in a Public Speaking Course," *College Teaching* 62, no. 2 (2014): 47–54, https://doi.org/10.1080/8756755 5.2013.855891.

13. Dwyer and Davidson, "Is Public Speaking Really More Feared Than Death?," 100.

14. K. E. Menzel and L. J. Carrell, "The Relationship between Preparation and Performance in Public Speaking," *Communication Education* 43, no. 1 (1994): 17, 24.

15. R. R. Behnke and C. R. Sawyer, "Milestones of Anticipatory Public Speaking Anxiety," *Communication Education* 48, no. 2 (1999): 165, 171.

16. J. C. McCroskey, *An Introduction to Rhetorical Communication* (Englewood Cliffs, NJ: Prentice-Hall, 1986), 31.

17. A. N. Finn, C. R. Sawyer, and P. Schrodt, "Examining the Effect of Exposure Therapy on Public Speaking State Anxiety," *Communication Education* 58, no. 1 (2009): 92–109, 104.

18. S. Beilock, *Choke: What the Secrets of the Brain Reveal about Getting It Right when You Have To* (New York: Atria, 2010), 244.

19. G. Fauville, M. Luo, A. Queiroz, J. Bailenson, and J. Hancock, "Nonverbal Mechanisms Predict Zoom Fatigue and Explain Why Women Experience Higher Levels than Men," *SSRN Electronic Journal* (January 2021), http://dx.doi.org /10.2139/ssrn.3820035.

20. C. Rodriguez and C. Telloian, "Zoom Anxiety is More Common Than You Think: Here's Why," *PsychCentral,* June 25, 2021, https://psychcentral.com/anxiety/zoom -anxiety-is-more-common-than-you-think-heres-why.

21. C. W. Choi, J. M. Honeycutt, and G. D. Bodie, "Effects of Imagined Interactions and Rehearsal on Speaking Performance," *Communication Education* 64, no. 1 (2015): 25–44, https://doi.org/10.1080/03634523.2014.978795.

22. Choi, Honeycutt, and Bodie, "Effects", 41.

23. J. Ayres, "Comparing Self-Constructed Visualization Scripts with Guided Visualization," *Communication Reports* 8 (1995): 193–99.

24. E. Nanou, "The 7 Best Apps to Beat Your Fear of Public Speaking," MUO, April 21, 2021, https://www.makeuseof.com/apps-to-beat-fear-of-public-speaking.

25. C. R. Sawyer and R. R. Behnke, "State Anxiety Patterns for Public Speaking and the Behavior Inhibition System," *Communication Reports* 12 (1999): 34.

26. D. D. Deiters, S. Stevens, C. Hermann, and A. L. Gerlach, "Internal and External Attention in Speech Anxiety," *Journal of Behavior Therapy and Experimental Psychiatry* 44, no. 2 (2013): 143–49, https://doi.org/http://dx.doi.org/10.1016/j .jbtep.2012.09.001.

27. C.-F. Hsu, "The Relationships of Trait Anxiety, Audience Nonverbal Feedback, and Attributions to Public Speaking State Anxiety," *Communication Research Reports* 26, no. 3 (2009): 237–46, 244.

## Chapter 3

1. See C. G. Christians, "Primordial Issues in Communication Ethics," in *The Handbook of Global Communication and Communication Ethics*, ed. R. S. Fortner (Hoboken, NJ: Blackwell, 2011), 5: "For cultural relativism, morality is a social product. Whatever the majority in a given culture approves is a social good. Since all cultures are presumed to be equal in principle, all value systems are equally valid. Cultural relativity now typically means moral relativism. Contrary to an ethnocentrism of judging other groups against a dominant Western model[,] other cultures are not considered inferior[,] only different."

2. *Black's Law Dictionary*, 9th ed. (2009), s.v. "plagiarism."

3. See N. Granitz and D. Loewy, "Applying Ethical Theories: Interpreting and Responding to Student Plagiarism," *Journal of Business Ethics* 72 (2007): 293: "Through online paper mills (http://www.cheater.com, http://www.schoolsucks .com), Google searches, as well as access to library databases, students literally have a world of information at their fingertips."

4. N. P. Lewis and B. Zhong, "The Personality of Plagiarism," *Journalism and Mass Communication Educator* 66 (December 2011): 327; J. M. Stephens, M. F. Young, and T. Calabrese, "Does Moral Judgment Go Offline When Students Are Online? A Comparative Analysis of Undergraduates' Beliefs and Behaviors Related to Conventional and Digital Cheating," *Ethics and Behavior* 17 (July 2007): 233–54.

5. United States National Park Service, "History Continued," *Statue of Liberty National Monument*, August 14, 2006, http://www.nps.gov/stli/historyculture /history-continued.htm (accessed May 16, 2013).

## Chapter 4

1. J. Stewart, *Bridges Not Walls*, 4th ed. (New York: Random House, 1986), 181.

2. G. D. Bodie, D. Worthington, M. Imhof, and L. O. Cooper, "What Would a Unified Field of Listening Look Like? A Proposal Linking Past Perspectives and Future Endeavors," *International Journal of Listening* 22 (2008): 105. For more on this, see also B. R. Burelson, "A Constructivist Approach to Listening," *International Journal of Listening* 25 (2011): 27–41. Burelson describes listening as "a process that involves the interpretation of messages that others have intentionally transmitted in an effort to understand those messages and respond to them appropriately" (27).

3. L. K. Steil, "Listening Training: The Key to Success in Today's Organizations," in *Listening in Everyday Life: A Personal and Professional Approach*, ed. M. Purdy and D. Borisoff (Lanham, MD: University Press of America, 1997), 215.

4. Steil, "Listening Training," 215.

5. O. Hargie, *Skilled Interpersonal Communication: Research, Theory and Practice* (New York: Routledge, 2011), 179–81.

6. Hargie, *Skilled Interpersonal Communication*, 180; J. D. Boudreau, E. Cassell, and A. Fuks, "Preparing Medical Students to Become Attentive Listeners," *Medical Teacher* 31 (2009): 22–29.

7. Study by TCC Consulting (San Francisco), undertaken between 1987 and 1997.

8. M. K. Johnston, J. B. Weaver, K. W. Watson, and L. B. Barker, "Listening Styles: Biological or Psychological Differences?," *International Journal of Listening* 14 (2000): 36; E. Langer, "Rethinking the Role of Thought in Human Interaction," in *New Directions in Attribution Research*, vol. 2, ed. H. Hurvey, W. Ickes, and R. Kidd (Hillside, NJ: Erlbaum 1980), 35–38.

9. Johnston et al., "Listening Styles," 37.

10. K. W. Watson and L. L. Barker, *The Listening Style Inventory* (New Orleans: SPECTRA, 1985).

11. K. Watson, L. Barker, and J. Weaver, "The Listening Styles Profile (LPP16): Development and Validation of an Instrument to Assess Four Listening Styles," *International Journal of Listening* 9 (1995): 1–13.

12. Johnston et al., "Listening Styles," 37.

13. G. Artyushina and O. A. Sheypak, "Mobile Phones Help Develop Listening Skills," *Informatics* 5, no. 32 (2018): 1–7; S. Parasuraman, A. T. Sam, S. W. Lee, B. L. Chik Chuon, and L. Y. Ren, "Smartphone Usage and Increased Risk of Mobile Phone Addiction: A Concurrent Study," *International Journal of Pharmaceutical Investigation* 7, no. 3 (2017): 125–31.

14. S. Turkle, *Reclaiming Conversation: The Power of Talk in a Digital Age* (New York: Penguin Books, 2015).

15. M. Kho and S. Ting, "Oral Communication Apprehension in Oral Presentation among Polytechnic Students," *Human Behavior Development & Society,* 22, no. 2 (2021): 17–26.

## Chapter 5

1. See D. Paul-Pertaub, M. Slater, and C. Barker, "An Experiment on Public Speaking Anxiety in Response to Three Different Types of Virtual Audience," *Presence* 11, no. 1 (2002): 69: "The smaller the size of the audience, the more the interaction approximates a conversational paradigm."

2. For more on using demographics to craft messages, see D. Therkelsen and C. Fiebach, "Message to Desired Action: A Communication Effectiveness Model," *Journal of Communication Management* 5, no. 4 (2001): 376.

3. K. T. Jones, "Instructor's Corner #2: What Presidential Speeches Can Teach Us about Audience Analysis," *Communication Currents* 10, no. 3 (June 2015), https://www.natcom.org/communication-currents/instructors-corner-2-what-presidential-speeches-can-teach-us-about-audience: "Good audience analysis begins with a clear demographic assessment—age, sex, religion, socio-economic status, etc. From this basic assessment, the speaker develops a psychological profile of the audience that identifies beliefs, attitudes and values."

4. Human Rights Campaign, "Sexual Orientation and Gender Identity Definitions," https://www.hrc.org/resources/sexual-orientation-and-gender-identity-terminology-and-definitions, last visited October 9, 2021.

5. GLAAD, "Transgender FAQ," https://www.glaad.org/transgender/transfaq, last visited December 18, 2021.

6. S. Sokol, "Pope Francis: Attacks on Jews Are Anti-Semitism, as Are Attacks on Israel," October 28, 2015, http://www.jpost.com/Diaspora /Jews-Catholics-celebrate-50th-anniversary-of-Nostra-Aetate-430321.

7. Although Obama and Romney often spoke about middle-class job creation and economic growth, they rarely mentioned the existing poverty rate. See, for example, B. C. Calvan, "Little Mentioned on Trail, Poverty Widening in US," *Boston Globe*, September 10, 2012, http://www.bostonglobe.com/news /politics/2012/09/09/for-advocates-country-poor-presidential-campaign-gives -little-clarity-addressing-poverty/sZhd9i4Z0gMGahFKxknDXM/story.html.

8. A. Chozick, "Middle Class Is Disappearing, at Least from Vocabulary of Possible 2016 Contenders," *New York Times*, May 11, 2015, http://www.nytimes .com/2015/05/12/us/politics/as-middle-class-fades-so-does-use-of-term-on -campaign-trail.html?_r = 0.

9. Common ground is critical not only because it enhances a speaker's credibility but also because it makes a speech easier to understand. See S. R. Fussell and R. M. Krauss, "Understand Friends and Strangers: The Effects of Audience Design on Message Comprehension," *European Journal of Social Psychology* 19 (1989): 510.

10. For more, see J. S. Tuman, *Communicating Terror: The Rhetorical Dimensions of Terrorism*, 2nd ed. (Thousand Oaks, CA: Sage, 2010), 113: "Another audience-centered question the creator of the speech may ask is 'Has the audience heard the speech message before?' This is also known 'prior exposure' . . . and it deals with whether the audience has already been exposed to the speech message and has formed some kind of opinion or position in response."

11. For more on this speech, go to http://www.americanrhetoric.com/speeches /tedkennedytruth&tolerance.htm.

12. See J. White, "Edward Kennedy's 1983 Speech at Liberty Articulated View of Faith," August 25, 2009, https://baptistnews.com/article /edwardkennedys1983speechatlibertyarticulatedviewoffaith/#.XEDi8VxKg2x.

## Chapter 6

1. S. Liu, "Catching FIRE: Seven Strategies to Ignite Your Team's Creativity," *Quality Progress* 47, no. 5 (2014): 18–24.

2. M. Christova, H. Aftenberger, R. Nardone, and E. Gallasch, "Adult Gross Motor Learning and Sleep: Is There a Mutual Benefit?" *Neural Plasticity* 2018 (August 2018): 1–12. https://doi.org/10.1155/2018/3076986.

3. Illumine Training, "How to Make a Mind Map," 2015, https://www.illumine.co.uk /resources/mind-mapping/how-to-make-a-mind-map.

4. B. Kirchner, "Mind-Map Your Way to an Idea: Here Is One Approach to Rooting Out Workable Topics That Move You," *Writer* 122, no. 3 (2009): 28–29.

5. B. Aston, "Mapping Software of 2021," *Digital Project Manager,* March 1, 2021, https://thedigitalprojectmanager.com/mind-mapping-software.

6. C. Frey, "2017 Mindmapping Software Trends Survey," https:// mindmappingsoftwareblog.com/wp-content/reports/2017_MMS_Trends_Survey _Report.pdf.

7. J. F. Wilson and C. C. Arnold, *Public Speaking as a Liberal Art*, 3rd ed. (Boston: Allyn and Bacon, 1974), 70–71.

## Chapter 7

1. R. D. Rieke and M. O. Sillars, *Argumentation and Critical Decision Making*, 5th ed. (New York: Addison Wesley Longman, 2001), 136.

2. E. O'Carroll, "After a 'Post Truth' Presidency, Can America Make Facts Real Again?" *Christian Science Monitor,* February 4, 2021, https://www.csmonitor.com/Science/2021/0204/After-a-post-truth-presidency-can-America-make-facts-real-again.

3. A. Guess and A. Coppock, "Does Counter-Attitudinal Information Cause Backlash? Results from Three Large Survey Experiments," *British Journal of Political Science* 50 (2020): 1497, 1515.

4. J. C. Reinard, *Foundations of Argument* (Dubuque, IA: Brown, 1991), 113.

5. E. Brynjolfsson, L. M. Hitt, and H. H. Kim, "Strength in Numbers: How Does Data-Driven Decisionmaking Affect Firm Performance?" working paper, April 22, 2011, http://ssrn.com/abstract = 1819486.

6. Brynjolfsson, Hitt, and Kim, "Strength in Numbers"; J. Livingston, "The Secret of Successful Business Is Data-Driven Decision-Making," CIO, October 3, 2017, www.cio.com/article/3229853/cio-role/the-secret-of-successful-business-is-data-driven-decision-making.html.

7. K. Bierce, "The Rise of the Data-Driven Nonprofit," *Philanthropy News Digest,* January 22, 2021, https://philanthropynewsdigest.org/columns/techsoup-pnd/the-rise-of-the-data-driven-nonprofit.

8. H. Howard, S. Huber, L. Carter, and E. Moore, "Academic Libraries on Social Media: Finding the Students and the Information They Want," *Information Technologies and Libraries* 37, no. 1 (March 2018): 8.

9. American Library Association, *State of America's Libraries Special Report: COVID-19,* April 2021, https://www.ala.org/news/sites/ala.org.news/files/content/State-of-Americas-Libraries-Report-2021.pdf.

10. J. P. Biddix, J. C. Chung, and H. W. Park, "Convenience or Credibility? A Study of College Student Online Research Behaviors," *Internet and Education* 14 (2011): 176.

11. S. Miller and N. Murillo, "Why Don't Students Ask Librarians for Help? Undergraduate Help-Seeking Behaviors in Three Academic Libraries," in *College Libraries and Student Culture: What We Now Know,* ed. L. Duke and A. Asher (Chicago: American Library Association, 2012), 53.

12. Association of College and Research Libraries, *Academic Library Impact on Student Learning and Success* (Chicago: Association of College and Research Libraries, 2017): 13–15.

13. Reinard, *Foundations of Argument,* 115.

14. N. Pastore and M. W. Horowitz, "The Influence of Attributed Motive on the Acceptance of a Statement," *Journal of Abnormal and Social Psychology* 51 (1955): 331–32.

15. National Center for Education Statistics, *Fast Facts: Distance Learning,* https://nces.ed.gov/fastfacts/display.asp?id = 80, last accessed November 12, 2021.

16. J. Moody, "The Coronavirus and College This Fall," *U.S. News and World Report,* July 27, 2021, https://www.usnews.com/education/best-colleges/slideshows/what-the-coronavirus-means-for-the-college-experience-this-fall

17. A. J. Head, *Learning the Ropes: How Freshmen Conduct Course Research Once They Enter College*, Project Information Literacy Research Report, December 5, 2013, 10, 13, http://www.projectinfolit.org/uploads/2/7/5/4/27541717/pil_2013 _freshmenstudy_fullreportv2.pdf.

18. K. McLaughlin, "America's Local Newspapers Might Be Broke—but They're More Vital Than Ever," *Guardian*, September 11, 2017, https://www.theguardian.com /us-news/2017/sep/11/inequality-local-news-outlets-journalism-media-reporting.

19. "Defenseless: Investigating the Only State Without Public Defenders," *ProPublica*, 2021, https://www.propublica.org/series/defenseless.

20. C. Allison et al., "An Analysis of Student Internet Usage and Its Impact on the Infrastructure of a School's Information Technology Services," May 6, 2016, http://csis.pace.edu/~ctappert/srd2016/2016PDF/d7.pdf

21. K. Soria, J. Fransen, and S. Nackerud, "Beyond Books: Academic Benefits of Library Use for First-Year College Students," *College and Research Libraries* 78, no. 1 (January 2017): 8–22; Primary Research Group, *The Survey of American College Students: Who Goes to the College Library and Why?*, April 2009.

22. C. Petrov, "25+ Impressive Big Data Statistics for 2021," *Techjury*, November 1, 2021, https://techjury.net/blog/big-data-statistics/#gref.

23. Poorvu Center for Teaching and Learning, "Scholarly vs. Popular Sources," 2021, https://poorvucenter.yale.edu/undergraduates/using-sources/principles-citing -sources/scholarly-vs-popular-sources.

24. M. J. Metzger, A. J. Flanagin, and L. Zwarun, "College Student Web Use, Perceptions of Information Credibility, and Verification Behavior," *Computers and Education* 41, no. 3 (November 2003): 271–90.

25. D. Westerman, P. R. Spence, and B. Van Der Heide, "A Social Network as Information: The Effect of System Generated Reports of Connectedness on Credibility on Twitter," *Computers in Human Behavior* 28, no. 1 (2012): 199–206.

26. W. L. Lym, "Tempting Students with Scholarly Research: Breaking the Fast-Food Research Diet," *College Teaching* 57 (Fall 2009): 237.

27. B. Swire-Thompson and David Lazer, "Public Health and Online Misinformation: Challenges and Recommendations," *Annual Review of Public Health*, 41 (2020): 433–51.

28. O. G. El Jassar, I. N. El Jassar, and E. Kritsotakis, "Assessment of Quality of Information Available Over the Internet About Vegan Diet," *Nutrition and Food Science*, 49, no. 6 (2019): 1142–1152.

29. K. D. Boatright and M. L. Sperry, "Accuracy of Medical Marijuana Claims Made by Popular Websites," *Journal of Pharmacy Practice*, 33, no. 4 (2020): 457–64.

30. N. Yu, Q. Xu, S. Chen, and Y. Song, "Are You Passing Along Something True or False? Dissemination of GMO Messages on Social Media," *Public Understanding of Science*, 30, no. 3 (2021): 285–301.

31. American Bar Association, "Obtaining and Protecting Domain Names," September 26, 2016, https://www.americanbar.org/groups/business_law /safeselling/domains.

32. D. Pinsky, "8 Smart Tips for Choosing a Winning Domain Name," *Forbes*, April 10, 2017, https://www.forbes.com/sites/denispinsky/2017/04/10/domain /#6f885f244b4f.

33. M. Walker and K. E. Matsa, "News Consumption Across Social Media in 2021," *Pew Research Center,* September 20, 2021, https://www.pewresearch.org /journalism/2021/09/20/news-consumption-across-social-media-in-2021.

34. G. L. Ciampaglia and F. Menczer, "Misinformation and Biases Infect Social Media, Both Intentionally and Accidentally," *The Conversation,* June 20, 2018, https:// theconversation.com/misinformation-and-biases-infect-social-media-both -intentionally-and-accidentally-97148.

35. S. Brown, "MIT Sloan Research About Social Media, Misinformation, and Elections," October 5, 2020, https://mitsloan.mit.edu/ideas-made-to-matter /mit-sloan-research-about-social-media-misinformation-and-elections.

36. A. R. Brown, "Wikipedia as a Data Source for Political Scientists: Accuracy and Completeness of Coverage," *PS: Political Science and Politics* 44, no. 2 (2011): 339.

37. Brown, "Wikipedia," 340.

38. C. Royal and D. Kapila, "What's on Wikipedia, and What's Not . . . ?," *Social Science Computer Review* 27, no. 1 (2009): 146.

39. *Wikipedia,* s.v. "Wikipedia: Academic Use," last edited February 17, 2021, https:// en.wikipedia.org/wiki/Wikipedia:Academic_use.

40. BBC, "How Do Search Engines Work?" Bitesize, accessed December 22, 2018, https://www.bbc.com/bitesize/articles/ztbjq6f.

41. J. Johnson, "Global Market Share of Search Engines," *Statista,* October 8, 2021, https://www.statista.com/statistics/216573/worldwide-market-share-of -search-engines.

42. M. Naudascher, "Conducting Interviews Over Zoom? Here Are Some Tips," *International Journalists Network,* April 5, 2021, https://ijnet.org/en/story /conducting-interviews-over-zoom-here-are-some-tips.

43. N. Ndugga and S. Artiga, "Extreme Heat and Racial Health Equity," *Kaiser Family Foundation,* September 8, 2021, https://www.kff.org/policy-watch/extreme-heat -racial-health-equity.

44. J. L. Lawless and R. L. Fox, *Girls Just Wanna Not Run: The Gender Gap in Young Americans' Political Ambition* (Washington D.C.: Women & Politics Institute, March 2013), ii.

## Chapter 8

1. K. E. Rowan, "A New Pedagogy for Explanatory Public Speaking: Why Arrangement Should Not Substitute for Invention," *Communication Education* 44, no. 3 (1995): 236, 241.

2. American Institute of Mathematics, "$E_8$ and Physics," site visited December 20, 2021, https://aimath.org/E8/e8andphysics.html.

3. J. Maddox, "A Further String to the Believers' Bow," *Nature,* 398, no. 6730 (April 29, 1999): 797.

4. C. Heath and D. Heath, *Made to Stick: Why Some Ideas Survive and Others Die* (New York: Random House, 2007), 110–11.

5. Heath and Heath, 111.

6. C. C. Mann, *1491: New Revelations of the Americas before Columbus* (New York: Knopf, 2005), 345–49.

7. J. A. Herrick, *Understanding and Shaping Arguments* (State College, PA: Strata Press, 2011), 44.

8. T. Li, "Privacy in Pandemic: Law, Technology, and Public Health in the COVID-19 Crisis," *Loyola University Chicago Law Journal* 52 (2021): 792.

9. D. Gershgorn, "21 States Are Now Vetting Unemployment Claims With a 'Risky' Facial Recognition System," *OneZero,* February 3, 2021, https://onezero.medium .com/21-states-are-now-vetting-unemployment-claims-with-a-risky-facial -recognition-system-85c9ad882b60

10. Li, 781–82.

11. J. Schuppe, "Undercover Cops Break Facebook Rules to Track Protesters, Ensnare Criminals," *NBC News,* October 5, 2018, https://www.nbcnews.com /news/us-news/undercover-cops-break-facebook-rules-track-protesters-ensnare -criminals-n916796.

12. *Cambridge Dictionaries Online*, s.v. "Zoroastrianism," accessed January 31, 2007, http://dictionary.cambridge.org.

13. M. Boyce, *Zoroastrians: Their Religious Beliefs and Practices* (London: Routledge, 1979), 2.

14. Boyce, 2.

15. Ontario Consultants on Religious Tolerance, "Zoroastrianism," ReligiousTolerance .org, March 24, 2005, http://www.religioustolerance.org/zoroastr.htm.

16. J. Ma and M. Pender, *Trends in College Pricing and Student Aid* (New York: College Board, 2021), 11.

17. J. Reinard, *Foundations of Argument* (Dubuque, IA: Brown, 1991), 111.

18. Ma and Pender, *Trends in College Pricing*, 13.

19. W. R. Fisher, *Human Communication as Narration: Toward a Philosophy of Reason, Value, and Action* (Columbia: University of South Carolina Press, 1987).

20. K. Houston, "Food Truck Stolen From Local Business Students," *8 News Now*, December 12, 2021, https://www.8newsnow.com/news/local-news/food-truck -stolen-from-local-business-students.

21. 8 NewsNow Staff, " 'Amigo Taco' Food Truck Returned to Family Days After It Was Stolen," *8 News Now,* December 14, 2021, https://www.8newsnow.com/news/local -news/amigo-taco-food-truck-returned-to-family-days-after-it-was-stolen.

22. C. Dean, "In Road-Building, Black Soldiers Defied Prejudice," *New York Times*, July 24, 2012, D4.

23. C. McCombie, "Explaining Bitcoin to the Masses: A Glass Box Analogy," *CoinTelegraph,* May 22, 2016, https://cointelegraph.com/news/explaining -bitcoin-to-the-masses-a-glass-box-analogy.

24. Rowan, "New Pedagogy," 245.

25. N. Shute, "How Analogies Can Make Complex Science Clear," *Science News,* November 15, 2021, https://www.sciencenews.org/article/how-analogies-can -make-complex-science-clear.

26. Shute.

27. Shute.

28. "New Data from Virginia Tech Transportation Institute Provides Insight into Cell Phone Use and Driving Distraction," Virginia Tech Transportation Institute, July 29, 2009, https://vtnews.vt.edu/articles/2009/07/2009-571.html.

29.  "Can Abstract Imagery Tell a Story?" *Art 21,* 2021, https://art21.org/read /conversation-starter-can-abstract-imagery-tell-a-story.

## Chapter 9

1.  J. C. McCroskey, *An Introduction to Rhetorical Communication,* 5th ed. (Englewood Cliffs, NJ: Prentice Hall, 1986), 185.
2.  J. C. McCroskey, "The Effects of Disorganization and Nonfluency on Attitude Change and Source Credibility," *Speech Monographs* 36 (March 1969): 13–21; and H. Sharp Jr. and T. McClung, "Effect of Organization on the Speaker's Ethos," *Speech Monographs* 33 (June 1966): 182–83.
3.  D. Leung, "Electronic Whiteboard Options for Online Lectures," *Teaching Hub,* September 23, 2020, https://teachinghub.as.ua.edu/faculty-blog/large-courses /electronic-whiteboard-options-for-online-lectures-ipad-zoom-or-blackboard -collaborate-ultra.
4.  D. Taylor, "America's Bald Eagle Population Has Quadrupled," *New York Times,* March 25, 2021, https://www.nytimes.com/2021/03/25/climate/how-many-bald -eagles-united-states.html.
5.  C. S. Hemphill and J. Suk, "The Law, Culture, and Economics of Fashion," *Stanford Law Review* 61 (March 2009): 1147–99, 1158, 1168.
6.  A. Arora, P. Dahlstron, E. Hazan, H. Khan, and R. Khanna, "Reimagining Marketing in the Next Normal," *McKinsey & Company,* July 19, 2020, https://www.mckinsey .com/business-functions/marketing-and-sales/our-insights/reimagining-marketing -in-the-next-normal.
7.  K. Cartier, "New Exoplanet Telescope Detects Its First Two Planets," *Eos* 99 (September 25, 2018), https://doi.org/10.1029/2018EO106663.

## Chapter 10

1.  P. Bizzell and B. Herzberg, *The Rhetorical Tradition* (New York: St. Martin's Press, 1990), 429; K. K. Campbell, *The Rhetorical Act,* 2nd ed. (Belmont, CA: Wadsworth, 1996), 264–65.
2.  L. T. Yearwood, "Being Homeless Cost Me $54,000," *New York Times,* January 2, 2022, p. 10.
3.  A. Mehta, "Where Do Your Online Returns Go?" *TED@UPS,* July 2018, https:// www.ted.com/talks/aparna_mehta_where_do_your_online_returns_go.
4.  S. Colbert, "Quotes," *Goodreads,* https://www.goodreads.com/quotes/143405 -wikipedia-is-the-first-place-i-go-when-i-m-looking, site last visited, January 12, 2019.
5.  B. Cowgill, V. Perez, E. Gerdes, A. Sadda, C. Ly, W. Slusser and A. Leung, "Get Up, Stand Up, Stand Up for Your Health! Faculty and Student Perspectives on Addressing Prolonged Sitting in University Settings," *Journal of American College Health* 69 no. 2 (2021): 198–207.
6.  M. al-Sharif, "The Drive for Freedom," Speech, Oslo Freedom Forum, May 8, 2012, http://www.oslofreedomforum.com/speakers/manal-al-sharif.html.
7.  S. Ride, "Shoot for the Stars," May 25, 2012, http://eloquentwoman.blogspot .com/2012/05/famous-speech-friday-sally-rides-shoot.html.
8.  R. Clark, *Einstein: The Life and Times* (London: Hodder and Stoughton, 1973), 26.

## Chapter 12

1. J. R. Biden, Jr., "A Proclamation on National Black History Month, 2022," The White House Briefing Room, January 31, 2022, https://www.whitehouse.gov /briefing-room/presidential-actions/2022/01/31/a-proclamation-on-national-black -history-month-2022.

2. G. Washington, "Proclamation—National Day of Thanksgiving," October 3, 1789, *The American Presidency Project,* https://www.presidency.ucsb.edu/documents/ proclamation-day-national-thanksgiving.

3. Online Etymology Dictionary, "Jam," https://www.etymonline.com/word/jam, accessed February 22, 2022.

4. The Equality Act, H.R. 5, 116<sup>th</sup> Congress (2019–2020), *CONGRESS.GOV,* https:// www.congress.gov/bill/116th-congress/house-bill/5.

5. Rev. Dr. D. Wiley, *The Equality Act: Hearing on H.R. 5, Before the Committee on the Judiciary,* 116<sup>th</sup> Congress, April 2, 2019, https://docs.house.gov/meetings/JU /JU00/20190402/109200/HHRG-116-JU00-Wstate-WileyD-20190402.pdf.

6. K. Yoshino, *The Equality Act: Hearing on H.R. 5, Before the Committee on the Judiciary,* 116<sup>th</sup> Congress, April 2, 2019, https://docs.house.gov/meetings/JU /JU00/20190402/109200/HHRG-116-JU00-Wstate-YoshinoK-20190402.pdf.

7. See, for example, K. Murdock, "Recovering the Classical in the Common: Figures of Speech in 'A Scandal in Bohemia,'" *Minnesota English Journal* 47 (2012): 85–89; "Figures of Speech," ChangingMinds.org, http://www.changingminds.org /techniques/language/figures_speech/figures_speech.htm; and J. I. Liontas, "Exploring Figurative Language across the Curriculum," Wiley Online Library, January 18, 2018, https://doi.org/10.1002/9781118784235.eelt0755.

8. Politicians often use antithesis in their speeches. See, for example, Q. Zhou and B. Kazemian, "A Rhetorical Identification Analysis of English Political Public Speaking: John F. Kennedy's Inaugural Address," in "Critical Discourse Analysis, Rhetoric, and Grammatical Metaphor in Political and Advertisement Discourses," special issue, *International Journal of Language and Linguistics* 4, no. 1 (2015): 10–16, https://doi.org/10.11648/j.ijll.s.2016040101.12.

9. For more on metaphors, see B. Forgács et al., "Metaphors Are Physical and Abstract: ERPs to Metaphorically Modified Nouns Resemble ERPs to Abstract Language," *Frontiers in Human Neuroscience* 9 (February 2015): 28, https:// doi.org/10.3389/fnhum.2015.00028.

10. C. R. Jorgensen-Earp and A. Q. Staton, "Student Metaphors for the College Freshman Experience," *Communication Education* 42, no. 2 (1993): 125.

11. L. Matthews, "Here's the Full Transcript of Angela Davis's Women's March Speech," *ELLE,* January 21, 2017, https://www.elle.com/culture/career-politics /a42337/angela-davis-womens-march-speech-full-transcript.

12. J. L. Stringer and R. Hopper, "Generic *He* in Conversation?," *Quarterly Journal of Speech* 84, no. 2 (1998): 209–21; D. Cameron, *Feminism and Linguistic Theory* (New York: St. Martin's Press, 1985), 68.

13. C. Cottier, "People Have Used They/Them as Singular Pronouns for Hundreds of Years," *Discover,* January 4, 2021, https://www.discovermagazine.com/mind /people-have-used-they-them-as-singular-pronouns-for-hundreds-of-years.

14. Cottier, "People Have Used They/Them."

15. M. Tavits and E. Pérez, "Language Influences Mass Opinion Toward Gender and LGBT Equality," *PNAS* 116, no. 34 (August 20, 2019): 16781.

16. For more, see F. E. Likis, T. L. King, P. A. Murphy, and B. Swett, "Intentional Inconsistency as Gender-Neutral Language Evolves," *Journal of Mid-Wifery & Women's Health* 63, no. 2 (March/April 2018): 155–56.

## Chapter 13

1. Research has shown that along with desensitization (relaxation, deep breathing, visualization) and cognitive restructuring (identifying what causes your anxiety and developing coping strategies), *learning, knowing,* and *practicing* your speech are the best ways to reduce speech anxiety. For more, see T. Docan-Morgan and T. Schmidt, "Reducing Public Speaking Anxiety for Native and Non-Native Speakers: The Value of Systematic Desensitization, Cognitive Restructuring, and Skills Training," *Cross Cultural Communication* 8, no. 5 (2012): 16–19. For more on speech preparation, see H. Liao, "Examining the Role of Collaborative Learning in a Public Speaking Course," *College Teaching* 62, no. 2 (2014): 47–54.

2. See, for example, *Merriam-Webster,* s.v. "nuclear," accessed February 26, 2022, www.merriam-webster.com/dictionary/nuclear. See also M. Reed and J. Lewis, *The Handbook of English Pronunciation* (Malden, MA: Wiley-Blackwell, 2015).

3. J. S. Tuman and the Reverend P. Levine, personal communication, 1976.

4. S. Uono and J. Hietanen, "Eye Contact Perception in the West and East: A Cross-Cultural Study, *PLoS One* 10, no. 2 (2015), https://doi.org/10.1371/journal.pone.0118094.

5. N. Hadjikhani, "Look Me in the Eyes: Constraining Gaze in the Eye-region Provokes Abnormally High Subcortical Activation in Autism," *Scientific Reports* 7, no. 1 (2017): 3163, https://doi.org/10.1038/s41598-017-03378-5.

6. D. Matsumoto and H. S. Hwang, "Body and Gestures," in *Nonverbal Communication: Science and Applications,* ed. D. Matsumoto, M. Frank, and H. S. Hwang, 75–96 (Thousand Oaks, CA: Sage, 2013), 75.

7. V. Manusov, "Perceiving Nonverbal Messages: Effects of Immediacy and Encoded Intent on Receiver Judgments," *Western Journal of Speech Communication* 55, no. 3 (1991): 236.

8. For more on gestures, see A. Hostetter, "When Do Gestures Communicate? A Meta-Analysis," *Psychological Bulletin* 137 (2011): 297–315.

9. For more on co-speech gestures, see L. Marstaller and H. Burianova, "The Multisensory Perception of Co-Speech Gestures: A Review and Meta-Analysis of Neuroimaging Studies," *Journal of Neurolinguistics* 30 (2014): 69–77.

10. J. K. Burgoon and B. A. LePoire, "Nonverbal Cues and Interpersonal Judgments: Participant and Observer Perceptions of Intimacy, Dominance, Composure, and Formality," *Communication Monographs* 66 (1999): 107.

11. S. Kapp, "Stimming, Therapeutic for Autistic People, Deserves Acceptance," *Spectrum,* June 25, 2019, https://www.spectrumnews.org/opinion/viewpoint/stimming-therapeutic-autistic-people-deserves-acceptance.

12. Much of the original research on proxemics was pioneered by anthropologist Edward T. Hall: E. T. Hall, *The Hidden Dimension* (New York: Doubleday, 1966). See also M. L. Patterson, "Spatial Factors in Social Interactions," *Human Relations* 21 (1968): 351–61.

13. Patterson, "Spatial Factors," 351–61; J. K. Burgoon et al., "Relational Messages Associated with Nonverbal Behaviors," *Human Communication Research* 10 (1984): 351–78.

14. E. T. Hall, *Hidden Differences: Doing Business with the Japanese* (New York: Doubleday, 1987).

15. Communication scholars note that other elements of physical appearance—such as physiognomy, hair color, and height—can also affect how audiences respond to speakers. For more, see J. K. Burgoon, L. K. Guerrero, and V. Manusov, "Nonverbal Signals," in *The Sage Handbook of Interpersonal Communication*, 4th ed., ed. M. L. Knapp and J. A. Daly, 239–80 (Thousand Oaks, CA: Sage, 2011), 241.

16. L. J. Smith and L. A. Malandro, "Personal Appearance Factors Which Influence Perceptions of Credibility and Approachability of Men and Women," in *The Nonverbal Communication Reader*, ed. J. A. DeVito and M. L. Hecht (Prospect Heights, IL: Waveland Press, 1990), 163.

## Chapter 14

1. E. Bohn and D. Jabusch, "The Effect of Four Methods of Instruction on the Use of Visual Aids in Speeches," *Western Journal of Communication* 46 (1982): 253–65.

2. H. E. Nelson and A. W. Vandermeer, "The Relative Effectiveness of Several Different Sound Tracks Used on an Animated Film on Elementary Meteorology," *Speech Monographs* 20, no. 4 (1953): 261–67.

3. See, for example, Ş. Y. E. Seçer, M. Şahin, and B. Alci, "Investigating the Effect of Audio Visual Materials as Warm-Up Activity in Aviation English Courses on Students' Motivation and Participation at High School Level," *Procedia: Social and Behavioral Sciences* 199 (August 2015): 120–28, https://www.sciencedirect.com/science/article/pii/S1877042815044985.

4. See, for example, A. Kumar et al., "Students' Views on Audio Visual Aids Used during Didactic Lectures in a Medical College," *Asian Journal of Medical Science* 4, no. 2 (2013): 36–40.

5. J. Park and J. Zuniga, "Effectiveness of Using Picture-based Health Education for People with Low Health Literacy: An Integrative Review," *Cogent Medicine* 3, no. 1 (2016), https://www.tandfonline.com/doi/full/10.1080/2331205X.2016.1264679.

6. To watch a video presentation of Freeman Shen's TED talk on autonomous electric vehicles, go to https://www.ted.com/talks/freeman_h_shen_a_future_with_fewer_cars.

7. In a study examining student learning and retention of information, it was determined that memory retention was greatest for information extracted from visual materials. See P. Baggett and A. Ehrenfeucht, "Encoding and Retaining Information in the Visuals and Verbals of an Educational Movie," Technical Report No. 108-ONR, Institute of Cognitive Science, University of Colorado, 1981, 1. See also M. A. Defeyter, R. Russo, and P. L. McPartlin, "The Picture Superiority Effect in Recognition Memory: A Developmental Study Using the Response Signal Procedure," *Cognitive Development* 24, no. 3 (2009): 265–73.

8. To watch a video presentation of Molly Wright's TED talk on how children can thrive in life, go to https://www.ted.com/talks/molly_wright_how_every_child_can_thrive_by_five.

9. V. Nikolaeva, "15 Best Presentation Software for 2021," *GraphicMama* (2022), https://graphicmama.com/blog/presentation-software-2021.

## Chapter 15

1. National Telecommunications and Information Administration, "Nearly a Third of American Employees Worked Remotely in 2019, NTIA Data Show," September 3, 2020, https://www.ntia.gov/blog/2020/nearly-third-american-employees-worked-remotely-2019-ntia-data-show.

2. M. Iqbal, "Zoom Revenue and Usage Statistics (2020)," *LISA Learning,* September 7, 2020, https://lsiaal.org/zoom-revenue-and-usage-statistics-2020.

3. N. Anderson, "The Post-Pandemic Future of College? It's On Campus and Online," *Washington Post,* September 28, 2021, https://www.washingtonpost.com/education/2021/09/28/post-pandemic-university-online-classes.

4. T. Telford, "Corporate America is Coming Around to Remote Work. But More Big Changes Lie Ahead," *Washington Post,* January 15, 2022, https://www.washingtonpost.com/business/2022/01/15/remote-work-omicron.

5. R. van der Kleij, R. M. Paashuis, and J. M. Schraagen, "On the Passage of Time: Temporal Differences in Video-Mediated and Face-to-Face Interaction," *International Journal of Human-Computer Studies* 62, no. 4 (2005): 539.

6. N. Kock, "Media Richness or Media Naturalness? The Evolution of Our Biological Communication Apparatus and Its Influence on Our Behavior toward E-Communication Tools," *IEEE Transactions on Professional Communication* 48, no. 2 (2005): 121.

7. N. Kock, "Information Systems Theorizing Based on Evolutionary Psychology: An Interdisciplinary Review and Theory Integration Framework," *MIS Quarterly* 33, no. 2 (2009): 407.

8. See T. M. Wells and A. R. Dennis, "To Email or Not to Email: The Impact of Media on Psychophysiological Responses and Emotional Content in Utilitarian and Romantic Communication," *Computers in Human Behavior* 54 (2016): 1–9.

9. J. K. Burgoon et al., "Testing the Interactivity Principle: Effects of Mediation, Propinquity, and Verbal and Nonverbal Modalities in Interpersonal Interaction," *Journal of Communication* 52, no. 3 (2002): 662.

10. A. Lyons, S. Reysen, and L. Pierce, "Video Lecture Format, Student Technological Efficacy, and Social Presence in Online Courses," *Computers in Human Behavior* 28, no. 1 (2012): 182.

11. Burgoon et al., "Testing the Interactivity Principle," 662.

12. W. Turmel, *Ten Steps to Successful Virtual Presentations* (Alexandria, VA: ASTD Press, 2011), 8.

13. Z. Guo et al., "Improving the Effectiveness of Virtual Teams: A Comparison of Video-Conferencing and Face-to-Face Communication in China," *IEEE Transactions on Professional Communication* 52, no. 1 (2009): 1–16.

14. L. MacLellan, "How to Get More Comfortable with Public Speaking on Zoom—or Anywhere Else," *Quartz at Work,* March 9, 2021, https://qz.com/work/1977974/how-to-conquer-a-fear-of-public-speaking-on-zoom-or-anywhere-else.

15. Kock, "Media Richness," 121.

16. J. M. Denstadli, T. E. Julsrud, and R. J. Hjorthol, "Videoconferencing as a Mode of Communication: A Comparative Study of the Use of Videoconferencing and Face-to-Face Meetings," *Journal of Business and Technical Communication* 26, no. 1 (2012): 66.

17. J. Gendelman, *Virtual Presentations That Work* (New York: McGraw-Hill, 2010), 35–36.

18. Van der Kleij, Paashuis, and Schraagen, "On the Passage of Time," 523.

19. R. F. Adler and R. Benbunan-Fich, "Juggling on a High Wire: Multitasking Effects on Performance," *International Journal of Human-Computer Studies* 70, no. 2 (2012): 156.

20. R. Riedl, "On the Stress Potential of Videoconferencing: Definition and Root Causes of Zoom Fatigue," *Electronic Markets,* (December 6, 2021), https://doi.org/10.1007/s12525-021-00501-3.

21. J. Bailenson, "Nonverbal Overload: A Theoretical Argument for the Causes of Zoom Fatigue," *Technology, Mind, and Behavior* 2, no. 1 (February 23, 2021), https://doi.org/10.1037/tmb0000030.

22. Bailenson, "Nonverbal Overload."

23. E. Cores, M. Anthenuis, A. Schouten, and E. Kramer, "Social Attraction in Videomediated Communication: The Role of Nonverbal Affiliative Behavior," *Journal of Social and Personal Relationships* 36, no. 4 (2019): 1221, https://doi.org/10.1177/0265407518757382.

24. Turmel, *Ten Steps*, 125–26.

25. T. Koike, M. Sumiya, E. Nakagawa, S. Okazaki, and N. Sadato, "What Makes Eye Contact Special? Neural Substrates of On-Line Mutual Eye-Gaze: A Hyperscanning fMRI Study," *eNeuro* 6, no. 1 (January/February 2019): 2, https://doi.org/10.1523/ENEURO.0284-18.2019.

26. Bailenson, "Nonverbal Overload."

27. T. J. Koegel, *The Exceptional Presenter Goes Virtual* (Austin: Greenleaf Book Group Press, 2010), 98.

28. Guo et al., "Improving the Effectiveness," 3.

29. C. A. Noble, "From China's Great Wall to Hollywood's Great Spy: The Story of Military Smokes and Obscurants," in *Aerosol Science and Technology: History and Reviews*, ed. D. S. Ensor (Research Triangle Park, NC: RTI International, 2011), 377.

30. Turmel, *Ten Steps*, 8.

31. Turmel, *Ten Steps*, 93.

32. S. Stockman, *How to Shoot Video That Doesn't Suck* (New York: Workman, 2011), 12–13, 120.

33. Gendelman, *Virtual Presentations That Work*, 66.

34. R. McCammon, "Is There Proper Etiquette for Videoconferencing?," *Entrepreneur*, November 2011, 20.

35. Turmel, *Ten Steps*, 93.

36. Koegel, *Exceptional Presenter*, 114.

37. Stockman, *How to Shoot Video*, 41.

38. Stockman, *How to Shoot Video*, 150.

39. Y. Shkorko, "Online Communication: Doubts About Evolutionary Mismatch." *Frontiers in Sociology* (February 14, 2022), https://doi.org/10.3389/fsoc.2022.78844.

## Chapter 16

1. See, for example, Vote.gov, at https://vote.gov.

2. Flag-folding etiquette is detailed by the American Legion at http://www.legion.org /flag/folding (accessed March 23, 2010).

3. U.S. Code, title 4, chapter 1, sections 3 and 8(d), via Cornell Law School, https:// www.law.cornell.edu/uscode/text/4/chapter-1 (accessed March 2, 2019).

4. D. Russakoff, "Building a Career Path Where There Was Just a Dead End," *Washington Post*, February 26, 2007, A1. In 2013, Per Scholas was recognized for inclusion in the S&I 100 list, recognizing nonprofits that provide high-impact solutions to America's problems. For more, see http://www.socialimpactexchange .org/exchange/si-100.

5. For more, see Editorial Board, "A Football Player's Safe Exit," *New York Times*, March 21, 2015, http://www.nytimes.com/2015/03/22/opinion/sunday/a-football -players-safe-exit.html?_r = 0.

6. N. Chokshi, "Lucid Motors Beats Tesla in Range, Going 520 Miles on a Charge, the E.P.A.Says," *New York Times*, September 16, 2021. See also F. Markus, "The Lucid Air is the 2022 MotorTrend Car of the Year," *MotorTrend*, November 15, 2021, https://www.motortrend.com/news/lucid-air-2022-car-of-the-year.

7. D. M. Fraleigh and J. S. Tuman, *Freedom of Speech in the Marketplace of Ideas* (New York: St. Martin's Press, 1997).

8. J. S. Tuman, *Communicating Terror: The Rhetorical Dimensions of Terrorism*, Second Edition (Los Angeles: Sage, 2010), 197–201.

9. K. E. Rowan, "A New Pedagogy for Explanatory Public Speaking: Why Arrangement Should Not Substitute for Invention," *Communication Education* 44 (July 1995): 236–50.


## Chapter 17

1. R. E. Petty and J. T. Cacioppo, *Communication and Persuasion: Central and Peripheral Routes to Attitude Change* (New York: Springer-Verlag, 1986).

2. J. K. Clark, A. T. Evans, and D. T. Wegener, "Perceptions of Source Efficacy and Persuasion: Multiple Mechanisms for Source Effects on Attitudes," *European Journal of Social Psychology* 41, no. 5 (2011): 596–607; R. L. Holbert, R. K. Garrett, and L. S. Gleason, "A New Era of Minimal Effects? A Response to Bennett and Iyengar," *Journal of Communication* 60, no. 1 (2010): 25.

3. Petty and Cacioppo, *Communication and Persuasion*, 7.

4. I. M. Handley and B. M. Runnion, "Evidence That Unconscious Thinking Influences Persuasion Based on Argument Quality," *Social Cognition* 29, no. 6 (2011): 677.

5. Handley and Runnion, "Evidence," 669.

6. Holbert, Garrett, and Gleason, "New Era of Minimal Effects?," 25.

7. M. B. Wanzer, A. B. Frymier, and J. Irwin, "An Explanation of the Relationship between Instructor Humor and Student Learning: Instructional Humor Processing Theory," *Communication Education* 59, no. 1 (2010): 5.

8. S. Greenberg et al., "Nudging Resisters toward Change: Self-Persuasion Interventions for Reducing Attitude Certainty," *American Journal of Health Promotion* 32, no. 4 (2018): 997–1009, https://doi.org/10.1177/0890117117715295.

9. M. A. Yeh and R. D. Jewell, "The Myth/Fact Message Frame and Persuasion in Advertising: Enhancing Attitudes toward the Mentally Ill," *Journal of Advertising* 44, no. 2 (2015): 161–72.

10. X. Wang, F. Chao, G. Yu, and K. Zhang, "Factors Influencing Fake News Rebuttal Acceptance During the COVID-19 Pandemic and the Moderating Effect of Cognitive Ability", *Computers in Human Behavior* 130 (2022): 107174, https://doi.org/10.1016/j.chb.2021.107174.

11. M. Sherif and C. I. Hovland, *Social Judgment, Assimilation, and Contrast Effects in Communication and Attitude Change* (New Haven, CT: Yale University Press, 1961), 195–96.

12. Sherif and Hovland, *Social Judgment, Assimilation, and Contrast Effects.*

13. D. K. O'Keefe, *Persuasion: Theory and Research* (Newbury Park, CA: Sage, 1990), 36–37.

14. Petty and Cacioppo, *Communication and Persuasion,* 81.

15. A. H. Maslow, "A Theory of Human Motivation," *Psychological Review* 50 (1943): 370–96; V. Packard, *The Hidden Persuaders* (New York: Pocket Books, 1964).

16. M. Rokeach, *Understanding Human Values* (New York: Free Press, 1979), 2.

17. J. S. Tuman, "Getting to First Base: Prima Facie Arguments for Propositions of Value," *Journal of the American Forensic Association* 24 (Fall 1987): 86.

18. M. Rokeach, *Beliefs, Attitudes, and Values: A Theory of Organization and Change* (San Francisco: Jossey-Bass, 1968).

19. J. Hornikx and D. J. O'Keefe, "Adapting Consumer Advertising Appeals to Cultural Values," *Communication Yearbook* 33 (2009): 38–71.

20. D. Hample and J. M. Hample, "Persuasion about Health Risks: Evidence, Credibility, Scientific Flourishes, and Risk Perceptions," *Argumentation and Advocacy* 51 (Summer 2014): 17–29; S. Benjamin and K. Bahr, "Barriers Associated with Seasonal Influenza Vaccination among College Students," *Influenza Research and Treatment* (2016), https://doi.org/10.1155/2016/4248071.

21. T. Haelle, "Dangerous Flu Comeback Expected Atop COVID this Winter, *Scientific American,* January 25, 2022, https://www.scientificamerican.com/article/dangerous-flu-comeback-expected-atop-covid-this-winter1.

22. J. Cannon and J. Niederdeppe, "Understanding Audience Beliefs and Values is Essential for Successful Organizational Health Policy Change," *American Journal of Health Promotion* 36, no. 3 (February 14, 2022): 575, https://doi.org/10.1177/08901171211070953.

23. Rokeach, *Beliefs, Attitudes, and Values,* 3.

24. M. Fishbein and I. Ajzen, *Belief, Attitude, Intention, and Behavior: An Introduction to Theory and Research* (Reading, MA: Addison-Wesley, 1975).

25. K. Gallagher, "Using 'Make & Take Quizzes' to Improve Exam Performance and Engage Students in Effective Study Strategies," *Teaching of Psychology* 49, no. 2 (2022): 124, https://doi.org/10.1177/0098628320957991.

26. M. Allen, "Comparing the Persuasive Effectiveness: One- and Two-Sided Message," in *Persuasion: Advances through Meta-Analysis,* ed. M. Allen and R. W. Preiss (Cresskill, NJ: Hampton Press, 1998), 96.

27. R. Hamill, T. Wilson, and R. Nesbit, "Insensitivity to Sample Bias: Generalizing from Atypical Cases," *Journal of Personality and Social Psychology* 39 (1980): 578–89.

28. C. Hoyt, "The Sources' Stake in the News," *New York Times*, January 17, 2010, WK8.

29. L. Grossman, "A Star Is Born," *Time*, November 2, 2015, 30–39.

30. A. Monroe, *Principles and Types of Speech* (New York: Scott, Foresman, 1935).

31. Monroe, *Principles and Types of Speech*.

32. K. Zambon, "Facebook Whistleblower Encourages Students to Demand Transparency from Social Media Companies," Georgetown University Medical Center, February 11, 2022, https://gumc.georgetown.edu/gumc-stories/facebook -whistleblower-encourages-students-to-demand-transparency-from-social -media-companies.

## Chapter 18

1. J. C. Reinard, *Foundations of Argument* (Dubuque, IA: William C. Brown, 1991), 353–54.

2. Aristotle, *On Rhetoric*, trans. G. A. Kennedy (New York: Oxford University Press, 1991), 1378a.

3. J. C. McCroskey and J. J. Teven, "Goodwill: A Reexamination of the Construct and Its Measurement," *Communication Monographs* 66, no. 1 (1999): 92.

4. S. Wheaton, "Missouree? Missouruh? To Be Politic, Say Both," *New York Times*, October 13, 2012, A1.

5. A. Blanc, "Why Research Will Prevail in a Post-Fact World," *MHTF Blog*, May 18, 2018, https://www.mhtf.org/2018/05/18/why-research-will-prevail-in-a-post -fact-world.

6. H. Flesher, J. Ilardo, and J. Demoretcky, "The Influence of Field Dependence, Speaker Credibility Set, and Message Documentation on Evaluations of Speaker and Message Credibility," *Southern Communication Speech Journal* 34 (Summer 1974): 400.

7. J. C. McCroskey, "A Summary of Experimental Research on the Effects of Evidence in Persuasive Communication," *Quarterly Journal of Speech* 55 (April 1969): 172.

8. McCroskey, "A Summary of Experimental Research," 175.

9. N. Sattar and N. Forouhi, "More Evidence for 5-a-Day for Fruit and Vegetables and a Greater Need for Translating Dietary Research Evidence to Practice," *Circulation* 143, no. 17 (April 27, 2021): 1655, https://doi.org/10.1161/CIRCULTIONAHA .121.053293.

10. R. E. Nisbett and L. Ross, *Human Interference: Strategies and Shortcomings of Social Judgment* (Englewood Cliffs, NJ: Prentice Hall, 1980).

11. D. Hample and J. Hample, "Persuasion About Health Risks: Evidence Credibility, Scientific Flourishes, and Risk Perception," *Argumentation and Advocacy*, 51 (Summer 2017): 17.

12. "Editorial: Success! California's First-in-the-Nation Plastic Bag Ban Works," *San Jose Mercury News*, November 13, 2017, https://www.mercurynews. com/2017/11/13/editorial-success-californias-first-in-the-nation-plastic -bag-ban-works.

13. J. Curtin, "Ireland Can Lead Charge in War against Plastic," *Irish Times*, January 31, 2018, https://www.irishtimes.com/opinion/ireland-can-lead-charge-in-war -against-plastic-1.3374066.

14. "In Just One Year, Israel Halves Plastic Bags Found in the Sea," UN Environment, February 6, 2018, https://www.unenvironment.org/news-and-stories/story /just-one-year-israel-halves-plastic-bags-found-sea.

15. J. McWhorter, "College Has Become the Default. Let's Rethink That," *New York Times*, April 7, 2022, p. A27.

16. P. Noonan, "Same Russia, Different War," *Wall Street Journal,* March 26–27, 2022, p. A15.

17. M. DeLisi et al., "Violent Video Games, Delinquency, and Youth Violence: New Evidence," *Youth Violence and Juvenile Justice* 11, no. 2 (2013): 138.

18. B. Kiviat, "How to Create a Job," *Time*, March 29, 2010, 18.

19. S. Callahan, "The Role of Emotion in Ethical Decision Making," *Hastings Center Report* 18, no. 3 (1988): 9.

20. G. Anders, *Health against Wealth: HMOs and the Breakdown of Medical Trust* (Boston: Houghton Mifflin, 1996), 108–9.

21. K. Witte and K. Morrison, "Examining the Influence of Trait Anxiety/Repression-Sensitization on Individuals' Reactions to Fear Appeals," *Western Journal of Communication* 64 (Winter 2000): 1.

22. P. A. Mongeau, "Another Look at Fear-Arousing Persuasive Appeals," in *Persuasion: Advances through Meta-Analysis*, ed. M. Allen and R. W. Preiss (Cresskill, NJ: Hampton Press, 1998), 66.

23. Mongeau, "Another Look."

24. J. Dillard, "COVID Suggests that Fear Itself Not Sufficient for Health Messaging," *Social Science Space,* February 16, 2022, https://www.socialsciencespace.com/ 2022/02/covid-suggests-that-fear-itself-not-sufficient-for-health-messaging.

25. S. Ali and S. Ganapati," Argumentation Tactics and Public Deliberations," *Administrative Theory and Praxis* 42 (2019): 550, https://doi.org/10.1080 /10841806.2019.1627840.

26. D. Westen, "Health Care Reform: It's How You Say It," *StarTribune*, July 1, 2009.

27. Yale Project on Climate Change Communication, "What's in a Name? Global Warming vs. Climate Change," May 2014, http://environment.yale.edu/climate -communication-OFF/files/Global_Warming_vs_Climate_Change_Report.pdf.

28. D. Rocklage, D. Rucker, and L. Nordgren, "Persuasion, Emotion, and Language: The Intent to Persuade Transforms Language via Emotionality," *Psychological Science* 29 no. 5 (2018): 749–60.

29. J. G. Hodge Jr. and D. Campos-Outcalt, "Legally Limiting Lies about Vaccines," *Jurist*, November 17, 2015, http://jurist.org/forum/2015/11/hodge-campos -vaccines-speech.php.

30. "Off-Base Camp: A Mistaken Claim about Glaciers Raises Questions about the UN's Climate Panel," *Economist*, January 23, 2010, 76–77.

31. W. DeJong and L. Wallack, "A Critical Perspective of the Drug Czar's Antidrug Media Campaign," *Journal of Health Communication* 4 (1999): 155–60; D. R. Buchanan and L. Wallack, "This Is the Partnership for a Drug-Free America: Any Questions?," *Journal of Drug Issues* 28, no. 2 (1998): 329–56.

32. A. Lang and N. S. Yegiyan, "Understanding the Interactive Effects of Emotional Appeal and Claim Strength in Health Messages," *Journal of Broadcasting and Electronic Media* 52, no. 3 (2008): 432–47.

## Chapter 19

1. Aristotle, *On Rhetoric*, trans. G. A. Kennedy (New York: Oxford University Press, 1991), 1358a–b.
2. Aristotle, 7, 47.
3. See D. J. Ochs, *Consolatory Rhetoric: Grief, Symbol, and Ritual in the Greco-Roman Era* (Columbia: University of South Carolina Press, 1993).
4. S. Railton, "The Toast of the Evening," *Mark Twain in His Times*," 2012, https://twain.lib.virginia.edu/onstage/speeches.html.
5. W. D. Hansen and G. N. Dionisopoulos, "Eulogy Rhetoric as a Political Coping Mechanism: The Aftermath of Proposition 8," *Western Journal of Communication* 76, no. 1 (2012): 26.
6. To review some of Twain's famous after-dinner speeches, see B. Blaisdell, ed., *Great Speeches by Mark Twain* (Mineola, NY: Dover, 2013).

## Chapter 20

1. B. R. Patton and K. Giffen, *Decision-Making Group Interaction*, 2nd ed. (New York: Harper & Row, 1978), 2.
2. R. Kroichick, "Stanford's Haley Jones Keeps Her Team Calm as It Chases Second Straight NCAA title," *San Francisco Chronicle,* March 30, 2022, https://www.sfchronicle.com/sports/college/article/Stanford-s-Haley-Jones-keeps-her-team-calm-as-17037955.php.
3. I. Janis, *Victims of Groupthink* (Boston: Houghton Mifflin, 1972).
4. B. Kennedy, "The Hijacking of Foreign Policy Decision Making: Groupthink and Presidential Power in the Post 9/11 World," *Southern California Interdisciplinary Law Journal* 21 (2012): 637.
5. W. E. Watson, K. Kumar, and L. K. Michaelson, "Cultural Diversity's Impact on Interaction Processes and Performance: Comparing Homogeneous and Diverse Task Groups," *Academy of Management Journal* 36 (1993): 590–602.
6. K. D. Benne and P. Sheats, "Functional Roles of Group Members," *Journal of Social Issues* 1, no. 4 (1948): 41, 49. For a modern look at types of roles for group members, see A. N. Novak, C. M. Mascaro, and S. P. Goggins, "Virtual Play and Communities: The Evolution of Group Roles in Electronic Trace Data," in *Proceedings of the 2012 iConference on Culture, Design and Society* (New York: ACM, 2012), 490–91, http://dl.acm.org/citation.cfm?id = 2132260.
7. The reflective-thinking process was developed from the ideas of John Dewey, an American philosopher who was interested in problem solving.

## Chapter 21

1. A. Blair, "Making and Remaking the Political: Lessons from the U.S. Experience of Civic and Political Engagement in the Teaching of Political Science," *Learning and Teaching in Politics and International Studies* 37, no. 4 (2017): 486–99.
2. J. Kahane, E. Hodgin, and E. Eidman-Aadahl, "Redesigning Civic Education for the Digital Age: Participatory Politics and the Pursuit of Democratic Engagement," *Theory and Research in Social Education* 44, no. 1 (2016): 1–35.

3. R. Putnam, "Bowling Alone: America's Declining Social Capital," *Journal of Democracy* 6, no. 1 (1995): 65–78.

4. Putnam, "Bowling Alone," 67–68.

5. Putnam, "Bowling Alone," 66–67.

6. R. Jones et al., *American Democracy in Crisis: Civic Engagement, Young Adult Activism, and the 2018 Midterm Elections* (Washington, DC: PRRI, 2018), 17–18.

7. L. Buchanan, Q. Bui, and J. Patel, "Black Lives Matter May Be the Largest Movement in U.S. History," *New York Times,* July 3, 2020, https://www.nytimes.com/interactive/2020/07/03/us/george-floyd-protests-crowd-size.html.

8. J. Madden, M. Oliver, and M. Yang, "Pro-choice Demonstrators Rally Across the U.S. Over Expected Reversal of Roe v. Wade—As it Happened," *The Guardian,* May 14, 2022, https://www.theguardian.com/us-news/live/2022/may/14/abortion-protests-us-roe-v-wade-politics-live-updates.

9. E. Silverman, J. Moyer, and J. Heim, "Crowds Protest at Supreme Court After Leak of Roe Opinion Draft," *Washington Post,* May 3, 2022, https://www.washingtonpost.com/dc-md-va/2022/05/03/protests-roe-v-wade-supreme-court.

10. Points of Light, *Civic Life Today: A Look at American Civic Engagement Amid a Global Pandemic,* September 22, 2020, 4.

11. Points of Light, 10.

12. K. Zezima, "Is It Possible to Resurrect Civility amid a Tsunami of Toxicity? This Group Is Trying," *Washington Post,* January 11, 2019, https://www.washingtonpost.com/national/is-it-possible-to-resurrect-civility-amid-a-tsunami-of-toxicity-this-group-is-trying/2019/01/11/7ccbba7c-15c6-11e9-90a8-136fa44b80ba_story.html?utm_term = .26b58ed44105.

13. T. Van Green, "Republicans and Democrats Alike Say It's Stressful to Talk Politics with People Who Disagree," *Pew Research Center,* November 23, 2021, https://www.pewresearch.org/fact-tank/2021/11/23/republicans-and-democrats-alike-say-its-stressful-to-talk-politics-with-people-who-disagree.

14. K. Ronayne, "Kennedy Warns of Dangers to Democracy, Won't Talk Kavanaugh," AP News, September 28, 2018, https://apnews.com/c9c39fedd46f4b00bb642ef8c7b34624.

15. American Psychological Association, "Stress in America: Coping with Change," February 15, 2017, https://www.apa.org/news/press/releases/stress/2016/coping-with-change.pdf.

16. A. Fleming, "Why Social Media Makes Us So Angry, and What You Can Do about It," *Science Focus,* April 2, 2020, https://www.sciencefocus.com/the-human-body/why-social-media-makes-us-so-angry-and-what-you-can-do-about-it.

17. D. Nield, "Social Media Is Training Us to Unleash More Moral Outrage and Vitriol, Study Reveals," *Science Alert,* August 17, 2021, https://www.sciencealert.com/social-media-networks-are-training-us-to-express-more-outrage-online.

18. J. Haidt, "Why the Past 10 Years of American Life Have Been Uniquely Stupid," *Atlantic,* April 11, 2022, https://www.theatlantic.com/magazine/archive/2022/05/social-media-democracy-trust-babel/629369.

19. Haidt, "Why the Past 10 Years."

20. H. R. Gilman, "For Democracy to Survive, It Requires Civic Engagement," *Vox,* January 31, 2017, https://www.vox.com/polyarchy/2017/1/31/14458966/democracy-requires-civic-engagement.

21. P. Levine, *We Are the Ones We Have Been Waiting For* (New York: Oxford University Press, 2013), 3.

22. M. Bridgman et al., "Encouraging Civic Engagement on College Campuses through Discussion Boards," accessed May 17, 2019, https://www.mesacc.edu/community-civic-engagement/journals/encouraging-civic-engagement-college-campuses-through-discussion.

23. Blair, "Making and Remaking the Political," 489.

24. L. O'Leary, "Civic Engagement in College Students: Connections between Involvement and Attitudes," *New Directions for Institutional Research* 162 (2014): 55, 61.

25. L. Wray-Lake, C. DeHaan, J. Shubert, and R. Ryan, "Examining Links from Civic Engagement to Daily Well-Being from a Self-determination Theory Perspective," *Journal of Positive Psychology* 14, no. 2 (2019): 166–77.

26. Bridgman et al., "Encouraging Civic Engagement."

27. J. Huddleston, "Free Speech in the Age of Political Correctness: Removing Free Speech Zones on College Campuses to Encourage Civil Discourse," *Alabama Civil Rights and Civil Liberties Law Review* 8 (2017): 279–94.

28. G. Leef, "One State Shows How to Get Rid of Campus Free Speech Zones but Another Fumbles," *Forbes*, March 9, 2018, https://www.forbes.com/sites/georgeleef/2018/03/09/one-state-shows-how-to-get-rid-of-campus-free-speech-zones-but-another-fumbles/#700954311b4c.

29. G. Satell and S. Popovic, "How Protests Become Successful Social Movements," *Harvard Business Review*, January 27, 2017, https://hbr.org/2017/01/how-protests-become-successful-social-movements.

30. Kahane, Hodgin, and Eidman-Aadahl, "Redesigning Civic Education for the Digital Age," 7.

31. Kahane, Hodgin, and Eidman-Aadahl, "Redesigning Civic Education for the Digital Age," 2.

32. C. Mattos, "Women's March in Fresno, a Call for Inclusion and Justice," *Collegian*, January 22, 2018, http://collegian.csufresno.edu/2018/01/22/womens-march-in-fresno-a-call-for-inclusion-and-justice/#.XJfsEZhKjSE.

33. J. Kantor and K. Weise, "How Two Best Friends Beat Amazon," *New York Times,* April 14, 2022, https://www.nytimes.com/2022/04/02/business/amazon-union-christian-smalls.html.

34. J. Fallows, "Get Off My Lawn," *Atlantic*, April 2019, 14, 16, https://www.theatlantic.com/magazine/archive/2019/04/james-fallows-leaf-blower-ban/583210.

35. V. Strauss, "This Parkland Student Quickly Amassed More Twitter Followers Than the NRA," *Washington Post*, March 1, 2018, https://www.washingtonpost.com/news/answer-sheet/wp/2018/03/01/this-parkland-student-quickly-amassed-more-twitter-followers-than-the-nra-heres-what-shes-been-writing/?utm_term = .5ed0c8310bd0.

36. CNN Staff, "Florida Student Emma Gonzalez to Lawmakers and Gun Advocates: 'We Call BS,'" CNN, February 17, 2018, https://www.cnn.com/2018/02/17/us/florida-student-emma-gonzalez-speech/index.html.

37. NPR, "Emma Gonzalez: Fight for Your Lives, Before It's Someone Else's Job," March 25, 2018, https://www.npr.org/2018/03/25/596805330/emma-gonzalez-fight-for-your-lives-before-it-s-someone-else-s-job.

38. National Immigrant Justice Center, "Undocumented Yet Hopeful: Dreamer Sandy Rivera's Speech at the Indianapolis Women's March," January 30, 2018, https://immigrantjustice.org/staff/blog/undocumented-yet-hopeful-dreamer-sandy-riveras-speech-indianapolis-womens-march.

39. Our Children's Trust, "Kelsey Cascadia Rose Juliana," accessed March 21, 2019, https://www.ourchildrenstrust.org/kelsey.

40. K. Juliana, "Youth as Solutionaries: Active Hope Against Climate Catastrophe," TEDx Salem, April 11, 2017, https://www.youtube.com/watch?v = AfsemDEisxk.

41. H. Brueck, "A Mother in Flint, Michigan Collected More Than 800 Neighborhood Water Samples to Help Uncover the City's Lead Crisis," *Business Insider*, April 23, 2018, www.businessinsider.com/flint-water-crisis-crusader-leeanne-walters-wins-goldman-prize-2018-4.

42. "LeeAnne Walters Acceptance Speech, 2018 Goldman Environmental Prize," May 2, 2018, https://www.youtube.com/watch?v = 699wQ_s1hUY.

43. T. Lowery, "Oscars 2022: 8 Moments the Academy Awards Showed Up for the World," *Global Citizen,* March 28, 2022, https://www.globalcitizen.org/en/content/oscars-2022-ukraine-gender-lgbtq-disability.

44. N. Warne, "Being Young and Making an Impact," TEDx Teen, April 2011, www.ted.com/talks/ory_okolloh_on_becoming_an_activist/transcript. https://www.ted.com/talks/natalie_warne_being_young_and_making_an_impact/transcript?language = en.

45. C. Robinson, "Tent City for Homeless Headed to UW Campus," *Crosscut*, April 17, 2016, https://crosscut.com/2016/04/why-uw-is-thinking-of-hosting-a-tent-city.

46. Stacey Park Milbern's 35th Birthday, *Google Doodle,* May 19, 2022, https://www.google.com/doodles/stacey-park-milberns-35th-birthday.

47. M. Moore, "Read John Stewart's Full Testimony Supporting the 9/11 Victim's Fund," *New York Post,* June 12, 2019, https://nypost.com/2019/06/12/read-jon-stewarts-full-testimony-supporting-the-9-11-victims-fund.

**abstract**   A summary of an article's contents, often included in library indexes.

**abstract word**   A term that refers to intangible things, like feelings, ideals, concepts, and qualities. An abstract word is general and can be confusing and ambiguous for an audience. To say "I have a pet" is less informative than saying "I have a gray tabby cat."

**academic research**   The study of a topic by experts who have education and experience in the topic area. An expert's academic research is generally reviewed by other authorities in the field.

**action-oriented listening**   A style of listening in which the listener focuses on immediately getting to the meaning of a message and determining what response is required. Action-oriented listeners indicate a preference for messages that are direct, concise, and error-free.

***ad hominem* (personal attack) fallacy**   An error in reasoning in which the speaker tries to compensate for a weak argument by targeting an opponent's character through unsubstantiated claims, rather than focusing on the relevant issues.

***ad populum* (bandwagon) fallacy**   An error in reasoning in which the speaker tries to persuade an audience to accept an argument by claiming that a fact is true because a large number of people believe that it is true. Another form of this logical fallacy (often used in advertising and marketing) is to imply that because many people are engaging in an activity, everyone should engage in the activity. Bandwagoning is unethical if speakers fail to provide well–reasoned support for their claims.

**advanced search**   A search-engine feature that allows users to limit their searches by date, language, country, or file format, as well as to prioritize search terms based on their location on a web page.

**age**   A demographic consideration that affects an audience's response to and understanding of a speaker's message. For example, avoiding popular culture references that are too old or too young for an audience is a good way to take age into consideration.

**agenda-driven listening**   Focusing only on the mechanics of delivering one's speech without acknowledging the audience's questions and comments.

**algorithm**   A formula used by search engines to sort the list of results generated by a keyword search.

**analogy**   A comparison of two things—one that is familiar to an audience and one that is less familiar—that is based on their similarities and that helps listeners use their existing knowledge to absorb new information.

**anaphora**   A repetition of a word or phrase at the beginning of successive phrases, clauses, or sentences. It is used to emphasize, clarify, and deliver a rhetorical sense of style.

**antithesis**   Clauses set in opposition to one another, usually to distinguish between choices, concepts, and ideas.

**appeal to tradition fallacy**    An error in reasoning in which the speaker tries to persuade an audience to believe that a practice or policy is good by claiming that people have followed it for a long time.

**argumentative listening**    Focusing on a message only long enough to get material to feed one's own argument.

**arrangement**    The effective structuring of ideas to present them to an audience. It is one of the five classical canons of rhetoric.

**articulation**    Speaking that is crisp and clear so that listeners can distinguish separate words, syllables, and vowel or consonant sounds within words.

**asynchronous presentation**    See **prerecorded (asynchronous) presentation**.

**atlas**    A reference work that collects maps, charts, and tables relating to different geographic regions.

**attention-getter**    The material at the start of a speech that is intended to capture an audience's interest. The speaker can get an audience's attention by telling a story or an anecdote, offering a striking or provocative statement, building suspense, letting listeners know the speaker is one of them, using humor, asking a rhetorical question, or providing a quotation.

**attitude**    The audience's favorable or unfavorable feelings toward a speaker's thesis.

**audience analysis**    The process of learning about an audience's interests and backgrounds in order to create or adapt a speech to their wants and needs.

**audience size**    The number of people who will witness a speech.

**audience surveillance**    The speaker's analysis of an audience's nonverbal and verbal responses while listening to a speech.

**bandwagon fallacy**    See *ad populum* (bandwagon) fallacy.

**bar graph**    A graph that compares several pieces of information by showing parallel bars of varying height or length.

**beliefs**    The facts audience members consider to be true.

**biased language**    Words, phrases, and expressions that suggest prejudice against or preconceptions about other people, usually referring to race, ethnicity, gender, sexuality, religion, or mental or physical ability.

**body**    The main part of a speech. The body falls after the introduction and before the conclusion and includes all the main points and the material that supports them.

**body clock (chronemics)**    The time of day or day of the week when an audience will be listening to a presentation. An audience is more prone to distraction at certain times of the day, such as lunchtime, and certain days of the week, such as Friday.

**boomerang effect**    The act of pushing an audience to oppose a position even more vigorously than they did before, which often results from presenting a position that falls on the extreme end of their latitude of rejection. See also **latitude of rejection**.

**brainstorming**    A strategy for generating topic ideas by listing every idea that comes to mind—without evaluating its merits—in order to develop a long list of ideas quickly.

**brief example**   A short instance (usually a single sentence) that supports or illustrates a more general claim.

**categorical (topical) pattern**   A model for speech organization in which each main point emphasizes one of the most important aspects of the speaker's topic. This pattern is often used when a speaker's topic does not easily conform to the other speech organization patterns—spatial, temporal, causal, comparison, problem-cause-solution, criteria application, or narrative.

**causal pattern**   A model for speech organization that explains cause-and-effect relationships in which each main point is either an event that leads to a situation or a link in a chain of events between a catalyst and a final outcome.

**causal reasoning**   Arguing that one event has caused another.

**central route**   According to the elaboration likelihood model, one of two ways that audience members may evaluate a speaker's message. This route denotes a high level of elaboration—a mental process that involves actively processing a speaker's argument. See also **peripheral route**.

**channel**   The medium through which a source delivers a message, such as voice, microphone, radio, television, or Internet.

**chronemics**   See **body clock (chronemics)**.

**chronological (temporal) pattern**   A model for speech organization in which the speaker presents information in the order that events occurred, with each main point addressing a particular time within the chronology.

**circle graph**   See **pie chart (circle graph)**.

**citation**   The key information about a researched source, including author, author's credentials on the subject, title, publication date, and page numbers or URL.

**civic engagement**   Active public participation in political affairs and social and community organizations.

**classical canons of rhetoric**   According to Cicero, the five concepts that effective speakers must attend to while preparing a speech. These concepts are invention, arrangement, style, memory, and delivery.

**clincher**   A closing comment in a speech that leaves a lasting impression on listeners' minds. This comment or call to action should be as compelling as the speech's attention-getter and usually appears as the second element in a speech conclusion. To leave the audience thinking, a speaker can extend a story that was used at the start of the speech, relate a new story or anecdote, highlight the thesis, end with a striking phrase or sentence, or conclude with an emotional message.

**common ground**   The collection of beliefs, values, and experiences that a speaker shares with an audience. A speaker seeks to establish common ground with an audience, whether verbally or nonverbally, so that listeners will be more receptive to the speaker's message.

**common knowledge**   Widely known information that can be found in many sources and that does not require citation.

**comparison pattern**   A model for speech organization that discusses the similarities and differences between two events, objects, or situations. This pattern is especially useful when comparing a new subject to one that is known to the audience.

**comparison reasoning**   Arguing that two instances are similar enough that what is true for one is likely to be true for the other. If a speaker argues that U.S. residents will eventually accept mandatory health insurance because they accepted mandatory car insurance, the speaker is using comparison reasoning.

**competence**   Knowledge and experience in a subject. Referred to as *practical wisdom* by modern communication scholars.

**conclusion**   The final part of a speech, in which the speaker summarizes the main points and leaves the audience with a clincher, such as a striking sentence or phrase, an anecdote, or an emotional message.

**concrete word**   A specific word or phrase that suggests exactly what you mean. For example, to say a person was wearing a "dark blue suit" (which mentions a color) is more concrete than saying they were wearing "clothes."

**connotative meaning**   An association that comes to mind when a person hears a word. For example, saying "He tackled the project" brings to mind football and is a more vivid way to convey enthusiasm than saying "He was excited to start the project and tried to do a good job."

**constructive criticism**   Thoughtful and tactful suggestions for improvement that take into account what a speaker is trying to accomplish. Speakers can use these kinds of suggestions to make improvements for future presentations.

**content-oriented listening**   Focusing on the depth and complexity of information and messages. Content-oriented listeners are willing to spend more time listening, pay careful attention to what's being said, and enjoy discussing and thinking about the message afterward.

**context**   The occasion, surrounding environment, and situation in which a speaker gives a presentation.

**coordination**   The connection of two or more ideas of equal weight and importance. In a well-organized speech, all points at the same level share the same significance. Each main point is coordinate with other main points, each subpoint with other subpoints, and each sub-subpoint with other sub-subpoints.

**core belief**   A deeply held viewpoint about the self and the world that is particularly immune to persuasion. See also **peripheral belief**.

**credibility**   The perception of an audience that a speaker is prepared and qualified to speak on their topic. Trustworthiness, dynamism, and goodwill are also elements of a speaker's credibility. See also **ethos (credibility)**.

**credible source**   An author or organization that can be reasonably trusted to be accurate and objective in presenting information.

**criteria-application pattern**   A model for speech organization that proposes standards for a value judgment that a speaker is making and then applies those standards to a related topic. For example, a speaker who argues that an area in her town should be considered a historic neighborhood would first establish criteria for determining that a neighborhood is historic, and second, explain how the area she is discussing meets those criteria.

**critical thinking**   The analysis and evaluation of one's own ideas and others' ideas based on reliability, truth, and accuracy.

**culturally relative**   The principle that ethics vary according to the norms of individual societies.

**culture (cultural background)**   The values, traditions, and rules for living that are passed from generation to generation. Culture is learned, not innate, and it influences all aspects of a person's life.

**decode**   To interpret a message by making sense of a source's verbal and nonverbal symbols. Decoding is performed by a receiver.

**defeated listening**   Pretending to understand a message while actually being overwhelmed by or uninterested in the subject matter.

**definition**   A statement that explains the essence, meaning, purpose, or identity of something.

**delivery**   A speaker's varied and appropriate use of vocal and nonverbal elements, such as voice, hand gestures, eye contact, and movement. It is one of the five classical canons of rhetoric.

**delivery reminder**   Instructions in a speaking outline that remind the speaker about body language, pauses, special emphasis, and presentation aids.

**demographics**   The characteristics of audience members, including age, gender, sexual orientation, race, ethnicity, disability status, group membership, occupation or academic major, religious affiliation, socioeconomic background, and political affiliation.

**demonstration**   A technique used in informative speeches that involves both physical modeling and verbal elements and that teaches an audience how a process or set of guidelines works.

**denotative meaning**   The literal dictionary definition of a word.

**description**   The use of words to paint a mental picture for audience members so that they can close their eyes and imagine what a speaker is saying.

**designated leader**   A person who is chosen by an authority figure to help a group move quickly forward with its mission.

**detailed outline**   A complete outline that is used to craft a speech. It contains full sentences or detailed phrases of all the elements of a speech, including attention-getter, main points, subpoints, sub-subpoints, and clincher. It is also referred to as a *working*, *full-sentence*, or *preparation outline*.

**diagram**   A drawing that details an object or an action and shows the relations among its parts.

**diction**   See **word choice (diction)**.

**dictionary**   A reference work that offers definitions, pronunciation guides, and sometimes etymologies of words.

**dictionary definition**   The meaning of a term as it appears in a general or specialized dictionary.

**direct quotation**   An author's exact words. Quotation marks must be put around quotations to avoid plagiarism.

**disability status**   A demographic category that relates to whether a person has a disability.

**disposition**   An audience's likely attitude toward a message. In most cases, an audience can be divided into three groups—sympathetic, hostile, and neutral.

**divergent thinking**    Employed in the brainstorming process of a speech, a path of thinking that generates diverse and creative ideas.

**elaboration likelihood model**    A dual-process theory that shows that audience members may evaluate a persuasive speaker's message according to two routes—the central and peripheral routes. See also **central route**, **peripheral route**.

**emergent leader**    A person who comes to be recognized as a leader by a group's members over time.

**encode**    To choose verbal or nonverbal symbols to organize and deliver one's message.

**encyclopedia**    A reference work that offers relatively brief entries that provide background information on a wide range of alphabetized topics.

**epideictic**    Praising or blaming (in speaking).

**ethical absolutism**    The belief that people should adopt a code of behavior and adhere to it in all situations. See also **situational ethics**.

**ethical audience**    An audience that exhibits courtesy, open-mindedness, and a willingness to hold the speaker accountable.

**ethical speech**    Language that incorporates ethical decision making, follows guidelines to tell the truth, and avoids misleading the audience.

**ethics**    A set of rules and values that are shared by members of a group and that help them guide conduct and distinguish between right and wrong.

**ethnicity**    The part of a person's cultural background that is usually associated with shared religion, national origin, and language.

**ethos (credibility)**    An appeal to ethics; the quality of being worthy of trust. Credible speakers win audience members' trust and persuade them to embrace their viewpoints by conveying a sense of their knowledge, honesty, trustworthiness, experience, authority, or wisdom.

**etymological definition**    An explanation of the linguistic origin of a term. It is useful when the term's origin is interesting or will help the audience understand the word.

**eulogy**    A speech that comments on the death of an individual, celebrates that person's life, and often shares personal reflections and stories about the deceased.

**evidence**    Information gathered from credible sources that supports a speaker's claims.

**evidence and reasoning**    See **logos (evidence and reasoning)**.

**example**    A sample or an instance that supports or illustrates a general claim.

**example reasoning**    Presenting specific instances to support a general claim and to convince listeners that the claim is reasonable or true.

**expert definition**    A statement that provides the meaning of a term as presented by a person who is a credible source of information on a particular topic.

**expertise**    The possession of knowledge necessary to offer reliable facts or opinions about a topic.

**expert testimony**    Statements made by credible sources who have professional or other in-depth knowledge of a topic.

**explanation**    An analysis of something that traces a line of reasoning or a series of causal connections between events.

**export (citations)**   To move source citations from a computer-based library index to a digital file.

**extemporaneous delivery**   Presenting a speech using a speaking outline as a reference rather than reading it word-for-word.

**extended example**   A detailed narrative that serves as a sample or an instance to support or illustrate a general claim.

**external noise**   A distraction in the external speech environment that disrupts communication between source and receiver. For example, a speech might be drowned out by a fleet of jets roaring overhead. Also known as an *external distraction*.

**eye contact**   The act of looking directly into another person's eyes. This occurs between a speaker and an audience as they are speaking or listening.

**fact claim**   A statement that asserts that something is true or false. For example, "Animal experimentation is necessary for human survival."

**fallacious (faulty) reasoning**   Faulty, and thus unsound, reasoning in which the link between a claim and its supporting material is weak.

**false dilemma fallacy**   An error in reasoning in which the speaker incorrectly claims that there are only two possible choices to solve a problem, that one of them is wrong or impractical, and that the audience should therefore support the speaker's solution. This fallacy can usually be detected when listeners know that there are more than two choices.

**false inference**   Presenting information that leads an audience to an incorrect conclusion.

**fear appeal**   An argument that arouses fear in the minds of audience members. It is a form of pathos.

**feedback**   An audience's verbal and nonverbal responses to a source's message.

**figurative analogy**   An analogy in which the two entities being compared are not in the same category.

**figurative language**   Words and phrases that employ certain techniques to describe claims or ideas in order to make them more clear, memorable, or rhetorically stylistic. It is also referred to as *figures of speech*. See also **anaphora**, **antithesis**, **metaphor**, **simile**.

**fixed-response question**   A survey question that provides a set of specific answers for the respondent to choose from. Examples include true/false, multiple-choice, and select-all-that-apply questions.

**flowchart**   A diagram with text labels that demonstrates the direction of information or ideas or illustrates the steps in a process.

**forum (location)**   The setting where an audience will listen to a speech.

**freedom of expression**   The right to share one's ideas and opinions free from censorship.

**free speech zones**   Specific spaces on campus that are set aside for the expression of students' opinions.

**full disclosure**   A speaker's acknowledgment of any potential conflicts of interest in the topic.

**full-text source**   The complete text of a published article that can be accessed through a link on a library's online periodical index.

**functional definition**   An explanation of how something is used or what it does.

**gender identity**   "One's innermost concept of self as male, female, a blend of both or neither," as defined by The Human Rights Campaign.

**gender-neutral term**   A word that does not suggest a particular gender.

**gender stereotype**   An oversimplified, often distorted view of what it means to be male, female, or any other gender.

**gesture**   A hand, head, or facial movement that emphasizes, pantomimes, demonstrates, or calls attention to something.

**goodwill**   Friendly or helpful feelings toward another person. Good speakers want what is best for their audience rather than what would most benefit themselves.

**graph**   A visual representation of the relationship among different numbers, measurements, or quantities. See also **bar graph**, **line graph**, **pie chart (circle graph)**.

**group dynamics**   The ways in which the members of a group relate to one another and view their functions.

**groupthink**   The tendency of group members to accept ideas and information uncritically because they have strong feelings of loyalty or single-mindedness.

**half-truth**   A statement that deceives an audience by stating part of the truth but mixing it with a lie.

**hasty generalization**   An error in reasoning that occurs when a speaker bases a conclusion on limited or unrepresentative examples.

**hearing**   Passively receiving messages without trying to interpret or understand them.

**heterogeneity**   Diversity among members of a group.

**heteronormativity**   A worldview promoting heterosexuality and heterosexual relationships as the norm and the only natural way of expressing sexuality.

**hierarchy of needs**   A theory that people's most basic needs must be met before they can focus on less essential ones. Psychologist Abraham Maslow's hierarchy of needs begins with physiological needs and is followed by safety needs, social needs, self-esteem, and self-actualization needs.

**homogeneity**   Similarity among members of a group.

**hostile audience**   A group of listeners who oppose a speaker or a speaker's message and resist listening to the speech.

**hypothetical example**   An imagined example or scenario that a speaker presents to help an audience follow a complicated point.

**imagery**   Mental pictures or impressions painted with vivid language.

**imagined interaction**   The mental delivery of a speech to an audience. The speaker practices delivering a speech silently and pictures a positive interaction with the audience (such as applause).

**implied leader**   Someone with preexisting authority or skills who is likely to be recognized as a leader by a group, even if leadership has not been formally assigned.

**impromptu delivery**   Generating the content of a speech in the moment, without advance preparation.

**inductive reasoning**   Generalizing from facts, instances, or examples and then making a claim based on that generalization. If people have two bad experiences in a row at the same restaurant, they might conclude that they will always have a bad experience at that restaurant.

**informative purpose**   The intent to educate and increase an audience's understanding and awareness of a topic. It is one of three possible rhetorical purposes: to inform, to persuade, or to mark a special occasion.

**interactive listening**   The process of a receiver filtering out distractions, focusing on the speaker(s), and communicating that they are paying attention.

**interference**   See **noise (interference)**.

**internal noise**   A thought that distracts a sender or receiver from processing and retaining a message. Also known as *internal distraction*.

**internal preview**   A short list of ideas that summarizes the points that will follow. Using an internal preview in a speech gives the audience an advance warning of what is to come.

**internal summary**   A quick review of what has just been said in a speech's main point or subpoint. It is used to help an audience remember a particularly detailed point.

**interruptive listening**   Consistently interrupting a person who is speaking. Both audience members and speakers can be guilty of interruptive listening, either by interjecting questions or comments before a speaker is finished speaking or by cutting off an audience member who is asking a question.

**interview**   A conversation conducted to gather information for research or audience analysis. A speaker interacts with experts or select members of a future audience and records their responses. The interview can be conducted in person, by phone or email, or online.

**introduction**   The beginning of a speech. It gains the audience's attention, presents the thesis statement, builds common ground with the audience, establishes speaker credibility, and previews the speech's main points.

**invention**   The use of a variety of techniques and sources to gather and choose ideas for a speech. It is one of the five classical canons of rhetoric.

**jargon**   Specialized or technical words or phrases that are familiar only to people who work in a specific field or belong to a specific group.

**keyword**   An important word or term that relates to a topic, including a synonym of the word. Keywords are often used in online or database searches.

**latitude of acceptance**   The range of positions on a given issue that are acceptable to an audience.

**latitude of rejection**   The range of positions on a given issue that are unacceptable to an audience.

**lay testimony**   Statements about a topic that are made by persons with no special expertise in the subject they are discussing.

**legally protected speech**   The expression of any opinion in public without censorship by the government. When speakers use legal protection as a guiding principle for a speech—telling or withholding information based on whether the law allows it—they can technically stay within the bounds of what is lawful but still speak unethically.

**line graph**   A graph that compares the relationships between two elements by plotting data points on vertical and horizontal axes and connecting the points with a line.

**listening**   Actively receiving and processing messages to understand their meaning and remember their content.

**literal analogy**   A comparison based on similarities between two entities in the same category.

**loaded language fallacy**   An error in reasoning in which the speaker tries to persuade an audience by using emotionally charged words to convey a meaning that is not supported by factual evidence.

**location**   See **forum (location)**.

**logos (evidence and reasoning)**   An appeal to logic; the sound reasoning that supports a speaker's claims and makes an argument more persuasive to an audience.

**main point**   A key idea that supports a thesis and helps an audience understand and remember what is most important about a speaker's topic. Main points are supported by subpoints. See also **subpoints**.

**marking a special occasion**   Honoring a person or an event by entertaining, inspiring, or emotionally moving an audience. It is one of three possible rhetorical purposes: to inform, to persuade, or to mark a special occasion.

**mediated communication**   The transmission of a message through either a mechanical or an electronic medium.

**mediated presentation**   A speech that is transmitted through technology rather than to an audience face-to-face.

**memory**   The process of preparing and practicing a speech to ensure confident and effective delivery. It is one of the five classical canons of rhetoric. Although this canon originally referred to learning a speech by heart, today using notes and other memory aids is usually preferred.

**message**   The verbal or nonverbal ideas that a source conveys to an audience through the communication process.

**metaphor**   A comparison of unlike objects that identifies one object with another. For example, "Her adviser was a *fount of knowledge*."

**mind mapping**   Generating topic ideas by writing down an initial word or phrase and then surrounding it with additional words, pictures, and symbols to create an interconnected map of ideas.

**mobile audience**   Listeners who will be strolling by, stopping for a moment to listen, or drifting off to get on with their day. Mobile audiences might be found at an exhibitor's booth, on a town common, or on a city sidewalk.

**moderator**   The person who introduces the participants in a panel discussion and facilitates the discussion.

**monotone**   Unchanging in pitch or tone.

**motivated sequence**   A model for persuasive speech organization that inspires people to take action. This popular organizational pattern was developed by Alan Monroe and has five main points: attention, need, satisfaction, visualization, and action.

**multitasking**   Engaging in several different activities at once, often including the use of technological devices. This speech distraction is more likely to occur among audience members when the speaker is presenting from a remote location.

**narrative**   An anecdote (a brief story) or a somewhat longer account that a speaker tells to share information and capture an audience's attention. In informative speeches, the story can be a personal remembrance, a humorous anecdote, or a serious account of an event that happened in someone else's life.

**naturalness**   The extent to which a communication medium matches the features of face-to-face interaction.

**needs**   Objects that an audience desires or feelings that must be satisfied.

**nervous listening**   Talking through silences in conversation due to discomfort with conversational lapses or pauses.

**neutral audience**   A type of audience that has neither negative nor positive opinions about a speaker or message.

**noise (interference)**   External or internal phenomena that disrupt communication between a source and a receiver. External sources include nearby loud noises, and internal sources include the wandering thoughts of the source or receiver.

**nonbinary**   Refers to gender identity. Not identifying as exclusively male or female.

**nonlistening**   Failing to pay attention to what one is hearing and thus failing to process, understand, and retain the message.

**nonverbal delivery skills**   The use of physical behaviors—eye contact, gestures, physical movement, proxemics, and personal appearance—to deliver a speech.

**nonverbal symbol**   A means of conveying a message without using words. Examples include hand gestures, eye contact, and facial expressions.

**objectivity**   The quality of being impartial. In research, credible sources show objectivity when they avoid bias—that is, prejudice or partisanship.

**observational capacity**   The ability to witness a situation for oneself, thus increasing reliability.

**omission**   A form of false inference that deceives an audience by withholding important information.

**open-ended question**   A survey question that invites respondents to give answers of their own choosing, rather than offering them a limited set of responses.

**outline**   A written means of organizing a speech by using complete sentences or briefer phrases. An outline includes the main ideas of a speech's introduction, body, and conclusion.

**outlining**   Organizing the points of a speech into a structured form that lays out the sequence and hierarchy of a speaker's ideas.

**panel discussion**   A form of group presentation in which group members engage in discourse with one another while being observed by an audience.

**panelist**   A participant in a panel discussion.

**panning**    A form of nonverbal delivery in which a speaker looks at and surveys all audience members. When panning, the speaker looks back and forth across the audience, pausing and making extended eye contact with an individual listener for a few moments before moving on to do the same with another listener.

**paraphrasing**    Restating someone else's ideas in one's own words and giving appropriate credit to the original source.

**pathos**    An appeal to emotion; an attempt to persuade an audience by creating an emotional response.

**pausing**    Leaving strategic gaps of silence between the words and sentences of one's speech.

**paywall**    A system that allows access to an online article to paid subscribers only.

**peer review**    The evaluation of an author's professional work by other experts in a particular field.

**people-oriented listening**    Investing time and attention in communication because of an interest in supporting one's friends and strengthening relationships. People-oriented listeners notice the mood and body language of speakers and express more empathy toward them.

**periodical**    A publication that appears at regular intervals—for example weekly, monthly, quarterly, or annually, including scholarly journals and newsmagazines.

**peripheral belief**    A viewpoint that is not held as closely or as long as a core belief and that may be open to persuasion. See also **core belief**.

**peripheral route**    According to the elaboration likelihood model, one of two ways that audience members may evaluate a speaker's message. Those who follow this route do not actively process the message (low elaboration) but are instead influenced by tangential cues, such as attractiveness of the speaker, flashy presentation aids, or certain aspects of the speaker's delivery. See also **central route**.

**personal appearance**    The impression that speakers make on an audience through their clothing, jewelry, hairstyle, grooming, and other elements of their appearance.

**personal attack fallacy**    See *ad hominem* **(personal attack) fallacy**.

**persuasive purpose**    The intent to strengthen listeners' commitment to an existing belief, encourage listeners' to consider or adopt a new position, or promote a particular action. It is one of three possible rhetorical purposes: to inform, to persuade, or to mark a special occasion.

**persuasive speech**    Language that aims to influence audience members' beliefs, attitudes, or actions by employing strategic discourse and calling for the audience to accept fact, value, or policy claims.

**physical movement**    The bodily activity that a speaker engages in while giving a presentation.

**pie chart (circle graph)**    A graph that arranges information to resemble a sliced pie to clarify how proportions and percentages relate to one another and add up to a whole.

**pitch**    How high or low a speaker's voice is.

**plagiarism**  The presentation of another person's words or ideas as one's own.

**policy claim**  A statement that advocates that organizations, institutions, or members of the audience should take action. For example, "Anyone opposed to animal experimentation should join an activist organization, such as the Humane Society."

**political affiliation**  A person's political beliefs and positions.

*post hoc* **fallacy**  An error in reasoning that incorrectly states that a second event is caused by the event that immediately preceded it.

**power wording**  The rewording of evidence in a way that supports one's own claim but misrepresents a source's point of view. It is considered unethical.

**precise evidence**  Specific dates, places, numbers, and other facts that are presented as supporting materials.

**prerecorded (asynchronous) presentation**  A speech that is recorded by the speaker for later viewing by one or more audiences.

**presentation aid**  Anything beyond the speech itself that a speaker uses to help listeners help understand and remember the message. Presentation aids include materials that can be seen, heard, or touched.

**presentation software**  A computer program that enables users to create, edit, and present information, usually in a slide-show format. It is sometimes referred to as *slideware*.

**presentation time**  The length of time that a speaker has to deliver a speech.

**preview**  A brief statement of the main points that a speaker will be developing in a speech. The preview tells audience members what to expect and helps them visualize the structure of a speech.

**prior exposure**  The extent to which an audience has already heard a speaker's message, which affects the audience's interest or belief in what the speaker is saying.

**problem-cause-solution pattern**  A model for speech organization that identifies a problem, explains the problem's causes, and proposes one or more solutions, which often include asking an audience to support a policy or take a specific action.

**processing**  Thinking about the meaning of the verbal and nonverbal components of a message that one is receiving. Processing is the first step in effective listening.

**projection**  The act of "booming" one's voice across a speaking forum to reach all audience members.

**pronunciation**  The way that a person says words as they typically sound in the language or dialect of their speech.

**proxemics**  The use of space and distance between a speaker and an audience.

**quotation book**  A reference work that contains famous or notable quotations on a variety of subjects.

**race**  A common heritage based on the genetically shared physical characteristics of people in a group.

**rate of delivery**  The speed at which a person speaks while giving a presentation.

**real-time (synchronous) presentation**  A speech that is delivered directly to the audience as the speaker presents the message from a remote location.

**receiver**    The person who processes a message to perceive its meaning.

**recency**    The state of having just happened, or timeliness. Because of society's many and rapid changes, newer evidence is generally considered more reliable and credible than older evidence.

**references**    A list of all the sources cited in a speech, often included at the end of a detailed outline. May also be referred to as a list of works cited or a bibliography.

**reference work**    A compilation of background information on major topic areas that is useful for doing exploratory research or discovering a specific fact.

**reflective-thinking process**    A five-step strategy for group decision making that includes defining the problem, analyzing the problem, establishing criteria for solving the problem, generating possible solutions, and selecting the best solution.

**relaxation strategy**    A technique that can be performed before giving a speech to help reduce muscle tension and negative thoughts. Relaxation strategies include deep breathing and tensing and releasing one's muscles.

**religious orientation**    A person's set of religious beliefs, which can shape how the individual responds to a speech.

**representative example**    An instance that is typical of the class it represents. For example, a speaker who is arguing that Americans are tired of corrupt politicians might cite instances of like-minded Americans from several regions rather than from only one or two states.

**research**    The process of gathering information from libraries, quality online sources, and interviews with authorities on a topic to increase a speaker's credibility and understanding of the topic.

**research librarian**    A career professional who is hired to assist students and faculty with their research.

**research objective**    A goal that a speaker wants to accomplish through research.

**research plan**    A strategy for finding and keeping track of the information (in books, periodicals, websites, and other sources) that a speaker might use to prepare a presentation.

**retention**    The ability to remember what one has heard. It is the second step in effective listening and is directly related to how much attention someone pays during an event. The more attentive a listener is, the more information will be remembered.

**reversed causality**    A situation in which what appears to be an effect of an event is actually the cause of the event.

**rhetoric**    The craft of public speaking.

**rhetorical purpose**    The speaker's intended primary goal for the speech. There are three possible rhetorical purposes for a presentation: to inform, to persuade, or to mark a special occasion.

**rhetorical question**    A question that a speaker expects listeners to answer in their heads. It is used to capture an audience's attention and lead them to think about a speaker's topic.

**scaled question**    A survey question that measures the intensity of a respondent's feelings on an issue by offering a range of fixed responses. These can take the form of a numerical scale (for example, the numbers one to ten) or a list of options ("strongly agree," "agree," "neutral," "disagree," or "strongly disagree").

**script**   A typed or handwritten document that contains the entire text of a speech.

**search engine**   A specialized online program that continually visits web pages and indexes what is found there. Users enter a search term, and the engine provides access to relevant web pages. Examples include Google, Bing, Yahoo!, and Baidu.

**sexist language**   Language that reveals a bias against any gender identity.

**sexual orientation**   A demographic characteristic related to attraction; includes people who are heterosexual and people who are part of the LGBTQ community.

**shared meaning**   A common understanding with little confusion and few mis-interpretations among speakers and listeners. Achieving shared meaning is a priority of the transactional model of communication.

**signpost**   A word or phrase within a sentence that informs the audience about the direction and organization of a speech.

**sign reasoning**   Arguing that a fact is true because indirect indicators are con-sistent with that fact. For example, a speaker might argue that the United States is in a recession, supporting that claim with evidence that people are taking out more payday loans.

**simile**   A comparison of objects that uses the word *like* or *as*. For example, "My grandmother's lap was *as soft as a pillow*."

**situational audience analysis**   The process of learning about an audience's inter-ests and backgrounds just before or during a speech. It is usually conducted when speakers discover that the makeup of an audience is different from what they expected or when the audience appears to be confused, lost, or hostile.

**situational characteristics**   Factors in a specific speech setting that a speaker can observe or discover before giving the speech. Examples include audi-ence size, time, location (forum), and audience mobility.

**situational ethics**   The belief that ethical behavior can vary depending on the situation at hand, especially when those circumstances are extreme or unusual. See also **ethical absolutism**.

**slippery slope fallacy**   An error in reasoning in which the speaker argues against a policy with the assumption (without proof) that the first policy will lead to a second, undesirable outcome. For example, "If we legalize mari-juana, that will be the first step toward legalization of all drugs, which would create a public health catastrophe."

**small group**   A limited number of people (three or more) gathered for a specific purpose.

**social judgment theory**   A theory stating that receivers decide to accept or reject a persuasive thesis by comparing it to their own position on the issue.

**social media**   Online communication methods that allow users to both create and access material or participate in social networking. Information that is posted on social media is often not reviewed by editors or other readers, so speakers should proceed with caution before using it in a speech.

**socioeconomic status**　A measure of the financial resources, education, and occupation of people compared to other individuals.

**source**　In models of communication, a person with an idea to express who creates and sends a message to receivers.

**spatial pattern**　A model for speech organization in which the main points represent important aspects of a topic and are thought of as adjacent to one another in location or geography. A speaker who is discussing historical sites in a state's three largest cities might use a spatial pattern of organization.

**speaking outline**　A type of outline that uses brief phrases, keywords, or abbreviations to represent the speaker's key ideas and give reminders of delivery guidelines.

**specific purpose**　A concise phrase that states the rhetorical purpose and objective of a speech.

**speech anxiety (stage fright)**　The nervousness that a person experiences before giving a speech. It can take a variety of forms, including butterflies in the stomach, sweaty palms, dry mouth, nausea, hyperventilation, and panic.

**speech critique**　Written or oral feedback following a presentation that identifies the presentation's main points and objectives, discusses strengths and weaknesses, and offers suggestions for improvement.

**stage fright**　See **speech anxiety (stage fright)**.

**stationary audience**　Listeners who are relatively motionless (sitting or standing) during a speech. Classrooms, lecture halls, and conference rooms generally house stationary audiences.

**statistic**　A piece of numerical data that helps a speaker quantify points and helps an audience understand how often a given situation occurs.

**stereotype**　A generalization based on the false assumption that the characteristics displayed by some members of a group are shared by all members of that group.

**strategic discourse**　The process of selecting arguments that will best achieve a speaker's rhetorical purpose in an ethical manner.

**straw person fallacy**　An error in reasoning in which the speaker replaces an opponent's real claim with a weaker claim that can be more easily refuted. For example, if a mayor proposes adding bike lanes to a city's main streets but the city council argues that it would be too expensive to add bike lanes to every street in the city, the city council is committing this fallacy (the mayor proposed adding bike lanes only to main streets, not to every street).

**style**　A speaker's choice of language that will best express their ideas to the audience. It is one of the five classical canons of rhetoric.

**subordination**　The act of making one thing secondary to another thing. This principle of outlining dictates the hierarchy in the relationship of main points and supporting materials. Each subpoint must support its corresponding main point, and each sub-subpoint must support its corresponding subpoint. In an outline, supporting points are written below and to the right of the point they support. See also **subpoint, sub-subpoint**.

**subpoint**　An idea that is gathered from brainstorming and research and that explains, proves, or expands on a speech's main points.

**sub-subpoint**   An idea that is gathered from brainstorming or research and that explains, proves, and expands on a speech's subpoints.

**summary**   A brief review of a speech's main points. It is used in the conclusion of a speech to help audience members remember what they have heard.

**superficial listening**   Pretending to pay attention while actually succumbing to internal or external noise, such as wandering thoughts, cell phones, or conversation.

**supporting material (supporting points)**   The examples, definitions, testimony, statistics, narratives, and analogies that develop and support the claims made in a speaker's main points.

**survey**   A set of written questions that a speaker asks audience members to answer in advance of the presentation.

**symbolic expression**   The use of nonverbal symbols to express a message.

**sympathetic audience**   An audience that already agrees with a speaker's message or holds the speaker in high esteem and will respond favorably to the speech.

**symposium**   A method of group presentation in which group members take responsibility for delivering different parts of the presentation.

**synchronous presentation**   See **real-time (synchronous) presentation**.

**takeaway**   A memorable phrase or sentence that captures the essence of a speech and can be repeated at key points in the speech.

**taking evidence out of context**   Selectively choosing from a source's data or statements and presenting the information in a manner that is inconsistent with the source's beliefs or conclusions.

**temporal pattern**   See **chronological (temporal) pattern**.

**testimony**   Information on a topic that is provided by other people. Testimony is often gathered from sources researched in a library, found online, or recorded in an interview.

**thesis statement**   A single sentence that sums up a speech's main message and reflects the speaker's narrowed topic and rhetorical purpose. All the different parts of a speech, such as the main points and subpoints, should tie into the thesis statement. It is also referred to as the *central idea* or *topic statement*.

**time-oriented listening**   A style of listening in which listeners are concerned with managing, conserving, and protecting their time. Time-oriented listeners see time as a precious resource to be conserved and protected, so may exhibit impatience and rush interactions.

**tone**   The high and low qualities of a person's speaking voice. Moderate tonal variety is preferable to using a single tone which is usually either low and mumbling or high-pitched and annoying. See also **monotone**.

**topic**   The subject of a speech. Speakers should choose a topic that is based on their own and their audience's interests and knowledge level, as well as their ability to cover the topic during the allotted time frame.

**topical pattern**   See **categorical (topical) pattern**.

**top-level domain**   The designation at the end of a web address that at one time indicated the site sponsor's affiliation—for example, commercial (.com), nonprofit (.org), educational (.edu), government (.gov, .uk), and network

(.net). The top-level domain can no longer be used to determine whether an online source is credible, as websites can now choose from a variety of suffixes. Therefore, when using websites for research purposes, the credibility of the person or organization that created the site must be assessed.

**transaction**    A communicative exchange in which all participants continuously send and receive messages.

**transition**    A sentence that indicates you are moving from one idea to another in a speech.

**trustworthiness**    The characteristic of exhibiting honesty and fairness. Often seen as one component of a speaker's ethos.

**two-sided argument**    An argument in which the speaker acknowledges an opposing argument and then uses evidence and reasoning to refute that argument.

**unprocessed note taking**    Writing down a speech word-for-word without thinking about what is being said. Unprocessed note taking hampers retention.

**value claim**    A statement that attaches a judgment—such as deeming something good, bad, moral, or immoral—to a subject. For example, "Animal experimentation is inhumane."

**values**    Core conceptions about what is desirable for an individual's own life and for society. Values guide people's judgments and actions.

**verbal chart**    Words arranged in a certain format, such as a bulleted list or columns, to explain ideas, concepts, or general information.

**verbal clutter**    Extraneous words that make a presentation hard to follow.

**verbal delivery skills**    The use of one's voice to deliver a speech effectively. A speaker should consider volume, tone, rate of delivery, projection, articulation, pronunciation, and pausing.

**verbal filler**    A word or phrase, such as *you know* or *like*, that a speaker uses to fill uncomfortable silences.

**verbal symbol**    A spoken, written, or recorded word that a source uses to convey a message.

**verbal tic**    A sound, such as *um* or *ah*, that speakers use when searching for a correct word or when they have lost their train of thought.

**visualization**    A method of easing speech anxiety in which the speaker imagines giving an extremely well-received speech.

**vivid language**    Attention-grabbing and descriptive words and phrases that appeal to the senses.

**volume**    The loudness or softness of a speaker's voice when delivering a speech.

**word association**    A method for generating topic ideas in which one idea leads to another, then another, and so on, until the speaker generates an appropriate topic.

**word choice (diction)**    The selection of language for a speech that considers the audience, occasion, and nature of one's message in order to make the speech more memorable and engaging.

**yearbook**    A reference work that is updated annually and contains statistics and other facts about social, political, and economic topics.

# INDEX